A User's Guide to German Cultural Studies

Social History, Popular Culture, and Politics in Germany
Geoff Eley, Series Editor

A History of Foreign Labor in Germany, 1880–1980: Seasonal Workers/Forced Laborers/Guest Workers
    Ulrich Herbert, translated by William Templer
Reshaping the German Right: Radical Nationalism and Political Change after Bismarck
    Geoff Eley
The Stigma of Names: Antisemitism in German Daily Life, 1812–1933
    Dietz Bering
Forbidden Laughter: Popular Humor and the Limits of Repression in Nineteenth-Century Prussia
    Mary Lee Townsend
From Bundesrepublik *to* Deutschland: *German Politics after Unification*
    Michael G. Huelshoff, Andrei S. Markovits, and Simon Reich, editors
The People Speak! Anti-Semitism and Emancipation in Nineteenth-Century Bavaria
    James F. Harris
The Origins of the Authoritarian Welfare State in Prussia: Conservatives, Bureaucracy, and the Social Question, 1815–70
    Hermann Beck
Technological Democracy: Bureaucracy and Citizenry in the German Energy Debate
    Carol J. Hager
Society, Culture, and the State in Germany, 1870–1930
    Geoff Eley, editor
Paradoxes of Peace: German Peace Movements since 1945
    Alice Holmes Cooper
Jews, Germans, Memory: Reconstruction of Jewish Life in Germany
    Y. Michal Bodemann, editor
Exclusive Revolutionaries: Liberal Politics, Social Experience, and National Identity in the Austrian Empire, 1848–1914
    Pieter M. Judson
Feminine Frequencies: Gender, German Radio, and the Public Sphere, 1923–1945
    Kate Lacey
How German Is She? Postwar West German Reconstruction and the Consuming Woman
    Erica Carter
West Germany under Construction: Politics, Society, and Culture in Germany in the Adenauer Era
    Robert G. Moeller, editor
A Greener Vision of Home: Cultural Politics and Environmental Reform in the German Heimatschutz *Movement, 1904–1918*
    William H. Rollins
A User's Guide to German Cultural Studies
    Scott Denham, Irene Kacandes, and Jonathan Petropoulos, editors

A User's Guide

to

German Cultural Studies

Edited by
SCOTT DENHAM,
IRENE KACANDES, *and*
JONATHAN PETROPOULOS

Ann Arbor

THE UNIVERSITY OF MICHIGAN PRESS

Published in the United States of America by
The University of Michigan Press
Manufactured in the United States of America
♾ Printed on acid-free paper

2000   1999   1998   1997   4   3   2   1

A CIP catalog record for this book is available from the British Library

Library of Congress Cataloging-in-Publication Data

A user's guide to German cultural studies / edited by Scott Denham,
   Irene Kacandes, and Jonathan Petropoulos.
        p.   cm. — (Social history, popular culture, and politics in Germany)
   Includes bibliographical references and index.
   ISBN 0-472-06656-0 (pbk. : acid-free paper). — ISBN 0-472-09656-7
(cloth : acid-free paper)
      1. Germany—Civilization—Study and teaching—United States.
   2. Popular culture—Germany—Study and teaching—United States.
   3. Art and state—Germany.   4. Political culture—Germany.   5. Arts,
   Modern—20th century—Germany.   I. Denham, Scott D.   II. Kacandes, Irene,
   1958–   .   III. Petropoulos, Jonathan.   IV. Series.
   DD67.U74   1997
   943'.007'2073—dc21   97-4768
                                                                                 CIP

To our parents

Contents

Preface   xi

Part 1. Why German Cultural Studies?   **1**

Chapter 1. German Cultural Studies: What Is at Stake?   3
Irene Kacandes

Part 2. What Is German Cultural Studies?   **29**

Chapter 2. Interrogating Germanness:
What's Literature Got to Do with It   31
Angelika Bammer

Chapter 3. Who's Afraid of Cultural Studies? Taking
a "Cultural Turn" in German History   45
David F. Crew

Chapter 4. Multiculturalism and the Study
of German Literature   63
Arlene A. Teraoka

Chapter 5. Cultural Studies and Foreign Policy
in a Strategic Alliance, or Why Presidents
of the United States Should Learn German   79
Jeffrey M. Peck

Part 3. Who Practices German Cultural Studies?   **91**

Chapter 6. Learning to Stop Hating Germans:
The Challenge of Journalistic Objectivity   93
Deidre Berger

Chapter 7. Born Later: On Being a German Germanist
in America   113
Christian Rogowski

Chapter 8. Asking the Questions/Telling a Story   127
Norma Claire Moruzzi

Part 4. What Was "German" in the Past?   **137**

Chapter 9. Bach Revival, Public Culture, and National
Identity: The *St. Matthew Passion* in 1829   139
Celia Applegate

Chapter 10. A Nation for the Masses: Production
of German Identity in the Late-Nineteenth-Century
Popular Press   163
Kirsten Belgum

Chapter 11. Consumer Culture Is in Need of Attention:
German Cultural Studies and the Commercialization
of the Past   181
Alon Confino

Chapter 12. Colonial Legends, Postcolonial Legacies   189
Susanne Zantop

Part 5. What Is "German" Now?   **207**

Chapter 13. "Seit die Juden weg sind . . .": Germany,
History, and Representations of Absence   209
Omer Bartov

Chapter 14. Schinkel and the Politics of German Memory:
The Life of the Neue Wache in Berlin   227
Wallis Miller

Chapter 15. Stones Set Upright in the Winds
of Controversy: An Austrian Monument against War
and Fascism   257
John Czaplicka

Chapter 16. Economic Influences on Constructions
of German Identity   287
Robert Mark Spaulding

Chapter 17. Living with Which Past? National Identity
in Post-Wall, Postwar Germany   297
Laurence McFalls

Chapter 18. Dis-Membering the Past: The Politics
of Memory in the German Borderland   309
Daphne Berdahl

Chapter 19. How American Is It? The United States
as Queer Utopia in the Cinema of Monika Treut   333
Gerd Gemünden

Part 6. How Do We Mediate the German Case to the Public?   **355**

Chapter 20. The Future of Auschwitz: A Case for the Ruins   357
Michael R. Marrus

Chapter 21. The First Draft: Writing History
for the General Public   367
Timothy W. Ryback

Chapter 22. Who Owns the Past? The Surrender
of the Berlin Document Center 377
Geoffrey J. Giles

Part 7. Teaching German Cultural Studies **389**

Chapter 23. Translation in Cultural Mediation
and Pedagogy 391
A. Leslie Willson

Chapter 24. Cultural Studies, the Eighteenth Century,
and the Uses of the German Classics 399
Burkhard Henke

Chapter 25. Interdisciplinary Teaching with the Case
Study Method 417
Louis L. Ortmayer

Chapter 26. Teaching Students and Teachers of German
Cultural Studies 431
Richard M. Hunt

Chapter 27. The Pragmatics of Studying the "German"
at the Turn of the Century 439
Sander L. Gilman

Part 8. Tools **449**

Chapter 28. "How to . . ." Classroom Handouts 451
A. How to Read a Poem *(Judith Ryan)* 452
B. How to View a Building *(Wallis Miller
and Scott Denham)* 456
C. How to View a Film *(Gerd Gemünden)* 458
D. How to Listen to Western Music *(Jean H. Leventhal)* 461
E. How to View a Painting *(Jonathan Petropoulos)* 464
F. How to Read a Play *(Christian Rogowski)* 467
G. How to View Performance *(Heidi Gilpin)* 469
H. How to Read a Novel *(Scott Denham
and Irene Kacandes)* 474
I. How to Read History *(Omer Bartov)* 477
J. How to Read Statistics *(Laurence McFalls)* 479
K. How to Use an Archive *(Geoffrey J. Giles)* 483

Chapter 29. German Cultural Studies Course Syllabi:
Sources and Examples 489
A. German Studies and the General Culture Course:
The Stanford Curriculum *(Russell A. Berman)* 491
B. Culture and Society in Weimar and Nazi Germany:
Harvard University Core Program *(Richard M. Hunt)* 497

C. The Rapprochement of History and Anthropology
in Germany (University of Chicago)
(Daphne Berdahl and Drew Bergerson)   502
D. Survivors, Victims, and Perpetrators: The Literature
of the Holocaust (University of Texas at Austin)
(Irene Kacandes)   508

Chapter 30. German Cultural Studies and the Internet   515
Daniel E. Rogers

Chapter 31. Practicing German Cultural Studies   521
A. Directories, Resources, Journals   521
B. Funding and Agencies   522

Chapter 32. Selected, Annotated Bibliographies
on German Cultural Studies and on Cultural Studies
in General   529

Notes on Contributors   537

Index   545

Preface

This volume provides a broad overview of German cultural studies. By *German cultural studies* we mean an interdisciplinary project that has developed out of "German studies" as it has been variously practiced in the United States for the last twenty-five years or so. German studies approaches have been increasingly influenced by the field generally referred to as "cultural studies," derived in part from British theorists associated with the Birmingham Centre for Contemporary Cultural Studies, in part from Continental critical theory, and highly influenced by North American contexts and praxis. Our term *German cultural studies* thus means to draw attention to a transformation that has already taken place and to point out a trajectory for future change. The first part of our title, "A User's Guide," signals that this overview is offered as an invitation, not a prescription. Indeed, this is a guide, not an instruction manual or even a survey, because cultural studies does not constitute a new discipline. Rather, it is best described as an interdisciplinary field in which certain questions and methods converge, providing us with sometimes conflicting sets of practices beyond the scope of a single discipline. Such a definition disallows the introduction of a new orthodoxy. We also call this volume "A User's Guide" because it aims for practical consequences; its essays and supporting material serve the goal of curricular and research development.

Through introductory and linking comments by the editors, essays by expert practitioners, and a unique section devoted to pedagogical tools, the book illustrates what kinds of questions get asked in cultural studies; demonstrates how these questions are approached by scholars in the German context; describes the relations between German cultural studies and other fields; and, finally, explores how successful teachers bring cultural studies into the classroom. The progression over the course of the book from theoretical issues to case studies to practical applications allows readers to personalize its use: to proceed either start to finish for a structured introduction to German cultural studies or to skip selectively to topics of greatest interest. Whereas a general reader might be most interested in parts 4, 5, and 6 dealing with historical and contemporary issues, students might turn first to parts 1, 2, and 3, introducing the field and its practitioners. Teachers and advanced graduate students of German or other foreign cultures might be more curious about parts 7 and 8, which offer essays on teaching German cultural studies, concrete pedagogical aids for interdisciplinary work, annotated bibliographies, sample syllabi, and sources of institutional support. Students and teachers will also be interested in the individual essays' works cited, which offer guidance to further reading. Not all readers will need or want the same things from this volume. Therefore, the book ranges from basic, definitional information to material that takes the debate about cultural studies to new ground.

This is an auspicious moment for the publication of *A User's Guide to German Cultural Studies.* First, the resurgence of nationalism provides relevance for the volume's central concern with the construction of national identity. Second, the rise of neo-Nazism and right-wing extremism as well as the recent anniversary of the close of World War II have drawn attention to Germany again. Third, and closer to home, the concern about shrinking enrollments in the humanities—especially in foreign language programs—has caused numerous university German departments to consider a German studies curriculum as a recruitment tool. But, even in schools in which neither student taste nor budget cuts prompt realignments, realignments are occurring in response to changes in the object of study. Central Europe has been transformed dramatically in the last decade, and academics are shifting what and how they teach about this region. The essays and pedagogical materials in this volume provide needed models and concrete aids for effecting such curricular transformations. And, finally, *A User's Guide to German Cultural Studies* is timely because there is an increasing demand for multicultural education. Our book constitutes a contribution to precisely such an education.

To date the German case has generally been absent from discussions and celebrations surrounding cultural studies in the North American academy. This is to the impoverishment of cultural studies, since the German case proves a fertile ground for interdisciplinary work. Indeed, the German-speaking world has spawned not only some of the most extreme contrasts between products of culture—the clichéd though endlessly fascinating Beethoven-Hitler dichotomy—but also approaches to culture that are methodologically sophisticated. Whereas the names Theodor Adorno, Hannah Arendt, Walter Benjamin, Peter Gay, Sander Gilman, Max Horkheimer, Andreas Huyssen, Biddy Martin, Alexander and Margarethe Mitscherlich, George Mosse, Peter Paret, Carl Schorske, Fritz Stern, and James Young may be as familiar to the U.S. cultural studies crowd as are the names Roland Barthes, Roger Darnton, Natalie Zemon Davis, Jacques Derrida, Michel Foucault, Clifford Geertz, Stephen Greenblatt, bell hooks, Lynn Hunt, Gayatri Spivak, and Raymond Williams, the issues that occupy scholars of German culture are mostly unknown. A first goal of this book, therefore, is to showcase work in German cultural studies. We hope to bring to the attention of a wider audience the ways that the peculiarities of German history have elevated levels of self-scrutiny among scholars of German culture—and of criticism when self-scrutiny is lacking. More particularly, we hope to show why certain subjects have been privileged sites of German cultural studies and others have not.

One such privileged site has been "identity." As numerous essays in this volume demonstrate, the construction, contestation, and representation of individual and national identities have been a locus of activity in German cultural studies. Distant as well as more recent German history offers clues for why this might be the case. The relatively late founding of the German nation-state, the violent imposition of racial criteria for citizenship by the National Socialists, and the division of the nation-state into multiple countries after World War II are just a few of the landmark events that show why the definition of *German* is so problematic and therefore of abiding interest to cultural scholars.

While we maintain that sophisticated interdisciplinary work on questions like the construction of identity has an important tradition in the German sphere, paradoxically, such scholarship has often been hidden within traditional disciplinary boundaries. As a result of the particular development of the German university system in the nineteenth century and this system's tenacity as a model, historians generally have been ill aware of advances in literary study, political scientists of developments in historiography, and scholars in the humanities of progress in social science fields. Methodological self-reflection on the part of literary scholars, historians, and political scientists has usually been addressed only to others within the same field. Happily, this situation has begun to change, at least in the North American context. More journals are publishing truly interdisciplinary work, and some recent departmental hirings have also been cross-disciplinary.

In support of this trend a second goal of this volume is to provide a place in which various types of scholars and advanced students can become acquainted with work on German subjects that cuts across disciplinary lines. The volume's contributors include not only historians, an art historian, an architectural historian, an anthropologist, film and literary scholars, economic and cultural historians, and political scientists but also academics in interdisciplinary programs such as Humanities, Women's Studies, and Social Studies. Furthermore, the inclusion of journalists (Deidre Berger of National Public Radio and Tim Ryback, who has written for the *New Yorker,* the *Atlantic Monthly,* and *ARTnews*) illustrates the editors' commitment to initiating dialog between academics and those who mediate our subjects to the public at large. We consider this mediation part of the cultural studies project too. While the several established scholars in this volume were some of the pioneers in German studies over the last quarter-century, the many younger scholars here demonstrate the viability of cultural studies research and teaching for the decades to come.

The genesis of this book provides additional insight into cultural studies. It not only shows how substantially *A User's Guide to German Cultural Stud-*

ies differs from volumes of conference proceedings; it also makes clear a model for true collaborative, interdisciplinary work among scholars from different fields. The idea for the volume grew out of a German Studies Association panel on "Teaching German Studies Interdisciplinarily," which the editors (a Germanist, a comparative literature scholar, and a historian of Germany with substantial training in art history) organized in 1993. Despite its Sunday morning time slot, the panel was greeted enthusiastically, as was a booklet of syllabi for interdisciplinary German studies courses that was distributed after the conference, and so we began to think about methodically addressing key theoretical and practical issues in German studies. We commissioned the essays in the volume to do just this. About two-thirds of the contributors attended a symposium on "German Studies as Cultural Studies," supported with major funding from the DAAD (Deutscher Akademischer Austauschdient; German Academic Exchange Service) and Davidson College, where first versions of essays were presented and discussed at length. An important feature of this conference was roundtable discussion, during which all participants debated what constitutes a cultural studies praxis and what it has to offer the study of things German. The essays were revised for publication, read and commented on by all three editors, and returned to the authors for further revision. The essays speak to one another because their authors have done just that—and always with the common concerns of interdisciplinary ways of thinking and cultural studies modes of questioning in mind. A sense of the negotiating process can be gleaned from the editors' comments introducing individual sections and essays. These "bridge texts" not only link the essays to one another but, perhaps more important, challenge as well as frame; they position the essays in numerous discussions about the efficacy and limitations of cultural studies. They point out agreements and disagreements. By modeling debate, they invite the reader to participate actively in the dialog.

Dialog notwithstanding, even the many voices that constitute this book could not address all the topics of German cultural studies. This attests foremost to the breadth of the field, but it is also true that the editors were unable to find writers on some topics that should have been included. Despite general agreement that "German" cultural studies concerns itself with a large section of Central Europe, former African and Polynesian colonies, German immigrants and refugees in Australia and North and South America, and ethnic Germans in Eastern Europe, the majority of essays center on topics and issues related to the nation-state Germany. To be sure, essays such as Teraoka's on multiculturalism, Belgum's on German emigrants, Zantop's on postcolonialism, and Czaplicka's on Austria do point to this larger definition of *German,* but there could have been countless others. In a different vein, though the disciplinary home bases of our contributors is broad indeed, it could have been broader still. How would a theologian or a psychiatrist or a philosopher approach German cultural studies? Yet a third type of absence in this volume is that of premodern periods. Burkhard Henke argues persuasively for the inclusion of the German "long eighteenth century" in cultural studies, but, surely, times even earlier than the eighteenth century should be investigated for their cultural production. By mentioning these "gaps" here, we highlight that this book aspires not to an exhaustive role but, rather, to a catalytic one. We hope that it will launch numerous additional studies that will expand the work begun with this volume.

This volume would not have been possible without the aid and support of numerous individuals and organizations. We would first like to thank those colleagues—administrators, staff, and fellow faculty—at our home institutions who lent both tangible and intangible support with patience and smiles. No such broad collaboration could have taken place without the almost endless photocopying, faxing, and telephoning paid for by Dartmouth College, Davidson College, and Loyola College in Maryland. We would like to thank particularly the community of Davidson College for the extraordinary Southern hospitality extended to us and our contributors during the "German Studies as Cultural Studies" symposium of March 1995. A special word of thanks is due to Cheryl Branz at Davidson, whose help was instrumental to both the symposium and this book. Second, we would like to express our appreciation to Heidrun Suhr, Barbara Motyka, and especially Gottfried Gügold of the New York DAAD office for their encouragement and generous financial support. We want to acknowledge the many members of the profession who were invited to contribute essays and who, though unable to write for the volume, expressed enthusiasm and offered valuable suggestions. We would like to single out Peter Hohendahl and Patricia Herminghouse for leading the productive roundtable discussions during the Davidson symposium. The volume would not exist without the intense collaboration of its many contributors. Their energetic commitment to improving the profession inspired us to work as hard as necessary to coordinate this project. Our thanks go out as well to the University of Michigan Press series editor Geoff Eley, whose early words of encouragement and criticism helped shape the book, and to our editor Susan Whitlock, for her exuberance and advice. Beatrice and Evelyn Denham were cooperative longer than any children should have to be while their dad was stowed away in his office. And, finally, but most especially, we would like to thank our respective spouses, Cathy Denham, Philippe Carrard, and Kimberly Petropoulos, who proved to be the most intelligently critical yet loyal and supportive fans any team could hope to have.

Part One

WHY GERMAN CULTURAL STUDIES?

Part 1 contains a single contribution that offers background to the issues that permeate this volume. Kacandes's piece, however, does not constitute a standard introduction. Introductory material—a survey of how the book is put together, how it was conceived, and to whom it is directed—is contained in the preface. And introductions to themes raised by individual essays will be found in the headnotes to the eight parts and the bridge texts between essays. Kacandes's essay aims, rather, to contextualize the cultural studies project as a whole. It also describes the convergence of German studies with cultural studies into a new area of endeavor that she and the team behind this book propose is most appropriately called "German cultural studies." In offering her description of cultural studies as a field, Kacandes relies extensively on British and North American traditions. The idea that cultural studies contributes to our general social welfare resonates throughout her piece. Her apparent frustration about scholars' inability to collaborate to date is tempered by her assessment that this is starting to change and that cultural studies can and will make a difference.

CHAPTER 1

German Cultural Studies: What Is at Stake?

Irene Kacandes

Margaret Atwood's dystopic novel of the United States in the near future, *The Handmaid's Tale* (1986), begins by throwing us directly into the nightmare world of its nameless protagonist-narrator, but it ends about a century and a half after the main events with a section called "Historical Notes." Here the reader gets "a partial transcript of the proceedings of the Twelfth Symposium on Gileadean Studies, part of the International Historical Association Convention, held at the University of Denay, Nunavit, on June 25, 2195" (299). The transcript records the introduction by a "Professor Maryann Crescent Moon of the Department of Caucasian Anthropology" and the talk by a "Professor James Darcy Pieixoto, Director of the Twentieth- and Twenty-first-Century Archives at Cambridge University." In other words, Atwood offers a creative projection of what we scholars will be doing in two hundred years. Atwood herself has stated that she added the epilogue in order to communicate a number of things about Gilead that the novel's protagonist, the Handmaid herself, could not have known and also to show her optimism that Gilead, like the Third Reich, would not last forever (Ingersoll 217). The "Historical Notes" certainly accomplish these tasks. But Atwood is being a bit duplicitous in her explanation. The epilogue functions more compellingly to extend the totalitarian themes of the novel, illustrating how Atwood does *not* want us to read it. She dislikes these late-twenty-second-century scholars and their attitudes. Thus, though we can locate helpful information in the scholar's talk about the origins of the text (recorded onto cassette tapes, presumably after the Handmaid's escape from the household but before actually leaving Gilead), the ironic tone in which these facts are communicated, like the witty place and personal names, carries a message for readers about scholarly work.

The scholars at the conference show no interest in what the Handmaid actually tells, indicated in part by their obsession with the historical identity of her Commander; Pieixoto's hypotheses about this take up the greater part of his talk. He concludes:

> This is our guesswork. Supposing it to be correct—supposing, that is, that Waterford was indeed the "Commander"—many gaps remain. Some of them could have been filled by our anonymous author, had she had a different turn of mind. She could have told us much about the workings of the Gileadean empire, had she had the instincts of a reporter or a spy. What would we not give, now, for even twenty pages or so of print-out from Waterford's private computer! However, we must be grateful for any crumbs the Goddess of History has deigned to vouchsafe us. (Atwood 310)

This passage and others mean to lead readers to the conclusion that these scholars have missed the point. Their implicit and explicit criticisms of the Handmaid gloss over her pain, over her trauma, over her story—to their minds: "crumbs"! They miss all the insights her tale *does* provide "about the workings of the Gileadean empire," because they seem interested only in historically verifiable fact, in the most limited political and military events and their agents. Atwood leaves readers with the intriguing proposition that we who historically "precede" the tale could be superior exegetes to those who come after it (and us), *if* we are able to grasp what is important—that is, if we are able to realize that twenty pages of a computer printout would *not* reveal more about a culture than a lengthy personal narrative of an individual's interactions with her society. When the professor finishes his speech, the audience applauds, and the novel concludes with the query: "Are there any questions?" (311). Yes, plenty, readers say to themselves, beginning with: why did Atwood include this epilogue anyway?

Moreover, why does an essay on German cultural studies begin with a Canadian author's novel about a dystopic North America? I propose Atwood's "Historical Notes" as a kind of morality tale for those of us who are currently struggling with university curricular reform. In universities and colleges across North America the humanities and social sciences are losing ground to the traditionally named natural sciences, the so-called hard sciences. At my own "liberal arts" institution, the number of entering students declaring interest in the humanities and social sciences has dropped noticeably. On the federal scene the National Endowment for the Arts (NEA) and the National Endowment for the Humanities (NEH) continue to come under attack in budget and morality debates. Luckily for all of us, like Atwood, some intellectuals are sounding the alarm to look at what we are doing to ourselves in the academy and beyond. This is to be welcomed, for, as Gerald Graff has argued: "if the public furor over political correctness has shed more heat than light, it has at least proved that the gap between American culture and the ivory tower has closed. . . . Today's academic disputes . . . *mirror* broader social conflicts over race, ethnicity, and privilege" (9; emph. added). It is a good thing that the general population discusses what goes on in universities, and it is certainly also a good thing that academics engage issues currently being debated in the public arena.

For part of what is wrong with Atwood's scholars of the twenty-second century is that they do not see the connection between their scholarship and their society. In placing intellectual and social distance between themselves and Gilead, they fail to see the privileges and sexism in their own world. The novel's readers, on the other hand, are supposed to notice that it is the woman who introduces the male featured speaker (who, among other things, then makes sexist jokes) and that this Professor Pieixoto is director of the archives at Cambridge University (UK). In other words, it is still white, male professors from England who command the greatest respect, or at least get the prestigious jobs and plum speaking engagements. Furthermore, these scholars, male and female alike, seem blind to the limitations of their scholarly method: they simply do not uncover cultural knowledge by reading the Handmaid's tale. Even though Atwood suggests that a Gilead would come to an end, should we be concerned about her depiction of a totalitarian society based in one of the oldest homes of academia in North America, Cambridge, Massachusetts?[1] And should we be concerned that the culture that comes after it is still fundamentally sexist and probably racist? That is to say, should we be concerned about the possibility that we humans do not learn from history, even from its most gruesome chapters?

Recent events certainly imply that we should. The perpetration of ethnic cleansing in areas of the former Yugoslavia, increasing right-wing extremist violence in the United States, the worldwide tidal wave of refugees, continued persecution of would-be democratic reformers in the People's Republic of China, and recurring attacks against nonethnic Germans in the newly unified Germany provide some alarming evidence that humankind will hardly survive into, never mind through, the twenty-first century if we fail to learn more about culture: about the ways it informs and shapes human behavior both among members of one community large or small and also, even especially, in contact across communities. Nearly all societies in the world today are pluralistic; no society is truly monocultural, despite claims by some tyrants and ordinary bigots that it is so and despite familiar repressive actions to impose the pretended monoculturalism. Dwindling and contaminated natural resources, increasing populations, and new political demands confront contemporary societies with questions and problems for which we are still insufficiently prepared. And yet, while there remains much to learn about specific cultures and how individuals and communities imbibe, express, and shape culture, some thinkers have made significant progress in analyzing complicated cultural processes.

One set of developments from inside academia that holds promise has been broadly grouped under the rubric *cultural studies*. As is the case in many developing fields, the term has proliferated in conferences, book and course titles, academic press catalogs, and department or program names without clear definition. Indeed, cultural studies has been heralded and maligned by many who are frustratingly vague about the field they claim to praise or criticize. Like the recent debates on multiculturalism, critiques of cultural studies have been confusing and often vicious, fueled by emotions and polarized ideological presuppositions rather than intimate knowledge of the field's origins and internal developments. For some in today's academy, to title a book "German Cultural Studies" is a polemical act to which they will want to respond with hostility, perhaps by not reading it, perhaps by attacking it directly. But such reactions only reinforce the logic of this volume: to provide some clarifications and illustrations of methodology for the purpose of *facilitating reasoned debate*. Like Gerald Graff, the members of the team behind this book do not locate the problems of the American academy in controversy but, rather, in the ubiquitous American *fear of controversy,* which in turn leads to imposition or attempted imposition of one's own opinion as the only correct one (see Graff 8).[2] Therefore, in providing some background on cultural studies and a provisional framework for German cultural studies, I aim to spark the transformation spelled out in this volume's title: that readers will become *users,* employing this essay and those that follow as a departure point for continued exploration and debate.

Cultural Studies: Some Contours

In 1990 Stuart Hall, one of the founding fathers—and they were mainly fathers—of cultural studies, wrote that, "cultural studies is not one thing; it has never been one thing" ("Emergence" 11). Perhaps the most useful clues this nondefinition offers us are *not one* and the plural form *studies*. Because of this plural, I would modify Geoff Eley's helpfully compact definition of *cultural studies*—"a set of proposals with which to think" (24)—to: *sets* of proposals with which to think. The need to use these plurals becomes obvious upon even the most cursory consideration of the sources for cultural studies. As an academic endeavor its practices derive from the works of scholars as diverse as Hoggart, Williams, and their colleagues at the Birmingham Centre for Contemporary Cultural Studies; Adorno, Horkheimer, and the Frankfurt School; such poststructuralists as Barthes, Foucault, and Bourdieu; rediscovered marxists like Gramsci, Benjamin, and Althusser; and North American scholars who emphasize identity politics and popular culture. One immediately perceives that cultural studies claims a genealogy of partly incompatible and even antithetical views about the nature of culture, its production and consumption. While I do not intend to give a historical overview of the development of cultural studies—

this has been done well elsewhere—I would like to approach my task of orienting the reader by surveying some contours that seem to dominate the terrain of this field and to be most germane to the kind of cultural studies demonstrated in this volume.[3] The most prominent contour might rightly be cultural studies' relation to disciplinarity.

1.   Cultural Studies and Traditional Disciplines

Shaping the relationship of cultural studies to traditional disciplines has been what Lynn Hunt evocatively calls the "bad odor" of discipline itself since the 1960s and particularly since Foucault's investigations into the nature of power and institutions (Hunt 2). The negative side of what might be considered the neutral division of labor and taxonomic activity—that is, of "disciplines"—is revealed in the inevitable connection to power and control. Significantly, what may be said to distinguish the books identified most closely with the launching of cultural studies from previous works by the same authors and from other studies produced at the same time is their refusal to follow single disciplinary pursuits. Roland Barthes's *Mythologies* (1957), Richard Hoggart's *Uses of Literacy* (1958), Raymond Williams's *Culture and Society* (1958) and *The Long Revolution* (1961), and E. P. Thompson's *Making of the English Working Class* (1963) use lessons learned from literary analysis, history, social theory, anthropology, and more, and yet each speaks a critique of these disciplines. Over the years, then, cultural studies has developed into a "bricolage," with no distinct methodology of its own, since it "draws from whatever fields are necessary to produce the knowledge required for a particular project" (Nelson et al. 2; also see Gilman 202). Furthermore, "to do something interdisciplinary," Barthes reminds us, "it's not enough to choose a 'subject' (a theme) and gather around it two or three sciences. Interdisciplinarity consists in creating a new object that belongs to no one" (qtd. in Clifford 1). An additional response to the traditions of disciplinarity has been the preponderance of collaborative work in cultural studies. Indeed, collaboration aids greatly in approaching the polysemous, if not elusive, concept of "culture," to turn to the other component in the name of our field (see Pratt 63).

2.   Culture as an Object of Study

Like the diversity indicated by the plural form *studies,* the broad semantic range of the word *culture* points us toward some features of the field itself. Though this very broadness poses almost insurmountable intellectual challenges—Williams has claimed: "I've wished that I had never heard of the damned word. I have become more aware of its difficulties, not less, as I have gone on" ("Politics" 154)—it also spurs creativity through freedom. Richard Johnson flaunts the word's adaptability when he says: "I fly culture's flag . . . and continue to use the word where imprecision matters" (qtd. in Brantlinger 37).

Webster's relevant definitions of the word *culture* already begin to demonstrate just how diverse the concept is: from the pedagogical ("the act of developing the intellectual and moral faculties") to the personal ("acquaintance with and taste in fine arts, humanities, and broad aspects of science as distinguished from vocational and technical skills") to the epistemological ("integrated pattern of human knowledge, belief, and behavior that depends upon man's capacity for learning and transmitting knowledge to succeeding generations") to the communal ("the customary beliefs, social forms, and material traits of a racial, religious, or social group") (*Webster's Ninth Collegiate Dictionary*). A foundational move of the cultural studies project was a refusal to equate *culture* with *high culture*. Indeed, Raymond Williams provocatively proclaimed that culture is "ordinary." One of the ways in which Williams perceived culture as ordinary is production: it "is made and remade in every individual mind" ("Culture Is Ordinary" 4). But this belief in personal agency, it should be pointed out, conflicts with the Frankfurt School's culture industry thesis: that mass culture is saturated with imposed meaning and that individuals are highly manipulable.[4] The Birmingham School achieved a kind of synthesis between the starting points of Williams, on the one hand, and Adorno and Horkheimer, on the other; as Stuart Hall explains, British cultural studies "defines 'culture' as *both* the meanings and values which arise amongst distinctive groups and classes, on the basis of their given historical conditions and relationships through which they 'handle' and respond to the conditions of existence; *and* as the lived traditions and practices through which these 'understandings' are expressed and in which they are embodied" ("Two Paradigms" 527). This recognition of culture as a social signifying practice accords with similar concerns in ethnography, a field on which cultural studies has drawn extensively for inspiration and methodology. For ethnographers culture "is always relational, an inscription of communicative processes that exist, historically, *between* subjects in relations of power" (Clifford 15). In sum, in taking culture as its object of study, cultural studies engages "the political, economic, erotic, social, and ideological"; it "entails the study of all the relations between all the elements in a whole way of life" (Nelson et al. 14). While on a practical level such a project can never be completed, cultural studies proponents continue to aim for the whole picture in reaction to the demarcation and decontextualization of traditional academic disciplines.

3.   Texts and Contexts

Taking culture as an object of study profoundly affects how we think about and value "text" and "context." As Brantlinger has pointed out:

On the one hand, for those in literary fields, culture is by any definition a beyond-the-text, if by text is understood a work of literature taken in isolation from history and society—that is, pried loose from its contexts. On the other, the stress on culture—"culturalism," as it is sometimes called—involves a rejection or at least revision of the old base/superstructure paradigm in Marxist theory as well as of the more sharply "causal" and reductive features of other literary and social theories such as psychoanalysis and structuralism. The cultural studies trend has been away from formalist literary criticism, history, and the isolated social science disciplines toward forms of "ethnographic" analysis. (36)

Brantlinger makes it perfectly clear that cultural studies is averse to disciplinary practices that hold that texts are interpretable in and of themselves. But, to point to one of the excesses in some cultural studies treatises, it would be foolish to think that context or culture could be seriously analyzed without careful attention to text. In their enthusiastic proclamation of how different cultural studies is from what has gone on before, Nelson, Treichler, and Grossberg injudiciously declare that, "although there is no prohibition against close textual readings in cultural studies, they are also not required" (2). Even a cursory look at their own anthology will show that convincing cultural studies projects contain careful—close—reading of some kind of text. The definition of what counts as worthy of being studied (text) has surely been shifted by cultural studies, but the value of careful analysis has not (see Turner 87–130). I suggest that it is more fruitful and accurate to say that designating culture as the object of analysis has redirected the vectors of academic endeavors, precipitating an inward turn: practices of self-scrutiny (academia as a culture [McCabe, qtd. in Brantlinger 36]); and an outward one: connecting texts with contexts, disciplines with one another, and the academy with society at large.

4.   Cultural Studies and the Political

In a broad sense cultural studies is interested not only in "the political" as an object of study, that is, in investigating politics in relation to the other elements that constitute a culture; it is also interested in interrogating its own practice as a political act. Cultural studies practitioners recognize themselves and what they do as interwoven with the fabric of contemporary culture. Thus, cultural studies is "political," since it posits its own intellectual work as making a difference (Nelson et al. 6). To return to the pluralism with which I began this review: though cultural studies is an open project, "it does matter whether cultural studies is this or that. It can't be just any old thing which chooses to march under a particular banner. . . . [T]here is something *at stake*" (Hall, "Theoretical Legacies" 278).

One of the ways in which cultural studies tries to make a difference is by showing just what is "at stake" in the world around us, that is, by naming and investigating categories that are inherently relevant to contemporary societies. Theoretical concepts that have occupied center stage in much of the work that comes under the cultural studies umbrella include: articulation, conjuncture, gender, habitus, hegemony, identity, ideology, power, race, representation, and sexuality. From its central concerns it is clear that cultural studies has learned from and often intersects with fields like African-American studies, ethnography, feminist theory, gender studies, lesbian and gay studies, new historicism, and some aspects of poststructuralist literary theory. It would be important to specify in conjunction with such lists that, though cultural studies, especially in its nascent stage, was closely associated with marxism and the New Left, its strongest proponents insist that it cannot and should not be identified with any one political position (see Hall, "Theoretical Legacies" 278). Nonetheless, cultural studies (along with other fields and universities in general) has been charged by undiscriminating critics, among other things, with the politicization of the classroom. The accusation is a patently false one in the sense that the classroom has always been a political space in which power and ideology are contested. But this assessment would be correct if it were meant to point to the way cultural studies refuses to let the category of the political—that is, of waging and contesting power—become invisible. Internal struggles around questions of gender and race have put and kept the interrogation of power on the cultural studies agenda (see hooks 124; Hall, "Theoretical Legacies" 282–83; During 15–16). One of the particularly poignant contributions of British cultural studies in this regard has been its strong commitment to pedagogy, not only in general but also in its associations with the Open Universities, offering higher education opportunities to individuals who in previous eras never would have done postsecondary work.

5.   Popular Culture and the Canon

One aspect of the charge of cultural studies' politicization of the classroom is the idea that cultural studies rejects "canons," that is, the texts that traditionally have structured any given discipline. Based on the previous brief forays into culture as an object of study and the role of the political, I wager that such an accusation arises in reaction to cultural studies' interest in cultural artifacts more broadly defined than standard canonical texts and in reaction to cultural studies' rejection of the notion of completely disinterested analysis; aesthetics exists as a category, to be sure, but not in an apolitical vacuum. Although I concentrate here on the example of the literary canon, similar arguments can be constructed for canons of other fields, such as history, political science, philosophy, and religion, to mention just a few.[5] Casting a brief glance at the popular culture/literary canon debate allows a review of the contours of cultural studies singled out earlier and demonstrates the value of rejecting preconceived ideas about cultural studies. Since the various dimensions of this issue have been in the public forum so frequently, an adumbration of the controversy should suffice.

Any approach to a cultural object that does not consider that object in relation to the society in which it was produced *and* to the society in which the analysis takes place would be alien to cultural studies. The object in itself does not have inherent aesthetic or intellectual properties. Rather, societies label objects with designations such as "beautiful," "transcendent," "good," and "truthful," and one type of cultural studies project would be to question what is invested in those designations. Alternately, cultural studies has been particularly associated with the analysis of—and I use the term as a convenient shorthand only—popular culture. This is not because there is anything necessarily more appropriate about analyzing less hegemonic forms of cultural production but, rather, because, at least since Williams's articulation of the idea in *Culture and Society,* cultural studies has been concerned with "the everyday terrain of people, and with all the ways that cultural practices speak to, of, and for their lives" (Nelson et al. 11; also see Brantlinger 37). Furthermore, it is often easier to detect the dynamics of authority by focusing on what is contested by a society rather than on what is accepted by one. Thus, some of the most notable works in cultural studies to date have dealt with the cultural practices of marginal groups (e.g., Hebdige's work on lower-class British youth), with popular art forms (e.g., Radway's work on popular romance), and with the mass media (e.g., Modleski's work on soap operas).

On the other hand, cultural studies is not nor should be defined (at least not exclusively) by its object of study. Were literature departments to make a wholesale commitment to popular literature, they would still not be "doing cultural studies," for they would probably be asking the wrong questions. Nelson, Treichler, and Grossberg point in the right direction when they explain that:

> Cultural studies does not require us to repudiate elite cultural forms—or simply to acknowledge with Bourdieu (1984), that distinctions between elite and popular cultural forms are themselves the products of relations of power. Rather, cultural studies requires us *to identify the operation of specific practices,* of how they continuously reinscribe the line between legitimate and popular culture, and of what they accomplish in specific contexts. (13; emph. added)

Thus, cultural studies does not "exclude" the canon—though some people believe this and use it as a reason to dismiss the cultural studies project.[6] What cultural studies has proposed is that we ask (different) questions of the canon.

A cultural studies approach to the canon would foreground, in Dominick LaCapra's phrase, "how implausible it is to maintain that texts simply read themselves" (129; also see Lennox 167). To offer one brief concrete example, in approaching a canonical text, say Schiller's *Wallenstein,* the question is not: what are the aesthetic qualities of this work that make it part of Arnold's "the best that has been thought and written"? But, rather: what are the qualities of this text admired by readers in the late eighteenth and nineteenth centuries that made them think of it as expressing absolute "beauty" or "truth" in a way that they believed transcended the historical moment in which it was written or in which it was being read? The distinction between these two questions is critical to understanding the spirit of cultural studies.[7] Again, the cultural studies project does not assume that the text "is" beautiful (or truthful, good, etc.); it asks why the text was, and perhaps still is, *considered* beautiful and by whom. It might also ask how beauty functioned as a category for a particular culture at a particular point in time. What cultural forms were excluded by this definition? Further: if a text was in the canon, what did that mean about who read it, when, and why? What historical, political, or institutional forces might have pushed a text out of the canon at a later point in time?

A different but related investigation of canonical texts might begin with the question of how knowledge that a text is part of the traditional literary canon affects the way it is read. Inversely, one can ask what aspects of the text might resist or undermine its being read as canonical. In this spirit we as teachers must not only acknowledge but also expose the fact that our very act of putting a book (film, video, piece of music) on a syllabus itself functions as a kind of canonization for our students. We need to help our students become aware of their own reading practices. In summary one could say that cultural studies by no means denies the existence of canons; rather, it asks: what is the cultural, ideological, and political work that canons do? Along such lines of questioning, so-called high literature via the study of canons undoubtedly has a place in a cultural studies curriculum.[8]

Though the notion of cultural studies we are putting forth in this volume disallows definition per se, I would like to conclude this section with a capacious description to complement the two concise ones with which I began:

> cultural studies is an interdisciplinary, transdisciplinary, and sometimes counter-disciplinary field that operates in the tension between its tendencies to embrace both a broad, anthropological and a more narrowly humanistic conception of culture. Unlike traditional anthropology, however, it has grown out of analyses of modern industrial societies. It is typically interpretive and evaluative in its methodologies, but unlike traditional humanism it rejects the exclusive equation of culture with high culture and argues that all forms of cultural production need to be studied in relation

to other cultural practices and to social and historical structures. Cultural studies is thus committed to the study of the entire range of a society's arts, beliefs, institutions, and communicative practices. (Nelson et al. 4)

German Studies as German Cultural Studies

So far there has been little dialogue between North American practitioners of cultural studies and German scholars, broadly speaking. One indication of this is that in the largest compendium to date of cultural studies essays there are no contributions focusing on German topics (see Grossberg et al.). Similarly indicative of the distance between the two fields, numerous commentators from "within" German studies have argued that (most of) their colleagues in their home disciplines are behind the times with respect to theoretical developments like cultural studies.

In the late 1980s the DAAD (Deutscher Akademischer Austauschdienst; German Academic Exchange Service) sponsored a series of conferences to discuss "new approaches" to German studies. In each of the three published volumes that resulted, one finds lamentations about the "belatedness"—a seemingly perennial German problem—of response to theoretical developments in other fields and calls to vigorous interdisciplinary endeavors in the German field. For example, historians Michael Geyer and Konrad Jarausch offer the following criticism of their discipline:

> German History has not only given little credit to the country's proverbial poets and thinkers, but it has also been stunningly negligent in considering "texts" and their meaning as historical artifacts. Yet we are told, second- and third-hand, that German thought ever since the eighteenth century was deeply concerned, even obsessed with problems of signification. German historiography, in other words, has desisted from reflecting on its own and its subjects' condition which had experienced, time and again, the collapse of language in the face of "reality." The origin of German history and its continuous fascination with linguistic realism appear, in this light, as efforts to neutralize an unmasterable and unspeakable present—the rapid succession of political ruptures in which one regime of signification followed the other. ("Future of German Past" 247)

Geyer and Jarausch's view of the historical profession reminds us of the portrait of Atwood's twenty-second-century scholars, who do not know how to glean cultural knowledge from the texts around them and who resist interrogating themselves.

In a similarly critical vein Peter Hohendahl summarizes the proceedings of the literary conference by citing Germanists' "adherence to a rather rigid definition of its legitimate field of study in terms of the traditional extrinsic/intrinsic opposition" (228). Hohendahl continues:

> In spite of the widespread assault on literary studies during the years of the student movement, the majority of German departments in this country have continued to define their programs in terms of the accepted literary canon, adding civilization and film courses in the margins to make the program more appealing to a new generation of students. With respect to the centrality of the literary canon, new critics and (old) historicists tend to agree, since both their projects are based on notions of ultimately self-evident aesthetic and moral values expressed in the German literary tradition. (228–29)

But Hohendahl, like the other participants at the Germanists' conference, is sanguine that this attitude is already changing on the part of some within the field: "The idea of a self-confined literary tradition appears to be a decisive marker; proponents of interdisciplinary German Studies no longer adhere to this doctrine" (229). Thus, these proceedings mark a shift from criticism of the past and resistant colleagues to the forward-looking "reconceptualization of German Studies as a critical and interdisciplinary set of activities" (Taubeneck 220).[9]

Despite the sincerity and intelligence of these analyses and proposals, it is in itself symptomatic of the "German" problem that no one remarked on the fact that literary scholars (*GermanistInnen*), historians (*HistorikerInnen*), and political scientists (*PolitikwissenschaftlerInnen*) assiduously conducted and published their deliberations separately.[10] Despite the ubiquitous calls for interdisciplinarity, there was no self-reflection—at least not in the published record—on the common training of all participants at each conference.[11] This should be attributed at least in part to the continuing vigor of the disciplinary model.[12] Even when discussing interdisciplinarity, one does so from within a discipline. Of course, the German government's willingness to fund three separate conferences also contributed to this odd state of affairs.

By insisting in this volume on the term *German cultural studies,* the participants in this project are trying to honor the great amount of conceptual work accomplished in the past under the rubric "German studies."[13] But we are also trying to accelerate the gains of the present moment in the reconceptualization of the field by explicitly linking German studies with the now long and rich development of the field of cultural studies. To date there has been little circulation of the term *German cultural studies* to designate an interdisciplinary field investigating topics in German culture distinct from German studies.[14] We are promoting this new term for practical and polemical reasons, cognizant that naming is not an innocent act. German history offers a superfluity of lessons in the ideological power of names, not the least of which is the invention of the concepts "German," "Germans," and "Germany."[15] An example even closer to the academic orientation of this book is the sometimes sinister path of the development of *Germanistik* (German literary studies, called by some "Germanics" in the North American academy), from Herder's and the Grimm Brothers' original insistence on the existence of a specifically German spirit that was expressed in certain artistic forms to the gradual development of an academic field called *Germanistik* to the Nazi-mandated transformation of *Germanistik* into *Deutschkunde* (something like *Germanology*) and then into *Deutschwissenschaft als Organ des deutschen Selbstverständnisses* (the science of Germanness as an agent of German self-understanding).[16] It is precisely because of the burden of such pasts, to paraphrase Bate, that a new term has a particular appeal for those of us who occupy ourselves with "things German."

But, if we are promoting a new term, it must not be just to rename what we are already doing nor just to cash in on the current excitement and popularity of a dynamically developing new field. We have already had to parry colleagues' charges of following fashion.[17] Name changes surely should only follow or accompany structural curricular changes. And modifications in how we teach and conduct our research should respond to ontological and epistemological transformations outside the academy. So what will it take for German studies to become German cultural studies, and why should that happen now?

First of all, it should be noted that the DAAD-sponsored conferences of the late 1980s, and a series of others that I do not have space to mention here, demonstrate that at least a portion of the profession *is engaged already* in the self-examination Geyer and Jarausch charged was lacking more widely.[18] As Hohendahl pointed out, German literary scholars in fact have begun to restructure their curricula fundamentally. What I and the team behind this book propose as the differentiating criterion between German studies as it has been practiced in the last decades and what we want to call German cultural studies is *interdisciplinarity,* as opposed to what has been most in evidence to date: *multidisciplinarity.* In working toward genuinely interdisciplinary approaches to problems, a first step clearly involves getting the literary scholars and the political scientists and the historians—even some "outsider" journalists—into the same room. This was a foundational principle in preparing this volume and, it appears, of some other recent colloquia such as the "Cultural History" conference held at Harvard University's Center for European Studies in spring 1994.[19] But this is not sufficient. Nor will it be sufficient to add new objects to the corpus, a comic book to the literature or history course reading list, so to speak.[20] In actually meeting together and in looking at new (and old) objects of inquiry, we must also reconsider to whom we are addressing ourselves (see hooks 128). Furthermore, we must take "other projects and questions seriously enough to do the work—theoretical and analytical—required to understand and position specific cultural practices. *This interdisciplinarity thus poses difficult questions:* what and how much must be learned from other fields to enable us sufficiently to contextualize our object of study for a given project?" (Nelson et al. 15; emph. added). To avoid dilettantism teachers and scholars must work hard to reeducate themselves about other disciplinary practices. Finding the time to do this kind of reeducation is difficult, given increasingly heavy teaching loads and continuing demands for specialization and publishing in almost all American institutions of higher learning.[21]

In attempting this kind of hard work with uncertain outcomes, we should prepare for discomfort; longtime practitioner of cultural studies Stuart Hall testifies that: "cultural studies has drawn the attention [to] itself, not just because of its sometimes dazzling internal theoretical developments, but because it holds theoretical and political questions in an *ever irresolvable but permanent tension*. It constantly allows the one to irritate, bother, and disturb the other, without insisting on some final theoretical closure" (Hall, "Theoretical Legacies" 284; emph. added). If we rely on Hall's experience, we must "resist the quest for harmony" (comment attributed to Isabel Hull, in Link 456)—a quest that seems to haunt the interstices of discussions among scholars of German to date. In addition to preparing for creative tension, we might learn from cultural studies that, in reconstituting our field, we will inevitably set up new hierarchies (see Hohendahl 231) and that these new relations must themselves be interrogated to avoid new orthodoxies (see During 20; Turner 4). Peck surely has this lesson in mind when he observes: "we can see how the realignments in our own discipline—between *Germanistik* and German Studies—set up new arrangements of power. In short, we are in the process of remapping our discipline—with the emendation, however, that in these disciplinary realignments we will take into account from the beginning the meaning of our collaboration and coexistence with those who administrate power, such as tenure committees and editorial boards" (182). By embracing a cultural studies model, we embrace Proteus. "Creative tensions" that arise from studying one problem will undeniably take on a different form in approaching another. In other words, we must realize that cultural studies does not offer *a* theory that we can just transfer to the German cultural context; each new cultural context will itself suggest a particular methodological constellation (see Nelson et al. 7; also Turner 1, 4, 11).

Fortunately, there are numerous signs that we are now moving in these directions. The German Studies Association continues to grow; there is an impressive array of disciplines represented at the annual conferences, even if cross-disciplinary attendance at panels remains limited. And the organization's journal, the *German Studies Review,* prints diverse types of analyses, including some that are truly interdisciplinary. *New German Critique* and *German Politics and Society* maintain high standards in publishing fine interdisciplinary articles. Some undergraduate German literature departments have been transformed—and not just in name—into interdisciplinary programs.[22] The first graduate students with genuinely interdisciplinary training are completing their dissertations (e.g., at Duke and the University of Michigan), and, while it is still too early to know their fate on the job market, it is encouraging to know that a few university departments are making cross-disciplinary appointments.[23] We hope that the publication of this volume will support and further such transformations.

It would be misleading, however, to end this section on a triumphal note. Though I am cautiously hopeful about our ability to transform our profession into a politically engaged, intellectually rigorous new field—and working on this volume has only made me more hopeful—I feel a responsibility to point out some of the ways in which the disciplinary model continues to undermine efforts at change. Even as recently as 1994, one notices a distinct ambivalence in calls to interdisciplinarity. Numerous examples of this ambivalence can be located in the report of the proceedings of a conference on *Germanistik*.[24] Although it appears that there were several excellent papers presented at this gathering, it is discouraging to note that, once again, Germanists were talking about interdisciplinarity among themselves.[25] To my mind, the most worrisome point of "universal agreement" that emerged from the conference runs as follows: "enhanced interdisciplinarity and multiculturalism must not entail the loss of cultural heritage(s) which gave rise to *Germanistik* in the first place" (McCarthy, "Prospects" 3). Among other things, what I read in this dictum is that, while departments may find it necessary to "add" material to the curriculum, they must be careful not to "replace" what we already know, love, and teach.[26] To be sure, transformations already effected by new approaches to the humanities are evidenced in this statement through the inclusion (and presumed acceptance, if not embrace, by conference attendees) of the ideas of "interdisciplinarity" and "multiculturalism," as well as through the curious "(s)" added to "heritage." But the overall message can only be read as a warning: don't throw out the baby with the bathwater. The specter of popular culture is still lurking, goes the argument: if we teach *Flugblätter* (pamphlet literature), songs, movies, novels by Turks, we won't have enough time for Goethe. Furthermore, despite that fragile "(s)," the statement implies that there is one great cultural heritage; we all agree on what it is because we all love it; and we have got to protect it, because its loss could be precipitated by those interlopers, interdisciplinarity and multiculturalism.

My other example stems from the Harvard conference previously cited, at which, fortunately, multidisciplinary representation was not a problem. While I find *very* much in the proceedings that makes me sanguine about the possibility of substantive change in the direction of German cultural studies as we are proposing it here, there are specters of accusation in the rhetoric of the introduction of the published proceedings that lead me to believe that we still need to serve as watchdogs to ourselves. Since Czaplicka, Huyssen, and Rabinbach present this part of their argument as a frontal attack on cultural studies—"which simply has not yet delivered the goods" (5)—I quote at length:

> Premature anti-disciplinarity is a major problem when it leads to the abandonment of the archive and the object, to ignoring traditional cultural forms, to the shunning of close reading, and to the forgetting of anything but the currently or formerly popular. . . .The reservations expressed (and often heard at the conference) by historians and literary critics who insist on some grounding in "disciplinarity" are not entirely inappropriate. Rather than problematizing and working through traditional dichotomies such as text/context, high culture/low culture, fact/fiction, or modernity/postmodernity, cultural studies all too often simply reverses the plus and minus signs in the name of transgression and subversion. . . . Postmodernity and its concerns with the important issues of gender, class, race, and sexuality is [*sic*] seen as a panacea while all the ills of the world are blamed on modernity and Eurocentrism. (5–6)

The most disturbing strategy of this passage is its setting up of strawmen—and presumably strawwomen. Which are the cultural studies projects that "all too often" engage in antidisciplinarity and reversal of values for the simple sake of transgression? Who writes them? Is this a pitchfork thrown at our colleagues in American studies? A covert appeal for Eurocentrism? If so, let us agree that promotion of our field need not come at the expense of another.

While the authors' points about "premature anti-disciplinarity," careful documentation, and close reading are well-taken, they need not have expressed their views in confrontational prose that is itself negligent about documenting the facts.[27] There is no doubt that shabby pieces of scholarship have been published under the rubric "cultural studies," as unsubstantial work has been published under "history," "literary criticism," or "political science." But to counter celebrations of cultural studies with denigrations is also simply to reverse the plus and minus signs. Furthermore, rhetorical exaggeration invites scrutiny of one's own scholarship. The authors should cite the works that call postmodernity a "panacea" and that blame Eurocentrism for "*all* the ills of the world." When produced, these studies should be decried. There is a place for polemics, and my own essay has been written intentionally in a polemical vein. If we are to take the next step, however, we must begin by granting one another respect (at least until it is proved unwarranted), and we must back up our positions with careful documentation, clear definitions of terms, close readings, and appropriate rhetoric. These were our guidelines for contributions to *A User's Guide to German Cultural Studies*. Such guidelines represent an effort to take "other projects and questions seriously enough to do the work required," the task called for by Nelson, Treichler, and Grossberg and mentioned earlier. In a spirit of collegiality I want to emphasize that my critique of one passage in the Czaplicka, Huyssen, Rabinbach introduction is not intended as a dismissal of this insightful piece nor of this extremely useful and sophisticated special issue. Rather, it is an effort to warn us that we should fall neither into Hull's harmony trap nor into the disrespect and self-righteousness traps.

What Is at Stake?

Mary Louise Pratt points to three historical processes that should resonate loudly for those of us who teach cultural studies: globalization, democratization, and decolonization (59). James Clifford is gesturing at the same phenomena as Pratt (and as Atwood, for that matter, albeit in a very different form), when he writes in his introduction to the influential *Writing Culture* (1986):

> We ground things now, on a moving earth. There is no longer any place of overview (mountaintop) from which to represent the world. Mountains are in constant motion. So are islands: for one cannot occupy, unambiguously, a bounded cultural world from which to journey out and analyze other cultures. Human ways of life increasingly influence, dominate, parody, translate, and subvert one another. Cultural analysis is always enmeshed in global movements of difference and power. However one defines it, and the phrase is here used loosely, a "world system" now links the planet's societies in a common historical process. (22)

That the nature of the world has changed, and that we are irrevocably linked to one another, may seem so self-evident as to not warrant mention. And yet we endanger ourselves and all others if we refuse this knowledge and carry on as we have to date.

It would be inexcusably chauvinistic to argue that nowhere in the world is the case for cross-cultural understanding as clear as in contemporary Germany. But surely it is accurate to say that recent events in Central Europe demonstrate the greater and greater implausibility of monoculturalism—precisely because of the disastrous consequences of the search for it. Unification of the two Germanies has only sharpened the questions: what is German? how do we live together? how do we live with our neighbors? With the collapse of Western and Eastern postwar hegemonies and the emergence of "Europe" as an ever more unified political and economic entity, not only the internal but also the external balances of power are shifting; Germany can neither be an island nor survey the rest of the world from the mountaintop, to borrow Clifford's metaphors. As Geyer and Jarausch summarize, "Most Germans experienced the collapse of communism and the reunion of the German states as a partly exhilarating, partly frightening return of history" ("Great Men" 263). In other words, Germany must "participate" in history once again, and not the least frightening aspect of that participation is the forced encounter with diversity. Precisely at a moment when many Germans want to claim some sort of positive cohesive national political identity, events like the influx of hundreds of thousands of refugees, the fiftieth anniversary of the defeat of the Nazis in World War II, and even the release of Spielberg's epic film of the Holocaust remind them of things they might rather put behind them; neither the past nor the present will allow the Germans to retreat into isolationism.[28]

What are the consequences of such events for scholars of the German scene? Clearly, there is no going back: "Even if traditionalists reclaim some ground in the current culture wars, the very conditions for the old verities, canons, and methods are gone and the effort to restore them takes on an artificial and, in the Prussian image, 'reactionary,' antimodern quality." In the case of historiography, Geyer and Jarausch remind their colleagues, surely American "tutelage" is over and it is time to move into "a future that will have a different past" ("Great Men" 266, 267, 269).

American Germanists would do well to follow similar advice. Not only because, if cultural studies is right, the historical and the literary are inexorably linked. But, even more self-interestedly, because the old ways are simply of little interest to the vast majority of American students. If Germanists have led the way in thinking about German studies, this has been at least in part as a reaction to declines in enrollments of German language and literature courses. And, indeed, initial discussions of German studies were launched in the early 1970s in a period of diminishing student interest (see Lützeler 139). Despite a brief surge following the fall of the Berlin Wall, numbers are once again dropping ("Result" 2). Clearly, *Nazis* and the *Holocaust* still attract large numbers to German history courses and to the literature departments, where courses that include the Third Reich are offered—a phenomenon that should be investigated as much for what it says about American culture as for what it may reveal about German culture.[29] On the other hand, the increasingly widespread student suspicion of the viability as well as the efficacy of acquiring *Bildung* (cultivation) through reading "the classics" has shrunk most other German department courses (Seeba 146).

External pressures such as major political realignments and the market of student interest certainly offer compelling motivation for change. But not to be discounted or ignored are real pressures from within, Pratt's "democratization." While the first decades of the postwar era found German departments and historians of German history populated with various persuasions of German "émigrés," that is simply no longer the case. Although burgeoning student bodies at German public universities from the 1970s to the present account for a new generation of German academics in the United States, a comparison of North American department rosters now and twenty years ago (or a look at the roster for this volume) reveals that those of us who teach things German come from varied ethnic backgrounds and are mainly trained in this country. If not quite as multicultural as, say, a current faculty of English, we are no longer all native German speakers. Many of us like to be "clear up front" and assert with Sander Gilman: "I am not a German, nor do I wish to be one" (192). One of the consequences of the substantial presence of those who, like myself, first came to German out of academic interest rather than "very specific personal motivation," as Hinrich Seeba points out, is that we are "not restricted by either a positive or a negative identification with German society" (146). But this is not to say that our subject positions have no impact on what and how we teach. There is a critical—in the many senses of the word—role for native Germans (Austrians, Swiss) in American academic departments.[30] And, as Arlene Teraoka, Jeffrey Peck, and others have suggested, we can use our difference and our displacement (from one another and from those who teach our subjects in German-speaking countries) to teach us and others new things (see Teraoka 189; Peck 183). Sara Lennox, taking her cue from feminist theory, similarly argues for the multiple values of diversity: "Since we are not unitary subjects—we also inhabit contradictory locations and are subject to conflicting pressures—as historical agents we have the option of taking various political stances and defending various political positions, in our literary analysis as well as in more obvious forms of political practice. Openly declaring our allegiances is one form of accountability to our comrades, brothers, and sisters" (167). It is precisely the issue of difference and politics that leads me to my final point.

What, then, do Atwood, Pratt, Clifford—cultural studies—have to do with the study of German? If Pratt is right, and globalization, democratization, and decolonization continue to be the forces that shape our world most dramatically, any and all of us who teach about other cultures, and who by virtue of that teaching are ourselves bi- or multicultural, are poised to make the *biggest* contribution to our students' ability to deal with the "real" (i.e., multicultural) world. As Pratt argues, the fact that peoples everywhere are learning English should not be interpreted as the triumph of English but as the sovereignty of being "fluent" in more than one language/culture.[31] Rather than apologize about our trafficking in another culture, then, we need to make the case most strongly to our students and our administrations "that this is no time to be monolingual." We need to present German cultural studies as "an especially hospitable space for the cultivation of multilingualism, polyglossia, the arts of cultural mediation, deep intercultural understanding, and genuinely global consciousness" (Pratt 62). Along these lines, it is imperative to point out that, no matter how governments and cultural commentators tried or try to portray the common denominator, the reality of Germany (as of any other large social unit) is diversity; Switzerland and Austria offer poignant cases, which German scholars should explore more often. We also need to remind ourselves that, regardless of Luther's stunning achievement, even "the German language" is not one (see Seyhan). Our very subject positions, as Americans (Germans, Jews, Australians, Dutch, Japanese, Greeks, Israelis, Italians—hyphenated or not) teaching about German culture in the United States, thematize the ubiquity of intercultural negotiations. What we have to do is question ourselves, what we are doing, and the connection of our work to the society in which we live, so that we do not become Atwood's scholars of the twenty-second century. The essays in this volume demonstrate that, fortunately, many of us are already engaged in this process.

NOTES

1. Note that Mexico has an older tradition.

2. For a similar line of thought, see Geyer and Jarausch: "It is not postmodern thought, but the manicured unwillingness to think which destroys higher education" ("Great Men" 256).

3. For information on the history of cultural studies, readers are referred foremost to During's excellent introduction to his anthology *The Cultural Studies Reader* (1–25); to Brantlinger's *Crusoe's Footprints,* particularly chaps. 1–2; and to the introduction to Grossberg, Nelson, and Treichler's compendium, *Cultural Studies* (1–22). While my review of cultural studies here constitutes neither a history nor an exhaustive survey, it *is* meant to orient readers who are beginning their exploration of the field; that is to say, its content is intentionally basic. Additional further reading is suggested in the annotated bibliography on cultural studies in the last section of this volume. My topographical metaphors are meant to echo recent turns to anthropology and geography for analytical paradigms (e.g., Peck).

4. See Adorno and Horkheimer; also During's helpful remarks (29–30); and Burns's analysis (108).

5. On the assumed politicization of today's university and the "leftist" rejection of traditional literary canons, see Howe. For a general theoretical discussion of the function of canons in today's academy written by a historian, see LaCapra.

6. Despite the charges against U.S. educational institutions, it should be noted that, for better or for worse, today's high school and college students "are apparently reading pretty much the same things their parents did" (Applebome, B8; newspaper article based on a recent surveys by the College Board and the Modern Language Association). This confirms Barbara Herrnstein Smith's statement three years prior, that "teachers still assign, explicate, and celebrate works by those still-honored writers whose portraits still adorn department halls and office walls" (6).

7. To offer a "concrete" example of the former position: in his defense of the traditional Western literary canon Irving Howe anthropomorphizes the university as follows: "The university is saying to its incoming students: 'Here are some sources of wisdom and beauty that have survived the centuries. In time you may choose to abandon them, but first learn something about them'" (44). A cultural studies approach might modify his contention by suggesting to students: "Here are some texts that have been consid-

ered sources of wisdom and beauty by Western elites over the centuries. You may choose to consider them so too, but first learn something about what values and ideologies were reinforced by granting them transcendent stature."

8. One critic even goes so far as to assign the study of canons exclusively to the field of cultural studies (see Riffaterre 71).

9. There remains, unfortunately, much ambivalence toward interdisciplinarity within the profession. See my analysis later in this essay.

10. Each conference, as mentioned earlier, was sponsored by the DAAD. The literary scholars met in conjunction with the annual meeting of the German Studies Association in Philadelphia in October 1988 and published their results the following spring in the *German Quarterly,* a journal with an almost exclusively literary focus, received at the time by all members of the American Association of Teachers of German ("Germanistik as German Studies: Interdisciplinary Theories and Methods" 62.2 [Spring 1989]). The political scientists and sociologists met similarly in conjunction with the annual meeting of the American Political Science Association in Atlanta in September 1989 and published their results in a special issue of the *German Studies Review,* the official journal of the German Studies Association and one of the few journals that truly does publish articles written from a variety of disciplinary as well as interdisciplinary perspectives ("DAAD Special Issue" 13 [1990]). The historians met last at the University of Chicago in October 1989, and published their deliberations under the title "German Histories: Challenges in Theory, Practice, Technique" in *Central European History,* probably the most important English-language journal of German history (22.3–4 [September–December 1989]; note that, despite the date, the issue actually appeared in 1990, and thus there are additional comments reflecting on how the events of fall 1989 in Germany affect the analyses offered and the future course of German historiography).

11. This is not to say there was no self-reflection on this issue at all. Jere Link, in his protocol of the historians' debate, for example, does comment on insiders and outsiders, though with regard to theoretical orientation, rather than disciplinary training. Specifically, he mentions the general agreement among participants that "old 'fixities' had to be re-evaluated in the light of post-modern challenges" and, further, that "all who might have disagreed were outside the room" (444).

12. For one emblematic example of the power of the disciplinary model, consider the title of a study on the establishment of *Germanistik: Eine Wissenschaft etabliert sich 1810–1870* (A Science Establishes Itself, 1810–1870), ed. Janota. The reflexive verb makes it seem as if the discipline comes into being of its own will.

13. It cannot be stressed enough how extensively and intelligently much of the debate about German studies has been waged in this country over the course of at least the last twenty-five years (cf. Lützeler 139–40). (For some of the most helpful components of the written record, see the annotated bibliography of German studies included in the last part of this volume. The 1989 *German Quarterly* issue already mentioned is particularly helpful for its plurality of views and subtlety of argument. Of similar value, see Trommler, though it is curious that this volume obviously intended a mainly German audience.) On the other hand, it should be noted that these discussions took place almost exclusively among *GermanistInnen,* that is, among scholars trained in the study of German literature and philology. Dialogue among historians and political scientists about interdisciplinary pursuits is a much more recent phenomenon. The reasons for this divergent

interest can be traced in great part to the unequal fortunes of the respective fields in the American academic and cultural scene. For an overview of the development and status of the study of German literature in the United States, see Seeba; and, for that of German history, see Geyer and Jarausch ("Great Men"). On possible reasons for disinterest on the part of historians, see Crew's essay in this volume.

14. The most notable exception is the recent book published by Oxford UP in a series on foreign cultural studies: *German Cultural Studies* (ed. Rob Burns; see also Jones's unrelated use [155]). The team behind the Oxford book draws almost exclusively on the Frankfurt School and secondarily on British cultural studies to guide their cultural history. In any case we are not trying to claim coinage of the term but, rather, to disseminate it.

15. The bibliographic record on these topics is vast. Useful places to begin include Gilman (esp. 200); Peck (180); Seeba; Wagner; Adorno; and the essays in this volume, especially that by Bammer and those in pts. 4 and 5.

16. See Seeba (esp. 144–46) and the volumes edited by Janota and Vosskamp.

17. Historians of German seem particularly eager to make the charge of "trendiness." For one particularly caustic accusation, see Barkin (249). And for an eloquently persuasive response, see Geyer and Jarausch ("Great Men") and the essay by Crew in this volume. See also Canning's careful explication of attitudes toward contemporary theory in relation to the writing of German women's history.

18. The DAAD, in fact, has sponsored quite a large number of conferences; to name just a few of those that took place in 1994: Wellesley College, University of Arizona, and Vanderbilt University; this last will be discussed briefly in this essay.

19. In March 1995 more than half of the eventual contributors to this volume gathered at Davidson College for a conference on "German Studies as Cultural Studies." Early drafts of papers were presented, and, most important, several multiple-hour sessions were dedicated to general discussion; we struggled as a group to conceptualize what German cultural studies might be. Significantly, many participants excitedly agreed that they would have to modify their arguments in light of these discussions. Indeed, a few reconceptualized their projects altogether. The papers delivered at the Harvard conference were published in *New German Critique,* no. 65 (Spring–Summer 1995).

20. For this reason I find both the models of "ersetzen" (replacing) and "ergänzen" (adding) (see Timm 2), inadequate roadmaps for the future direction of the field; neither affects nor effects structure.

21. On the specter of dilettantism, see Taubeneck 225. On the pressures of teaching loads and specialization, see Arnold.

22. See the syllabus for the introductory class in German studies at Stanford University in the last part of this volume.

23. To cite just two examples: although it was not a new hiring, the Germanic Studies Department (formerly Germanic Languages) at the University of Texas at Austin recently voted to appoint Peter Jelavich (from the History Department) to an official position on the Budget Council, the departmental governing board; Scott Spector has a joint appointment at the University of Michigan at Ann Arbor in History and Germanic Language and Literature.

24. "Prospects for Change—Changing Prospects," held at Vanderbilt University,

13–16 October 1994. A summary report on the conference was published in the winter 1994–95 bulletin of the AATG (American Association of Teachers of German); a fuller report and essays from the conferences were subsequently published in book form; see McCarthy and Schneider. For an analysis of this report and other expressions of anxiety, fear, and loss in the profession, see Kacandes.

25. See list of participants in McCarthy and Schneider (165–66). Note also that, of the thirty-nine participants listed, nearly all were affiliated with major research universities; three taught at liberal arts colleges and four at regional state universities.

26. This subscribes to the dichotomy of *ergänzen* and *ersetzen* I criticize in note 20.

27. There is only a single footnote to this passage, citing the infelicitous statement from the Nelson, Treichler, Grossberg introduction about close reading not being required by cultural studies approaches that I, too, criticize in previous pages (see Czaplicka et al. 6 n. 2; and Nelson et al. 2).

28. On Germans' desire to put the past behind them and their longing for a positive identification, see Jones (156). On Germans' complicated and overwhelming reactions to *Schindler's List,* see Denham; and Geyer and Jarausch ("Great Men" 265).

29. See Henke's essay in this volume.

30. See Rogowski's essay in this volume.

31. Pratt makes these points specifically about the field of comparative literature. But once we acknowledge the multicultural nature of any given society—an acknowledgment with which I foregrounded this introduction—her argument applies to the study of that culture as a whole as well; the genuine analytic study of any society will therefore reveal its diversity, just as the investigation of any individual will reveal that individual's multiple subject positions. It should be noted that Pratt offers her argument as a way to distinguish comparative literature from cultural studies (63). But in this effort I am even less interested than she is in policing the fences (her metaphor [see 58, 60]). For it seems to me that, clearly, the approach to literature she is prescribing falls under the purview of cultural studies.

Works Cited

Adorno, Theodor W. "Was ist deutsch?" In *Bundesrepublikanisches Lesebuch,* ed. Hermann Glaser. Munich: Carl Hanser, 1978. 335–46.

Adorno, Theodor W., and Max Horkheimer. "The Culture Industry: Enlightenment as Mass Deception." In *The Cultural Studies Reader,* ed. Simon During. London and New York: Routledge, 1993. 30–43.

Applebome, Peter. "Class Notes." *New York Times,* 1 March 1995, B8.

Arnold, Herbert. "Germanistik in a Liberal Arts Setting." In *Germanistik Weltweit? Zur Theorie und Praxis des Disziplinrahmens,* ed. Eitel Timm. Munich: iudicum, 1992. 118–27.

Atwood, Margaret. *The Handmaid's Tale.* Boston: Houghton Mifflin, 1986.

Barkin, Kenneth. "Bismarck in a Postmodern Age." *German Studies Review* 18.2 (1995): 241–52.

Barthes, Roland. *Mythologies.* Paris: Seuil, 1957. Selected and trans. Annette Lavers. New York: Hill and Wang, 1987.

Bate, W. Jackson. *The Burden of the Past and the English Poet.* Cambridge, MA: Belknap Press of Harvard UP, 1970.

Brantlinger, Patrick. *Crusoe's Footprints: Cultural Studies in Britain and America.* New York and London: Routledge, 1990.

Burns, Rob, ed. *German Cultural Studies: An Introduction.* Oxford: Oxford UP, 1995.

Canning, Kathleen. "German Particularities in Women's History/Gender History." *Journal of Women's History* 5.1 (1993): 102–14.

Clifford, James. "Introduction: Partial Truths." In *Writing Culture: The Poetics and Politics of Ethnography,* ed. James Clifford and George E. Marcus. Berkeley, Los Angeles, and London: U of California P, 1986. 1–26.

"Cultural History/Cultural Studies." *New German Critique* 65 (Spring–Summer 1995).

Czaplicka, John, Andreas Huyssen, and Anson Rabinbach. "Introduction: Cultural History and Cultural Studies: Reflections on a Symposium." *New German Critique* 65 (Spring–Summer 1995): 3–17.

Denham, Scott. "Schindler Returns to Open Arms: *Schindler's List* in Germany and Austria." *German Politics and Society* 13.1 (Spring 1995): 135–46.

During, Simon, ed. *The Cultural Studies Reader.* London and New York: Routledge, 1993.

Eley, Geoff. "What Is Cultural History?" *New German Critique* 65 (Spring–Summer 1995): 19—-36.

"German Histories: Challenges in Theory, Practice and Technique." *Central European History* 22. 3–4 (September–December 1989).

German Studies Review 13 (1990). DAAD special issue.

"*Germanistik* as German Studies: Interdisciplinary Theories and Methods." *German Quarterly* 62.2 (Spring 1989).

Geyer, Michael, and Konrad H. Jarausch. "The Future of the German Past: Transatlantic Reflections for the 1990s." *Central European History* 22.3–4 (1989): 229–59.

———. "Great Men and Postmodern Ruptures: Overcoming the 'Belatedness' of German Historiography." *German Studies Review* 18.2 (1995): 253–74.

Gilman, Sander L. "Why and How I Study the German." *German Quarterly* 62 (1989): 192–204.

Graff, Gerald. *Beyond the Culture Wars: How Teaching the Conflicts Can Revitalize American Education.* New York and London: Norton, 1992.

Grossberg, Lawrence, Cary Nelson, and Paula A. Treichler, eds. *Cultural Studies.* New York and London: Routledge, 1992.

Hall, Stuart. "Cultural Studies and Its Theoretical Legacies." In *Cultural Studies,* ed. Lawrence Grossberg, Cary Nelson, and Paula A. Treichler. New York and London: Routledge, 1992. 277–94.

———. "Cultural Studies: Two Paradigms." In *Culture/Power/History: A Reader in Contemporary Social Theory,* ed. Nicholas B. Dirks, Geoff Eley, and Sherry B. Ortner. Princeton: Princeton UP, 1994. 520–38.

———. "The Emergence of Cultural Studies and the Crisis of the Humanities." *October* 53 (1990): 11–23.

Hebdige, Dick. *Hiding in the Light.* London: Routledge, 1988.

Hoggart, Richard. *The Uses of Literacy: Changing Patterns in English Mass Culture.* 1958. Reprint. New York: Oxford UP, 1970.

Hohendahl, Peter U. "Interdisciplinary German Studies: Tentative Conclusions." *German Quarterly* 62 (1989): 227–34.

hooks, bell. "Culture to Culture: Ethnography and Cultural Studies as Critical Intervention." In *Yearning: Race, Gender, and Cultural Politics*. Boston: South End P, 1990. 123–33.

Howe, Irving. "The Value of the Canon." *New Republic,* 18 February 1991, 40–47.

Hunt, Lynn. "The Virtues of Disciplinarity." *Eighteenth-Century Studies* 28.1 (1994): 1–7.

Ingersoll, Earl G., ed. *Margaret Atwood: Conversations*. Princeton: Ontario Review P, 1990.

Janota, Johannes, ed. *Eine Wissenschaft etabliert sich 1810–1870*. Tübingen: Max Niemeyer Verlag, 1980.

Jones, Michael T. "Identity, Critique, Affirmation: A Response to Hinrich C. Seeba's Paper." *German Quarterly* 62 (1989): 155–57.

Kacandes, Irene. "What's L—— Got to Do with It? Love, Literature, and Languishment in the Language Department." Modern Language Association Convention, Chicago, December 1995.

LaCapra, Dominick. "Canons, Texts, and Contexts." In *Learning History in America: Schools, Cultures and Politics,* ed. Lloyd Kramer, Donald Reid, and William L. Barney. Minneapolis and London: U Minnesota P, 1994. 120–38. Also in LaCapra, *Representing the Holocaust: History, Theory, Trauma*. Ithaca: Cornell UP, 1994. 19–41.

Lennox, Sara. "Feminist Scholarship and Germanistik." *German Quarterly* 62 (1989): 158–70.

Link, Jere. "The Play of German Histories: Protocolling the Debate." *Central European History* 22.3–4 (1989): 444–57.

Lützeler, Paul Michael. "Letter from the Editor." *German Quarterly* 62 (1989): 139–40.

McCarthy, John A. "Report: DAAD Symposium on '*Germanistik* in the USA: Prospects for Change—Changing Prospects.'" *AATG Newsletter* 30.2 (1994–95): 3–4.

McCarthy, John A., and Katrin Schneider, eds. *The Future of Germanistik in the USA: Changing Our Prospects*. Nashville: Department of Germanic and Slavic Languages, 1996.

Modleski, Tania. *Loving with a Vengeance: Mass-Produced Fantasies for Women*. New York and London: Methuen, 1984.

Nelson, Cary, Paula A. Treichler, and Lawrence Grossberg. "Cultural Studies: An Introduction." In *Cultural Studies,* ed. Lawrence Grossberg, Cary Nelson, and Paula A. Treichler. New York and London: Routledge, 1992. 1–22.

Peck, Jeffrey M. "There's No Place like Home? Remapping the Topography of German Studies." *German Quarterly* 62 (1989): 178–87.

Pratt, Mary Louise. "Comparative Literature and Global Citizenship." In *Comparative Literature in the Age of Multiculturalism,* ed. Charles Bernheimer. Baltimore: Johns Hopkins UP, 1995. 58–65.

Radway, Janice. *Reading the Romance: Women, Patriarchy, and Popular Literature*. Chapel Hill: U of North Carolina P, 1984.

"Results of the MLA's Fall 1995 Survey of Foreign Language Enrollments." *MLA Newsletter* 28.4 (Winter 1996): 1–2.

Riffaterre, Michael. "On the Complementarity of Comparative Literature and Cultural Studies." In *Comparative Literature in the Age of Multiculturalism,* ed. Charles Bernheimer. Baltimore: Johns Hopkins UP, 1995. 66–73.

Seeba, Hinrich C. "Critique of Identity Formation: Toward an Intercultural Model of German Studies." *German Quarterly* 62 (1989): 144–54.

Seyhan, Azade. "Language and Literary Study as Cultural Criticism." *ADFL Bulletin* 26.2 (1995): 7–11.

Smith, Barbara Herrnstein. "Introduction: The Public, the Press, and the Professors." In *The Politics of a Liberal Arts Education,* ed. Darryl J. Gless and Barbara Herrnstein Smith. Durham and London: Duke UP, 1992. 1–11.

Taubeneck, Steven. "Voices in the Debate: German Studies and *Germanistik.*" *German Quarterly* 62 (1989): 220–26.

Teraoka, Arlene A. "Is Culture to Us What Text Is to Anthropology? A Response to Jeffrey M. Peck's Paper." *German Quarterly* 62 (1989): 188–91.

Thompson, E. P. *The Making of the English Working Class.* New York: Vintage, 1963.

Timm, Eitel. "Einführung." In *Germanistik Weltweit? Zur Theorie und Praxis des Disziplinrahmens,* ed. Eitel Timm. Munich: iudicum, 1992. 1–5.

Trommler, Frank, ed. *Germanistik in den USA: Neue Entwicklungen und Methoden.* Opladen: Westdeutscher Verlag, 1989.

Turner, Graeme. *British Cultural Studies: An Introduction.* Media and Popular Culture 7. New York and London: Routledge, 1992.

Vosskamp, Wilhelm. "Für eine systematische Erforschung der Geschichte der deutschen Literaturwissenschaft." *Deutsche Vierteljahrsschrift für Literaturwissenschaft und Geistesgeschichte* (1987): 1*–6*. Special issue on "Von der gelehrten zur disziplinären Gemeinschaft."

Wagner, Richard. "Was ist deutsch?" In *Dichtungen und Schriften,* ed. Dieter Borchmeyer. Vol. 10 (Bayreuth, Späte weltanschauliche Schriften). Frankfurt a.M.: Insel Verlag, 1983. 84–103.

Williams, Raymond. "Culture Is Ordinary" (1958). In *Resources of Hope: Culture, Democracy, Socialism,* ed. R. Gable. London: Verso, 1989. 3–18.

———. *Culture and Society, 1780–1950.* 1958. Reprint. Harmondsworth: Penguin, 1963.

———. *The Long Revolution.* 1961. Reprint. London: Penguin, 1965.

———. *Politics and Letters: Interviews with* New Left Review. London: New Left, 1979.

Part Two

WHAT IS GERMAN CULTURAL STUDIES?

The essays in this section continue the work of Kacandes's introduction by offering definitions of what German cultural studies can and should be. They sketch out the kinds of questions that need to be asked, and they expose past and current resistances to these inquiries. Some resistance can be traced to specific events in German history: thus, the path to nationhood could be cited as a cause for intransigence and narrowness in defining "Germanness," and the burden of the National Socialist past could provide an explanation for the reluctance on the part of scholars to engage in analysis that is new, experimental, or playful. Other obstacles to cultural studies practice can be located in the particularly tenacious disciplinarity fostered by the nineteenth-century German university system. As Kacandes has suggested, interdisciplinarity offers a touchstone for the difference between German studies and German cultural studies. Crew and Teraoka pry open the disciplinary vise by exposing the histories of their respective disciplines of history and Germanistik. *Bammer and Peck propose new "objects" of study that invite new strategies of investigation. In pointing out what German cultural studies should be, Bammer, Crew, Peck, and Teraoka are in fact mapping the terrain.*

CHAPTER 2

Interrogating Germanness:
What's Literature Got to Do with It?

Angelika Bammer

In this essay Angelika Bammer introduces the interrogation of "Germanness" to be continued by Arlene Teraoka. Working from the premise, which she shares with Teraoka, that a unified German culture is a construction rather than an accurate reflection of historical or contemporary reality, Bammer approaches hegemonic German culture from the opposite direction. Specifically, Bammer proposes precisely the Germanness of German literature as the issue to be explored. Bammer locates territory on which traditional German literary studies (Germanics) can converse with cultural studies, by suggesting we begin calling the former "by its true name," that is, by acknowledging its expressly political agenda. "German literature," Bammer points out, existed before a nation called "Germany" did, thus serving as a prime example of Benedict Anderson's thesis that the conception of a nation exists before the political entity. Even though the claim that German literature expressed a specifically German soul was contested by those who believed literature was a transnational phenomenon, it was the nationalist position that imbued the scholarly discipline called Germanistik. *What the task of teachers of literature then becomes, Bammer proposes, is "to identify the Germanness of German literature, while at the same time countering the notion of 'German' as an exclusive category, a unitary entity."*

Bammer embeds her investigation in observations about contemporary German (leftist) denials of nationalist sentiment. As a native German herself, though one who has been "displaced" (a concept with which Bammer has become associated), she is sensitive to Germans' attempts at eluding their past. But the way forward, she suggests (drawing on James Young's distinction between monuments and memorials), is not by erecting a monument and disengaging from that which it represents but, rather, by creating a memorial, a place or occasion or activity in which groups of people deliberately enact certain memories. Bammer cleverly suggests that literature taught as an interrogation of Germanness along these lines can function to help us "engage with one of the more urgent social and political issues in contemporary Germany and beyond: the issue of cultural identity, its relationship to ethnicity and place, and its bearing on public imagination."

Bammer's essay grounds these highly theoretical questions in the concrete pedagogy of the academy, suggesting actual titles of literary works that could be used in a college "Introduction to German Literature" class pursuing the topic of Germanness she finds so urgent. She thereby illustrates how questions asked of one type of cultural production (such as those Young asks of Holocaust memorials) can be fruitfully asked of another (i.e., those Bammer herself asks of literature). In these respects Bammer's essay enacts several of the goals we set for this volume: how theory and scholarly research inform pedagogy and how different types of cultural production inform and shape one another.

The shift in emphasis from *Germanistik* to German studies, many feared, would inevitably, in the institutional practice of American academic life, diminish the study of (German) literature. German studies was supposedly more scientifically objective, its data more verifiably hard. Literature, in comparison, was subjective, impressionistically soft, without much evidentiary value. Thus, as enrollments in the waning 1980s ebbed, anxieties in many an American German Department rose as faculty and advanced students, trained as literary scholars, made efforts to retrain, borrowing tools from social science colleagues and adding numbers, charts, and graphs to newly designated German studies courses. In the process the status of literature often changed from object of analysis to dispensable means of illustration. To its adherents, meanwhile, it became a kind of guilty love.

My argument, in brief, is that this was neither a necessary nor a good move and that it was based on a wrong notion of what both German and literary studies were about. Indeed, it seems all but self-evident that literature is not only not dispensable but that an engagement with literature is critical to the very enterprise of German studies. What is called for—and this was the intent of German studies' multidisciplinary base—is not a *dismissal* of literature but, rather, a rethinking of its use. For, I would argue, the agenda of German studies is defined precisely by what the collected body of German literature is inevitably also always about: the cultural construction of an understanding of Germanness and the critical interrogation of that concept.

German studies (the study of things German) is, on the most general level, an inquiry into what *German* means: who and what is German? how so and why? This is also, on a certain level, what much of German literature is about. It, too, in countless instances—from the work of Heinrich Heine to that of Thomas Mann, from the writings of Bettina von Arnim to those of Saliha Scheinhardt—asks about the who and what. But, most insistently, literature probes the how so and why: how are the attachments formed that constitute our sense of identity within social formations, and what can cause us to detach? What does it mean to a person to be included in or excluded from a particular group? What does it *feel* like to be called German or to be denied that name? The objective of literature is subjectivity. And, so, it asks what German means in the particular experience of specific subjects and how it can mean differently depending on what has been done to them in that name. Literature, one could say, represents meaning in terms of love and loss; it weighs history on the scales of memory.

In *The Texture of Memory: Holocaust Memorials and Meaning* James Young posits that "the sites of memory are many and diverse, deliberate and accidental. They range from archives to museums, parades to moments of silence, memorial gardens to resistance monuments, ruins to commemorative fast days, national malls to a family's Jahrzeit candle" (viii). As Young's readings of Holocaust memorials in five countries (Germany, Austria, Poland, the United States, and Israel) proceed to show, "the motives of memory are never pure" but always bent toward certain ends (2). Acts of remembrance are, therefore, always also acts of testimony to these ends and to the particular set of interests informing them. How Germany remembers the Holocaust and the forms German Holocaust memorials take are different from the forms of memory and memorials in Poland, Israel, or Austria. Young's approach and its implications for engaged cultural practices are useful, I submit, for a reconsideration of how we use literature when we teach courses within national tradition structures, such as courses on German literature. The customary practice of focusing on questions of literature leaves the *German* in German literature unexamined, even as it is assumed. My proposal, therefore, would be to put it up for critical scrutiny. Such a move might yield historical insight about the Germanness in question, or, conversely, the national designation might dissolve into conceptual irrelevance. Either way, the process of critique would allow the assumptions on which academic course and department structures are still based to operate on a more reflected and conscious level.

The distinction between monument and memorial could be put in passive/active terms: a monument is an impassive and, in that sense, neutral marker of an experience or event that a people, or group, wants to remember; a memorial is a deliberate, hence engaged, enactment of particular memories. If memorials, then, as Young defines them, are the sites where remembering is enacted and monuments the concrete objects to which the act of memorializing is attached, then a people's literature—the acts, names, and events it emplots in the form of collected stories—can be seen as a monument to that people in this sense, a reenactment of what Young calls "collected memory" (*Texture* xi). Put another way, a body of literature defined in national terms could be seen as a monument to the myth of the nation it represents. The individual instance of the public evocation of this myth in the form of, say, a course in German literature could thus be seen as a national memorial in Young's terms: an occasion for "groups of people . . . to create a common past for themselves" by telling their "constitutive narratives . . . of the past" (6–7).

Memorials pose problems when they purport to speak for a collectivity divided in its remembering. When the event or experience being remembered is something some would rather forget, the memorial can generate a crisis. Predictably, therefore, in post–World War II/post-Holocaust Germany, national memorials generate national crises of memory almost every time they come up.[1] The crisis is generated by the ambivalence of memory for a people for whom the collective mandate to remember what they did is in tension with the desire to forget it. Even more fundamentally, however, the crisis is already inherent in the very assumption of such a thing as a *national* memory. For, on a level of unconsciousness so deep that it is almost inaccessible, the very legitimacy of the nation in the name of which a given memory is invoked has been, for the collectivity of Germans after 1945, deeply suspect.

One response to this ambivalence of national memory is to pretend the thing in question (Germany) doesn't really exist. One avoids referring to it by name, calling it, instead, simply and generically, the "Federal Republic" or, acronymically, the "BRD." Another is to insist that it is not what it is (a state) but something else (a culture). This latter move has the double advantage of making the thing in question, Germany, appear more noble and benign, defined by matters of mind and aesthetics rather than by power and affairs of state. For, unlike a state, a culture is not represented by the apparatuses of power through which a nation manifests itself (immigration laws, a military, and such). It trafficks more in the sublime. In post-1945 West Germany both of these responses—denial and sublimation—were typical. While young people professed not to know their national anthem or recognize their flag (it looked, after all, so much like Belgium's), the presentation of Germany to the world as culture became a central part of state affairs.[2] In the process the nationally bounded category "German" was transmuted into a broader, non–nationally defined realm of culture of which Germans were a part. By means of shifting definitions, Germany could disappear . . . and reappear as *Geist*.

There is much to be gained from such a move. Indeed, arguments for a transnational, global ("world") literature have repeatedly been advanced—and at critical moments forcefully so—by precisely those thinkers and scholars with whom those of us who aspire to the status of progressive intellectuals are most likely to sympathize: names like Erich Auerbach, with his 1952 essay "Philology and *Weltliteratur*";[3] Hans Magnus Enzensberger, from his early essay "Bin ich ein Deutscher?" (Am I a German?) (1964) to his 1993 work *Aussichten auf den Bürgerkrieg* (Prospects for a Civil War);[4] Peter Sloterdijk, with his 1989–90 work *Versprechen auf Deutsch: Rede über das eigene Land* (Promising in German: A Speech about One's Own Country); or Günter Grass, with virtually everything he has ever written, come to mind.

On the face of it this is the obviously progressive, namely antinationalist, strategy. And in the force field of rising ethnic nationalisms, it is a position we certainly want and need to strengthen. Yet what makes me uneasy is my suspicion that part of the comfort of this position lies precisely in the fact that it gets around the very ambivalence at the heart of German memory that so often lies like a pall over Germans' engagement with Germanness. To get at, rather than around, this ambivalence in order to address the dilemmas it perceives, I therefore propose a different (and less comfortable) strategy. What I propose is to take up the very Germanness we might be inclined to leave behind: acknowledge it, name it, and then interrogate it about its effects and assumptions. For, only in so doing, I believe, will we be able to see the relationship between German as a culture and Germany as a state with the requisite degree of critical clarity. Moreover, by positing the Germanness of things German (including German literature) as a question to be explored, instead of assuming it as given or pretending it isn't there, we engage with one of the most urgent social and political issues in contemporary Germany and beyond: the issue of cultural identity, its relationship to ethnicity and place, and its bearing on public legitimation.

The prevailing assumption is that the raising of such questions marks a radical (cultural studies) break with conventional (literary) approaches to (German) literature, a break that is often seen as the fault line between German studies and *Germanistik*. Questions of identity, power, and ideological formations tend to be regarded as the purview of cultural studies, while textual strategies—questions of narrative structure or language, for example—are seen as literary concerns. If, however, one looks at the history of *Germanistik* and its nineteenth-century roots, it becomes evident that the so-called cultural studies approach actually engages with a foundational tradition of the discipline of *Germanistik:* the debate over whether German literature is defined in German (i.e., national-political) terms or in terms of its medium, its literariness.

The history of modern Germany is a perfect case in point for Benedict Anderson's thesis that the idea of the nation precedes the fact of the nation-state.

German literature existed before Germany did. Indeed, after earlier thinkers and scholars such as Martin Opitz, Johann Christoph Gottsched, Friedrich Nicolai, Gotthold Ephraim Lessing, and Johann Gottfried Herder had set the stage,[5] the construction (or, as it had to be put, "discovery") of a German nation that could—and eventually would—be consolidated into state form became, in the nineteenth century, a central task of German literature and literary scholarship. At the core of the institution of a German literary tradition—indeed, of the very notion of such a tradition itself—is thus an expressly political agenda: the creation of a nation that would figure as a recognized power in the world.

The ethnic culture position, according to which (German) literature was an expression of a (the German) people's soul, or *Geist,* was advanced with the conviction born of the particular German variant of Romantic nationalism. The stuff out of which to fashion Germany was literally gathered together on all sides in collections of folk literature, myths, and histories such as *Des Knaben Wunderhorn* (1805–8) by Achim von Arnim and Clemens Brentano; *Die deutschen Volksbücher* by Joseph Görres; and *Deutsches Volkstum* (1810), compiled by the founder of the German *Turner* movement, Friedrich Ludwig Jahn. Pride of place among these compilers of the textual material of German national culture undoubtedly belongs to Jacob and Wilhelm Grimm, whose publications literally span the history of modern Germany. Their *Kinder- und Hausmärchen* (1812–15) was followed by *Deutsche Sagen* (1816–18), which was followed by Jacob's *Deutsche Grammatik* (1819–37) and Wilhelm's *Deutsche Heldensagen* (1829): in 1835 there followed again a jointly authored work, *Deutsche Mythologie.* Their lifework, however, was the monumental— and, to this day, authoritative—*Deutsches Wörterbuch,* which began publication in 1852 and was completed (provisionally), generations later, in 1961. The publication of the first histories of German literature in the early nineteenth century, such as August Koberstein's 1827 *Grundriss der Geschichte der deutschen Nationalliteratur* and, a year later, Wolfgang Menzel's *Die deutsche Literatur,* provided scholarly corroboration for the case already made materially by the collections of literary texts—namely, that Germany had a long and strong literary tradition on which to base its claim to (cultural) nationhood.

Not that the goal of nationhood was an uncontested agenda. Then, as now, there were differing points of view. There were those, like Novalis, for example, who pushed beyond the boundedness of separate nations toward the vision of a shared European culture.[6] In the work of Friedrich and August Wilhelm Schlegel the ambivalence toward the national(ist) cultural agenda that was to mark the history of their century becomes particularly clear. Friedrich Schlegel's Vienna lectures on the *Geschichte der alten und neuen Literatur,* delivered in 1808 and 1812, are a good example. For with a fundamental uneasiness that reverberates to our time, finding echoes in the work of successor thinkers like Erich Auerbach, Schlegel struggles with the dilemma created by literature's dual role: simultaneously representing and transcending its native culture. Literature, *as literature,* is a transnational phenomenon with national variants, he insists. Yet he maintains the ethnic culture claim in his description of world literature as, in sum, the collective expression of individual, national particularities.[7]

In this early, nineteenth-century round of debate the national(ist) position won out. Now, in the waning twentieth century, in the wake of German unification, the debate over Germanness and its meaning (does it signify cultural, ethnic, or state affiliation or some combination of these three?) is again alive and predictably rife with controversy. Yet, while echoes of the earlier arguments abound, the nationalist position is no longer as respectable as it once was. The very magnitude of its victory under National Socialism undermined its continued claim. Within the social spectrum of contemporary Germany, therefore, it has largely been displaced onto xenophobic acts and slogans on the streets.

What does this have to do with teaching literature? The issue, as I see it, is how to identify the Germanness of German literature and at the same time counter the notion of German as a unitary category. This is what I take as the structuring principle of our work in German cultural studies. For only by at once identifying and deconstructing the category "German" can we interrogate the often unexamined notions of national identity, ethnicity, and race underlying nationally defined structures such as "German literature" and the exclusions they imply. Moreover, if courses taught within such structures introduce students to complex, nonunified, even contested, notions of Germanness, these students will be more able to read the canonical tradition for what it is: a never-quite-settled, and often unsettling, negotiation of the very national category such traditions assume as foundational.

Let us take, for example, an "Introduction to German Literature" course and consider the difference it might make if, instead of the conventional survey of canonical texts in chronological (and/or genre-defined) order, we selected readings on the basis of their potential yield for an interrogation of the category "German" posited in the very course title. We could begin with a play by Georg Tabori, perhaps *Weisman und Rotgesicht* (White Man and Redface; premiered in the Akademietheater, Vienna, in the spring of 1990). Next, we could read Jurek Becker's novel *Jakob der Lügner* (*Jacob the Liar*), first published 1969 in the German Democratic Republic; then a shorter, poetically dense prose narrative by Herta Müller, perhaps *Barfüssiger Februar* (Barefoot February [1990]). Finally, we could read Vera Kamenko's 1978 autobiographical narrative, *Unter uns war Krieg* (War among Us). These readings would provide the basic structure of the course.

What is German about these texts? There is nothing—at least at first reading—inherently or obviously German about their textual form (plot structure, character development, form of narration, and such). (Although this would be a question to which we would return throughout the course: can we identify something German about the textual form of a given work; is there a national inflection to literariness?) If not in form, then, are they German on the level of content? Are the stories they tell German stories? Are the issues they raise German issues?

Weisman und Rotgesicht is a play about an older Jewish man, his invalid daughter, and a man who claims to be Native American. They happen to meet somewhere in the American West (in a place that could be the setting for a Wim Wenders film) and proceed to debate—and, finally, argue over—who of them has an identity, who has a history, what it matters to have one or the other (or neither or both). It is about the relationship between identity and history, I would say. These are, undoubtedly, eminently German concerns; at the same time, they are obviously not just German. *Jakob der Lügner* is set in Nazi-occupied Poland in 1943–44. It is the story of the story—the "lie"—that Jakob Heym invents to keep the inhabitants of his ghetto alive in the limited space of time between annihilation and liberation. It is also a metanarrative reflection on fiction itself, its power and limitations. For Jakob's stories (stories attributed to a nonexistent radio he makes up) keep hope and the ghetto alive for a while, yet they are ultimately unable to sustain them. Only the narrator, and his memory and tale, in the end survive. *Barfüssiger Februar* begins and ends with a woman's arrival in a winter-cold land, with descriptions of a never-named Germany that echo the language and poetic mood of Else Lasker-Schüler. For, like Lasker-Schüler, the narrator of Herta Müller's text feels foreign in this land that should be hers by tradition of birthright. In between the scenes of her arrival in Berlin, Müller's text describes the narrator's life before urban Germany in rural Rumania. *Unter uns war Krieg,* finally, tells Vera Kamenko's story of coming to Germany as a so-called guest worker in the early 1970s. After she is convicted of manslaughter in the beating death of her child, she is imprisoned and deported back to Yugoslavia.

These are stories about Germany but not solely German stories. What is most irreducibly and unequivocally German about them is the language in which they are told. This, then, would be where our inquiry would begin: with the proposition that Germanness resides in the German language. Contemporary studies of nationalism, such as Benedict Anderson's by now classic *Imagined Communities,* analyze the correspondences between a national vernacular, the experience of a national identity (the "community" of Anderson's title), and the apparatus of a nation-state. Poets and writers take up these correspondences also, even if in different ways. They render the abstractions of nation or culture vivid as we experience them. For the nation in whose name we are identified— or identify ourselves—informs the texture of our daily lives. Indeed, it literally lives in us: in the way our mouths form words, the way our ears hear sounds, the way our minds and hearts respond. Even Virginia Woolf, in *Three Guineas*

(1938), her most passionately antinationalist work, acknowledges the powerful hold of our native country on our feelings. Even as we repudiate it rhetorically, its claim to our allegiance remains, embedded deep in the unconscious reaches of our psyche. Thus, she follows her famous internationalist manifesto ("as a woman I have no country. As a woman I want no country. As a woman my country is the whole world") with the recognition that, even as she tries to reject it, "still some obstinate emotion remains, some love of England [could we substitute *Germany* here?—A. B.] dropped into a child's ear by the cawing of rooks in an elm tree, by the splash of waves on a beach, or by English voices murmuring nursery rhymes" (Woolf 109).

In thus taking up the issue of the relationship between nation, language, and state, our hypothetical "Introduction to German Literature" class would engage with a defining tradition in the history of the meaning of Germanness. Indeed, this is a relationship we can trace from the etymological origins of the word *deutsch*[8] through nineteenth-century struggles to substantiate German claims to nationhood to contemporary, postnationalist attempts to reconceptualize those very claims.[9] A common thread throughout this history is the identification of German with, and as, language. And it is precisely this identification that texts like the ones that I proposed—*Weisman und Rotgesicht, Jakob der Lügner, Barfüssiger Februar,* and *Unter uns war Krieg*—simultaneously reenforce and unsettle.

Tabori, born in Hungary to a Jewish family and exiled by Nazism in 1933, lives in Austria and Germany, where he is an integral part of the contemporary cultural scene. He writes his plays in English, and they are translated into German by Ursula Grützmacher-Tabori.[10] Is he a German writer? Or is it she? Or do the plays *become* German as they become part of the German cultural public sphere? If Tabori counts as German, even though his language of writing is not, who else could be so claimed? Perhaps Shakespeare?

What, then, of Vera Kamenko, who is not German and does not consider herself such but writes in German, moreover, in a German that breaks Germanness apart to disclose its intractable resistance to the foreignness that she, her Turkish companion, and her Yugoslavian child represent? Or Herta Müller: Rumanian born but ethnically and culturally (at least, in part) German? Assimilated into German citizenship upon her 1987 move to West Berlin on the basis of her ethnicity, she writes in what reviews unfailingly laud as true—or, as they put it, "pure"—German. What does this mean? What makes it pure? What of those (ethnic) Germans who speak no German? Or those who are linguistically (and perhaps culturally) German, like many second- or third-generation German Turks, but aren't German by blood-line conventions? What is the weight of language here?

And, finally, what of Jurek Becker, already a well-known writer in the GDR before he was expelled to the West in the wake of the 1976 Biermann affair? Becker's status as a German writer has never been in question. And yet German, like Joseph Conrad's English, is not native to him. Born to a Polish-Jewish family in 1937, Becker's mother tongues were Yiddish and Polish; he didn't learn German until after 1945, when he and his father were liberated from the concentration camp Sachsenhausen and settled in East Berlin. Becker writes in German but in a German that is, in the Brechtian sense, made strange, as it is inflected by the Yiddish tradition it salvages and reinscribes into the literary landscape of contemporary Germany.

Reading these texts not as *minority* literature but as exemplars of the range of *German* literature, a primary focus of our inquiry would be on what these texts do with and to language and how, in the course of this work, they negotiate concepts of Germanness. Not only, I believe, would such readings force us to be deliberate in our definition of what *German literature* means; they would also enable us to test the validity and implications of theses like that of Deleuze and Guattari who claim that minority, or as they put it, "minor" literature is not marginal, in the end, but the most vital and vibrant (even if suppressed) life force of a given literary culture. In the process we would take up the question of translation—what is literally and figuratively "carried across"—in the moves among and between cultures: what is lost, what is displaced, and how all involved are transformed. (We might, in this context, even read parts of *Jakob der Lügner* in the excellent English translation by Melvin Kornfeld or a section of Tabori's play in the English "original.")

By way of conclusion I return to my initial suggestion that, if we can think of a national literature as a monument to the nation it represents, then we could consider the particular instance of a German literature course as a form of German memorial. What kind of memorial, then, would we want it to be? What we would want to avoid, I would think, is a course in which, as in conventional museums, the past is on display as fact, its claim to authority implied in its embalmed pastness. This is the kind of monumental, antiquarian use of history that Nietzsche scorned as an abuse because it abstracts agency into already scripted narratives whose meaning has been set. What we need, rather, are representations of history that free it of the past to enable agency in the present. As models for such dynamic approaches to the representation of history, I would take work like that of memorial artists such as Shimon Attie, Norbert Radermacher, or Maya Lin, the architect of the Vietnam Memorial in Washington, DC. Attie, for example, projects slides of places and people from the past that no longer exist—a Jewish bookstore or Jewish residents from 1930s Berlin—onto the sites in the present where they used to be then. We see both at once. In a similar installation in the Neukölln district of Berlin, Radermacher also used light beam–triggered slide projections to remind passersby of the sites of Nazi violence their daily activities traverse. While Attie and Radermacher bring the past to light in the present, as it were, Maya Lin's memorial to the American war in

Vietnam brings the present to the past by inviting visitors to bring token items from their everyday lives now—photos, flowers, anniversary cards, saved mementos of the deceased—to the site of a war that, in memories and emotions, lives on.[11] The work of artists such as these that witnesses the past in the present and positions the present in relation to the past is particularly suggestive as a model for how we might use literature when we teach, particularly in German studies courses. For they present different moments in time as separate yet inseparably linked, contextualizing the one in light of the other and, in so doing, historicizing both. They thus remind us that history cannot be seen in solely unidirectional terms, in which we begin in the past and go forward from there. Instead, we sometimes need to begin in the present and go backward from here.[12]

To return, then, to my imagined course and the framing question I put thus—is this (works by writers such as Georg Tabori, Herta Müller, Vera Kamenko, and Jurek Becker) German literature?—I would answer yes. But the reasons for this yes are arguably not self-evident. To make them so, to bring the reasons forth as evidence, as it were, would be the purpose of such a course. For, to paraphrase James Young, "the best German memorial . . . may not be a single memorial at all—but simply the never-to-be-resolved debate over which kind of memory to preserve, how to do it, in whose name, and to what end" (*Texture* 21). I wholeheartedly agree.

NOTES

1. Young defines the dilemma of German national memory as "that of a nation tortured by its conflicted desire to build a new and just state on the bedrock memory of its horrendous crimes" (*Texture* 22).

2. In a deliberate attempt to counter the Nazi casting of German identity in nationalist political terms, (West) Germany's postwar representation of itself to the international community of nations was defined in terms of culture. The explicit foreign policy goal of the newly founded Federal Republic after 1949 was to construct a new, antinationalist foundation on the basis of which to establish not only a new state but also a new set of relations with other states. The answer to this mandate was culture. Cultural policy as a key dimension of international relations thus became a central part of the operations of the federal Auswärtiges Amt (Foreign Affairs Office). (Not coincidentally, it was in 1919, in the wake of World War I, that a Cultural Affairs Division was first established in the Auswärtiges Amt. That same year the forerunner of what in 1932 was to become the first Goethe Institute, the Deutsche Akademie, was founded on private initiative in Munich.) Under Ralf Dahrendorf, state secretary in the Auswärtiges Amt between 1969 and 1978, this emphasis on cultural representation became official state foreign policy. As part of this process, the Goethe Institutes, which had been founded anew in 1952 on a redefined basis, negotiated a structural alliance with the Auswärtiges Amt that marked the beginning expansion of their international network. To their original

mission ("Zur Pflege der deutschen Sprache im Ausland" [care of the German language abroad]) an express foreign cultural policy dimension (the "Förderung der internationalen kulturellen Zusammenarbeit" [support of international cultural cooperation]) was added at this time.

3. As Maire and Edward Said put it in their brief translators' introduction, Auerbach's concept of "Weltliteratur" (harking back to and building on that of Goethe) is "a visionary concept for it transcends national literatures without, at the same time, destroying their individualities. . . . [It] is not to be understood as a selective collection of world classics or great books . . . but rather as a concert among all the literature produced by man about man" (Auerbach 1).

4. Enzensberger has consistently urged Germans to take seriously the psychological power of the *idea* of the nation-state, which compels even—or perhaps particularly—when it no longer has a material reality. While his earlier essays, such as "Bin ich ein Deutscher?" (1964), are still shadowed by the specter of Nazi Germany and marked by the desire to shed German identity like a skin that has been outworn, his more recent elaborations on the subject, such as *Aussichten auf den Bürgerkrieg,* respond to the alarming rise of racist, antisemitic, and xenophobic actions in Germany in the late 1980s and early 1990s by assuming Germanness, with all its responsibilities.

5. Martin Opitz's *Buch von der deutschen Poeterey* (1624) set out to demonstrate the fact that German was as literary a language as Italian, English, or French and that the literature it produced could rightfully hold its own alongside its European rivals. Gottsched and Lessing then argued the merits of standards based on national difference. The former, notably in his 1730 *Versuch einer Critischen Dichtkunst vor die Deutschen,* attempted to create a legitimating foundation of aesthetic norms on the basis of which German writing could support a world-class literature. The latter, most explicitly in the seventeenth letter of his *Briefen, die neueste Literatur betreffend* (1759–65), scornfully countered, meanwhile, that in his normative drive Gottsched had lost the very sense of the specificity—the essential Germanness—of the language in question. Friedrich Nicolai, one of Lessing's two coeditors of these letters on German literature (the other was Moses Mendelssohn), went on to document this specificity of the language of German culture with the publication of the *Allgemeine deutsche Bibliothek* (1765–96). Moreover, with the compilation of German literature in the *Deutsche Bibliothek,* Nicolai helped lay the empirical foundation of the claim to a German national literary tradition on which German culture, and the emergent German nation, of his time could build. Herder, finally, came full circle in *Fragmente über die neuere deutsche Literatur* (1867–68), when he linked the individual work of art not just to the *Geist* of the times but to the *Geist* of a particular nation.

6. This transcendent vision of unity-in-difference was itself severely bounded, of course, by its exclusively Christian terms.

7. Earlier, in one of his most famous aphoristic fragments, published in the journal *Athenäum,* which he coedited between 1798 and 1800 with his brother, August Wilhelm, Friedrich Schlegel had taken a much sharper, more unambiguous view: "Die Deutschen, sagt man, sind, was Höhe des Kunstsinns und des wissenschaftlichen Geistes betrifft, das erste Volk in der Welt. Gewiss; nur gibt es sehr wenige Deutsche" (qtd. in Martini 1977, 325).

8. The meaning of *deutsch* (Old High German, *diutisc*) arose out of the dynastic struggles and territorial disputes between East and West Francia: it designated the clan languages spoken in East Francia and, by extension, those who spoke them. These languages had in common a substantially Germanic base, as opposed to the Romanized lingua franca of West Francia (*theodisca lingua* was the administrative term for the native Frankish tongue within the realm of Charlemagne's empire). "Deutschland," in other words, was the land of those who spoke German. Thus, as the historian Mary Fulbrook points out, "Germany is probably unique among modern European states in having a name derived not from a tribe or territory, but from a spoken language" (Fulbrook 13).

9. For a representative sampling of nineteenth-century nationalist arguments and their relation to language, one could begin with Herder (e.g., his *Abhandlung über den Ursprung der Sprache* or *Von deutscher Art und Kunst* [1772 and 1773, respectively]), proceed through Fichte's landmark *Reden an die deutsche Nation* of 1807–8, and conclude with Richard Wagner's polemic "Was ist deutsch" (written in 1865 and published in 1878). For perspectives on twentieth-century postnationalist Germanness and its relation to language, one could read Hannah Arendt (e.g., selected letters from her correspondence with Karl Jaspers, such as her letter of 1 January 1933 and Jaspers' response), T. W. Adorno (perhaps, most pertinently in this case, his 1966 response to Richard Wagner, "Auf die Frage: 'Was ist deutsch?'" or his essay "Wörter aus der Fremde" of 1959), and, for a contemporary, postunification, view, Peter Sloterdijk's 1990 work *Versprechen auf Deutsch: Reden über das eigene Land.*

10. Having assumed from the name that Ursula Grützmacher-Tabori was Georg Tabori's wife, I was informed by Veronika Nowag-Jones, a longtime collaborator and close friend of Tabori's, that the translator's actual name is Ursula Grützmacher. She is not his wife but adds *Tabori* as a professional acknowledgment of the fact that they are, in part, joint authors.

11. For a documentation of Attie's work, see Attie. For a discussion of the work of both Attie and Radermacher in the larger context of Holocaust memorials, see Young, *Art of Memory*. For an analysis of Lin's Vietnam Veterans Memorial in the context of cultural memory, see Sturken.

12. For a sustained and unfailingly thought-provoking, critical reflection on what historicizing history might mean, I would refer particularly to the work of Agnes Heller. See, for example, chaps. 19 and 20 ("History Retrieved?" and "Is Progress an Illusion?") in her 1982 work *A Theory of History;* and chap. 7 ("On the Railway Station") in her 1983 work *A Philosophy of History in Fragments.*

WORKS CITED

Adorno, Theodor W. "Wörter aus der Fremde" ("Words from Abroad"). Trans. Shierry Weber Nicholsen. In vol. 1 of *Notes to Literature,* ed. Rolf Tiedemann. New York: Columbia UP, 1991. 185–99.

———. "Auf die Frage: 'Was ist deutsch?'" In *Stichworte: Kritische Modelle 2.* Frankfurt a.M.: Suhrkamp, 1969. 102–12. Trans. Thomas Y. Levin. "On the Question: 'What Is German?'" *New German Critique* 36 (Fall 1985): 121–31.

Anderson, Benedict. *Imagined Communities: Reflections on the Origin and Spread of Nationalism.* Rev. ed. London and New York: Verso, 1991.

Attie, Shimon. *The Writing on the Wall: Projections in Berlin's Jewish Quarter.* Heidelberg: Edition Braus, 1994.

Auerbach, Erich. "Philology and *Weltliteratur.*" Trans. Maire and Edward Said. *Centennial Review* 12.1 (Winter 1969): 1–17.

Becker, Jurek. *Jakob der Lügner.* Frankfurt a.M.: Suhrkamp, 1982. Trans. Melvin Kornfeld. *Jacob the Liar.* New York: Harcourt Brace Jovanovich, 1975.

Deleuze, Gilles, and Felix Guattari. *Kafka: Toward a Minor Literature.* Trans. Dana Polan. Minneapolis: U of Minnesota P, 1986.

Enzensberger, Hans Magnus. "Bin ich ein Deutscher?" *Die Zeit,* 12 June 1964, 9.

———. *Aussichten auf den Bürgerkrieg.* Frankfurt a.M.: Suhrkamp, 1993.

Fulbrook, Mary. *A Concise History of Germany.* Rev. ed. Cambridge: Cambridge UP, 1992.

Heller, Agnes. *A Theory of History.* London: Routledge and Kegan Paul, 1982.

———. *A Philosophy of History in Fragments.* Oxford and Cambridge: Basil Blackwell, 1983.

Kamenko, Vera. *Unter uns war Krieg. Autobiografie einer jugoslawischen Arbeiterin.* Berlin: Rotbuch-Verlag, 1978.

Martini, Fritz. *Deutsche Literaturgeschichte.* 17th rev. ed. Stuttgart: Alfred Kroner Verlag, 1977.

Müller, Herta. *Barfüssiger Februar: Prosa.* Berlin: Rotbuch-Verlag, 1987.

Sloterdijk, Peter. *Versprechen auf Deutsch: Rede über das eigene Land.* Frankfurt a.M.: Suhrkamp, 1990.

Sturken, Marita. "The Wall, the Screen, and the Image: The Vietnam Veterans Memorial." *Representations* 35 (Summer 1991): 118–42.

Tabori, Georg. "Weisman und Rotgesicht." Trans. Ursula Grützmacher-Tabori. *Theaterstücke II.* Frankfurt a.M.: Fischer Taschenbuch Verlag, 1994.

Woolf, Virginia. *Three Guineas.* New York and London: Harcourt Brace Jovanovich, 1966.

Young, James. *The Texture of Memory: Holocaust Memorials and Meaning.* New Haven and London: Yale UP, 1993.

———. *The Art of Memory: Holocaust Memorials in History.* Munich and New York: Prestel-Verlag, 1994.

CHAPTER 3

Who's Afraid of Cultural Studies?
Taking a "Cultural Turn"
in German History

David F. Crew

For those who have commented on the indispensability of theory to history, David Crew has rendered invaluable service. His article on "Alltagsgeschichte" (the history of everyday life) in the special issue of the Journal of Central European History, *for example, stands out as an important contribution to the possibilities of postmodernist scholarship. Crew, who has also recently edited the well-received volume* Nazism and German Society, 1933–45, *is widely respected for his judgment on scholarship treating modern Germany. After impressive early work in social history, including a social history of Bochum during the half-century prior to World War I, Crew, like many historians, shifted his focus to cultural topics. This is not to imply that he has been a "conjuncturist": David Crew has, in fact, been a pathbreaker, providing thoughtful reflections on new methodologies and fields of inquiries.*

The following essay reflects his experience as a theorist and arbiter. Like Kacandes, Crew covers some basic ground, justified by the audience of historians to whom he partly addresses this essay. Many historians of Germany—though by no means all—have come into an awareness of cultural studies rather later than literary scholars. Crew provides lucid explanations of the new categories and terms; summarizes recent accomplishments in cultural studies, especially as they apply to Germany; and maps out potentially fruitful fields of study. He sees special promise in the methods and queries of feminist historiography and gender studies as well as in the history of daily life. In rendering this service, Crew shows a striking ability to reach out and make connections. This is especially noteworthy with respect to nationality, as he surveys schol-

arship not only in the United States but also in the United Kingdom and on the Continent. While appreciating distinctions in national scholarly cultures—for example, the Germans' relative reluctance to embrace the linguistic turn—Crew recognizes academia's increasingly global character.

Crew also reaches out beyond his own field of history. In undertaking a diplomatic mission on behalf of fellow historians, Crew communicates to those in other fields what historians have accomplished and, conversely, relates information from disciplines such as literature and anthropology to the historical community. His belief in his undertaking—most notably, cross-disciplinary communication, the identification of worthwhile scholarly projects, and the creation of precise and comprehensive theoretical constructs—makes him a very effective ambassador. Ultimately, David Crew argues for a cultural studies that is more historical: where there is greater focus on the development of popular culture and a subtler appreciation of "the complexities and contradictions of the social and cultural practices and milieux." In pointing out the tremendous potential of projects with these goals, Crew assures historians and the rest of us that there is little to fear.

It would be wrong simply to conflate "cultural studies" with the "new cultural history" or with the "linguistic turn" in the human sciences, more generally. These are distinct, if often overlapping, discourses. Yet, on the planes of theory and methodology, these three discourses force historians to face similar questions. For the purposes of this discussion, then, *cultural studies* will act not only as the designation of a specific field but also as a shorthand reference to the larger challenge posed by "poststructuralism" and "postmodernism" to the current and future practice of writing German history.[1]

But What Is Cultural Studies?

Cultural studies may not be "a unified body of work, set of practices, or even an easily defined academic subject" (Franklin et al. 4–5),[2] but it can, nonetheless, be identified, first, by its preferred subjects (which, however, many historians have often regarded as marginal, residual, or simply "soft options")—that is, leisure, entertainment, media, popular culture in general; second, as an important site for attempts to go beyond the limitations of economistic-materialistic and structuralist approaches (nonmarxist as well as marxist) to the

questions of interest and identity formation; and, third, by the theoretical influences shaping the field. These theories, methodologies, and "philosophies,"
which can conveniently, if perhaps too easily, be labeled *poststructuralism, deconstruction,* and *postmodernism* are quite diverse. They extend from femi-
nist/gender studies through literary criticism and cultural anthropology and include the work of, for example, Michel Foucault, Antonio Gramsci, Pierre
Bourdieu, and Michel de Certeau. These various theoretical approaches have
collectively moved the discourse in and on cultural studies much beyond the
largely allergic, top-down reaction of the Frankfurt School (although here we
should not forget to mention Walter Benjamin as a notable exception to the generally negative appraisals of modern "mass culture" presented by the Frankfurt
School). We are now confronted with a much richer, contradictory, and fascinating picture of cultural consumers as also producers of culture—in the sense
that consumption is now regarded also as an act of production of meaning and
significance—that no longer allows us to read the reception of modern cultural
products and practices solely in terms of their intended purposes.[3]

Where Is Cultural Studies?

If one browses through university bookstores or scans department course offerings, especially those in English departments in this country, cultural studies currently appears to be everywhere. Cultural history has also become a significant presence in certain fields and time periods of French, British, and
American historical research and teaching. French historians working on the
early modern period and the history of the French Revolution have certainly
been pioneers in taking the "cultural turn," as mention of only the most well-
known studies amply testifies: that is, the work of Roger Chartier, Robert Darnton, Natalie Davis, Simon Schama, and Lynn Hunt.[4] In England the work of the
Birmingham Centre for Contemporary Cultural Studies (CCCS) has been pivotal in the development of a British cultural studies, although here the direct focus has been post-1945 British society.[5] Nineteenth-century British social history bears the indelible imprint of two towering figures—E. P. Thompson and
Raymond Williams—and their insistence on the importance of "culture" and
"experience." British social historians, like Gareth Stedman Jones, have also
begun to explore the possibilities of a linguistic turn, and Judith Walkowitz's
work on narratives of sexual danger in late Victorian London is clearly influenced by Foucault.[6]

Until quite recently, however, German historians have shown very little
interest in taking the linguistic turn, experimenting with retrospective cultural
anthropology or more generally engaging in the project of "reading the signs"
(Samuel).

Why?

1. We can point, first of all, to the continuing influence of a mandarin academic tradition of "high culture" that dismisses mass culture as mindless and debased. This posture reflects and reproduces the historical divisions and confrontations and "the vehement debate which accompanied the expansion of mass culture in Germany" in the 1920s and again in the 1940s and 1950s (Widdig 18; von Saldern, "Massenfreizeitkultur").[7]
2. The *Strukturgeschichte* (social structural history) exemplified by the work of the so-called Bielefeld School, which has played such an important role in constructing a distinctive German variant of social history since the 1960s, has been quite uninterested in the kind of cultural history that is now a well-embedded fixture of British and French historical writing. Indeed, until very recently *Strukturgeschichte* has been actively hostile to new approaches, such as *Alltagsgeschichte* (history of everyday life), that have attempted to address the need for a more "cultural" approach to German social history.
3. Some German historians have also objected to the ethical problems of postmodernist theory, arguing that German history is "too serious" and, especially under Nazism, has been too murderous to allow German historians to "play" the kinds of cultural/language "games" that the French can afford.[8]

Overall, this means a general tendency to abhor the suggestion that German historians should begin to shift their attention to "the historical analysis of representation as opposed to the pursuit of a discernible, retrievable historical 'reality'" (Canning, "Feminist History"). There are, however, unmistakable, if rather dispersed, signs of an impending change in recent work on German history, even if these are still often confined to the margins of academic life. While intellectual and art historians have been engaged in the construction of an impressive and still growing body of research on modernist high culture, some German social historians have begun to explore the history of mass culture, popular leisure, and entertainment. A recent issue of *WerkstattGeschichte,* for example, edited by Inge Marssolek and Adelheid von Saldern, has attempted to introduce its readers to a variety of "historiographische Experimente" with subjects and approaches, such as popular clothing fashions in the Weimar Republic and the semiotics of urban advertising, that indicate the willingness of at least some younger German historians to investigate the possibilities of cultural studies and the "new cultural history."[9] Dagmar Kift's recent collection of essays on popular entertainment, Heide Schlüpmann's work on early German cinema, and Patrice Petro's book on Weimar cinema all offer new and, in the case of both Schlüpmann and Petro, gendered perspectives on the ways in which the emerging mass culture in Germany was "read" and "appropriated" by its consumers. Wolfgang Sachs's somewhat earlier book on the cultural significance of the motorization of German society has recently been translated into English.

Von Saldern and Marssolek are at present also directing a fascinating research project at the University of Hannover on the history of listening to radio and "gender regimes" in the Third Reich and in the German Democratic Republic (GDR) during the 1950s (Marssolek et al.; see also Lacey). Von Saldern has herself recently published some pioneering articles on mass/popular culture, including a consideration of "Kulturelle Praxisformen im Dritten Reich" (Forms of Cultural Praxis in the Third Reich [see also von Saldern, "Kunst"]). Franz Bokel's recent dissertation examines "Third Reich Celebrities as Mediators between Government and People." And Kaspar Maase has introduced us to the reception of American rock music in the early Federal Republic. A new journal, *Historische Anthropologie. Kultur. Gesellschaft. Alltag* (Historical Anthropology. Culture. History. Everyday Life), has begun to provide an important forum for discussion of the "cultural turn" in German historical research, as did the first in a new series of "Göttinger Gespräche zur Geschichtswissenschaft" (Göttingen Conversations on Historical Studies), which brought Roger Chartier together with Rudolf Vierhaus for an intensive discussion of "cultural history between the 'linguistic turn' and the return of the subject" and "the reconstruction of historical 'life-worlds.' Themes and problems of modern cultural-historical writing" (the titles of Chartier's and Vierhaus' contributions, respectively).[10]

All of these recent departures in the direction of "cultural studies/cultural history" have steadfastly refused to regard popular/mass culture as merely a residual or marginal category but have, instead, begun to show us how popular culture can be read in ways that challenge and expand some of the more limited notions of what is and what is not "political" as well as reminding us that in nineteenth- and twentieth-century German history "popular culture" has itself been the subject of highly political attempts to control, to channel, or simply to repress those features regarded as degraded or dangerous by various state agencies (including most notably the expanding state welfare apparatus) as well as moral reformers and other self-appointed cultural "authorities." Indeed, these approaches to popular culture see it as a new and highly contested "public sphere" that, after 1933, the Nazis attempted to colonize and control.[11] As Adelheid von Saldern observes, "Mass culture became a 'terrain of contestation' not only between workers' organizations and bourgeois-dominated institutions but also within the bourgeoisie itself" ("Hidden History" 35; see also Schlüpmann, Guckel, Radloff). This way of looking at popular culture clearly challenges "Habermas's formally circumscribed understanding of the public sphere as a kind of magic circle of liberal proceduralism" (Eley, "Cultural Socialism" 3).

German History and Cultural Studies/New Cultural History?

There at least five important zones in which traffic across the border between cultural studies and German history has either already begun to move or certainly can and should be encouraged in the future. The most important crossing points have been provided by recent discussions of class, mass politics/mass culture, "society," subjectivity/human agency, and narratives.

1. Class

Recent work on the history of women and gender has made it difficult to see politics as an expression of objective economic or social positions and interests. Kathleen Canning has shown, for example, that the nineteenth-century German labor movement constructed its class interests and identities around the ideal of the skilled, male industrial worker ("Gender and Politics"; and "Feminist History"). This "language of class" marginalized or excluded women as well as several other groups of allegedly backward workers whose identities and interests conflicted with the socialist image of the "true" proletarian— Catholics, Poles, the unskilled, the unorganized, the rough, and the unrespectable. Rather than seeing class-consciousness as an expression of "objective" economic or social interests, we might more usefully begin to think of class as one among several possible ways of describing, ordering, organizing, and making sense of the often diverse and contradictory realities of workers' everyday lives and experiences. In Germany, between 1880 and 1933, class languages had to compete with many other social and political languages— Catholicism, nationalism, liberalism, Nazism—which ordered the same social facts in quite different ways and gave them other meanings and significance.

Alf Lüdtke has, for example, recently suggested that the Nazis' "language of labor" expressed meanings attached by ordinary workers to work that the marxist language of class did not ("Ehre"). Walter Benjamin had drawn attention, in the mid-1930s, to the Nazis' "aestheticization of politics" in the form of huge meetings and marches or mass sporting events. But Lüdtke suggests that these mass spectacles should not obscure the power of the less dramatic, everyday use of symbols by the Nazis. Lüdtke focuses, in particular, upon the rich symbolism surrounding and representing manual work. He contends that even workers who had supported the Social Democrats or Communists during the Weimar Republic displayed ambivalent attitudes toward the Nazi regime after 1933. The Nazis attempted to exploit this "skeptical acquiescence" with a "symbolic offering" in the form, for example, of Nazi insistence on the importance of "German quality work" and "the dignity of labor," enduring cultural icons in German society that could engage the sympathies of a wide range of ordinary Germans, from factory engineers to skilled workers, regardless of their former political persuasions. The Nazis frequently used the written or spoken word to communicate their image of the dignity of labor, but they also mobilized nonverbal, sensual, visual images—for example, photographs of laboring bodies—which, as Walter Benjamin recognized, could be infinitely replicated and circulated to a mass audience. The readers for whom these words and images were intended were, however, primarily men. The labor that the Nazis attempted to dignify and through which industrial workers constructed their own identities and self-esteem was paid wage labor performed by the skilled, strong bodies of German men, not the unpaid housework of German women. By offering male German workers new forms of recognition, new status, new opportunities, and new hopes, the Nazi regime facilitated these workers' acceptance of and participation in the construction of the murderous Nazi regime.

2.   Mass Politics/Mass Culture: Gender and Genre

Eve Rosenhaft has recently suggested that gender, understood "not as the qualities attributed to empirical individuals but as a system of organizing social perception in which sexual difference is pivotal" is central to an understanding of the discourses of mass politics and mass culture (159, 161–64). Bernd Widdig contends that the development of these discourses in the late nineteenth and early twentieth centuries "follows an overriding pattern in German modernist culture of conceptualizing crowds and masses as feminine entities which threaten to destroy male autonomy" (14; see also Theweleit). World War I, the German Revolution (1918–19), and the German inflation of 1923 greatly accelerated fears of a "massification" of German society that would transform "formerly distinct entities into larger and larger numbers, which causes the single entity to lose its former value and its distinctiveness" (15; see also Tatar, "Fighting" and *Lustmord*). The image of the "New Woman" reinforced anxieties about conventional gender differences and fears that gender identities were becoming increasingly unclear and unstable in the Weimar Republic. But if the rise of the masses threatened masculine identities, "the cultural forms that characterized the new mass society had a particular appeal or utility for women" (Rosenhaft 163). Women (and young people) were the most important element(s) of the early filmgoing audiences, and the filmmakers began to shape their products in ways they thought would appeal to women. Melodrama became a particularly popular genre, and film melodrama appears, in turn, to have influenced the modes of address and visual narration adopted by other Weimar mass media such as photojournalism (Rosenhaft 164–65; Petro 26). Rosenhaft suggests that this intertextuality can also be observed in the language of the political extremes—Nazism and communism—for whom melodrama was the preferred form of political address (168–69). But we need to know much more about the ways in which popular modes of seeing and reading cultural products invaded politics and/or were appropriated by political practices.[12]

3. "Society" and   4.   Subjectivity/Human Agency

If attempts to write the history of politics or culture with reference to their underlying "social determinations" have been seriously challenged by the postmodernist claim that "'individual' and 'society' are not real 'objective' entities, but historical and normative creations" (Joyce 83), then a postmodernist approach to German history would shift our attention to the ways in which society and the categories it constitutes—class, identity, the individual—were formed by the discourses and practices of the past (Canning, "German Particularities" 105).[13] But German historians are, quite understandably, disturbed by the ethical implications of a linguistic turn that might have the effect of erasing recognizable notions of the individual subject. As Peter Jelavich puts it: "the horrors of the Nazi era hover over every conceptualization of the German past. Within that context, it is hard to avoid the conclusion that a denial of human agency exculpates the perpetrators of these deeds, while a denial of subjectivity amounts to silencing the voices of the murdered" ("Contemporary" 376). Of course, simply insisting on the importance of human agency will not resolve the dilemma created by appropriations of discourse analysis that deflate "the illusion of autonomous agency/subjectivity" only to succumb to "the vision of discourse as singularly determinant of subjects and their experiences" (Canning, "Feminist History" 397). After the linguistic turn can there be "no history of the victims but only a history of the construction of victimization" (Benhabib 113)?[14] Kathleen Canning suggests that focusing upon the (female) body "as a complex site of inscription and of subjectivity/resistance" ("Feminist History" 397)[15] may be one way to understand how subjects "can . . . be constituted by discourse without being determined by it" (Benhabib 110). I think that historians will also need to expand and refine their vocabulary if they are to convey "the multiple everyday ambiguities of 'ordinary people' making their choices among the various greys of active consent, accommodation, and non-conformity" (Peukert 243). Instead of thinking in terms of a polarized spectrum of possibilities leading from domination to resistance, we should also recognize those kinds of "hiding in the light" that can, in the youth subcultures described by Dick Hebdige, "convert the fact of being under surveillance into the pleasure of being watched." This politics of metaphor "deals in the currency of signs and is, thus, always ambiguous" ("Hiding" 35; see also Lüdtke, "Geschichte und Eigensinn"). Historians also need to acknowledge the importance of symbolic and expressive needs as well as material and instrumental interests and to explore symbolic practices through the use of more unorthodox sources—photographs, for example—and nonverbal forms of expression such as the "body language" of German workers (Crew, *"Alltagsgeschichte"* 396, 399; see also Berliner Geschichtswerkstatt).

5. Narratives

For at least the past thirty years modern German historical writing has been structured by some of the strongest narratives and counternarratives of any postwar Western European historiography. The notion of a German *Sonderweg* (special path) leading from Bismarck to Hitler was soon challenged by Eley and Blackbourn's call for the "normalization" of modern German history, and their critique was followed by Detlev Peukert's brilliant attempt to understand Nazism and the Third Reich as one pathological, but possible, outcome of Germany's "crisis of classical modernity." Each of these attempts to rethink Germany's past has made it more and more difficult to accept "a concept of reality which is monolithic, linear and does not allow for plural realities" (Lindenberger and Wildt 85). Few German historians are ready to embrace the view "that there are neither fixed meanings nor privileged positions from which truth might be known" (Caplan 266). But the exponents of *Alltagsgeschichte* have certainly voiced their dissatisfaction not only with the old narratives but also with the "'old' way of writing history [that has] lost its power to convince, its capacity to 'fabricate the real' by narrating it" (Lindenberger and Wildt 85). Especially in its use of oral history, *Alltagsgeschichte* has defied the "professional/academic" historian's assertion of a monopoly of historical knowledge. *Alltagsgeschichte* has, indeed, attempted "to dissolve altogether the conventional construction of the historian as the sole narrator, the creator of a single monologue" (77–78). But, while it is certainly important to retrieve the stories and voices suppressed or ignored by previous narratives of German history, we also need to know how homogenization, suppression, and silencing achieved their effects in past history itself as well as in the histories written about the past (see, e.g., Geyer).

Conclusions

At this point German historians' engagement with the issues raised by cultural studies/cultural history is quite uneven—much weaker, for example, in the corpus of research on the *Kaiserreich* (the Second Empire) than on Weimar, Nazi Germany, or the postwar Federal Republic. It remains to be seen exactly how cultural history or *Alltagsgeschichte* will influence the construction of a social history of the GDR (see, e.g., Kaelble et al.) The majority of German historians are probably still untroubled by the "postmodernist challenge" or simply unaware of its existence. Even German women's history and gender studies remain remarkably innocent of "the acute sense of 'epistemological crisis' that has accompanied the feminist interrogation of established categories, narratives, and chronologies in Britain and the United States" (Canning, "German Particularities" 104).

But the task, as Lynn Hunt has rightly suggested, is not only to bring cultural studies into history but also to make cultural studies more historical (*New Cultural History* 22). This can be done in at least two ways.

First, we must historicize the discussion of cultural studies by reconstructing the historical emergence, development, and reception of popular/mass cultural practices and products. This dimension is by no means a completely blank slate; the history of German cinema is, for example, one of the best researched fields in modern German cultural history (see Frieden et al.; Fehrenbach). But even here there is still much to be learned about the everyday meanings and uses of the cinema in the past (see Kinter). Much less attention has been paid to the other modern mass media: records, radio, photography (see, e.g., May; Tagg; and Lüdtke, "Industriebilder" 431–50). And, though film history has shown that we need to pay particularly close attention to gender in our discussions of cultural production/consumption, we also need to know how class, religious, ethnic, regional, and other identities affected the ways in which modern cultural products/practices were read, seen, and heard (see Franklin et al.).

Second, historicizing the discourse of cultural studies could also expand and deepen the critique of the vocabulary of cultural studies that has already begun to develop within the field itself (see Schiach). Neither *mass culture* nor *popular culture* nor *working-class culture* nor *commercial culture* adequately reflects the complexities and contradictions of the social and cultural practices and milieux these terms claim to describe. It is symptomatic that cultural studies has itself increasingly turned, instead, to another category, "everyday life." It is probably on this terrain, where German historians have been genuine pioneers, that historical and cultural studies have the best chance of meeting in the future (During 24–25).

NOTES

1. It is likewise important to point out that there is considerable disagreement about what each of these individual terms actually describes. *Postmodernism* is, for example, "a complex, disputed and elusive concept" and "the very categories, assumptions and tenets of post-modernism and its frequently related phenomenon, post-structuralism, are far more problematical and contested than often assumed by those historians embracing the 'linguistic turn'" (Kirk 222, 221).

2. Geoff Eley describes cultural studies as: "a still-emergent cross-disciplinary formation [which] comprises a varying miscellany of influences—sociologists, literary scholars, and historians in Britain (but interestingly rather few anthropologists); mass communications, film studies, literary theory, reflexive anthropology in the USA, with a supportive institutional context in programs in Women's Studies, American Culture, and so on" (Eley, "Is There a History" 32). My comments in this essay were originally formulated in response to a panel on "Learning from Cultural Studies" at the German Studies Association annual meeting in Dallas, Texas, October 1994. They still bear the imprint of that earlier concentration on cultural studies, but I have tried here to encompass what may more generally be called the challenge of the "cultural turn" in the human sciences.

3. See, for example, Fiske, *Reading* and *Understanding;* Willis; Hebdige, *Subculture* and *Hiding;* Chambers; "Scholarly Controversy"; Denning; Butsch; and Appadurai.

4. For a recent overview, see McMillan; see also Stewart; and Hunt, "Objects."

5. Simon During provides an excellent orientation to the work of the CCCS in his introduction to *The Cultural Studies Reader.*

6. A representative sample of work in cultural studies in the United States can be found in Grossberg, Nelson, and Treichler.

7. See also "Gegen die Kulturreaktion"; on the 1920s, see von Saldern, "Hidden History"; on the 1950s, see Maase, Fehrenbach, "Fight"; and Poiger.

8. Kenneth Barkin suggests, for example, that "the stakes are higher in German history; there is less room for French intellectual gymnastics" (246); see also the response to Barkin (Geyer and Jarausch, "Great Men").

It should, however, be emphasized that scholars of German history in North America have, so far, devoted much more attention to the problems of poststructuralism, postmodernism, and the linguistic turn than have their colleagues in Germany itself. Indeed, most German historians in the Federal Republic appear to be relatively uninterested in participating in the kind of debates that have recently engaged their North American counterparts. But see Jelavich, "Poststrukturalismus."

9. See especially Heinze; Guckel-Seitz, "Stadtreklame"; see also Birkefeld and Jung.

10. See, for example, Lüdtke, "Industrie-Bilder"; and Minkmar. The first meeting of the "Göttinger Gespräche" was held at the Max Planck Institut für Geschichte, Göttingen, 16 June 1994.

11. Miriam Hansen points out that American and German reactions to the early cinema were quite different; whereas cinema and its audience became the locus of considerable cultural anxiety, at least for the cultivated/educated elites, moral authorities, and state officials in Germany, early cinema was received much more positively in the United States, as a new medium of popular education and enlightenment (see also Kuhn). The education/enlightenment side of the debate on German cinema was, however, by no means absent.

12. In his book *Aufstand der Bilder. Die NS-Propaganda vor 1933,* for example, Gerhard Paul acknowledges the growing importance of photography in Nazi electoral propaganda but contents himself with the observation that "photography recommended itself to Nazi propaganda because it was endowed with a greater degree of concreteness and sensuousness than the written and spoken word" (die Fotografie empfahl sich der NS-Propaganda, da ihr im Gegensatz zum geschriebenen und gesprochenen Wort ein

höheres Mass an Konkretheit und Sinnlichkeit zuerkannt wurde). Paul makes no attempt to locate photographic languages within any broader field of contemporary cultural practices nor to explore the various, complex ways in which such political "pictures" might have been "read" (including, certainly, readings that frustrated, even rejected, the political intentions of the authors) by the audiences to whom they were directed (146). Considerably more successful in both of these respects is Alf Lüdtke, "Industriebilder-Bilder." For a discussion of the contradictions between the KPD's attempts to instrumentalize "melodramatic" representations of working-class "everyday life" in the Weimar welfare state and the satisfaction of readers' own needs see my article "A Social Republic? Social Democrats, Communists and the Weimar Welfare State."

13. See also Eley, "Is All the World a Text?"; and Burchell et al. A fundamental text announcing the linguistic turn in feminist historiography is Scott, *Gender and the Politics of History;* for German history, more specifically, see Canning, "Feminist History."

14. One of the few serious attempts to apply discourse analysis to German sources can be found in von Saldern et al., "Exkurs."

15. In this connection Thomas Balistier's *Gewalt und Ordnung. Kalkül und Faszination der SA* deserves to be better known.

WORKS CITED

Appadurai, Arjun, ed. *The Social Life of Things: Commodities in Cultural Perspective.* Cambridge: Cambridge UP, 1986.

Balistier, Thomas. *Gewalt und Ordnung. Kalkül und Faszination der SA.* Münster: Westfälisches Dampfboot, 1989.

Barkin, Kenneth. "Bismarck in a Postmodern Age." *German Studies Review* 18.2 (May 1995): 241–51.

Benhabib, Seyla. "Subjectivity, Historiography, and Politics: Reflections on the Feminism/Postmodernism Exchange." In *Feminist Contentions. A Philosophical Exchange,* ed. Seyla Benhabib, Judith Butler, Drucilla Cornell, and Nancy Fraser. New York and London: Routledge, 1995. 107–25.

Berliner Geschichtswerkstatt, ed. *Alltagskultur, Subjektivität und Geschichte: Zur Theorie und Praxis von Alltagsgeschichte.* Münster: Westfälisches Dampfoot, 1994.

Birkefeld, Richard, and Martina Jung. *Die Stadt, der Lärm und das Licht: Die Veränderung des öffentlichen Raumes durch Motorisierung und Elektrifizierung.* Seelze (Velber): Kallmeyersche Verlagsbuchhandlung, 1994.

Bokel, Franz. "'Great Days' in Germany: Third Reich Celebrities as Mediators between Government and People." Ph.D. diss., Department of Germanic Languages, U of Texas at Austin, 1995.

Burchell, Graham, Colin Gordon, and Peter Miller, eds. *The Foucault Effect: Studies in Governmentality.* Chicago: U of Chicago P, 1991.

Butsch, Richard. "Mass Culture: Terrain for Collective Action?" *International Labor and Working-Class History* 39 (Spring 1991): 33–34.

Canning, Kathleen. "Feminist History after the 'Linguistic Turn': Historicizing Discourse and Experience." *Signs* 19.2 (Winter 1994): 368–404.

————. "Gender and the Politics of Class Formation: Rethinking German Labor History." *American Historical Review* 97.3 (June 1992): 736–68.

————. "German Particularities in Women's History/Gender History." *Journal of Women's History* 5.1 (Spring 1993): 102–14.

Caplan, Jane. "Postmodernism, Poststructuralism and Deconstruction: Notes for Historians." In "German Histories: Challenges in Theory, Practice, Technique," ed. Michael Geyer and Konrad Jarausch. Special issue of *Central European History* 22 (1989): 260–78.

Chambers, Iain. *Popular Culture: The Metropolitan Experience.* London and New York: Routledge, 1986.

Chartier, Roger. *The Cultural Uses of Print.* Princeton: Princeton UP, 1987.

Crew, David F. "*Alltagsgeschichte:* A New Social History 'From Below'"? In "German Histories: Challenges in Theory, Practice, Technique," ed. Michael Geyer and Konrad Jarausch. Special issue of *Central European History* 22.3–4 (September–December 1989): 394–407.

————. "A Social Republic? Social Democrats, Communists and the Weimar Welfare State." In *Between Reform and Revolution: Studies in the History of German Socialism and Communism from 1840 to 1990,* ed. David E. Barclay and Eric D. Weitz. Providence and Oxford: Berghahn Publishers, forthcoming.

Darnton, Robert. *The Great Cat Massacre and Other Episodes in French Cultural History.* New York: Vintage Books, 1985.

Davis, Natalie Zemon. *Society and Culture in Early Modern France.* Palo Alto: Stanford UP, 1975.

Denning, Michael. "The Ends of Ending Mass Culture." *International Labor and Working-Class History* 38 (Fall 1990): 63–67.

During, Simon. "Introduction." In *The Cultural Studies Reader,* ed. Simon During. London and New York: Routledge, 1993. 1–28.

Eley, Geoff. "Cultural Socialism, the Public Sphere, and the Mass Form: Popular Culture and the Democratic Project, 1900–1934." Paper prepared for the conference "Past and Present: The Challenge of E. P. Thompson," Princeton University, 22–23 April 1994.

————. "Is All the World a Text? From Social History to the History of Society Two Decades Later." In *The Historical Turn in the Human Sciences,* ed. Terrence J. McDonald. Ann Arbor: U of Michigan P, 1996. 193–243.

————. "Is There a History of the Kaiserreich?" In *Society, Culture, and the State in Germany, 1870–1930,* ed. Geoff Eley. Ann Arbor: U of Michigan P, 1996. 1–42.

Fehrenbach, Heide. *Cinema in Democratizing Germany: Reconstructing National Identity after Hitler.* Chapel Hill: U of North Carolina P, 1995.

————. "The Fight for the 'Christian West': German Film Control, the Churches and the Reconstruction of Civil Society in the Early Bonn Republic." *German Studies Review* 14 (1991): 39–63.

Fiske, John. *Reading the Popular.* Boston: Unwin Hyman, 1989.

————. *Understanding Popular Culture.* Boston: Unwin Hyman, 1989.

Franklin, Sarah, Celia Lury, and Jacki Stacey, "Introduction 1. Feminism and Cultural Studies: Past, Presents, Futures." In *Off-Centre: Feminism and Cultural Studies,* ed. Sarah Franklin, Celia Lurey, and Jackie Stacey. London: HarperCollins Academic, 1991. 1– 20.

Frieden, Sandra, et al., eds. *Gender and German Cinema: Feminist Interventions.* Providence and Oxford: Berg, 1993.

"Gegen die Kulturreaktion. Was ist Kulturbolshewismus!" *Kulturwille* (Leipzig) 5–6 (May– June 1931): 82–87.

Geyer, Michael. "Historical Fictions of Autonomy and the Europeanization of National History." In "German Histories: Challenges in Theory, Practice, Technique," ed. Michael Geyer and Konrad Jarausch. Special issue of *Central European History* 22.3–4 (September–December 1989): 316–42.

Geyer, Michael, and Konrad Jarausch. "Great Men and Postmodern Ruptures: Overcoming the 'Belatedness' of German Historiography." *German Studies Review* 18.2 (May 1995): 253–73.

Grossberg, Lawrence, Cary Nelson, and Paula Treichler, eds. *Cultural Studies.* London and New York: Routledge, 1992.

Guckel, Sabine. "Von 'Kinderseelen und ungebildeten Volksmassen'. Filmreform und Lehrfilmkino in Hannover zwischen 1912 und 1925." In *Stadt und Moderne: Hannover in der Weimarer Republik,* ed. Adelheid von Saldern. Hamburg: Ergebnisse, 1989. 285– 306.

Guckel-Seitz, Sabine. "Stadtreklame als Text: Die(se) Geschichte mit der Semiotik." *WerkstattGeschichte* 7.3 (April 1994): 31–42.

Hansen, Miriam. "Early Silent Cinema: Whose Public Sphere?" *New German Critique* 29 (1983): 147–84.

Hebdige, Dick. "Hiding in the Light: Youth Surveillance and Display." *Hiding in the Light. On Images and Things.* New York and London: Routledge, Comedia, 1988. 17–36.

————. *Subculture: The Meaning of Style.* London and New York: Methuen, 1979.

Heinze, Karen. "'Schick, selbst mit beschränkten Mitteln!': Die Anleitung zur alltäglichen Distinktion in einer Modezeitschrift der Weimarer Republik." *WerkstattGeschichte* 7.3 (April 1994): 18–30.

Hunt, Lynn, ed. *The New Cultural History.* Berkeley: U of California P, 1989.

————. "The Objects of History: A Reply to Philip Stewart." *Journal of Modern History* 66.3 (September 1994): 539–46.

————. *Politics, Culture, and Class in the French Revolution.* Berkeley: U of California P, 1984.

Jelavich, Peter. "Contemporary Literary Theory: from Deconstruction Back to History." In "German Histories: Challenges in Theory, Practice, Technique," ed. Michael Geyer and Konrad Jarausch. Special issue of *Central European History* 22 (1989): 360–80.

————. "Poststrukturalismus und Sozialgeschichte—aus amerikanischer Perspektive." *Geschichte und Gesellschaft* 21 (1995): 259–89.

Jones, Gareth Stedman. *Languages of Class: Studies in English Working Class History, 1832–1982.* Cambridge: Cambridge UP, 1983.

Joyce, Patrick. "The End of Social History." *Social History* 20.1 (January 1995): 73–91.

Kaelble, Hartmut, Jürgen Kocka, and Hartmut Zwahr, eds. *Sozialgeschichte der DDR.* Stuttgart: Klett Cotta, 1994.

Kift, Dagmar, ed. *Kirmes-Kneipe-Kino. Arbeiterkultur im Ruhrgebiet zwischen Kommerz und Kontrolle (1850–1914).* Paderborn: Ferdinand Schöningh, 1992.

Kinter, Jürgen. "'Durch Nacht zum Licht': Vom Guckkasten zum Filmpalast. Die Anfänge des Kinos und das Verhältnis der Arbeiterbewegung zum Film." In *Kirmes-Kneipe-Kino. Arbeiterkultur im Ruhrgebiet zwischen Kommerz und Kontrolle (1850–1914)*, ed. Dagmar Kift. Paderborn: Ferdinand Schöningh, 1992. 119–46.

Kirk, Neville. "History, Language, Ideas and Post-modernism: A Materialist View." *Social History* 19.2 (May 1994): 221–41.

Kuhn, Annette. *Cinema, Censorship and Sexuality, 1909–1925*. London and New York: Routledge, 1988.

Laccy, Kate. *Feminine Frequencies: Gender, German Radio, and the Public Sphere, 1923–1945*. Ann Arbor: U of Michigan P, 1996.

Lindenberger, Thomas, and Michael Wildt. "Radical Plurality: History Workshops as a Practical Critique of Knowledge." *History Workshop Journal* 33 (1992): 73–99.

Lüdtke, Alf. "'Ehre der Arbeit': Industriearbeiter und Macht der Symbole. Zur Reichweite symbolischer Orientierungen im Nationalsozialismus." In *Arbeiter im 20. Jahrhundert*, ed. Klaus Tenfelde. Stuttgart: Klett-Cotta Verlag, 1991. 343–94. Translated in an abridged version as "The 'Honor of Labor': Industrial Workers and the Power of Symbols under National Socialism." In *Nazism and German Society, 1933–1945*, ed. David F. Crew. London: Routledge, 1994. 67–109.

———. "Geschichte und Eigensinn." In *Alltagskultur, Subjektivität und Geschichte: Zur Theorie und Praxis von Alltagsgeschichte*, ed. Berliner Geschichtswerkstatt. Münster: Westfälisches Dampfoot, 1994. 139–56.

———. "Industriebilder-Bilder der Industriearbeit? Industrie und Arbeiterphotographie von der Jahrhundertwende bis in die 1930er Jahre." *Historische Anthropologie* 1 (1993): 394–430.

Maase, Kaspar. *Bravo Amerika. Erkundungen zur Jugendkultur der Bundesrepublik in den fünfziger Jahren*. Hamburg: Junius Verlag, 1992.

Marssolek, Inge, Adelheid von Saldern, Daniela Münkel, Monika Pater, and Ute C. Schmidt. "Zuhören und Gehörtwerden. Radiogeschichte und Geschlechterordnung im Dritten Reich und in der DDR der fünfziger Jahre." Zwischenbericht. Historisches Seminar, Universität Hannover, February 1995.

May, Rainhard. "Die Schallplatte als 'Kult-Mittel.'" In "Arbeiter und Massenkultur. Wandlungen im Freizeitverhalten der zwanziger Jahre." *Mitteilungen aus der kulturwissenschaftlichen Forschung* 15.30 (March 1992): 182–225.

McMillan, James F. "Social History, 'New Cultural History,' and the Rediscovery of Politics: Some Recent Work on Modern France." *Journal of Modern History* 66.4 (December 1994): 755–72.

Minkmar, Nils. "Vom Totschlagen kostbarer Zeit. Der Gebrauch des Kinos in einer Industrieregion (1900–1914)." *Historische Anthropologie* 1 (1993): 431–50.

Paul, Gerhard. *Aufstand der Bilder. Die NS-Propaganda vor 1933*. Bonn: Verlag J. H. W. Dietz Nachf., 1990.

Petro, Patrice. *Joyless Streets: Women and Melodramatic Representation in Weimar Germany*. Princeton: Princeton UP, 1989.

Peukert, Detlev. *Inside Nazi Germany: Conformity, Opposition and Racism in Everyday Life*. New Haven and London: Yale UP, 1987.

Poiger, Uta G. "Rebels with a Cause? American Popular Culture, the 1956 Youth Riots, and the New Conception of Masculinity in East and West Germany." In *The Amer-*

ican Impact on Postwar Germany, ed. Reiner Pommerin. Providence and Oxford: Berghahn Books, 1995. 93–124.

Radloff, Silke. "Filmkultur und gesetzliche Reglementierungen. Am Beispiel des Reichs-lichtspielgesetzes von 1920." Master's thesis, Universität Hannover, 1988.

Rosenhaft, Eve. "Women, Gender, and the Limits of Political History in the Age of 'Mass Politics.'" In *Elections, Mass Politics, and Social Change in Modern Germany: New Perspectives,* ed. Larry Eugene Jones and James Retallack. Cambridge: Cambridge UP, 1992. 149–73.

Sachs, Wolfgang. *Die Liebe zum Automobil. Ein Rückblick in die Geschichte unserer Wünsche.* Reinbek bei Hamburg: Rowohlt, 1984. Translated as *For the Love of the Automobile: Looking Back into the History of our Desires.* Berkeley, Los Angeles, and Oxford: U of California P, 1992.

Samuel, Raphael. "Reading the Signs: II. Fact-Grubbers and Mind-Readers." *History Workshop Journal* 33 (1992): 220–51.

Schama, Simon. *Citizens: A Chronicle of the French Revolution.* New York: Knopf, 1989.

Schiach, Morag. *Discourse on Popular Culture.* Cambridge: Polity Press, 1989.

Schlüpmann, Heide. *Unheimlichkeit des Blicks. Das Drama des frühen deutschen Kinos.* Frankfurt: Stroemfeld/Roter Stern, 1990. 189–243.

"Scholarly Controversy: Mass Culture." *International Labor and Working-Class History* 37 (Spring 1990): 2–40.

Scott, Joan. *Gender and the Politics of History.* New York: Columbia UP, 1988.

Stewart, Philip. "This Is Not a Book Review: On Historical Uses of Literature." *Journal of Modern History* 66.3 (September 1994): 521–38.

Tagg, John. *The Burden of Representation: Essays on Photographies and Histories.* Minneapolis: U of Minnesota P, 1993.

Tatar, Maria. "Fighting for Life: Figurations of War, Women and the City in the Work of Otto Dix." In "Cultural Transformation and Cultural Politics in Weimar Germany," ed. John Czaplicka. Special issue of *German Politics and Society* 32 (Summer 1994): 28–57.

Tatar, Maria. *Lustmord: Sexual Murder in Weimar Germany.* Princeton: Princeton UP, 1995.

Theweleit, Klaus. *Männerphantasien.* 2 vols. Frankfurt a.M.: Verlag Roter Stern, 1978.

Thompson, E. P. *The Making of the English Working Class.* New York: Vintage Books, 1963.

von Saldern, Adelheid. "The Hidden History of Mass Culture." *International Labor and Working-Class History* 37 (Spring 1990): 32–40.

———. "Kulturelle Praxisformen im Dritten Reich. Die Geschichtswissenschaft vor neuen Aufgaben." In *Kulturaustreibung. Die Einflussnahme des Nationalsozialismus auf Kunst und Kultur in Niedersachsen. Eine Dokumentation zur gleichnamigen Ausstellung,* ed. Hinrich Bergmeier and Günter Katzenberger. Hamburg: Dolling und Galitz Verlag, 1994.

———. "'Kunst für's Volk': Vom Kulturkonservatismus zur nationalsozialistischen Kulturpolitik." In *Das Gedächtnis der Bilder: Ästhetik und Nationalsozialismus,* ed. Harald Welzer. Tübingen: Edition Diskord, 1995. 45–104.

————. "Massenfreizeitkultur im Visier: Zu den Deutungs- und Einwirkungsversuchen während der Weimarer Republik." *Archiv für Sozialgeschichte* 33 (1993): 21–58.

von Saldern, Adelheid, with Karen Heinze and Sybille Kuster. "Exkurs. Eine Sensation stösst ins Leere: Gertrud Polley im Mittelpunkt eines Diskurses." In *Neues Wohnen: Wohnungspolitik in Hannover der zwanziger Jahre.* Hannoversche Studien: Schriftenreihe des Stadtarchivs Hannover, vol. 1. Hannover: Hahnsche Buchhandlung, 1993. 69–94.

Walkowitz, Judith R. *City of Dreadful Delight: Narratives of Sexual Danger in Late-Victorian London.* Chicago: U of Chicago P, 1992.

WerkstattGeschichte 7.3 (April 1994).

Widdig, Bernd. "Cultural Dimensions of Inflation in Weimar Germany." In "Cultural Transformation and Cultural Politics in Weimar Germany," ed. John Czaplicka. Special issue of *German Politics and Society* 32 (Summer 1994): 10–27.

Williams, Raymond. *Culture and Society: 1780–1950.* Harmondsworth: Penguin, 1958.

————. *The Long Revolution.* Harmondsworth: Penguin, 1961.

Willis, Paul. *Common Culture: Symbolic Work at Play in the Everyday Cultures of the Young.* Milton Keynes: Open University P, 1990.

CHAPTER 4

Multiculturalism and the Study of German Literature

Arlene A. Teraoka

In this essay Arlene Teraoka casts her critical eye upon German resistance—historical, contemporary, and scholarly—to the notion of multiculturalism. At the heart of her argument is a companion critique to David Crew's of the historical profession in the previous essay. Germanistik, *the study of German literature and philology, was and, as Teraoka and Bammer before her point out, to a great extent still is a discipline that has traditionally used literature as a tool of cultural hegemony. Germanists have generally operated on the principle that there is one unified German culture whose preservation and dissemination it is their job to promote. This professional chauvinism mirrors an attitude in the society at large that "Germanness" is a stable notion, a concept that numerous contributors in this volume, along with Teraoka, also critique. Thus, Trinh Minh-ha's statement "'I' is not unitary, culture has never been monolithic" could serve as an epigraph for the whole volume. In a German cultural studies context the pluralistic fabric of German society, both past and present, must be accepted as a given.*

Teraoka is a particularly appropriate individual to offer an analysis of the Eurocentrism common among both Germans and Germanists. Born in Hawaii of Japanese ancestry, she is one example of the younger generation of Germanists in the United States who came to the subject through intellectual curiosity (in her case, the German philosophical tradition) rather than through ethnic or other personal connections. A self-described "cultural outsider" in her field, she has dedicated her scholarly and pedagogical energies to interrogating German literature in the contexts of race, class, and gender. Her particular interest in so-called Gastarbeiterliteratur *(guest worker literature) has led her to useful insights into minority/majority interactions in society at large. Her discussion here offers a wise warning to proponents of American multi-*

63

cultural society, as well as of German multicultural study, not to reduce individuals to their ethnicity.

Teraoka's essay draws our attention to the way that Germans and Germanists have continued to resist conceptions of "German" culture as an inherently unstable entity, even though discussions of multiculturalism have begun in Germany. Traditional, hegemonic notions of German culture continue to undermine genuine transformation in our conception of what is German, as, for example, in the interkulturelle Germanistik *movement. On the other hand, Teraoka sees promise in the next generation of scholars, especially in the United States, for whom "a multicultural scholarly perspective comes close to second nature." One site of great transformative potential is the foreign language classroom. That German cultural studies and truly interdisciplinary work is still not the norm in American academia, however, is indicated by Teraoka's essay itself. The reader will notice that it is situated within the terms and premises of a now long line of discussions among Germanists alone. This discussion has not cut across disciplinary borders to include historians, political scientists, artists, journalists, etc. The polemical tone of Teraoka's essay reveals both her frustration that the conservative faction of American* Germanistik *still controls the terms of the debate and her sense of urgency about the field's need to move in a cultural studies direction.*

"'I' is not unitary, culture has never been monolithic." Thus writes the Vietnamese filmmaker Trinh Minh-ha, now resident in the United States, in an essay on the complexities of representing Others (76). The observation is especially pertinent to American scholars of German literature, whose field has been dominated until rather recently by male, German-born intellectuals striving to protect their national culture from the taint of political history (Schmidt). Despite the existence of a now unified German nation, the "I" that studies things German has become even more richly divided, and the culture that is "German" remains more than ever a conflicted, contested domain inhabited by various racial, ethnic, and national groups. That there exists a unified and unifying German culture; that our primary task is to preserve this tradition for new generations of readers; even that we study works of literature—at present these seemingly fundamental tenets can no longer be assumed to constitute the basis of our disciplinary identity.

A crucial factor contributing to this ideological disunification is the movement within the American academy known as *multiculturalism.* Encompassing a wide range of efforts by scholars in women's studies, postcolonial studies, and ethnic studies, the term denotes a powerful challenge to a monocultural curriculum, a Eurocentric humanism, that disguises itself as "the best that has been thought and known in the world" (Matthew Arnold) while promoting primarily the values and interests of Western bourgeois males (qtd. in West 21). Demands are raised that we recognize the hegemonic function—the exercise and preservation of class, racial, and gender privilege—performed by the notion of a universal culture and that we attend to other voices with different values and expressions. Further, the recognition of the partiality of the Western canon is not to result simply in the tolerant addition of new works and authors; rather, as Richard Brodhead urges, the very terms of our understanding must be changed and enriched (47). In this regard Cornel West observes, though not without a critical eye, the significant shift in sensibilities that has occurred among many artists and critics: away from monolithic, homogeneous, universal views of culture, toward discourses of diversity, multiplicity, the particular, and the contingent (19).

Unlike other scholarly reforms whose social agendas might be less explicit, the curricular changes demanded by multiculturalism have come about as a direct result of political pressures external to the American university. The strongest force derives from the actual multicultural nature of U.S. society: by the year 2000 over 40 percent of public school children will come from minority groups or the underclass, and 75 percent of the labor force will consist of women and people of color (Mohanty 197–98). Growing minority enrollments in colleges and universities have already led to the perceived "breakup of a white, middle-class constituency as the mainstay of college education" (Geyer 501). The typical American university of the 1990s supports a number of disciplines and departments—women's studies, ethnic studies, gay and lesbian studies—that originated in the civil rights and women's movements of the 1960s; deeper roots still can be found in the global process of decolonization in the wake of World War II, which marked, as West notes, the end of the "Age of Europe" (20). As proponents of multiculturalism often insist, the world itself is multicultural: the end of the Cold War, the development of a complex global economy, political and economic migration, the growth of the Pacific rim—these and other developments have resulted in a general decentering of Europe and the West in political-economic and especially intellectual terms.

Multiculturalism in the university thus represents only the latest consequence of a global revolution in the postwar period that seeks to dismantle Eurocentrist hegemony in all areas of life. Scholarly efforts to develop categories of race, class, and gender as critical terms of analysis; new social histories and subaltern studies that focus on the experience of marginalized and oppressed groups; the emergence and prominence of women and minority writers, artists, and scholars; legal requirements of equal opportunity and affirmative action goals in colleges and universities; the dominance of marxist, poststructuralist, psychoanalytic, and feminist theories that destabilize familiar texts and traditional modes of understanding; heated debates over the educational value and ideological function of "Great Books" courses in Western civilization;[1] and, most recently, the rapid success of cultural studies, a multidisciplinary and overtly political mode of analysis that investigates everyday cultural practices within larger systems of power (Brantlinger; Bathrick; Grossberg et al.; During)—these developments within the academy pose deep threats to the "monocultural, ethnoracial Eurovision" that had become institutionalized practice by the middle of the twentieth century (Goldberg 4; also see Geyer 505–10).[2]

To all of this the field of German studies has been slow to respond. Part of the discipline's inertia can be attributed to historical factors; the influx of talented European émigrés fleeing German fascism helped to create a strong scholarly profile for American *Germanistik* while, at the same time, institutionalizing the notion of the autonomous work of art and the ideal of a pure research untouched by politics (Trommler, "Einleitung" 20–22; Schmidt). The insistence on "suprapolitical autonomy" (Schmidt 297), an oppositional stance within the context of European fascism, however, took on a culturally conservative function in the decades after World War II: this has manifested itself in a variety of ways, including a resistance to innovations from English or French theory, an insular attitude that promotes the continued privileging of German as the language of professional discourse, and the loyal preservation of the canon of German literary works (by largely white, bourgeois, Protestant male authors) in the face of emerging demands for the inclusion of texts by women, working-class, or ethnically non-German writers.[3]

To be sure, major innovations in the discipline, which began to define itself at that time as German studies, occurred in the wake of the student movement in the late 1960s and early 1970s. As Michael Jones points out, the antiwar movement forged a new generation of politically committed, oppositionally minded scholars who, armed with marxist and feminist theories, opened the field to aspects of German culture beyond the national literary canon (155–56). Institutional markers for this juncture include the establishment of the leftist journal *New German Critique* in 1973, the feminist organization Women in German in 1974, and the interdisciplinary German Studies Association (first as the Western Association of German Studies) in 1976. It was during this decade of intellectual ferment that American scholars of German began to pursue research areas and approaches—among them feminism, Jewish literature, GDR literature, and film—that distinguish German studies even today from *Germanistik* in the Federal Republic of Germany.

Notwithstanding the mildly euphoric nostalgia that the baby-boom/student movement generation of American Germanists (those born between the mid-1940s and the early 1950s who are now well situated within the discipline) might feel toward the period of the late 1960s, Anna Kuhn reminds us that the student movement had little impact on *Germanistik* except at places like the University of Wisconsin (Madison) or Washington University (St. Louis) (98). In her words the German literary canon has remained unchanged, still dominated by male writers, traditional genres, and linear history, still resistant to marginal groups and to feminism; contemporary German studies in the United States is strongly invested in the "elitist patriarchal story of the *Bildungsbürgertum*" masquerading under the banner of eternal values (Kuhn 100). Although Kuhn's assertion of the ideological and institutional petrification of American *Germanistik* may seem harsh, it is true that scholars working in nontraditional areas or with theoretical approaches drawn from other fields still face misunderstanding or ostracization by their colleagues. (Thus, graduate students at the 1994 conference of Women in German asserted that only professors with the security of tenure could afford to pursue work in cultural studies; they themselves were afraid they would not be marketable.)

In keeping with the conservative nature of American *Germanistik* as a whole, then, the impact of multiculturalism on its disciplinary practices has been disappointingly limited. I see its influence mainly in two areas. First, the youngest generation of German studies practitioners, those receiving their Ph.D. degrees in the 1990s or currently pursuing graduate work, has been and is being trained in an academic climate strongly defined by multiculturalist ideas. These students take as canonical such minority and postcolonial critics as Gayatri Spivak, bell hooks, and Henry Louis Gates, all of whom have risen to prominence relatively recently within the academy. Frequently, new German studies scholars develop their intellectual paradigms, for example, from the work of Edward Said, whose *Orientalism* (1978) demonstrated the interdependence of scholarly knowledge and imperialist politics; from Gilles Deleuze and Félix Guattari's *Kafka: Toward a Minor Literature* (1986; French orig., 1975), on the subversive political possibilities of "minor" art; from Benedict Anderson's *Imagined Communities* (1983) on cultural-historical constructions of nationhood; or from the writings of Clifford Geertz or James Clifford on the political and poetic foundations of ethnographic texts—not to mention the immensely rich work in feminist theory on the category of gender. Works from fields such as philosophy, political science, and anthropology have become an indispensable part of current academic discourse in literary studies, and issues such as ethnicity, nationalism, colonialism, and gender have moved to the forefront of scholarly interest. For scholars trained today, then, the goal of impartial, disinterested reading has long been debunked. As Sara Lennox points out, the last two decades of theory have taught us that reality is always constructed and that every textual reading is positioned, partial, and political (166–67). Our students learn—to paraphrase some of Jeffrey Peck's points—to think of culture as emergent and contingent rather than absolute and uniform, of the self not as homogeneous or monolithic but as relational and inventive ("Going" 129), and of texts as embedded in relations of power that evolve along gender, class, racial/ethnic, national, and other lines of difference. Sensitized to Eurocentric and patriarchal, essentializing, and normative patterns of thought, this is a generation for whom a multicultural scholarly perspective comes close to second nature.

The other site of multiculturalist impact has been the German language classroom. Recently, foreign language educators have once again pointed prophetic fingers at the drastic decline of enrollments in German classes across the country—a loss of tens of thousands of students in the last twenty-five years, a decrease of more than 40 percent that Van Cleve and Willson describe as American *Germanistik* "sliding silently toward oblivion" (ix). Like the oppositional atmosphere of the early 1970s that created a German studies responsive to broader concerns of politics, history, and culture, the current crisis is also enrollment driven. But, whereas German studies once attempted to reclaim its lost ground through curricular changes—the addition of culture courses and courses in translation that met student demands for social and political relevance—the present slide cannot be halted by winning back our former constituency. Faced by a steady drop in enrollments, particularly in the number of students studying the language because of their German ancestry, German studies is now being forced to rethink its practices and premises in order to attract a new and "foreign" clientele: students of color.

The creation in 1989 of a task force and in 1993 of a standing committee on minority participation by the American Association of Teachers of German (AATG) represents the only major disciplinary effort thus far to confront the challenges created by a multicultural society for departments of German. In a statement of its mission the AATG Committee for the Recruitment and Retention of Minorities affirmed the diversity of American citizens and recognized the organization's "responsibility to ensure the study of German by a diverse American population taught by a profession whose members themselves reflect the racial and ethnic composition of our nation" (Peters et al. 97). Statistics on minority participation in German language classrooms offer a dismal picture indeed: over 98 percent of German teachers are of Caucasian background; less than 1 percent are black or Hispanic, compared to 8 percent in colleges and universities nationwide; 39 percent of college and university German faculty were born in Europe. Moreover, about 90 percent of German teachers in the United States face classes with few or no blacks or Hispanics, although students from these backgrounds make up over 25 percent of all elementary and secondary school populations (Peters 6; Van Cleve and Willson 90; Schulz). But, as laudable as the professional efforts are to increase the numbers of minority students and faculty in German classrooms, the focus on representative numbers, and the strategies suggested to attain them, reflect characteristic problems in multiculturalist thinking.

Concerned teachers of German often suggest that, in order to increase the presence of minorities in the field of German, we should teach about minorities in Germany: by presenting German society as multiracial and multicultural, by discussing xenophobic and racist violence, by exposing our students to the experiences of minorities (ideally expressed in their own words), we can instill tolerance and promote cultural understanding. By teaching about minorities in Germany, the general argument runs, we give our minority students something they can identify with and respond to, thereby attracting increasing numbers of them to the study of German (Peters 8). But such assumptions reduce our students—as well as the minority writers we have them read—to their ethnic and racial backgrounds while ignoring other, perhaps more relevant aspects of their identities such as class, age, gender, sexuality, or religion. There is, in fact, little reason to assume that black American students would find May Ayim or Alev Tekinay more relevant to their lives than Büchner or Heine or that the experiences of blacks and Hispanics in the United States and of Turks and Italians in Germany are more similar than they are different.

Rather, the issue is not a matter of demographics but one of rethinking the nature, goals, and habits of our discipline; the key is not what or whom we teach but how. A multicultural classroom does not mean simply diversifying our students according to race but, more important, interrogating the monocultural, nationalistic, and essentialist attitudes of our discipline. It does not mean just adding women and minority writers to the curriculum but raising the issue of white male (German) identity as a social and ideological construction.[4] A minority teacher of German may still be heavily invested in hegemonic assumptions of high German culture; one can teach the poems of the Afro-German May Ayim (Opitz) from a perspective that accepts the cultural centrality of white male German poets; or, alternatively, one can teach Goethe, Schiller, Heine, Brecht, *and* Ayim in a way that foregrounds the implicit historical constructions—and thus the contingent and politicized nature—of German identity enacted in their works. This process lays bare the question of the very definition of "German" literature and culture as a historical, class- and gender-based phenomenon, a project that requires the responsible engagement of all professionals in German studies, from experts in foreign language pedagogy to scholars of canonical German literature. The problem is not just that German departments have practiced the study of German language and literature as that of a homogeneous culture, as Frank Trommler aptly observes ("Multiculturalism"), but that German departments have *not* engaged in the analysis of how works of German literature have themselves created, sustained, and sometimes undermined the notion of German culture and German national identity as homogeneous. In short, the task is not to promote minorities so much as to analyze the construction and the continued assumptions of a monocultural, monolingual German identity.

Similar problems can be recognized in German political discussions on the status of minorities. Here it is especially difficult for American scholars of German studies, as well as for American students, to sympathize with the idea of a German nation that defines its citizenship in biological terms. From an American point of view the German practice of *jus sanguinis* is restrictive and exclusionary; equally surprising is the absence of antidiscrimination legislation. Since "race" and "racism" are strongly, if not exclusively, associated with National Socialism in German political discourse, these words are almost never used to speak about the present treatment of Germany's minority groups. But, as Ute Gerhard argues, the equation of racism with Nazism helps to hide real racist tendencies in contemporary German society. Not race but culture or ethnicity is seen to distinguish and separate groups; thus, culturalism, the insistent recognition and promotion of cultural difference, a new racism in effect, can present itself as adamantly antiracist (Gerhard 246–47).

Introduced in Germany in 1980 for the commemoration of the "Tag des ausländischen Mitbürgers" (Day of the Foreign Fellow Citizen), the word *multiculturalism* has moved from the evangelical academies, the alternative *Stammtische,* and Green Party politics to become a slogan serving the needs of a broad political spectrum (von Dirke 516; Leggewie 7). At one end the political scientist Claus Leggewie envisions a German republic in which it would be normal to find citizens of Turkish background with Islamic beliefs (ix); at the other we find threatening images of a "racially mixed-bred society" (the Bavarian minister of the interior Edmund Stoiber), a "goulash population" (Siegbert Alber, vice president of the European Parliament) in which Germans would disappear, a country reduced to ethnic ghettos and crippled by civil disorder (qtd. in Geissler 158; Schiffer). Frank-Olaf Radtke distinguishes four versions of multiculturalism: (1) a "programmatic-pedagogical multiculturalism" that promotes attitudes of respect and tolerance; (2) a "culinary-cynical multiculturalism" that appreciates the art, music, and cuisine of other cultures; (3) a "demographic-instrumental" form that argues for immigration as the solution to the social and economic collapse made inevitable by Germany's low birthrate; and (4) the "reactive-fundamentalist multiculturalism" of foreign groups who reclaim an "authentic" cultural identity within an unwelcoming and repressive society. All of these variants work to reinforce the petrification of ethnic differences—to reduce individuals to their ethnicity, to maintain discrimination and lines of demarcation between groups, and to distract attention from the political and material conditions that support a hierarchy privileging native Germans ("Marktwirtschaft" 43–47; also see Radtke, "Multikulturalismus"; Leggewie xi–xii; von Dirke).

Missing from the German discussions is a sense of the fluidity, contingency, and multiplicity—the constructed, contradictory, and changing nature—of social identity. Instead, German debates surrounding multiculturalism seem to focus on a search for the optimal manner of regulating the interaction of cultures understood as fixed objects. What constitutes "Turkish," for example, or "German" identity and how such identities are constructed and maintained are never questioned; only the possible modes of their coexistence are addressed. Even Leggewie, who defines the "correct" (*richtig*) version of multiculturalism in terms of a society without a hegemonic cultural center, envisions different and discrete ethnic groups existing in an "aggregate state" (xiii). The Turkish-German writer Zafer Şenocak, in contrast, argues for a heterogeneous, or hybrid, notion of identity with "gaps . . . through which the Other, the foreign, can enter and exit"—"not the mummification of traditional identities, but virtuoso movement among viewpoints and perspectives" (*Atlas* 14–15).[5]

Not coincidentally, the introduction of the concept of multiculturalism into German politics coincided with the emergence in the late 1970s and early 1980s of a migrants' literature produced by Germany's foreign residents (Weigel 188). (By 1980 the foreign population of the Federal Republic of Germany had reached 4.5 million, or 7.5 percent of total residents; 1.5 million Turks, the majority of them unemployed dependents, constituted by far the largest group of non-Germans.) A similar phenomenon occurred in the United States, as increased numbers of minority artists and intellectuals fueled the momentum of multiculturalism within American cultural life. But, while minority scholars occupy positions within the most prestigious of American universities and colleges and while the works of minority writers (among them the Nobel Prize winner Toni Morrison) are vigorously promoted by university and trade presses in the United States, minority scholars are virtually nonexistent within the German academy, and minority writers of German literature have been for the most part overlooked by Germanists in Germany. Related to the relative absence of minority intellectuals in the Federal Republic is the lack of a developed critique of Eurocentrism, one of the foundations of American multiculturalist discourse; as a result, even educated Germans take American multiculturalism as a movement promoting the "half-education" of "women and blacks, the ugly and the dumb" (*Frankfurter Allgemeine Zeitung,* qtd. in Gumbrecht 1074; also see Diederichsen 31–33; Henningsen 843–45).

Unfortunately, such factors have hindered the treatment of minority literature by scholars of German literature. At the 1990 International Congress of Germanists in Japan an important effort was made by Heidrun Suhr to inject American feminist theories of race, class, and gender into German literary discourse. Citing works by Teresa de Lauretis, Elly Bulkin, Trinh Minh-ha, Gayatri Spivak and others, Suhr noted that there is no comparable discussion of the constructed nature of social identity in Germany; for this very reason, she argues, minority writing in German deserves special attention ("Heimat" 73). As Suhr implies, the historically ingrained notion of an essential German identity rooted in biological heritage and a fixed cultural tradition has kept its hold on *Germanistik.* The resistance to the idea of identity as constructed and changing rather than essential and timeless carries over into the reluctance of Germanists to direct serious attention to the German-language literature written by minority authors; the fiction of German society as monocultural and homogeneous, with its minority populations considered permanently foreign and non-German, results in the categorization of minority literature as not really German literature and thus outside the proper purview of *Germanistik*.

The task of dealing with minority or multiculturalist issues has consequently fallen to others in Germany, notably to scholars engaged in the field of German language study (*Deutsch als Fremdsprache*). The Gesellschaft für Interkulturelle Germanistik (Society for Intercultural Germanistik), founded in 1984, for example, has devoted itself to questions concerning the pedagogical and hermeneutic significance of the diverse cultural backgrounds of international students of German. Alois Wierlacher, founding president, defines intercultural *Germanistik* as a field "that takes seriously the hermeneutic diversity of worldwide interest in German-speaking cultures, and that looks upon the variety of cultural perspectives on German literature not as a handicap or weakness but as a source of better—because multiperspectival—textual understanding" (x). This definition, however, locates cultural diversity *beyond* the borders of Germany, so that multiple perspectives and interests are brought from elsewhere to bear upon the study of its literature. As Karen Jankowsky points out, intercultural *Germanistik* recognizes the foreign as something outside, not within, German society—more specifically, as something separate from, not an integral part of, German identity. In effect, Wierlacher's statement upholds a view of culture as unified, homogeneous, and monolithic; fixed for all time, German literature is only to be better understood, not put in question, not challenged as a historical and political concept, not constructed anew for and by a multicultural readership (for other critiques, see Zimmermann).

In addition, there were the efforts in the early 1980s by Irmgard Ackermann and Harald Weinrich at the Institut für Deutsch als Fremdsprache (Institute for German as a Foreign Language) in Munich to promote literary texts by foreigners—the first response of scholars of German language and literature to multiculturalism within German society. While the important anthologies edited by Ackermann brought German minority literature to a broad audience, Ackermann and Weinrich's projects were nonetheless flawed by a lack of self-reflection regarding their own cultural biases and power.[6] Their arguments to legitimize minority literature as an area of study emphasized its authenticity rather than its artistry, pointed approvingly to the high quality of French- and English-language literature coming from former colonies, and praised the oral forms of storytelling as an antidote to the ills of advanced industrial society. Such characterizations reduced minority writing to documents of minority experiences (necessarily ones of disappointment, anger, and protest) while dismissing any expectation of aesthetic quality; equated ethnic minorities in Germany with formerly colonized peoples in Africa, thereby aligning Germany with grander European empires; and cast Turks and other minorities as premodern folk. In their effort to promote minority literature, in short, Ackermann and Weinrich reinforced the political hierarchy that places German culture above the exotic cultural expressions of non-Germans; neither they nor the scholars of intercultural *Germanistik* have allowed the force of multiculturality to destabilize traditional notions of Germanness.[7]

In the United States the emergence of minority discourse as a field of literary study, the nationally publicized Western culture debate at Stanford University, and the outpouring of publications, discussions, and initiatives on multiculturalism in the late 1980s and 1990s shaped the response of many German studies scholars to recent political developments in Germany. To be sure, the fall of the Berlin Wall, German reunification, and xenophobic violence against resident foreign populations and asylum seekers reopened questions of German identity on both sides of the Atlantic. But, among American scholars of German studies working within a multiculturalist context, the political reconceptualization of Germany has offered a renewed opportunity to dislodge *Germanistik* from its base in national identity and to envision a field of study with "open borders" (Peck, "Institution" 317–18).

Not surprisingly, the issue of German minority literature has taken major precedence in these efforts to develop German studies from a multicultural perspective. Pursuing the question "What's the difference?" Jeffrey Peck promotes German studies as a "heterogeneous interdisciplinary field . . . which calls attention to its own divergent interests and ideologies disseminated across disciplinary and national borders" ("Methodological" 206). As Peck argues, heterogeneity and difference define us at every level; they characterize German literature and German culture, the identities, interests, and ideologies of Germanists, the methods and the very definition of *Germanistik*. Furthermore, if minority discourse exposes "the way difference has been submerged, excluded, or simply ignored" in the construction of a unified national or disciplinary identity (207), it becomes a constitutive, if not the definitive, feature of current attempts to rethink *Germanistik*. Reading minority literature self-consciously as *German* literature, for example, exposes and explodes interpretive presuppositions that otherwise go unchallenged: that the authors we read share a common (Judeo-Christian and Germanic) literary tradition; that their works are accessible to us through methods of literary interpretation rooted in French, German, or Anglo-American theory; that our ethnic, cultural, or national identities, as well as our moral and political beliefs, are irrelevant to our critical tasks as literary scholars. At stake are the very definition of "German" culture and—concomitantly—our own disciplinary identity as "Germanists," for it has become amply clear that our understanding of Germanness can no longer be based on a nationalism defined in terms of historical continuity, ethnic and cultural commonality, or linguistic uniformity. Rather, German literature, German culture, and German identity must be understood as fundamentally unstable constructions, the products of highly politicized historical processes in which scholars of *Germanistik* and German studies necessarily participate.[8]

Working within an academic culture sensitized to issues of racial, ethnic, cultural, and gender identity, German studies practitioners in the United States have become more cognizant of the differences entailed by their own positioning vis-à-vis "the German." Jeffrey Peck, above all, has called repeatedly for greater self-reflection regarding the many factors that separate German studies scholars from one another and from Germanists in Germany and for the recognition and cultivation of these points of difference as critical strengths. Increasingly, scholars of German studies are growing more comfortable with their diverse Americanness: consciously choosing English rather than German as their professional language of discourse, creatively appropriating methodologies from other disciplines (thereby cultivating even further structures of hybridity within German studies), developing areas of research—in social history, cultural studies, gender studies, minority discourse, or film—that are clearly not part of the traditional disciplinary repertoire of *Germanistik.*

In these efforts many German studies practitioners, rather than assimilating themselves into the projects of German *Germanistik,* are seeking to make their own identities and their differences explicit, productive, and constitutive of new knowledge. (Indeed, for many of us our multiple differences from traditional notions of what is German preclude any serious attempt at assimilation.) The recognition that *Germanistik* as practiced in the Federal Republic does not define our center—that the privilege and exclusionary priority claimed in the notion of "indigenous *Germanistik*" (*Inlandsgermanistik*) can be rejected by those who refuse to be assigned to, and circumscribed by, a marginalized "foreign" position (*im Ausland*)—this is a difference that multiculturalist thinking has made in the American field of German studies. It is only through this radical disprivileging of points of view rooted in essentialized notions of identity that German studies can become a field of study truly responsive and responsible to the students of a multicultural world.

NOTES

A slightly different version of this essay appeared in German translation as "Deutsche Kultur, Multikultur: Für eine Germanistik im multikulturellen Sinn," in *Zeitschrift für Germanistik* 6 (1996): 545–60.

1. The most publicized and invigorating of these debates occurred at Stanford University in 1988 (Pratt). Guillory offers a sophisticated critique from the Left of liberal-pluralist attempts to open the canon.

2. The seriousness of the challenge posed by these trends can be gauged by the vehe-

mence of the defenders of the Western canon (e.g., Bennett; Bloom; Hirsch). Conservative cultural critics basically see a coalition of feminists, gays, marxists, and blacks attacking traditional standards of rationality, truth, and excellence in order to advance their political ideology (see, e.g., Searle). Arthur and Shapiro provide a useful collection of views from all sides.

3. The isolationism of American *Germanistik* was first discussed in a provocative article by Sammons in 1976.

4. I adopt this point from Erickson (104). Consider also Gerald Graff's notion of "teaching the conflicts." For German studies scholars a particularly relevant example of an attempt to investigate whiteness as a category is bell hooks's analysis of Wim Wenders's *Wings of Desire;* see also Morrison's discussion of the construction of whiteness and American identity.

5. See also the explorations of Afro-German identity in Oguntoye, Opitz, and Schultz.

6. The volumes are *Als Fremder in Deutschland* (1982), *In zwei Sprachen leben* (1983), and *Türken deutscher Sprache* (1984), all published by Deutscher Taschenbuch in Munich. See Suhr for a useful survey of the history and development of minority literature in Germany ("Ausländerliteratur").

7. My criticisms of Ackermann and Weinrich are presented in greater detail elsewhere (Teraoka, *"Gastarbeiterliteratur"*); also see Suhr, "Ausländerliteratur"; and Adelson, "Migrants.'" Minority writers have themselves vigorously protested the manner in which they are treated by German critics and scholars; see the essays by Rafik Schami, Yüksel Pazarkaya, Zafer Şenocak, Suleman Taufiq, Jusuf Naoum, and Aras Ören, in Ackermann and Weinrich.

8. For analyses of the constructed nature of "German" and "Turkish" identity in German literary and political discourse, see Adelson, "Opposing"; Teraoka, "Talking" and "Turks"; and Şenocak, *War Hitler.*

WORKS CITED

Ackermann, Irmgard, and Harald Weinrich, eds. *Eine nicht nur deutsche Literatur: Zur Standortbestimmung der "Ausländerliteratur."* Munich: Piper, 1986.

Adelson, Leslie A. "Migrants' Literature or German Literature? TORKAN's *Tufan: Brief an einen islamischen Bruder." German Quarterly* 63 (1990): 382–89.

———. "Opposing Oppositions: Turkish-German Questions in Contemporary German Studies." *German Studies Review* 17 (1994): 305–30.

Anderson, Benedict. *Imagined Communities: Reflections on the Origin and Spread of Nationalism.* London: Verso, 1983.

Arthur, John, and Amy Shapiro, eds. *Campus Wars: Multiculturalism and the Politics of Difference.* Boulder: Westview, 1995.

Bathrick, David. "Cultural Studies." In *Introduction to Scholarship in Modern Languages and Literatures,* ed. Joseph Gibaldi. New York: MLA, 1992. 320–40.

Bennett, William J. *To Reclaim a Legacy.* Washington: National Endowment for the Humanities (NEH), 1984.

Bloom, Allan. *The Closing of the American Mind: How Higher Education Has Failed*

Democracy and Impoverished the Souls of Today's Students. New York: Simon & Schuster, 1987.

Brantlinger, Patrick. *Crusoe's Footprints: Cultural Studies in Britain and America*. New York: Routledge, 1990.

Brodhead, Richard H. "An Anatomy of Multiculturalism." *Yale Alumni Magazine*, April 1994, 45–49.

Clifford, James. *The Predicament of Culture: Twentieth-Century Ethnography, Literature, and Art*. Cambridge: Harvard UP, 1988.

Clifford, James, and George E. Marcus, eds. *Writing Culture: The Poetics and Politics of Ethnography*. Berkeley: U of California P, 1986.

Deleuze, Gilles, and Félix Guattari. *Kafka: Toward a Minor Literature*. Trans. Dana Polan. Minneapolis: U of Minnesota P, 1986.

Diederichsen, Diedrich. "PC zwischen PoMo und MuCu: Ein Erfahrungsbericht." *Neue Rundschau* 103.3 (1992): 23–39.

During, Simon, ed. *The Cultural Studies Reader*. London: Routledge, 1993.

Erickson, Peter. "Profiles in Whiteness." *Stanford Humanities Review* 3.1 (1993): 98–111.

Geertz, Clifford. *The Interpretation of Cultures*. New York: Basic, 1973.

Geissler, Heiner. "Meise zu Meise? Plädoyer für eine 'multikulturelle Gesellschaft.'" *Der Spiegel*, 26 March 1990, 155–73.

Gerhard, Ute. "'Fluten,' 'Ströme,' 'Invasionen': Mediendiskurs und Rassismus." In *Zwischen Nationalstaat und multikultureller Gesellschaft: Einwanderung und Fremdenfeindlichkeit in der Bundesrepublik Deutschland,* ed. Manfred Hessler. Berlin: Hitit, 1993. 239–53.

Geyer, Michael. "Multiculturalism and the Politics of General Education." *Critical Inquiry* 19 (Spring 1993): 499–533.

Goldberg, David Theo. "Introduction: Multicultural Conditions." In *Multiculturalism: A Critical Reader,* ed. D. T. Goldberg. Oxford: Blackwell, 1994. 1–41.

Graff, Gerald. "Teach the Conflicts." In *The Politics of Liberal Education,* ed. Darryl J. Gless and Barbara Herrnstein Smith. Durham: Duke UP, 1992. 57–73.

Grossberg, Lawrence, Cary Nelson, and Paula A. Treichler, eds. *Cultural Studies*. New York: Routledge, 1992.

Guillory, John. "Canon, Syllabus, List: A Note on the Pedagogic Imaginary." *Transition* 52 (1991): 36–54.

Gumbrecht, Hans Ulrich. "Die Hässlichen und die Dummen? Der amerikanische Multikulturalismus und seine Kritiker." *Merkur* 45 (1991): 1074–79.

Henningsen, Manfred. "Der heilige Mauritius und der Streit um die multikulturelle Identität des Westens." *Merkur* 46 (1992): 834–45.

Hirsch, E. D., Jr. *Cultural Literacy: What Every American Needs to Know*. Boston: Houghton Mifflin, 1987.

hooks, bell. "Representing Whiteness: Seeing *Wings of Desire*." *Yearning: Race, Gender, and Cultural Politics*. Boston: South End, 1990. 165–71.

Jankowsky, Karen. "'German Literature' Contested: The 1991 Ingeborg Bachmann Prize Debate." Modern Language Association Convention, San Diego, December 1994.

Jones, Michael T. "Identity, Critique, Affirmation: A Response to Hinrich C. Seeba's Paper." *German Quarterly* 62 (1989): 155–57.

Kuhn, Anna. "Canon as Narrative: A Feminist Reading." In *Rethinking Germanistik: Canon and Culture,* ed. Robert Bledsoe et al. New York: Lang, 1991. 91–104.

Leggewie, Claus. *Multi Kulti: Spielregeln für die Vielvölkerrepublik.* Berlin: Rotbuch, 1990.

Lennox, Sara. "Feminist Scholarship and Germanistik." *German Quarterly* 62 (1989): 158–70.

Mohanty, Chandra Talpade. "On Race and Voice: Challenges for Liberal Education in the 1990s." *Cultural Critique* 14 (Winter 1989–90): 179–208.

Morrison, Toni. *Playing in the Dark: Whiteness and the Literary Imagination.* New York: Vintage, Random, 1993.

Oguntoye, Katharina, May Opitz, and Dagmar Schultz, eds. *Farbe bekennen: Afrodeutsche Frauen auf den Spuren ihrer Geschichte.* Berlin: Orlanda, 1986. Trans. as *Showing Our Colors: Afro-German Women Speak Out.* Trans. Anne V. Adams. Amherst: U of Massachusetts P, 1992.

Peck, Jeffrey M. "Going Native: Establishing Authority in German Studies." *German Studies Review* 13 (1990): 127–33.

———. "The Institution of Germanistik and the Transmission of Culture: The Time and Place for an Anthropological Approach." *Monatshefte* 79 (1987): 308–19.

———. "Methodological Postscript: What's the Difference? Minority Discourse in German Studies." *New German Critique* 46 (Winter 1989): 203–8.

Peters, George F. "Dilemmas of Diversity: Observations on Efforts to Increase Minority Participation in German." *ADFL Bulletin* 25.2 (1994): 5–11.

Peters, George F., et al. "Report and Recommendations of the AATG Committee for the Recruitment and Retention of Minorities in German." *Die Unterrichtspraxis* 26.1 (1993): 97–98.

Pratt, Mary Louise. "Humanities for the Future: Reflections on the Western Culture Debate at Stanford." In *The Politics of Liberal Education,* ed. Darryl J. Gless and Barbara Herrnstein Smith. Durham: Duke UP, 1992. 13–31.

Radtke, Frank-Olaf. "Marktwirtschaft, Multikulturalismus und Sozialstaat: Zur politischen Ökonomie der Bürgerrechte." In *Die multikulturelle Versuchung: Ethnische Minderheiten in der deutschen Gesellschaft,* ed. Doron Kiesel and Rosi Wolf-Almanasreh. Frankfurt a.M.: Haag und Herchen, 1991. 39–57.

———. "Multikulturalismus: Ein Gegengift gegen Ausländerfeindlichkeit und Rassismus?" In *Zwischen Nationalstaat und multikultureller Gesellschaft: Einwanderung und Fremdenfeindlichkeit in der Bundesrepublik Deutschland,* ed. Manfred Hessler. Berlin: Hitit, 1993. 91–103.

Said, Edward W. *Orientalism.* New York: Vintage, Random, 1979.

Sammons, Jeffrey L. "Some Considerations on Our Invisibility." In *German Studies in the United States: Assessment and Outlook,* ed. Walter F. W. Lohnes and Valters Nollendorfs. Madison: U of Wisconsin P, 1976. 17–23.

Schiffer, Eckart. "Der Koran ist nicht Gesetz." *Der Spiegel,* 30 September 1991, 53–59.

Schmidt, Henry J. "What Is Oppositional Criticism? Politics and German Literary Criticism from Fascism to the Cold War." *Monatshefte* 79 (1987): 292–307.

Schulz, Renate A. "Profile of the Profession: Results of the 1992 AATG Membership Survey." *Die Unterrichtspraxis* 26.2 (1993): 226–52.

Searle, John. "The Storm over the University." *New York Review of Books,* 6 December 1990, 34–42.

Şenocak, Zafer. *Atlas des tropischen Deutschland.* Berlin: Babel, 1993.

———. *War Hitler Araber? IrreFührungen an den Rand Europas.* Berlin: Babel, 1994.

Suhr, Heidrun. "Ausländerliteratur: Minority Literature in the Federal Republic of Germany." *New German Critique* 46 (Winter 1989): 71–103.

———. "'Heimat ist, wo ich wachsen kann': Ausländerinnen schreiben deutsche Literatur." In *Begegnung mit dem "Fremden": Grenzen, Traditionen, Vergleiche,* ed. Eijiro Iwasaki. Proceedings of the Eighth International Congress of Germanists, Tokyo, 1990. Vol. 8. Munich: iudicium, 1991. 71–79.

Teraoka, Arlene A. "*Gastarbeiterliteratur*: The Other Speaks Back." *Cultural Critique* 7 (Fall 1987): 77–101. Rpt. in *The Nature and Context of Minority Discourse,* ed. Abdul R. Janmohamed and David Lloyd. New York: Oxford UP, 1990. 294–318.

———. "Talking 'Turk': On Narrative Strategies and Cultural Stereotypes." *New German Critique* 46 (Winter 1989): 104–28.

———. "Turks as Subjects: The Ethnographic Novels of Paul Geiersbach." In *Culture/Contexture: Explorations in Anthropology and Literary Studies,* ed. E. Valentine Daniel and Jeffrey M. Peck. Berkeley: U of California P, 1996. 195–213.

Trinh T. Minh-ha. *When the Moon Waxes Red: Representation, Gender and Cultural Politics.* New York: Routledge, 1991.

Trommler, Frank. "Einleitung." In *Germanistik in den USA: Neue Entwicklungen und Methoden,* ed. F. Trommler. Opladen: Westdeutscher Verlag, 1989. 7–43.

———. "Multiculturalism: A Moral Frontier for German Studies?" German Studies Association Conference, Dallas, September 1994.

Van Cleve, John, and A. Leslie Willson. *Remarks on the Needed Reform of German Studies in the United States.* Columbia, SC: Camden, 1993.

von Dirke, Sabine. "Multikulti: The German Debate on Multiculturalism." *German Studies Review* 17 (1994): 513–36.

Weigel, Sigrid. "Literatur der Fremde—Literatur in der Fremde." In *Hansers Sozialgeschichte der deutschen Literatur vom 16. Jahrhundert bis zur Gegenwart,* ed. Rolf Grimminger. Vol. 12. Munich: Hanser, 1992. 182–229, 740–44.

West, Cornel. "The New Cultural Politics of Difference." In *Out There: Marginalization and Contemporary Cultures,* ed. Russell Ferguson et al. New York: New Museum of Contemporary Art; Cambridge: MIT P, 1990. 19–36.

Wierlacher, Alois. "Einleitung." In *Das Fremde und das Eigene: Prolegomena zu einer interkulturellen Germanistik,* ed. A. Wierlacher. Munich: iudicium, 1985. vii–xv.

Zimmermann, Peter, ed. *"Interkulturelle Germanistik": Dialog der Kulturen auf Deutsch?* Frankfurt a.M.: Lang, 1989.

CHAPTER 5

Cultural Studies and Foreign Policy in a Strategic Alliance, or Why Presidents of the United States Should Learn German

Jeffrey M. Peck

What sort of practical results can come from cultural studies? More specifically, what kinds of political insights can cultural studies offer the world outside the academy? Can current events be analyzed in a cultural context? Jeffrey Peck answers these question in several ways. A shift from an analysis exclusively concerned with the literary text to contexts, nonliterary, and even nonaesthetic "texts" or events has taken place in recent decades in humanities and literature departments in the United States. Peck makes contemporary theories concrete by analyzing Clinton's visit to Berlin in the summer of 1994. He shows how the analytical tools of those trained in close reading—"philologists" in an earlier situation, "cultural studies practitioners" now—can be put to use in areas usually understood to be in the purview of the political scientist or historian. But beyond "reading" a nonliterary text, Peck sees this kind of analytical practice, judiciously informed by anthropological, historical, poststructural, and other methodologies, as key to the proper understanding of culture in general. The ability to interpret cultural-historical events astutely and critically, Peck proposes, is absolutely necessary for those who study foreign policy or who are diplomats themselves. That Peck proceeds somewhat self-consciously in this essay shows that disciplinary boundary crossings for analyzing events as text are still considered transgressive.

In an ideal world educators would wish for all citizens to be competent judges of their own societies and informed critics of others'. But for Peck's students at Georgetown University's School of Foreign Service the capacity for a clear-headed understanding of culture—beyond polls, policy briefs, interest rate differentials, or arms control agreements—is imperative. He uses an analysis of a key political event as a primer for applying the ideas of Clifford Geertz and Michel Foucault. He shows what it means, pragmatically, to deconstruct a dense complex of meanings. He brings to bear current theoretical terms such as alterity, multicultural, *and* thick description, *for example, in a clear and useful context. Peck does all this with the dual personae of both pedagogue and researcher. Society's leaders outside the academy first learn their fields within it. Cultural studies methods can and should give our future policy makers, economists, and scientists the tools for understanding the world they help shape.*

As traditional *Germanistik* was transformed into a discipline that included what has come to be called, in the United States, German studies, the study of culture has become a central academic activity. A paradigm shift has taken place that has moved analytic and interpretive practices from an exclusive focus on the literary text, often using formal or aesthetic criteria, to the contexts that produce or surround texts, events, or representations. Anthropology and the critical reinscription of "writing culture" developed in interpretive ethnography has had without a doubt the strongest influence on pushing literary studies (the next developmental stage after literary criticism) toward cultural studies (Clifford and Marcus). As a literary-turned-cultural critic, I seized upon President Bill Clinton's speech in Berlin in the summer of 1994 as a decisive opportunity to apply what I had been theorizing—namely, to interpret a cultural-historical event in all of its signifying potential.

On a gloriously sunny day, 12 July 1994, President Clinton spoke at the Brandenburg Gate in Berlin. He declared to the throngs of Americans and Germans from East and West (an estimated fifty thousand), "Amerika steht an Ihrer Seite, jetzt und für immer" (America is on your side, now and forever). He concluded his speech dramatically, first in English then in German: "Nothing will stop us. Everything is possible. Berlin is free. Nichts wird uns aufhalten. Alles ist möglich. Berlin ist frei." Perhaps one should not be too hard on Clinton for spouting such banalities; he had a hard act to follow: John Kennedy's "Ich bin ein Berliner" speech has gone down in history and become an epigram for the United States' commitment to Germany at the height of the Cold War. Unfortunately, and surprisingly, for a politician highly sensitive to the symbolic potential of such a moment and to the media, Clinton's speech seemed flat and empty, no matter how forcefully and loudly he spoke. Clinton is not the rhetorician Kennedy was, nor does the Cold War hang over Germany or German-U.S. relations and give a leader of Clinton's status the opportunity to make such a mark in history. To be fair however, Clinton's brief eight-and-a-half-minute speech did strike a timely chord when he warned the Germans about the evils of racism and xenophobia.

The focus on Clinton should, of course, not neglect German chancellor Helmut Kohl, who preceded him. The cheers that greeted Clinton's appearance contrasted with the more subdued response to Kohl, whose rise to the podium was also marked by jeers and boos. The chancellor's brief statement concluded, "Die Brücke über den Atlantik hat bisher vor allem unserer gemeinsamen Sicherheit gedient. Ich wünsche mir von Herzen, dass auch die anderen Fahrbahnen der Brücke rasch ausgebaut werden; die wirtschaftlichen, die wissenschaftlichen und vor allem auch im kulturellen Bereich" (Up until now the bridge across the Atlantic has above all served our common security. I wish with all my heart that other roads on that bridge will be quickly extended: in economics/business, scholarship/science, and above all in the *cultural* realm" [my emph.]).

While Chancellor Kohl's statement might be read cynically as a use of "culture" as compensation for the absence of "serious" political issues after the fall of the Berlin Wall, the unification of Germany, and the end of the communist threat, it is still fruitful to analyze the contents of both his and Clinton's speeches for how they construct a strategic alliance of culture and foreign policy. I want to discuss how we as critics, specifically cultural critics, can use such scenarios for interesting and rich analysis. It seems to have been Samuel Huntington, a well-known Harvard political scientist, who has drawn greater public attention to the question of culture, especially from social scientists, by framing this discussion in more serious terms in his now often quoted (and severely critiqued) essay in *Foreign Affairs* (see also Ajami). I, too, have become aware of the positive potential of the relationship between humanists and policy makers for a neglected sphere of study, namely, culture and foreign policy.[1] While I and my social scientist colleagues may be uneasy bedfellows, I think Clinton's speech serves as a site (to use Foucault's very appropriate term) where cohabitation, although sometimes tense, is at least possible and even productive.

This site I propose for analysis includes not only Bill Clinton's speech at the Brandenburg Gate but also many aspects of the Clintons' visit to Berlin. Defining my subject of analysis in this way permits greater insight into the intersection of culture and foreign policy, with the two linked through attention to the symbolic, discursive, and semiological readings of this cultural-political event as a kind of text. I use the term *text* here in anthropologist Clifford Geertz's sense as a literal *text*ure of signs, practices, and actions that can be read for their meaning. These events are not, especially in politics and the media, coincidental or haphazard, but *sinnvoll*—full of meaning—in the German sense.

And I think that those of us who are trained as philologists, as readers and translators of texts in the broadest sense, have to make more out of our skills as meaning makers through the interpretations that we construct. The potential theorizing to which I allude—and which can be identified with poststructuralist thought and the field now called cultural studies—provides, I think, a language or a framework of analysis to study such events. I am aware at the outset that many readers will counter my claims by saying that the interpretation I offer with attendant reflection on its hermeneutics is superfluous, a trumped-up critical apparatus to legitimize observations that are actually rather obvious. This criticism may be an appropriate one. Nevertheless, the obvious is not immune to serious analysis, reflective theorizing, or purposeful systematization that frame it as a problem to be recognized and explained, even solved. As we humanists like to note, social scientists are often expending serious time empirically proving what also seems obvious, proclaiming answers that we would like to think we have already interpreted through subjective and interpretive methods. Moreover, the theories used for analysis in cultural studies have an important pedagogical function: to teach students, especially those in political science, international relations, and policy studies, that culture and cultural studies have an important place in their education. Cultural studies may in fact account for or explain events, practices, behaviors, or actions that more traditional social scientific analysis either neglects, ignores, or cannot adequately lay claim to. By the same token traditional *Germanistik* is limited (and most assuredly disinterested) in its ability to account for the political, social, and economic interests shaping present-day Germany.

It is, in fact, this nebulous realm in between the humanities and the social sciences called "culture" in which precise definition is slippery and methodology so eclectic as to be often useless. And yet *political culture,* a term actually linking political science and cultural studies, becomes ever more appealing to those in the literature disciplines whose traditional expectations—until German studies developed—were to read primarily literary texts. Fortunately, the terms *literary, text, context,* and *culture* have overflowed their disciplinary, intellectual, and academic boundaries to such a degree that critics of all kinds are running in as many directions as the migrants and asylum seekers who are also transgressing national borders. In both cases there are authorities trying to hold check on any attempt to open up traditional territories to new and different influences. More attention needs to be given to cultural studies as a disciplinary designation connoting a much broader corpus of questions than its narrower Birmingham School origins. But openness and cross-fertilization require interested parties and democratic forums. I offer this essay in the hope that this volume becomes a catalyst for such exchange.

I would like, therefore, to move to the concrete. Using a word that has been sorely misrepresented and misunderstood, allow me to *deconstruct* what in and of itself is not a historic moment but symbolically was played out in a variety of settings that inscribe or construct this event with meanings far beyond any literal connotation. As a literary critic whose discipline's roots go back to philology, the love of the word, let me start with language and its transformation into discourse, which I would define most simply as language situated in a specific social context. The message of Clinton's speech spoken in German was not received by the crowds with great enthusiasm or surprise. That "Berlin remains free" was so obvious at this point in the political development of Germany and Europe that the significance of the statement was clearly to be found in the German language, actually in its force as a performative, in which to state is also to *do* something, that is, to perform (see Austin). This effort on Clinton's part— apparently one American reporter commented that he brought out his college German, and one German journalist noted that his pronunciation was far better than Kennedy's—was without a doubt meant to parallel the latter's words at the Schöneberger Rathaus in 1963. But the value of the event was clearly Clinton's exploitation of the discursive moment to use the language not only of his hosts and that of Kennedy but to signal commitment to the German people by taking advantage of the tradition that had already been established. In addition, walking from the Reichstag through the Brandenburg Gate, Clinton gave his speech on the side of the edifice facing east, as does the Quadriga on the gate's top. Many Easterners were pleased that Clinton spoke "from the East" and mentioned their "gentle revolution." He was laying claim to new territories and surely welcoming them into the Western fold.[2] Of course, neither Reagan nor Bush could make this gesture when speaking in Berlin. Moreover, neither could allow himself the freedom of being linked to the Democrat Kennedy, whose place in history was in part established by a short German phrase. Thirty years later the crowd, at least the Americans present, were so attuned to the symbolic significance of the event that Clinton's German phrase was a letdown rather than a surprise. It was precisely the expectation raised by a precedent that had been set by Clinton's own heroic model, JFK, that undercut the well-meaning words. Clinton's words were mere signs without a referent, floating signifiers, that connoted a reality that had already taken place and no longer meant much to the assembled crowd. While it is expected of a president to speak at such an occasion, Clinton's words rang rather hollow and left the audience frustrated rather than satisfied. While Clinton's ability, unlike Kennedy's, to pronounce the umlauts in *für* and *möglich* may be compared to Pavarotti hitting a high *C,* and, as an ironic *Spiegel* reporter humorously notes, perhaps a Southern accent lends itself better to German than upper-class Bostonian, Clinton's speech was in the journalist's words "ein Triumph . . . als Arie, nicht als Rede" (a triumph . . . as an aria, not as a speech) (Widman 27).

But let us not be too hard on Clinton. His invocation of racism, xenophobia, and what is called in theory "alterity," the question of otherness and difference, was another matter. Striking a high note that had already been voiced by American politicians, Clinton was exploiting his privilege of being the leader of *the* multicultural society par excellence to warn his German friends about intolerance. Perhaps aware of the limitations of his political rhetoric, comments on a topic that had filled U.S. newspapers (and gotten somewhat carried away) and inspired fears in the United States of a Nazi resurgence were bound to get a response. In a venue that allowed Helmut Kohl to bask in the glory of his political successes, which had led to German reunification, Clinton's empty rhetoric may have been fodder for Kohl's own political ambition and foreign policy, but it certainly did hit a raw chord about Germany's inability to cope with the heterogeneity of its new society, whether political and social, as represented by the East Germans, or racial, religious, and ethnic, as represented by the so-called *Ausländer* (foreigners).

Clinton's most powerful step in a direction that one loosely could call "multicultural" was a less grandiose, albeit equally dramatic and symbolic, visit—namely, his appearance that afternoon at the most famous of European synagogues, the Oranienburger synagogue, now known as the Neue Synagogue–Centrum Judaicum in the former East Berlin. In fact, there were more of Clinton's American staff assigned to this visit than to the Brandenburg Gate. This part of his Berlin visit could, of course, be interpreted cynically as a crude political ploy to win favor back home with the "Jewish vote" or, more generously, as a further criticism of Kohl and the Germans' persistent difficulty in dealing with the past and this past's intrusion into the present. The Neue Synagoge–Centrum Judaicum was a project of the East Berlin Jewish Community with the support of the GDR government and, one shouldn't forget, the help of American benefactors. It was described in 1988 in a brochure of the time as "ein internationales Zentrum der Begegnung, der Bewahrung jüdischer Kultur und Tradition und der Forschung zum antifaschistischen Widerstandskampf, als Stätte des ehrenden Gedenkens und der Mahnung" (international meeting center, for the preservation of Jewish culture and tradition and for research into the antifascist resistance, as a memorial site for remembrance) (*Damit die Nacht* 74). The last five years have seen swift changes in the synagogue itself and the adjoining building housing the Neue Synagoge–Centrum Judaicum that includes a library and a gallery. The synagogue was officially dedicated in May 1995 (ten months after the Clintons' visit). Drawing hordes of people, the Oranienburgerstrasse, with the synagoge complex, its many restaurants, the club Tacheles, and even the prostitutes who line the street, has become very popular. Always, as one observer noted, "ein Ort der Geschichte," this entire "site of history" has been transformed since unification as merely a street with the ruins of a synagogue and some offices into a richly textured terrain: Tacheles quite literally as a half-ruined building in a surreal landscape that looks like a battle zone, Cafe Oren, where hip, usually non-Jewish Berliners and tourists eat

"Jewish food" (actually Israeli/Middle Eastern), a site of pilgrimage for Jews visiting Germany, and the site where East Berlin's Jewish community finds itself still in a tense relationship within the greater Berlin Jewish community dominated by West Berlin Jews (located in the Fasanenstrasse on the other side of town).

This "thick description" (as Clifford Geertz calls it) is meant only to situate the Clintons' visit to the synagogue in a complex topography that is variegated with the history of not only German-Jewish life in general but also the religious, economic, cultural, and now social tensions between East and West Berlin. The Clintons' appearance at the synagogue was also, according to an informant in the Jewish community, a site of controversy between the U.S. government officials planning the visit and the German government's representatives. There was a fascinating tug-of-war between the West German Jewish community and the Americans strangely mediated by former East Germans from the synagogue. Apparently, in the advance stages of the planning Kohl's people were not as enthusiastic about Clinton's visit to the synagogue as the Americans, and the list of memorial sites where Clinton was to appear was altered many times. The details of the negotiation merit mention: the Americans suggested the synagogue, and the Germans replaced it with the Neue Wache, for example; the Americans accepted the Neue Wache with the synagogue; then the Germans eliminated the synagogue and replaced it with the Neue Wache and the Pergamon museum; then the Americans excluded both and left the synagogue.[3] The juxtaposition of the Neue Wache and synagogue is significant when one takes into consideration the outcry against honoring German soldiers from World War II that is represented in that monument and the obvious message incorporated in its replacement by a Jewish synagogue substantially destroyed during *Kristallnacht.* It was clear at least to the Americans from Clinton's team that a visit to the synagogue was very significant to this particular American president.

While Clinton himself or even his advance people might not have understood the interwoven histories of this specific cultural landscape, they recognized the significance of an American president making a gesture toward the U.S. and world Jewish community. Clinton's visiting a site sentimental to some for its connection to the destruction of German Jewry, rather than the Jewish community in West Berlin, represented a commitment against intolerance not only toward Jews and foreigners in Germany but beyond. This synagogue was symbolically overladen with the genocide of the Jews in Germany and other parts of Europe. Therefore, Clinton was demonstrating by his presence and attention the solidarities that exist in the United States rather than in Germany, between an American Baptist president and his fellow Americans who also happen to be Jewish (in contrast to the German term *jüdische Mitbürger* [Jewish fellow citizens]). For a person like Clinton, educated at Georgetown University and at Yale Law School, his familiarity (and Hillary Rodham Clinton's) with Jews was reflected in their comfort in a synagogue. Helmut Kohl has rarely been seen, at least publicly as a politician, in a synagogue and yet did not miss the chance to appear at a German-American event equally as symbolically laden as Bitburg (fig. 1).

U.S. politicians, especially those of the Clintons' generation, are simply more comfortable in diverse religious settings than their German counterparts. Living, growing up, and being educated in the U.S. system has given the Clintons, as all Americans, certain advantages in dealing with different races, ethnicities, and religions. This was the import of his speech at the Brandenburg Gate. This is what an American president, even with the problems that exist in the United States, can say to the Germans. Kohl's visit to the synagogue, in other words, was clearly influenced by the Americans.

Unlike the U.S. press, most German newspapers paid little attention to the synagogue visit, mentioning it only briefly, if at all. The local Berlin *Tagesspiegel* gave it a paragraph and in its extended analysis even published a picture of the Clintons at the temple. Apparently, holy objects were laid out specifically for a photo opportunity with the Clintons. Although Clinton's advance team may have been sophisticated in the methods of the media and how important a well-placed menorah or ritual object might look in front of the president, they did not seem to be aware of the more personal machinations transpiring behind the scenes between the West and East Berlin Jewish communities regarding access, proximity, and inclusion in the entourage. There was, of course, to be parity in the numbers of people present from both parts of the Berlin Jewish community, but that the synagogue and Centrum were located in East Berlin provided an obvious advantage to the Easterners. Ultimately, the Clintons' visit to the synagogue took on greater symbolic value than even his speech at the Brandenburg Gate, his presence at the Lichtenberg base to dismiss the American brigade, or even Hillary Rodham Clinton's speech at the John F. Kennedy School, which indeed was one of the high points of the trip for those who heard her speak. The synagogue visit went beyond mere political rhetoric and provided a substantive message about problems that still exist and need to be seriously addressed: xenophobia, racism, and antisemitism. These comments in particular did not have the impact on the Germans that Kennedy's words did because, unlike Kennedy's message about solidarities, Clinton's admonitions about multiculturalism only reflected disunity and lack of agreement between Germans and Americans.[4] Clinton's visit to the Neue Synagoge was the closest he came to emulating John Kennedy. His presence at this particular synagogue was a symbol of solidarity with the persecuted. What Kennedy performed linguistically, Clinton effected symbolically in a rather different discursive form.

I have offered in brief a reading of an American president in Berlin. What

Fig. 1.   Bill Clinton and Helmut Kohl at the Neue Synagoge–Centrum Judaicum. (AP/Wide World Photos.)

was announced as a "historische Rede" (historical speech) left most professional commentators and the general audience disappointed. But there is no question that the fact of the visit itself, what can be called the performative moment, exactly where Clinton went along with the rhetorical force of his discourse, made the visit overall more *sinnvoll* than it appeared at first glance. Thousands of tickets—as if to a sporting event or rock concert—were printed and handed out, pupils were let out of school early, and in the rush toward the Brandenburg Gate on that hot summer afternoon there was excitement and euphoria (fig. 2). Did anyone really expect a historic speech? I doubt it. But what they did get was a narrative, indeed what is called a "master narrative," of a Democratic president continuing a precedent and tradition of America's commitment to Germany (and, as I have shown, to Jews and other minorities), even if the politics of Kohl's Social Democratic opponent Rudolf Scharping (trailing badly in the polls at that time) was more akin to Clinton and Kennedy than to Bush and Reagan.

This master narrative has clearly been political or at least been seen that way for many decades. Perhaps this is because of the overriding influence of the Cold War and the apparent power of states, institutions, and elites to dominate the discourse of academics and policy makers to set the disciplinary terrain in such a way as to privilege "political analysis." Witness the governmental funding of critical languages for national security or the creation of area studies programs at major universities. But Clinton's speech has shown, enhanced by this brief cultural analysis, that there may be a potential new master narrative called culture. Is this what Kohl was referring to in his speech? Is the discussion of such matters the impetus for the newly formed German-American foundations such as the German-American Academic Council Foundation or even the Centers of Excellence? If cultural critics have learned anything from poststructuralist and hermeneutic debates, it is the all-encompassing influence of context, of sites, and of place in production of meanings. Culture, whether or not artificially opposed as high and low, does not exist outside or inside, above or below, the important political events of the day. It is, in point of fact, the terrain (as the Oranienburgerstrasse) upon and through which all political activities take place. It is a network, and a discursive one at that, of intertwined signs, significations, and symbols woven together in such a way as, paradoxically, to create constantly shifting patterns, as if a kaleidoscope could be constructed of colorful threads rather than chips of glass. Clinton's speech and, even more, his visit to the synagogue at the moment it took place are replete with such threads that become rewoven and sometimes re-entangled in a contexture in which meaning is made, whether these meanings were intended or not (for the media or for political capital). Hermeneutic wisdom (precisely that legacy of German philosopher Friedrich Schleiermacher who taught at the Humboldt University located approximately between the Brandenburg Gate

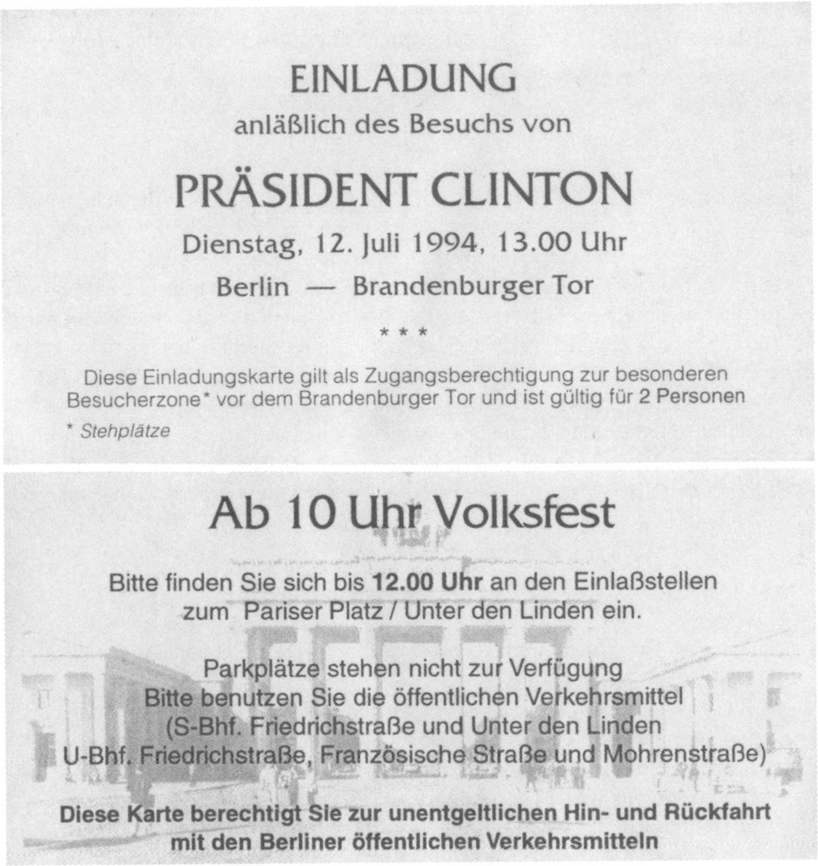

EINLADUNG

anläßlich des Besuchs von

PRÄSIDENT CLINTON

Dienstag, 12. Juli 1994, 13.00 Uhr

Berlin — Brandenburger Tor

* * *

Diese Einladungskarte gilt als Zugangsberechtigung zur besonderen
Besucherzone* vor dem Brandenburger Tor und ist gültig für 2 Personen

* Stehplätze

Ab 10 Uhr Volksfest

Bitte finden Sie sich bis **12.00 Uhr** an den Einlaßstellen
zum Pariser Platz / Unter den Linden ein.

Parkplätze stehen nicht zur Verfügung
Bitte benutzen Sie die öffentlichen Verkehrsmittel
(S-Bhf. Friedrichstraße und Unter den Linden
U-Bhf. Friedrichstraße, Französische Straße und Mohrenstraße)

**Diese Karte berechtigt Sie zur unentgeltlichen Hin- und Rückfahrt
mit den Berliner öffentlichen Verkehrsmitteln**

Fig. 2.   Ticket to Clinton speech at the Brandenburg Gate, 12 July 1994.

and the Oranienburger synagogue) posits that meanings always supersede the words or texts originally spoken or written. To ask whether Clinton's speech was historic is perhaps the wrong approach. Culture is such a contexture, and the Clintons' visit generated material and symbolic meanings that need not only be the limited subject matter of content analyses by reporters or editors. Cultural studies of the kind I offer here might bring some new perspectives to how meanings get made and how texts and cultures get *trans*lated, how meanings get moved from place to place. I have returned to the origins of cultural studies, at least for me, to philology and hermeneutics, in a new sense. And I think for cultural studies and foreign policy there may be no better place to start.

NOTES

1. I teach at the Center for German and European Studies located in the School of Foreign Service at Georgetown University. The center, one of three such "Centers of Excellence" funded by the German government, is truly interdisciplinary. Five faculty make up its core in the fields of politics, international relations, literary and cultural studies, history, and economics; students are required to take graduate courses in all five areas. The School of Foreign Service itself is known for its international relations and policy curriculum, which is now being complemented by courses in cultural studies.

2. I want to thank Christian Rogowski for sharing with me his interpretation of Clinton's position at the Brandenburg Gate. I gratefully include it in my essay.

3. On the symbolically freighted Neue Wache, see Miller's essay, in this volume.

4. I appreciate Klaus Milich's reading of this essay; he drew my attention to this point.

WORKS CITED

Ajami, Fouad. "The Summoning." *Foreign Affairs* 72.4 (September–October 1993): 3–9. Response to Huntington.

Austin, J. L. *How to Do Things with Words.* 2nd ed., ed. J. O. Urmson and Marina Sbisà. Cambridge: Harvard UP, 1962, 1975.

Clifford, James, and George Marcus, eds. *Writing Culture: The Poetics and Politics of Ethnography.* Berkeley: U of California P, 1986.

Damit die Nacht nicht wiederkehre: Gedenken an die faschistische Pogrommnacht vom 9. November 1938. Berlin: Verband der jüdischen Gemeinden in der DDR, 1988.

Geertz, Clifford. *The Interpretation of Cultures.* New York: Basic Books, 1973.

Huntington, Samuel. "The Clash of Civilizations?" *Foreign Affairs* 72.3 (Summer 1993): 22–49.

Widman, Carlos. "Makellose Arie für die Berliner." *Der Spiegel,* 18 July 1994, 27–29.

Part Three

WHO PRACTICES GERMAN
CULTURAL STUDIES?

Cultural studies opens up the question of identity itself. As the previous section demonstrates, German cultural studies necessarily explores the construction of "Germanness." In part 3 the authors interrogate themselves *by asking why they do what they do and how who they are may affect not only their choice of career and specialization but also the performance of their jobs. Investigation of one's subject positions and the concomitant rejection of the idea of perfectly objective scientific inquiry are integral to cultural studies approaches. Hoggart's and William's working-class backgrounds profoundly influenced their early books and shaped the conception of the Birmingham Centre for Contemporary Cultural Studies. But it was perhaps the insistent voices of women and people of color that made interrogation of identity a critical part of cultural studies. Feminist theory, African-American studies, and, later, gender, postcolonial, and queer studies have all problematized the relationships between anatomy and identity; that is to say, they offer a critique of essentialist notions of difference. Thus, cultural studies concerns itself with demonstrating that* woman, man, white, black, straight, queer, American, Jewish, British, *or* German *must be scrutinized as constructions without minimizing differences among us—and these kinds of investigations are what follow in this part.*

CHAPTER 6

Learning to Stop Hating Germans: The Challenge of Journalistic Objectivity

Deidre Berger

The sound of Deidre Berger's actual voice is probably familiar to most readers of this volume. As a correspondent for National Public Radio (NPR), American audiences have heard her perceptive reporting of contemporary German events for more than ten years. In "Learning to Stop Hating the Germans: The Challenge of Journalistic Objectivity" we "hear" Deidre Berger's voice in print, as she shares with us how the radio broadcast news gets put together. The product of a reporter's activity is shaped by the constraints of the medium, the requirements of editors and specific shows, and reporters' and editors' knowledge of what interests the American radio audience. Berger's inclusion of the transcript of an actual report and her explanation of what did and did not make it onto the air reveal some of the differences between oral and written media.

Berger takes us through several important events in recent German history from her perspective, sharing how her own preconceptions were transformed by the people she met and her efforts to understand German culture from a German's position. Her awareness of her own bias and her efforts to consider how it affects her ability to "report" the news echo the importance in cultural studies of reflection on one's own subject positions in selecting, researching, and teaching any given topic. Similarly, Berger emphasizes how much her work is shaped by her sense of the audience. Her starting point is always ultimately how little Americans know about the contemporary German scene and how frozen our attention has been on National Socialist Germany. This is a somber point that academics should consider when transforming curricula and planning future research projects.

Berger's main tool in this essay, the personal anecdote, has played a cen-

tral role in cultural studies. A "moment" regarded in myriad dimensions can be an efficient guide to cultural knowledge. Berger is a captivating storyteller, as any "cultural broker" (her term) must be. This essay invites us to consider how cultural knowledge circulates in an age of mass media. Cultural studies in the large definition we are trying to promote in this volume is not limited to the classroom and academic symposia. In the global village we need to promote discussion among all the villagers.

Working as a journalist forces a continuing confrontation with personal prejudice and social bias. And these, in the case of Germany, tend to extremes. Since the two world wars there have been dozens of horrifying civil and regional wars. Still, for countless Americans, Germany remains the ultimate metaphor of evil, the frightening reminder of the fragility of civilization.

Ideally, those who shape the crucial images that define our knowledge of the outside world are objective and single-minded in the pursuit of truth and justice. But journalists, too, are products of the prevailing assumptions and outlook of their own culture. It is difficult for them to suspend prejudices against a society. Even when they try, they are reporting to audiences who remain unchanged by direct contact. I try to transmit to my audience the discoveries I have made through my exposure to German culture. This may stimulate curiosity and open some minds. But the recounting of personal experience cannot replace personal experience. Time and space constraints also limit reporters' chances to convey the personal impressions or analysis that cast perspective on news events.

Far-right-wing ideology is on the rise throughout the Western world. For more than a decade Jean Marie Le Pen has consistently scored between 10 and 15 percent of the French vote in nationwide elections. In Austria the charismatic right-wing politician Jörg Haider received more than 20 percent of the vote in the 1995 national elections, despite his refusal to retract comments praising former members of the Waffen-SS for sticking to their "politically incorrect" convictions. In Italy the neofascist party briefly entered a Center-Right government coalition. In the United States a man on the fringes of the far-right-wing militia movement was most likely responsible for the bombing of a government building in Oklahoma City, which killed over a hundred people. But it is the politically disorganized German neo-Nazi movement that continues to generate the most public interest, perhaps because few journalists can be indifferent to the emotional impact of young Germans in black leather jackets and boots, draped and tattooed with Nazi paraphernalia.

Outside of Germany another legacy survives: the image of the Germans as a fearsome nation of arrogant, duty-bound, obedience-loving racists, who are only held in check by their economic and military interdependence with the West. The image of the enemy from VE-Day 1945 has been frozen in time for many Americans. Modern German culture is not well-known, and since World War II there have been too few German cultural representatives on a popular level—such as rock stars, filmmakers, or writers—to change significantly the enemy image. The most positive attribute of modern Germany for many Americans is the high quality of its consumer and technical products.

These layers of preconceptions, misconceptions, and ignorance on the part of the journalist and the audience create inevitable problems. Reports on all aspects of German culture—politics, economics, art, and everyday life—are colored by this inherent subjectivity. The dilemma for foreign journalists is to translate a story from a foreign cultural context into a context familiar to readers, listeners, or viewers, without distorting the event's significance for the principal parties involved.

When there is not a conscious attempt to do this, reports can end up revealing more about the journalist's attitudes and opinions than about the culture on which he or she reports. For instance, a U.S. reporter in Europe might write a story about unemployment that focuses on the battle of some politicians to reduce corporate taxes. The story might not reflect, however, that these politicians are in the minority, as Continental European countries often favor public spending programs as the chief method to fight unemployment. Such a story would reveal the reporter's personal feelings that tax reduction is the most important job creation tool and that Europeans create their own unemployment problems by not applying this tool properly. This, in turn, reinforces possible preconceptions of American readers that Europe's social market system is inferior to a U.S.-style market economy. Instead of reporting on the approach taken by a foreign culture, the journalist has transferred prevailing cultural assumptions from one culture to another.

Cultural distortions can also arise in editorial offices through the selection of story topics. If there is relatively high unemployment in the United States, affecting an upcoming presidential campaign, editors might ask for reports on unemployment problems elsewhere. But conditions that create an explosive political problem in one country may not disturb a different electorate. European governments often stay in power despite relatively high unemployment because of generous unemployment benefits and retraining programs. The series could be interesting but only if reporters explain the different cultural contexts. Otherwise, the audience gets the false impression that unemployment is just as much a political problem in country X as in the United States.

Numerous factors determine the final mix of information in a given newspaper article or television or radio program. At National Public Radio, for instance, story ideas stem from reporter suggestions, requests from programs (often based on ideas culled from newspaper stories), and daily news meetings at which editors and producers generate ideas and coordinate coverage of breaking news.

Some reports can be planned. Every month I prepare a list of upcoming and potentially newsworthy events in Germany (conferences, state visits, seminars, etc.). Then I discuss the list with my editor to decide whether I should be sent to certain events or if background reports need to be prepared in advance. I also write a monthly political summary to keep my editors informed of trends and directions in German politics and economics. Feature ideas occasionally come from NPR producers who read an interesting article about Germany, but I suggest most of the topics for longer features. There are foreign editors on duty around the clock, so I can always call to report on breaking news. Through the news agencies my Washington editors often know more quickly than I do about events in Germany. They then call me, or I call them, to discuss the news and put it in context. We make a joint decision on what coverage is necessary and what is technically possible. It is not always possible in foreign countries to go quickly to the site of breaking news to get interviews and sound, so initial reports on a situation might be quite short. The poor quality of available broadcast facilities also could mean short reports.

The editors are then responsible for convincing the producers of the upcoming news show to broadcast the report. Longer feature reports that require more work are rarely assigned until a specific program has agreed to broadcast the report. Personal relations between an editor and producers can also affect his or her ability to "sell" a report to a program. Producers must also consider how to keep a listener's interest, varying the content with shorter and longer pieces, serious and humorous pieces, reporter features and host interviews.

The list of variable factors influencing the decisions on reports is long. When a piece is assigned, reporters are often given approximate time lengths for the final report. Editors and producers make this decision based on experience as well as on available broadcast space. After years of reporting, I also have a sense of how long I can sustain interest in a topic. At the last minute other breaking news or an unexpectedly long report may cause my report to be shortened due to overall time constraints.

But, in any case, the report is much shorter than a comparable print story because of the expense and therefore brevity of airtime in broadcasting. This forces the exclusion of innumerable observations, subtle details, and background information. The art of broadcasting is to telegraph to the listener or viewer concepts, ideas, and information in a comprehensible and balanced manner. Good radio and TV reports compensate for the lack of detail by conveying a sensory immediacy to events.

An example is a report I wrote after the death in January 1996 of François

Mitterand on his relationship to Germany. I was present at Mitterand's last major speech as president of France, which he delivered in Berlin on 8 May 1995. Already gravely ill, Mitterand spoke fluidly, and with great emotion, about French-German reconciliation. When he died, I recalled how moved I had been by the speech and how much it seemed to sum up his vision for Europe. A foreign editor at NPR agreed that Mitterand's relationship to Germany warranted a separate report. The following report was broadcast on 9 January 1996 on "Morning Edition":[1]

> French socialist François Mitterand, and German conservative Helmut Kohl, were an unlikely pair. But their common conviction in European unity . . . to keep the peace in Europe . . . created a lasting political friendship. Yesterday, Chancellor Kohl called Mitterand's death a deep loss:
>
> KOHL [German; original quote not given here]
>
> Kohl said François Mitterand was a great European, a great French patriot, and a loyal friend of our country.
>
> In 1984—shortly after he came to power—Mitterand boldly made a gesture of reconciliation toward France's centuries-old enemy, Germany. He invited Kohl to visit the WWI battlefield at Verdun, where the French fought the Germans. At the site, they spontaneously clasped hands, a symbolic moment for both nations. After several years in office, Mitterand had decided that European unity was only possible if France and Germany were reconciled. Bruno Schoch is a political scientist at the Hessen Institute for Peace and Conflict Research.
>
> SCHOCH [English]: HE KNEW THAT MAINTAINING FRENCH INFLUENCE IN EUROPE IS POSSIBLE ONLY TOGETHER WITH GERMANY. AND THAT IS THE REASON WHY HE WAS SO STRONG IN HIS GERMAN-FRENCH ENGAGEMENT . . . BECAUSE EVERYBODY KNOWS, IF THE GERMAN-FRENCH NUCLEUS DOESN'T WORK AS A MOTOR OF THE ENGINE OF EUROPEAN UNIFICATION, SO WE WILL HAVE NO UNIFICATION PROCESS.
>
> Still, Mitterand had a lingering mistrust of German political goals . . . He hoped the European Union would finally balance power within Europe between Germany and France. At first, he opposed German unification . . . because he thought Germany would become too powerful. Bruno Schoch:
>
> SCHOCH [English]: THEN HE ACCEPTED THE UNIFICATION, BECAUSE HE COULDN'T STOP IT, FRANCE WASN'T STRONG ENOUGH, AND HE COULDN'T COUNT ON GORBACHEV, AND THE SECOND POINT HE ALWAYS STRESSED. . . . HE WAS CON-

VINCED THAT THE GERMANS AFTER 40 YEARS OF DEMOC-
RACY HAVE CHANGED.

Mitterand deliberately chose Berlin as the site of his final speech as French
president. He spoke last May, shortly before relinquishing his office. In
highly personal remarks, marking the fiftieth anniversary of the end of
World War II, he talked about his experiences as a German prisoner of
war, and the help he got from ordinary Germans. Then, he praised German soldiers. Mitterand spoke through an interpreter.

MITTERAND (English interpreter): THEY WERE BRAVE. THEY AC-
CEPTED THE LOSS OF THEIR LIVES FOR A BAD CAUSE. BUT
THEIR GESTURE IN FACT HAD NOTHING TO DO WITH THAT.
THEY WERE DEFENDING THEIR COUNTRY.

(*sound of loud applause*)

There were tears in many eyes . . . when the ailing Mitterand finished his
speech . . . walking slowly but erect toward his chair. Chancellor Kohl
embraced him. Mitterand's speech was later criticized by many French
as too pro-German. But the larger question is what will happen to
French-German friendship . . . and to European unity . . . when both
François Mitterand and Helmut Kohl have left the political stage. I'm
Deidre Berger in Frankfurt.

At the last minute there were several small cuts in the script for time reasons. I
had to cut out the fact that Mitterand invited the Eurocorps, which includes German soldiers, to march on the Champs d'Elysées on 14 July 1994. This was interesting, but the example of Mitterand and Kohl at Verdun had already made
the larger point about French-German reconciliation. I had to reduce the extract
from Mitterand's speech to his praise of German soldiers, taking out his explanation for the praise:

SO I THINK WE HAVE TO REALIZE THAT. WE ARE BUILDING EU-
ROPE. WE ALL LOVE OUR OWN COUNTRIES. LET US REMAIN
FAITHFUL TO OURSELVES. LET US LINK THE PAST WITH THE
FUTURE. WE CAN PASS THE BATON ON TO THOSE WHO COME
AFTER US WITH SECURITY AND PEACE.

And in the final paragraph I dropped a thought about a possible weakening of
Franco-German relations under President Jacques Chirac.

Still, the report could highlight several components of Mitterand's legacy:
reconciliation between France and Germany and the vision of European unity
that tied him to Kohl. Hearing Kohl's voice in German and the applause for Mitterand in Berlin, the listener could sense the strength of the link between the
two countries.

What such a report could not do is illuminate the complexity of that link. There are hundreds of city partnerships between French and German cities, but many French citizens continue to fear renewed German dominance in Europe. The comment that Mitterand's Berlin speech was criticized within France as too pro-German was an understatement. His comments about learning to respect average Germans during the war years, the resulting conviction that the age-old hatred between two neighboring countries must end, and his respect for German soldiers serving their country caused a furor among the French intelligentsia. I could barely touch on the seeming contradiction of a man emphasizing good French-German relations but opposing unification. That would have required more analysis of the numerous contradictions in Mitterand's political behavior as well as historical background on French and German roles in Europe. And that is more detail than I can assume interests a broad U.S. audience in the context of a radio broadcast, given the lack of European history education in U.S. schools and the general disinterest in foreign topics, except during moments of crisis.

The German Self-Image: Rabta—
Reaction to International Pressure

In the German case cultural translation is complicated by the country's obsession with its international image. There are weekly television programs in Germany with foreign correspondents and daily summaries in radio and print of articles on Germany in the foreign press. Prominent German columnists periodically complain about "Germany bashing" by foreign reporters. It is essential for foreign journalists to be aware of the Germans' concern with their image abroad to evaluate the significance of specific news stories. For instance, the German government is highly sensitive to reports that in any way touch on the country's Nazi past, such as arms shipments to areas of tension.

Whether or not it is justified after fifty years of peace, Germany is held to higher moral standards on numerous political issues than other countries. This was the background of the international outrage against the unscrupulous dealings of the German businessman, Jürgen Hippenstiel-Imhausen, who smuggled plans and parts for a chemical weapons factory through a network of dummy companies in Hong Kong and other locations to Rabta, Libya. The deal was morally reprehensible, and illegal, even by Germany's lax standards on technology export. But German government officials were still furious when U.S. columnist William Safire characterized the affair as "Auschwitz-in-the-Sand."[2]

Safire's column, which prompted an immediate press conference on the part of the Bonn government, did two things: it implied the entire transaction had the tacit approval of the German government, as did Auschwitz, and that Germans were still capable of committing the horrible kind of atrocities they did at Auschwitz. The story was no longer just about a criminal business transaction. The Bonn government considered its honor as a reliable NATO partner and democratic ally to be at stake. Instead of admitting the serious loopholes in its export regulations, Bonn denied all knowledge of the matter, although it later admitted that some officials had known about the situation long before the story made headlines. The government's initial news conferences on the affair revolved more around the treatment of the story in the foreign press than about legal action being taken against Imhausen and other German companies involved in the deal.

Even after the government started prosecuting the case, the focus remained on Germany, despite reports of other questionable arms deals in the United States, France, and Britain. It is journalistically "sexier"—that is, assumed by editors to be of interest to a larger audience—when a German company, rather than a U.S. firm, can be traced to factories of death. Many foreign journalists come to Germany with the suspicion that nothing has changed in fifty years and pounce on opportunities to prove their underlying assumptions.

In this case the media probably created a distorted impression in the United States that Germany was the major culprit in the dissemination of deadly weapons technology to countries such as Libya and Iraq. But international press attention was also a powerful tool in bringing about a change in German export laws for dual-use technology. The Rabta story transformed the role of foreign journalists from one as cultural brokers to catalysts for change, through news reports that created outside pressure on the Germans to take action.

Changing Perceptions: Dresden— Justified Revenge or Pointless Suffering?

I came to Germany believing the United States had fought a just war against a merciless aggressor. I assumed that the vanquished Germans had recognized the error of their ways and would view the war similarly. It did not take long for me to realize how differently the Germans perceived the war years.

One of the first stories I produced shortly after coming to Germany was a fortieth-anniversary account of the bombing of Dresden the nights of 13 and 14 February 1945. Before the report Dresden meant little more to me than yet another German city that had been bombed in the attempt to defeat Hitler.

In the process of preparing my report, I interviewed a woman who was outside the city center the night carpet bombing raids set Dresden on fire, producing furnace-like temperatures that created an instant inferno. She retold the gruesome minutes and hours of those two days as if in a trance; her tale succeeded in transporting me to the banks of the Elbe in those moments when the sky turned red, the river filled with victims trying to escape the flames, and the stench of burning human flesh permeated the air. When dawn broke she had set off in search of her parents, stumbling without orientation through the rubble of no longer recognizable streets. Everywhere there were macabre scenes of corpses burned beyond recognition, often stacked in piles like logs in a fire. The woman reached into a long-sealed-up cavity of memories, speaking for nearly an hour with the eloquence and drama of a trained actress. And I listened, spellbound, to one of the most remarkable accounts I have ever heard of the impact of war. Suddenly, the bombing was no longer an abstract military action carried out against an enemy but a questionable act of war carried out against civilians.

My report of the bombing was no doubt influenced by this extraordinary interview and by the seeming lack of military justification for the bombing. For the first time I began to question the basic assumption upon which I had been taught World War II history: that every means was justified if it helped shorten the days of the Third Reich. I realized that many Germans considered the Dresden attack a case of unwarranted brutality and revenge on the part of the Allies.

Some months after the report was broadcast, in an interview with a former Jewish concentration camp prisoner, I acquired yet another perspective on the bombing. Lise Scheuer witnessed the burning of Dresden during her shift as a slave laborer at a factory in Freiberg, about thirty miles from Dresden. One day the air raid sirens went off. Normally, the slave laborers were not allowed into the air raid shelters, but this time they were rushed to the basement. Lise hid behind the curtains to look out the windows, more curious than afraid of the unusual order to go into the shelters. In the distance she saw a red sky and knew Dresden was burning. Her feelings were ambivalent. She was anguished by the untold levels of human suffering brought on by the flames but joyful at the fiery evidence that the Allies were coming closer to winning the war, which could mean her eventual liberation. If the great German cultural center of Dresden is burning, she thought, the end of the war cannot be long in coming. I learned from Lise that the bombing could not be judged alone on its legal and ethical merits. The flattening of Dresden and other cities gave the persecuted Nazi victims hope, a promise of survival.

The construction of reality, in the attempt to reconstruct history, is a highly subjective process. A journalist tries to weld personal accounts to factual information in order to capture a moment in time. The bias of the sources, as well as the experiences and emotions of the journalist, decisively color the resulting synthesis. The account is again filtered through the lens of the reader, listener, or viewer, whose attempt to focus on another culture is influenced by personal and social attitudes. And the longer a journalist lives in another culture, the greater the gap with the audience at home who does not have the experience of direct exposure. For those convinced that German civilians got their due punishment in the bombing raids, the story of the firestorm in Dresden will have little impact; the grim details might even reinforce convictions of justifiable retribution.

A journalistic recapitulation of historical events for a popular audience should not attempt to settle historical disputes or to even scores but, rather, to refresh memory and to present a more complete picture than may have been possible at the time of the event. A comprehensive overview can bring shades of understanding into the often black-and-white popular perception of history.

Dealing with the Past: The War Generation

During the year following my arrival in Germany I did a series of interviews on the end of World War II in Germany, for a report on the fortieth anniversary of the 8 May capitulation. One of my interview partners, a teacher in Detmold, was a young soldier during the war. He had the valuable capacity to recount his thoughts at the time, without the reflections and judgments of the intervening forty years. "In the beginning," he told me, "we thought Hitler was the great peacemaker. We thought he would finally bring peace to the middle of Europe."

I was astounded. I had never before heard a plausible defense of the German position. Indeed, nineteenth- and early-twentieth-century Europe had been a nearly ceaseless, turbulent battlefield of power politics. Germany as a nation had trouble paying the punishing reparation payments stipulated in the Versailles treaty ending World War I. Suddenly, I could grasp at least some reasons for the enormous support for Hitler, at a time when the consequences of racism were unclear to many. If I made no attempt to understand another perspective, I realized I could only produce a one-sided account weighted with facts that supported my preconceptions. Still, I often found it difficult to accept the war accounts of German suffering, when they were told without mention of the simultaneous persecution, torture, and murder by the Nazis of millions of innocent people.

One notable exception was a woman who described to me her flight from Pomerania to the Western Allied zones during the last months of the war. I was not aware of the human toll of the forced resettlement of ethnic Germans. Tens of thousands lost their lives during the treks westward. The woman talked about her hunger and desperation trying to find food for her son and elderly mother. She then described her rape by a Soviet soldier. There was no bitterness, but shame still hung over her account forty years later. She did not realize the extent of the crimes against the Jews, she said, until she watched the American miniseries "Holocaust," which was broadcast in Germany in 1979. And then she started crying. She was deeply ashamed, she said, for the entire German people, and for herself, and expressed her deep apologies for what had happened.

But this open acknowledgment of German responsibility for Nazi atrocities has not happened often during my interviews with older Germans. Most commonly, I encounter people who say they did not know what had happened to the Jews until the war was over. This confused me enormously at the beginning, especially as a half-million Jews lived in Germany before the Nazi takeover. Even the smallest villages had their *Judengasse* (Jew Alley). Most Germans had witnessed or had heard of the dispossession and deportation of their Jewish neighbors. Millions of German soldiers who had witnessed atrocities had home leave during the war. German children were told to behave themselves, or they would end up in Dachau. How could the genocide of the Jews have remained a secret?

I interviewed novelist Heinrich Böll shortly before his death. After the interview was over I told him I was Jewish and that I tried to repress my feelings of suspicion, and even hatred of the Germans, in order to learn German and acclimate myself to the culture. Still, I shared, even without my asking, many people instantly volunteer to me, "I didn't know." I asked Böll if it were true that most Germans did not know what was happening to the Jews. He put his hand on my shoulder and shook his head. "Of course many people knew, but it doesn't matter. The point is, they could have known, but they didn't want to know. They repressed the truth." Then he looked up at me. "Ach, Mädchen," he said sadly, "it won't be easy for you to live here."

So it was true, but it was also not true. It took many years for me to understand the layers of defensiveness and repression veiling the German memory of the Holocaust. Many never attempted to confront the past, and they evaded their children's questions.

Dealing with the Past: Children of the War Generation

During the 1992 trial of war criminal Josef Schwammberger I met a teacher who had brought his seventh-grade class to observe the court proceedings. It was a day when a survivor of the Przemsyl ghetto talked about the inhuman conditions in the ghetto and the arbitrary sadistic violence of ghetto commander Schwammberger. I later visited the class to discuss with the students what they had experienced. The children were too young, or too shy, to articulate their feelings easily. But it was obvious that most had never heard about Nazi crimes in such detail, and they were shocked. The trial came at a time when far-right-wing political parties and skinhead movements were gaining ground in Germany, even among high school and junior high school students. Some of the children thought the neo-Nazi movement would be less attractive to teenagers if students learned more details about the Holocaust.

During lunch the teacher talked about his own family background. His father was a Nazi and had fought in the war with distinction, receiving an Iron Cross. He was wounded, losing an eye. The Holocaust was never discussed in the family. The teacher was a student in the 1960s, when many young people in Germany started confronting their parents about their role in the Third Reich. He, too, tried to discuss the subject with his parents, without success. The times were different, they said, and you could not understand that now.

The only option was to learn more about the Holocaust on his own initiative. He tried to expand scanty course material, teaching his students as much as possible about the crimes of the Nazis. The tension with his father remained. Father and son never reconciled. The son was struck by two keepsakes his mother refused to throw away following his father's death: his Iron Cross and his glass eye. At that moment he knew his mother was still not prepared to face the truth about her husband. And he knew he had to accept her inability to deal with the family past.

Many Germans could not, and still cannot, accept the ambivalence that to have fought honorably in a dishonorable war is not necessarily an honorable act. They cannot understand that their children judge them by the courage they had or did not have after the war to confront their own role in the Third Reich. Many in the second and third postwar generations are even less willing to accept responsibility for the deeds of their parents and grandparents.

These Germans, of course, are products of a not-so-distant past. They are children of parents who left them alone with their questions and anger. They are children of parents who knew nothing, because they did not even ask, dutifully respecting the unspoken taboo surrounding the Holocaust. They are children of families that continue to believe there were merits to Hitler's Germany, grandchildren of men and women who think Europe would have been a better place if the Germans had successfully liquidated the Jews, vanquished the Russians, and seized power over the Continent.

And some are children of parents who never had the chance to ask, because their parents were killed in the war, on the battlefield, in civilian bombing raids, or during the westward trek to Germany. For instance, a German journalist today working in Cologne was a small child when his father was killed in battle. His mother fled with the family from the oncoming Soviet army to western Germany. From an early age he kept running, running from the father who was a follower of Hitler, running from the silence of the father who was not there. He quickly moved up the career ladder, propelled by an enormous drive to achieve, to stay in motion, to not stop and think.

And then one day the Berlin Wall fell. The barrier to visiting his father's grave in eastern Germany was gone. Yet he waited, consumed by work, pushing away thoughts of confronting the father who was never a father, the father who was a Nazi, the father who was probably a murderer, the father who was a part of him. He waited until he could wait no longer.

First, he went to his cousin's house, the beautiful older cousin he had never forgotten, despite the decades of separation. Together they went to the cemetery, both for the first time. And then an inexplicable, feverish force took hold of him. He had no sense of time, only of place, of being near his father for the first time since he was two years old. He started running through the large cemetery he had never seen, losing contact between his feet and the earth, flying through the rows with the certainty of a homing pigeon zeroing in on its destination. He did not stop until he reached his father's grave. He flung himself on the gravestone, sobbing, inconsolable, the small child grieving over the loss of the father. For nearly a half-century he had postponed mourning; he had sealed his heart from the sadness of losing a father, terrified of unsealing his emotions about a shattered idol. It was a wrinkle in time, fifty years that lasted a moment. It was a reconciliation with a man who could not be forgiven, a peace that could not be made, a love betrayed.

This was a moment that for me captured the German postwar trauma. After the Allies spread news of the Holocaust and sentenced a few top Nazi officials and industrialists, Nazi crimes became an issue of the past. The perfunctory denazification process did little to provoke personal or social confrontation. At home and with friends stories were often related about the war years. But in public there was virtually no discussion of the feelings of betrayal Hitler left behind or of the nation's shattered psyche. Instead, Germans poured their energy into reconstructing their cities and economy and rebuilding an identity as democrats.

In the late 1960s children began interrogating their parents about their role in the war. It was an acrimonious debate, punctuated by guilt accusations, which stirred in some the militancy that led to the founding of the Red Army Faction. Others, like the high school teacher, gave up their attempts at personal reconciliation, pouring their energy, instead, into community work. A book by psychologists Alexander and Margarethe Mitscherlich, *Die Unfähigkeit zu trauern* (*The Inability to Mourn*), became a best-seller.

The journalist's belated acknowledgment of his father as a father, and not just as a Nazi, is a sign that mourning is a long process. Fifty years later some Germans are finding the strength to come to terms with their ambivalent heritage. A film producer in Hamburg made a movie in 1994 about the children of Nazis called *Das Schweigen brechen* [Breaking the Silence]. Her father was also a top-ranking Nazi. She told me she understood people's reluctance to have their family stories filmed. She, too, felt a deep sense of shame. "I would have liked to have had a father in the resistance, but I did not," she said. "I have to live with this."

The attempt to live with the past is an ongoing process, part of the evolution of memory. The death of the film producer's father is an inalterable fact. But the woman's response to the event is variable. It is a process of shifting perspectives, brought on by external forces such as the greater access for Germans since unification to Nazi documents and internal forces such as the gradual disappearance of the war generation whose members repressed their knowledge of Nazi crimes. Journalism affects and is affected by these shifting perspectives.

Story Context and Audience:
20 July—the Myths of Resistance

A controversial debate erupted in Germany in the spring of 1994 about German resistance and the 20 July 1944 plot to kill Hitler. Children and grandchildren of executed plotters angrily attacked the director of the Berlin resistance museum for including information on communist-directed resistance. The wounds of forty years of division were reopened, with a highly charged discussion about the postwar myths of resistance. West and East Germany both seized on accounts of resistance to legitimize their forms of government after the war, with the officers and diplomats of the 20 July plotters seen in the West as the founding fathers of democracy, while East Germany regarded the communist World War II resistance fighters as the founders of socialism. There was also heated discussion about the goals and plans of the 20 July plotters and the refusal of Britain and the United States to support the German resistance.

From experience I knew it was best to reduce the story to its basics for an American audience: who were the resisters, what were their motives, and why did it take so long for the army to rebel against Hitler? I also wanted to stress that the resisters were largely motivated by a desire to save Germany as a nation rather than human rights concerns to save the Jews and other Nazi victims. I did not know the motivation of the plotters until I started researching the story, assumed my audience also knew nothing, and thought listeners would be interested in what I had discovered. This observation was of lesser importance in German accounts, which stressed the debate about postwar resistance myths.

I decided to focus on an account of the failed plot and an elaboration of motives. This could be seen as pandering to the interests of the audience; I had to assume, however, that most of my listeners did not have the same degree of knowledge about the plot as Germans, who studied it in school and who publicly commemorate the event every year. So I felt it was justified in this instance to report the story differently than my German colleagues.

Even when an audience is better informed, emotional reactions to history influence audience receptivity. The debate in the United States about a planned Smithsonian exhibition on the bombings of Hiroshima and Nagasaki, which was ultimately canceled, illustrates the difficulty Americans also have in confronting their past. When we are not willing to acknowledge the immense degree of suffering the bomb inflicted on Japanese civilians, whatever military justifications there may have been for the command, how great is the interest of an American audience in the suffering of German civilians during the war? If the interest is limited chiefly to scholars, the story is not news for a general U.S. audience, even if it is a recurrent front-page story in Germany. In Germany journalists consider it their responsibility to educate their audience. U.S. journalists, however, emphasize information more than education. In our attempt to expand knowledge of foreign cultures we must respect the limits of our audience to absorb information completely alien to their own frame of reference.

German Division: Reports across the Wall

Before unification the two Germanies were obsessed with proving the superiority of their respective systems. I was reporting for an audience who a priori accepted the viewpoint of its democratic ally, West Germany. But I could not have reported about the unification process without trying to convey the East German viewpoint as well. Reducing the story to one of freedom triumphing over authoritarianism would have been historically unjust.

My first visits to communist East Germany in the mid-1980s brought little enlightenment. The East Germans were guarded in their comments to Westerners. They proudly pointed to achievements like full employment, low crime, and full daycare. In the back of my mind I balanced these factors against the lack of political freedom, travel restrictions, the omnipresence of the secret service, and the grimness of East German cities.

On a gray October day in Leipzig in 1989, shortly before the collapse of the Wall, I first glimpsed another world and another reality. I visited a children's author whose name had been given to me by the dissident group New Forum. He talked to me about the group's attempts to force fundamental reforms of the socialist system, introducing a limited amount of private enterprise and more individual freedom. He drove me to the social center directed by his wife, in a dilapidated turn-of-the-century villa, on the grounds of a once prosperous factory. It was twilight as we waited in the car for his wife to finish work. The crumbling architectural remains of Leipzig's once prosperous past were silhouetted against the red-gray sky.

In this setting he began to talk more openly, of his move from West Germany to East Germany out of love for the woman who became his wife. As a children's author, he had fewer censorship problems than many of his colleagues. He said his personal happiness blinded him for a long time to the deprivations of freedom.

I gestured to the crumbling facades and neglected construction sites outside the car and asked if it was depressing to live in such an environment. He was surprised at first by the question, then he stared hard, as if blinders had been lifted from his eyes: I no longer notice, he said. I guess it does look appalling to an outsider. But it has been a gradual deterioration process, over many years, and I no longer notice the decay.

Through the self-critical observations of the writer I could begin to construct a picture of daily life inside East Germany. Looking through my eyes, the writer saw a different world than the one to which he had become accustomed. And through his eyes I could begin to apprehend the contours of what I had considered to be the shadowy terrain of communism.

The next day I took the train from Leipzig to Berlin. I cautiously began a conversation with a petite blonde woman sitting in my compartment. She was carefully attired, wearing light slacks, a pink polyester sweater, and the oversized plastic glasses popular at the time in East Germany as an emblem of Western fashion. She talked of her job as a vocational schoolteacher, of her family, of her pride in the socialist system she had helped create. East Germany was a just society, she said, and that was more important than the material advantages of a Western lifestyle. She could not believe the rumors of corruption in the East German leadership that had already started making the rounds. She felt the money that Bonn paid to East Germany to ransom political prisoners was hard currency direly needed and sensibly invested in the economy.

Nevertheless, she found the constant shortages exasperating, especially for clothes in the small sizes she needed. She asked me if the situation were better in West Germany. I somewhat thoughtlessly said it was also hard in West Germany to find clothes styled for smaller women, so I tried to buy clothes in France and Italy. If I had considered my words for just a moment, I would have realized I was describing the equivalent of a trip to the moon.

Her beliefs had already been rubbed thin in past months by the unfolding criticism of the communist system. My answer seemed to snap the last threads of faith. Tears welled up in her eyes: What did we do wrong? she asked. We tried to give our children a better world. We worked hard, we did what we thought was right. And when I hear you talking about traveling to Paris to buy the right-size clothes—.

I realized my mistake. I tried to reassure her that life in the West also had its problems and that I could appreciate the attempts made by socialism for a better society. But it was too late; I had unwittingly stirred embers of doubt. Later, when dissident groups uncovered the extent of fraud and corruption among the East German leadership, I often thought of the woman on the train, especially when I read about party members who committed suicide out of despair over the destruction of the world they had built.

Nowhere did I more deeply sense this reaction of betrayal than on the night the Wall fell in Berlin. Like a dike bursting under the relentless pressure of floodwaters, the checkpoints on the Wall were opened, and the East Germans poured through, thronging the normally quiet residential streets nearby. They took over the West Berlin streets, making their way to the legendary Kurfürstendamm, Berlin's Champs d'Elysées. It was a surreal atmosphere, a mixture of the unexpected and the fantastic. For me the West Berlin backdrop was trusted, familiar. But the actors were disoriented, without cues, bewildered by the transformation of a once imaginary stage into concrete pavement, stone buildings, flashing neon signs, pulsating disco rhythms, and unfamiliar aromas of foreign cuisines.

I met two young East German couples wandering down the street where I was staying with friends. One of the women was a teacher who could speak some English. I brought them back to the apartment to do a phone interview with NPR. The woman described her sense of amazement that she was walking around West Berlin as if it were the most normal occurrence in the world. She knew it would bring changes in her life, but she could not begin to imagine what kind and in what way.

My West Berlin friends brought out a bottle of champagne and together with the East Berliners toasted the unification of the city after twenty-eight years of division. Then I asked the East Berlin teacher about her first impressions: Something very odd happened just before you met us, she said. For years I have collected white dishes. Wherever I saw a cup or plate, I would buy it. Plain white dishes are difficult to find in East Germany—most of the tableware is covered with atrocious ornamentation. In a street around the corner from here, I suddenly saw a store window with tableware. I went up for a closer look, and saw the store sold nothing but white dishes, in all sorts of patterns and shapes. I have spent years of my life collecting something that has no value.

Her attempt to be different, to create an individual environment of beauty in protest against the drab uniformity of everyday life in East Germany, had lost much of its meaning. For her, and for seventeen million East Germans, a process of mental and spiritual fragmentation began that has splintered personalities, broken apart relationships, and redefined the priorities of an entire society.

Balancing Cultural Distortion

Whenever I return to the United States, friends and acquaintances repeatedly ask me how I can live in Germany. I try to explain that I do not personally experience antisemitism or animosity toward foreigners. I tell them about the postwar generation of Germans, many of whom fight with determination and resolve against racism and the Nazi legacy; their actions, however, rarely translate into news events on which I can report. Even when this is possible, I must be careful to remain alert to manifestations of racism in Germany, ranging from right-wing attacks on foreigners to concentrated passport checks at airports for passengers with darker skin. And then I explain further that racism is only one aspect of life in German society. My everyday reality is infinitely more complex, consisting of exposure to people from all walks of life and to topics as diverse as flood management and interest rates.

For a short period following the fall of the Berlin Wall, it was easy to interest a U.S. audience in the issues affecting modern Germany. The bloodless revolution leading to unification created a far more positive image of Germany in the United States than had been possible in the decades following World War II. Yet the outburst of right-wing extremism that followed unification, as well as a temporary economic boom, stirred concerns about how unified Germany would deal with its increased political and economic power.

The perpetual question about my residence in Germany has made me realize the limits of my reporting. Even when I strive to overcome personal antipathy and produce balanced reports, the selection of topics inevitably distorts the culture as it is experienced by Germans. And the prejudices of an audience limit the subjects and degree of information it is willing to absorb. Furthermore, journalistic accounts can only transmit isolated aspects of a society, rarely portraying events within the larger context of the culture in which they occur.

On a given day the German front-page headlines might deal with spiraling health care costs, high unemployment figures, German-Israeli relations, a state government scandal, and personal rivalries within one of the political parties. None of these stories directly affect either a U.S. audience or U.S. security interests, so I would not report on them. There might be a back-page story, however, on U.S. plans to close a base in Germany. If I report on the plans, it is certainly news, also in Germany. Yet it is an event that is of secondary importance to Germans, except perhaps for local residents who will be affected by the closing. I am reporting news of interest to a U.S. audience and, hence, ignoring social and political issues being discussed in Germany. Reporters can occasionally do longer, more impressionistic reports on the state of a society to balance daily news reporting, but there are only rare chances to do so.

This does not release foreign journalists from the responsibility to strive for objective, balanced reporting. The awareness of the distortions inherent in the selection of information is the first step in counteracting a slanted perspective. Contact with a broad cross-section of members of a foreign society also helps journalists confront personal bias. Despite flaws in the news-gathering process, journalists can make a difference, expanding boundaries of knowledge, instead of cementing prejudices.

Germany has a chilling past that must not be forgotten. Certain cultural traits that still exist enabled the Nazis to take power. When I meet Germans, I unconsciously continue to divide them into those I think I might have trusted during the war and those who might have been Nazis. Still, through extensive personal exposure I have learned to stop hating Germans on principle. A once faceless and feared culture has acquired more realistic contours, helping me transmit the multidimensional images needed for a more meaningful global village.

NOTES

1. This is the text of an actual radio broadcast. Its written form displays some conventions used in broadcasting. For example, ellipses and commas show where the reporter plans to pause. And copy in capital letters indicates where tape of another's voice will be inserted in the journalist's report. Readers are invited to notice how different a written version of an oral report strikes us when we read it as opposed to its (intended) oral performance when we hear it.

2. "The German Problem," *New York Times,* 2 January 1989, A23.

CHAPTER 7

Born Later: On Being a German Germanist in America

Christian Rogowski

As Deidre Berger's sense of how to do her job is influenced heavily by her experience of living in Germany as an American, so too is Christian Rogowski's approach to German cultural studies informed by his subject position as a German living in the United States. It is clear to Rogowski that the key element in the rich mix that is German history and culture is "the German catastrophe." The facts of National Socialism and the Holocaust stand in marked contrast to the enlightened and idealistic values so often articulated in German and by Germans but also force us engage with the clichéd German icons of high culture, the scenic landscape, the coziness, and all the rest we know to be "good" about German Central Europe. This contrast produces ferment and demands analysis. Germans themselves are students of their own culture and their own Germanness and find themselves "subject to multiple tensions": professional, private, and emotional. Rogowski's essay here, a touching personal account of how he came to "study the German," in Gilman's words, puts forward a sophisticated analysis of the role of the native scholar in foreign cultural studies work.

    Working from dramatist Botho Strauss's image of "ever-widening rings of memory around that unique birthplace of ours: German National Socialism," Rogowski tries to get at the nature of his role as a young German-born teacher and scholar of German studies working in the United States. Those without direct personal ties to midcentury Germany, "nonnatives," we could say, do not necessarily exist in the orbit of National Socialism the way that Strauss and Rogowski say they themselves do. Helmut Kohl's significant phrase, the "Gnade der späten Geburt" (the mercy of having been born later), which has been used and misused recently by so many in German politics and historiography, is at

the center of Rogowski's analysis of his and his generation's situation as Ger-
man Germanists working in the North American academy today. His critical
insights expose this phrase in all its ambivalence and complexity.

Rogowski is a teacher and scholar at Amherst College, a model of the
American liberal arts college, a type of institution in which breadth of knowl-
edge and faculties of critical inquiry, rather than specific skills for future em-
ployment, have special value and are encouraged. In this environment he finds
himself able to offer his students at once "a perspective grounded upon lived
experience, the experience of growing up in a culture marked by constant and
complex renegotiation of often conflicting tendencies," and—given Americans'
own repressed traumatic history (of slavery, of relations with Native Americans,
of the bomb)—the model of how to learn and to "render productive the specters
of a problematic past." He in no way equates these radically different histories;
instead, he says simply, and with hope, that we can learn from one another. Like
it or not, our own personal and national histories are necessarily a part of that
learning process.

"We have to keep alive, at all cost, the ability to differentiate."
—Alexander Kluge

1. Introduction

Thomas Brasch's film *Der Passagier—Welcome to Germany* (1988) features a
survivor of the Shoah returning to Germany in order to shoot a film detailing
the remarkable story of his survival and escape. Now a successful director for
American television, Cornfield (played by Tony Curtis) is interviewed upon his
arrival in Berlin by a German journalist about his film project. In response to
the question whether the film will be made in German or in English, Cornfield
remarks with a hint of sarcasm, "Can you imagine this movie being made in
anything, any other language than the language of the murderers?" Much as I
may like to think of my own culture as that of "Dichter und Denker" (poets and
thinkers), I have to acknowledge that history has indelibly, and for good reasons, rendered Germany into the country of "Richter und Henker" (judges and
hangmen) in the American popular imagination.

How, then, do I view my position as a German pursuing German studies
in the United States? Although I can only speak for myself, I would argue that

what follows touches on issues with which every German scholar working in this country is confronted.

2. Narratives

As someone working in German studies, I am a member of a community that seeks to understand a particular cultural legacy and to preserve a kind of cultural memory. I use *German* here in a broad sense to refer to the culture of German-speaking Central Europe that historically encompasses, but is not restricted to, the territories and cultures of the current Federal Republic of Germany, Austria, and parts of Switzerland. In light of recent developments in German studies the definition of German culture also has to include the traditions of ethnic Germans outside of the geographical area thus specified, such as the Volga Germans or the Germans in Rumania. To this one needs to add the rich and complex history of German emigration, especially to the United States, as well as the tragic heritage of Germans who, on account of political or racial persecution, found themselves forced into exile around the world. Moreover, postcolonial theory requires an awareness of the colonial legacy in African and Asian territories formerly, however briefly, under German control. German studies, then, encompasses a wide geopolitical terrain, stretching from Stockholm to South-West Africa, from Shanghai to Santa Monica.

German studies, conceived along the lines of cultural studies, "entails reorienting scholarly attention from the literary work of art to the construction of collective cultural identity" (Berman 9). Cultural identities are constructed above all through a narrativization of experience. We tell stories about ourselves in order to understand where we came from, where we are, and where we are going. The aim of German studies is to "analyze the German national narrative" (Geisler), understood here in the most comprehensive terms. The various constituencies that make up German culture, as it is defined here, have been engaged in producing a wide variety of narratives in many divergent areas. What all these narratives have in common, and what makes them German, is that they are all disrupted: in general terms there is the lingering legacy of national fragmentation, encapsulated in a history marked by a seemingly endless series of cataclysmic conflicts, such as the Reformation and the Peasants' Revolt, the Thirty Years' War, the tensions between Prussia and Austria, the Napoleonic occupation, the failed revolution of 1848 and belated unification under the kaiser in 1871. Franco Moretti has traced what makes German history both unique and tragic back to "the destructive heritage of the religious wars of early modern Europe" (Moretti 250–51), which rendered Germany different from other European nations. In the twentieth century there is the collapse of the *Kaiserreich* in the revolution following World War I, the failure of the Weimar Republic, the dictatorship of the Third Reich, the genocide of the Holocaust, the experience of renewed war, defeat, displacement, and division:

> No other industrial power has ever been on the brink of socialist revolution, or under fascist rule: Germany has experienced *both,* as if to reveal a hidden and fatal bifurcation of Modernity—a truly tragic choice lying beneath that ordinary administration to which Western countries had grown used. (Moretti 252–53)

This problematic legacy of crisis and disruption has profoundly affected all constituencies that partake in German culture. To pursue German studies, then, involves an attempt to analyze a disrupted national narrative and to find out how and why the multiple catastrophes of German culture came about.

As a German, I am deeply implicated in this configuration, whether I like it or not. I share with all Germans who were "born later," after the multiple catastrophes, and in particular after the Holocaust, the problem of fashioning a personal and national identity, a narrative, if you will, for myself out of a tainted legacy: this legacy cannot be embraced wholeheartedly but cannot be rejected in wholesale fashion either. For Germans who, like me, live and work abroad this predicament involves a constant process of complex and potentially endless negotiations.

3.   Identities

What is it that makes me identifiable as a German? When I was seventeen, I participated in a group trip to Poland, where, among other things, I visited the site of the former concentration camp Stutthof near Gdansk. I do not remember much about the visit, other than vague recollections of the melancholy and pensive mood that overcame me as I walked around past empty barracks and torture chambers. To the best of my knowledge Stutthof was not a major camp; none of the large-scale, quasi-industrial genocide took place there. Yet it is a site of terror and remembrance that shocks one into a realization of the terrible weight of German history. As we were about to leave, I walked past a little boy sitting on a rock by the wayside. Just as I had passed him, I could hear him hiss, "deutsches Schwein!" after me—in German, my language, the language of the murderers. In retrospect I can understand the boy's invective as a spontaneous expression of powerless outrage at what he must have seen and thought. All of a sudden I found myself in the position of being the object of undifferentiated discrimination, since I personally had done nothing wrong that would warrant such a verbal assault. On the contrary, through my visit, it could be argued, I had shown my good intentions to confront my nation's problematic past. Yet it was obvious that for that boy at that time a distinction between "good" and "bad" Germans did not, and could not, exist. As far as I can remember, actually I had done nothing that identified me as a German. Walking alone, I had certainly not spoken within the boy's earshot. I did not dare to respond. All I could do was stand there, defiled and defenseless.

This experience of defenselessness is one I think I share with all Germans when abroad: no matter how we wish to see ourselves, we find ourselves subject to the image that others make of us. Many young Germans consider this predicament an unfair imposition: why, they ask, should they, who had nothing to do with what happened over a generation ago, be held accountable for things in which they were not themselves personally involved? Some even altogether reject any confrontation with the problematic legacy of the Third Reich and the Holocaust as irrelevant. In Germany, German studies needs to combat an increasing ignorance and indifference among young people concerning our nation's past. The challenge there is to counteract, on the one hand, a pervasive thoughtless hedonism of the majority and, on the other, the potential emergence of neo-Nazi tendencies among an alienated and disenfranchised minority. The task of the academic discipline of *Germanistik* is to ensure an awareness of our national cultural legacy, in all its complexity and richness, all its splendor and disgrace: our nation's memory has to remain alert to the German catastrophe and its implications.

Most Germans of my generation and those younger see themselves as enlightened, cosmopolitan, open-minded citizens of a reasonably stable and well-functioning democracy. Many, in fact, argue that questions of national identity are largely irrelevant for their self-definition: they don't define themselves primarily as Germans but, rather, as Europeans or as members of the industrialized West. They dismiss the obsession with German national identity as myopic and highlight the broadly international cultural identity that many Germans have adopted for themselves over the past decades. At home, in the German-speaking countries, this self-image may work quite well. Yet when we go abroad we find that, as far as other countries are concerned, we are viewed primarily according to preconceived notions of what makes us German. No matter how we wish to define ourselves, others will tend to see us in terms of stereotypes, largely negative, about Germans. As a German abroad, one has to learn to live with stereotypes perpetuated by personal prejudice and the media: whereas I may place myself in a complex tradition that includes Hölderlin, Büchner, Brecht, and Joseph Beuys, to most Americans Germany, if not associated with Neuschwanstein and Lederhosen, equals Hitler, Holocaust, authoritarianism, and narrow-minded efficiency. In the United States one often encounters ignorance and indifference concerning the history and culture of German-speaking Central Europe. The task of German studies abroad is to help create an awareness of the richness and complexity of German culture, without downplaying its profoundly problematic history. Most Americans know little or nothing about Germany, Austria, or Switzerland beyond, perhaps, a handful of touristy clichés or negative stereotypes from Nazi movies. All the symposia on Heiner Müller and Anselm Kiefer, I know, will not undo the effects of history, the shocking documentaries, the mediated images from countless Nazi films, and the mindless nightly doses of "Hogan's Heroes" on syndicated television.

4.   Rings of Memory

In a passage from *Paare, Passanten* (Couples, Passers-by), a volume of essayistic prose vignettes first published in 1981, the German dramatist Botho Strauss attempts to articulate the predicament of his own generation, those born at the end or in the immediate aftermath of the Third Reich:

> As we grow older, we inscribe ever-widening rings of memory around that unique birthplace of ours: German National Socialism. The distance increases, but we can never escape from this concentric determination. Those who emerged from the excesses of our century will never experience a phase of life when they can avoid an inner relationship with their origin; their origin is in truth the secret middle-point, indeed the prison, of all their intellectual and spiritual strivings. They may often resist this connection with all their strength. At times the connection seems to mature, to become more confident, more casual even. Just consider all the attempts by artists to render the appropriate element of candor to our historical moods: they range from Expressionist hyperbole to psychoanalytic metamorphisms, from documentary drama to obscene allegorical cabaret. Yet no real solution, no dissolution of the connection to history, has ever been attained. The only release would be the death of history, the cancellation of memory by means of a total presence of the mass media, in which everything is mere appearance, a mere fleeting aesthetic impression. (171)[1]

Strauss employs a complex—indeed, partly contradictory—dual metaphor to describe the psychic legacy of National Socialism: on the one hand, the German catastrophe is the anchor, the "secret middle-point" from which all creative and intellectual, all political and personal, efforts emanate and to which such efforts return; on the other, it demarcates the space in which such efforts take place, a "prison" from which Germans are unable to escape as long as historical memory is operative.

Strauss has in mind primarily the activities of the politicized generation of the so-called student revolution of the 1960s. In the final analysis their efforts to create a clean slate and to insist on a radical democratization of West German society in Strauss's assessment turn out to be subject to a "concentric determination." No matter how ostensibly unrelated their initiatives were to the problems of German history, they remained gestures aimed at a "coming to terms with the past" (*Vergangenheitsbewältigung*).

5.   Contexts

German studies in the United States currently finds itself in the midst of a variety of conflicts. The U.S. academy is being put under increasing pressure to justify what it does to a public highly suspicious of the critical impulses that have emerged in the last two decades and that call into question many of the suppositions that underpin the official self-image of Americans. At the same time, economic pressures threaten to erode the very concept of a liberal arts education on which the American university system is founded. In the humanities the hitherto suppressed voices of minorities (social, sexual, ethnic, or racial) have emerged, which present a challenge to the status quo. As universities come under attack from the political Right, the humanities are the first to feel the pressure. All foreign language educators find themselves under threat of being turned into "merely auxiliary service personnel" (Debevec Henning 23). German studies, subject to stereotypical perceptions as an unduly difficult and problematic discipline, faces the peril of being among the most marginalized disciplines in the humanities, a field that is itself marginalized. In many ways German studies finds itself in a defensive, and partly defenseless, position.

My position as a German in this context is subject to multiple tensions. On the most fundamental level I have to acknowledge that I am a kind of economic migrant: I came here attracted by the educational opportunities offered by the U.S. graduate school system. I stayed here because of job prospects. In a climate of dwindling resources and a rapidly shrinking job market, U.S.-born Germanists may very well regard me as an intruder who deprives them of a job. My generation finds a situation quite unlike the one that welcomed the various waves of emigrants in the nineteenth and early twentieth centuries from German-speaking Central Europe that have enriched and enlivened German studies in this country. German studies has been characterized in the past decade or so by an increased Americanization (Koepke 62) and what has been termed a feminization of the profession (Nollendorfs 6): the proportion of American-born scholars and of women has increased in the field. In a recent polemic John Van Cleve and A. Leslie Willson argued that the crisis of American *Germanistik* is primarily attributable to the predominance of German-born scholars who sought to transpose their own rigid and narrow-minded notions of scholarly enterprise without any regard for the profoundly different sociocultural context in which our discipline is embedded in the United States. It is important that German studies in the United States develop in ways distinct from those on the European Continent, in response to the different and rapidly changing academic, social, and political conditions in this country. An increased openness to such differences in perspective will be highly fruitful to *Germanistik* everywhere. Our field needs to be responsive to the intellectual and theoretical developments that emanate from U.S. academia. It also needs to reflect the interests and concerns of all its constituencies. This implies that German-born scholars like me will in all likelihood play a less prominent role. At the same time, a certain presence of natives of German-speaking countries, as people who have experienced in their upbringing the constellations outlined by Botho Strauss, is essential for the health of the field. While many of the most productive impulses in German studies have come and continue to come from American scholars, I think that native speakers still have something unique and useful to offer.

6. Born Later

In chronological terms I belong to the tail-end of the second generation affected by National Socialism, the children of those who lived through Nazi dictatorship and war, although in terms of age and my cultural outlook I am perhaps closer to the third generation, that of the grandchildren who grew up with U.S. television and British pop music rather than ration cards and chewing gum. I thus partake of what West German chancellor Helmut Kohl, in a remarkable phrase he coined, has labeled the "Gnade der späten Geburt," the merciful historical contingency that, so he argued, spared those during or after the Third Reich the often painful moral decisions to which were subject those who lived as adults under Hitler's dictatorship.

The notion of the "mercy of having been born late," I propose, is prone to a wide range of ambivalences. For one thing it potentially allows virtually all Germans who lived through National Socialism the status of victim—perpetrator, bystander, and fellow traveler alike. Moreover, it has turned out that the concept is readily evoked to silence any criticism on the part of young Germans of the generation of their parents and grandparents. Uncomfortable questions are all too easily countered with the admonition that the young cannot possibly imagine what it meant to live through those years. In this fashion any criticism of the most problematic phase of German history, and any probe into the complicity, through action or indifference, of individuals with a criminal regime is automatically stripped of legitimacy. We who may wish to know more seem compelled to concede that we have no right to pass judgment. What appears as a humble and generous gesture on the part of Germany's most important statesman thus easily turns into a tool for the suppression of critical inquiry. In evoking historical coincidence as an expediency, Chancellor Kohl in fact arrogated to himself the authority to absolve, as it were, several generations of Germans of concrete historical responsibility, himself included. It is surely no coincidence that Kohl made his famous dictum in 1984 during a state visit to Israel (Kaes 239).

I am born later in more ways than one. One of my earliest childhood memories is that of my father collapsing on the living room floor and trembling with the convulsions of an epileptic fit. I must have been ill then, since a make-shift bed had been prepared for me on the living room sofa. This is why I was there to observe, in a mixture of terror, fascination, and utter incomprehension, my father lose what little control he had over his own body. During the war my father had received a head wound that paralyzed the right half of his body. He was twenty-one years old. After the war he had to go to court to have this affliction, outwardly very similar to hereditary epilepsy, recognized as a war injury. For the past five decades my father has been a war invalid, in full possession of his mental faculties but physically handicapped, limping on his right leg and unable to use his right arm. My mother married him during the war despite—or perhaps even because of—his injury, in an effort, it seems, to bestow a core of meaning, through selfless devotion to nurture and care, to her existence in the chaos around her. Both my parents come from parts of Germany that after the war were, as it was put then, "placed under Polish and Soviet administration," respectively. Under difficult circumstances as displaced persons, they raised two children, my brother and my sister, first in the Soviet occupation zone and then, after a dramatic escape to the West, in the Federal Republic. I, their third child, was born long after the war into a world of suburban security and *Wirtschaftswunder* prosperity, yet the war has always been physically and mentally present in my perception of life.

What I bring to German studies is the *Erfahrungsdruck,* the pressure of my personal experience of growing up in Germany. The legacy of National Socialism to me remains of fundamental importance to my definition of myself as a German. Far from being the source of relief, being born later represents a challenge that necessitates constant negotiations. Reaching adolescence in the early 1970s, I am also born later with regard to the political upheavals of the 1960s. I was too young to participate in the student movement, yet my socialization took place against the backdrop of an intensely politicized culture, including the protests over the German involvement in the Vietnam War, the frenzy over German left-wing terrorism, and the debate over the deployment of U.S. nuclear missiles on German soil.

Growing up in West Germany in what could still be called the postwar period, I was placed in an extraordinary situation masquerading as normalcy. A peculiar dynamic of family life in the wake of historical catastrophe provided the backdrop to my socialization. As Eric Santner has observed, "the ghosts, the revenant objects—of the Nazi period," the undealt-with and repressed issues of guilt and personal responsibility, created a peculiar psychopathology of the family (35). I inherited the mess of German history in the form of the messed-up family dynamics from the 1950s to the 1970s. I am, quite literally, the son of *Kriegsbeschädigte,* of those "damaged by war," whose traumatic experiences obliquely affect the way they deal with the new realities. My parents clearly saw, and still see, themselves as victims of circumstances beyond their control. Though they may bear little, if any, personal responsibility for what happened, it is clear that they have never been willing to address questions of collective responsibility. The trauma of their own victimization has rendered them incapable of mourning the suffering of victims of a different kind. For instance, they and many others in their generation do not seem to experience the near annihilation of the German-Jewish symbiosis as a source of bereavement. The burden of carrying our nation's shame has thus fallen on subsequent generations. I therefore find myself in a situation in which I am called upon to undertake the "tasks of mourning," the *Trauerarbeit,* that my parents have been unable to perform (Santner 31). Perhaps my interest in things German reflects a compulsion to search for a wholeness that was absent from my upbringing. Any thoughtful German of my generation finds him- or herself in a position akin to Walter Benjamin's Angel of History: we find ourselves searching for a lost—and irretrievable—wholeness.

7.   Horizons

Living in this country has substantially altered and enhanced my perspective on my cultural and historical legacy. The longer I live in the United States, the more I realize that the quest for an understanding of a problematic legacy is something that cannot be performed by Germans alone, nor can it be carried out for us only by American Germanists. The process is interactive and involves a methodological shift away from the traditional models of philology and literary history that predominate in German *Germanistik.*

Both Americans and Germans find themselves in a situation that calls for an increased ability to negotiate difference in manifold ways. Difference and identity are constructed through a narrative ordering of the world into inside and outside, self and other. Alterity and identity are the products of complex mediations that can fruitfully be analyzed with the help of interdisciplinary methodologies developed in international literary criticism. Cultural studies provides tools for exploring alterity. To quote Jonathan Culler:

> A particular virtue of literature, of history, of anthropology is instruction in otherness: vivid, compelling evidence of differences in cultures, mores, assumptions, values. At their best, these subjects make otherness palpable and make it comprehensible without reducing it to an inferior version of the same, as universalizing humanism threatens to do. (187)

The process of mediation needs to be carried out by representatives of all parties involved. Germanists from the German-speaking countries thus play an important role in German cultural studies in this country but primarily as interlocutors and colleagues in combination with our American colleagues.

I see my role as that of a participant in this quest, as a mediator between German culture, as defined here, and American culture. Historically, Germany and the United States have always been intricately linked. In demographic terms there have been the various waves of immigration to this country. There are, indeed, more people of German extraction in the United States than of any other nation. In intellectual terms there is a mutual indebtedness that cuts across the centuries. Modern sensibility is indelibly shaped by contributions emerging from the German tradition. To be sure, much of this intellectual legacy is fraught with profound problems or owes its impact partly to the troubled history of the German-speaking countries.

Living and working in the United States has made me aware of a multitude of traditions that are largely obscured or ignored by the traditional academic training I received in Germany. As someone living abroad, I see developing "foreign cultural literacy" (Berman 10) not only as an aim I pursue in my teaching of American students but also as something I continue to strive toward myself. My focus as a scholar has widened, shifting from primarily literary concerns to issues that involve a large spectrum of high and popular culture. As a teacher, I am confronted with the constant challenge of making a different mode of experience accessible to my American students. I have found my research and teaching evolving along interdisciplinary lines. The pursuit of German studies as cultural studies for me thus necessitates a redefinition of my various roles: in the classroom I strive to be a facilitator who helps students to develop their own intellectual skills. In my scholarship the reorientation of my discipline in many ways implies that one remains a student of sorts, constantly learning and responding to ever new aspects and materials.

Germany, the problematic heart of Europe, has always been the site in which the tensions characteristic of Western civilization have manifested themselves most clearly and most destructively. In this context the German cultural heritage is of interest to American students on a fundamental existential level: as human beings, we are all born later; all our lives are determined by the multiple catastrophe of Central European civilization that culminated in the excesses of two world wars, the disgrace of National Socialism, and the unspeakable horrors of the Holocaust. We are also born later with regard to other historical circumstances that continue to haunt us. In the United States events such as the Civil Rights movement and the anti–Vietnam War protests have occasioned a recognition of a wide range of problematic aspects of American history: for instance, the enslavement of blacks is acknowledged as a comprehensive crime against humanity, the westward expansion of the United States is redefined in terms of the genocide of the Native American population, and the ethical implications of the bombings of Hiroshima and Nagasaki are discussed with increased fervor and candor. Much as Germany can learn a great deal from the United States concerning a multicultural and pluralistic democracy, the United States can learn a lot from Germany concerning the challenge of rendering productive the specters of a problematic past. For several decades Germans have been faced with a legacy of devastation, guilt, and shame, and they have met this challenge, on the whole, with a remarkable degree of success. As human beings, we all have a lot to learn from German history, a history marked by conflict and catastrophe, by resilience and hope.

What I have to offer, apart from—I would hope—a modicum of professional expertise, is a perspective grounded upon lived experience, the experience of growing up in a culture marked by constant and complex renegotiation of often conflicting tendencies. To be sure, my life and my work will remain grounded on the "concentric determination" of which Botho Strauss speaks. Yet I look forward to continuing to participate in an unending and challenging process of mediating and redefining cultural difference. In my work as a teacher and a scholar I wish to help broaden the horizons of my American students, colleagues, and friends. As I continue to learn, I likewise hope that my own horizon continues to expand.

NOTES

1. I wish to thank my colleague Donald O. White for his help in translating this dense, and somewhat cryptic, passage.

> Unser Älterwerden kreist in immer erweiterten Gedächtnis-Ringen um unsere einzigartige Geburtsstätte, den deutschen Nationalsozialismus. Der Abstand vergrössert sich, doch können wir aus der konzentrischen Bestimmung niemals ausbrechen. Für diejenigen, die aus dem Exzess des Jahrhunderts hervorgingen, wird es keine Lebensphase geben, in der sie nicht erneut zu diesem Ursprung sich innerlich verhielten, so dass er eigentlich das geheime Zentrum, ja Gefängnis all ihrer geistigen (und seelischen) Anstrengungen bildet. Gegen die Verbindung wird zuweilen krampfhaft aufbegehrt, zuweilen scheint sie selbst zu reifen, souveräner, lockerer zu werden. Was ist allein im künstlerischen Bereich nicht alles versucht worden, um unseren geschichtlichen Stimmungen den jeweils wahrheitsgemässen Ausdruck zu liefern; das reicht vom expressionisten Schwulst bis zur psychoanalytischen Metamorphotik, vom Dokumenten-Drama bis zur obzönen Revue der Embleme. Eine wahre Lösung, ein Sich-Lösen-Können wurde nicht erreicht. Nur der Tod der Geschichte selbst kann uns befreien, nur die Erledigung der Erinnerung durch die totale Gegenwart der Massenmedien, in der alles bloss Erscheinung, bloss ästhetisches Vorüberziehen ist.

WORKS CITED

Berman, Russell A. "Global Thinking, Local Teaching: Departments, Curricula, and Culture." *ADFL Bulletin* 26.1 (1994): 7–11.

Culler, Jonathan. "Excerpts from the Symposium on 'The Humanities and the Public Interest,' Whitney Humanities Center, April 5, 1986." *Yale Journal of Criticism* 1 (Fall 1987): 187.

Debevec Henning, Sylvie. "The Integration of Language, Literature, and Culture: Goals and Curricular Design." *Profession* 93 (1993): 22–26.

Geisler, Michael. Oral contribution to discussion, German Studies Workshop, Williams College, 7 May 1994.

Kaes, Anton. *From Hitler to Heimat: The Return of History as Film.* Cambridge, MA, and London: Harvard UP, 1989.

Koepke, Wulf. "Germanistik als eine deutsch-amerikanische Wissenschaft." In *Germanistik in den USA. Neue Entwicklungen und Methoden,* ed. Frank Trommler. Opladen: Westdeutscher Verlag, 1989. 46–65.

Moretti, Franco. *Signs Taken for Wonders: Essays in the Sociology of Literary Forms.* London and New York: Verso, 1988.

Nollendorfs, Valters. "Out of Germanistik: Thoughts on the Shape of Things to Come." *Die Unterrichtspraxis* 27.1 (1994): 1–10.

Santner, Eric L. *Stranded Objects: Mourning, Memory, and Film in Postwar Germany.* Ithaca and London: Cornell UP, 1990.

Strauss, Botho. *Paare, Passanten.* 1981. Reprint. Munich: Deutscher Taschenbuch Verlag, 1984.

Trommler, Frank, ed. *Germanistik in den USA. Neue Entwicklungen und Methoden.* Opladen: Westdeutscher Verlag, 1989.

Van Cleve, John, and A. Leslie Willson. *Remarks on the Needed Reform of German Studies in the United States.* Columbia, SC: Camden House, 1993.

CHAPTER 8

Asking the Questions/Telling a Story

Norma Claire Moruzzi

Because of the inherently political nature of cultural studies, its practitioners have developed a self-awareness that is evident in their scholarship. Fully disinterested scientific inquiry is simply a myth, and the notion of stumbling upon topics serendipitously provides only a partial answer. In "Asking the Questions/Telling a Story" Norma Moruzzi ponders why Hannah Arendt became the focus of her scholarly research. She probes beyond her initial answer that Arendt "made sense" to her, asking why that might be. For both women, Arendt and Moruzzi, Europe and America represent worlds personally lost and gained. Desire for self-knowledge led Moruzzi to German cultural studies, and her essay demonstrates how these intellectual modes of inquiry provide a framework for personal growth. Though cultural studies in the United States to date has been dominated (especially in university programs and scholarly conferences) by topics related to the United States and the English-speaking world, the example of Arendt is but one small reminder that the so-called foreign cultures offer vital areas of investigation for Americans as well.

In the lyrically written pages that follow the reader can discern a thread running through Moruzzi's negotiations with her own multicultural identity, Arendt's confrontations with the ways she fit and did not fit into Germany—and, specifically, German academia—and Rahel Varnhagen's interaction with the German world a century earlier. But it would be an injustice to all three women if the reader reduced the life's work of each to their inherited ethnic identities, as Arlene Teraoka warns in her essay. There is, rather, as Moruzzi makes clear, a dialectical process at work: the personal informs the scholarly and the scholarly the personal. Moruzzi herself represents a numerically small, younger generation of scholars whose formal education proceeded almost exclusively along interdisciplinary lines: her undergraduate major at Amherst College was a self-designed combination of English and political science, and she chose to do her graduate work at Johns Hopkins specifically because it is one of the few uni-

versities that actually encourages interdisciplinary work at the graduate level between its social science and humanities faculty. Moruzzi's Ph.D. degree is in political science, with a specialization in political theory, and her current appointment at the University of Illinois at Chicago is in political science and women's studies. In her scholarly work and teaching she aims to bring a historical perspective to theoretical debates, especially to those debates involving the politics of social and cultural identity.

The exercise of "personal criticism," the genre of using one's own autobiography as part of one's scholarly production, has come under attack from many camps. Given that it is perhaps least accepted within conservative fields like political science, Moruzzi's contribution here wields even greater polemical force. Arendt's own full-length study reveals that she herself did not wholly realize why she needed and wanted to study Varnhagen. Unfortunately, the world in which Arendt lived did not support the same kind of self-reflection and connection between the personal and the scholarly. Moruzzi's model here should be a reminder to us as teachers that we need to help our students ask themselves what motivates their learning. Personal predilections may not be the end point, but, as Moruzzi demonstrates, they provide a powerful intellectual launch if engaged reflectively and creatively.

This essay is about the relationship between intellectual and personal identity, about the patterns of scholarship and those that inflect our lives. In its details it is very much an essay about my experience. As a meditation on more general themes, however, its range is intended to be more extensive.

Sometimes people ask me, "Why Arendt?" Why this particular intellectual preoccupation, when so many others are available? There are several answers to this question, more or less complete, depending on the circumstances. The simplest, and maybe the most accurate, is that she makes sense to me. By now it is hard to determine to what degree she makes sense because she has shaped the way I think; I first picked up *The Origins of Totalitarianism* when I was sixteen. I have been reading Hannah Arendt's writing on and off ever since, a circulation of interest and surprise that has been going on for more than half my life. Given this relationship, the more intriguing question may be, why did Arendt make sense to me in the first place? Why did this particular individual's writing strike me as the best possible way to think about the world in which we live?

It's a world we both have lost and gained. For Arendt, a German-Jewish intellectual who wrote and published most of her important works of political theory in English in the United States, the lost world was obviously the cultural landscape of Europe; the world she gained, proverbially the "New World," was the place she landed as a refugee after having fled Nazi Germany for France in 1933 and France for the United States in 1941.[1] But for me, a postwar child born to first- and second-generation immigrants who believed the Old Worlds were well behind us, history's shadow casts a different shape. Firmly fore-shortened, minimized by the cheerful lighting of a consumer paradise, the shadow of history seemed barely to fall beyond one's feet. Mostly a matter of recipes and childhood mythology, history was not something that was supposed to get in your way. In our house my mother never called herself a refugee, although that is certainly what she was when she arrived in New York in 1938. At sixteen she and her younger sister had been shipped out of Germany to live with American relatives whom they had never met. Together, they set out to become Americans; when my grandparents did arrive a year later, their daughters would only speak English with them. German was part of the history they felt lucky to have been able to leave behind, a shadow my mother felt she mostly could do without. She got on with her life. When she married my Italian American, lapsed Catholic father, mixing ethnicities and religions, they were happy that this was so. They felt free.

For me, ironically, the shadow grew longer. Maybe it was just the passage of time, the shifting of perspective that accompanies the slow turning of the world. Raised as Americans, free to make of ourselves what we wanted, my brother and I pursued different paths: he working to build the present, I fascinated with questions of the past. The absence of certain parts of our personal history shaped my own life. At sixteen, finished with high school, I left home to spend a year on a kibbutz in Israel where my mother's sister lived. As a doctor, she had moved there somewhat skeptically years before, after she had married a fellow German-Jewish refugee, who was also a Zionist pioneer and a distant relative. On the kibbutz I worked in the cow shed and read everything I could get my hands on. Mostly, I depended on my aunt and uncle's library. After I had pulled out Salinger, Rousseau, de Sade, and Kazantzakis, my aunt handed me *The Origins of Totalitarianism.* I think she thought it might keep me busy for a while.

While I was living on the kibbutz, people used to ask me if I were Jewish, and my answer kept changing. In the beginning I said no. I was as Jewish as I was Catholic, having been raised in neither religion but, instead, with the American credo of self-creation. When a double line of my classmates had marched down the hill from the public elementary school to the church that held their catechism classes and I had been one of what seemed like the few to walk straight home, I certainly had known I wasn't Catholic, and it didn't occur to me that being Jewish was any different. My family did not practice any religion except a fairly secularized Unitarian-Universalism. We had not had any religious initiations, and we did celebrate Christmas—so had my mother when she was growing up—although when we were very small my parents tried a system of giving us one present a day for several days, on the pedagogical theory that too much Christmas buildup was overstimulating for the very young. We were proud to be a mix. But I looked like my mother, who looked like her sister, and people knew I was her niece. They were skeptical when I said I wasn't Jewish, and one day someone asked me if I were ashamed of it. Of course not! But it suddenly dawned on me that religious practice had nothing to do with it; at least in Israel, being Jewish was a matter of blood.

I suppose I had known that I was legally Jewish according to religious law, because Jewish national identity is passed on through the mother's line.[2] Nonetheless, I had clung to my mongrel assurance that performance mattered more than pedigree. Now, somewhat confused but accommodating to local custom, I switched my answer. But saying I was Jewish provoked a new set of problems: people expected me to be familiar with holidays and rituals about which I knew nearly nothing. I was suddenly shockingly ignorant about what before I had been proud to know a little. Frustrated, I revised my answer again: when asked if I were Jewish, I gave the somewhat unwieldy but accurate answer that I was Jewish through my mother and let it go at that.

Yet I remained puzzled. What exactly did it mean to be Jewish? What did it mean for me to be Jewish? The whole question seemed to me to be completely confused, not just in my own case but also in its larger, theoretical ramifications. My secular, modernist-rationalist kibbutznik relatives almost entirely rejected Jewish religious identification. For them Jewish identity seemed to be a national identity based on a valorization of history and an almost blood tribal bond. The more religious Jews, whom the kibbutzniks looked upon with varying degrees of dislike and contempt, at least seemed to think that Judaism had to be linked to certain actions and traditions; their emphasis on spiritual practice struck me as possibly more enlightened than my relatives' faith in blood. Jewish identity did involve choices, but they seemed to be split between the rituals of a spirituality I hadn't been raised to practice and adherence to a Zionist nationalism I didn't necessarily believe. In the midst of this quandary my aunt lent me Arendt's book, and I started reading history.

At the time I didn't finish it, but I made my way through the first volume on antisemitism and well into the second volume on imperialism. Arendt's work on European Jewish history opened up to me a whole new way of thinking. Specifically, it allowed me to place my own questionable Jewish identity within the context of a variegated historical narrative, instead of finding myself simply confronting the most blunt of that narrative's end results. For Arendt the evolution of European Jewish identity was central to the story of European identity in general and to the development of the nation-state in particular. Contemporary Jewish alternatives were themselves as much the products of the tradition of the nation-state as of the traditions of Judaism. Reading Arendt's compelling and elaborate account of European Jewry's troubled relationship with political emancipation and cultural self-identification, I also came to realize that for me, as for my mother, Jewish identity had a lot to do with being German.

And what did that mean? For postwar children German identity could be a confusing mix of Beethoven, marzipan, and death camps. Unlike most other sizable American ethnic groups, there wasn't even an available immigrant identity; the various and powerful German-American clubs and organizations had been disbanded or outright banned during World War I. German cultural identity, including German-Jewish identity, was something that had to be reconstituted out of a broken past and an anomalous present.

This peculiar lack of historical presence wasn't true of my father's Italian background. We weren't raised to think of ourselves as especially Italian, but we could go to Boston and walk by the house in the North End in which my father was born. For my father a reasonably satisfactory continuity with the Old World existed, something that was, after all, less possible for my mother, the refugee. The quaint traces of cultural practice that are for the second generation the signs of ethnicity are for the first generation still the remnants of a defining loss. For the refugee the memory of that loss is confounded because it is mixed with relief: under the circumstances that necessitate flight, almost any place is better than where you have been—the past a stigma to be shed, the present a process of restive assimilation. Nonetheless, the distant memories of childhood always remain the most familiar. My mother was not the only one to say she could never go back—and not only because her childhood home was destroyed in a direct hit near the end of the war. One of her duties as a U.S. Army nurse had been to act as an interpreter for German prisoners; when they would ask her where she learned her good German, she lied. "In school," she said, "in Cincinnati."

So I, a generation removed, went back to Germany instead. In part, at least, I went to study Arendt. A German friend was studying with a Jewish professor who had finished the war in the United States and who had decided, with the strength of age, to return to teach the new generation. He was running a seminar on Hannah Arendt and a study group arranged in the old-fashioned way, with Sunday afternoon meetings at his home and evening gatherings with his venerable friends. I had been reading Arendt through college, her writing on philosophy as well as on history and politics, but what I now began to appreciate was her intellectual tone. Both passionate and rigorously disciplined, her voice was historically definite while broadly conversant. Again, she made sense to me, the perspective from which she chose to "think what we are doing," her famous phrase from the prologue to *The Human Condition,* so oddly appropriate to my own intellectual queries. Certainly, we were of different minds and more than a generation apart. But, whereas other intellectuals seemed to me to presume the limits of their version of a project, a discipline, or a world, Arendt offered a complex affirmation of difference and critique. Although I would learn to question the value of her hierarchies and the validity of her distinctions, her writings taught me how to think of social (and of course political) identity as a complex set of historical constructions, both determinate and mutable. She had also become a model of stylistic practice; her habit of easily incorporating serious discussions of literature within her social theory a relief from the relentless specialization of much academic writing. By the end of my year in Germany I knew that when I returned to the United States to go to graduate school I would write on Hannah Arendt.

I did, and I continue to do so. But maybe the most honest use we make of others is of the dead, and at some point I became curious about Arendt's own enunciation of a voice, her modeling of another's life as autobiography. After she finished her university degree, Arendt's first independent scholarly project was an investigation of the German Romantics, which became a book on the Jewish salon hostess Rahel Varnhagen.[3] In writing Rahel's story "as she herself might have told it," Arendt tried on another's voice while detailing that other's story. Although by the end of her text Arendt reverted to her own clearly enunciated style, her experiment with the muffled interiority she held to be characteristic of Rahel served its purpose. Narrating a version of Rahel's story in an approximation of her voice, Arendt could reclaim a precedent for her own experience as a German-Jewish woman troubled by the difficult personal realities of assimilation. In Rahel Varnhagen's own writings Hannah Arendt discovered a sensibility that insistently created itself, a woman both seduced by the aura of gentile patrician glamour and yet resolutely uncontained by the limitations of its norms. If in her mature work Arendt herself rejected Rahel's introverted personal style, she nonetheless had already found in Rahel an important cultural and textual precedent.

A connection with the past enables the future. In June 1993 my mother, her sister, and I traveled to Würzburg, the city where they were born. We had all been visitors there before: my aunt in the 1950s, myself during my year in Germany before graduate school, my mother after that. But this trip was in the nature of a pilgrimage. That winter both my father and my uncle had died, after long illnesses; for all of us, but especially for my mother and my aunt, the circumstances of the present had once again been terribly changed, and it seemed the right time to return to an earlier lost past. Together, we retraced paths that were familiar to them. They told stories, and they pointed out sites: the park paths along which they had walked to school; the street where my aunt was bitten by a dog; the bakery to which their mother sent for baking pastries too large to fit into their own oven; the exact place where their house had stood; the exact location of their grandmother's house, my grandfather's mother, and the only member of the family to die in Theresienstadt. We spoke freely among ourselves, but neither my mother nor my aunt would ever admit, or boast, in conversations with anyone else that they had lived in this city before.

Certain silences still hold, but it is sometimes easier to find the voices that filled them. My mother's cousin rediscovered, translated into English, and distributed a family history put together by one of the uncles. Originally written in German by a man spending his retirement in postwar London and reflecting the preferences of the family snob, this brief document nonetheless provides a fairly complete account of the extended family and their life in Würzburg both before and after the turn of the century. My mother still keeps, but will not catalog, the extensive collection of her own mother's family photographs. They are perfectly ordinary scenes of swimming, dress-up parties, and picnic outings—now perfectly foreign. As remnants of another life, the family relics are hoarded, which also means they are hidden away. My aunt thinks they should be thrown out. So far they have been preserved but denied as history: images of a life displaced in space and time; artifacts of ambivalent significance; evidence not yet erased but seemingly, so far, destined for oblivion.

I certainly wasn't reading Arendt during our journey to Würzburg. In fact, I was reading *Obabakoak,* a recent novel first published in the almost nearly lost tradition of written Basque. But once I was back in the United States I returned again to Arendt's work, reviewing her own inquiry into European Jewish lives, a focus that I eventually narrowed to Arendt's early writing on Rahel Varnhagen. In Rahel, Arendt had found a precedent for her own self-conscious construction of a German-Jewish cultural and intellectual identity. In telling Rahel's story, she also answered certain questions for herself, questions about the relationship between an individual and a distantly formative past. At a farther, mongrelized remove perhaps I have found, through reading Hannah Arendt, a way of answering somewhat similar questions for myself.

All scholars, all readers, find themselves at times considering such questions. To some extent each answer is highly specific. But it is also true that we learn from one another and that considerations of diverse experience often reveal a surprising commonality. The inconsistencies of my own background encouraged me to pursue themes that cross disciplines and to discover the value of the kind of historically informed investigations of social identity and its aesthetic representations that are now termed *cultural studies.* I didn't set out to be an interdisciplinary scholar or to do cultural studies. Nonetheless, it usually seemed to me that the most effective methodology was an eclectic one, the most compelling questions those that acknowledged a wide range of ramifications and contradictions.

In an increasingly global world I have found that the most satisfactory route between two intellectual points often involves an extended detour through adjoining territory. Cultural studies does not necessarily mean traveling without an intellectual map. But it can mean questioning the boundaries we tend to draw for ourselves between disciplines, between categories, and between the familiar and the unknown. This exploration is a demanding process, one that involves careful preparation beforehand and scrupulous attention throughout. As is true, however, of all worthwhile journeys, intellectual and otherwise, getting there is really half the fun.

NOTES

This essay is dedicated to the four people who made it possible: my mother, Leonore Frank Moruzzi; my aunt, Heddy Frank Blum; my friend, Pia Bungarten; and my teacher, Friedrich Friedmann.

1. Hannah Arendt is usually described as the only woman political theorist who is definitely accepted into the canon of political philosophy. She wrote classic, groundbreaking studies of totalitarianism (*The Origins of Totalitarianism* and *Eichmann in Jerusalem*) and important works on the distinction between the public and the private spheres in the Western political tradition (*The Human Condition*), European Jewish identity (*The Jew as Pariah* and *Rahel Varnhagen*), and social and political revolutions (*On Revolution*), as well as numerous assorted essays and a final, unfinished analysis of the distinctions between thinking, willing, and judging in the tradition of political philosophy (*The Life of the Mind*). For those less familiar with her life and her writing, a very brief biography follows. Those whose interest is piqued can refer to Elizabeth Young-Bruehl's biography, *Hannah Arendt: For Love of the World,* Elzbieta Ettinger's essay on Arendt and Heidegger, and, of course, to Arendt's own texts.

Hannah Arendt was born into a middle-class, assimilated Jewish family in the German city of Königsberg (now the Russian city of Kaliningrad) in 1906. At eighteen she became a student at the University at Marburg, where she had a brief but very significant affair with her married and much older teacher Martin Heidegger. At the end of her first year of study she transferred to Heidelberg, where she completed her doctorate in philosophy under the supervision of Karl Jaspers, writing on the conception of love in the writings of Augustine. She then moved to Berlin and began working on a project on the German Romantics that eventually became her book on the German-Jewish salon hostess Rahel Varnhagen. Before the manuscript was finished, however, Arendt left Germany for France, where she found work as a coordinator of Jewish refugee programs and then, with her mother and second husband, Heinrich Blücher, left France for the United States.

In New York she worked as an editor, taught part-time, published in small journals, and worked on her first major work of political theory, the three-volume study of *The Origins of Totalitarianism,* which was published in 1951. This book established her as an important scholar and led to her first university faculty appointment, at Berkeley in 1955. Over the rest of her life she published substantial, original analyses on a variety of political topics, yet, although she was affiliated with many of the country's major research universities, she did not settle down at any particular one. She died in 1975 at her home in New York City, the epigraph page for the third and last volume of her unfinished book, the one she referred to as her return to philosophy, in her typewriter.

2. I specify national identity under religious law, since my mother's Jewishness (as opposed to her perhaps questionable Judaism) makes me and my brother automatically eligible for Israeli citizenship, even though we have never been through any kind of religious training or community observance. Thus, Judaism does not simply rely on mothers to pass on cultural continuity through adequate domestic supervision but also recognizes them as the only fully reliable parent through whom to trace a child's ethnicity. As my uncle rather gleefully pointed out to me, fathers aside, you always know who the mother is.

3. Within German literary studies Rahel Varnhagen (b. Rahel Levin [1771–1833]) is such a well-known figure that she is typically referred to only as "Rahel," a practice that at least avoids confusion with her diplomat husband, Karl Varnhagen. She is one of the best-known examples of a small group of bourgeois Jewish women who established salons in nineteenth-century Berlin and briefly helped define their era's cosmopolitanism. Rahel herself seems to have tried to escape her Jewishness through romantic alliances with non-Jewish men and through conversion. Although Rahel may be best known for promoting the Goethe cult, Arendt was primarily interested in her as an example of an especially sensitive, frank, Jewish feminine personality, a woman preoccupied with her existence as a Jew in relation to the gentile German aristocracy.

WORKS CITED

Arendt, Hannah. *Eichmann in Jerusalem: A Report on the Banality of Evil.* New York: Viking, 1963.
———. *The Human Condition.* Chicago: U of Chicago P, 1958.
———. *The Jew as Pariah: Jewish Identity and Politics in the Modern Age.* New York: Grove, 1978.
———. *The Life of the Mind.* New York: Harcourt Brace Jovanovich, 1978.
———. *On Revolution.* New York: Viking, 1963.
———. *The Origins of Totalitarianism.* New York: Harcourt Brace Jovanovich, 1973.
———. *Rahel Varnhagen: The Life of a Jewish Woman.* Trans. Richard and Clara Winston. New York: Harcourt Brace Jovanovich, 1974.
Atxaga, Bernardo. *Obabakoak.* Trans. Margaret Jull Costa. New York: Pantheon Books, 1992.
Ettinger, Elzbieta. *Hannah Arendt/Martin Heidegger.* New Haven and London: Yale UP, 1995.
Young-Bruehl, Elisabeth. *Hannah Arendt: For Love of the World.* New Haven: Yale UP, 1982.

Part Four

WHAT WAS GERMAN IN THE PAST?

A central issue in this volume involves the creation of national identity, precisely because historically this process has been intimately linked to culture. As the four essays in part 4 illustrate, culture is defined very broadly so as to encompass high and low registers, both inside and outside of Germany. Indeed, the authors are highly invested in the interplay between the elitist and the popular. This breadth is also evident in the contributors' eclectic sources. Applegate, who explores the role of music in the still burgeoning national consciousness of the early nineteenth century, utilizes materials that range from memoirs and newspaper accounts to present-day critical and anthropological theory. This diversity also characterizes Belgum's analysis of the popular nineteenth-century periodical Die Gartenlaube *and Confino's program for studying tourism. Zantop looks at the way postcolonial studies calls us to reassess Germany's own colonial legacy. All four authors affirm the potential of popular culture as a subject—especially for those who are creative with their sources and make use of interdisciplinary methodologies. Furthermore, their essays are valuable because they show why cultural activities were important for contemporary figures and why they continue to be so for scholars today.*

CHAPTER 9

Bach Revival, Public Culture, and National Identity: The *St. Matthew Passion* in 1829

Celia Applegate

Music is one of the most readily identifiable components of German culture, both from within and without. It is therefore particularly appropriate that we include an extended analysis of a moment in which music played a critical role in the search for consensus about German national identity. As a cultural historian with broad interests and author of an influential study on Heimat, *Celia Applegate focuses her musical acumen on a specific event—the 1829 revival of Bach's* St. Matthew Passion—*as a means of exploring the cultural and social climate in the Prussian capital. Applegate is concerned here primarily with the influence of individuals and institutions on the shaping of public taste. This event signaled the arrival of Felix Mendelssohn as "the maestro of past masters until Wagner, leader of a self-consciously German musical culture." Moreover, the performance of the elaborate Bach piece required the cooperation of local musical groups; the participation of the Berlin Singakademie illustrates the institutional foundations needed to effect a change in popular taste and national culture. Just as Theodore Ziolkowski has shown in his important 1990 study that German Romanticism had institutional foundations, Applegate demonstrates how the Singakademie provided the necessary talent and publicity to carry off this epochal event.*

While Applegate utilizes many resources that fall within the purview of traditional musicology—the memoirs of the principles, the critical press notices, and the literature within the field are all consulted—her portrayal also relies on several primary and theoretical sources that signal a cross-disciplinary approach. Early on in the essay, for example, she establishes the social milieu that delimited the sphere of those involved in this early Bach revival. Her

139

discussion of the Bildungskreise (educated circles) provides a social history of music that goes considerably beyond traditional reception histories. Applegate's interdisciplinary research leads her to examine the response of figures in a wide range of fields: critics such as E. T. A. Hoffmann and scholars such as historian Gustav Droysen are among those who comment on the 1829 concert. With respect to theory Applegate's analysis is informed by art historian Michael Baxandall and anthropologist Clifford Geertz, as she explores the nexus between artists and the public, offering hypotheses about process and structure.

Celia Applegate's study of the 1829 Bach revival shows how a specific event can be opened up, or, to use her term, "unraveled," so as to gain insight into not only music history but also a broader civic and national consciousness. This essay is an excellent example of the kind of study Kacandes calls for in the introduction on canon formation, that is, on the numerous historical, ideological, social, and in this case musical factors that lead to a cultural product's designation as "beautiful" and "great." In focusing on contemporary responses and subsequent reflections regarding a truly momentous event, she is provided with a wealth of information to analyze. Her explication reveals the way that an interdisciplinary cultural studies approach can be utilized in a field that was for many years somewhat isolated from the scholarly mainstream. Applegate's essay here is of interest not only to musicologists but also to those who care about nineteenth-century German history, cultural institutions in general, and the processes by which aesthetic views and tastes are molded within specific national, class, religious, and political contexts.

What used to appear to us as a dream, to be realised in far-off future times, has now become real: the "Passion" has been given to the public, and is everybody's property.
  —Fanny Mendelssohn (qtd. in Hensel, *The Mendelssohn Family*)

On 21 February 1829 a prominent notice in the leading musical journal of Berlin, the *Berliner Allgemeine musikalische Zeitung,* invited readers to "an important and happy event," a performance of "The Passion according to St. Matthew by Johann Sebastian Bach" under the "direction of Herr Felix Mendelssohn-Bartholdy." The notice, written by editor Adolf Bernhard Marx and reprinted with additional commentary over the next few weeks, described the *Passion* as the "greatest and holiest work of the great composer." The performance, Marx wrote, "would open the gates of a temple long shut down." "We are called," he continued, "not to a festival of art, but to a most solemn religious celebration [*zu einer religiösen Hochfeier*]." And Berliners answered the call. On 11 March 1829, the date of the first performance, the hall of the Berlin Singakademie was filled; close to a thousand people were turned away. Anybody who was anybody in Berlin came, from king and court to Hegel, Schleiermacher, and a host of other members of the Bürgertum of *Bildung und Besitz* (education and property). Goethe, unable to travel all the way from Weimar, nevertheless commented on the event in his correspondence with Karl Friedrich Zelter, director of the Singakademie. In the following months repeat performances took place in Berlin and in Frankfurt. In the following years the score was published for the first time, and more performances took place in Breslau, Stettin, Königsberg, Kassel, and Dresden. The reputations of Bach and his Passion were soon unshakably established and, with them, the foundations laid for the construction of a national canon of German musical genius.[1]

In the context of a volume devoted to something called "German cultural studies," this particular event has a number of overlapping claims to our attention. First, the impact of the performance on contemporary Germans—in its planning stages, its execution, and its repercussions—raises the issue of the "contingencies" of cultural value and evaluation, how certain objects come to be regarded as good, beautiful, worth the time it takes to look, listen, read, or perform them (Herrnstein Smith). Indeed, the overwhelming importance that contemporaries attributed to this potentially ordinary event—the revival of a dusty, rather ponderous, unusually difficult piece of church music—poses the kind of mystery that an eclectic and heterodox field like cultural studies takes particular delight in unraveling. For music historians, of course, there has been nothing in the least mysterious about this event or its place in the scheme of things. A conservative estimation reckons it a "milestone in the concert life of Germany, indeed of the world" (Riemann 251). Others have called it a "music-historical great deed," "an event whose meaning for the music history of the nineteenth century cannot be overestimated," an "overwhelming event," an epochal moment reflecting "the brilliant genius of an individual" (Grossmann-Vendrey 28; Dahlhaus, intro.; Geck 5). The most enthusiastic accounts, notably that of the eminent musicologist Friedrich Blume, reckon it something of a miracle (290).[2] More concretely, the revival brought the choral and church music of Bach back into circulation, thereby affecting compositional practice, aesthetic philosophy, musical instruction, historical research, performance, and taste—and consolidating the nineteenth-century movement to revive old music, a movement that (again in Blume's vivid language) "has engulfed in waves the whole musical activity of the nineteenth and twentieth centuries" (290; see also Jacob 89).

Yet all of these considerations are largely retrospective ones that have bearing on the musical consequences of the Bach revival but do not explain why contemporaries put so much stock in their aesthetic experience of the *St. Matthew Passion* and, therefore, cannot explain the consequences of that enthusiasm, which exceed the reach of musical analysis. Barriers to a more broadly gauged analysis of the event qua event have been the expected disciplinary ones, grounded both in essential features of music and in influential traditions of musical scholarship. In regards to the first sort of barrier, music communicates meaning in far more elusive ways than either words or pictures, and, consequently, cultural historians have tended to leave the history of music to music historians, the experts in music's technical language. They, in turn, have until recently returned the favor by leaving the rest of history to the historians. This stand-off, born of a very nineteenth-century respect for the *wissenschaftlich,* or scientific, authority of each discipline, testified also to the success of generations of musicologists and aesthetic philosophers, especially German ones, in persuading everyone else of the universal and transcendental qualities of their musical subject. *Musikwissenschaft* (musicology) taught its practitioners that certain works were "masterpieces," that these works alone were worthy of serious study, and that the proper means by which to study them was musical analysis, or the demonstration of the masterpiece's inner coherence in strictly musical terms.[3] Such a methodology effectively shut off the conversation about historical context of any given musical work or event. With the importance of Bach established by means of analysis of harmonic usage and contrapuntal intricacies, why reviving Bach might have been important to nineteenth-century Germans becomes an issue of little moment.

But, if disciplinary paradigms have discouraged a more contextual examination of the 1829 Bach revival, then the kind of interdisciplinary work that goes under the rubric of cultural studies can make it possible. Music historians, historians, and music lovers alike should have a stake in understanding how and why certain pieces of music have value for us, and, while historical context does not provide the whole answer, it is an indispensable part of any answer. This brings me to the second major claim this event has on our attention, and that is its role in helping to shape the "unity of taste and judgment" that is the goal of any self-consciously national culture (Schulze 45). Speaking very generally, Mendelssohn and his contemporaries valued the *St. Matthew Passion,* among other things, because it seemed to them the very pinnacle of what German culture had achieved. The revival shows in microcosm how people put a national culture together. It promises, in other words, to give the concreteness of specificity to the general problem of national identity formation, how and under what circumstances national identities emerged in Europe, and what role the cultural artifacts of art, music, and literature played in that emergence.

Cultural studies has devoted increasing attention to the examination of the construction, contestation, and disintegration of national identities, in part because the flexibility and indeed the patent artificiality of national identities well suits a contemporary sense of reality—elusive, ever moving, more subjective than not, prone to bend and sway and change shape under the influence of power and political will. Not surprisingly, we see in the processes that created nation-states and people to live and die for them the perfect embodiment of our own sense of truth-as-deception, of talk of "reality" as just another ideology. One has only to read the writings of those who have over the past two hundred or more years sought to put into words what it meant to be German to see the play of fantasy and other forms of wishful thinking in all of them. Yet, at the same time, what can appear to us as a kind of cultural scavenger hunt—one of cobbling together disparate artifacts, characteristics, practices, and stories into a unity called German culture or German identity—was not a game for those who participated in it. (The twentieth century proves that, if nothing else.) By conceiving of the paradox of national identity in such terms, as culture that kills, cultural studies sets itself the daunting task of explaining how something so seemingly arbitrary and so remarkably recent in its formation could nevertheless have an unparalleled power to persuade people, to move them to action, and indeed to constitute their sense of reality (Anderson). To see how J. S. Bach's *St. Matthew Passion* became a quintessentially German thing is, I hope, a limited but fruitful way to isolate certain aspects of that power of national imagining.

Barbara Herrnstein Smith has written that understanding any act of literary or artistic evaluation—such as that by which Felix Mendelssohn, Adolf Bernhard Marx, and the Berlin public of 1829 judged Bach's *St. Matthew Passion* a work of transcendent beauty and profundity—involves "articulating an estimate of how well that work will serve implicitly defined functions for a specific implicitly defined audience, who are conceived of as experiencing the work under certain implicitly defined conditions" (13). Those critical assumptions would seem to suggest that we can reach an understanding of *why* these people valued the music by investigating just these aspects of their historical condition—why they thought making music was important, who they were, and how they made music. In the remainder of this essay I will consider each of these issues in turn, beginning with the question of audience and moving from there to consider the conditions and, finally, the purposes of performing Bach in Biedermeier Berlin.

The literal audience for these three performances consisted of, to use the succinct phrase of Eduard Devrient, Felix Mendelssohn's friend and the baritone who sang the role of Jesus in the performance, "the educated circles [*Bildungskreise*] of Berlin" (Devrient 62). If we take Herrnstein Smith's concept of audience to include those who performed and promoted the music as well, we would need to expand those circles slightly to include a handful of professional musicians who might or might not ordinarily be considered among the

Gebildete (cultivated people).[4] The music historian Martin Geck would also include in the performance's audience all of "Protestant Germany" (60), and, if that seems a bit too embracing, then one could alternatively propose to include all those who read the north German and the musical press, all those who went to coffeehouses and talked about the latest events, and all those who corresponded with their friends and relatives in the "educated circles" of Berlin.

One might be tempted to characterize this collection of people who cared about Bach simply as "middle-class," but that would be neither accurate nor enlightening. The actual audience in the hall of the Singakademie included plenty of titled aristocrats, starting with, as indicated at the outset, Frederick William III, nor would Devrient or anyone else have expected otherwise of a performance aimed at the educated circles of the city. As William Weber has sensibly pointed out, music historians need to be more conscious of the difficulties involved in pinning the label *middle-class* onto musical audiences, musical patronage systems, and especially musical styles throughout the nineteenth century. Despite the eventual decline of aristocratic influence in modern Europe, aristocrats remained important, even dominant, figures in the musical world of the nineteenth century, especially in Germany ("Muddle").[5] Weber suggests that what one is really talking about is an elite, a *haute bourgeoisie,* or "second aristocracy, who made up the core of the 'middle-class' public in concert and opera life" (179). But, as a number of social historians of the German scene have pointed out, this kind of elite, united by wealth and status, if not by title or outlook, was more likely to be found in the capital cities of France and England than in the Biedermeier backwaters of north Germany. Devrient's phrase *educated circles* refers not to the wealthy as such but, rather, to people who had had the opportunity to pursue the rigorous course of higher education in *Gymnasium* and university; practically speaking, it encompasses officeholders in the state bureaucracy and, closely linked, doctors, clergy, academics, and lawyers. Members of the Prussian nobility might form part of this group, particularly if they lived in Berlin, though one ought not to expect them to share all attitudes of the *Bildungsbürgertum.* Because of the protracted educational and apprenticeship requirements for these positions and the meager salaries attached to them, they were "virtually closed to the least fortunate members of society, relatively open to intermediate groups, but most accessible to those from families already inside" (Sheehan 515).

These were men and women, moreover, whose place in society was not at all ambiguous, not at all in flux, and, indeed, subject to an increasingly extensive process of bureaucratic rationalization. They were in that way quite unlike the audiences that Weber identifies as typical for the midcentury Parisian musical scene, whose social position was "vague" and fluctuating and who nervously cast about for ways to secure their status and prove their claims to participation in the elite. These status insecurities enhanced music's importance in

Paris not because people thought music especially beautiful or elevating but because it had a marvelous capacity to cover over awkward moments in the conversation. Weber quotes a journalist from 1840 saying that "music was necessary in the salons because people were too uneasy to talk all evening; the arts are the only point of cohesion possible between so many persons of varied rank and different wealth, who find themselves at the same gatherings and carry there the same desire to distinguish themselves" ("Muddle" 179). In contrast, audience silence in Berlin had very little to do with social awkwardness and everything to do with an emerging consensus about the profoundly transcendent nature of musical expression. To make further sense of that, we must turn from the audience itself to the musical institutions this audience had nourished and now represented, institutions in which audiences "experienced the work" (to use Herrnstein Smith's terms again) and, consequently, through which musical evaluation of a certain sort could emerge.

Just as the term *middle-class* tells us little about the audience of the late eighteenth and nineteenth centuries, so too is the term *musical institution* inadequate. I find it useful instead to look upon musical institutions in the German lands over the half-century preceding the Bach revival as marked by their increasing participation in the public sphere, as Habermas classically conceived of it—that "sphere of private people [coming] together as a public" (27). For Habermas what defined the public sphere was the kind of talk that went on in it, talk in which arguments, not status, determined decisions. This "rational-critical discourse" was made necessary and sensible by the circumstances of an advancing market culture, which drew people and objects out of a hitherto meaningful context, that of court and church, and threw them into an inherently meaningless sphere of commodity exchange. The process of "profaning," of stripping things and relations of previously held values, required, in Habermas's conception of it, that "private people . . . determine . . . meaning on their own (by way of rational communication with one another)" (37). Habermas suggested that people became accustomed to such talk in coffeehouse disputes about the value of this or that piece of recently published literature but that such habits of judgment could apply to any aspect of the artistic, social, or political realm.

Habermas was not writing a historical account at all, let alone of musical culture, but many of the elements of his account of the emergence of the public sphere have resonance for things musical. First is the undeniable attenuation in the course of the eighteenth century of the connections between music and church, music and court. A number of other forms of patronage and use came to the fore in that century, at first in imitation of court pageantry and church solemnity but soon evolving into something other, something different. The rise of the public concert and of concert societies to sponsor and organize them happened differently in England, France, and the German-speaking countries, with varying degrees of state and aristocratic control. But the intrusion of market forces into the practices of making music occurred throughout Europe. Music performed in a public concert or composed for public performance was music commodified, music repackaged as a commercial product—and the musicians transformed into employees or some species of independent producer.[6] The commodification of music through the growth of public concerts was, of course, slow to develop: concerts in the eighteenth century were often simply gatherings of the sponsor's family and friends, and methods of advertising and ticket sales were of limited effect (see Hanson; Mahling; Pinthus; Salmen; Weber, "Music"). But music publishing, as it developed first in England and then on the Continent, was a powerful motor, servicing a growing market of domestic performance and contributing to the professionalization of practicing musicians. As in industrialization itself, all the aspects of the musical marketplace—publishers, concerts, amateur duet playing, and so on—reinforced and encouraged one another, eventually becoming a self-sustaining set of products and desires.

But, to follow Habermas further, music dissociated from close connection to court festivities or church calendars was also music divested of its significance, at least for that instant in which the transformation took hold. For the very fact of a musical performance that took place in an eating establishment or a guild hall or a semiprivate salon made it accessible to new kinds of judgment. An obvious and early sign of changes in the contextual significance of music was reporting on musical events in the press—a development that began in Prussia in the second half of the eighteenth century and reached a level of sophistication by the second decade of the nineteenth century with the advent of critics such as E. T. A. Hoffmann, A. B. Marx, and Ludwig Rellstab (Burnham; Pederson; Rehm). Writing about music in the press marked it as part of a larger arena of secular cultural activity, which, though still formally linked to the court, was actually devoted to the education and entertainment of Prussians or Berliners more generally. A typical review, like one from the *Haude- und Spenersche Zeitung* concerning an 1819 performance of Cherubini's "Lodoiska," began with a framing reference to the birthday of "our beloved Crown Prince" but was largely devoted to commentary on the singers, especially the much admired Anna Milder (rptd. in Rehm 46–47). With his merely passing concern with the patronizing authority, his concentration on personalities and competing artistic styles, and, above all, his tone of up-to-the-minute reportage, the reviewer wrote with the legitimacy not of kingly approval but of public attention. By 1829, when A. B. Marx began beating the drum in his *Berliner Allgemeine musikalische Zeitung* for the *St. Matthew Passion,* the readers of Berlin's cultural press could encounter efforts to influence their judgment on musical matters ranging from mocking satire to high-minded exhortation. What all press reports shared was precisely that effort to persuade, which was simultaneously a claim that musical meanings were matters of public consequence. Likewise, musical scholarship, which first developed in the late-eighteenth century in the German lands, signified music's participation in the bourgeois public sphere. Although it would seem to have little immediate connection to the growing musical marketplace, either as cause or effect on it, musical scholarship attested to a self-conscious distance from the music itself, which was no longer taken for granted as an accompaniment to royal grandeur or an act of homage to God but, rather, treated as something to be understood on its own terms and imbued with intrinsic significance.

Finally, the most powerful marker of music's entrance into the public world of self-constituting people was the centrality of voluntary associations to the organization of musical life from the late eighteenth century on. In the absence of much in the way of representative political institutions, voluntary associations more or less constituted the public sphere in late-eighteenth- and early-nineteenth-century Germany. Though their political practices were either nonexistent or covert, these discussion groups, reading societies, museum clubs, historical associations, and the like did compensate for a stultified political public and did establish the personal relationships that would be exploited in a politics yet to develop. Further, to paraphrase Habermas, they provided forums for private persons to put reason to use, a capacity they, not coincidentally, shared with the press. Musical associations consisted of groups that performed music for themselves, groups that performed music for others, and groups that organized musical performances as such. By the end of the nineteenth century the range was even greater, from those devoted to specific composers to those promoting music in general, especially German music. But the dominant characteristic remained constant and one common to voluntary associations as a social type: men, and some women, amateurs in spirit if not always in actuality, organized as free individuals on the principle of self-cultivation and self-constitution. Only within such a context are the variations of values that nineteenth-century people began to attribute to music conceivable. Or, to put the case otherwise, the musical association—the voluntary gathering of music lovers—allowed a free play to musical meanings, which would have been impossible within a performance practice restricted to church and court.

Musical associationalism, along with all the other features of music as a public activity that I have touched upon, made the 1829 revival of the *St. Matthew Passion* into the culminating event of the 1828–29 musical season in Berlin and, by extension, made it into an archetypical concert of the modern period. The Bach revival was grounded in the scholarship cum public advocacy of Johann Nikolaus Forkel (1749–1818), organist, music director, professor at University of Göttingen, and author of the first *Allgemeine Geschichte der Musik* (Comprehensive History of Music) (which, despite its title, never made it past the sixteenth century).[7] Forkel was a prolific commentator on the music of the past, a man with an encyclopedic approach to the interpretation of musical culture, conscientious and hardworking rather than inspired, yet finally famous for his production of the first biography of J. S. Bach. Published in 1802, the study addressed itself to "patriotic admirers of the art of music" (a phrase that we might read as homologous to the public as a whole) and provided the fullest and most worshipful account to date of Bach's contributions as "player, teacher, and composer," the latter chiefly of keyboard works (Forkel xvi; Mintz 202–3).[8] Forkel's appreciation was by no means unanticipated; it came, for instance, hard on the heels of a series of articles on eighteenth-century music, published anonymously in the widely read *Allgemeine musikalische Zeitung* of Leipzig.[9] But Forkel made converts and stirred up even broader public interest. He had had, moreover, extensive contact with Bach's sons, Carl Philipp Emanuel and Wilhelm Friedemann, in the preparation of the text. Their contributions to the study helped to make it authoritative. Interest in Bach among the German-speaking public had begun.

At the same time, the Bach legacy began to flourish among amateur musicians and musical educators embedded in the growing number of musical associations. Among these the choral society represented the most organized expression of voluntary music making in this period, and Berlin was home to the earliest of the German choral societies, the Berlin Singakademie, founded in 1793 as an outgrowth of Karl Friedrich Fasch's singing class for wealthy bourgeois women (Eberle, Schünemann, Bollert). Fasch had been a colleague of C. P. E. Bach in Potsdam and thus claimed a direct descent from the master himself. His successor in the post of director, Karl Friedrich Zelter, was even more of a Bach enthusiast. Right up to the time of the 1829 Passion revival, he led the group, now some three hundred members strong, in regular performances of Bach motets and cantatas.

Zelter, moreover, claims our attention as the very model of a modern musical man. From 1806 until his death in 1832 he organized musical life in Berlin into a system that linked amateur to professional, bourgeois to noble, preparation to performance, money and status to talent, supply to demand, revival and tradition to creation and innovation, music to art, and art to the state, in mutually reinforcing and porous relations. The extent of his activities was, to use one scholar's understatement, "uncommonly large": directing the Singakademie, founding a school for instruction in singing, founding a school for instruction in instrument playing, founding a *Liedertafel* (men's glee club), winning a place for a musician (himself, at first) in the Prussian Academy of Arts, serving as professor of music at the University of Berlin, founding an Institute for School and Church Music, and maintaining an extensive correspondence with Goethe as, in effect, his musical representative (Nitsche 11–14). As the Goethe connection also illustrates in a somewhat different fashion, Zelter made his work consonant with the goals of the Prussian reformers, with whom he closely associated himself. By so doing, he obtained for music a place among those human activities, the cultivation of which was seen as necessary to the well-being of the state. Zelter ensured music a role in Prussian public life, one that in his conservative plan tied the fortunes of professional and amateur music making to those of the state but at the same time tied them to the marketplace and to the instabilities of public taste.

The 1829 revival of the *St. Matthew Passion* was not, strictly speaking, Zelter's idea, but it took his system to bring it off. A double chorus, a double orchestra, an array of competent soloists, a large performing space, a respectably sized audience—none of these things was lying around Unter den Linden with nothing better to do in 1829. Large-scale concerts were notoriously difficult to put together until well into the nineteenth century: one has only to read an account of Beethoven's travails in staging the premier of the Ninth Symphony, of all things, to realize the challenges (Hanson 82–108). The sorts of obstacles that plagued Beethoven—rivalries among musicians, censors, changes in venue and too-small spaces, poor timing late in the season, inadequate high-level patronage, low ticket prices—were all superable within Zelter's system. What prevented Zelter's Berlin from playing a more prominent role in European concert life was something that never slowed down Beethoven, and that was a limited vision (Zelter's own) of music's possibilities.[10] This is the point in the narrative at which other aspects of the evolving musical institutions of the era allied with the Zelter system, exploiting its possibilities, compensating for its weaknesses, expanding its reach.

Enter Felix Mendelssohn. There are a number of ways to explain Mendelssohn's role in this event, but, if we stick to the structural, then we must see him as a representative of a further element of the emergent musical culture of the era, the cultivation of musical performance and traditions within the private sphere of the family. Certainly, part of the success of Zelter's system was its capacity to connect to and mobilize those forces, in effect to bridge the gap between public and private spheres, much as the Prussian reformers hoped to do in other aspects of the state's existence. Zelter's relationship with the Mendelssohn family was a case in point. Two of the Mendelssohn children, Fanny and Felix, sang in the Singakademie; Zelter taught Felix Mendelssohn, often visited the Sunday musicales and other gatherings in the family home, and arranged for the Mendelssohns to give an important collection of Bach cantata manuscripts to the Singakademie (Jacob 20–24; Hiller 149; Geck 18). Zelter was Felix Mendelssohn's route to an honorable career in music (something only gradually emerging as a possibility at the time), and Felix, with his exceptional talents, wealthy background, and gathering aura of genius, was somehow proof of the efficacy of Zelter's musical system, the wunderkind to be paraded in front of Goethe. The revival of the *St. Matthew Passion* neatly demonstrated the particular talents of each. Berliners could acknowledge, on the one hand, the flash of inspiration from Zelter's prodigy, who had had the idea to revive the piece in the first place, and, on the other, the remarkable performative capacities of Zelter's institutions.[11] Felix emerged from the salon into the public eye, and Zelter could garner praise for having provided the wings so that his protégé could fly.

The wings came in the form of competent and willing performers. Felix Mendelssohn persuaded Zelter to put the singers and the hall of the Singakademie at his disposal, and from that dispensation followed all the others: the orchestra, the soloists, and to a great extent the audience, many of whom were drawn in by the web of acquaintance stretching among the Mendelssohns, their salon guests, the Singakademie members, Zelter's other acquaintances, and so on—stretching in other words, across the length and breadth of educated Berlin. Fanny Mendelssohn described how the academy members' initial astonishment at the Matthew Passion ("their faces became very long with surprise at the existence of such a work, about which they, the members of the Berlin Academy, knew nothing") quickly turned into enthusiasm: "the members of the academy themselves spread such a favourable report about the music and such a general and vivid interest was created in all classes, that on the very day after the first advertisement of the concert all the tickets were taken" (Hensel 171–72).

But what made the concert so modern was the degree of media attention that accompanied it. The *St. Matthew Passion* had its own publicist in the person of Adolf Bernhard Marx, founder and editor of the *Berliner Allgemeine musikalische Zeitung* and the creator of his own school of Hegelian music criticism (Burnham; Pederson; Wallace). Marx first heard the *Passion* at the Mendelssohn house in 1823 and wrote in his memoirs that he was so moved by it that "day and night I could not separate myself from it." "Here, here," he continued, with Hegelian abandon "is the full realization of an Ideal of composition" (Marx 86–87). "Naturally," he concluded, "I told everyone about it." His correspondence and journalism over the next years were sprinkled with calculated references—something in the order of teasers—to this buried treasure. The media blitz proper began in April 1828 in his feuilleton. While ostensibly promoting a newly published edition of Bach's B Minor Mass, Marx coyly switched to verse: "Ich gedachte in der Nacht, Dass ich den Mond sähe im Schlaf;/Als ich aber erwachte, Ging unvermuthet die Sonne auf!" (I thought I saw the moon one night, as I lay in repose;/Though when I woke, surprisingly the sun arose!). Then, announcing the impending publication of "the greatest work of our greatest master, the greatest and holiest musical work of all peoples, the great Passion music of Matthew the Evangelist by Johann Sebastian Bach," Marx exclaimed "What wondrous times break forth!" (*BAMZ* [1828] 131–32). When it became clear that the piece would actually be performed,

Marx devoted no fewer than six consecutive issues of the *BAMZ* (21 February–28 March) to proclaiming the coming event. When it was all over, he devoted nearly as much space to extolling the performance.

Finally, the figures of Mendelssohn and Marx together remind us that what was at stake in the institutions of a self-consciously progressive musical culture was their capacity to make possible the career open to talent—that deceptively simple and fundamentally important legacy of the Enlightenment and French Revolution to practical men of the nineteenth century. In Marx's and Mendelssohn's cases the stigma that talent might erase was less estate as such than religion, that is to say, their birth as Jews, which no one, least of all themselves, ever forgot, even after conversion to Christianity. Felix Mendelssohn's father Abraham (the fifth of Moses Mendelssohn's six children who grew to adulthood) had begun his family's drive to conversion and full assimilation by abruptly arranging for Fanny and Felix, the two eldest children, both under fifteen at the time, to become Lutheran Protestants. One may speculate that by 1820 the musical talents of both had become evident, and Abraham was attempting to remove all obstacles to Felix's full acceptance as a musical prodigy. After all, any fame that young *Jewish* prodigies achieved was always accompanied by slighting remarks about the loyal support of their "coreligionists," packing the concert hall, applauding inappropriately loudly, generally showing undue enthusiasm for the (implied) minor talent of the performer.[12] Zelter himself wrote to Goethe in October of 1821 that he intended to bring his young protégé to visit the great man in Weimar, and, if one is in any doubt about whether Felix's recent conversion had anything to do with this honor, one has only to read the infamous letter: "Tomorrow early I start for Wittenberg with a pupil of mine, Herr Mendelssohn's son, a lively boy of twelve. . . . The pupil is a good and pretty boy, lively and obedient. To be sure, he is the son of a Jew, but no Jew himself. The father, with remarkable self-denial, has seen to it that his children learn something, and educates them properly. It would really be *eppes rores* [a remarkable thing] if the son of a Jew turned out to be an artist" (qtd. in Mendelssohn 19; Mendelssohn-Bartholdy 3). Living surrounded by such remarks, and worse, it is hardly surprising that, according to Devrient, Felix's Jewishness should have been very much on his mind as he contemplated the upcoming performance of Bach's masterpiece: "'And to think,' said Felix triumphantly, standing still in the middle of the Opern Platz, 'that it should be an actor and a Jew that gives back to the people the greatest of the Christian works'" (Devrient 57). We can imagine, if not know for certain, what sort of opportunities an unconverted Felix Mendelssohn would have missed, whether he would have been Zelter's "best pupil," to whom the eminent man would be willing to lend performers and reputation. It is likely in any case that conversion made Mendelssohn's extraordinary talent visible, audible, palatable, to his contemporaries and useful to Mendelssohn himself, not just in making a career but in proving that, yes, a Jew could be an artist and a German. Was it a private satisfaction, or was it public knowledge—I suspect the former—that Felix revived the *St. Matthew Passion* on the centenary not only of its first performance but also of the birth of Moses Mendelssohn?

The emergent institutions of the musical public—associations, publishing businesses, scholarship, journalism, salons—explain how the *St. Matthew Passion* performance was possible but not why it was successful; why, in other words, the music became valuable to the Berliners/Prussians/Germans then and later. Success was reflected in the repeat performances, first in Berlin and then in numerous other north German cities. It was reflected in the way in which the *Passion* became—and still is—the annual culmination of the Singakademie's performance season. It was reflected in the attention devoted to the initial performance in contemporary journals, correspondence, and memoirs, as though to have an opinion on Bach's Passion was a marker of inclusion in the *Bildungsbürgertum*. It was reflected in Felix Mendelssohn's subsequent career as maestro of past masters and, until Wagner, leader of a self-consciously German musical culture. But we can only explain this success by looking more closely at those "implicitly defined functions" this particular piece of music served, or, to put it otherwise, at why this music seemed suddenly just right to people, a more-than-adequate expression of values they already held and were in the process of constructing.

In speculating on this final set of issues, I think it important to clarify that, by focusing on "implicit functions" of the piece and the performance, I do not mean to rule out the possibility that people simply found the music beautiful, hence played it and listened to it and valued it. This was certainly the case, at one level, and much has already been written about why, precisely, the *St. Matthew Passion* is so beautiful, what about its harmonies and melodic gestures strikes the ear with such pathos, what about its combination of chorus, chorale, recitative, and aria creates such drama, what in its musical totality so moves us. Formal analysis takes one deep into the music but perhaps not so far into the culture that played the music. Implicit functions might, at the other extreme from aesthetic formalism, indicate a reduction of the music to an instrumental plane of action, in which it serves only to reinforce certain social norms, like bourgeois self-control (hence, perhaps, the silence in the concert hall?), or certain relationships, like monarch to subject (hence, perhaps, the presence of the Prussian king?). But I do not wish to pursue such interpretative strategies either, for they are rarely able to account for the aesthetic force of the music in question nor the complexities of its craft. Avoiding both instrumental reductionism and aesthetic formalism, I hope to speak in conclusion of music's general representational or ideational function, its capacity, in Clifford Geertz's words, to "materialize a way of experiencing, bring a particular cast of mind out into the world of objects, where men [*sic*] can look at it" (100). Geertz argues that understanding the cultural significance of art is "always a local matter," by which he means that it always involves understanding the preoccupations, the interpretive "equipment," and the kinds of "discriminations" (in this case, skills of hearing) held collectively by members of the culture (97, 102). Relying on art historian Michael Baxandall, Geertz further asserts that the experience of art depends on a kind of cooperation between the artist and public, in which "the public does not need . . . what it has already got" but, rather, something that deepens, enriches, and perhaps ultimately changes its perception of the world.[13]

Explaining all this is, as Geertz's proposals always are, a tall order, complicated in this case by the triangular relationship between the artist whose work is being revived, the artists who conceived and carried out the revival, and the public. We are looking for a shared understanding between the latter two parties but one that would seem necessarily to be limited in certain ways by the first, in this case J. S. Bach, as well. The task of explaining the cultural significance or function of the *St. Matthew Passion* in 1829 is thus infinitely complex, involving as it does an array of aesthetic, intellectual, and religious attitudes held by a variety of people from two distinct eras, in various degrees of agreement with each other. In broad outline, then, let me suggest, and then briefly elaborate, that the power of the *St. Matthew Passion* of 1829 was its capacity to make both audible and visible the idea of a German community. It may thus serve as a particular instance of what Jacques Attali asserts has been the central feature of tonal music from the eighteenth century until the twentieth, its "attempt to make people believe in a consensual representation of the world" (Attali 46). For Attali that attempt anticipates the work of political economy and is essentially manipulative. I would prefer to restore some human agency to this conception. People of this place and time chose to imbue music with a peculiarly great capacity to express their collective belonging, in an attempt, to paraphrase Attali, to represent their belief in the consensual representation of the people that they called the nation. "We must," wrote A. B. Marx in 1826, referring in this case to the symphonic works of Haydn, Mozart, and Beethoven, "know them if we are to identify our times and ourselves" (qtd. in Pederson 96).

Marx in particular, but others as well, immediately recruited the *St. Matthew Passion* to their progressive new vision of music's importance, a vision that centered on the future of the German people as a cultural community—and possibly, though rarely explicitly, as a political one. People who wrote about the piece at the time frequently used a trope of newness to express what was special about it: Marx's first full-length description of the piece, on 28 February 1829 in the *Berliner Allgemeine musikalische Zeitung,* began with the sentence "After a hundred year intermission, this greatest and most holy work of music has arisen, and like the first morning sun after the fogs of the flood it announces a new shining day" (33). Likewise, Felix Mendelssohn's friend, the young Gustav Droysen, wrote in a Berlin feuilleton after the performance that "it is given to art to make a great beginning, whose influence will be felt over a long time" (*Berliner Conversations-Blatt* 205). "I felt," wrote another, "that a new, hitherto unknown creation [*Kunstwelt*] had opened up before me" (J. W. Loebell; qtd. in Geck 46). Such language was deliberately paradoxical in its references to something most decidedly old, and, while one could explain it simply as consciousness of a new appreciation for an old work, their sense of inception seems more far-reaching than that would suggest. In his account of the contexts for the 1829 performance of the *St. Matthew Passion,* Martin Geck has emphasized the role of the literary and intellectual leaders—Humboldt, Hegel, the Schlegels, Schleiermacher, and so on—who flocked to the Mendelssohn salons and in whose presence music could emerge as "participant in the ideas of the times" (Geck 64). The *St. Matthew Passion,* as Geck urges us to see it, was for Germans an *Ideen-Kunstwerk,* a piece of art so rich in meaning as to warrant the kind of serious reflection usually reserved for higher theological or philosophical pursuits. The trope of newness, then, expressed a hope that people were poised on a new era of cultural flowering, which would gather the genius of the past and take it into the future.[14] Since 1823 Marx had waged a campaign in the pages of his journal for German music's claim to musical—and, by extension, moral—leadership of Europe, a campaign in which the revival of the *St. Matthew Passion* was the final, triumphal move.[15] This set of attitudes about music's importance was accompanied by a reappraisal of Kant's aesthetics and an odd deployment of Hegelian categories that involved ignoring what few and generally wrongheaded things Hegel actually said about music. It manifested itself in a growing consensus that music could be deeply serious, not simply pleasing, entertaining, or, worse, frivolous. Its practical consequence was the growth of concerts in which audiences were expected not just to keep quiet in the presence of the artwork but to exert intellect and heart together to achieve a higher understanding. In short, what was new were the expectations German audiences began to have of music as art and as idea, expectations that the *St. Matthew Passion* answered particularly well.

Though not without effort. Very few of the few cognoscenti who were aware of the existence and the dimensions of the *St. Matthew Passion* believed that Berliners, or anyone else for that matter, would accept it. Zelter was notoriously reluctant to help Mendelssohn put it on, claiming that the music was suitable only for private enjoyment and that the public, in contrast, would find it tedious (Devrient 55–58). Georg Nägeli, in the midst of a scheme to publish a gallery of Bach's compositions, wrote an article explaining why it would be incomprehensible to the public (Geck 22). Part of the achievement of Felix Mendelssohn was anticipating the eventual reaction of his contemporaries to the *St. Matthew Passion* and pushing on despite, or because of, the difficulties the piece offered. Indeed, difficulty became a key concept in the positive reception of the piece, for, the more difficult and demanding the piece, the more profound and lasting the experience, for performers and audience alike: "Stern is Sebastian, to be sure, and serious," wrote one Bach-struck listener, "but in such a way that along with the immense seriousness of the material, the deep suffering, the lamentation, the woe, the remorse, the penance, the brightness and joy of life breaks through most wonderfully."[16] William Weber has written of the bifurcation of musical taste in the early nineteenth century into "extremes of levity and seriousness" (16–17). Although self-consciously serious music was initially incapable of attracting an audience, Weber argues that by 1848 its promoters had "fashioned the values for seriousness and learning which were eventually to become the basic tenets of European concert life." Mendelssohn's revival anticipated all that, perhaps even began it, although on this point one would find considerable dispute. He made it the most fashionable thing in Berlin to have, literally, suffered through the "passion music" that Eastertide, so that even Heine, for whom Felix served as a kind of hated alter ego, felt he had to make veiled and ironic reference to having been there (Heine 269).

But that brings us, finally, to why this difficult and old-fashioned piece of music so paradoxically made people feel that they were greeting the future. To enlarge upon claims I have made throughout, the piece "worked" because of an overwhelming identification that its audience made between Bach, Protestant Christianity, and being German. By 1829 Bach's stature as the old man of German music and the embodiment of a whole set of qualities that Germans identified as peculiarly their own (gruffness, diligence, thoroughness, profundity, earthiness, tenderness, sublimity) was beginning to be well-established, certainly in northern Germany, to a lesser extent in southern Germany and hardly at all in Vienna and Paris. One minor but revealing example may suffice. When the young Felix Mendelssohn took his teenage trip to France in order to test the extent of his musical talent by holding it up to the judgment of people not intimates of the Mendelssohn salons, he appointed himself an ambassador of Bach's genius, playing Bach's music at every opportunity and singing the praises of his beloved "Sebastian" to all the musicians he met (Mendelssohn). On the whole Felix was disappointed with the Parisian musical scene, which he found frivolous and superficial. He shared this sensibility with his German contemporaries; it illuminates the differences in cultural style between Berlin and Paris as well as anything.[17] The anecdote further illustrates that, already in 1825, love of Bach was becoming a marker of a distinctively German musical taste. A half-century later Berlioz remembered his amazement at the German love for Bach's recitative; by then Wagner had himself placed Bach near the beginning of the German musical tradition that culminated in himself.

Although Mendelssohn's admiration for Bach sprang as much from family tradition and local influence, Bach's growing prominence in the north German public eye owed more to J. N. Forkel's 1804 biography. Interestingly, Forkel's estimation of Bach's German genius had little to do with Bach's Protestantism. The preface to the book, a paean to Bach and to the German cultural nation, contained nothing about his religious music and only passing references to his religious profession as cantor of the Thomaskirche in Leipzig. Bach's works, according to Forkel, were "a priceless national patrimony," which "all who hold Germany dear are bound in honour to promote," but Bach's genius resided entirely in his keyboard and instrumental works (xxv). Bach was celebrated in the first flush of his revival as the inventor of the true rules of harmony: "what joy it is," wrote J. K. F. Triest in 1801, "to know that the greatest, most profound harmonist of all time to date, a man whose work excelled everything that Italy, France, and England had done for pure music, . . . was a German. . . . With a spirit like Newton's, he embraced everything that had previously been known about harmony . . . so that he properly should be viewed as the greatest law-giver of harmony who has yet appeared" (Mintz 205). Bach first entered the national culture as the embodiment of Enlightenment rationalism, the musical spirit of a deistic, rather than a Protestant, universal order.

But by the 1820s the Protestant significance of Bach's reputation dominated public expressions of his meaning for Germans. A. B. Marx's publicity was steeped in Protestant language, albeit overlaid with Hegelian historicism.[18] I have already quoted Marx's repeated use of the phrase *religiöse Hochfeier* to describe the upcoming event as well as his somewhat heavy-handed Noah/Christ imagery of the early reviews of the work. Marx was ever intent on explaining its true religiosity without yet losing sight of the Forkelian formulation of Bach as national treasure. Bach's Passion music had to be rescued not only from the dismissive rationalism of the Enlightenment but also from the austere prescriptions of contemporary church reform movements, which tended to condemn Bach's cantatas and Passion music as inappropriately individual and expressive.[19] In 1954 the musicologist Donald Mintz wrote that the transformation of Bach from Newtonian harmonist to a kind of pious romantic nationalist has a significance "so great as to be difficult to measure" (201). But here the perspective of nonmusical history is surely useful. Between Forkel and Marx lay a series of consciousness-shaking events in German society, particularly as measured in Berlin. Defeat, reform, and restoration all had an impact on Bach's reputation, until it emerged late in the 1820s to express not a de-nationalized Bach but, rather, the continuing importance of the Christian narrative to the unfolding of a German essence. For Bach to be the complete national hero Marx and his contemporaries needed to place him again in a religious frame, recover not just his emotionalism (as those wedded to the classical-to-romantic scheme tend to emphasize) but also his piety, his Protestantism, his Christology.[20] Indeed, Mendelssohn's interpretation of the Passion music was not, as common (mis)understanding would have it, a romantic one but, rather, a Protestant one, in which he brought out the "dramatic profile of the Passion story," cutting mainly those arias and recitatives that slowed down the action (Geck 36–41). Mendelssohn understood the obvious, that the primary significance of the music was religious, but, knowing that, he also chose to perform it in a secular space, with performers from secular organizations, to an audience gathered under secular auspices.[21] In a letter to his friend Franz Hauser he wrote that the singers performed "as if they were in a church," and Fanny too described how the scene of the performance seemed "like a church, the most profound silence, the most joyous devotion" (Geck 42; Hensel 234). But it was not a church or a church service, and in that resemblance, which contains also a distance, a transformation, and a drawing together, lies the significance of the performance.

Bach and Protestantism, Protestantism and the German cultural nation, Bach and the German cultural nation—the performance brought them all together, literally performed them. The key to this coming together of history, religion, and culture was the chorus itself, so crucial to Bach's musical rendering of the Passion narrative and at the same time to placing the narrative and its art in its Berlin context. Emphasis on "participation" (*Theilnahme*) of the community is a red thread that runs through the newspaper reviews, letters, and memoirs of the event. The choruses and chorales represented the *Volk* of the Christian story, lamenting, angry, guilt laden, who were given voice by the members of the Singakademie, themselves representatives of the Berlin, Prussian, and German communities, whether sitting in the audience or not. Contemporary accounts collapsed these communities together or, rather, understood them as an artistic whole. Johann Wilhelm Loebell, professor of history at the military academy in Berlin and later at the University of Bonn, wrote the very next day to his friend Ludwig Tieck that "in this moment my soul is overflowing with the Passion music of Sebastian Bach, which we have just experienced not once but twice here in Berlin, with the most extraordinary and unexpected enthusiasm of the public as a whole" (qtd. in Geck 46). He went on to speak of the music of chorus and chorale, the voice of the "believing community," which, following Schleiermacher, he saw as the embodiment of Christian belief in this world. For the music critic Ludwig Rellstab the unprecedented enthusiasm of the public for this performance, its "participation" in it, reiterated and reembodied the participation of the crowds in the Passion story. Had there not been such public participation in this "highest work that German art has brought forth," thought Rellstab, then the whole tradition of German art would have suffered for it (*Vossische Zeitung;* qtd. in Geck 51–53). For another twenty-year-old and friend of Mendelssohn's, Johann Gustav Droysen, it was "extraordinarily important that in Berlin in our time Bach's Passion music has again been brought to the attention of the public, . . . not the music of a forgotten, alien time . . . but rather the music of a free, evangelical belief of all those who trust in

God. . . . It belongs not to art and history alone but rather, as with all great art, to the community, to the people (*Berliner Conversations-Blatt;* qtd. in Geck 58–59).

Friedrich Blume wrote of this generation's enthusiasm for Bach that it was "spontaneous," that it existed "for no readily discernible reason," and found an explanation in the "enthusiastic soul of Romanticism" discovering "Bach the Romantic" (298). Such statements, which are common in accounts of this event, tantalize us with the incompleteness of their explanation. The 1829 performance of the *St. Matthew Passion* seized the imagination of a society in the grip of a transition that all perceived but none understood, a society inclined to view its sense of an era's passage in terms of the aging of great individuals, a society obsessed with its relation to its past, the meaning of which was up for grabs, a society caught between its various and only sometimes compatible attachments to state, enlightenment, faith, and personhood. That the idea of the nation, so vague and so promising, would seem attractive under such circumstances is hardly surprising. Mendelssohn's performance of the *St. Matthew Passion* could serve as a synthetic enactment of the Germanness of its audience, a moment when disparate elements of that elusive, contested quality came together in peculiarly satisfactory ways. Many paths of public and private cultural activity led to it, and many more—transformed, to some extent redirected—led from it. As a synthesis, it endured nearly intact until Wagner performed his destructive magic on the musiconational sensibilities of Germans. To disentangle the elements of that synthesis is to understand something of that society, of its cultural practices, and, perhaps, of music itself.

NOTES

1. This brief account, versions of which can be found in nearly every music history text that deals with the nineteenth century, is in this case drawn largely from the relevant chapter in Eberle and the superb account and documentary collection of Martin Geck.

2. There are, of course, exceptions to this tendency. In the same journal ten years earlier Donald Mintz acknowledged that "the revival of interest in the music of the time of Bach" was "perhaps merely marginal notes in the musical history of the 19th century" and then proceeded to make much of it (201).

3. To survey some of the important critiques of the purely analytical approach to music history, one might begin with Kerman's critique of musical analysis ("How" 1980) and go from there to his essays on the future of musicology (*Contemplating* 1985) and to the historical and theoretical work of Leo Treitler (1989), Susan McClary (1991), and Richard Leppert and McClary (1987). See also Katherine Bergeron and Philip V. Bohlman's analysis of canon formation in music history (1992).

4. Some of the more impecunious ones would fit better into the *Kleinbürger*, or artisanal, category, though none, I suspect, would still consider themselves servants. Most of the performers, however, were what contemporaries nonpejoratively called *Dilettanten*, which is to say that they certainly would have been members of the *Bildungsbürgertum*. A few of the soloists (especially Anna Milder-Hauptmann, the soprano) were closer to what we would recognize as stars, well-paid and highly praised members of the Royal Opera.

5. Weber is especially impatient with the persistent influence of the venerable text by Leo Balet, on the "embourgeoisement" of German art, music, and literature, which simply pins "middle-class labels on works of art throughout German culture of the time," with no real social-historical justification (181).

6. The situation for opera is different; most of the material summarized here refers chiefly to nonoperatic performances.

7. This little regarded work, then or now, was most famously dismissed by Karl Friedrich Zelter as a history of music that "came to an end just where the history of music begins." See the translator's introduction to the 1920 edition of Forkel's somewhat better regarded Bach biography (xi).

8. Forkel was not familiar with the vocal works, which made their way into the nineteenth century by other routes.

9. Under the title "Bemerkungen über die Ausbildung der Tonkunst in Deutschland im achtzehnten Jahrhundert" (Remarks on the Development of the Art of Music in Eighteenth-Century German), Johann Karl Friedrich Triest had credited Bach with having laid the foundations of the music of the future by his mastery of the science of harmony. The editor of the *AMZ*, Friedrich Rochlitz, was himself a pivotal figure in the Bach revival (Mintz 204–6; Reimer 20–24).

10. He is notorious for influencing Goethe against the music of Beethoven and Schubert—a reputation that may need to be revisited.

11. How Felix actually got the idea is another story. His family had an unbroken connection to the Bach legacy and a lively interest in Bach manuscripts as they came available. Felix's maternal great-aunt Sara Itzig Levy had been student and patron of J. S. Bach's two sons, C. P. E. and W. F. Bach; his mother, Leah Salomon, had been a student of one of J. S. Bach's pupils; she, in turn, made sure her children were learning Bach preludes and fugues from the time they first sat at a keyboard.

12. Louis Spohr, for instance, described a performance in 1804 of the young Meyerbeer, which "drew a crowd of his co-religionists"; Marx's own *Berliner Allgemeine musikalische Zeitung* published a review of an 1824 concert of the Jewish prodigies Louise and Ferdinand David, at which the "loudest applause" came from their "co-religionists, the Israelites" (Spohr 58; *BAMZ* 1824, 189).

13. The gradually more and more favorable reception of Beethoven's music in the last decade of the eighteenth century might be an example of the kind of paradigmatic shift in a cultural system that some art can prompt. See the new book by Tia DeNora, *Beethoven and the Construction of Genius.*

14. This kind of confidence existed alongside an equally strong, maybe stronger, sense of nostalgia—a depressing feeling that the time of the greats was passing. The deaths of Beethoven and Goethe filled a number of German artists, including Mendelssohn, with melancholy despair, or so they said.

15. See especially Pedersen, although she has the usual fixation on Marx's championing of Beethoven's symphonies and misses the significance of the Passion revival to her argument.

16. Johann Wilhelm Loebell to Ludwig Tieck (qtd. in Geck 46–47).

17. In a letter to his mother from Paris he wrote, "The salons (although I hadn't expected too much from them) are *ennuyant,* and care for nothing besides frivolous music and coquetteries, nothing serious and solid"—for example, Bach. He calls Rossini "maestro Windbag" and generally finds nothing musically admirable about Paris, the acknowledged "home town of music" in that period (Elvers 34–38).

18. Marx's account of the Bach revival in his memoirs is characterized by a relentless and certainly self-conscious echoing of scriptural and Protestant language, including— in his justification for why he felt compelled to spread the word about Bach—the Lutheran phrase, that "ich gar nicht anders konnte" (I could do no other) (Marx 87).

19. Justus Thibaut, author of the astonishingly successful *Über die Reinheit der Tonkunst* (1825), was already part of a "Palestrina Renaissance" in church music. The book generally distanced itself from Bach's music, without actually condemning it. For perspectives on earlier conflicts between Bach and the Pietists, see Irwin (29–40); and Mintz (210–15).

20. Of relevance here is the literature on the politics of Protestantism in the early nineteenth century. See especially Besch 1950; Pinson 1934; and Hoover 1986. On the pietistic revival among aristocrats in Frederick William III's court, see Clark 1993.

21. It is worth noting that in Vienna during this same period the performance of church music in secular spaces was often prohibited by the censors.

WORKS CITED

Anderson, Benedict. *Imagined Communities.* Rev. ed. London: Verso, 1991.

Attali, Jacques. *Noise: The Political Economy of Music.* Trans. Brian Massumi. Minneapolis: U of Minnesota P, 1985.

Balet, Leo. *Die Verbürgerlichung der deutschen Kunst, Literatur und Musik im 18. Jahrhundert.* Strassburg and Leipzig: Heitz, 1936.

Bergeron, Katherine, and Philip V. Bohlman, eds. *Disciplining Music: Musicology and Its Canons.* Chicago: U of Chicago P, 1992.

Berliner Allgemeine musikalische Zeitung (BAMZ), 1824–30.

Berliner Conversations-Blatt für Poesie, Literatur und Kritik, 1829.

Besch, Hans. *J. S. Bach: Frömmigkeit und Glaube.* Vol. 1: *Deutung und Wirklichkeit, Das Bild Bachs im Wandel der deutschen Kirchen- und Geistesgeschichte.* Kassel: Bärenreiter-Verlag, 1950.

Blume, Friedrich. "Bach in the Romantic Era." *Musical Quarterly* 50 (1964): 290–306.

Bollert, Werner. *Sing-Akademie zu Berlin.* Berlin: Rembrandt Verlag, 1966.

Burnham, Scott. "Criticism, Faith and the Idea: A. B. Marx's Early Reception of Beethoven." *Nineteenth Century Music* 13 (1990): 183–92.

Clark, Christopher. "The Politics of Revival: Pietists, Aristocrats, and the State Church in Early Nineteenth-Century Prussia." In *Between Reform, Reaction and Resis-*

tance: Studies in the History of German Conservatism, ed. Larry Eugene Jones and James Retallack. Providence, R. I. and Oxford: Berg, 1993. 31–60.

Dahlhaus, Carl, ed. *Studien zur Musikgeschichte Berlins im frühen 19. Jahrhundert*. Regensburg: Bosse, 1980.

DeNora, Tia. *Beethoven and the Construction of Genius: Musical Politics in Vienna, 1792–1803*. Berkeley: U of California P, 1995.

Devrient, Eduard. *Meine Erinnerungen an Felix Mendelssohn Bartholdy und seine Briefe an mich*. Leipzig: J. J. Weber, 1869.

Eberle, Gottfried. *200 Jahre Singakademie zu Berlin*. Berlin: Nicolai, 1991.

Elvers, Rudolf, ed. *Felix Mendelssohn: A Life in Letters*. Trans. Craig Tomlinson. New York: Fromm, 1986.

Forkel, J. N. *Johann Sebastian Bach: His Life, Art, and Work*. Trans. Charles Sanford Terry. London: Constable, 1920.

Geck, Martin. *Die Wiederentdeckung der Matthäuspassion im 19. Jahrhundert: die zeitgenössische Dokumente und ihre ideengeschichtliche Deutung*. Regensburg: Bosse, 1967.

Geertz, Clifford. "Art as a Cultural System." *Local Knowledge*. New York: Basic Books, 1983. 94–120.

Grossmann-Vendrey, Suzanne. *Felix Mendelssohn Bartholdy und die Musik der Vergangenheit*. Regensburg: Bosse, 1969.

Habermas, Jürgen. *The Structural Transformation of the Public Sphere: An Inquiry into a Category of Bourgeois Society*. Trans. Thomas Burger. Cambridge, MA: MIT P, 1991.

Hanson, Alice M. *Musical Life in Biedermeier Vienna*. Cambridge: Cambridge UP, 1985.

Heine, Heinrich. *Briefe*. Vol. 1. Mainz: Kupferberg, 1948.

Hensel, Sebastian. *The Mendelssohn Family: From Letters and Journals*. Trans. Carl Klingemann. London and New York: Harper and Bros., 1882.

Herrnstein Smith, Barbara. *Contingencies of Value: Alternative Perspectives for Critical Theory*. Cambridge, MA: Harvard UP, 1988.

Hiller, Ferdinand. *Felix Mendelssohn Bartholdy: Briefe und Erinnerungen*. Cologne: DuMont-Schauberg, 1878.

Hoffmann, E. T. A. *E. T. A. Hoffmann's Musical Writings*. Ed. David Charlton. Trans. Martyn Clarke. Cambridge: Cambridge UP, 1989.

Hoover, Arlie. *The Gospel of Nationalism*. Stuttgart: F. Steiner, 1986.

Jacob, Heinrich Eduard. *Felix Mendelssohn and His Times*. Trans. Richard and Clara Winston. Englewood Cliffs, NJ: Prentice-Hall, 1963.

Kerman, Joseph. *Contemplating Music: Challenges to Musicology*. Cambridge, MA: Harvard UP, 1985.

———. "How We Got into Analysis and How to Get Out." *Critical Inquiry* 7 (1980): 311–31.

Leppert, Richard, and Susan McClary, eds. *Music and Society: The Politics of Composition, Performance, and Reception*. Cambridge: Cambridge UP, 1987.

Mahling, Christoph-Hellmut. "Zum 'Musikbetrieb' Berlins und seinen Institutionen in der ersten Hälfte des 19. Jahrhunderts." In *Studien zur Musikgeschichte Berlins im frühen 19. Jahrhundert*, ed. Carl Dahlhaus. Regensburg: Bosse, 1980. 127–284.

Marx, A. B. *Erinnerungen aus meinem Leben.* Berlin: O. Jahnke, 1865.

McClary, Susan. *Feminine Endings: Music, Gender, and Sexuality.* Minneapolis: U of Minnesota P, 1991.

Mendelssohn, Fanny. Letter to Carl Klingemann, 22 March 1829. In *The Mendelssohn Family: From Letters and Journals,* ed. Sebastian Hensel. London and New York: Harper and Bros., 1882. 169.

Mendelssohn, Felix. *Letters.* Ed. G. Selden-Roth. New York: P. Elek, 1945.

Mendelssohn-Bartholdy, Karl. *Goethe and Mendelssohn.* Trans. M. E. von Glehn. 1872. Reprint. New York: Haskell House, 1970.

Mintz, Donald. "Some Aspects of the Revival of Bach." *Musical Quarterly* 40 (1954): 201–21.

Nitsche, Peter. "Die Liedertafel im System der Zelterschen Gründungen." In *Studien zur Musikgeschichte Berlins im frühen 19. Jahrhundert,* ed. Carl Dahlhaus. Regensburg: Bosse, 1980. 11–26.

Pederson, Sanna. "A. B. Marx, Berlin Concert Life, and German National Identity." *Nineteenth Century Music* 18 (1994): 87–107.

Pinson, Koppel. *Pietism as a Factor in the Rise of German Nationalism.* New York: Columbia UP, 1934.

Pinthus, Gerhard. *Das Konzertleben in Deutschland.* 1932. Reprint. Baden-Baden: Verlag Valentin Körner, 1977.

Rehm, Jürgen. *Zur Musikrezeption im vormärzlichen Berlin: Die Präsentation bürgerlichen Selbstverständnisses und biedermeierlicher Kunstanschauung in den Musikkritiken Ludwig Rellstabs.* Hildesheim and New York: Georg Olms, 1983.

Reimer, Erich. "Nationalbewusstsein und Musikgeschichtsschreibung in Deutschland, 1800–1850." *Archiv für Musikwissenschaft* 27 (1993): 17–31.

Riemann, Hugo. *Geschiche der Musik seit Beethoven, 1800–1900.* Berlin: Spemann, 1901.

Salman, Walter. *Das Konzert: Eine Kulturgeschichte.* Munich: Beck, 1988.

Schulze, Hagen. *The Course of German Nationalism, from Frederick the Great to Bismarck, 1763–1867.* Cambridge and New York: Cambridge UP, 1991.

Schünemann, Georg. *Die Singakademie zu Berlin 1791–1941.* Regensburg: Bosse, 1941.

Sheehan, James. *German History, 1770–1866.* Oxford and New York: Oxford UP, 1989.

Spohr, Louis. *The Musical Journeys of Louis Spohr.* Trans. Harry Pleasant. Norman: U of Oklahoma P, 1961.

Treitler, Leo. *Music and the Historical Imagination.* Cambridge, MA: Harvard UP, 1989.

Wallace, Robin. *Beethoven's Critics: Aesthetic Dilemma and Resolutions during the Composer's Lifetime.* Cambridge: Cambridge UP, 1986.

Weber, William. "Mass Culture and the Reshaping of European Musical Taste, 1770–1870." *International Review of the Aesthetic and the Sociology of Music* 8 (1977): 5–21.

———. "The Muddle of the Middle Classes." *Nineteenth Century Music* 3 (1979): 179–85.

———. *Music and the Middle Class: The Social Structure of Concert Life in London, Paris, and Vienna.* London: Holmes and Meier, 1975.

CHAPTER 10

A Nation for the Masses:
Production of German Identity
in the Late-Nineteenth-Century
Popular Press

Kirsten Belgum

Kirsten Belgum has, from her earliest work, been interested in challenging the traditional canonical notions of what earns the label "literature." For example, her dissertation on nineteenth-century German realism—a topic examined by a long line of eminent Germanists—includes a wide range of texts: works by certified "great author" Thomas Mann; canonical German realists Theodor Storm, Paul Raabe, and Theodor Fontane, whose familiarity is primarily limited to a German readership; and works by German authors less frequently found on graduate reading lists, such as Gustav Freytag, Max Kretzer, and Eugenie Marlitt. The fact that these last three authors were among the most popular of their day but have been ignored by academics for most of this century is a sign that canon building runs the risk of losing touch with the reading habits of a previous era. To understand a society and its culture, Belgum believes, we must consult the whole variety of texts it produced—texts of diverse styles and with disparate audiences. Cultural studies transforms literary studies through its examination of varied texts.

The idea of challenging the canon is closely tied to methodological issues. In studying nineteenth-century Germany, Belgum turns here to the popular press. The diversity of material in popular illustrated magazines has encouraged her to find new interpretive approaches to studying written culture. She borrows from the fields of history, geography, political science, anthropology, and iconography. Although cultural studies practitioners who cross disciplinary boundaries often lack a complete familiarity with those other disciplines,

163

it is precisely the attempts to mobilize multiple methodologies that yield rich analyses, as Belgum's essay here demonstrates.

How and why groups of people come to identify themselves as they do are central questions for cultural studies projects. Likewise, we know that identity politics, whether factionalizing or unifying, plays important roles in the discourse around us every day. In the following essay Belgum looks closely at an important public voice for the idea of a culturally unified German nation: the late-nineteenth-century bourgeois journal Die Gartenlaube, *which was Germany's most widely distributed and read magazine of the era. She shows how this representative example of the popular press helped Germans develop a national identity more modern than any before. The identity she finds articulated here is* modern *in several ways: it is expansionist, imperialist, self-assured, racialist if not necessarily racist, progressive, and liberal. This essay helps us understand the importance that the colonial enterprise took on for Germans, even though German colonialism may seem insignificant compared to that of other European powers. Belgum's essay shows us some ways in which the trope of constructing the German nation beyond its accepted borders within Europe had been rehearsed during and, more important, before Germany's acquisition of actual colonies.*

The present student of culture studies the watching and looking of peoples in order to discover how in their turn they discover and invent a tale of identity with which to keep out the cold.

—Fred Inglis, *Cultural Studies*

The popular press of any era provides the student of culture with a rich representation of various identities. The success of a periodical publication depends on its ability to win over a substantial and consistent share of the reading market. This in turn means the publication has to provide its readers with attractive material on a regular and dependable basis. In other words, the popularity of the press is a measure of its ability to present readers with identities that are readily understandable and acceptable. In the nineteenth century the magazine that was most effective in helping the German reading public "discover and invent a tale of identity" was the extremely popular weekly illustrated family magazine *Die Gartenlaube* (The Arbor). As a successful mediator of cultural identities, the *Gartenlaube* was ideally situated to participate in the construction of national identity for a people who lacked a unified state and for whom the extent of the nation was disputed.[1]

This weekly magazine was founded in 1853 by Ernst Keil, who as publisher and editor had been an active proponent of liberal politics prior to and during the middle-class revolution of 1848. In the reactionary political climate after the revolution, Keil remained dedicated to the two liberal goals of democratic freedoms and national unification.[2] His objective was to entertain and educate German readers to political maturity and to further the liberal cause of national unity.[3] Keil's *Gartenlaube* began with a circulation of 6,000 in 1853. By the 1860s it was distributed to all parts of Germany as well as to German colonists in the United States, Brazil, and Australia. With its selection of serialized fiction, biographical sketches, essays on topics from culture and nature, and a wide array of illustrations, it became the first German periodical to gain a mass following. By 1875 the *Gartenlaube* had a circulation of 385,000 and a readership in the millions.[4]

The period of the magazine's extraordinary growth also brought momentous social and political changes, such as industrialization, urbanization, and mass emigration, that affected conceptions of the German nation. Although these decades preceded the political organization of antisemitism in Germany as part of party platforms, they did witness an increase in racialist language, and this occasionally crept into essays in the magazine that dealt with German identity. Most important, the rise of the *Gartenlaube* paralleled the gradual emergence of Prussian domination in German politics, Bismarck's wars (1864 against Denmark, 1866 against Austria, and 1870 against France), and the founding of the German Empire in 1871. In the 1870s this popular magazine had to define the nation against the backdrop of a German state with disparate regions that had only recently been united and that did not include all German-speaking territories.[5]

The genius of Keil's magazine and the key to its success was its ability to attract men and women, young and old, readers from different social classes. Above all, it appealed to Germans from a wide range of geographical areas and cultural traditions. This essay considers one aspect of the construction of national identity in the *Gartenlaube:* its treatment of regional specificities and mass emigration as concerns of the German nation. The popular magazine, as a mediator of information and images, created a spatial vocabulary of the nation on several levels. It familiarized its readers with geographical terrains and could shape these places according to its own interests. More than that, the *Gartenlaube* generated a national space in the minds of its readers that was not limited by political boundaries. The *Gartenlaube* helped establish a definition of the German nation as a community in space that both preceded the nation-state and stood in an uneasy alliance with it after 1871. In the process the magazine itself became an important space for national imagining.[6]

Representing a National Space

Geographical education was central to the *Gartenlaube*'s stated goal of enlightening the German people.[7] The magazine provided a summary on a regular basis of various peoples, traditions, costumes, and landscapes of German lands. The insistent portrayal of an internal German geography began quite early, in the third year of its publication, with a series entitled "Land und Leute" (Land and People), which appeared regularly over several decades and which took an ethnographic approach to describing regional landscapes and customs. The *Gartenlaube* systematically unified its version of the nation by appealing to the commonalities and interrelationships among these various locales. Essays regularly described local festivals, such as wedding ceremonies and harvest celebrations, as well as dialect, culinary specialties, the details of regional dress (of men, women, and children), games, music, dance, houses, and professions. The magazine summarized the purpose of these introductions to regional cultures as explicitly national: "It is a satisfying task to offer them to the German people as newly won treasures, since we can never become acquainted with enough lovely and good things about our fatherland, in order to always hold it in greater and holier esteem" (1864, 502).[8]

Each sketch of local culture varied in emphasis, yet all adhered to a standard style and content. The fourteenth essay in the "Land and People" series illustrates this format. In presenting the region of Betzingen, near Tübingen, it begins by noting the beauty of a Sunday morning in late May. It then describes the approach to the village including the geological formations, their larger context (this range is "the last terrace step before the Swiss Alps"), and the names and spatial orientation of landmarks ("on the farthest left side in the east . . . the Hohenstaufen, . . . on the farthest right side in the west the Hohenzollern" [1864, 438]).[9] The essay describes the people of this area first from their external appearance; the characterization of traditional peasant dress takes up six long paragraphs, itemizing such details as the variety of colors, fabrics, patterns, and dimensions of the women's bodices and accompanying accessories, with regional names. A discussion of the social significance of this traditional dress—that is, that nonvirgins may not wear the white apron—is followed by a lengthy description of important customs and celebrations: for marriage, baptism, burial, Christmas, egg hunting, cock dancing, and the "Karz," a winter courting ritual. The essay also discusses the history of the region, praising the local population's resistance to the French in 1796, tracing costumes back to medieval times and the residents themselves back to the last great migration of peoples before the Middle Ages (fig. 1).

Like other essays in the series, this one combined two strategies in presenting a local culture to the *Gartenlaube* readers as part of the German nation.

Betzinger Bauern am Sonntagmorgen nach der Kirche.
Originalzeichnung von Theodor Pixis in München.

Fig. 1. **Betzinger peasants Sunday after church. (Reproduced from *Die Garten-laube* [1864]: 437.)**

On the one hand, the presentation speaks the language of scientific objectivity. It categorizes this space and orients the reader with typologies (of geographical formations) and names (of mountains and articles of clothing). The accompanying illustration of young women and men in the village allows the reader to verify the descriptive detail with a visual presentation. The essay affirms its authority to report by noting which things were witnessed directly ("we were able to convince ourselves with our own eyes") or based on local testimony ("about that we gathered no information") or historical documents ("a charter of Emperor Maximilian I from Worms from 17 September 1495") (440).[10] It insists on comprehensive description when it lists customs (such as the winter courting tradition) that would not have been visible in late May, the time of the narration.

On the other hand, the description contains numerous points for reader identification. It begins with positive associations ("What a wonderful feeling") and repeatedly affirms the pleasing character of the place: mountains with forests and rocks lie "in the richest glow"; villages "glisten and sparkle under the beautiful spring sky" (438–39).[11] It employs similes and metaphors from common experience (a mountain "that spreads out its lowest layers like a petticoat") to make this landscape and its culture recognizable. Finally, even in its difference this region is made familiar. The relationships between the sexes, the problems of morality, are said to be "just like in the city." This presentation does not look down on rural life in Betzingen but, rather, through contrast and comparison, argues that it is just as "complicated" as urban existence. Regional events (such as the occupation of the French) tie the history of the region to national history. Both are characterized as an unbroken chain of tradition. In other words, in a variety of ways the *Gartenlaube* makes a connection between this place and the national whole.

These lessons in German geography generated a common national identity by familiarizing readers from various German lands with other German regions. The magazine's presentation of regional spaces in this series included a diverse cross-section of the national geography: from the islands in the North Sea to Bavaria, from the Black Forest to the Spree River. In addition, many of these contributions were from the outer boundaries of the German lands— Schleswig and Holstein, Alsace, the Alps. Recently, Dennis Rumley and Julian Minghi have noted that cultural geographers have moved away from a morphology of geographical regions to a discussion of their symbolic value (4). They have suggested that peripheral geographical regions or boundaries can even be central to the social and political meaning of a space (296). For nineteenth-century German nationalists the perimeter was important to defining the national space. In his influential poem "What Is the German's Fatherland?" (1813) Ernst Moritz Arndt insisted that none of the German regions alone

(Swabia, Prussia, the Rhineland, Styria, etc.) could satisfy the call for a German homeland. Arndt concluded his list of German lands with the hope "Where'er resounds the German tongue, Where'er its hymns to God are sung" and the demand "All Germany shall be the land!"[12]

Almost three decades later Heinrich Hoffmann von Fallersleben wrote the most famous and enduring geographic definition of the German nation. The first stanza of Hoffman von Fallersleben's poem used Arndt's strategy (although in abbreviated form) to identify Germany by its geographical regions, as a place bounded by rivers and a coast in the west, east, south, and north: "from the Maas to the Memel, from the Etsch to the Belt."[13] Giving the disparate German lands political coherence was a major issue for German nationalists throughout the century. It is not surprising that a liberal magazine like the *Gartenlaube* appealed to this geographical tradition of defining the German nation. As in Hoffmann von Fallersleben's poem, the magazine's discussion of German boundary regions established a perimeter that circumscribed, and thus figuratively protected, a stable national center.

The *Gartenlaube*'s preoccupation with frontier regions was not limited to those territories that were part of the German Empire of 1871. After the founding of the nation-state, the magazine went beyond the political boundaries of the state to insist on the larger category of the cultural and linguistic national entity. The magazine responded to one of the main dilemmas of nineteenth-century German nation building, the inclusion or exclusion of Austria. Prussia's quick and decisive military victory over Austria and its southern German allies in 1866 gave military support to the smaller German solution that eventually led to Bismarck's unification of Germany in 1871 without the German areas of Austria.[14]

This exclusion of a large German-speaking region, however, was not accepted as a given or as a national good by all members of the German nation. The *Gartenlaube* and its editorship insisted on the membership of German Austrians in the definition of a cultural German nation. In the first year of the empire (1871–72) the magazine published six essays on Tyrol, an ethnically German region that was not part of the German empire.[15] Between 1881 and 1901 it published thirty-seven articles on Tyrol and its people. Occasionally referring to such regions as "the lost (betrayed, deserted) brother tribe" (*der verlorene [verrathene, verlassene] Bruderstamm*), the magazine adhered to a definition of the nation that transcended territorial disputes or political boundaries. This definition of a cultural, ethnic community viewed the nation as an archaic and thus eternal entity.[16] Although the *Gartenlaube* never called for a political incorporation of this region into the empire, the magazine became a compensatory visual space for the nation that existed in the imagination and outside political reality.

Beyond the Borders of the Nation: Emigrants and Explorers

From its beginnings the *Gartenlaube* supported the founding of a political state to encompass and represent the nation, yet it consistently generated conceptions of national identity that stood in contrast to the state. Another prominent example of this was its discussion of German emigration. During the first decades of the magazine's existence (1853–73) Germany experienced two great waves of emigration.[17] In the years of the first wave of emigration, which lasted from 1846–57, the *Gartenlaube* published eight essays on the lot and fate of German emigrants. Another thirteen essays and notices appeared between 1863 and 1874, roughly coinciding with what has been called the second peak in the nineteenth-century wave of emigration. As a magazine interested in the welfare, as well as unification, of the German people, the *Gartenlaube* was dedicated to protecting emigrants as members of the national community from the perils that threatened them.

Before the founding of the empire, the *Gartenlaube* functioned as a mouthpiece for emigrant concerns and as advisor to German emigrants. It repeatedly published essays that warned its German readers about pitfalls and potential hazards of emigration, advising them not to sign vague, dubious contracts and not to believe the oral promises made by agents in harbor towns. Other notices brought attention specifically to false promises made by foreign governments that were trying to lure German emigrants to their countries.[18] Many of the pieces about conditions German emigrants would encounter in specific countries ended with the appeal to other publications, such as daily papers to print the same information and thus disseminate it among Germans as far as possible. An extensive essay by Friedrich Gerstäcker on the problems facing emigrants granted permission for reprinting the essay, something that was otherwise often explicitly prohibited by the magazine (1863, 361). The *Gartenlaube* lamented the lack of a unified state that could protect the interests of Germans abroad (1862, 590–91). As Gerstäcker asserted, "The absurdity that is the German Federation cannot be considered for it [the protection of German emigrants]" (1863, 363).[19] By informing the unwary German emigrant, the press assumed responsibilities of the state and thus shaped itself as an alternative national voice.

A major concern of the *Gartenlaube* was that Germans who leave their homeland not lose their identity. This included concern with their loss of language and culture but, first and foremost, with their understanding of themselves as Germans. According to the magazine's various contributors, emigrants carried their nationality with them into the new country and might keep it forever. Even much later generations, those born in the new country, were identified as "our countrymen" (*unsere Landsleute*) (1885, 531). In 1864 one author argued for a "German-patriotic" (*deutsch-patriotisch*) stance for emigrants that included teaching German language and customs in the new country (1864, 351). Another essay from the same year praised a group of emigrants who expressed eternal loyalty to German identity: "And rest assured that we will remain, in our house and hearts, upstanding Germans!" (1864, 87).[20] In an essay from the 1880s about German emigration to Australia an author bemoaned the fact that Germans were threatened with losing their "Nationalität" by being submerged into the general English population (1885, 532). In the view of the *Gartenlaube* the nation could and should be exported to places outside the borders of Germany even after a unified German nation-state existed.

Given this notion of national purity, it is not surprising to find that the magazine uniformly praised its "Landsleute" as the best newcomers to other countries. Essay after essay suggested that the work ethic and skill of the Germans made them the most desired immigrants. (1862, 456; 1863, 361–64). "Again we have proof that foreign nations always look for Germans whenever they want to fill a position of responsibility with someone" (1863, 304).[21] But even more notable than the comparison of Germans with other European immigrants in these new countries was the way in which the Germans were discussed in the context of their new country and culture.

In order to understand the role in defining a national space that the *Gartenlaube* set for itself, let us consider its presentation of German emigration to one country.[22] In essays about Brazil, German emigrants confront a foreign nature, obstacles such as jungles, raging rivers, and mosquitoes. In all of these discussions nature is presented as strange, perplexing, and fascinatingly exotic for the nineteenth-century German reader. The extensive narration of encounters with this aspect of Brazil is not as revealing as what is missing from the characterization of the travelers' and emigrants' experience there. The essays rarely include encounters with other humans who might confront the German narrator and thus the German readers with *their own difference*. The reader gains the odd impression that these Germans are the main residents of this new place. There are scattered references to an unspecified landlord or slaves, characters who for lack of detailed description remain disembodied and unreal. Non-German inhabitants, be they native Indians or descendants of earlier immigrants, are for the most part absent, or at best a decorative backdrop to letting the German define and identify him- or herself in the context of the foreign landscape and in dealing with its challenges. The characterization of German emigrant life in "Christmas Memories from Brazil" by Alfred Waeldler, for example, focuses exclusively on attempts to maintain German cultural traditions.[23]

German exploration of foreign lands plays a similar role in the *Gartenlaube* to that of emigration. Articles glorify the work of German specialists in charting new global territory. The title of an essay from 1875 indicates the German perspective that dominates in such articles. "The White Spots on our Maps" (Die weissen Flecken unserer Landkarten) describes Brazil as a place deserving the interest and attention of researchers, a place in need of present-day exploration. Although a list of previous explorers is included, Brazilians themselves are absent from the essay. The only locals who appear are "natives" (*Ureinwohner*) recommended as an ideal object of study for German ethnographers. Brazil is cited as a source not only of valuable raw materials for industry but also of items for modern scientific investigation; its forests yield treasures of glorious woods, textile fibers and oils for German industry, products for German medicine, and new species for the natural sciences.[24] As in the essays about German emigration to Brazil, this foreign, distant terrain becomes a space to be occupied and explored by German experts.

In the illustration accompanying one essay the *Gartenlaube* reader sees three individuals measuring and charting an otherwise open wilderness (fig. 2). The most pronounced of the figures in the image is the author (and illustrator) himself, Keller-Leuzinger (1875, 477). This illustration receives the following elucidation:

> The researcher cannot find a more beautiful or pleasant setting, as our illustration shows him, with the sextant or rather the reflection-circle in his hand and ready to measure the height of the sun. Underneath the massive branches of a Uauassé palm (Attalea) a lightweight table is set up which holds the carefully tended chronometer. The gaze is cast afar from the high shore across the wide river and its islands crowned with palms. (1875, 479)[25]

Via description and illustration the *Gartenlaube* reader is included in the action of the researcher ("the gaze is cast afar") and in the conclusion that Brazil is a geographical space lacking scientific analysis and systematized knowledge. As Mary Louise Pratt has shown, European travel writing, beginning with the Enlightenment, often saw its task in categorizing and organizing knowledge about these "unknown" places (15–37). In our context of German national identity this reportage reaffirms the readers' confidence in the German *Volk* and discourages any questioning of German culture and traditions as they come in contact with those of other peoples and places. Indeed, as the author exhorts his audience to visit this wonderful, exotic, "uncharted" Brazil, this terrain even becomes the ideal space for German tourism (1875, 479).

A later essay by the same author on the construction of a road in an inland area of Brazil also emphasizes the German experts whose knowledge and technical skill are key to completing the project.[26] Again, this essay praises the capabilities of the German engineers as it erases the local individuals and their competencies and skills.[27] There is no mention of the residents of this area or the usefulness of the road nor even of the local crews who no doubt made its completion possible. Instead, we hear of the determination with which these

Vorbereitungen zu astronomischen Beobachtungen in Brasilien.
Originalzeichnung von J. Keller-Leuzinger.

**Fig. 2. Preparations for astronomical observations in Brazil. (Reproduced from
Die Gartenlaube [1878]: 477.)**

Germans struggled against the foreign elements and succeeded. The work, frustrations, existences of non-Germans are invisible for the *Gartenlaube* reader. In descriptions of the German people encountering a new place, the strength and determination of the German *Volk* took center stage. The characterization of Germans abroad enabled the *Gartenlaube* to affirm a catalog of national virtues that included technical skill, industriousness, and tenacity.

Despite the liberal, mainstream tendency of the *Gartenlaube,* it was not immune to racial typologizing, to the idea of superiority through racial purity. The author of one essay suggested that German emigrants to Brazil, no matter what their number, would lose their racial identity: the ships that drop them off "would do nothing more than deposit an element that would be lost to its motherland on those southern shores, so that it might brazilianize itself, i.e., serve as dung for a mixed race, which is prohibited from ever playing a substantial role in the great drama of peoples" (1864, 350).[28] This characterization clearly implies the inferiority of people who lose their traditional identity. The racialist language of this author was not the norm for the *Gartenlaube,* but it does reveal the popular magazine's susceptibility to contemporary racial definitions of the nation.

By the middle of the nineteenth century the nation could not be understood without the context of other parts of the world. To be sure, the geography of German-speaking Europe was the main focus of this liberal magazine's attempt to define the nation as a cohesive entity. Yet, in the rest of the world as well, Germanness was not only defended and preserved but also constructed. In this geographical view of the nation the world was both a potential extension of the nation and a stage upon which the German nation could play.[29] The reality of German emigration and the eventual issue of German colonialism near the end of the century presented challenges to an ethnically and geographically defined national identity.[30] The popular press met these challenges by incorporating distant lands into a cohesive national imagination. The fact that the *Gartenlaube* included German emigrants in its definition of the German nation, even after the founding of the German Empire in 1871, was perhaps more than anything else a response to the unprecedented emigration that challenged the concept of a geographically stable nation.

Although the landscape of the nation was one means to understanding and arguing for a nation-state, true membership in the nation was not limited or affected by a person's place of residence. Membership in the German nation, as Rogers Brubaker has demonstrated, was historically tied to a person's ethnic identity or origin. Furthermore, if national identity was based on a sense of eternal and lasting ethnic identity, it could and should extend beyond the limits of traditional political borders. The *Gartenlaube*'s presentation of Germans outside the boundaries of German lands demonstrates that, although local geography was an important point of departure for defining the nation, when necessary, the nation could be transported to other places, thus expanding the national space. In the age of mass emigration and European imperialism the flexibility of a spatial nation was an important addition to the traditional notion of a national homeland.[31]

With its discussion of national geography the *Gartenlaube* contributed to the historical process of nation building, which must be distinguished from the political state building Bismarck achieved in 1871. Even after the founding of the nation-state in 1871, the magazine continued to imagine the German nation as something larger than the specific state boundaries of the empire; the landscape of the nation potentially included all regions of the world where Germans lived and worked. The German nation was identified as existing not merely within the nation-state but wherever and as far as the pages of the *Gartenlaube* reached. This inclusive definition had a dual implication for the press and for the construction of national identity. It enabled the popular magazine to address all of its readers—that is, potentially any German speaker anywhere in the world—as part of the German nation it was in the process of describing. At the same time, the popular family magazine could define itself as a national publication, because it reached a national audience.[32]

The presentation of an understandable geography was not the only recurrent approach of the *Gartenlaube* and popular magazines like it to defining the nation. The repeated narration of a common national past and the commemoration of national heroes were central to a process of legitimizing the nation that occurred in the popular press.[33] Industrialization and competitive commercialization were also celebrated as signs of the modern capabilities and future strength of the German people and the empire after 1871. But the prevalence and persistence of geographical images suggest that they were a mainstay in the popular construction of German identity. The enthusiastic response to the work of a contemporary sociologist, Wilhelm Heinrich Riehl, including his volume entitled *Land and People,* like the *Gartenlaube* series, also indicates the broad interest in the geography of the nation.[34] This preoccupation suggests an ideological component to space.

Some recent theoretical notions from other disciplines have helped me articulate an interest in illustrated magazines that goes beyond deciphering the representations of self the press presented to an identity-hungry nation. Edward Soja's insistence on a spatial understanding of cultural meaning can challenge those of us used to working with narrative meaning to broaden our conception of the construction of identity (10–43). Simon Schama has recently shown how the elements of landscapes in various periods and cultures have captured human imagination and have generated collective myths of identity. In late-nineteenth-century Germany the *Gartenlaube* was an important vehicle for this kind of spatial imagination. It proffered identities not as reflections, nor as concrete, realistic alternatives to lived reality, but as a space of textual and visual compensation.[35] With readerships that gradually grew to mass dimensions, institutions of communication, such as the popular press, constituted a political space in their own right that competed with other political institutions (such as the state) in constructing national identity. Through its distribution of a national vocabulary the press itself became an important national space.

One role of cultural studies must be to take seriously cultural and ideological elements of identity that have stood in opposition to state-sanctioned political identity. Precisely because it combines interpretive tools and theoretical insights from a variety of fields, cultural studies enables us to explore the diverse processes involved in the construction of identity, the ties between cultural imagination and lived reality. The geographical presentation of the German nation in the popular press can help explain the central role the press, as a cultural institution, played in the nineteenth-century discussion of national identity. It should encourage us to look at the press as a formidable partner in the construction of national identity in other times and places, including our own.

NOTES

1. My other work on the visual and narrative construction of national identity in this periodical includes a range of topics: from its discussion of modern technology and its dissemination of images of national monuments to the incorporation of women readers into a national audience through serialized romance novels.

2. For a concise discussion in English of German liberalism and the "national question" around 1848, see Langewiesche.

3. Especially in the first two and a half decades of its publication the *Gartenlaube* routinely celebrated liberal traditions of the nineteenth-century student fraternities (*Burschenschaften*) and the historical figures from the barricades of 1848. Some of these instances are mentioned in the antisemitic discussion of the magazine by Zang (16–26). Despite its initial self-characterization as an apolitical publication: "Fern von aller raisonnirenden Politik und allem Meinungsstreit in Religions- und andern Sachen, wollen wir Euch in wahrhaft guten Erzählungen einführen in die Geschichte des Menschenherzens und der Völker" (Far from all political debates and disagreements in religious and other matters we want to introduce you to truly good stories about the history of the human heart and the world's peoples) (1853, 1), the *Gartenlaube* was clearly perceived by its contemporaries to be a liberal magazine.

4. Circulation statistics are available in Barth (cols. 184–86).

5. John Breuilly provides a clear introduction in English to the complicated history of the national idea in nineteenth-century Germany.

6. My interest in the institution of the press has been inspired by Benedict Anderson's thesis concerning the role of print capitalism in the ability of a community of readers to imagine themselves as a unified, homogeneous entity.

7. This objective was stated on the first page of the first issue of the *Gartenlaube* (1853, 1).

8. "Sie dem deutschen Volke als neuerworbene Schätze darzubringen, ist eine erfreuliche Arbeit, denn wir können nicht Liebes und Gutes genug von unserem Vaterlande kennen lernen, um es immer höher und heiliger zu halten."

9. "Gleichwie dieses die letzte Terassenstufe vor den Schweizeralpen ist"; "Auf der äussersten Linken im Osten schliesst der Hohenstaufen mit seinem öden Gipfel, auf der äussersten Rechten im Westen der Hohenzollern mit seinen luftigen Spitzen das Gemälde ab."

10. "Doch haben wir uns mit eigenen Augen . . . überzeugen können"; "davon ist uns keine Kunde geworden"; "eine Urkunde des Kaisers Maximilian I. aus Worms vom 17. September 1495."

11. "Welch ein Wohlgefühl;" "im reichsten Glanze"; "glänzen und blitzen unter dem schönsten Frühlingshimmel."

12. English translation quoted in Snyder (144–46).

13. This characterization clearly included German Austrians in the idea of the German nation. Peter Alter points out that this conception of a greater Germany (*Grossdeutschland*) was still prevalent among the large majority of German nationalists in the 1830s and 1840s. Other authors of the 1840s, such as Max Schneckenberger and Nikolaus Becker, wrote in more explicitly chauvinistic tones about a geographical centering of Germany. Their impassioned lyrics about defending the Rhine River as German made no attempt to hide an anti-French aspect of defining the nation. In the context of their time, however, these songs were all tied to the predominantly liberal goal of establishing a unified German nation-state based on liberal principles and often with no concern for the authority of existing German kingdoms and principalities (Alter 107).

14. Langewiesche outlines the political groups at midcentury that favored either the greater German (*grossdeutsch*) nation-state that would include the German-speaking parts of the Hapsburg Empire or the smaller German (*kleindeutsch*) nation-state under the leadership of Prussia (73–77).

15. *Gartenlaube* articles on Tyrol appeared, entitled "Tirol: Aus hoher Region" (Tyrol: From the High Region) (1871, 144 ff.); "Tirol: In den Gletscherspalten" (Tyrol: In the Crevasses) (1872, 61 ff.); "Aus den Tiroler Bergen" (From the Tyrolian Mountains) (1872, 143 ff.); "Der Bregenzer Wald" (The Forest of Bregenz) (1872, 188 ff.); "Bei den Granatenklauber" (With the Garnet Gatherers) (1872, 505 ff.); "Das Jagen" (Hunting) (1872, 534 ff.).

16. For a thorough discussion of the role of ethnicity in national identity, see Smith.

17. For a history of German emigration, see Bade.

18. Examples of this included discussions of Peru (1867, 815–16), Chile (1868, 496), and Venezuela (1869, 690).

19. "Das Unding des deutschen Bundes kann dabei [beim Schützen der deutschen Auswanderer] natürlich nicht in Betracht kommen."

20. "Und seien Sie versichert, dass wir in Haus und Herzen treue, redliche Deutsche bleiben!"

21. "Wieder haben wir den Beweis, dass fremde Nationen sich immer nach Deutschen umsehen, wenn sie eine Vertrauensstelle mit irgend wem besetzen wollen."

22. Although actual emigration to Brazil paled in comparison with that to the United States, it was nonetheless the second most popular destination for German emigrants. According to Klaus J. Bade, 89 percent of German emigration between 1847 and 1914

was to the United States, and only 2 percent was to Brazil (Bade 270). This fact, combined with the much more "foreign" and exotic character of the Brazilian geography, climate, and culture, made it an intriguing place for the magazine's exploration of German identity abroad.

23. "Weihnachts-Erinnerungen aus Brasilien." This example of the transmission of German culture to other parts of the globe is a story (published at Christmas time, 1879) of a German who had spent fourteen years in Brazil (1879, 848–52). "Drüben im Lande der Palmen feiert man auch Weihnachten, aber das ist nur ein schwacher Abglanz der Weihnachtslust, welche hier von Jung und Alt empfunden wird" (Over there in the land of palms Christmas is also celebrated, but that is only a faint reflection of the Christmas joy that is felt here by young and old) (1879, 848). The assertion of Brazilian inadequacy compared to German traditions runs throughout the essay, as in the problems of creating a Christmas tree in the tropics and complaints about the absurdly hot Christmas weather.

24. "Die Schätze, welche die unermesslichen Wälder an den Ufern jener Riesenströme des Amazonas, Orinoco und Parana heute noch bergen, und wodurch unserer Industrie ganz neue Materialien an prächtigen Hölzern, textilen Fasern, Farbstoffen, Harzen, Oelen, unserer Heilkunde neue Arzneimittel an die Hand gegeben werden könnten, die Aufschlüsse, welche den Naturwissenschaften aus einem eingehenderen Studium wenig bekannter Thierformen erwachsen würde" (1875, 478).

25. "Schöner und angenehmer kann es der Forscher, wie unsere Illustration ihn darstellt, mit dem Sextanten oder vielmehr dem Reflexionskreise in der Hand und im Begriffe, eine Sonnenhöhe zu messen, wohl nicht treffen. Unter den gewaltigen Wedeln einer Uauassú-Palme (Attalea) wird da der leichte Tisch aufgeschlagen, der die sorgsam gehüteten Chronometer trägt. Weithin schweift der Blick vom hohen Ufer über den breiten Strom und seine palmengekrönten Inseln."

26. "Ein Strassenbau und die Anlage einer deutschen Colonie in Brasilien, II" (Construction of a Road and the Layout of a German Colony in Brazil, II), by F. Keller-Leuzinger (1884, 299– 301).

27. Keller-Leuzinger proclaims that German engineers, "who led the great work to its happy conclusion in the course of seven years" (welche die grosse Arbeit im Laufe von sieben Jahren glücklich zu Ende führten), had been called in to construct the road after the French had proved incapable of the task (1884, 299).

28. "Sie würden nichts weiter thun, als ein dem Mutterlande verlorenes Element an jenen Südgestaden absetzen, damit es sich brasilianisire, d.h. als Dünger für eine Mischlingsrace diene, der es versagt ist, jemals eine erhebliche Rolle in dem grossen Völkerdrama zu übernehmen."

29. A similar argument has been made about *National Geographic* and the United States. See Lutz and Collins.

30. There is not enough space here to discuss adequately the representation of German colonial involvement by the popular press. I do address this in a larger work in progress on the *Gartenlaube* and images of the nation. In his work on "Colonial Space" in German South West Africa, John Noyes discusses the discourse of colonialism in literature of the late nineteenth century.

31. A detailed examination of German geographical magazines could no doubt also yield fascinating insights into the use and importance of geography for the presentation

of national identity. An important and popular geographical magazine, *Globus,* first published in 1862, followed the fate of German emigrants in America, Australia, and elsewhere. Like the *Gartenlaube,* it advocated the maintenance of German culture abroad.

32. This dual claim was summarized in a statement from the first issue of 1861. The editorship announced that the *Gartenlaube* had reached a circulation of 100,000 and that it was the first periodical publication in Germany to do so. It then went on to credit this mass distribution to the German content and national sentiments of the magazine (1861, 1).

33. This could certainly be considered part of what Eric Hobsbawm has called the national "invention of tradition."

34. This book, as part of Riehl's three-volume *Natural History of the German People* published between 1851 and 1855, went to twelve editions. See Schama (112–16).

35. Soja quotes Foucault's statement that some colonies may function not so much as illusions for social identity but as compensation (16). This image has inspired me to think of about the institution of the mass media in a new light.

WORKS CITED

Alter, Peter. *Nationalismus.* Frankfurt: Suhrkamp, 1985.

Anderson, Benedict. *Imagined Communities: Reflections on the Origin and Spread of Nationalism.* 2d ed. New York: Verso, 1991.

Bade, Klaus J. "Die deutsche überseeische Massenauswanderung im 19. und frühen 20. Jahrhundert: Bestimmungsfaktoren und Entwicklungsbedingungen." In *Auswanderer—Wanderarbeiter—Gastarbeiter: Bevölkerung, Arbeitsmarkt und Wanderung in Deutschland seit der Mitte des 19. Jahrhunderts,* ed. Klaus J. Bade. 2 vols. Ostfildern: Scripta Mercaturae Verlag, 1984. 1:259–99.

Barth, Dieter. "Das Familienblatt—ein Phänomen der Unterhaltungspresse des 19. Jahrhunderts: Beispiele zur Gründungs- und Verlagsgeschichte." *Archiv für Geschichte des Buchwesens* 15 (1975): cols. 121–316.

Breuilly, John. "The National Idea in Modern German History." In *The State of Germany: The National Idea in the Making, Unmaking and Remaking of a Modern Nation-State,* ed. John Breuilly. New York: Longman, 1992. 1–28.

Brubaker, Rogers. *Citizenship and Nationhood in France and Germany.* Cambridge: Harvard UP, 1992.

Die Gartenlaube. Leipzig: Ernst Keil Verlag, 1853–78; Leipzig: Ernst Keil Nachfolger, 1878–89.

Hobsbawm, Eric J. "Introduction: Inventing Traditions." In *The Invention of Tradition,* ed. Eric Hobsbawm and Terence Ranger. Cambridge: Cambridge UP, 1983. 1–14.

Inglis, Fred. *Cultural Studies.* Oxford: Blackwell, 1993.

Langewiesche, Dieter. "Germany and the National Question in 1848." In *The State of Germany. The National Idea in the Making, Unmaking and Remaking of a Modern Nation-State,* ed. John Breuilly. New York: Longman, 1992. 60–79.

Lutz, Catherine A., and Jane L. Collins. *Reading National Geographic.* Chicago: U of Chicago P, 1993.

Noyes, John. *Colonial Space: Spatiality in the Discourse of German South West Africa, 1884–1915.* Chur: Warwood, 1992.

Pratt, Mary Louise. *Imperial Eyes: Travel Writing and Transculturation.* New York: Routledge, 1992.

Rumley, Dennis, and Julian V. Minghi, eds. *The Geography of Border Landscapes.* New York: Routledge, 1991.

Schama, Simon. *Landscape and Memory.* New York: Knopf, 1995.

Smith, Anthony D. *The Ethnic Origins of Nations.* Oxford: Blackwell, 1986.

Snyder, Louis L., ed. *Documents of German History.* New Brunswick: Rutgers UP, 1958.

Soja, Edward M. *Postmodern Geographies: The Reassertion of Space in Critical Social Theory.* New York: Verso, 1993.

Zang, Hermann. *Die "Gartenlaube" als politisches Organ: Belletristik, Bilderwerk und literarische Kritik im Dienste der liberalen Politik 1860–1880.* Coburg: Rossteutscher, 1935.

CHAPTER 11

Consumer Culture Is in Need of Attention: German Cultural Studies and the Commercialization of the Past

Alon Confino

Alon Confino, trained in history, crosses disciplinary boundaries in his work with the ease and pleasure reminiscent of the subjects of this article: tourists. Yet his intent is not mere amusement. He seeks a rigorous treatment of this important historical phenomenon and, therefore, utilizes a wide variety of available resources: from exhibition catalogs and periodicals aimed at the masses to the archives of professional associations and the scholarly undertakings of sociologists. These sources enable Confino to explore the nexus of tourism and consumer culture in late-nineteenth-century Germany.

Confino is able to situate his eclectic cultural history in the recent literature produced by scholars in other national fields—from Simon Schama and his erudite investigations of Dutch material culture to Rosalind Williams and her study of mass consumption in nineteenth-century France. But the German field, Confino notes, is lacking in studies of consumer culture. This shortcoming is surprising in light of the German people's economic success (and concomitant material rewards) as well as their penchant for expressing themselves through their practices as consumers. Confino's focus on tourism makes it evident that this behavior, which the Germans entered into with such enthusiasm as to become world leaders, provides a subject that is tremendously rich in its interpretive potential. Confino, then, merges high and low cultural sources in this engaging study of a quintessentially German activity.

The study of consumer culture has recently made important headway in the United States, France, and Britain, though in Germany it still remains on the historiographical sidelines. This essay draws attention to the potential of the topic of consumer culture for understanding German history and identity by exploring the commercialization of the past in modern Germany. This investigation requires a research object linking consumer society to modern perceptions of the past. I have therefore chosen to focus on tourism, for tourism is a child of consumer society and a fundamental social practice through which people construct ideas about the world—and about the past. To illustrate my argument regarding the fundamental nexus in Germany between consumer culture, tourism, and perceptions of the past I have decided to focus on the period before 1914, namely, on the prehistory of German mass tourism and mass consumption. For, if consumer culture, through tourism, shaped Germans' perceptions of the past before 1914, we can readily understand the significance of this topic to German history as the twentieth century progressed.

I

In 1911 the Berlin Zoologischer Garten hosted a successful exhibition, whose cultural significance was obscured by its dreary name, the Internationale Ausstellung für Reise- und Fremdenverkehr (International Travel and Tourism Exhibition). European countries and the German states were asked to represent in large pavilions their industrial and technological achievements, natural and historical sites, and common ways of life. Small request indeed! These were (and still are), after all, the very elements of modern identity and habitat. Judging by the throngs of visitors, the participating countries succeeded in communicating their identity to the public in clear and familiar images and symbols. Particularly popular among visitors were reconstructions of past environments. At the entrance to Württemberg's pavilion, for example, stood a life-size mannequin of a woman dressed in a Black Forest *Tracht,* the traditional dress. Inside were a Black Forest *Kaffeestube* and a wine cabinet from Esslingen. There visitors, seated at peasant wooden tables, were waited on by *Tracht*-dressed blonde Swabian women. On the walls hung tiles of old peasant art and colorful peasant pottery. This assemblage of objects was meant to appeal to an urban public that viewed folklore with the same fascination it viewed foreign countries. Berliners were enchanted by the *Trachten,* which, after all, were about as common in the street of the metropolis as traditional dress of an African tribe (*Schwäbische Merkur*).

There was something inherently modern in the Berlin exhibition: the fashioning of modern identities through tourism and consumer culture. The exhibition followed a familiar model (on a reduced scale) of world exhibitions, which developed after 1851 in the British Great Exhibitions, the French Expositions Universelles, and the American World Fairs (Greenhalgh). Walter Benjamin's observation that "world exhibitions were places of pilgrimage to the fetish Commodity" was also true for the modest Berlin tourism exhibition (165). In these spaces of entertainment everything was a commodity, including the nation and the past. The Württemberg exhibit in Berlin, for example, was a site to display concisely what was construed as the essence of Swabianness and an invented Swabianness at that: the proudly displayed Betzinger *Tracht* was a tradition invented after 1861 (*Trautes Heim,* 58–60).

The exhibition in Berlin was designed to arouse people's desire to travel to other places, to experience unknown pasts. The display of Württemberg's identity to attract foreign tourists is interesting in itself. Even more intriguing for scholars is the decision of the Association for Tourism in Württemberg and Hohenzollern (Württembergisch-Hohenzollerische Vereinigung für Fremdenverkehr) to use tourism as a means of cultivating local identity among Württembergers themselves. Opened in 1912, the Swabian Exhibition for Travel and Tourism (Schwäbische Landesausstellung für Reise- und Fremdenverkehr) was significantly larger than Württemberg's pavilion in Berlin. It featured, among other displays, a *Schwarzwald Kaffeestube* and a *schwäbische Trinkstube.* The exhibition catalog, a handsome booklet of one hundred pages, read like a guide for "how to become a Swabian in several easy steps" (*Bunte Blätter*). It included sections about history, landscape, art, *Trachten,* wines, and cuisine.

That seventy thousand people visited the exhibition and thousands more read the catalog (published in sixty thousand copies) should raise the historian's curiosity. Why were Württembergers attracted to a space of entertainment that could easily be derided as commercial and artificial, that merely reproduced the reality outside the exhibition? Why drink a *Viertele* and eat *Spätzle* in the exhibition's *Stüble,* an artificial environment constructed especially for the event, when a "real" *Wirtschäftle* existed just around the corner? What did merchant Herbst mean when he observed at the closing ceremony that the Swabian exhibition allowed people "to get to know one's own *Heimat* and to appreciate its worth" (*Schwäbische Kronik*)?

We can do more than speculate about the meaning of the Swabian exhibition—and, more generally, of tourism and consumer culture—for the making of German identity. Gustav Ströhmfeld, the official writer of the tourist associations of Stuttgart and Württemberg, an organizer of the Swabian exhibition and editor of its catalog, observed as early as 1910 that tourism is a matter of culture, "and one cannot create culture, for it is the outcome of a glorious development . . . the sum of world-shaking events, it is history. . . . [People travel] because [in traveling] they find a link to the past. . . . In this sense, tourism is a problem of culture" (*Gedenkschrift,* 19). He further articulated his views in an essay "The Tasks and Duties of the Cultivation of Tourism" ("Aufgaben und Pflichten der Fremdenverkehrspflege"). He argued that the essence of tourism was to accomplish national integration and to raise national consciousness: "We therefore look forward to the increase of tourism not only from the point of view of economic advantage, for we are entitled to hope for a national advantage: as the Germans actively embrace *Heimat* feelings [*Heimatgefühle*] and national belonging [*nationale Zusammengehörigkeit*], so will our German Empire grow stronger from within" (*Aufgaben,* 70).

The notion that tourism was a fundamental cultural practice was shared outside political centers such as Berlin and Stuttgart. Around 1900 tourist associations (*Fremdenverkehrsvereine*) were founded across Württemberg in small, provincial localities. A veritable "identity market" developed, in which communities strove to gain revenues and attract tourists by marketing their landscape, folklore, and past. Significantly, the competition in "the market of the past" led to close working relationships between tourist associations and historical associations (*Geschichtsvereine*). The commercialization of the past in this period was obviously not unique to Württemberg. All over Germany local communities attempted to attract tourists by marketing their past as worthy of a visit. Thus, the inauguration in Scheessel (Lower Saxony) in 1913 of the new local *Heimat* museum included a *Heimatfest* and an exhibition of *Heimatkunst* material objects. The program in the local hall featured traditional local dances and a play about peasant life; tickets were available at prices between 75 pfennigs to 1.50 marks. The entire event attracted overwhelmingly tourists from Hamburg and Bremen who came by train to "experience" how their ancestors had lived. The town, by putting its past on the market, generated revenues. And the local newspaper observed philosophically: "unfortunately, such *Heimatfeste* and profit [*Geldverdienen*] hang these days closely together" (*Zevener Zeitung*).

II

Gustav Ströhmfeld insightfully understood eighty years ago that the relations between consumption, tourism, and the past are fundamentally a problem of culture. Scholars of consumer society have understood this as well. They have explored the symbolic elements of consumer culture and material objects and the role of cultural commodities as belongings that help people construct identities. As Grant McCracken forcefully argues, consumers "use the meaning of consumer goods to express cultural categories and principles, cultivate ideals, create and sustain life-styles, construct notions of the self, and create (and survive) social change" (xi). Simon Schama's magisterial study *The Embarrassment of Riches* shows how the "lust for consumption" in seventeenth-century Dutch society was simultaneously a source of national pride and anxiety (304). Schama demonstrates how the Dutch constructed from the riches of their society—from food, drink, tobacco, household goods, and other commodities—a national identity that reconciled abundance with civic consciousness.

Yet historians of Germany, it appears, have not followed Ströhmfeld's lead. An evaluation of the historiography of German consumer culture is unfortunately short and uneventful, for until very recently historians have neglected the topic. This is best demonstrated in recent studies about the German bourgeoisie, such as the three volumes edited by Jürgen Kocka (1988). This distinguished study does not include even one contribution about consumption and consumer culture. Arguably, it is impossible to understand the social, political, cultural, and economic making of any bourgeoisie without discussing habits, perceptions, and values of consumption. The topic of consumer culture is thus one of the most under-researched and promising fields of inquiry in German cultural studies. Theodore Zeldin, a historian of France, wrote that "the consumer . . . has yet to find a historian" (epigraph, in Williams).[1] The British, French, and American consumers have found in recent years their historians, but the German consumer is still waiting.

Moreover, consumer culture has always been inextricably connected to national identity. But, while Germany has developed since the last third of the nineteenth century into an industrial powerhouse, the relations between the "world of goods" and German identity have remained a terra incognita (see Douglas and Isherwood). Charles Maier has recently argued in his study of the "historians' dispute" (*Historikerstreit*) that "West German nationhood meant production. Nor was this a new phenomenon" (8). But he neither develops this argument nor connects consumer culture before and after 1945 to problems of German identity. In *A German Identity, 1770–1990* Harold James explores the connections between economic development and German identity. After the mid-nineteenth century, he argues, the performance of the economy "became crucial to Germans' view of themselves" (216). But in the book the scope of this intriguing idea is limited because he focuses on the reactions of intellectuals to the fluctuations of German economy, not on how Germans constructed meanings through consumer goods and activities. Significantly, the entries "consumption" and "consumer" do not appear in the book's index.

At this point the intrigued scholar may justifiably ask, how exactly should one explore the relations between national identity and consumer culture? This field of inquiry is wide open for a multitude of research topics. Let me suggest briefly three. The first concerns the ways in which Germans changed the representations of the past as a result of consumer culture. In Scheessel and at the travel exhibitions, history and tourism converged as the portrayal of the past became a business enterprise. How did tourist associations change and invent historical attractions to remain competitive in the "market of the past"? How did the organizers in Scheessel "improve" their past to attract the upper-class tourists from Hamburg in search of an "authentic" German past?

A second topic shifts our view from the institutions of tourism to the role of tourism as a shaper of a shared, and partly invented, German national past. Behind the activity of tourists and tourist associations was the idea that it was necessary to cultivate the German past. But what kind of a past? A myth of origins for the immemorial nation? A past that reconciled regional and national identities? And whose past? Only the idealized rural past displayed in the Black Forest *Kaffeestube?* And which pasts were to be obliterated on the way?

These questions became increasingly important after 1918, when the petite bourgeoisie and working class began for the first time to travel on a regular basis. And these questions obviously remained significant during the Third Reich, when the Nazis took tourism extremely seriously. They used the tourist and leisure organization Kraft durch Freude (Strength through Joy) to inculcate ideology and to win tacit consent for the regime. How, then, did these social and political changes shape the representation of the past in tourist attractions? More important, how were relations of power in German society expressed in and formed by touristic representations of the past?

The third topic turns to the tourists themselves and explores how tourism and consumer culture shaped the historical consciousness of Germans. Did the travel exhibitions nourish a sentiment of the German present as an extension of the past or as inherently different from it? Or did they foster among Germans ahistorical notions that entailed anachronisms and a flattening of the inherent difference between past and present—both of which constitute elements of any myth of origins? If tourism did emphasize the essential alienation between past and present, in what ways, then, was the past relevant in German society?

An investigation of the mental world of German tourists and how they constructed perceptions of the past is a difficult project that demands a great variety of sources. The archive of the newly founded Institut für Tourismus at the Free University of Berlin has invaluable material. Other essential sources are tourist travel guides: famous ones such as *Baedecker* and, no less important, those published in local and provincial communities. Documents of local, regional, and national tourist associations are an excellent source to tap tourists' motivations and institutional initiatives. Professional tourist journals, such as *Archiv für Fremdenverkehr,* contain a wealth of information. Other significant sources, which present a particular methodological challenge for historians, are tourist images: posters, postcards, advertising material, and images from travel guides, to list some of the available iconographic sources. All images are a fundamental source for understanding the collective mentality of people in the past. Tourist images have played a significant role in marketing a conception of the past; when they succeed, they are desired by many consumers.

III

The topic of consumer culture is in need of attention. Think of the following proposition: when individuals reply that they wish for no presents for Christmas, we think either that they are insincere or that they depart from normal standards of society to the point of being deviants or eccentrics.[2] We live in a world of an insatiable desire for goods. Mass consumption and consumer culture have been a constitutive element of modernity, of mass culture and popular culture, of the making of gender, class, religious, regional, and other German identities. This world of material and immaterial goods (such as the past) should be embraced by German cultural studies.

Moreover, consumer culture and tourism can do more than simply introduce cultural studies into the mainstream of German history; these topics can also transform cultural studies into a more historical discipline. A major contribution of the new cultural history has been the notion that the past is culturally constructed, politically contested, and open to various interpretations by different groups in society. This notion has been helpful in thinking about the German past. What is often missing in studies about the construction of the past in, say, a museum or a film is the connection between the representation of the past and the reception or rejection of this past. Thus, studies focus on cultural institutions (such as a museum) rather than on the cultural habits that are associated with and practiced in the museum. They focus on cultural products and less on cultural processes. In short, the study of representation is taken as an equivalent to doing cultural studies. But, as William James observed, "a belief is a habit of action."[3] The past should be explored not only as a representation but as a sociocultural mode of action. This essay illustrates that it is possible to explore how German perceptions of the past evolved into a "habit of action" by focusing on two of the most celebrated social practices of modernity—consumption and tourism.

Our profession is concerned with thinking about the past and about culture and with discriminating among these ideas. For most of us traveling is a favorite pursuit. And even those of us who dislike traveling do so nonetheless. When we think about the connections between the past and travel we might remember the words of John Stuart Mill: "In history, as in traveling, men usually see only what they already had in their minds; and few learn much from history, who do not bring much with them to its study" (qtd. in Newman 49). By associating consumer culture and perceptions of the past, we can enrich our world both as historians and as tourists.

NOTES

1. Williams's book, although interesting, cannot satisfy the consumer either.
2. I borrow this example from the excellent study by Campbell (235).
3. I am indebted to Allan Megill for this citation.

WORKS CITED

Benjamin, Walter. "Grandville or the World Exhibitions." In *Charles Baudelaire: A Lyric Poet in the Era of High Capitalism*. Trans. Harry Zohn. London: NLB, 1973.

Bunte Blätter aus Württemberg und Hohenzollern: Ausstellungs-Katalog. Stuttgart: Würrtembergisch-Hohenzollerischen Vereinigung für Fremdenverkehr, 1912.

Campbell, Colin. *The Romantic Ethic and the Spirit of Modern Consumerism*. Oxford: Blackwell, 1993.

Douglas, Mary, and Baron Isherwood. *The World of Goods: Toward an Anthropology of Consumption*. New York: Basic Books, 1978.

Greenhalgh, Paul. *Ephemeral Vistas: The Expositions Universelles, Great Exhibitions and World's Fairs, 1851–1939*. Manchester: Manchester UP, 1988.

Kocka, Jürgen, ed. *Bürgertum im 19. Jahrhundert*. 3 vols. Munich: DTV, 1988.

James, Harold. *A German Identity, 1770–1990*. London: Weidenfeld and Nicolson, 1989.

Newman, Gerald. *The Rise of English Nationalism: A Cultural History, 1740–1830*. New York: St. Martin's, 1987.

Maier, Charles. *The Unmasterable Past. History, Holocaust, and German National Identity*. Cambridge: Harvard UP, 1988.

McCracken, Grant. *Culture and Consumption: New Approaches to the Symbolic Character of Consumer Goods and Activities*. Bloomington: Indiana UP, 1990.

Schama, Simon. *The Embarrassment of Riches*. Berkeley: U of California P, 1988.

Schwäbische Kronik, 11 July 1912.

Schwäbische Merkur 156 (3 April 1911); 162 (6 April 1911).

Ströhmfeld, Gustav. *Gedenkschrift des Vereins für Fremdenverkehr in Stuttgart e.V. zur Feier seines 25 jährigen Bestehens 1885–1910*. Stuttgart: Munz and Geiger, 1910.

———. *Aufgaben und Pflichten der Fremdenverkehrspflege*. Stuttgart: Published by the Württembergisch-Hohenzollerische Vereinigung für Fremdenverkehr, 1911.

Trautes Heim. Heitere Gefühle bei der Ankunft auf dem Lande. Bilder Schwäbischen Landlebens im 19. Jahrhundert: Katalog zur gleichnamigen Ausstellung im Württembergischen Landesmuseum, Stuttgart 1983. Tübingen: n.p., 1983.

Williams, Rosalind. *Dream Worlds: Mass Consumption in Nineteenth-Century France*. Berkeley: U of California P, 1982.

Zevener Zeitung, 26 August 1913.

CHAPTER 12

Colonial Legends, Postcolonial Legacies

Susanne Zantop

While postcolonialist studies have been central to recent endeavors in American, British, and French cultural studies, the investigation of the German colonial period and its legacy are only now coming to be recognized as a key component to understanding German national identity. Though it is true that some German historians made an effort to interrogate the colonialist past as early as the 1960s, German society seems to have ignored the implications of colonialism and colonialist thinking until the recent outbreaks of xenophobia.

In this essay Susanne Zantop suggests that contemporary Germany pays a high price for continued ignorance of its colonial legacy: she singles out the violent attacks against asylum seekers in Hoyerswerda in 1991 as representative of the literally thousands of apparently racially motivated incidents in the years since unification. These are likely to continue, Zantop implies, until Germany recognizes itself as the immigrant nation it in fact is. White ethnic Germans must learn that peoples of color are sometimes Germans too. As Zantop argues further, German "xenophobia" is part of a larger pattern of racism that includes, but by no means is limited to, the Holocaust.

Previous justifications for ignoring German colonialism are anchored in the brief life of official German colonies themselves (1884–1918). But Zantop points out that not only were there much earlier colonialist endeavors, but, perhaps even more important, the idea of colonies—"colonial fantasies" is Zantop's phrase—"pre-dated, accompanied, and followed" actual colonialism. Like the other writers in part 4, Zantop looks to various sources to trace these fantasies, sources from "high" culture (like the writings of Herder or Enzensberger) and "popular" culture (feature films). Like the other writers, too, she combines close reading of a text (defined broadly) with inquiry into a specific historical context. What Zantop discovers in disparate and yet ideologically linked historical moments is "triangular thinking" (a concept she borrows and extends from Katrin Sieg), which allows Germans to create an identification and alliance with oppressed peoples (e.g., black Africans or Native Americans) against an "oppressor" (e.g., the United Kingdom or the United States) without recognizing their own participation in oppressive practices. This playing down of German imperialist involvement continues today. Finally, Zantop, like Bammer, is suspicious of some contemporary German leftist intellectuals' anti-imperialist rhetoric. They too are engaging in centuries-old triangular thinking, which looks for and finds blame with others. Instead of too little Eurocentrism, Zantop provocatively suggests, there is perhaps not enough. That is to say, Germany must look at itself in the context of Europe, recognizing that it, too, has a colonial legacy that will not dissipate until it is acknowledged and worked through.

Susanne Zantop is particularly prepared to conduct such a study. As a native of Germany, she has lived for extended periods in Spain, Latin America, and the United States. Her graduate studies in Comparative Literature focused on Spanish as well as German and on history as well as literature. Her investigation of power structures has been honed through publications on German women writers and the colonial imagination. She has most recently published a monograph titled Colonial Fantasies *and coedited a volume on German postcolonialism,* The Imperialist Imagination.

One of the most disturbing events in postwar and post-Wall Germany has been circumscribed by the name of a small East German town, Hoyerswerda. In September 1991 a gang of young skinheads in Hoyerswerda terrorized several hundred asylum seekers, most of them from Africa and Asia, who had been living in shelters waiting for their status as political refugees to be recognized. After suffering five nights of attacks with stones, bottles, and explosives, the besieged foreigners moved out, while a mass of ordinary citizens of all ages, men and women, looked on—approvingly, at times even gleefully. Accounts and pictures of that event, which was followed by a series of further assaults against so-called *Ausländer* all over Germany in the months thereafter, sent shock waves through the country. What was the cause of these outbreaks of "neuer Fremdenhass," this *new* xenophobia, as *Der Spiegel* called it? Hadn't Germans proven, in over forty years of democratic interaction, that they were able to get along peacefully not just with one another but with "others" as well? Hadn't the new Germany been the model of hospitality, providing refuge to the oppressed

from all over the world? The answers to these pressing questions came with surprising speed and surprising uniformity: "Wir sind keine Fremdenhasser" (We
are *not* hostile to foreigners), a Social Democratic deputy said (*Der Spiegel* 40,
30 September 1991, 31). He and other commentators blamed the "excesses"
against foreigners on economic pressures, that is, on the fears and tensions resulting from an avalanche of impoverished peoples seeking refuge and jobs in
a recently united yet economically unstable Germany—and, by implication, on
the victims themselves. As for the skinheads, analysts agreed that they were
mostly underprivileged youths from broken homes, outcasts themselves, who
just needed someone further down the social ladder on whom to vent their
anger. In both cases responsibility and guilt rested with "them," not "us." But
what about the gleeful onlookers?

Racism was not considered a factor, at least not immediately. Any allegations that the hostilities were racially motivated were quickly brushed aside:
"How can there be racism if there are so few blacks?" "How can there be racism
after the Holocaust?" were the most widely heard responses. Few of the economic or sociopsychological explanations by the xenophobia experts took into
account the fact that the vast majority of victims were not just foreigners but
also people of color and that in several instances they were not even foreigners
but Germans—African Germans, Turkish Germans, German Gypsies—of
color. When these Germans of color finally spoke out, when they "showed their
colors," as the title of a recent publication put it (Opitz et al.), it became obvious that, while economic competition for scarce jobs may have contributed to
increasing tensions, race, or rather racism, provided the common link in all reported incidents. In the words of Sheila Mysorekar, one of the approximately
three thousand members of the newly founded "Initiative Black Germans" (Initiative Schwarze Deutsche): "For White Germans, Black stands for *Ausland,
Fremde,* non-German. . . . That's why there is supposedly no racism here, just
'xenophobia.' . . . Basically Germans have not progressed one step beyond
colonial times" (*Der Spiegel* 52, 23 December 1991, 56–57).

I

It is this connection between unacknowledged racism and un-worked-through
colonialism that I want to explore in this essay. To my mind it characterizes the
German "postcolonial" condition and directs the Germans' "postcolonial gaze"
(Lützeler) outward rather than inward. Collective amnesia produces statements
such as: "We are not an immigration country" in the face of centuries of de facto
immigration from the east, southeast, and south. It surfaces in utterances such
as "We are not racists" or "There is no such thing as a Black German," despite
evidence to the contrary (see Ayim). It also forms the basis for what has been
dubbed the "colonial legend": the conviction that the Germans were model col-

onizers who were deprived of their rightful colonial possessions by envious British; that they were kinder, gentler colonial masters, who were to live on as such in the memories of their grateful former subjects, particularly their "loyal" *askari* (Jacob 73; Solf 49–58). The *Brockhaus Konversationslexikon* of 1966 still finds it necessary to allude to that special relationship when it defines *askari* as "native African soldiers in colonial armies, e.g., the colored soldiers of the protective force [*Schutztruppe*] in German East Africa. They remained loyal to their leaders during World War I" [sie hielten während des 1. Weltkriegs zu ihren Führern, 1: 789, 1]. Apart from the fact that any form of the word *Führer* in 1966 had an ominous ring, the cryptic sentence "They remained loyal to their leaders" resonates with the legend of benign and enduring patriarchal relations among colonizer and colonized. This legend is the legacy not just of thirty years of German colonialism but of close to three hundred years of colonial fantasizing.

Indeed, the colonial fantasies that predated, accompanied, and followed colonialism produced the mind frame, or screen, that has been hampering a critical self-assessment to date. Colonial fantasies created what Katrin Sieg calls a "triangulated communicative structure" ("Ethnic Drag" 6). She defines this as a "theatre of identity in which the brown-white relationship pivots on an absent third party"; in other words: in which an alleged blood brotherhood between "Germans" and "Indians," for example, or the denunciation of U.S. imperialism obscures and displaces an exploration of the genocide perpetrated on Jews, the racism extended to dark-skinned *Ausländer,* or Germany's share in international corporate expansionism. While Sieg locates these triangular structurations in post-Holocaust Germany and links them directly to a desire for redemption (she uses the term *Wiedergutmachungsfantasien* [fantasies of absolution and restitution]), my own research suggests that they were present much earlier (*Colonial Fantasies*). In fact, triangular relationships with unnamed or absent third parties were constitutive of the German (and possibly not just German) colonialist imagination from the eighteenth century onward.[1]

Despite the brevity of the German colonial period—Germany held colonies in Africa (Togo, Cameroon, German East Africa, German Southwest Africa), Asia (Kiaochow), and the Pacific (German New Guinea, German Samoa, the Mariana, Caroline, and Marshall Islands) from 1884 to 1918—colonialism as an ideology was much more deeply ingrained than scholars have led us to believe.[2] The brevity and belatedness of the colonial period, which went hand in hand with the belatedness of German statehood, led to a curious mix of national and colonial myths in the minds of not just chauvinist nationalists but many liberal bourgeois. Involuntary colonial abstinence—the approximately three hundred small and medium-sized principalities that constituted "Germany" up to the nineteenth century did not have the financial, naval, or military power to acquire colonies—relegated the "colonial idea" to the powerful realm of desire and fiction. Antagonism and rivalry with the more developed colonizing powers France and England produced a sense of Germany as the underdog, the late-comer, in need of outdoing its peers. And the loss of the German colonies as a result of a lost war, with all its humiliating circumstances, generated revenge thinking: to reverse the "robbery" of German possessions became a national goal in the 1920s and 1930s, if only in theory (Smith 232–33; Schmokel).[3] The sense of insignificance as a nation, of having had no share in the "partition of the world," combined with the trauma of failed "German" ventures in the past, such as the short-lived occupation of South American territories by the Welser merchant house of Augsburg in the 1500s or the establishment of an African colony and a Caribbean slave trading post by the Great Elector of Prussia in the late 1600s (Schück),[4] nurtured the desire for another chance. This desire for reprieve was further enhanced by the "premature" decolonization from above in 1918–19, after which Germans sought to disprove British allegations, published in the *Blue Book,* that Germans were particularly cruel colonizers who deserved to be deprived of their colonies.[5] German colonialism in sum, therefore, was much more an imaginary configuration than a political stance. As such, it could develop unhampered and unchecked by colonial realities. It could become legendary and persistent.

The enforced abstention from imperialism, furthermore, created a special role for German "armchair colonialists": that of critical bystander who felt free to denounce and condemn the atrocities committed by others. It fostered a moral high ground, a sense of "difference," and a desire for action—"we" would not repeat the mistakes that "they" had made. This outsider status kept Germans from taking a good look at their own investment in colonialism and the politics of race, both before and after the actual acquisition of colonies in the 1880s. The unnamed "third" in the colonial triangles were, more often than not, the German onlookers themselves.

If the lack of colonies (the missed chance) and the loss of colonies (the "Versailler Diktat") colored the pre- and immediate postcolonial situation in Germany, respectively, the Holocaust profoundly affected "postcolonial" thinking in contemporary Germany.[6] As Sara Lennox has proposed, "the German focus on the Holocaust as the central and unavoidable fact of German history might occlude Germans' view of European colonialism and their own complicity as Europeans in it" ("Postcolonial" 5). And indeed, by embracing Europeanness as a means to escape a burdensome national identity, German intellectuals after 1945 often failed to examine the nationalist-colonialist legacy handed down by that very Europe. They preferred to concentrate instead on the imperialist practices of the United States, thereby (re)assuming the triangulated positionality many Germans had espoused in the past.

II

Triangular thinking occurred in different historical constellations and took various forms. An early example can be found in Herder's *Briefe zur Beförderung der Humanität* (Letters for the Promotion of Humanity) of 1793–97. In the tenth collection Herder launches his most extended critique of European colonialism to date. His tortured syntax seemingly implicates Germans as well:

> About Spanish cruelties, British avarice, and the cold insolence of the Dutch—celebrated in heroic epics during the delirium of conquest— books have recently been written which do them so little honor that if there were a spirit of European community anywhere except in books, *we* would all have to be ashamed before most peoples of the earth of *our crimes against humanity.* Show me one country where Europeans arrived and did not become guilty of sinning against its unarmed, trusting people through restrictions, unjust wars, avarice, lies, oppression, diseases and harmful gifts, perhaps for centuries to come! (234; emph. added)[7]

Yet the letters immediately preceding and following Herder's colonialist invective modify his wholesale condemnation of an all-encompassing European enterprise. While the old Germans were indeed implicated in colonial expansion ("The old Prussians were annihilated; Lithuanians, Estonians, and Latvians under poorest conditions still curse, in their hearts, their oppressors, the Germans" [234]), contemporary Germans are innocent. In letter 113, in the enclosed poem "Der deutsche Nationalruhm" (German National Glory), and in letter 115, Herder reiterates Germans' childlike innocence, their outsider position in Europe ("We Germans are the poor youth, the weak child" [222]). In their innocence and weakness the Germans resemble the colonized Indians and the enslaved Africans. If the first glory of a nation is innocence, the second, Herder says, is moderation:

> The second glory is moderation.
> The Hindus' and Peruvians' pain,
> The rage of Blacks, the roasted Montezuma
> Of Mexico: all call to heaven still
> Begging to be avenged!—
> Believe me, friend, no Zeus with his choir
> Of gods will visit a people, that
> Burdened with guilt, blood and sins
> and gold and diamonds, sits down to dine!
> He joins instead the frugal meal
> Of quiet Ethiopians *and Germans.*
> (225)[8]

Political weakness thus translates into moral strength. Zeus will reward with his presence not the "greedy" English nor the "cruel" Spaniards but the "quiet Ethiopians and Germans." As a noncolonial (non)nation, Germans have not heaped guilt on their heads. It is colonial Spain and the "new Carthage," merchant England, that merit Herder's particular scorn, and so would the "poor, guiltless Germans" (251), should they follow the British footsteps. Significantly, the reiteration of Germany's colonial innocence appears next to a short characterization of Las Casas's indictment of "Spanish atrocities." Like other German observers of his time, Herder overlooks the cruelties committed by German conquistadors in the sixteenth century included in Las Casas's report (Zantop, *Colonial Fantasies* 1), focusing instead on the moral depravity of the other European colonial powers.

Curiously, France does not enter the equation, although in the eyes of Herder's contemporaries France's cultural and political "imperialism" constituted a major threat for Germany's burgeoning revival as a *Kulturnation*.[9] By pointing to the past and present colonial powers, Spain and Britain, and by associating Germany with the colonized, Herder thus establishes two overlapping colonial triangles with absent thirds. The European triangle does not name the true "culprit" as far as Germany is concerned: France. Nor is France mentioned in the transatlantic triangle that pits colonial powers against "Negroes" and "Indians"—although France, at the time, was involved in a major colonial battle on the island of Saint-Domingue (the "Haitian Revolution"), where England was siding with the rebelling blacks for its own imperialist purposes. By associating the Germans with the colonized rather than with European colonizers, Herder suggests that Spain and England are just stand-ins for that colonial power that threatens Germany most—its immediate neighbor across the Rhine, France.

The focus on England and Spain as perpetrators and Germans as innocent victims, in the same league as Africans and Native Americans, furthermore distracts from the curious combination of ideological anticolonialism and colonialist practice that the emerging power on German soil, Prussia, was engaging in, in its attempt to round out and "colonize" its newly acquired territories and populations. Bernd Fischer aptly characterizes the anticolonialist colonialism of the national project, which he finds operative in Herder, Fichte, and Kleist's concept of nation, as a clash between "the myth of anti-colonial self-liberation and self-determination and a decidedly colonialist politics towards the interior and towards the exterior" (228). The triangulated communicative structures that suggest Germany's elevated moral stature and desire for emancipation serve to preclude any critical examination of that internal contradiction. The fantasy Herder's triangulated construction suggests is a fantasy of national vindication.

III

More insidious, overdetermined forms of triangulation can be observed in Germany's immediate postcolonial period, the years from 1920 to 1945. In the 1941 film *Ohm Krüger,* which narrates the struggle of the Boers against the

British between 1899 and 1902, for example, Hans Steinhoff creates a complicated set of overlapping configurations that position Germans as moral judge
and avenger in one. While, on the surface, the film adheres to historical facts,
it generates in its viewers a total identification with the plight of the Boers, who,
in their rustic blond patriarchal probity, resemble any generic Germans of *Blut
und Boden* Heimat films. The film makes no attempt at historical contextual-
ization but concentrates the action on British atrocities and Boer suffering: how
greedy and devious British imperialists drive the peaceful settlers to armed resistance, destroy their homes through a scorched-earth policy, and imprison
their women and children in concentration camps, where they are left to die
from starvation and typhoid fever. As Ohm Krüger reminds his (German) audience, future peoples are called upon to avenge this massacre of the innocent:
"England, England, you will be judged!" (*Ohm Krüger* 329). At the end of the
film the camera moves over an apocalyptic landscape "reminiscent of Goya's
Horrors of War" (347), while a chorus of voices curses England. The scene of
the horrors dissolves into the face of blind Ohm Krüger turned visionary who
prophesies the end of all wars—"when the war for justice is over":

> And yet, I believe: so much blood cannot have been shed in vain; so many
> tears cannot have been vainly cried, and so much heroic courage cannot
> have been in vain. For if world history has any meaning, it can only be
> this: A new future of all peoples founded on the profound longing for
> peace, which will eventually come when the war for justice is over. (348)

Throughout the film Britain is portrayed as a "poisonous spider" (328)
building a spiderweb empire and preying on innocent victims. As Ohm
Krüger's disembodied voice admonishes his spectators:

> and truth must be said, and it cries to the heavens. Wherever there is a na-
> tion on this globe pursing its work peacefully and achieving prosperity and
> recognition, there, one day, appears the Brit and steals away from it the
> fruits of its industry. *What happens to us now* happened to the Irish, the In-
> dians, the Egyptians. And it will happen to many more people—even *you*
> will recognize this. (327; emph. added)

The wording of this speech establishes an association with the present of
1941, the war years, and the planned attack on England. The cinematic technique of dissolve used at this point in the film further underscores these connections, as it leads from the scenes of desolation of the past to the future, which
is the present: Ohm Krüger speaks directly to "us," the heirs to that struggle.[10]
In this particular colonial triangle Germans are thus the unnamed third: the
Boers are their stand-ins, their brothers (Hake 19); hence, the Germans must

avenge the British atrocities perpetrated on Boer families. Not surprisingly, the film premiered on 4 April 1941—seven days before German war planes bombed Coventry (Rentschler 253).

By focusing on the British as cruel empire builders and keepers of concentration camps, the film evokes and obliterates Germany's own colonial wrongdoings, the extermination campaign directed at the Hereros during the Herero and Nama uprisings in 1904–7, during which the Africans were also interned in concentration camps or directly massacred (Drechsler). Woodruff Smith describes the "orgy of killing" following the defeat of the main Herero army thus:

> Trotha [the commander of the expeditionary force] himself actively sought to wipe out the Herero by refusing to negotiate with them, authorizing his troops to kill Herero on sight, and issuing a notorious extermination order to shoot or exile every Herero man, woman, and child. . . . By 1906, of the eighty thousand Herero who had lived in Southwest Africa before the war, less than twenty thousand remained; most of these were confined in concentration camps at the coast to be used for cheap labor. (Smith 64–65)

The film's insistence on British atrocities shifts attention away from Germany's colonial past at a time when Germany was, again, involved in racist orgies. By discrediting the present "owners" of Southwest Africa, it seeks to reverse the *Blue Book* verdict according to which Germans were morally unfit to administer colonies. And it provides an implicit justification for the current war effort, which is thus recast as a "revenge" campaign against the British for having deprived Germans of their rightful possessions.

The Africans, the original sufferers of colonial policies, are relegated to the role of stereotyped sidekicks, described in the script as: capricious, greedy, vain like "children" or "women" (*Ohm Krüger* 100; Hake 14, 20), "bloodthirsty," "fanatic" (*Ohm Krüger* 107), "wild," "barbaric," like predatory animals, moving in the dark and voicing inarticulate piercing screams (96–97); an undefined inchoate intoxicated mass, dancing to the beat of the drums (97). They are corruptible, have not "learnt" anything, and have remained heathens, despite the missionaries' efforts (102)—in short, they are caricatures of the "savages" of early travel literature, whose function in the film is merely symbolic. Since the Boers assume their place as colonial victims and are, in turn, displaced by Germans resolved to be no longer Britain's victims but her judges and executioners, the Africans are doubly marginalized. In a way the film is not even "about" Africa or colonialism but, instead, renegotiates European power relations in colonialist terms. It suggests, in the twisted logic of Nazi ideology, that "we" the Germans no longer want to be "the slaves" of Europe, as the Hitler Youth leader in the early Nazi propaganda film *Hitlerjunge Quex* (1933) put it[11] and as Ohm Krüger reiterates it now: "it can't be the Lord's will that a whole people should live in slavery!" (20).

The second absentee in this triangular construction are the Jews.[12] Significantly, Cecil Rhodes, gold-greedy imperialist (62), is played by Ferdinand Marian, whom German viewers of the 1940s would have recognized as the power-greedy Süss Oppenheimer of the film *Jud Süss* (1940). The British are ironically referred to as the "chosen people" (91). The name of the English concentration camp in the film, Irenenburg, resonates with the name of a concentration camp at Berlin's outskirts, Oranienburg, which must have been familiar to many viewers.[13] Like the casting of Englishmen as concentration camp founders and merciless executioners, the simultaneous and paradoxical association of Englishmen with Jews *and* with Germans[14] serves above all both to rewrite German colonial history and to overwrite Germany's current racist policies: On 22 June Operation Barbarossa initiated the invasion of the Soviet Union. The notorious *Einsatzgruppen* followed, liquidating Jews and other "undesirables." On 31 July "Göring order[ed] Heydrich to prepare a 'comprehensive solution' of the Jewish question," as Eric Rentschler laconically notes, when he discusses the close proximity of the film's premiere to political events (256). In the autumn the SS set up an installation for mass executions in Sachsenhausen near Oranienburg. If viewed against this political backdrop, the film's function as a means of distraction becomes apparent—distraction from the true perpetrators, from the true victims, from the atrocities themselves. It is a fantasy of revenge and national assertiveness dressed up as a fantasy of reckoning.

Despite their profound historical and ideological differences, the two moments of triangulation I have characterized so far share common features. Both associate Germans with victimhood, a status they aspire or seek to redress. Both divert from self-analysis and the analysis of actual historical conditions by pointing to other historical moments and other agents and by creating self-serving identifications: those of Germans with Africans/Indians and Germans with Boers (the victims); or of British with Jews (the aggressor); of Jews with Africans (the *Untermenschen*). Through these identifications Germans claim for themselves a position as outsider and moral arbiter. In Herder's text this moral superiority is based on political weakness and supposed innocence; in Steinhoff's film it is derived from the "moral obligation" incurred when the German Reich failed to help the Boers (the famous *Krüger-Depesche*). Germany *must* intervene on behalf of the downtrodden Boers (who, as the film fails to inform, were released from the camps in 1902, after the Peace of Vereeniging, and were given royal subsistence grants to reconstruct their lives).[15] In both, the triangulated structure is thus a smokescreen that permits rewriting one's own place in history in Manichaean ways. If there are only perpetrators or victims, masters or slaves, guilty or innocent, bad or good, the choices are, of course, limited. And who wants to remain the underdog?

IV

As I suggested before, the postcolonial situation in Germany after 1945 was radically different from that of other former colonial powers. The war experience and the Holocaust had eclipsed or repressed any recollections of previous relations with the colonized. Until the late 1960s Germany's colonialism was not a topic of inquiry, at least not in West Germany, which supposedly used "the claim that there was no colonial legacy" as a justification for "penetrating Africa by neocolonialist methods," as the East German historian Horst Drechsler states (*Südwestafrika* 8). While polemical statements such as these must be read within the context of Cold War competition—the communist East blamed the capitalist West for ignoring the colonial legacy, the West blamed the East for not addressing the Holocaust legacy—it is true that the *Aufarbeitung* (working through) of Germany's colonial past took considerably longer in the West than in the East.[16] The lack of access to the archives of the German Imperial Colonial Office in East Berlin may have accounted in part for this uneven interest in the past. Yet the reluctance to explore the ramifications of Germany's colonial legacy also had deeper reasons, as recent studies suggest (Bley; Campt et al.; etc.).

In part, of course, the lack of interest had to do with the fact that Germany's colonial period was so far removed in time that Germans, unlike the British or the French, could enter the period of decolonization seemingly *unbelastet*—unburdened by the past—as the editor of the *Entwicklungspolitische Korrespondenz,* Helmut Bley, points out (9). No former colonial subjects would challenge that perception by presenting their side of the story and reminding Germans of colonial abuses. Furthermore, as the critique of German imperialism/neocolonialism was raised, above all, by the communist East and by left-wing intellectuals, West German conservatives (the government, the business interests, even the academies) could dismiss it as partisan and refuse to engage it (Bley 10).[17] To the postwar German government interested in establishing good (business) relations with African nations, a critical approach to the colonialist legacy, furthermore, seemed counterproductive. Only with respect to South Africa and its approximately thirty thousand German-speaking settlers, Bley suggests, could a sense of continuity develop, since past and present interests overlapped. As a consequence, "the reluctance to engage in the imperialist legacy and the acute, spontaneous siding with white minorities in Southern Africa, particularly Namibia, [created] an apologetic, euphemizing treatment of colonialism in the media" (11)—if colonialism was mentioned at all. "As late as 1965 a journalist who attacked the colonial legend on [West German] TV received death threats; whoever mentioned parallels between the genocide of the Hereros and that of Jews and Poles abroad was confronted with the censors of the Foreign Office," Bley reports (15). It thus seems that beyond economic reasons for repressing the legacy there were also ideological ones: the need to see the Holocaust as unique, as a historical aberration rather than as part of a historical continuum that included the racial theories preceding colonialism and the race policies of colonial times.

The "blindness with respect to one's own violent traditions" (Bley 16) and the self-righteousness with which the colonial past was (mis)represented in the public until the 1980s, were, however, not limited to nationalist or reactionary forces. They extended to the intellectuals of the New Left as well. In their attempt to denounce (U.S.) imperialism, these intellectuals created, again, triangular structures with absent third parties: a moral high ground from which the critical German onlooker could analyze the colonialism of others, without investigating not just his own complicity in past and present colonialist endeavors but also the historical connections previously outlined.

Hans Magnus Enzensberger's 1966 essay "Las Casas, oder: Ein Rückblick in die Zukunft" (Las Casas, or: A View Back to the Future), which accompanied a new edition of the 1790 German translation of Las Casas's *Brevísima relación de la destrucción de las Indias* (The Devastation of the Indies: A Brief Account), is a case in point. Referring to the "genocide committed against 20 million people" (124) in the Americas, Enzensberger quickly points to other, comparable atrocities that occurred throughout history: "the extermination of the European Jews by the Germans, the Stalinist deportations, the destruction of Dresden and Nagasaki, the terror of the French in Algeria." All these have shown "even to the blindest," he affirms, "that all nations are capable of everything: and while the *Brief Account of the Devastation of the Indies* by the Spaniards is going to press again this year, *we, as witnesses, accessories, and accomplices* experience the devastation of the territories beyond India by the Americans" (128; emph. added). The terms Enzensberger employs are, however, imprecise and ahistorical. He establishes a connection between various moments in past and present history via the term *genocide*—which he dilutes by subsuming under it events as different as the Holocaust, the bombing of Dresden, the colonial battles in Algeria, or the war in Vietnam. Nor does he explain the nature of "our" complicity with U.S. imperialism. While he obliquely refers to modern structures of colonialism—the exploitation of natural resources and one-sided trading practices "legitimized" by developmentalism and "alliance for progress" rhetoric (129–32)—he does not explore to what extent German industrial interests were/are involved in that exploitation. In fact, German imperialism is not the issue. Enzensberger neither mentions an earlier instance of German colonialism right before his eyes, Las Casas's allegations directed at German conquistadors in the sixteenth century (85–91), nor German neocolonialist practices in Latin America during the Nazi years or after the war. Despite general affirmations to the contrary, the United States emerges as the only named imperialist power. While "the battle takes place before our very own eyes" (150), "we" are obviously not part of it.

Like Herder, Enzensberger is moved by moral outrage. His indictment of colonialism includes the whole "First World," yet his particular references transform Europe, and particularly Germany, into helpless onlookers of a global drama that unfolds across the oceans. The reference to the Holocaust as emblem of Germany's capacity for evil precludes an analysis of colonial/racist structures before and after that "event": Germany's share in the discourse of race in the eighteenth and nineteenth centuries, its participation in the international scramble for colonies in the late 1800s, the racial politics of its colonial administrations, the shift from Africa to the East as "colonizable" territory (illustrated by the shifting significance of the *Volk ohne Raum* slogan) during the Third Reich, neocolonialist tendencies in the postwar economy, persistent attitudes about race that now extend to Turks or other dark-skinned minority groups in Germany (Campt). In Enzensberger's triangulations the Jewish victims of the Holocaust become the stand-ins for Africans whom Germans had massacred in their attempt to secure colonial possessions; whereas the United States stands in for Germany as the new worldwide culprit. In the process the links between nineteenth-century racism, colonialism, and twentieth-century racism/antisemitism become obliterated. It is as if the Holocaust, by concentrating and absorbing all guilt Germans have incurred, had wiped out all memory of and connection with any other aspect of the past.

In her analysis of Enzensberger and the politics of the periodical *Kursbuch,* Sara Lennox explores the Eurocentric interests behind what she calls the "Third-Worldism" of the German radicals of the 1960s. "Without impugning the sincerity of New Left commitment to revolution in that heady time," she writes, "it is nonetheless possible to argue that the position of Enzensberger and many other radicals still retained a certain sort of Eurocentrism: no longer on the wrong side of history or peripheral to it, they could now imagine that their own efforts placed them in the world-historical vanguard that would soon transform the world." By "placing their intellectual skills at the service of the revolution outside of Europe" (188), they hoped to cleanse themselves from the moral reproach of passivity, of intellectualism without political practice, and to revitalize the failed class struggle in Europe. While I agree with Lennox that Enzensberger's writings "never escaped a European focus," I propose that it is not Eurocentrism that accounts for the self-serving triangularity of his critique of colonialism but, rather, his—admittedly unconscious—attempt to explain historical conditions in Europe by recourse to simplified metaphorical constellations in the former colonies. While he and others are quite willing to include themselves, that is, Germans, in attributions of global guilt (industrial nations as the oppressors, the "Third World" nations as the oppressed; the rich versus the poor), their global categories hide more than they reveal. They do justice neither to the differences among nations in the "Third World," or within these nations themselves, nor to the complex social and economic developments inside Germany. Instead of too much Eurocentrism in their work, there is not enough—not enough reflection about the relationship between colonial legends and realities in the colonies and the postcolonial legacy that even Germany must face.

NOTES

1. I do not make the distinction here between colonialist and imperialist. As I have explained elsewhere (intro., *Colonial Fantasies*), the distinctions elaborated by Said, Lenin, Hobson, Mommsen, and others seem academic when it comes to the fantasy life in which "imperialist" dreams of national expansion and a desire for founding colonies or settling abroad coalesce and mutually reinforce each other.

2. In her recent study of German colonialist film, Hake reiterates that commonly held view.

3. Thus, Ritter von Epp at the Wiener Reichskolonialtagung in May 1939 (Jacob 76).

4. In 1528 the wealthy Southern German merchant and banking company Bartolomä Welser, which had lent Charles V vast sums to finance his election as emperor of the Holy Roman Empire, negotiated a treaty for colonial possessions with the Spanish government. The Welsers were allowed to conquer, settle, rule, and exploit a hitherto unknown region—roughly the territory of today's Venezuela and part of Colombia. Charles V granted the Welsers the privilege, under Spanish sovereignty, to choose governors and military and administrative heads for the new acquisitions, to appropriate land for their own use, collect 4 percent of the profit that was to be transferred to the Crown, and retain the "fifth" for precious metals for three years. In exchange for these privileges the new rulers agreed to settle the colony within two years, found two settlements, erect three forts, and establish a functioning colonial administration. The Welsers had to return the colony to the Spanish Crown after a series of personal, administrative, and financial problems in 1555. In 1685 the Great Elector of Brandenburg-Prussia purchased a trading post on St. Thomas from the island's Danish "owners" in order to get his foot into the international slave trade. Prussia had "acquired" a small African colony, Gross-Friedrichsburg, on the Ivory Coast and now needed a trading base in the Caribbean. Yet both the Caribbean acquisition and the African fortress had to be relinquished in 1717 after repeated conflicts with Dutch, Danish, and French competitors. Further attempts to negotiate purchases or occupy islands by force were unsuccessful.

5. In the Versailles Peace Treaty dictated by the Allies (ratified on 10 January 1920) Germany had to relinquish all rights to its colonies (para. 119). On 3 March 1919, 414 deputies (even the Social Democrats, who had been opposed to colonialism in the beginning) in the Reichstag voted to oppose the loss of colonies; only 7 voiced support. They vehemently opposed what they called the "lie of colonial guilt" (*koloniale Schuldlüge*) and demanded that the colonies be returned to their rightful owners.

6. I put *postcolonial* in quotation marks because, strictly speaking, there is no postcolonial literature in postwar Germany, if one understands by this phrase writings by formerly colonized subjects who have moved to the "metropolis." As Sara Lennox has pointed out, "there are apparently no post-colonial texts in German, partly as a conse-

quence of German language policy in the colonies, which favored keeping the number of literate 'natives' deliberately small" (Lennox, "Post-Colonial Theory").

7. "Von den spanischen Grausamkeiten, vom Geiz der Engländer, von der kalten Frechheit der Holländer, von denen man im Taumel des Eroberungswahnes Heldengedichte schrieb, sind in unsrer Zeit Bücher geschrieben, die ihnen so wenig Ehre bringen, dass vielmehr, wenn ein europäischer Gesamtgeist anderswo als in Büchern lebte, wir uns des Verbrechens beleidigter Menschheit fast vor allen Völkern der Erde schämen müssten. Nenne man das Land, wohin Europäer kamen und sich nicht durch Beeinträchtigungen, durch ungerechte Kriege, Geiz, Betrug, Unterdrückung, durch Krankheiten und schädliche Gaben an der Unbewehrten, zutrauenden Menschheit, vielleicht auf alle Äonen hinab, versündigt haben!" (All translations are mine, unless otherwise noted.)

8.
> Der zweite Ruhm ist Mässigung. Es ruft
> Der Hindus und der Peruaner Not,
> Die Wut der Schwarzen und der Mexikaner
> Gebratner Montezuma rufen noch
> Zum Himmel auf und flehn Entsündigung!—
> O glaube, Freund, kein Zeus mit seinem Chor
> Der Götter kehrt zu einem Volke, das,
> Mit solcher Schuld- und Blut- und Sündenlast
> Und Gold- und Demantlast beladen, schmaust!
> Er kehrt bei stillen Äthiopiern
> *Und Deutschen* ein, zu ihrem armen Mahl.

9. To use the term *imperialism* for pre-imperial times is, of course, an anachronism. It is used here to characterize both the long-standing French cultural overprint and the more recent attempts of the Revolutionary forces to expand their territories across the borders.

10. In his book on Nazi film Eric Rentschler frequently comments on the function of this favorite technique of Nazi filmmakers (158 ff.).

11. A similar configuration emerged in the "hammer vs. anvil" speech von Bülow delivered before the Reichstag on 11 December 1899. The image of the Germans as the "slaves" of Europe, familiar to us from the Herder quotes, is a popular image throughout the nineteenth century.

12. On the absent Jew in German culture, see also Bartov's essay in pt. 5.—Eds.

13. By 1941 Oranienburg, one of the three largest camps in 1933, was closed; however, Sachsenhausen, on the outskirts of the Berlin district of Oranienburg, was becoming one of the centers for mass killings in 1941 (Gutman 3:1091, 4: 1321). In view of the deliberate slippages I outlined it might be possible to consider *Irenenburg* an indirect allusion to and displacement of Sachsenhausen by way of the discontinued Oranienburg concentration camp.

14. As Rentschler argues, the Jews were, to the Germans, "negativity incarnate" (159). For the purposes of the film the British are, too. As a power that establishes concentration camps and carries out total warfare against a people, they are also the mirror image of Germany.

15. See Thoman (62). The film also fails to provide information on all causes for the conflict. As Thoman notes, part of the responsibility for the war lay with the Boers and their intransigence toward the *Uitlanders*.

16. See the contributions to the series "Studien zur Kolonialgeschichte und Geschichte der nationalen und kolonialen Befreiungsbewegung," ed. W. Markov, which started in 1959 and includes studies by Kurt Büttner, *Die Anfänge der deutschen Kolonialpolitik in Ostafrika* (1959); Manfred Nussbaum, *Vom 'Kolonialenthusiasmus' zur Kolonialpolitik der Monopole. Zur deutschen Kolonialpolitik unter Bismarck, Caprivi, Hohenlohe* (1962); and Horst Drechsler, *Südwestafrika* (1966). In the West the historical investigation of colonialism did not take off until the late 1960s, with the series "Beiträge zur Kolonial- und Überseegeschichte," published simultaneously by Steiner (Stuttgart), Westdeutscher Verlag (Köln), and Atlantis (Zürich), 1966–.

17. Significantly, this repression of critique has its precedent: in the 1920s national-conservative forces had managed to blame the "left-wing" Weimar coalition under Vice-Chancellor and Finance Minister Erzberger for both the loss of war and the loss of colonies by claiming that Germany's responsibility for these losses were fabrications (*Kriegsschuldlüge, Kolonialschuldlüge*); a critique of colonialism to them was antipatriotic.

WORKS CITED

Ayim, May. "Das Jahr 1990. Heimat und Einheit aus afro-deutscher Perspektive." In *Entfernte Verbindungen,* ed. Ika Hügel et al., 206–20.

Bley, Helmut. "Unerledigte Kolonialgeschichte." *Deutscher Kolonialismus. Materialien zur Hundertjahrfeier.* Hamburg: EPK–Drucksache Nr. 1, 1983.

Campt, Tina, Pascal Grosse, and Yara-Colette Lemke-Muniz de Faria. "Blacks, Germans, and the Politics of Imperial Imagination, 1920–1960." In *The Imperialist Imagination,* ed. Friedrichsmeyer, Lennox, and Zantop (forthcoming).

Drechsler, Horst. *Let Us Die Fighting: The Struggle of the Herero and Nama against German Imperialism, 1884–1915.* Trans. Bernd Zollner. London: Zed Press, 1980.

———. *Südwestafrika unter deutscher Kolonialherrschaft. Der Kampf der Herero und Nama gegen den deutschen Imperialismus (1884–1915).* East Berlin: Akademie-Verlag, 1966.

Fischer, Bernd. *Das Eigene und das Eigentliche: Klopstock, Herder, Fichte, Kleist. Episoden aus der Konstruktionsgeschichte nationaler Intentionalitäten.* Berlin: Schmid, 1995.

Friedrichsmeyer, Sara, Sara Lennox, and Susanne Zantop, eds. *The Imperialist Imagination* (forthcoming).

Gutman, Israel., ed. *Encyclopedia of the Holocaust.* 4 vols. New York and London: Macmillan, 1990.

Hake, Sabine. "Mapping the Native Body: On the Colonial Film in the Third Reich." In *The Imperialist Imagination,* ed. Friedrichsmeyer, Lennox, Zantop (forthcoming).

Herder, Johann Gottfried. *Briefe zur Beförderung der Humanität,* 2 vols. Berlin and Weimar: Aufbau, 1971.

Hügel, Ika, Chris Lange, and May Ayim, eds. *Entfernte Verbindungen. Rassismus Antisemitismus Klassenunterdrückung.* Berlin: Orlanda Frauenverlag, 1993.

Jacob, Ernst Gerhard, ed. *Das koloniale Deutschtum. Ein Volkslesebuch.* Bayreuth: Gauverlag Bayerische Ostmark, 1939.

Lennox, Sara. "Post-Colonial Theory and German Studies." Talk delivered at NYU on Minority Discourse in Contemporary Germany and the United States, 14 October 1995.

―――. "Enzensberger, Kursbuch, and 'Third-Worldism': The Sixties' Construction of Latin America." In *"Neue Welt"/"Dritte Welt": Interkulturelle Beziehungen Deutschlands zu Lateinamerika und der Karibik,* ed. Sigrid Bauschinger and Susan L. Cocalis. Tübingen and Basel: Francke, 1994. 185–200.

Lützeler, Paul Michael. "Der postkoloniale Blick. Deutschsprachige Autoren berichten aus der Dritten Welt." *Neue Rundschau* 107.1 (1996): 54–69.

Ohm Krüger. Emil Jannings-Produktion der Tobis, dir. Hans Steinhoff, script by Harald Bratt and Kurt Heuser, based on motives from the novel "Man without People" by Arnold Krieger; original script, Berlin 1941.

Opitz, May, Katharina Oguntoye, Dagmar Schultz, eds. *Showing Our Colors: Afro-German Women Speak Out.* Trans. Anne Adams. Amherst: U Massachusetts Press, 1992 (trans. of *Farbe bekennen*).

Rentschler, Eric. *The Ministry of Illusion: Nazi Cinema and Its Afterlife.* Cambridge: Harvard UP, 1996.

Schmokel, Wolfe W. *Dream of Empire: German Colonialism, 1919–1945.* New Haven: Yale UP, 1964.

Schück, Richard. *Brandenburg-Preussens Kolonial-Politik unter dem Grossen Kurfürsten und seinen Nachfolgern (1647–1721).* Leipzig: Grunow, 1889.

Sieg, Katrin. "Ethnic Drag and National Identity: Performance, Multiculturalism, Xenophobia." In *The Imperialist Imagination,* ed. Friedrichsmeyer, Lennox, and Zantop (forthcoming).

Smith, Woodruff. *The German Colonial Empire.* Chapel Hill: U of North Carolina P, 1978.

Solf, Wilhelm. H. *Kolonialpolitik: Mein politisches Vermächtnis.* Berlin: Hobbing, 1919.

Thoman, Roy E. "The Boer War." In *Historical Dictionary of European Imperialism,* ed. James S. Olsen. Greenwood: Greenwood P, 1991. 62–63.

Zantop, Susanne. *Colonial Fantasies: Conquest, Family, and Nation in Precolonial Germany, 1770–1870.* Durham: Duke UP, 1997.

Part Five

WHAT IS "GERMAN" NOW?

Defining the "German" today entails thorough negotiation with historical, personal, political, and national identities. The seven essays in part 5 seek, with their own specific methods and through their particular subjects, to gain a better understanding of the nature of contemporary German self-definition. Cultures and politics of identity, the importance of alterity and difference, the position of the subject and the Other: these are issues at the center of cultural studies. The traumatic recent history of Germany has posed difficult questions of self-definition for those in the German cultural realm. Here Bartov explores how aspects of German identity and cultural production are defined by the absence of Jews in German society. Miller and Czaplicka both analyze how the public memory of the German—and also Austrian—catastrophe is constructed in the concrete examples of memorial architecture in Berlin and public art in Vienna, respectively. Spaulding looks at how the Germans' economic success can also serve as a positive defining characteristic. McFalls and Berdahl each look at loss and absence of the Wall—physically and as a trope of existence— and how such losses are used by eastern Germans to help them find new roles as members of the polity and the local community. Finally, Gemünden looks at German filmmaker Monika Treut's ways of defining herself and her characters through their relationships with the United States as Other and in their explorations of gender roles. These essays not only help us understand some aspects of contemporary German self-definition; they also show us why knowing who one is depends so much on knowing from whence one came.

CHAPTER 13

"Seit die Juden weg sind . . .": Germany, History, and Representations of Absence

Omer Bartov

No one would question that Germans have produced myriad representations of the National Socialist period and of the Holocaust. And yet the question of coming to terms with this past continues to haunt the national psyche. In his essay historian Omer Bartov attempts to address a crucial missing element from literary, filmic, and scholarly representations: the absence of Jews. Launching his argument from a seemingly unremarkable moment in a conversation with a young German colleague, Bartov discusses the issue of Jewish presence and absence in German history. During the Weimar Republic and the early years of the National Socialist regime, Bartov reminds us, numerous commentators decried the "overrepresentation" of Jews in certain areas of contemporary life. And, in fact, for their relative proportion of the overall population German Jews did occupy a higher percentage of positions in certain professions such as medicine and law and in the media and the academy. Thus, it is particularly ironic that current literary, cinematic, and scholarly treatments of that same period tend to efface the Jewish presence. Non-Jewish Germans, as Bartov points out, have often been depicted as victims of the tragedies of the period, and hence there is no representational room for the historical victims. Bartov finds it worrisome that one answer to the question "What is 'German' now?" seems to be: victims.

Though trained in Israel and England as a historian in a traditional empirical style, tinged with the enlightened marxism of his Oxford mentor, Tim Mason, Bartov has always been interested in the visual and literary arts. He is himself a twice-published novelist, in addition to his three books and numerous articles on the Wehrmacht and the Holocaust; he is conversant with contem-

209

porary literary critical theory (e.g., the work of Edward Said and Paul de Man) and with important developments in German cultural studies (e.g., the work of Eric Santer and Anton Kaes). Nonetheless, he has refrained from forays outside his traditional field in historical research until recently. In his latest book Murder in Our Midst: The Holocaust, Industrial Killing, and Representation, *as in this essay, Bartov uses various types of cultural evidence to probe his subject. As David Crew points out in his essay on the historical profession, such interdisciplinary efforts still remain rare among those trained as historians. Bartov considers himself a kind of double outsider, analyzing works by Germans from the perspective of a non-German and analyzing film and literature as a historian rather than as a film or literary critic. And, though Bartov does not reside in Germany, he, like Deidre Berger, uses an anecdote from personal contact with Germans to launch a reflection on contemporary German culture.*

Contemporary Germans' inability to empathize with Jews and minorities has roots in earlier periods as Zantop shows. Bartov questions here whether or not Germans have ever been able to recognize Jews as part of the fabric of German culture. To extend his argument to a recent development, there has been great controversy surrounding the creation of a Holocaust memorial near the Reichstag building in Berlin and the creation of a Jewish museum within the precincts of the Berlin Museum. That is to say, Germans have been challenged once again to remember that Jewish citizens have been and are a constitutive element of German culture. In the context of cultural studies it is also important to consider popular culture genres, such as television and the press. Despite substantial media attention given to the Third Reich and the Holocaust in Germany today, the representation of Jews remains limited. Bartov here explores this absence.

In 1987, during a conversation with a young German scholar, I remarked that, having spent a few months in Berlin, I had been struck by its distinctly provincial air as compared with other European capitals such as Paris and London. My friend sighed in agreement, adding that in the past Berlin, too, had of course been a much more vibrant and creative city but that, "seit die Juden weg sind" (since the Jews have been gone), it has lost its cosmopolitan atmosphere.

On the face of it this was a rather straightforward assertion, and at the time I gave it little thought, although I was slightly disturbed by my own instinctive agreement with it, which implied that I too believed that the Jews (as a distinctly different category from the Germans) had made city life more interesting. That, I conceded, was *my* prejudice. Subsequently, however, I realized that my friend's comment, perceived by him as a mere statement of fact, was anything but innocent of an ambiguous, multilayered, and quite prevalent perception of Jewish presence and absence in German history. To be sure, this complex set of attitudes about the role of Jews, and the impact of their absence (as distinct from the mechanism whereby this absence was produced), is rarely acknowledged or even perceived by many Germans. Indeed, even German filmmakers and novelists, that is, those concerned with creating verbal and visual representations for public consumption, as well as German historians of precisely the period during which Jews were transformed from a presence to an absence, that is, scholars, conventionally viewed as charged with constructing more "reliable" (if less popular) representations of the past, rarely seem to be aware of the implications this German-Jewish (negative) symbiosis has on their own work— and on that past with which it is concerned (Diner). And yet, perhaps precisely because of this lack of awareness, the representation of absence is arguably one of the most crucial tropes in German literary, cinematic, and scholarly representations of recent German history.

There is a major difference between the absence of representation and the representation of absence, although at the same time there may be close links between them (Said, chap. 5; de Man, chaps. 7, 9). In the case of postwar German representations of the past, and especially of the Nazi era and the period immediately preceding it, Jews are clearly underrepresented, except as opaque objects of Nazi ferocity. Although one cannot speak of a complete absence of representation, the gap between the prominent role of Jews in German society, culture, and xenophobia, on the one hand, and the marginal place they are awarded in postwar representations of that past, on the other, is quite striking. In view of the prevalent argument in Weimar and the early years of the Third Reich of Jewish *overrepresentation* in the professions, the media, and the intelligentsia, their current underrepresentation in representations of that past is only one of numerous ironies characteristic of recent German history and its various literary, cinematic, and scholarly reconstructions.[1] And, whatever we may say about the portrayal of Jews (or the lack thereof) in postwar German discussions of the past, it is obvious that little attempt has been made to grapple with the problems of representing the Holocaust. Indeed, one is hard put to think of any German film or work of fiction devoted to the Jewish experience of genocide,[2] while the much larger body of German scholarship on the subject has similarly concentrated exclusively on the German side, and especially on either the technical and bureaucratic or the political and ideological facets of genocide. While not absent, the victims remain anonymous and faceless; the evil, whatever the causes attributed to it, is in the deed (and its effects on the perpetrators), not in its application to individual human beings. This is a type of representation not unrelated to the Nazis' own perception and representation of the victims as constituting targets for their actions totally lacking individual identity. Of course, the Nazis organized genocide, while postwar German representations deplore it, but in the latter the event itself assumes an abstract quality, bereft of precisely that empathy that has in the past, as well as much more recently, been seen as central to the recreation of a historical period and to the "pleasure of narration" (Broszat, qtd. in Baldwin 78).

Not representing a phenomenon may have to do either with its perceived irrelevance to current preoccupations or with a sense of unease about its implications for the present. In other words, the absence of representation may be caused by two contradictory, though not necessarily mutually exclusive, factors: indifference and anxiety. They are contradictory because we are rarely anxious about things to which we are indifferent, yet they are not necessarily mutually exclusive because our indifference may be superficial and assumed, rather than a true reflection of our consciousness. We may train ourselves to feel indifferent toward an object, a person, or an event that would otherwise cause us profound anxiety. To cite just one example, also related to the present discussion by a series of ironic links, it can be argued that attitudes toward the "Arab Problem" within the pre-state Jewish community (*Yishuv*) of Palestine were characterized by that same absence of representation of Palestinian Arabs that can be seen in postwar Germany vis-à-vis the Jews. Having escaped the "Jewish Question" in Europe, the Zionists confronted what they called the Arab Problem by not confronting it at all. This was partly a conscious decision, motivated by rational political arguments, according to which this "problem" ought not to be dealt with before demographic equality or, even better, superiority had been achieved. But it was also rooted in a psychological reaction, whereby fear of Arab nationalism and a violent reaction to Jewish settlement in Palestine manufactured an assumed indifference to the issue, indeed, an argument that the problem that had caused this anxious reaction did not exist in the first place (Shapira).

Conversely, representations of absence may involve direct confrontation with an acknowledged vacuum or void, perceived as either perpetual or as having been created by the disappearance of previously existing objects and entities. Yet even in this case, by their own definition, such representations are not concerned with the creation of the vacuum (even if it is not an immanent condition) but with absence as such; with the void, not with the mechanism that had emptied a formerly occupied space. Now representing an absence, an emptiness, a no-thing, is almost a contradiction in terms, akin to representing silence or the ineffable or perfection—that is, the Absolute, which is, by definition, unrepresentable. And yet we know, of course, that, such aesthetic and philosophical assertions notwithstanding, humanity has rarely accepted such judgments; has, indeed, felt itself challenged to try nevertheless to represent precisely that which had been deemed unrepresentable. The Jews, after all, have a long tradition of representing God, who both by decree and by definition is not amenable to representation.

Yet what concerns me here is not the representation of the Absolute, at least not insofar as absolute Evil is excluded from this definition. Moreover, I am not especially interested in the absence of representation of the Jews, and especially the Holocaust, in Germany. For one thing this is such an obvious phenomenon as to merit, at best, only hopes or calls for change. For another this does not mean that postwar Germany has refrained from preoccupation with the reality and direct consequences of Nazi crimes, that is, the physical murder of millions of human beings. Indeed, anyone visiting Germany even for a relatively brief period will be struck by the amount of media attention given to Nazism, not excepting the genocide of the Jews. Rather, what interests me here is the representation of the absence itself, the representation of the ultimate result of Nazism's "success" in bringing about the "disappearance" of Jews from Germany (and Europe), and, by extension, the representation of the nature of postwar German society and culture as compared to prewar and pre-Nazi Germany, that Germany in which there had presumably been Jews who were "done away with," even if the information available about them is neither ample nor particularly accurate. Indeed, what appears to me most fascinating in this phenomenon is the manner in which postwar German representations of Jewish absence serve an apparently crucial need in German society and culture to identify, or empathize, with its own immediate predecessors and to perceive itself as the inheritor of a tragic history of (its own) victimhood and suffering.

In reality, of course, the Jews are not absent from postwar Germany, even if their numbers are much smaller than their meager share of the population of pre-1933 Germany and their cultural and intellectual contribution is similarly diminished. But in much of the German visual and literary representational universe they are seen as absent, to the extent that one may even find the Holocaust being described as "the end of European Jewry" (Hillgruber). This, in itself, is a significant conception of reality, since it implies that, whoever the Jews currently residing in Germany may be, they have little to do with *those* Jews who had become absent and with *that* world of which they had been part.

More important, however, is the implicit and wholly pervasive subtext of representations of absence in the German context. After all, everyone knows quite well (thanks not least to the media's preoccupation with the issue) where the Jews "went" and what happened to them once they got "there." It is also acknowledged that Germans, or at least some Germans, had had a great deal to do with this "disappearance." Hence, the question is not at all what brought about this absence or the fact that novels and films do not actually try to represent the process whereby this "happened" or that historians tend to concentrate on the mechanics rather than the human aspects of this "event." The question is, rather, what are the implications of German representations of the past from which the Jews are either absent or, in the rare cases in which they appear (just before they disappear), are represented as outsiders, as different, strange, indeed ephemeral beings, who are obviously about to disappear at any given moment precisely because they are not an inherent part of the reality reconstructed by the filmmaker, novelist, or historian. Moreover, it is necessary to inquire into the implications of such representations of Germany's destruction during the war and its suffering following the "capitulation," or "catastrophe," from which the Jews are once more almost wholly absent or, when they do appear, seem to have fared better than the average German during their long years of disappearance.

How does one deal with the question of absence? How does one come to terms with, or overcome, the absence of an object, an entity, a memory, that is known (if only perhaps vaguely and inaccurately) to have existed before, indeed, to have been seen by many as a far too pervasive presence? Does one lament the present condition (of absence), glorify past circumstances (of presence), and simultaneously decree that the process whereby the past was transformed into the present is a matter for a different, not unimportant, but nevertheless almost wholly unrelated discussion? My friend, of course, knew a great deal about the Holocaust. Yet he was sorry that the Jews were "gone," since Berlin had become much more boring compared to its glorious, if also tumultuous, past. Is there an implicit blame here of the absentees themselves, those eternal "Weggeher" who for some reason left Germany in the lurch? (Reitz 102, 145–46; qtd. in Santner 75, 80).[3] Is there a connection here between this sense of a past glory somehow diminished by the Jews' absence and the anger and frustration within the German public just before and after the end of the war that they were being punished for the crimes committed (by whom?) against the Jews?—that is, that the Jews (directly or by proxy) were destroying Germany? (Arendt; Engelmann 331–33; Bartov, *Hitler's Army* 169–70).

Absence, after all, has much to do with questions of guilt and innocence, justice and punishment, death and survival, just as it is related to the problem of distinguishing between fact and image, history and memory, the represented (object, person, event) and its representation. Absence, in this specific context, compels us to think about, and yet paradoxically also enables us to repress, the crucial distinction between perpetrators and victims, however much the boundaries between them are blurred and however great the overlap may sometimes be.

One of the greatest contributions of German thought and letters in the late eighteenth and nineteenth centuries was the introduction of the notion of empathy, or *Einfühlung,* both to representations of the individual and to the study of the past. While Romanticism insisted on the need to "look into" one's innermost feelings and passions, historicism sought to "feel oneself into" the past. Both the social and the human sciences and the arts are profoundly indebted to the conceptualization of and experimentation with these ideas by German philosophers, historians, writers, and artists. Yet it should be stressed that empathy is, by definition, exclusive. Only God (at least under certain circumstances) can empathize with all His creatures. For human beings, however, empathy begins with the self and is therefore deeply rooted in a narcissistic view of the world. This may greatly enrich our understanding of human psychology and history, but it may just as much distort one's perception of others. And if, as Ranke argued, "all nations are equal under God," they are not necessarily equal under the historian's gaze. Indeed, the very process of feeling oneself into history must establish clearly defined limits and boundaries in order not to degenerate into an impressionistic world history or a series of superficial platitudes, in which empathy wholly replaces knowledge and understanding. Moreover, since all nations, periods, and individuals are necessarily burdened (and motivated) by their own specific biases and prejudices, and since these biases and prejudices normally concern other nations, periods, and individuals, empathy must perforce also lead to antipathy, or at least to empathy with antipathy, without which understanding (*Verstehen*) would remain detached from the "reality" of the past.

Now, considering this intellectual heritage, as well as the traumatic events of the first half of this century, and especially the manner in which this period came to a catastrophic end—from which, of course, it nevertheless continued to flow, as it surely must—it is not surprising that postwar Germany has been so preoccupied with the recent past and that notions of empathy and understanding have been so central to both historical scholarship and literary and visual representation. This context helps us understand why much of this body of creative work has been concerned with the relationship between the nation and the individual, on the one hand, and with history's anonymous forces of destruction and the limitless misery, suffering, pain, and sorrow they had brought in their wake, on the other. The aura of tragedy that accompanies a great deal of postwar German fiction and film is rooted in a sense of betrayal and dashed hopes, unfulfilled aspirations and disillusionment from previously held beliefs, loyalty and falsehood, innocence and victimization (Kaes; Ryan). Politics and ideologies do not fare well in such representations; individuals and the nation (the "true" nation, the presumed conglomerate of culturally and ethnically related individuals constituting a historical, perhaps even an organic, entity, not the nation created by doctrine and coercion) are at the center of our empathy. Finally, such strong empathies and such a tragic context must necessarily engender boundaries and distance, detachment and animosity. When one's own suffering is not only great but also perceived as tragic, it is difficult to feel, or even notice, the pain of others not clearly included in this community of misfortune. In other words, empathy necessitates absence; the deeper our empathy, the more keenly felt is the pain; the more tragic the circumstances of our empathy, the more urgent is the need for absence. Hence, empathy and absence are as closely related as pain and indifference. Now, under conditions of a clear-cut confrontation between friend and foe, empathy with the friend will "naturally" make for hostility toward his foe. But under such perceived tragic circumstances as those of postwar Germany, where the cause for which sacrifices had been made was largely discredited, the foe can no longer fulfill this need. Since this conventional dichotomy cannot be maintained, the foe is replaced by a gaping absence, which continues to function as that with which one cannot empathize, and yet is clearly separated from the enemy, who must now be acknowledged as the true destroyer of evil.

The issue under discussion, however, is even more complex. It is not simply that the absent must take upon itself the role that the enemy can no longer fulfill. Rather, the absent is *known* to have been the victim, the true, innocent, "ideal" victim, the victim with whom one precisely *should* empathize, had one not already chosen oneself as the preferred object of empathy. This is, one might argue, only natural. Furthermore this absent victim cannot be deprived of the status of victim, since that status is openly acknowledged, even if it does not evoke empathy. Indeed, this other's victimhood *must* be emphasized and reiterated, not least because, being so clearly and evidently immense, it becomes a kind of measuring rod for one's own victimhood, just as that other's tragedy becomes a measuring rod for one's own. And yet, in this skewed universe of competing victimhood in which the rationale for self-empathy is founded on suffering, can one concede first place to another? According to this logic, the absent must become ever more abstract, precisely because its presence is both a fundamental obstruction to self-empathy—which is perceived as crucial to individual and national existence—and its precondition.

A few examples from three different areas of representation—namely, literature, film, and scholarship—must suffice to demonstrate this process. Let me begin with three important young writers who emerged in the Federal Republic in the aftermath of World War II: Heinrich Böll, Günter Grass, and Siegfried Lenz. All three had lived as children and teenagers in the Third Reich, and all had served in the military, although, while the slightly older Böll spent many years at the front, Grass and Lenz were conscripted only toward the end of the war, and the latter actually deserted from his unit, a fact never mentioned in the dust-jacket blurbs of his works.[4] There is little doubt that these writers were strongly preoccupied with German history and, in some of their best works, especially with the Nazi past. What interests me here in their oeuvres is not their literary merit, which I find to be considerable, but, rather, the manner in which they represented that past, what concerned them most about it, and what they chose to leave out. In other words, I am interested in presence and absence in their writing on Nazism and the connections between the two.

All three writers are strongly preoccupied with the fate of the unique, remarkable, or rebellious individual in the context of a violently conformist society. In this sense they are, of course, concerned with themselves but also, by way of extension, with the options and limitations of individual action, creation, and interaction. Thus, for instance, the protagonists of *Group Portrait with Lady* [*Gruppenbild mit Dame* (1971)], *The Tin Drum* [*Die Blechtrommel* (1959)], and *The German Lesson* [*Deutschstunde* (1968)] are all extraordinary in one way or another; surrounded by a conventional, conformist environment, they are constantly threatened by another extraordinary minority of uniquely evil individuals. No less important, all these types, the individualistic, the indifferent, and the evil, are caught in the throes of something that is beyond their comprehension and capacities, an upheaval of universal proportions, against which individualistic action is all the more remarkable because it is so utterly hopeless. Ultimately, all, or rather, all Germans, become victims of this anonymous force and are either physically or mentally destroyed by it. The others, the non-Germans who arrive at the scene following the catastrophe, if represented at all, are obviously outsiders to the tragedy and wholly incapable of grasping it.

What is notable about these works is not merely the fact that all Germans end up in them as victims but that there are no other victims but Germans. This is what I would call an absence of representation. Thus, for instance, in Böll's *The Train Came on Time* [*Der Zug war pünktlich* (1949)], the victim is the German soldier, the innocent, war-hating, music-loving, frightened young man who gets blown up by the Polish resistance. His is a tragic figure, because he is in the clutches of forces he cannot control and is destroyed by those with whom he in fact learns to sympathize, embodied in the figure of a Polish woman who is like him but works (with much greater conviction) for the other side. But another aspect of these literary texts seems of greater significance, namely, their manner of representing absence. What I would like to suggest is that these exceptional protagonists could in fact be easily replaced by those most obviously absent, namely the Jews. From the point of view of the regime and its followers, as well as from that of many other Germans, whether antisemitic, philosemitic, or, most commonly, indifferent, the Jews were the example par excellence of all that was exceptional, different, bizarre, in other words, unlike the rest, for better or for worse. They too were surrounded by a multitude of conformists and were hunted down by a minority of exceptionally committed, or at least extraordinarily obedient, servants of a regime sworn to their destruction and willing to further the careers of those who carried out its wishes. Yet in these novels we hardly ever encounter Jews, while we do hear a great deal about exceptional Germans. This is what I would call the representation of absence, since the absence of the Jews is represented by exceptional German protagonists, and the (fictional) existence of these protagonists makes possible the absence of the Jews. For, if we are to empathize with anyone during the Nazi period, and if we simultaneously insist that the focus of our empathies must be German (as defined by the Nazi regime, i.e., excluding former Jewish citizens), then it must be someone who has very similar qualities to those of the Jew (as perceived by German society).

This is not to say, of course, that such works are allegories of the fate of Jews in Nazi Germany, whatever else they may be allegories of (*The Tin Drum,* e.g., is arguably a mixed metaphor of both Hitler's and Germany's fate). I do not think that any of these writers consciously gave his protagonists perceived Jewish characteristics; rather, all of these works have a strong autobiographical element and are imbued with the writers' own sense of victimhood and singularity, which combines the Romantic notion of the artist with the specific details of their lives and times. Yet through this self-empathy, which in another way makes possible also empathy with the nation (in the sense of at least one righteous man in the city of Sodom), they need no longer empathize with their own, and their nation's, victims. Indeed, they thereby exclude those victims from the sphere of empathy altogether, since, as I have noted, empathy must by definition be exclusive rather than inclusive in order to have any meaning at all. Hence, the representation of absence acts as a crucial mechanism of empathic self-representation even under the most unlikely circumstances, such as those of persecution and genocide.

A later generation of German filmmakers was also greatly preoccupied with history (Kaes). Here I will also mention only three of the most prominent German directors of the 1970s and 1980s—Alexander Kluge, Edgar Reitz, and Rainer Werner Fassbinder—although many others come to mind, such as Hans-Jürgen Syberberg, Volker Schlöndorff, Helma Sanders-Brahms, Werner Herzog, and Wim Wenders. Here, too, I would like to focus only on one aspect of these filmmakers' work, that is, the interplay between presence and absence. Alexander Kluge's film *The Patriot* [*Die Patriotin* (1977–79)], about which I have written in greater detail elsewhere ("War"), is ostensibly about German history. Not surprisingly, it is a tale of tragedy and folly, hopelessness and despair, destruction and mutilation (of people, of landscapes, of history, of the film itself). As a fragmented pastiche of images and words, it is a truly postmodern work, an attempt to confront both the conventions of filmmaking and of German history. It remains, however, part of a postwar German tradition of representation in that it presents the Germans as victims of history and its anonymous, evil forces and in that it is innocent of any preoccupation with other victims. Considering the film's focus on World War II, the total absence of the Jews, whose own encounter with German history ended up in genocide, is especially blatant. Yet Kluge's insistence on digging up the past and revealing its hidden fragments is once more an exercise not merely in the absence of representation but also in the representation of absence. For the heavy emphasis on the centrality of death and destruction in German history creates a consistent subtext that must perforce make the informed (and who is not informed on this?) viewer think of the Holocaust, an event never explicitly mentioned in the film. Once again we find ourselves empathizing with the victims of an inexplicable, omnipotent power and especially with the unique, eccentric schoolteacher who has taken upon herself the task of remaking history, not by telling it as "it really happened" but by changing it so as to be able to tell it "as I would like it to have been." We can think of Kluge's protagonist as a survivor of the genocide who would greatly prefer *not* to tell the world what she had actually experienced—which she obviously cannot tell in any case, since no one can tell this tale without distorting it (Levi 82–85)—but, rather, to be able to change the past itself and thereby to transform it into a tale that *can* be told. I do not believe that this is the conscious subtext of Kluge's film; he truly empathizes with his heroic schoolteacher, as he does with the victims of Stalingrad—the German victims, not the Soviet ones—with whom he is so obviously obsessed. But this is nevertheless a representation of absence in the sense I have been developing here, since both Kluge and his viewers must, somewhere, be constantly thinking about the genocide of the Jews as they wind their way through the piles of human and material wreckage that constitute Kluge's view of the (German) past, in those same lands of (Jewish) ashes and erased memories that haunted Paul Celan.[5]

Edgar Reitz's view of history, as presented in the film *Heimat* (1980–84), is far less fragmented and apocalyptic than Kluge's, despite, or perhaps precisely because of, the fact that he claims to be much more preoccupied with memory than with history. The German (rural) memory of the past, according to Reitz, is simple, modest, warm, and tightly knit; it is enclosed upon itself, and there is little room in it for outsiders. Indeed, the outside intrudes only in the shape of war, foreign countries, modernity, and Jews. The war is where the community must send its sons; foreign countries are where some other sons go and are unrecognizably transformed, not for the better; modernity is what finally destroys the harmony of village life, community, and the family; and the Jews are an ephemeral existence, appearing only to disappear rapidly as a somewhat disturbing, ambivalent presence, provoking hostility and fleetingly witnessing intimacy of which they have no part. Reitz's is a simpler work, and its symbolism is never very subtle. And, since it is about German memory rather than history, and because it represents that memory as wholly turned upon itself, it leaves no room for those whom the Germans would rather forget or repress, that is, their victims. And yet it too is dependent for its own coherence not merely on an absence of representation but also on a representation of absence. Conscious of a context of prejudice and genocide, evil and complicity, it must escape to the environment of a remote, anachronistic village, finally connected to modernity only following World War II and the (obviously unfortunate) Americanization of Germany. And yet even in that distant location the film cannot completely ignore a presence that its own realistic and traditional technique (so unlike Kluge's) must somehow acknowledge. Hence, Reitz feels obliged to make room for a momentary appearance of the absent, if only in order to indicate that the absent remained absent for his protagonists even when they were actually there. He must make the point that the Jews had no role in German (rural) memory, precisely because he knows that German memory is inseparably tied with visions of genocide. Indeed, the major motivation of *Heimat,* as Reitz himself argued, was to give back German history to the Germans, after it was taken away from them by the American film *Holocaust*—that is, taken away from them by the Jews, who are the main protagonists of both *Holocaust* the miniseries and the historical event of Nazi genocide. I suggest that the absence of the Jews is the fundamental subtext of *Heimat,* its motivation and the unspoken arbiter of its content. Without this absence the film would have been nothing more than a sentimental, overlong tale of rural life in a Godforsaken province. It is that absence that gives it meaning, provides it with the context it so emphatically rejects. In this sense *Heimat* is a film not about memory but about amnesia, that is, about the absence of memory and all that can be remembered and must nevertheless be erased.

Rainer Werner Fassbinder seems to have been more concerned with representing Jews than any of his colleagues (Koch 246). Perhaps the most accomplished director of the New German Cinema, he also gained a fair measure of notoriety. His films have enjoyed wide success in many countries, including Israel; yet his representations of Jews make the most blatant use of antisemitic stereotypes of any prominent German filmmaker. I would argue that Fassbinder, however, is not in fact concerned with Jews. His protagonists, like those of all of these filmmakers and writers, are marginal yet exceptional individuals, simultaneously survivors and victims of a catastrophe. In *The Marriage of Maria Braun* [Die Ehe der Maria Braun (1978)], the main character, a truly heroic figure, survives all hardship and betrayal, only to be blown up in a gas explosion in her villa, which she had gained through hard work and determination. (One cannot avoid thinking of the implicit association made here with those other victims of gas never represented by the director.) In *Lili Marleen* (1980) yet another survivor of anonymous destruction (with whose well-known chiefs she had had a brief but glamorous association) fares much worse than the shadowy figures of Jews, who seem to be more capable of controlling the forces of evil, not least by their great fortunes. Indeed, as has been pointed out (Koch 254), the Jews appear to extract themselves from the Holocaust with little difficulty and to thrive once more, while the heroine, abandoned by her Jewish lover, is destroyed along with Hitler's empire. We, the informed viewers, may of course be thinking of Auschwitz as we watch the stylized fighting at the front. But the absence of genocide makes room for the presence of money-grubbing Jews, and the misfortunes of the heroine are linked to the dubious accomplishments of the Jewish survivors (of an unmentioned Holocaust). Ultimately, it is the power of the Jews that is at the background of German suffering, and it is the absence of the Jewish genocide that serves as a crucial precondition for the representation of German victimhood.

Finally, I extend my argument to a few words about the historians. German scholarship has produced a remarkable volume of work on the Holocaust. In this sense there is no room to speak of an absence. Yet it is worthwhile to examine the nature of this scholarship and the main focus of its concerns and lacunae. In this context I would like to mention three historians who have written extensively on the National Socialist regime: Martin Broszat, Hans Mommsen, and Andreas Hillgruber (Bartov, "Wem gehört"). Broszat's well-known plea for a historicization of National Socialism provides a good starting point for this brief discussion, since it touches directly on some of the issues with which I am concerned (in Baldwin). Broszat argued that there was a need to reintroduce the notion of empathy to the study of Nazism and to eliminate the distancing techniques and rhetoric employed in such writing, whose impact has been to diminish greatly the pleasure of writing and reading such history. That is, Broszat quite clearly called for what I claim had been present all along in German cinematic and literary representation of the period: German empathy for their own history and its protagonists. In his correspondence with Broszat, Saul Friedländer argued that it was still too early to approach Nazism in the same manner as one would, for instance, sixteenth-century France (Broszat and Friedländer 129–30). Yet, looking at this debate from the perspective of almost ten years, I am struck by the fact that Broszat's basic assumption—namely, that such empathy was lacking and, therefore, had to be reintroduced—was rather off the mark, since even among the historians empathy was never absent, even if it was wrapped in what he thought of as a kind of compulsory and unproductive detachment. To be sure, this empathy was expressed indirectly, in that German historians writing on Nazism, and even specifically on the Holocaust, had shown a complete inability to empathize with the victims, even while they did indeed distance themselves from the perpetrators (but not from the remaining, vast majority of Germans). This is precisely what I would term a representation of absence, since the absence of empathy for the Jewish victims of Nazism left enough room for—indeed, made necessary—empathy with the German victims and survivors, who, from the perspective of the Jewish and other political and "racial" enemies of the Reich, were in fact the (often complicit) bystanders. Hence, the absence of representation (of Jewish victims as objects of empathy) is closely linked to a representation of absence, whereby the impossible empathy for the Jews is directed at the Germans, those large multitudes who were neither direct perpetrators nor active resisters but, instead, either complicit or resistant bystanders. The need for empathy has been rightly seen by Broszat as a crucial component of the historian's craft. But those who are the most obvious objects of empathy cannot be accorded that emotion, because, being as they are outside the frame of reference of identification and intimacy, empathy for them would block the option of empathy for oneself, creating thereby an unbearable psychological burden. This is what makes the mechanism of representing absence through enhanced empathy for one's own fate as individual, group, and nation all the more urgent.

Broszat's essay was important because it pointed at some of the fundamental problems of absence and representation (though I do not believe that he was aware of the implications of his argument as previously outlined). Hans Mommsen's contribution to the debate was of a more technical nature, insisting on the "functionalist" aspects of the "Final Solution" and the "cumulative radicalization" of policies during the Third Reich that led to genocide ("National Socialism" and "Realization"). In one sense there is no empathy here at all, merely a detailed (and contested) interpretation of how a modern, bureaucratic, industrial state launches itself on the path to unprecedented mass murder. And yet here too absence and empathy constitute the fundamental subtext of the whole interpretative edifice. This could be gleaned momentarily from the expression of empathy made by Mommsen when writing on the "sober" mentality of German soldiers on the Eastern Front, which obviously also demonstrated sympathy for their fate ("Kriegserfahrungen"). Most of the time, however, the subtext of the argument can be gathered only through the intense effort to understand the psychology of the middle-ranking perpetrators, on the one hand, and from Mommsen's complete lack of interest in their victims, who serve merely as the (somewhat opaque) object of the former's thoughts and actions, on the other. The absence of any empathy with the victims is not a simple function of Mommsen's focus on the perpetrators; rather, it is a precondition for his interpretation, since any treatment of the victims as potential objects of empathy would strongly undermine the main thrust of the argument, which is, after all, based on the perpetrators' perception of reality. Having chosen that perspective, any discussion of reality from the perspective of the victims would seem a mere interference, an unnecessary complication, irrelevant to both the argument and its objects. Yet, of course, this too is a representation of absence, in that the only reason for our interest in the mentality and thought processes of such otherwise wholly uninteresting characters as Mommsen's functionaries is what they were actually doing. In other words, it is the absentees who are the raison d'être of the whole interpretative undertaking, even if they appear only as numbers and figures distorted through the Nazi prism.

Andreas Hillgruber, my final example, expressed great interest in the objects of the historian's empathy and identification, though his approach was much less subtle than Broszat's relatively sophisticated (and ultimately far more influential) argument. As I have noted elsewhere ("Historians"), there is a clear link between Hillgruber's insistence that the historian (meaning, of course, the German historian) *must* identify with the fate of the Wehrmacht's soldiers in the eastern provinces of the Reich, his assertion that if there is any tragic element in World War II it is to be found in the carving up of Germany and the division of the world between the two flanking, non-European superpowers, and his cool and detached essay on the "end of European Jewry." Hillgruber feels, just like Broszat, that the historian must empathize with his protagonists, and he is similarly quite incapable of seeing the Jews as his protagonists, let alone empathizing with them. More radically than Broszat, he chooses to identify with the soldiers, the population, and even some of the Nazi party functionaries of the areas in the East under threat of invasion by the Red Army. While it is crucial to his argument, the genocide of the Jews is explicitly and intentionally absented from his empathic portrayal of the last months of the war in the East. It is crucial not only because it is constantly present both in the mind of the historian and in the minds of his protagonists but also because it has to be removed so as to make empathy possible. It is there, but it is not there; it is relevant, but it is not relevant; it is a precondition for the events described, yet it is not discussed. And when, in the second essay of Hillgruber's volume, the focus is on the genocide of the Jews, the tone and style of writing undergoes a radical transformation, adopting the bureaucratic language and detached rhetoric that both Hillgruber and Broszat have found so detrimental to good historical writing (Hillgruber 95–96; Bartov, "Historians" 343–44). In this second essay there is no case to be made for the absence of representation but very much of the representation of absence, since, while Hillgruber is explicitly concerned with the manner in which the physical absence of the Jews was achieved, the Jews as protagonists deserving the scholar's empathy are wholly absent from it, until their existence is systematically and totally "ended," in stark contradiction to the Germans, whose continued existence makes it possible for them to remain victims of a tragedy.

Tragedy is an important term in this context. It implies, we assume, an event or a circumstance in which the malicious forces of history had distorted the individual's or the nation's (heroic, in part even well-intentioned) actions into a self-destructive process, entrapping the individual in an inexplicable, and inescapable, web of errors and horrors, disillusionment and despair. What is absent from such German representations of the past is the tragedy of others. Being the true precondition for Germany's own tragedy, that other tragedy must be represented as an absence, an unspoken, unexpressed, separate moment, that is both known and unknown to have constituted the essential starting point of the one tale with which Germans can wholeheartedly empathize: their own history. That other tragedy—which is, of course, radically different in that its objects were caught up not in the web of their own doings but in that of others—must serve as an unacknowledged model for comparison; one must constantly contend with the model and always avoid direct comparison. Even Ernst Nolte does not directly compare German and Jewish victimhood, preferring, much more conveniently, to use Stalin's victims for that purpose ("Historical Legend," "Past"). Hence, the representation of absence is a basic, and yet never to be articulated, precondition of German representations of the past and especially of the Nazi past. It is not confined to the sphere of literature, film, and scholarship. As my friend in Berlin had (quite unintentionally) shown me, it is an important element in many Germans' self-representation: the sense that something that had previously been there is gone and that, while this disappearance has had long-term cultural, political, and psychological consequences, it can nevertheless not be processed by way of empathy and understanding. The process whereby the Jews were made into an absence is therefore detached from the tragedy that this absence has meant for Germany, and that tragedy of Jewish absence is subsumed under the greater tragedy of German fate and history. In this case the Jews have played a double role in the tragic tales of modern German history—first by being there then by "going away."

NOTES

1. For a fascinating case of representation of absence by a converted Austrian Jew in the interwar period, see Bettauer; see further Noveck, "Kampf," 74–80; and Noveck, "Bettauer."

2. Agnieszka Holland's film *Europa Europa* (1991) is neither wholly German nor about the Jewish experience of the Holocaust but is concerned, rather, with a highly exceptional case.

3. Reitz notes: "With *Holocaust,* the Americans have taken away our history"; "the Jews, since time immemorial 'people who go away' [*Weggeher*], fit well into this American culture."

4. This information was given me by Lenz himself in a private conversation in 1981.

5. I refer here especially to Celan's poem "Engführung."

WORKS CITED

Arendt, Hannah. "The Aftermath of Nazi Rule." *Commentary* 10 (October 1950): 342–53.

Baldwin, Peter, ed. *Reworking the Past: Hitler, the Holocaust, and the Historians' Debate.* Boston: Beacon, 1990.

Bartov, Omer. "Historians on the Eastern Front: Andreas Hillgruber and Germany's

Tragedy." *Murder in Our Midst: The Holocaust, Industrial Killing, and Represen-tation.* New York: Oxford UP, 1996. 71–88.

————. *Hitler's Army: Soldiers, Nazis, and War in the Third Reich.* New York: Oxford UP, 1991.

————. "War, Memory, and Repression: Alexander Kluge and the Politics of Repre-sentation in Postwar Germany." *Tel Aviver Jahrbuch für deutsche Geschichte* 23 (1994): 413–32.

————. "Wem gehört die Geschichte? Wehrmacht und Geschichtswissenschaft." In *Vernichtungskrieg: Verbrechen der Wehrmacht 1941 bis 1944,* ed. Hannes Heer and Klaus Naumann. Hamburg: Hamburger Edition, 1995. 601–19.

Bettauer, Hugo. *Die Stadt ohne Juden.* 1922. Reprint. Frankfurt a.M. and Berlin: Ull-stein Verlag, 1988.

Böll, Heinrich. *The Train Was on Time (Der Zug war pünktlich* [1949]). Trans. Richard Graves. New York: Criterion, 1956.

————. *Group Portrait with Lady (Gruppenbild mit Dame* [1971]). Trans. Leila Ven-newitz. Harmondsworth and New York: Penguin, 1976.

Broszat, Martin. "A Plea for the Historicization of National Socialism." In *Reworking the Past,* ed. Peter Baldwin. Boston: Beacon, 1990. 77–87.

Broszat, Martin, and Saul Friedländer. "A Controversy about the Historicization of Na-tional Socialism." In *Reworking the Past,* ed. Peter Baldwin. Boston: Beacon, 1990. 102–32.

Celan, Paul. "Engführung." *Sprachgitter.* Frankfurt a.M.: S. Fischer, 1959. 55–64.

De Man, Paul. *Blindness and Insight: Essays in the Rhetoric of Contemporary Criticism.* 2d rev. ed. Minneapolis: U of Minnesota P, 1986.

Diner, Dan. "Negative Symbiosis: Germans and Jews After Auschwitz." In *Reworking the Past,* ed. Peter Baldwin. Boston: Beacon, 1990. 251–61.

Engelmann, Bernt. *In Hitler's Germany: Daily Life in the Third Reich.* Trans. Krishna Winston. New York: Schocken Books, 1986.

Grass, Günter. *The Tin Drum (Die Blechtrommel* [1959]). Trans. Ralph Manheim. Lon-don: Secker and Warburg, 1974.

Hillgruber, Andreas. *Zweierlei Untergang: Die Zerschlagung des Deutschen Reiches und das Ende des europäischen Judentums.* Berlin: Corso bei Siedler, 1986.

Kaes, Anton. *From Hitler to Heimat: The Return of History as Film.* Cambridge: Har-vard UP, 1989.

Koch, Gertrud. *Die Einstellung ist die Einstellung: Visuelle Konstruktionen des Juden-tums.* Frankfurt a.M.: Suhrkamp, 1992.

Lenz, Siegfried. *The German Lesson (Deutschstunde* [1968]). Trans. Ernst Kaiser and Eithne Wilkins. New York: Hill and Wang, 1972.

Levi, Primo. *The Drowned and the Saved.* Trans. Raymond Rosenthal. New York: Sum-mit Books, 1988.

Mommsen, Hans. "Kriegserfahrungen." In *Über Leben im Krieg: Kriegserfahrungen in einer Industrieregion 1939–1945,* ed. Ulrich Borsdorf and Mathilde Jamin. Rein-bek bei Hamburg: Rowohlt, 1989. 7–14.

————. "National Socialism: Continuity and Change." In *Fascism: A Reader's Guide,* ed. Walter Laqueur. 2d ed. Harmondsworth: Penguin Books, 1982. 151–92.

————. "The Realization of the Unthinkable: The 'Final Solution of the Jewish Question' in the Third Reich." In *The Policies of Genocide: Jews and Soviet Prisoners of War in Nazi Germany,* ed. Gerhard Hirschfeld. London: Allen and Unwin, 1986. 93–144.

Nolte, Ernst. "Between Historical Legend and Revisionism?" and "The Past That Will Not Pass." Both in *Forever in the Shadow of Hitler?* Trans. James Knowlton and Truett Cates. Atlantic Highlands: Humanities Press, 1993. 1–15, 18–23.

Noveck, Beth Simone. "Der Kampf um Wien: Sexuality and Politics in Hugo Bettauer's Vienna 1918–1925." Bachelor's thesis, Harvard College, 1991.

———. "Hugo Bettauer and the Political Culture of the First Republic." In *Austria in the Nineteen Fifties: Contemporary Austrian Studies,* ed. Günter Bischof and Anton Pelinka. New Brunswick and London: Transaction, 1995. 138–70.

Reitz, Edgar. *Liebe zum Kino: Utopien und Gedanken zum Autorenfilm, 1962–1983.* Cologne: Verlag Köln 78, 1984.

Ryan, Judith. *The Uncompleted Past: Postwar German Novels and the Third Reich.* Detroit: Wayne State UP, 1983.

Said, Edward W. *Beginnings: Intention and Method.* New York: Basic Books, 1975.

Santner, Eric L. *Stranded Objects: Mourning, Memory, and Film in Postwar Germany.* 2d ed. Ithaca: Cornell UP, 1993.

Shapira, Anita. *Land and Power: The Zionist Resort to Force, 1881–1948.* Trans. William Templer. New York: Oxford UP, 1992.

CHAPTER 14

Schinkel and the Politics of German Memory: The Life of the Neue Wache in Berlin

Wallis Miller

The guild of architectural historians has traditionally stood outside the academic mainstream not only because of the service role architectural historians play in practically oriented schools of architecture and design but also because of the varied association of scholars with local historic preservation groups, government sponsored building surveys, and expensive architectural tours for patrons. Wallis Miller's essay shows why architectural historians should be brought into the mainstream of academic culture. Architectural history adds a new dimension to cultural studies in terms of its message and its own methods. It can tell us a great deal about the meaning of places and space: how and why space was designed and constructed in a particular way and who influenced the decisions and paid the bills for structures that necessarily affect far more people and for far longer than many other creative endeavors. And the already interdisciplinary nature of the architectural historian's work—encompassing art, aesthetics, classics, history, engineering, semiotics, sociology, and economics, for example—can serve as both model and inspiration for some of the border crossings that we see as productive and necessary for the academy today.

We include Miller's essay here because it is such a useful example of architectural history done well. She provides a comprehensive description of a structure, Berlin's Neue Wache, and its compelling history. The kinds of questions she asks about this edifice are those that embody a cultural studies mode of thinking: concern with relationships between disparate entities, with the work of power and politics, with collective memory, and with a culture's response to trauma and dislocation. Miller's argument, like Omer Bartov's,

*demonstrates the persistent problems that Germans have encountered with ob-
jects of empathy. As in Bartov's piece, here too, the question "Which victims?"
finds perturbing answers.*

*Miller's entry into the Neue Wache comes via its architect Karl Friedrich
Schinkel. Her thesis is that Schinkel's original construction (1818) constitutes
an act of "renovation." Miller constructs notions of renovation to mean renewal and reinvigoration, but with an intact past, with a constant foundation
present. Schinkel's "renovation," necessarily, has to negotiate the past and incorporate it and the memory of it into a newly invigorated, forward-looking
structure. His work set the terms of the Neue Wache's subsequent renovations
(in a more traditional sense): during the Weimar Republic, the Third Reich, under Walter Ulbricht's East German regime, and, finally, in 1993 following
reunification. Miller's essay can teach us much about the nature of both renovation and memory. Her analysis of this key symbolic space shows the power—
analytical and pedagogical—of looking at such sites of public tension and commemoration.*

Since the beginning of the eighteenth century the instability of the Prussian/
German state has affected the shape of Berlin. Constant shifts in the boundaries
of the empire as well as in its ideology have forced countless architectural re-
definitions of the center of its capital. The decisions to preserve, renovate, or
replace Berlin's monuments have thus always been caught between considerations of their ideological impact and their effect on the body of historic documentation. Karl Friedrich Schinkel's Neue Wache grew out of this tension (fig.
1). It was originally designed and subsequently renovated at significant points
of change in German history: it was designed after the defeat of Napoléon and
renovated after World War I, modified during the Nazi period, and substantially
changed at three points after World War II: in the early years of the German Democratic Republic, at the height of the Cold War, and after reunification in 1993.
Consequently, its architecture has always borne traces of history consciously
transformed by the ideologies of the present.[1]

Given that the building has always been renovated as a memorial, it is no
surprise that it is the locus of a confrontation of history and ideology, or, more
precisely, a confrontation of history and memory and of the past and the
present. The mutual dependency within each of these pairs is revealed by the
fact that each member is often defined in terms of the other. In his study of history and memory the historian Jacques LeGoff describes memory as "the raw

Fig. 1. The Neue Wache viewed from Unter den Linden. (Karl Friedrich Schinkel, *Sammlung Architektonischer Entwürfe*, pl. 2. Photo courtesy of Princeton Architectural Press.)

material of history," while "history nourishes memory in turn, and enters into the great dialectical process of memory and forgetting experienced by individuals and societies" (xi). The two terms fluctuate between identical and independent states, in which history remains closest to the event itself, to the objective, and to a notion of truth, and memory is colored by experience, ideology, by the search for power (54), and by imagination. According to Vico:

> The Latins call memory *memoria* when it retains sense perceptions, and *reminiscentia* when it gives them back to us. But they designated in the same way the faculty by which we form images, which the Greeks called *phantasia,* and which we call *imaginativa;* for where we vulgarly say *imaginare,* the Latins said *memorare.* . . . Thus the Greeks say in their mythology that the Muses, the powers of imagination, are the daughters of Memory. (Qtd. in LeGoff 86)

The intimacy of memory and imagination implies a similar intimacy of past and present. These reciprocities are played out throughout the life of the Neue Wache, in its original design as well as in its renovations.

From the time of the first design phase to the present the Neue Wache has used these complex relationships as the means to portray first Prussian then German identity. As the Royal Guard House, the building stood on the boulevard Unter den Linden as one in a collection of early monuments to the public; after the dissolution of the monarchy, the building was repeatedly chosen as the site of a war memorial, first implicitly and later explicitly, of national scope. While each memorial mourned *human* death, it also marked the birth of a new type of government born out of *political* death. In each case the present was a product of the past. Consequently, as those in charge of the project worked to represent their history, they assumed the responsibility for representing themselves. The technique of renovation emerged as their means to reveal the complex relationships between past and present and between history and memory before the general public. Renovation did not merely allow the new design to erase the traces of the past, but it, by definition, "remodeled" and "imparted new vigor" to the past (*American Heritage Dictionary*); the new design had to respect, but not restore, the existing structure while accommodating it to the uses of the present. Literally, then, this architectural technique put the architectural forms of the past and the ideologies that motivated them in the context of a new design and new ideologies.

While the Neue Wache may have been ultimately selected as the site of German war memorials because of its ties with the Prussian origins of the modern German state and because of its location on the major ceremonial axis in the country's capital city, its renovation was not merely an artifact of the pragmatic requirements of the project. It was an ideological tool, as integral a part of identity as was the content of the memorial itself. This is not only relevant to the twentieth-century projects, whose explicit goal was to create a memorial, but to the original Neue Wache as well, which, I contend, its designer Schinkel likewise created as a renovated building.

Juxtapositions in German History

The Neue Wache was one of the first architectural signs of German pride after the defeat of Napoléon; King Friedrich Wilhelm III commissioned the project, which was built between 1816 and 1818, in order to express the public importance of the Prussian victory over the French as well as to provide himself with a guardhouse for his new residence across the street. Thus, the building formed a major part of the king's plan to transform the center of Berlin from a closed royal enclave, protected by the military, into an area open to the public. The nature of the Neue Wache project placed the military in the pivotal role of the agent who would unite the general public with the monarchy in the center of the city.

In 1816 King Friedrich Wilhelm III ordered the architect, painter, and set designer Karl Friedrich Schinkel (1781–1841) to replan the center of Berlin (see fig. 5). Schinkel had been appointed to the head of the royal building department (Geheimer Oberbaurat), one year earlier. This commission was an expression of the king's desire to build the recent Prussian victory into the design of its capital, Berlin. It was not merely a victory for the monarchy, however, but was perceived by all to be a victory won by the people as well. Until the Napoleonic Wars the military had been seen as a vehicle of the ruling aristocracy. It had been an adversary of the civilian population and had exploited their families and their possessions at will. The wars against the French fundamentally changed this relationship, and thus the relationship between the ruling class, the military, and its subjects, by providing the occasion for fundamental military reforms.

According to General Gerhard von Scharnhorst, an important military leader, strategist, and theoretician at the time, "When free citizens become soldiers and soldiers are free citizens, the state that they should defend, should be governed, [or] in other words, shaped by them."[2] As this new perception of the soldier radically changed the military's recruitment strategy, it affected the nature of the military's alliances to the public and the monarchy. Not surprisingly, however, it only had a moderate effect on the king. While he commissioned Schinkel to redesign the center of Berlin as a civic realm, the king was unwilling to release it completely to the public. Many of Schinkel's public commissions in Berlin, for the redesign of the city center (1816–41), the 1818–21 Schauspielhaus (National Theater), the 1822–27 Altes Museum (National Museum), the Friedrich-Werderische Church of 1824–30, the 1829–32 Packhof (customs buildings), the 1831–36 Bauakademie (Architecture Academy), as well as the Neue Wache, were manifestations of the king's attempt to exercise his sovereignty while recognizing the new significance of the public, represented by Schinkel himself.[3]

The king's correction to Schinkel's 1816 site plan (fig. 2), which ultimately determined the building's location, made it clear that there was a difference between his interpretation of the situation and that of Schinkel. Schinkel had placed the building to respond to the public space on the other side of Unter den Linden; the king slid the building to a position that clearly related it to his residence. Schinkel further expressed this tension in his design for the building. Rather than simply reinforce the military's allegiance to the monarchy, acted out in their function as the royal guard, Schinkel juxtaposed this function to the new relationship between the military and the general public by making his building out of two very different parts: he surrounded a guardhouse, designed as a Roman *castrum,* or fortress, with Greek porticoes at the front and the back.[4] In his description of the building he clearly separated the two elements. He began by talking about the "building itself": "The plan of this entirely freestanding building is more or less modeled on a Roman *castrum.* Whence the four massive corner towers and the interior court." Only after finishing his description of the *castrum* does he describe the portico as "attached or brought on to the front [*der vorne angebrachte Porticus*], resting on ten free columns and the connecting pilasters."[5]

The portico signified the public realm in Schinkel's urban works and allowed the Neue Wache to enter into a dialog with the two most recent civic structures: Knobelsdorff's 1741 Staatsoper, across the street, and Langhans's Brandenburg gate to the west, where Unter den Linden entered the city, built between 1788 and 1791.[6] Soon after, the Schauspielhaus (1817) and the Altes Museum (1823–24) joined the group. Schinkel's decision to place the Greek portico entry in front of the Roman *castrum* allowed him to exploit a simple architectural difference between exterior and interior, between Greek and Roman languages, and, in Alberti's terms, between ornament and structure.

Sometimes with subtlety, sometimes directly, Schinkel let the hybrid nature of the Neue Wache emerge in his descriptions and renderings of the building. In his description in the *Sammlung Architektonischer Entwürfe* (*The Collection of Architectural Drawings*) he makes no mention of the fact that the portico and the *castrum* towers are of the same material; he only mentions that the portico is made of sandstone from Saxony. This distinction becomes clear in his representation of the building (fig. 1), in which only the entire surface of the *castrum* is rendered as cut stone blocks and the portico is left blank.

The actual building was treated in a slightly more complicated way. While the front and the rear facades, including the *castrum* towers, were of the same stone, the *castrum* side walls were of brick. The distinction between the Royal

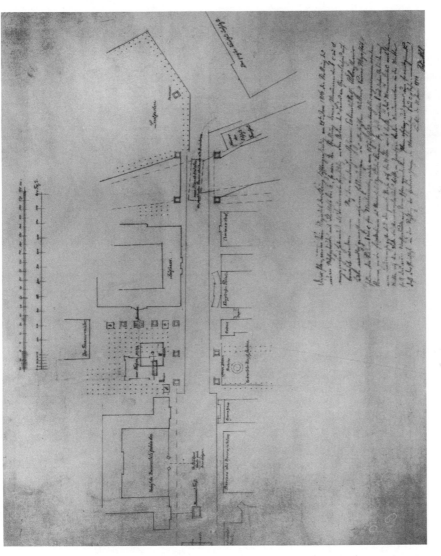

Fig. 2. Schinkel's second site plan for the Neue Wache, June 1816, as corrected by the king. The king's correction is centered on the site; Schinkel's hovers above it to the left. (Pundt, pl. 58; a negative of the original is located in the photo archive of the Stiftung Preussische Schlösser und Gärten Berlin-Brandenburg, Schloss Charlottenburg.)

Fig. 3.   The Neue Wache and Arsenal, around 1910. The statues of two of the four generals, but not the canons, are visible. (University of Kentucky, College of Architecture Slide Collection.)

Guard House and the public monument was brought to Unter den Linden by Schinkel's typical assignment of materials: the public faces—the portico and the *castrum* towers—were of a dignified stone; the "working facade" was of brick, thus bringing to the street the emblem of a function usually hidden from the public. While the portico was the backdrop for the public life—that is, the ritual of the changing of the guard and the continuous crowds strolling down Unter den Linden (fig. 3)—the interior was dedicated to the business of guarding the king. Schinkel even exploited the typical use of a courtyard within a *castrum;* in his project he used it "[to hide] the utility and service rooms from the square around the building" (Schinkel 35). One can therefore understand one of Schinkel's earlier designs as a more radical display of the tension between interior and exterior: its glass facade forced the internal activity, and not just its sign, out of hiding.[7]

Conquering the Guardhouse: The Temporal Nature of the Juxtaposition

The location of the building made sense as it was diagonally opposite the new royal residence across the street (see fig. 5). While the portico, framed with trees, was as much a backdrop for the king's view of his guard as it was for the public's, its relationship to the new palace was not so strong as to privilege the king's position, as did, say, his royal box in the theater. The king was simply a member of the public viewing the urban spectacle in the center of the city.

Schinkel's Neue Wache was the catalyst for a new urban scheme that was to transform the existing Berlin. But the resonance of the new scheme lay in making clear its conquest of the old city and thus the old order. The construction of an entirely new guardhouse would not have expressed this notion of conquest as well as the transformation of an old one. The old guardhouse—the Alte Wache—was located slightly to the east of the Neue Wache site, in the shadows of the Zeughaus, the arsenal (fig. 4). Since 1800 there were plans to replace the old "unsightly" military guardhouse (*die unansehnliche Kanonierwache*) with a new Royal Guard House (Forsmann 92). On the far side of the Alte Wache—which would become the site of the Neue Wache—lay the Grüner Graben (Green Moat), a part of the old fortifications from the mid-seventeenth century. The fortifications had not defended the Prussian monarchy merely against a military enemy; they prevented the expansion of the suburbs and, thus, of civilian territory. They were dismantled around 1700 by King Friedrich I and replaced by new fortifications, completed by 1736, that embraced a wider area. While the new walls allowed the suburbs and the civilian population to grow, the official justification for their new location was that they were to contain potential military deserters. Thus, they once again defended the monarchy against the civilian enemy, as they transformed a growing population into agents of the king.[8] In his site plan for the new guardhouse Schinkel defied the historic predominance of the royal defense line as he covered over the moat (fig. 5). His Neue Wache stood as the slightly, but significantly, displaced Alte Wache, the *castrum* representing the unadorned form of the old guardhouse, renovated with the new public garb (figs. 3, 4). The renovation represented what Schinkel hoped would be the transformation from Hohenzollern to civic Berlin and the birth of a new Prussian identity. The concept of renovation became the means to shape German memory—a construct founded on the tension between the present and the past—and thus it became an appropriate template for the subsequent projects on the site.

Renovation as a Representative Tool

How could the same building be used to serve the memory of the Weimar Republic, the Third Reich, the early German Democratic Republic, the German

Fig. 4. Jean Rosenberg, *Der Platz am Zeughaus*, 1780. The Alte Wache is the small building with the pyramidal roof on the right side of Unter den Linden, just behind the Arsenal. (Pundt, pl. 53; original source, Bildarchiv Preussischer Kulturbesitz.)

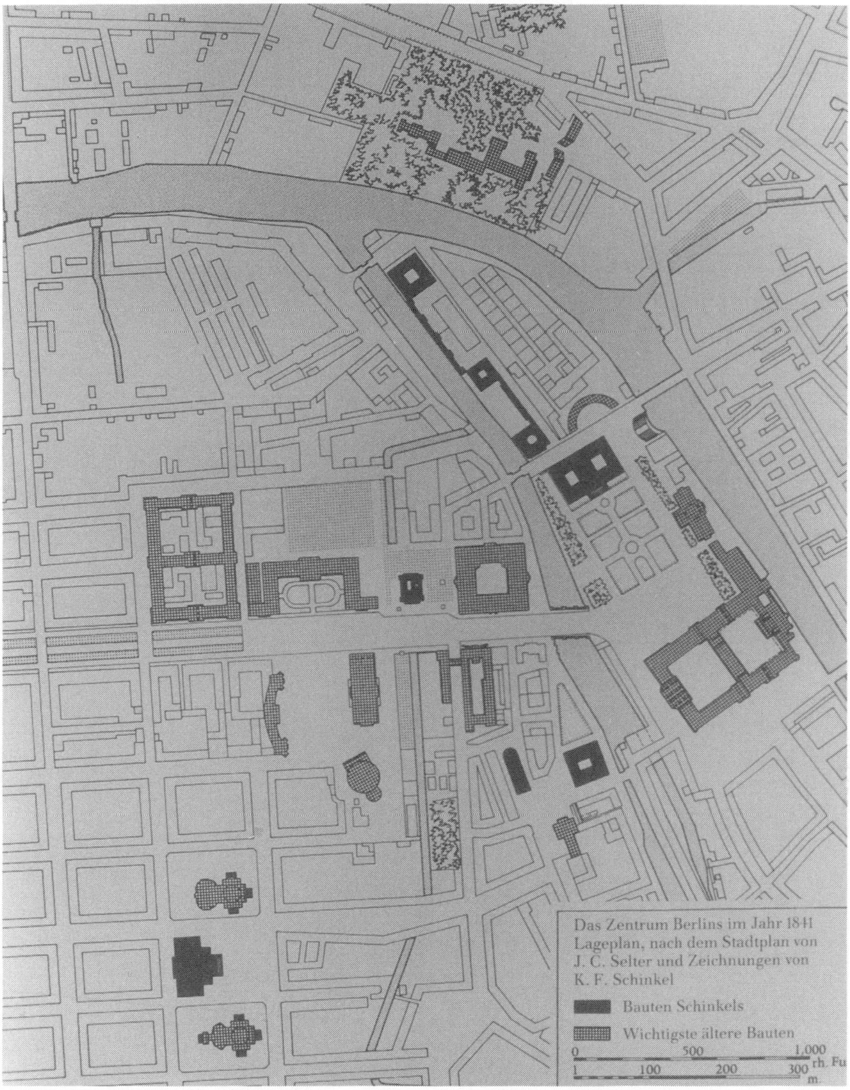
Das Zentrum Berlins im Jahr 1841
Lageplan, nach dem Stadtplan von
J. C. Selter und Zeichnungen von
K. F. Schinkel
Bauten Schinkels
Wichtigste ältere Bauten
0
500
1,000
rh. Fu
1
100
200
300
m.

Fig. 5. **Schinkel's plan of the center of the city, 1816–41. Schinkel's buildings are black; other important buildings are gray. One can see the vestiges of the moat above and to the right of the Neue Wache (the small rectangle at the center) and below, across Unter den Linden. (Drawn by James K. M. Cheng; Pundt, pl. 73.)**

Democratic Republic steeped in the Cold War, and a reunified Germany? Was an eternal respect for Schinkel and a wish to use his traces to preserve his presence in Berlin the sole basis for repeatedly using the shell of his guard building for a major memorial? As each new period of German history made the existing Neue Wache ideologically obsolete and demanded its renovation, there were many proposals for using the building as something other than a memorial as well as for other locations for a major war memorial. Each time, however, the Neue Wache and plans for a new memorial converged. Its location, its architectural value, and the fact that the building was one of the few that focused on the historic relationship between the military, the people, and the government contributed to the Neue Wache's desirability as a war memorial of national scope. That the renovation process, which focused on the interior, was not cumulative, but one in which a new project replaced its predecessor, explains how these very different states made use of a similar container to express their different attitudes toward the past.

Rather than simply weave the past and present into a new whole, each of these projects exploited Schinkel's architectural confrontation of the interior with the exterior. In many countries, however, national memorials and monuments provide a sense of continuity with the past, such as the Arc de Triomphe in France, and, in the United States, the Tomb of the Unknown Soldier and the Jefferson and Lincoln Memorials. Jefferson and Lincoln stand as *individual* representations of universally accepted values in the United States. The military memorials, both the Arc de Triomphe and the Tomb of the Unknown Soldier, represent a military generally perceived always to have been fighting on the "right" side.

In the case of the Tomb of the Unknown Soldier any doubt concerning military allegiance, as has been caused by the U.S. involvement in the Vietnam War, is deflected by the presence of the individual soldier, whose sacrifice for his country at the expense of his identity is the focus of remembrance at the site.[9] In turn, the potentially negative connotation of the Vietnam War has been isolated in a memorial specifically dedicated to that event. The Vietnam Veterans Memorial is the site where Americans could cast doubt on the correctness of *their* military involvement in the Vietnam War, thus assigning responsibility for the mistake to the U.S. government and, in turn, to themselves. But, again, the emphasis is on the memory of the individual soldiers who perished in battle. In reading each name, the viewer first identifies with the dead soldier and not with those who may have wrongly led him or her, and many others, to their deaths.

Germany certainly has its share of military memorials and monuments, but most, like the Vietnam Memorial, commemorate specific individuals, groups, or events. In Berlin Schinkel's monument on the Kreuzberg (1817–21), placed on the highest point on the military parade grounds near the Tempelhofer Feld (the field at Tempelhof), is one such example. With the construction of the Kreuzberg monument, the renaming of the rondel at the nearby Hallesches Tor, one of the city gates, to Belle-Alliance Platz (Square of Good Alliance), and the largest victory celebration ever in Berlin (some sixty thousand people attended), the Germans fully commemorated their victory over Napoléon (Mieck 476–77 and n. 103). The Siegessäule (Victory Column) could be seen as another example of the same kind. It was built in 1873 as a monument to the victory over Denmark, Austria, and France in the wars from 1864 to 1871 that provoked the founding of the Second Empire. Placed opposite the future site of the Reichstag, it seemed to transfer the sense of victory from the military to the people and their new country. The frieze covering the shaft was decorated with French canons, thus transforming the column into a figurative display of the trophies of victory.[10] One of these canons had, in fact, been dragged from the battlefield to the side of the Neue Wache (Tietz 20), where it assumed iconographic significance. This was reinforced by its position alongside similar canons confiscated earlier from the French, after the Napoleonic Wars. In front of all of them stood statues of the four generals who helped to win both those wars and an improved status for the civilian conscripts.[11] But cast over all of the canons was the shadow of the Neue Wache, which remained in the service of the king. The ambiguous role of the military was more subtly present around the Siegessäule, not only because this ambiguity was transferred, via the trophies of victory, from the Neue Wache back to the column but because the Siegessäule was based, so to speak, in the monarchy: it stood on nothing other than the Königsplatz (Square of the King).

In the twentieth century the association of civic identity with the military became even more problematic. Given the German defeat in both world wars, the Holocaust, and, for some, the short life of the German Democratic Republic, any plans to create a *central* memorial on this recent history would be difficult to realize. "After all," as James Young says in *The Texture of Memory:*

> while the victors of history have long erected monuments to their triumphs and victims have built memorials to their martyrdom, only rarely does a nation call upon itself to remember the victims of crimes it has perpetrated. Where are the national monuments to the genocide of American Indians, to the millions of Africans enslaved and murdered, to the Russian kulaks and peasants starved to death by the millions? They barely exist. (21)

Nonetheless, each German government in place after World War I, with the exception of the National Socialist government, seemed willing to shape national identity anew within a building that could not fail to evoke negative associations. Each decided to create a major memorial when it acceded to power and to locate the project in a renovated Neue Wache. Rather than designing a completely new structure, which would be a separate addition to those built in the past, or restoring an old one to its original state, which would seamlessly carry past associations into the present, each government made an architectural decision that forced it to juxtapose the present to the past and thus preclude any ideological continuity.

The Weimar Renovation

Schinkel's building was first renovated during the Weimar Republic, when it had become functionally as well as ideologically obsolete. The fall of the monarchy eliminated the need for a Royal Guard; the loss of the war made the celebration of victory on the building's exterior inappropriate. Heinrich Tessenow's winning entry in the 1930 competition to renovate the building as a "Memorial Site for those killed in the Great War" (*Gedächtnisstätte für die Gefallenen des Weltkrieges*) replaced the workspaces of the living guard with a space for the dead, carefully echoing what had existed there previously (fig. 6). Tessenow was an ambiguous, if important, figure in the German architectural community at the time, who situated himself between the avant-garde and the conservative factions of the profession. His buildings, many of which were residential, reflected his faith in mass production, while they assumed the simplified forms of a traditional German architecture (a *Heimatstil*). Although his new interior was a single cubic space, Tessenow metaphorically retained the essential feature of the guard's quarters: the separation of the guard from the urban life outside. The interior was completely sealed off from all sources of natural light except for a skylight, which echoed the presence of the old service courtyard. The side windows were filled with brick, laid in the same manner as was the rest of the original wall, literally making a seamless connection between new and old construction. Access to the building was reduced to three doorways sealed by iron gates, displaced artifacts of the fence that had previously surrounded the building outside to protect the guardhouse during the 1848 revolution. Tessenow's original intention further separated the guard from the public: he wanted to allow only visual access to the building except on special, that is, state-sanctioned, occasions.

The memorial objects consisted of a granite cube, two candelabra, a bronze tablet inscribed with the dates of World War I, and a series of wreaths: natural wreaths hung on the side walls and a silver wreath gilded in gold and platinum lay atop the granite cube, which Tessenow described as a sarcophagus. It was as if Tessenow had reached to the Winged Victories on the entablature of Schinkel's building and taken a wreath to place inside. But the wreath was not the laurel wreath of victory; it was the oak wreath of death (figs. 6, 7).

The significance of Tessenow's project can be best understood by looking at a project that was not selected but often publicized. Among the other five en-

Fig. 6. The interior of the Neue Wache in 1931, designed by Heinrich Tessenow. (*Streit um die Neue Wache* 67; original source, Berlin, Landesbildstelle.)

Fig. 7.   Installation of the wreath in the Tessenow project, 1931. (Tietz 51; original source, Berlin, Ullstein Bildarchiv.)

tries in the competition Ludwig Mies van der Rohe's project most directly challenged Tessenow's scheme (fig. 8): among the nine jury members five supported Tessenow, three supported Mies, and one supported Hans Poelzig.[12] Mies was one of Germany's best-known architects and a leader of the modern avant-garde movement in architecture, although he was less politically committed than most of its other members. A few years earlier he had completed Germany's pavilion at the world exhibition in Barcelona (1929), one of the most studied projects in the history of modern architecture, and, in 1930, replaced the marxist Hannes Meyer as director of the Bauhaus, the German avant-garde's school of design, then located in the city of Dessau. Mies boldly confronted the connection between the military and the German state after the horrible losses of World War I. His project opposed the Schinkel building in detail: it slid into, rather than engaged, the existing building. The interior was sealed off but not concealed from the exterior: the window apertures were to be filled with gray glass, not brick. This uneasy juxtaposition was also revealed to the public on the interior. Seated at a bench located at the periphery of the space, a visitor looked through the transparent marble veneer used to clad the walls and saw Schinkel's guardhouse exterior as a shell, a ghost, hovering around the new site for meaning. At the center lay not a wreath but the state, represented by the *Reichsadler* (imperial eagle) engraved in a slab of stone. The inscription surrounding it dedicated the memorial "to the dead" [*den Toten*].

Given the link between memorial and identity, one can see how death referred as much to the nineteenth-century German Empire as it did to the victims of the war. Mies's scheme made clear the tragic genesis of the new German republic, which, in turn, tainted the republic's nineteenth-century origins in Prussian victory and military strength. By comparison, Tessenow intended to leave the victorious nineteenth-century origins intact for the Weimar identity, by isolating death as a separate affair. Only Schinkel's laurel wreath of victory on the exterior entablature would be a part of the public landscape; Tessenow's oak wreath of death inside would remain in the precinct of state-controlled ritual.

Tessenow's proposal seemed to reiterate the tensions between the public and the state present in Schinkel's construction of Prussian identity. The monarchy had died, but a state removed from the public still occupied the interior space, as it had done for the past century. Both inside and out, however, every trace of the military had disappeared but one: Tessenow had placed an iron cross—the symbol of heroism—in the central portal, between the zone of the public and that of the state. The military's absence, except as it was represented by the iron cross, suggested its diminished importance and, thus, the death of the nineteenth-century configuration of Prussian society, which had, in the eyes of some, continued to shape German identity since 1871. This loss was the subject of Tessenow's memorial project.[13]

Fig. 8. Mies van der Rohe's design for the 1930 competition to renovate the Neue Wache into a War Memorial. This image is for another version of the project, in which the walls are marble, not glass. (Perspective drawing. Courtesy, The Mies van der Rohe Archive, The Museum of Modern Art, New York. Photograph © 1997 The Museum of Modern Art, New York.)

The public, however, did not allow the Neue Wache to remain a memorial to an obsolete identity. Consequently, the scheme was changed: the public metaphorically broke through the iron gates, cast the iron cross to the side, and claimed the interior of the building and, thus, the memory of the war as their own.[14] They no longer needed to be represented by the military in national consciousness; they were present in their own right. As the barrier between the public and the state dropped away in Tessenow's final scheme, the stone floor turned to paving, reminiscent of Berlin's streets.[15] The interior of the Neue Wache became a part of the public landscape and part of a living German memory.

The emphasis now was on the specific origin of the Weimar Republic, which confronted, rather than absorbed, the nineteenth-century origins of the modern German state. As in Mies's project, "remembering" in this version of Tessenow's project enabled Weimar Germans to determine who they were and out of what they came. It did not simply inform them about who they had been but were no longer. Mies's project, however, allowed the past to confront the present directly; for him it was the brutal irony of military victory and mass death that was a key part of the Weimar consciousness. By physically separating these two terms, Tessenow placed tragic death at the heart of the original victory, without tainting it.

Both, however, left the connection between death and identity open to interpretation. The abstract nature of the *Denkzeichen* (sign of contemplation), as it was called by the competition's organizers, refused to fix the meaning that death had for the German citizen. Inside the victorious symbols of a distant national past the choice to assume the role of mourner, victim, passive witness to an uncontrollable horror, or its agent was the result of the individual interpretation of each German who visited the project. This choice is essential to the definition of memory given by the historian Charles Maier in his book *The Unmasterable Past: History, Holocaust, and German National Identity:*

> Memory, as in Saul Friedländer's affecting memoir, mingles private and public spheres. Like some Verdian aria of renunciation set against a backdrop of war or rebellion, it conflates vast historical occurrences with the most interior consciousness. (149)

It is this particular conflation of public and private, this mechanism of memory formation, that worked with the architectural template provided by the renovation to negotiate a varied German history and connect memorial building to the construction of national identity in these two Weimar projects. In both cases the abstract *Denkzeichen* was the nucleus of a dual confrontation; at this site of contemplation the viewer situated him- or herself relative to both the recent and the distant national past. It was from deep within the interior, not on the exterior, that German memory and, thus, identity emerged.

The Neue Wache between Weimar and Reunification

The National Socialist regime only altered the building superficially, uniting the exterior and interior with funerary ornament and a military guard that turned the whole building into a heroic monument. The Allies' bombings of Berlin in World War II severely damaged the building. The portico partially collapsed, and fire gutted the interior, melting Tessenow's granite cube. The wreath went missing, allegedly removed for safekeeping. Although rumored to be in the West, it was never found (fig. 9). Until renovation plans for the building existed, the building's ruins served as a backdrop for banners that called for peace in the name of the Soviet government.

After a long debate over the building's future, the East German government stabilized and restored it in 1957, leaving the wartorn Tessenow sarcophagus in place for public view. In 1968, at the height of the Cold War and in preparation for its twentieth anniversary the next year, the government completely renovated the building, removing the objects of Tessenow's renovation but maintaining its structure. Inside a newly finished space, one found an eternal flame and tombs of the unknown soldier and the unknown resistance fighter, dedicated, as in 1957, "to the victims of fascism and militarism." Thus, the history of the use of the building during the existence of the German Democratic Republic is one of a shift from reminding viewers of the extensive destruction caused by a war produced by the West to being a memorial whose representational technique created a continuity with the victors of World War I. These changes, those produced by the National Socialist government and the war as well as the total erasure of the final East German project by the reunified German government, despite protest from many quarters, reveal a series of religious, political, and cultural associations that are beyond the scope of this essay but the subject of my other research concerning this building. Here my examples are confined to the moments in the history of the Neue Wache admitted into the memory of those who specifically transformed it into a *national* memorial after German reunification.

The Neue Wache in a Reunited Germany

Given the sharp ideological turn that followed reunification, the Neue Wache was again obsolete after 1990. Its most recent renovation was completed in 1993, when it was dedicated "to the victims of war and oppression" (fig. 10). The project entailed an interesting combination of ideology and history created by Chancellor Helmut Kohl and the director of the German Historical Museum,

Fig. 9.   1945 photo of the interior of the Neue Wache by Robert Capa. (Tietz 76; original source, Berlin, Landesbildstelle.)

Fig. 10. Exterior of the Neue Wache, 1995. (Photo courtesy of Frank Döring.)

Christoph Stölzl. They erased all of the traces of the East German projects and almost completely restored Tessenow's design, except for the granite cube and the wreath. This they replaced with a copy of Käthe Kollwitz's *Pietá* of 1937–38 (fig. 11).

Although it was actually created during the Nazi period, the *Pietá* was substantially a product of the post–World War I era. Kollwitz made the Expressionist sculpture to represent her mourning for her son, who was killed in the war. While contemporary to Tessenow's original design, the sculpture clearly had no place there. The power of Tessenow's design, according to Siegfried Kracauer in 1931, lay in the absence of representational figures. He said: "[The viewer] notices, thanks to the nature [of the details] that essential human qualities are represented in the space. They fill it more than figures would." Memory in Tessenow's scheme was generated by the interaction of individual members of the public with the architecture. Now, the personal memory that was once liberated by Tessenow's architecture is absent, having been cast by the state into a bronze mold.

The individual is only present in the documents of history. The announcement by the German government and the German Historical Museum of completed plans for the building produced a flurry of responses in newspapers, magazines, radio, television, and the streets. While some defended the project, most protested both the selection process for the design, which was not made public, and the design of the memorial itself. The discussion has continued to the present, its focus shifting from the building to the surroundings after the memorial's dedication on Volkstrauertag (People's Day of Mourning) in November 1993.

The most recent debate concentrates on a plan to reinstall the statues of nineteenth-century generals that stood around the building from Schinkel's time to the early days of the German Democratic Republic.[16] Many of the pre-dedication responses to the new project were compiled in two books: one published by the German Academy of Arts (*Streit um die Neue Wache*) and the other by the German Historical Museum (Stölzl) Both books debate the validity of erasing all traces of the East German memorials. The former, published when the project was nearly complete, consists of opinion pieces, in scholarly and journalistic form, written by cultural experts and a discussion held by the academy the previous March, when demolition was already under way. The latter is similar, but it replaces the academy discussion with a debate held in the German Bundestag on the subject, which occurred on 14 May 1993, when the project was well under construction.

Both are records of the possibility of individual response to the building, so cherished by Kracauer but replaced by the bronze figure in the new memorial. This possibility remains concealed in books that were published after the

Fig. 11. Interior of the Neue Wache, 1995. (Photo courtesy of Frank Döring.)

renovation was largely complete and whose covers are opened only by those with a specific interest in the building. The exclusion of individual response from the site of contemporary national memory and its relegation to the historical record are made all the more poignant by two facts. The academy book devotes most of its pages to essays and a discussion concerning the appropriateness of the use of the Kollwitz figure, a use that is not supported by the academy in its wish to have seen a full restoration of the Tessenow design. The other book was published by the very institution that, along with the chancellor, sanctioned the design of the current memorial.

The 1993 Neue Wache project poses as the integration of history and memory; it claims to have restored history in order to demonstrate the continuity of German memory. Because of the installation of the *Pietà,* however, it has in fact reconfigured Weimar history for use by a new German memory. That the *Pietà* in the Neue Wache is five times the size of Kollwitz's original is a sign of this reconfiguration; it shows that continuity between the memory of the Weimar period and the present can only be created by forcing a history transformed by imagination—by memory—into place.

Historical fact has not been completely transformed by the new design, however, and in its own right presents the unavoidable challenge to memory that completes the memorial project. The site of the struggle of history and memory against their forced identity is at the juncture of interior and exterior: the locus of the military and of ambiguity for both Schinkel and Tessenow. Here hang two bronze plates, German descriptions of the complete history of the building and of the victims of Nazi terror (fig. 12). They hang outside the "contemporary" site of memory, outside the Weimar reconfiguration. The 1993 project attempts to restore German memory to its pre-Nazi era state. But the facts of history, both those that record the oppression of the Nazi period and those that record all of the changes to the Neue Wache, frame the recreated Weimar juxtaposition of the recent and distant past. At the threshold it is historical fact that challenges the contemporary use of the Weimar memory; each German-speaking visitor must read and interpret these facts alone, before entering the building and confronting the fixed symbolism inherent in Kollwitz's figure of the *Pietá.* Engraved on bronze tablets, these records strangely echo Tessenow's original plan to list the dates of World War I in the bronze frame of the skylight. In the form of a historical document the site for individual contemplation has resurfaced at the threshold, and thus the possibility for memory has returned. Despite the official attempt to create national memory in this project by resisting the facts of history, this memory is dependent on the very documentation of these facts for its existence.[17]

It is the juxtaposition of interior and exterior established by Schinkel that prophetically anticipated the needs of German memory. This juxtaposition has allowed the German memory builders—willingly or not—to escape a search

Fig. 12.   Threshold of the Neue Wache, 1995. (Photo courtesy of Frank Döring.)

for unity and integrate the tensions between past and present, public and private, and history and memory, into the architectural landscape. The fact that the German national memorial has always taken the form of a renovation, or change, is itself an appropriate metaphor for the history of German national memory, a metaphor of which the name Neue Wache (*New* Guardhouse) has always been a trace.

NOTES

A shorter version of this essay was presented at the conference of the Society of Architectural Historians, April 1995, in Seattle. An abstracted version of this essay was presented at the European Conference of the Association of Collegiate Schools of Architecture (U.S.), May 1995, in Lisbon and will be published in the transcripts of that conference. Support for this research has been given by the University of Kentucky and its College of Architecture. I would like to thank the editors and John Czaplicka for their helpful comments.

1. In contrast to other literature concerning the Neue Wache, this essay looks at the entire history of the building: from the time of its first design to the present. Other texts, many of which are listed in the following pages, concentrate on individual stages of the building's existence.

Only the most recent works on the building look at several of its designs at once. But they either offer a description, rather than an analysis, of its history (e.g., Tietz) or analyze specific changes to the building over time, often to evaluate the most recent renovation. Dolff-Bonekämper focuses on the history of the building during the German Democratic Republic in order to call into question the viability of erasing the East German memorial if the country is truly a reunification of two states. Kosseleck looks at the same history in order to question the use of the Kollwitz sculpture. Specifically, he traces the history of the inscriptions and symbols in the interior of the building. Other articles in newspapers and magazines, some gathered by Stölzl, refer generally to the history of the building likewise to defend their opinions about the building's most recent changes.

2. "Wenn freie Bürger Soldaten werden und Soldaten freie Bürger sind, muss der Staat, den sie verteidigen sollen, auch von ihnen mitgetragen, also auch mitgestaltet werden" (qtd. in Dolff-Bonekämper 41). Scharnhorst's statue was one of four statues of important generals in the Napoleonic Wars that flanked the original building.

3. There are numerous sources that describe and analyze Schinkel's work because of his importance both to Germany and German architecture as well as to the history of modern architecture. Some are cited in this essay. The recent English edition of Schinkel's *Sammlung Architektonischer Entwürfe,* translated as *Collection of Architectural Drawings,* includes an extensive bibliography as well as essays by Schinkel scholars Rand Carter and Hermann Pundt. Other important English-language sources include: Bergdoll; Forster; and Pundt.

4. See Forssman's description of the building, which reinforces the theory that it is a hybrid: "Dem römischen Vorbild widerspricht allerdings die Öffnung durch einen

griechisch-dorischen Portikus" (The opening through a Greek-Doric portico contradicts, however, the Roman precedent [94]).

5. "Der Plan dieses, ringsum ganz freiliegenden Gebäudes ist einen römischen Castrum ungefähr nachgeformt, deshalb die vier festeren Eckthürme und der innere Hof." "Der vorne angebrachte Porticus, auf 10 freien Säulen und den damit in Verbindung stehenden Wandpfeilern ruhend" (Schinkel, 1).

Barry Bergdoll claims that the *castrum* was a synthesis of both the fortification architecture and the portico. "Known only from texts, he [Schinkel] imagined the *castrum* as a synthesis of the forms of fortification architecture—the pylons and parapets of city walls—and the honorific portico of civic architecture, in this case a baseless Doric order, traditionally the order whose 'masculine character was deemed appropriate for military functions.'" In addition, Bergdoll goes on to talk about Schinkel reinterpreting the "classical Greek architecture in relation to the building's dual military and commemorative purpose." Here he is referring to the portico (this is clear from the discussion that follows) as Greek, without telling the reader of its transition from a Roman element—as one can assume from his theory, that the portico was a part of the Roman Castrum—to a Greek element. His reference to the portico as Greek is more convincing if one accepts that the Roman *castrum* did not include the portico and that the building was a hybrid of two very different elements (51).

6. Forssman talks about the relationships between the porticoes—and thus the buildings—in more specific terms. After pointing out the Doric connection between the Neue Wache and the Brandenburg gate, he discusses the Neue Wache's relationship to the opera diagonally opposite: to the opera's Corinthian, the Neue Wache Doric sets "a more serious counterpart, very different in character" (94).

7. A description of this scheme can be found in Bergdoll (3).

8. It is unclear when the old fortifications were dismantled. They had certainly disappeared by 1713, the year of Friedrich I's death (Pundt 10–11). The newer fortifications had a commercial as well as a military function: they were also used as customs walls. Thus, they "protected" the monarchy from the civilian public in two ways. On the one hand, they tempered the influx of commercial goods, restricting the amount of commercial activity in the city. On the other, they allowed the state to profit from any additional trade that did occur. Both prevented the relative increase in the power of the commercial class in Berlin that would have been a consequence of an increase of independent trade with the areas outside the city. According to Hermann Pundt, "The customs wall had been completed by 1736 and produced drastic planning limitations for Berlin until its demolition more than one hundred years later" (18). Thereby, the city's civilian territory, not just its civilian activity, was naturally ripe for expansion.

9. Although both men and women have been American soldiers, I use the masculine *his,* given the fact that those guarding the tomb are almost exclusively, if not exclusively, men. Here the continuity between the living soldier and the dead one play an important role in creating memory at the site.

10. The metal frieze is rumored to have been fabricated from melted cannons, confiscated from the French. This would have transformed the column into a literal, if abstract, display of the trophies of victory.

11. The history of the statues of the generals is important to an understanding of the

ambiguous relationship between the military, the civilian populace, and the monarchy in the context of victory and defeat. An analysis of their selection, placement, and removal, however, is beyond the scope of this essay and has been undertaken elsewhere; see Dolff-Bonekämper; and Tietz.

12. One jury member (Hiecke, from the historic preservation commission) supported Poelzig's entry, and five supported Tessenow (Waetzold, director of the Berlin museums; Wilhelm Kreis, architect; Karl Scheffler, art critic; Walter Curt Behrendt, from the finance ministry; and adviser Rudelius, an adviser from the defense ministry). Edwin Redslob, an adviser; Martin Wagner, the city planning commissioner; and Martin Kiessling, the chairman of the commission and the director of the building department in the Prussian Ministry of Finance supported Mies. See Tietz (61).

13. While the renovation of the Neue Wache into a war memorial and the creation of a national memorial were topics of broad-based discussions during most of the Weimar period, it was the Prussian government that made the actual decision to implement the plans to renovate the Neue Wache. Immediately thereafter, the national government joined the Prussians in directing the renovation, as it was afraid that the public could accuse the Prussians of taking over the national war memorial project. While no one intended that the Neue Wache would be the national memorial, there were no other buildings at the time that served this purpose. See Tietz (21–25).

The continuity of Prussian and German history was particularly problematic here and was mentioned as such by several of the project's critics; see Tietz (61). Both Mies and Tessenow dealt with the issue of historical continuity: Mies, in a clearly critical fashion; Tessenow, mourning its loss in his original scheme.

14. In the published research on the subject there is no explanation for the literal cause of this change, only a footnote citing material in the Federal Archive in Koblenz. See Tietz (58 n. 94).

15. A description of the change in design from stone to a mosaic, similar to Berlin's streets is found in Tietz (52).

16. The future of the urban planning around the Neue Wache and the issues raised concerning militaristic representation is the subject of my further research.

17. Both James Young and Charles Maier see documentation as a possible memorial site. Young sees a record of the debates concerning the creation of a memorial as the possible site: "Though some, like the Greens, might see such absorption in the process of memorial building as an evasion of memory, it may also be true that the surest engagement with memory lies in its perpetual irresolution. In fact, the best German memorial to the Fascist era and its victims may not be a single memorial at all—but simply the never-to-be-resolved debate over which kind of memory to preserve, how to do it, in whose name, and to what end" (21).

For Maier one possible memorial site is the museum. In *The Unmasterable Past* he links the West German project for a German Historical Museum with national identity and argues for a—perhaps impossible—fragmentary presentation of German history, which would communicate the complexities of both historical events and historians' interpretations while not sacrificing coherence (121–59).

In both cases, however, the authors do not refer to the documentation of "raw facts," as I do in my discussion of the recent renovation to the Neue Wache, but, rather, to the

256   *A User's Guide to German Cultural Studies*

documentation of many different interpretations of those facts, much like those in the two books, by the German Academy of Arts and the German Historical Museum, mentioned earlier.

Works Cited

Bergdoll, Barry. *Karl Friedrich Schinkel: An Architecture for Prussia.* New York: Rizzoli, 1994.

Dolff-Bonekämper, Gabi. "Schinkels Neue Wache Unter den Linden. Ein Denkmal in Deutschland." In *Streit um die Neue Wache. Zur Gestaltung einer zentralen Gedenkstätte.* Berlin: Akademie der Künste, 1993. 35–44.

Forssman, Eric. *Karl Friedrich Schinkel Bauwerke und Baugedanken.* Munich: Schnell und Steiner, 1981.

Forster, Kurt W. "Schinkel's Panoramic Planning of Central Berlin." *Modulus* 16 (1983): 62–77.

Friedländer, Saul. *When Memory Comes.* Trans. Helen R. Lane. New York: Farrar, 1979.

Kosseleck, Reinhart. "Stellen uns die Toten einen Termin." In *Streit um die Neue Wache Zur Gestaltung einer zentralen Gedenkstätte.* Berlin: Akademie der Künste, 1993. 27–34.

Kracauer, Siegfried. "Zur Einweihung des Berliner Ehrenmals." *Frankfurter Zeitung,* 2 June 1931, evening, 1.

LeGoff, Jacques. *History and Memory.* Trans. Steven Randall and Elizabeth Claman. New York: Columbia UP, 1992.

Maier, Charles. *The Unmasterable Past: History, Holocaust, and German National Identity.* Cambridge: Harvard UP, 1988.

Mieck, Ilya. "Von der Reformzeit zur Revolution." In *Geschichte Berlins,* ed. Wolfgang Ribbe. Munich: C. H. Beck, 1988. 407–602.

Pundt, Hermann. *Schinkel's Berlin, A Study in Environmental Planning.* Cambridge: Harvard UP, 1972.

Schinkel, Karl Friedrich. *Sammlung Architektonischer Entwürfe.* Berlin: Ernst und Korn, 1866. Reprint. Trans. as *Collection of Architectural Drawings.* New York: Princeton Architectural P, 1989.

Stölzl, Christoph, ed. *Die Neue Wache Unter den Linden.* Berlin: Koehler und Amelang, 1993.

Streit um die Neue Wache. Zur Gestaltung einer zentralen Gedenkstätte. Berlin: Akademie der Künste, 1993.

Tietz, Jürgen. "Schinkels Neue Wache Unter den Linden." In *Die Neue Wache Unter den Linden,* ed. Christoph Stölzl. Berlin: Koehler und Amelang, 1993. 9–93.

Young, James. *The Texture of Memory.* New Haven: Yale UP, 1993.

CHAPTER 15

Stones Set Upright in the Winds of Controversy: An Austrian Monument against War and Fascism

John Czaplicka

John Czaplicka's essay on Austrian sculptor Alfred Hrdlicka's Monument against War and Fascism *highlights two important aspects that are central to the development of German cultural studies. The first is geographical, as Czaplicka underscores the broad and inclusive conception of "things German." Indeed, the exploration of developments in the German-speaking world outside the Federal Republic of Germany deserves recognition and should be high on the list of scholars' priorities. This urgency stems from the fact that, compared to Germany, much less has been written about Austria, German-speaking Switzerland, Liechtenstein, and other ethnic Germans in Europe and overseas. The experiences of the Austrians and the Swiss during the Third Reich and their subsequent attempts to come to terms with their various histories, for example, are in need of much study as recent public controversies have made apparent. Kirsten Belgum's and Susanne Zantop's essays in this volume also confirm the richness of scholarship on topics that had formerly been at the geographical margins of German studies. Because German cultural studies stresses connections, a scholarly enterprise that links different nationalities is to be encouraged.*

The second aspect of cultural studies underscored by Czaplicka's essay is the important contribution that art historians are making to the field. In particular, a number of earlier leftist scholars pursued the idea of a "social history of art," which made connections to other disciplines and proved so stimulating and influential that the effect was felt far beyond the field of art history. One can point to the interdisciplinary work of T. J. Clark, who wrote on nineteenth-century France, or Otto Karl Werckmeister, who has studied a wide range of German topics: both are remarkable for the way in which they incorporate concepts and material from history, political theory, sociology, and literary criticism. Art history has come a long way since the connoisseurship and formalist analyses of earlier generations.

John Czaplicka is part of a new wave of interdisciplinary art historians. Trained in both the United States and Germany, his scholarship reflects a keen awareness of the historical circumstances of his subjects. His studies of Weimar Germans' conceptions of the United States and Austrian émigré artists' experiences in the United States reflect this concern for broader social, political, and cultural contexts. Czaplicka has also played a leading role in organizing a number of important collaborative efforts. As the cochair of the Study Group of Twentieth-Century German Culture at Harvard's Minda de Gunzburg Center for European Studies and the guest editor of important issues of New German Critique *and* German Politics and Society, *Czaplicka has been a catalyst for cross-disciplinary dialog among those interested in modern German culture.*

Whatever writers write
is yes nothing compared to reality
yes yes they of course write that everything is horrible
that everything's spoiled and ruined and
that everything's catastrophic
and that there's no escape from it all
but everything they write is nothing against reality
reality is so bad
that it cannot be described
no writer has yet described reality
as it really is
that is the terrible thing
　　　　　—Professor Robert, in Thomas Bernhard's
　　　　　　　　　　"Heldenplatz"

On a rainy day in November 1988 and fifty years after the annexation of Austria by the Third Reich and the November pogrom against the Jews, on Vienna's Albertinaplatz not far from the Heldenplatz, where in 1938 Austrians had gathered by the hundreds of thousands to salute Adolf Hitler, a smattering of dignitaries representing Austria's Second Republic gathered to unveil an incomplete monument against war and fascism (fig. 1).[1] They uncovered a sculptural en-

Fig. 1. **Alfred Hrdlicka,** *Monument against War and Fascism,* **on the Albertinaplatz, Vienna, 1988. (Photo copyright Bettina Secker, Bad Honnef.)**

semble composed of twisted and tormented human figures created by the renowned and controversial sculptor, printmaker, and painter Alfred Hrdlicka. Cast in bronze or sculpted in limestone or Carrara marble, the elements of this work of art lie upon an ashlar pavement or stand on rough-hewn bases of granite quarried at the former Austrian concentration camp, Mauthausen (fig. 2). Referring both topically and allegorically to historical events, the artist employs the traditional artistic means of figurative sculpture to compose a public monument with a twofold purpose. His monument warns its beholders of the effects of war and fascism through the naturalistic images of a ravaged humankind that recall the reality of an Austrian past so horrible that "it cannot be described."

Both warning and reminding the beholder with images of a shattered and wretched humanity, the ensemble on the Albertinaplatz belongs to the German tradition of admonishing monuments (*Mahnmale*). Such markers erected in public places did not serve as mere memorials to the dead; rather, they made a lesson of the dead. These admonishing monuments erected to commemorate events such as the passing of a plague also dispensed with any pretense of the encomium that characterizes conventional civic monuments. Erected sometimes in a religious context, what *Mahnmale* commemorate are the past misdeeds that had led to catastrophe. These monuments admonished by way of negative exemplification. Hrdlicka's modern *Mahnmal* stands in this tradition as it admonishes by displaying the results of the Austrians' own involvement in the horrific crimes of the fascist regimes that ruled their country from 1934 to 1945.

The artistic means Hrdlicka has employed in his approach to the Austrian past and to address the Austrian present are sculptural and, to the extent that his work configures space, architectural (fig. 3). His intentions, for which the artistic object is a vehicle, are both to convey history and to influence it. These means and intentions suggest three sets of criteria by which one can analyze a monument such as the one that now stands on the Albertinaplatz. With regard to the artistic means the criteria are aesthetic, involving questions of materials, craftsmanship, style, and genre. With regard to the intentions the first set of criteria are historiographic, in that the monument seeks to "represent" a historical situation. The second set of criteria related to intentions are political, in that the monument is an agent of change in history.

From its inception this public monument was bound up with history and politics. Central to understanding this public work of art is thus an understanding of the history that inspired it and the historical context into which it was built. Its erection in the center of Vienna was an act of political agitation. Supported by public authority of the city government in the person of Vienna's mayor, Dr. Helmut Zilk, the artist was able to intervene in public space to help revise history and to reform a collective memory. This is the artist's stated purpose when he calls his work a "monument *against* war and fascism." One could

Fig. 2. Alfred Hrdlicka, *Monument against War and Fascism,* on the Albertinaplatz, Vienna, 1988. View through the "Gate of Violence" toward the "Street
Washing Game." (Photo copyright Bettina Secker, Bad Honnef.)

Fig. 3.   Alfred Hradlicka in his studio with part of the "Gate of Violence" in progress, 1988. (Photo copyright Bettina Secker, Bad Honnef.)

say that the artist in the modern stance of the resister and cautioner wants his work to become much more than a historical referent.

He sees himself and his work as an agent of history and one that is "tendential," or, expressed differently, politically engaged. The results of that engagement are expressed most forcefully in the rituals that begin to surround his work, the manner of its contemporary usage, and the way it is accepted or rejected over time—that is, in the history of its critical reception (*Rezeptionsgeschichte*). The first rituals and usage take place at dedications such as the one that took place in Vienna on 24 November 1988. Those ceremonies and demonstrations initiate a history of use and disuse by a receptive or nonreceptive public, which lend the monument multiple meanings, often ones unintended by the artist or the commissioners. The history of reception, however, begins even before the monument is built, at the time when the plans of the monument are made public. Through the *history* of ceremony and reception one traces transformations in the meaning of a monument that lend it the character of impermanence. It is formed by history. What remains, though, are the formed pieces of metal and stone, a permanent presence of the past, a reminder, a marker, a place to collect thoughts about that past. One engages the past through the monument; it helps form our image of history (*Geschichtsbild*).

I.   Into the Winds of Controversy

After the unveiling of the *Monument against War and Fascism* on that autumn day in 1988, a priest, a protestant minister, and a rabbi dedicated it in an ecumenical ceremony attended by the Austrian chancellor, Franz Vranitzky; the mayor of Vienna, Helmut Zilk; and the leader of the Jewish community in Vienna, Paul Grosz. Conspicuous in his absence from the solemn act was the Austrian president, Dr. Kurt Waldheim. There was a logic to his absence, for the president epitomized all that the monument was meant to oppose. Documents had resurfaced in 1986 that revealed details about Waldheim's "forgotten" service in the Nazi Wehrmacht during World War II. Though they did not place him at the scene of crimes against humanity, they, at least, located him in a chain of command that made him a facilitator, or an indirect perpetrator of the type the Germans and Austrians call a *Schreibtischtäter* (i.e., one who commits crimes from behind a desk). In this manner his personal history was linked to brutal antipartisan operations against civilian populations in Yugoslavia and in deportations to the camps from the Balkans.[2] By 1988 these revelations and his own evasiveness about them had so undermined his credibility as the moral arbiter of the nation that his presence at a state ceremony commemorating the victims of the Third Reich would have appeared hypocritical at best and cynical at worst.

Political supporters of Waldheim, such as the members of the conservative Österreichische Volkspartei (ÖVP; Austrian People's Party) and the right-ist Freiheitliche Partei Österreichs (FPÖ; Austrian Freedom Party), also stayed away from the dedication of Hrdlicka's monument, citing disagreements about its siting and irregularities in the manner of its commissioning.[3] Thus, these politicians effectively distanced themselves from what is arguably the most important political monument to be erected in Austria after World War II.[4] In fact, only a small crowd of about three thousand onlookers and demonstrators braved the cold drizzle on that November day to share the Albertinaplatz with dignitaries of the Sozialistische Partei Österreichs (SPÖ; Austrian Socialist Party), and large contingents of reporters and police. During this dedication and a second dedication to mark the completion of the monument in 1991, several incidents occurred that are worth recounting because they indicate the contemporary relevance and understanding of Hrdlicka's monument.

At one point during the initial dedication ceremony, a group of punks and the illegal occupants of vacant housing (*Hausbesetzer*) began unfurling a banner proclaiming, "The Führer went, the Aryanizers remain." Provoked by this, the police intervened violently and, according to some reports, brutally (Frank). Many demonstrators were roughed up; three were arrested, and one was badly injured as their banner was forcibly torn from them (J. H.). The crowd responded by rhythmically chanting again and again: "Stop it. Stop it. Police, Fascists. Police, Fascists." The *Hausbesetzer* came to protest with demands to provide housing for "over 10,000 homeless" and had distributed leaflets months before the ceremony that referred to the monument with the heading "Again more Baroque in Vienna!" In the earlier protest leaflets they described the "Hrdlicka-Monument" as "nothing more than a jewel in the crown of the mayor," referring to Helmut Zilk, the mayor of Vienna, who had ordered police to evacuate occupied houses and apartments by force, so that they could be torn down.[5] Later, during the dedication ceremony, police confiscated yet another banner emblazoned with: "Homosexual victims of the concentration camps are still waiting for their rehabilitation."

The overzealous police seemed all too willing to corroborate the punks' belief that a historical continuity existed in Austria with regard to the persecution of marginal groups. The punks brought attention to the fact that the harboring of prejudices against foreigners, Jews, Roma and Sinti (Gypsies), and other minorities, which had led to the rise of the fascists, had not gone out of style in contemporary Austria. In a sense they did nothing more than elaborate on the admonishment against such prejudice expressed by the monument. The published criticism of the *Hausbesetzer* included a phrase from Max Horkheimer that brought their protest to a point: "Whoever does not want to speak about capitalism, should also keep silent about fascism." This prescription, taken out of its original context, points to the traditional equation between antifascism and anticapitalism promulgated by the communist states of Eastern Europe, and, apart from its more obvious gist, thus brings up a thorny issue of the relationship of the monument to the ideology of antifascism. For their part the homosexuals had only tried to draw attention to the need to rehabilitate unrecognized victims of the Nazis. Not possessing the strong international political representation of the Jews, marginal groups such as the homosexuals, the Roma and Sinti, and the physically and mentally impaired had never been truly rehabilitated or properly recognized in Austria.[6] The lack of public concern with their fate in Austria under the Nazis raises the issue of the tolerance for such marginal groups in a democratic Austria.[7]

On 21 June 1991 another group of dignitaries dedicated the last figurative element in Hrdlicka's monumental ensemble, the "Death of a Hero." That day the punks did not reappear, but those concerned with homosexual rights returned in full force with a similar pink banner. This time the well-advised and disciplined police force tolerated peaceful demonstrations, in order not to confirm any suspected continuities with the past. Gay protesters were allowed to openly walk through the crowd and to pin pink paper triangles—similar to the ones worn by homosexuals in the concentration camps—on the breast of any willing bystander. The triangles bore a complaint that at once reminded of the past and related to the present: "The community of Vienna does not commemorate its homosexual victims here."[8] At the same ceremony the Kommunistische Partei Österreichs (KPÖ; Communist Party of Austria) had raised a banner high above the milling crowd of onlookers. Stenciled in the Gothic type preferred by the Nazis one read the slogan "Arbeit macht Frei" written as if along an arch, much in the same way it is inscribed above the gate into Auschwitz. A subscript to the slogan provided a contemporary gloss on the historical allusion, by proclaiming: "Haider's employment policy." This referred to a recent speech given by the modern demagogue and FPÖ politician, Jörg Haider, in which he extolled "Hitler's labor policy." By coincidence, on the day the monument was dedicated, Haider relinquished his office as the governor of Carinthia, a province of Austria, and Kurt Waldheim decided not to run for a second term.[9]

Demonstrations at the site of Hrdlicka's monument underline its contemporary relevance while lending it new meaning in the shifting winds of political controversy. Protest against ingrained discrimination and reactionary politics seems appropriate before a monument clearly delineating their results in tortured and disfigured human bodies, which, by virtue of their imperfection, offer marginal groups a rare opportunity for public identification. By the same token it was not surprising that, after such politically charged dedications, few dignitaries found their way to the monument to lay wreaths at this important site of public commemoration. A genuflection by "official" representatives before such a graphic rendering of the violence and intolerance that has characterized the history of the twentieth century might have too easily been viewed as a mere farce.

As an engaged artist who is highly critical of Austria's history of denial, Hrdlicka gauges the effectiveness of his work in part by such *political* responses. He views them as symptomatic and revealing. In fact, with his monument on the Albertinaplatz he had hoped to draw out the reactionaries and to further bait the scandal-mongering boulevard newspapers that largely dominated the press scene in Vienna during the 1980s.[10] That press had always obliged the hard-talking, hard-drinking, and hard-line leftist artist by politicizing the debates about his work, and the artist, for his part, seldom disappointed a press that thrived on the scandals they could conjure up from his political slogans and polemical statements. Unfortunately, this "political theater," as the pundits in Vienna call it, often digressed from serious and larger issues concerning Austria's history into local and ephemeral, political disputes or into the simple defamation of the artist and his supporters.[11]

The reactions to Hrdlicka's monument need to be seen against the background of the artist's involvement in the Waldheim controversy. While his monument was taking shape in his studio, Hrdlicka became a central figure among the intellectuals who organized to oppose Waldheim.[12] Even after Waldheim won the election, Hrdlicka continued to agitate against him. At one point in 1986 he designed a wooden horse wearing the cap of a Nazi stormtrooper that derived from an idea by the socialist politician and former Austrian chancellor, Fred Sinowatz. Sinowatz had noted ironically that it wasn't Waldheim but only his horse that had served in an SA cavalry unit.[13] On the day of Waldheim's inauguration the horse was rolled out into the square before the Cathedral of St. Stephen in Vienna and outfitted with loudspeakers that carried protests written and spoken by some of Austria's most famous writers and poets, including Peter Handke, Elias Canetti, and Erich Fried; after a reading of these texts, Hrdlicka himself emerged from the belly of the horse to hold *his* Speech to the Nation, one directed satirically against the unrepentant careerist, Nazi collaborator, and freshly baked president of the Austrian Republic. Hrdlicka's bit of agitprop theater did not insinuate that Waldheim was a criminal; it pointed, rather, to his convenient and well-trained careerist's ability to forget his past and to the miscasting of such a man to act as the highest representative of a country whose past needed confronting.

The monument against war and fascism wanted to stem the loss of memory Waldheim's case exemplified by commemorating a "reality . . . so bad" that, as some, such as the playwright Thomas Bernhard proposed, "it cannot be described." Thereby, it broaches issues such as the complicity of Austrians in the crimes of the Nazis or the patterns of intolerance of the fascist period that linger on in the programs of the "populist Right" in contemporary Austria. Most important, by directly approaching the brutal facts of history, Hrdlicka challenges Austrians to include the years of political dissolution, war, and defeat in a truly integral history of their country in the twentieth century. In the relationship between its parts and in the individual messages of its sculptural elements, the monument disturbs normative images of Austrian history, *Geschichtsbilder,* that allow the Austrians to be at ease with themselves and their history. Though seldom stated directly, at stake in the cultural-political controversy surrounding the monument was exactly that accepted and generally shared understanding of Austrian history in the twentieth century. Sadly, it seems, the demonstrators on the margins of the dedications in 1988 and 1991 might have understood this better than almost all the critics in the press.

What came into the center of the unruly political stage in 1988, the year of anniversaries and scandals, was the double-edged and contradictory reality about Austrian involvement in fascist crimes and in a war of aggression. In the late 1980s, and in conjunction with political controversy surrounding Waldheim, for the first time in Austria's postwar history intellectuals and engaged politicians mounted a broad and public challenge to the *Lebenslüge* (a lie that enables one to live further unencumbered by the past) by which many Austrians had lived since the end of World War II. The erection of the monument by Hrdlicka can be understood as part of that challenge to a culture of denial, which is rooted in a particular understanding of Austria's relation to fascism and to Nazi crimes and aggression.

That Austrian history cuts in two ways when the issue of fascism arises has been well documented and discussed by engaged Austrian historians and thus can be recounted easily in its broader features.[14] On one side of a historical ledger several events bear repeating. It is true that Austria was invaded by the Third Reich on 12 March 1938 to become the first victim of Nazi aggression. On 14 March the German government passed a law declaring the union (*Anschluss*) of Austria with the Third Reich. The official historical term employed when referring to this event is *Anschluss,* which has come to mean "annexation" but can also mean simply "affiliation." *Anschluss* was a euphemism of the Nazis. Thus, Austrians became the first "foreign" country under the Nazi yoke, and the Austrians became the first foreigners to suffer Nazi persecution. This understanding of Austria as a *victim* of the Third Reich was nurtured by the Allies themselves, who signed the Moscow Declaration on 1 November 1943, a document that described Austria as the first free country to be invaded by Hitler. The limited resistance movement in Austria also comes down on this side of the ledger; though composed mainly of communists and monarchists, it provided a convenient heritage to appropriate in the name of democratic Austria after World War II.[15]

But on the other side of the ledger stands, in the first place, the indigenous movement of the Austro-fascists, whose authoritarian reign began in 1934, four full years before the *Anschluss*. Though the "clerical-fascists," as they were called, never indulged in mass murder, they did dismantle the democratic institutions of the First Republic of Austria (1919–34), in favor of an authoritarian regime, and establish the first large-scale political detention camps. Furthermore, many Austrians who did not believe in the viability of the rump Austria left after the demise of the Hapsburg Empire in 1918—including even members of the Socialist Party—also longed to be united with a greater Germany and thus welcomed the annexation. The actual "invasion" of Austria was not resisted by force of arms or public insurrection. Finally, whether as true believers or careerists, great numbers of Austrians enlisted in Hitler's war machine or in the Nazi apparatus of persecution. They often served with great distinction.[16]

So while some Austrians were, to be sure, victims of the Nazis, others were perpetrators of or at least complicit in Nazi crimes against humanity. During the period of authoritarianism in Austria of 1934–45 Austrians came in all the shades of gray that were on the scale between the clear consciences of the resisters and the black souls of the enthusiastic perpetrators. In fact, by the end of the Nazi occupation one could say that, to varying degrees, most Austrians had been both victimized by the regime *and* complicit in its crimes.

In light of this mixed history of a nation Hrdlicka designed a monument to memorialize the victims and their persecutors as well as those straddling the fence. The uneasiness engendered by his monument derives from this admixture, which makes it unlike the monuments erected to the heroes of resistance in many socialist countries or the ones of mourning dedicated to victims of fascism in all countries. Hrdlicka refuses to praise famous men, to mourn fallen heroes, or even to separate thoroughly victim from perpetrator in his monument. In the monument on the Albertinaplatz, Austrian history is made to flow as a bloodied current, one that carries the human flotsam and jetsam to the surface for public reexamination.

II.   The Monument: Stones Standing Upright

In 1971 Hrdlicka designed a sculptural relief representing a workers' uprising against the Austrian fascist regime during the Austrian civil war of 1934. These are the artist's first plans for an antifascist monument. They demonstrate an inclusive understanding of "fascism" in Austria, consisting of both the indigenous Austro-fascists, who usurped power in 1934, and the Nazis, who invaded Austria in 1938.[17] This first monument was never realized. In 1978 the artist set about designing another antifascist monument, this time as his entry into a competition for the reconfiguration of the Stock-im-Eisen-Platz, the square next to the St. Stephen's cathedral of Vienna.[18] Hrdlicka won the competition with a multifigurative composition inspired by the persecution and martyrdom of the patron saint of the cathedral, Saint Stephen. Expanding on the attributes of this saint, the monumental ensemble would offer a medley of historical motifs: scenes of insurrectionist workers being shot, a Jew washing the streets of Vienna, and a dead mother and child standing for the civilian casualties of war. According to the artist, this work would have complemented Fischer von Erlach's *Pestsäule,* a baroque sign of atonement that had been erected in 1688 on the Graben in Vienna to commemorate the passing of the plague of 1679. The modern monument for the Stephansplatz would have commemorated "the passing of the brown plague" brought on by the Nazis and their Austrian sympathizers (Lewin 4:159–60). In the designs for this sculptural ensemble, which combined both topical historical references and allegorical figuration, one recognizes the germ of the monument that would later be erected on the Albertinaplatz.

Though the city's plans to erect an antifascist monument on Vienna's Stephansplatz were dropped after Hrdlicka won the competition, the artist continued to develop his ideas about such a monument in further designs and agitated vigorously for the monument's realization. His persistence paid off in the summer 1983, when the city of Vienna awarded him a commission to erect a monument against war and fascism on the Albertinaplatz.[19] Helmut Zilk, a powerful and popular member of the SPÖ and, at that time, the minister of cultural affairs in Vienna, provided the needed political backing. In close consultation with Hrdlicka, Zilk designated the Albertinaplatz as the site for the monument. By the summer of 1988, however, as the foundation for the monument was already being prepared, the project seemed doomed. Perhaps due to his high-profile engagement in the anti-Waldheim campaign, the conservative press and politicians attacked Hrdlicka and his project. After a concerted campaign to whip up public opinion, it seemed the monument had little popular support. In a press conference on 26 July 1988 Zilk, then mayor of Vienna, displayed his civil courage by reaffirming his support for the monument on the Albertinaplatz and by guaranteeing that the city would stand by its contractual obligations. Zilk took the moral high ground, arguing that a consensus *should* exist that such a monument was needed in Austria. Still, the public controversy continued and soon involved the whole spectrum of Austrian political groups from the local to the national level. For the most part the arguments aired against the monument reflected the rather provincial bearing of some politicians and the hard-headed party line of others; the objections to the monument were, for the most part, trivial and digressive, because they did not consider the monument itself. Still, they are worth a listing, since they illustrate how the political opposition grasped for straws in an attempt not to confront the politically delicate central message of Hrdlicka's ensemble.

An office and apartment building, the Philipphof on the Albertinaplatz, was destroyed by Allied bombers on 12 March 1945 in one of the last air raids on Vienna. The collapsing building buried almost two hundred people, who had sought shelter in its cellar. Their remains were never recovered. Concerned about disturbing the peace of this last resting place (*Totenruhe*), some of the critics from the conservative ÖVP questioned the appropriateness of the site for a monument. Zilk countered this objection, noting that a number of the same politicians had proposed an underground parking garage at the site some years before (press conf., 7). Conservative critics also suggested the Morzinplatz as a more appropriate location for a monument against fascism, because the Gestapo headquarters had been located there. To this serious counterproposal that carried the predicate of historical authenticity, the artist objected, noting that it would mean the banishment of his work to a less-trafficked space above an underground parking garage that was already "well marked " by concrete air ducts. From several sides came the recommendations to erect the monument on the Schwarzenbergplatz close by the Soviet memorial known to some Viennese—who did not share Hrdlicka's admiration for the liberation of Austria by the Red Army—as "The Monument to the Unknown Rapist." Again, the artist demurred. Yet another critic thought it better to return the Mozart Monument to the Albertinaplatz quickly, so as to prevent Hrdlicka from making a scandal permanent.[20] Hrdlicka held firm to his plans to build his monument on the Albertinaplatz at the center of the city, a site much frequented by tourists and Viennese and a site with its own checkered history.

The artist had chosen a square whose successive designations offer an abbreviated history of Austria early in this century. Once named after Archduke Albrecht, the antidemocratic field marshal in the service of the Hapsburgs, that central square was then dubbed "Revolutionsplatz" by the Socialists in Vienna after the dissolution of the empire. Finally, when the Austro-fascists removed the Austrian socialists from the Vienna municipal government in 1934, Revolutionsplatz became Albertinaplatz, taking its name from the world-famous museum that abuts it (Pellar). The *Monument against War and Fascism* provides a sense of closure to the earlier history of the Albertinaplatz. Unlike the succession of renamings, it completes that earlier history in a concrete fashion that allows the past to be almost palpably present.

The monument itself consists of five sculptural elements arranged on a pavement of granite ashlar (fig. 4). These recompose the urban square in a manner that lends it an irregular rhythm of solid and void and a clear orientation from the two posts of the "Tor der Gewalt" (Gate of Violence) (fig. 5) to the tall stele "Stein der Republik" (Rock of the Republic) (fig. 6). The calibrated dispersal of the elements on the large open square keeps the monument from dominating the space around it, an impression that is underpinned by the loose correlation of the open configuration to the triangular shape of the square and to the traffic flow across and around it. Hrdlicka has composed a "pedestrian monument" (fig. 1).[21] It is an open-ended work of art that invites its beholders to

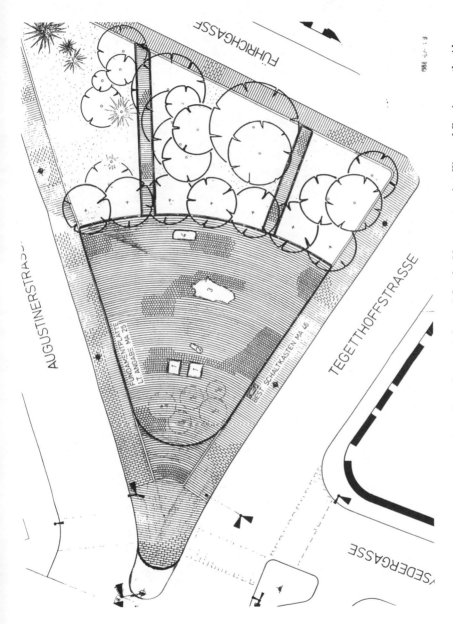

Fig. 4. Site plan (not representing minor placement changes) for the *Monument against War and Fascism*, on the Albertinaplatz, Vienna. (Vienna: Magistrat Wien, July 1988.)

Fig. 5.   Alfred Hrdlicka, "The Gate of Violence" (1991), from *Monument against War and Fascism,* on the Albertinaplatz, Vienna, 1988. (Photo: John Czaplicka.)

Fig. 6.   Alfred Hrdlicka, "Rock of the Republic," from *Monument against War and Fascism,* on the Albertinaplatz, Vienna, 1988. (Photo copyright Bettina Secker, Bad Honnef.)

perambulation and discursive interpretation. The many-sided, or plurifacial, sculptures composing it offer the beholder numerous angles of approach that allow multiple meanings to develop as one views and interprets the monument according to varying combinations of its elements or as a whole.

Walking around and through the complex configuration provides ocular experience of the first rank as the variegated surfaces of stone and metal change their pattern and color according to the shifting light of the stark Vienna sun. The artist has drilled, hammered, chiseled, and polished the stones, leaving their surfaces chipped, scratched, broken, or smooth depending on the manner of industrial or hand working. This results in a panoply of tactile sensations, among which a perception of brutal rawness would seem to dominate and, thereby, suggest power and violence. In considering the figures and their attributes carved in deep and shallow relief, one notes how they are left incomplete and fragmentary. The stones themselves describe no regular shape, and their jagged outlines suggest incompletion. Without symmetry, completion, or standard shape in its parts or an absolute ordering in its arrangement, the monument seems active in the manner of baroque sculptural compositions or the carving of Hellenistic reliefs. But, unlike these, Hrdlicka's agitated work is not subordinated to a program of architectural framing or to the grand axes of ceremonial routes in an urban design. Still, threaded through the monument's loose succession of elements is a programmatic aspect related to the history of Austria.

The sculptures are loosely arranged along a rough axis (fig. 1), so that the beholder may experience the monument as a succession of elements. This succession implies a sequential interpretation, or even a narrative, whose ultimate point is the tallest element in the composition, the "Rock of the Republic." The other elements seem set against the flat inscribed face of the stele, or, conversely, the stele stands as a "headstone" at the "back" of the monument, as if it not only provides a culmination point but also the coordinates of a life, by displaying name, dates of birth and death, and possibly even an epitaph.

According to the logic of the succession proposed by the loose alignment of elements, one enters through two asymmetrical posts called the "Gate of Violence." The posts consist of a rough-hewn block of Mauthausen granite over two meters in height topped by asymmetric and unfinished sculptures in Carrara marble. These marble blocks have been worked unevenly to produce reliefs in the round that tilt toward one another, leaving less than a meter separating them at their apex. Entering between them, one senses their mass and a constriction of space as well as one's own smallness. The artist also meant for the beholder to experience fear (Wodak 106–7).

The dramatic play of light on the carved marble surfaces of the gate reveals an entanglement of brutally disfigured bodies, the physical remnants of violence against humanity. On one side a rigid and uniformed tormenter administers a fatal injection to a crumpled and twisted mass of humanity that has been hacked, carved, and smoothed out of the marble (fig. 7). The tangled subjects of torture bring to mind photographs of concentration camp inmates that every educated Austrian must have seen. In costume and bearing their torturer could be a Nazi doctor. This sculpture also evokes the mass and technically facilitated murders of the handicapped, the mentally ill, of the Sinti and Roma, Jehovah's Witnesses, and homosexuals, of the Jews and Slavic peoples of different nationalities. More so, as the artist told me, the implements of torture should also bring to mind contemporary instances of bestiality and inhumanity.

Der Heldentod (The Death of a Hero) (fig. 8), on the opposite post of the gate, shows a horrific dismembering and violation of the human body. A child bursts forth from its mother's womb, and a fist plunges into the abdomen of a man as if to grab his entrails and rip them out. The helmeted head of a soldier lies overturned and discarded at the foot of a strident malformed figure. Bodies are intertwined and wrapped around the marble block. On the opposite side of the block in lower relief a strange helmeted soldier, wearing a gas mask and wielding a sword, stabs a man bent in agony. Such drastic mimetic scenes seek to make palpable the agony of soldiers dying at the front and of the civilians dying at home, but in their mode of exaggeration do so at risk of becoming caricatures of themselves. The "Gate of Violence" is about the horrific effects of violence perpetrated in war on the front and on the home front by fascist regimes. It is also about Austria's alliance with fascism and its subsumption into the Third Reich. Yet these sculptural images evoke more than they delineate. As the anachronistic combination of armor, sword, gas mask, and steel helmet suggest, they do not show specific historical events but, rather, display general instances of inhumanity during wartime and in a totalitarian system. In his figurative language the artist is polemical. He creates grotesque figures to engender and simulate horror. If this proposed effect is lost on the beholder, the figures become caricatures and may be valued only as kitsch.

Through the opening of the gate, meant to instill horror, one can approach the bronze sculpture of a bearded Jew with a yarmulke who scrubs the granite pavement on his hands and knees (fig. 2). At the arch of his back he rises no more than seventy or eighty centimeters from the pavement in the shadow of the massive gate, which dominates him. Any beholder who approaches the sculpture while standing erect assumes the pose of looking down at the massive and immovable Jew and in a dominant position similar to the one the Viennese assumed as they forced Jews into the streets in November 1938. The shift in the experience of the beholder from being diminished by the gate to looking down at the prostrate Jew is significant. It may remind one of the shifting borders between being oppressed and being complicit in oppression.

The bronze sculpture *Bei der Reibpartie* (The Street Washing Game) memorializes the peculiar manner of degradation the Viennese visited upon their Jewish compatriots in March 1938 after the *Anschluss.*[22] At that time "ex-

Fig. 7.   Alfred Hrdlicka, "The Gate of Violence" (detail of left post), from *Monument against War and Fascism*, on the Albertinaplatz, Vienna, 1988. (Photo copyright Bettina Secker, Bad Honnef.)

Fig. 8.   Alfred Hrdlicka, "The Gate of Violence/Heldentod" (1991), from *Monument against War and Fascism,* on the Albertinaplatz, Vienna, 1988. (Photo: John Czaplicka.)

ultant Nazi mobs ran riot. With the police standing idly by, S.A. men and Hitler Youth dragged well-dressed Jews off the sidewalks and forced them to clean 'Aryan' apartments. . . . Grotesque scenes took place on the streets. . . . Jews were made to scrub garbage-strewn cobblestones with toothbrushes . . . while crowds looked on and laughed; when they finished fresh garbage would be tossed down and the game would begin again" (Herzstein 53–54). The sculpture shows a Jew in a pose drawn directly from photographs in Austrian history books and films and, therefore, would be immediately recognizable to the Viennese.[23] Perhaps more than any other figure in the monument, the Jew has a historical specificity related to the open collaboration of the Viennese in Nazi acts of terror. Yet, not only does it refer to open complicity of Austrians; it also serves to admonish us that the most brutal crimes perpetrated by humanity often begin with acts that deny others dignity.

Because of the familiarity of this scenario and, perhaps, because of the direct indictment of the Viennese through this figure, the bronze Jew has become the most discussed element of Hrdlicka's monumental ensemble. It presents the Jew as a docile victim robbed of dignity and seems almost to conform with the caricatures of Jews used by the Nazis to construct their internal Other. The Jew is the only type Hrdlicka tries to characterize within the monumental ensemble, and his portrayal of the Jew with a skullcap and long beard comes dangerously close to stereotyping. This highly ambiguous figure has divided the Viennese Jewish community, many of whose members find it highly offensive.

One member of that remnant community thought the figure might even serve as an impetus for the incorrigible part of the populace who still harbored antisemitic sentiments. Others in that community saw it representing Ahasver, the eternal and wandering Jew. Paul Grosz, head of the Israelitische Kultusgemeinde in Vienna, interpreted it more in conformity with the artist's intentions. He expressed his "many grave doubts on account of the street-washing Jew" because it still evoked "painful memories" of degradation. Only after a discussion with the artist was he able to respond to the reservations of the Jewish community with a defense of the figure, which he thought would fulfill its function of admonishment ("Dokumentation"). The monument is not a memorial to the Jews; it is a reminder to the Viennese of the suffering they caused.

The question of the appropriateness of the street-scrubbing Jew arises because it too closely resembles Nazi caricatures of Jews. With his beard and skullcap, however, the Jew also recalls the Hassidim and the nineteenth-century shtetl culture, which many Jews abandoned by emigrating to Vienna. This traditional "ghetto type" responds to the fact that the culture completely destroyed in the Holocaust was exactly that of the East European Jews who lived in small towns and villages.

The next sculpture beyond the street-washing Jew displays a muscular forearm, powerful buttocks, and legs of a man emerging from one side of a tall limestone block, which is again set on a socle of Mauthausen granite (fig. 9). The head of a male figure lies unattended on the opposite side of the sculpture, where a hand emerges and grasps the other arm attached to the male torso as if to pull him down. The fragmentary emergence of human form from stone is entitled "Descent of Orpheus into the Underworld (Hades)," though it would seem to combine at least one other episode of the Orpheus myth, his beheading (because he had refused to honor Dionysus or because he had preached homosexuality after his emergence from Hades). The fearless mythical figure had descended into Hades to retrieve his love, Eurydice, but he lost her forever for disobeying the single condition placed upon him, that he should not turn to look at her until she was safely under the light of the sun. Orpheus, the singer and poet and the creative being who resisted, often appears in Hrdlicka's work and may represent the conflicted role of the artist.

Related to a series of ancient narratives, the Orpheus figure stands *pars pro toto* for the generic ideas that those narratives convey. These ideas have various historical and contemporary resonances. Certainly, in the monument Orpheus more generally embodies the concept of tragic resistance. He was punished for his actions against authority or for resisting the will of an authority. His punishment involved a dismemberment of the human body, a destruction of the wholeness of the vessel of our humanity. This was an inspiration to a modern artist like Hrdlicka, who sees "ravaged flesh" as "ideology" or, if one interprets this causally, as a *result* of ideology.

Understood allegorically, Orpheus stands for resurrection, resistance, and an ultimate demise of the body but not of the spirit (he continues to play his lyre even after being beheaded); in the combination of these meanings he has also been understood as a mythic prefiguration of Christ, who likewise descended into Hell. Thus, the mythic son of a muse in a Christological transformation can serve as a type of *ecce homo* figure with open relationship to political and social environment and to history. Within the framework Hrdlicka has provided the common concepts of resistance and sacrifice suggested by Orpheus point to an allegory of the Austrian resistance movement, but the artist himself has offered other, more site-specific layers of meaning to this element in his work. He tells us that the "descent" of Orpheus points to those civilians who entered the cellar of the Philliphof during a bombing raid in 1945. "These people were buried beneath the rubble and were suffocated or died of hunger," never again to emerge from their modern "Hades." On another plane, as the artist tells it, the setting up of Orpheus at this site was a wink to the Albertina, the State Opera, and the Theater Museum, Vienna's temples of the muses, which can all be seen from the monument (Wodak 106). Set in relation to the historical circumstances, the multiple meanings of this figure who resists, who succumbs but does not succumb completely, whose spirit lives beyond the dismembered body, open up wide possibilities for interpretation. The meanings may be ambivalent or even

Fig. 9.   Alfred Hrdlicka, "The Descent of Orpheus into Hades," from *Monument against War and Fascism,* on the Albertinaplatz, Vienna, 1988. (Photo copyright Bettina Secker, Bad Honnef.)

contradictory; the questions these contradictions might raise about humanity—about resistance, authority, victimization, or heroism and the gods—are generic ones relevant to almost any state in any historical era. Yet those questions were also posed in the extreme by the historical actions of the Nazis.

Closing the monument is the towering irregular stele called "The Rock of the Republic," which is inscribed with the Austrian "Declaration of Independence" from 27 April 1945, a document formulated by Austrians that marks the end of Nazi rule *before* the end of World War II and the beginnings of a new state in Austria.[24] The four figurative sculptures that precede it are, in a way, its historical preamble. Their disfigured and agitated rendering of humankind describe and allude to a bloodied and conflicted history that finds aesthetic and historical closure in the stele that embodies the founding of the Second Republic of Austria. Since its beginnings that republic has been largely a Republic of Denial, whose citizens have found a comforting refuge in their self-conceptualization as a nation of victims. Nonetheless, the liberties established by that same republic have allowed Hrdlicka's highly critical monument to a national rebirth to be built even while a president who had served the Third Reich held office. Hrdlicka himself sees the stele as a pivotal part of his work, for, from the terror and brutality of Austria's past history, a state based on tolerance and laws emerges to offer a future perspective (Wodak 107).

At this point one might draw a loose analogy between the artistic statement made by the artist and one made by the German philosopher Jürgen Habermas about Germany. In the midst of the *Historikerstreit* (historians' controversy) concerning the basis for reforming a national identity while coming to terms with an unmasterable past in Germany, Habermas wrote:

> The only patriotism that does not alienate us from the West is a patriotic commitment to constitutionalism. Unfortunately, a loyalty, one anchored in conviction, could be inculcated in the German nation only after—and by virtue of—Auschwitz. Whoever wants to suppress the blush of shame about this fact by resorting to slogans such as "obsession with guilt," whoever wants to summon the Germans back to a conventional form of their national identity, destroys the only reliable basis of our Western loyalty. (Qtd. in Maier 45)

Could one not read Hrdlicka's monumental statement to the Austrian nation along the same lines, relating the realization that the independence of Austria and its national identity separate from a greater German reich could only be secured after the admonishing experiences of war, Auschwitz, and the resolute oppression of the Third Reich? And isn't the belief in constitutionalism that was reinstated by the document whose text the "Rock of the Republic" bears exactly the beginning point for future Austrian state and identity? This text does not appeal to the emotions of the beholder as do the mimetic representations of the human body in the other elements of Hrdlicka's disjunct narrative. The Austrian state and identity begin to reconstitute themselves in the quiet abstraction of that declaration. It stands as the culmination of a vision of Austrian history that integrates the Nazi past and does not renounce responsibility for it.

Seen from a traditional perspective about memorials and monuments, few would argue that Hrdlicka's controversial ensemble is either beautiful or elevating. But beauty or elevation, two criteria derived from the Enlightenment's original and rational concept of a public monument, are simply inappropriate in the commemoration of oppression and violence perpetrated by the Nazis and Austro-fascists in Austria. And yet, critics have conceded that in its form and because of its central placement, the monument catches the eye of almost every passerby, which is something unusual for a public monument. Furthermore, once approached and recognized for what they are and understood for what they convey, the sculptural components of this complex and multifaceted ensemble offer their beholders, and especially the Viennese, cause for thought about uncomfortable historical and moral topics often left unbroached, conveniently forgotten, or relegated to the remote realm of some *past* history. One can understand Hrdlicka's work as admonishing stones set upright in the winds of political controversy.

NOTES

For their kind assistance in the research for this essay I would like to express my gratitude to Alfred Hrdlicka, Kurt Scholz, Richard Schmitz, Aaron and Sarah Rhodes, Richard Mitten, Rosa Mück, Konrad Oberhuber, Helmut Zilk, Andy Markovits, Alfred Gutmann, and Ursula Pasterk. I am indebted to Irene, Jonathan, and Scott for their editing and commentary.

Epigraph:

Professor Robert
Was die Schriftssteller schreiben
ist ja nichts gegen die Wirklichkeit
jaja sie schreiben ja dass alles fürchterlich ist
dass alles verdorben und verkommen ist und
dass alles katastrophal ist
und dass alles ausweglos ist
aber alles das sie schreiben
ist nichts gegen die Wirklichkeit
die Wirklichkeit ist so schlimm
dass sie nicht beschrieben werden kann
noch kein Schriftsteller hat die Wirklichkeit so beschrieben.

I have freely translated the text taken from the play *Heldenplatz* (115). The idea to employ this quote comes from Egon Schwarz's essay "Heldenplatz?"; his discussion of the parallel scandal in the Viennese "political theater" of 1988–89 offers a clear understanding of "literature's interdependence with its (political and social) environment" (330). More recently, the project of Ruth Wodak, Florian Menz, Richard Mitten, and Frank Stern on public commemoration in the media of Austria and Germany has been published as an excellent collection of essays, *Die Sprachen der Vergangenheiten: Öffentliches Gedenken in österreichischen und deutschen Medien* (1994). Their study centers on the Waldheim controversy and the year of anniversaries, 1988.

1. The monument was completed in 1991 with the addition of the last figurative sculpture, the *Heldentod*.

2. I am indebted to Robert E. Herzstein's invaluable *Waldheim: The Missing Years* for much of the information on the Waldheim controversy.

3. The best collection of the debates concerning the monument can be found in a documentation prepared by the SPÖ majority in the Vienna city government of 1988 (Sozialistische Fraktion im Wiener Landtag und Gemeinderat. Dokumentation Denkmal gegen Krieg und Faschismus von Alfred Hrdlicka [committee report], 1988, Rathaus Wien). The succinct and clear summation of these debates found in Wodak (105–14) confirmed many of the more general conclusions I have drawn from an incomplete personal documentation. My own interest in the demonstrations at the site of the monument stem from a realization of how incomplete any such documentation can be if it depends only on the printed reception in the press. The tendency among most reporters who engage in cultural-political criticism is to read the press notices and previous reports, scratch down a few notes, and construct a "new" report. Even reporters at the scene tend to focus only on the spectacle, the scandalous, and the unruly and thus offer little substantive analysis in their reports.

4. The dispute about the monument should not be seen only as a cultural-political adjunct to the Waldheim controversy but, as I argue here, as the first well-publicized, well-placed (in terms of the monument's siting), and well-conceived (on the part of the artist and members of the SPÖ) attempt to erect a permanent reminder of Austria's fascist past. Rachel Whitehead's proposed memorial for the Jews of Vienna on the Ruprechtsplatz may provide an aesthetically less problematic reminder, but its concentration on one group in Austria's history will leave it in the former ghetto, where it will stand.

5. The leaflet was first distributed in 1988 to protest the investment of money in a new monument by a libertine/sadomasochist initiative ("Unter Druck").

6. In June 1995 the Austrian coalition government of Social Democrats and conservatives finally voted to compensate the Jews, communists, and homosexuals who were sent to concentration camps and those who fled into exile to avoid persecution under the Nazis. Claimants would have to prove they were Austrian citizens. Only Austrians who returned after 1945 had already received some compensation, but marginal groups such as homosexuals had been excluded. Austria had avoided the question of compensation for most of the postwar period and claimed that the country was the first victim of Hitler's aggression. Only recently have political leaders publicly acknowledged that Austrians were also willing servants of Nazism.

7. Hrdlicka told me in an interview in June 1991 how pleased he was that a group of handicapped persons had also used the Albertinaplatz as a staging ground for their demonstration—a sign that his monument is being well received.

8. "Die Gemeinde Wien gedenkt hier nicht ihrer homosexuellen Opfer."

9. Yet since then Haider has held various political offices, and Waldheim still fights—most recently by publishing a book—to regain his credibility. Haider's most recent slip of the tongue came after a bomb attack by the radical right-wing on a Roma settlement in the Austrian province of Burgenland. He claimed that it was probably "the result of a gypsy feud." Later he retracted the statement and apologized to the public, a tactic—slip, retraction, and apology—that allows him to leave unsaid what he is saying and thus to encourage his far-right-wing supporters to remain firm behind him ("Bei Roma").

10. Related to the author in an interview with Hrdlicka, September 1989.

11. According Richard Mitten, in the summer months of 1988, during the high point of the controversy about the monument, forty-nine different political commentators had taken positions on its erection in ninety-two different articles (see Wodak 95).

12. He positioned himself on the side of the strong 46 percent minority that did not elect Waldheim, on the side of the leftist-intellectuals, the Jewish World Congress, and on the side of a purportedly ignorant and hostile international community. For his writings on this issue, see Lewin 203–4; see also the collection *Pflichterfüllung* as the presentation of an alternative Austria.

13. This relates to Waldheim's often repeated claim about his voluntary membership in the SA, or the Storm Troopers (not be confused with the SS). His membership he said was not in a Nazi organization but, rather, in a riding group only incidentally attached to the SA. The cynical response to this diplomatic phrasing was the joke about how not Waldheim but, instead, his horse had served in that unit.

14. The Austrians' peculiar unwillingness to deal with the aspects of their history I outline here has been the subject of many books and essays by those engaged historians. The Institut für Zeitgeschichte at the University of Vienna and the Dokumentationsarchiv des österreichischen Widerstandes have provided a home for the task of making Austrian history whole. Of the books on which I draw the most useful are: *Das Grosse Tabu;* Pelinka; Stourzh, *Vom Reich zur Republik;* and *Verdrängte Schuld, verfehlte Sühne.*

15. Within the resistance movement only the Communists and the Monarchists subscribed categorically to an independent Austria. The Austrian Communists (KPÖ), who had supported the idea of a greater Germany much as the Austrian Socialists (SPÖ), would begin to endorse the idea of an independent Austria and separate Austrian identity in 1936. The Monarchist, or Legitimist, Resistance, composed of the nobility, the clergy, and members of the officer corps, sought to maintain a historical continuity with the Hapsburg Empire (see Luza).

16. Rather than pointing out again that Adolf Hitler was Austrian or that his able lieutenants Adolf Eichmann and Ernst Kaltenbrunner were Austrian or noting the overrepresentation of Austrians in the administration of the death camps, it pays to look at the involvement of the larger population in organizations such as the Wehrmacht. The Waldheim controversy became so vehement not only because Waldheim was at least implicated in crimes against humanity but because his own past was, without a doubt, in certain ways similar to that of many Austrians in that he served the Third Reich as a "good" soldier. A good soldier, a good policeman, a good bureaucrat, a good Austrian, all served the Third Reich well. For a solidly researched view of Austrians in the Wehrmacht, see Manoschek and Safrian.

17. The concept of antifascism is used here only in this limited sense. The ideology of antifascism, the centerpiece of a national or international mission among the author-

itarian regimes of the former communist states of Central and Eastern Europe, was a state doctrine whose antagonist became all of the capitalist countries during the Cold War. Hrdlicka developed a complex relationship to this ideology, but this essay must restrict itself to the concept of antifascism as the artist concretely expressed it in his sculptural designs for public monuments.

Among the first artists to design antifascist monuments were the German sculptors Georg Kolbe and Richard Scheibe, who took part in a competition to erect such a monument in Halle in 1946.

18. The competition for a monument on St. Stephen's Square was part of the project for a new design of the square after the completion of the subway. Five artists were asked by the city of Vienna to take part in a competition (see Lewin, vol. 1, cat. nos. 143–49; and vol. 4, text nos. 83–87).

19. Hrdlicka received his commission for the monument against war and fascism on the Albertinaplatz on 30 August 1983. There is a published contract (Werkvertrag. a.Z1. MA 7– 888/83. 30. August 1983, Pr.Z. 2524. Magistrat der Stadt Wien). The Vienna city council unanimously approved the erection of the monument on the Albertinaplatz on 30 September 1983 (Auszug aus der Tagesordnung des Gemeinderates, 2524). See also *Dokumentation Denkmal gegen Krieg und Faschismus,* for further discussion of the monument at the level of the city council.

20. This was a monument to *Austrian* culture that in the late nineteenth century had won out over the proposition by the supporters of a greater Germany in Austria, who had envisioned a monument to Richard Wagner instead (Pellar 92–98). The pinnacle of absurdity in any serious discussion about a monument dealing with *Vergangenheitsbewältigung* was reached by the scandal-mongering newspaper *Kronen Zeitung,* which offered as a counterproposal a photograph of a Viennese beauty sniffing daffodils next to plans for an Old Vienna flower market on a tree-lined Albertinaplatz.

21. "Begehbares Denkmal" is a concept Hrdlicka first employed in referring to another antifascist monument he designed and erected for the city of Hamburg from 1983 to 1987.

22. One can speculate about why this form of degradation was preferred. Perhaps it derives from the resentment by a portion of the population that the Jews of Vienna played such a leading role in the business world, the professions, and the intellectual and cultural life of the city. The Nazis claimed the Jews did not work, that they only exploited other people; getting them out to scrub the pavement made them work. This useless work would find its analogue in the concentration camps, where *Arbeit macht Frei,* and the Jews were worked to death.

23. Though most Viennese recognize the figure, many tourists sat on the Jew's back before some uncomfortably sharp pieces of bronze were added.

24. Declaring the Anschluss null and void, the three newly reconstituted political parties of Austria issued a declaration of independence on 27 April 1945, with the permission of the Russian occupation troops (Bluhm 51–52).

WORKS CITED

"Bei Roma entschuldigt." *die tageszeitung,* 22 June 1996, 9.
Bernhard, Thomas. *Heldenplatz.* Frankfurt a.M.: Suhrkamp, 1995.

Bluhm, William T. *Building an Austrian Nation.* New Haven: Yale UP, 1973.

Das Grosse Tabu: Österreichs Umgang mit seiner Vergangenheit. Edition S. Vienna: Verlag der österreichischen Staatsdrückerei, 1987.

"Dokumentation Denkmal gegen Krieg und Faschismus von Alfred Hrdlicka." Committee Report of the Sozialistische Fraktion im Wiener Landtag und Gemeinderat. Vienna: Rathaus Wien, 1988.

Frank, Michael. "Eine Feier, bei der sich Gesinnungen enthüllen: Auseinandersetzungen mit Störern prägen in Wien die Einweihung von Alfred Hrdlickas umstrittenen Mahnmal." *Süddeutsche Zeitung,* 26–27 November 1988.

Herzstein, Robert E. *Waldheim: The Missing Years.* New York: Arbor House, 1988.

Hrdlicka, Alfred. Interviews with the author, 1989, 1991.

J. H. "Enthüllt, enthüllend: Alfred Hrdlickas Mahnmal auf dem Wiener Albertinaplatz." *Frankfurter Allgemeine Zeitung,* 28 November 1988.

Kronen Zeitung, 23 April 1986, 32–33.

Lewin, Michael. *Alfred Hrdlicka, das Gesamtwerk.* Vienna: Europaverlag in Zusammenarbeit mit der Galerie Hilge, 1987.

Luza, Radomir V. *The Resistance in Austria, 1938–1945.* Minneapolis: U of Minnesota P, 1984.

Maier, Charles. *The Unmasterable Past: History, Holocaust, and German National Identity.* Cambridge: Harvard UP, 1988.

Manoschek, Walter, and Hans Safrian. "Österreicher in der Wehrmacht." In *NS-Herrschaft in Österreich, 1938–1945,* ed. Emmerich Talos et al. Vienna: Verlag für Gesellschaftskritik, 1988. 331–60.

Pelinka, Anton. *Windstille: Klagen über Österreich.* Vienna: Medusa, 1985.

Pellar, Brigitta. *Albertinaplatz.* Vienna: Europaverlag, 1988.

Pflichterfüllung: Ein Bericht über Kurt Waldheim. Ed. "Neues Österreich." Vienna: Löcker Verlag, 1986.

Profil, 7 July 1986, n.p.

Schwarz, Egon. "Heldenplatz?" *German Politics and Society* 21 (Fall 1990): 33–47.

Stourzh, Gerald. *Kleine Geschichte des österreichischen Staatsvertrages.* Vienna and Cologne: Verlag Styria, 1974.

———. *Vom Reich zur Republik: Studien zum Österreichbewusstsein im 20. Jahrhundert.* Vienna: Atelier, 1990.

Unter Druck. 3. Vienna: Printmedium der "Libertine-Sadomasochismusinitiative Wien," 1988.

Verdrängte Schuld, verfehlte Sühne: Entnazifizierung in Österreich, 1945–1955. Munich: R. Oldenbourg, 1986.

Wodak, Ruth, Florian Menz, Richard Mitten, and Frank Stern, eds. *Die Sprachen der Vergangenheiten: öffentliches Gedenken in österreichischen und deutschen Medien.* Frankfurt a.M.: Suhrkamp, 1994.

Zilk, Helmut. Letter to the author, 15 September 1989.

———. "Zum Denkmal gegen Krieg und Faschismus auf dem Platz vor der Albertina." Press conference transcript, 26 July 1988.

CHAPTER 16

Economic Influences on Constructions of German Identity

Robert Mark Spaulding

Scholarly explorations of relationships between cultural characteristics and economic performance are not new. To cite perhaps the best-known example, Max Weber undertook such an investigation of Western European culture and economic development in his The Protestant Ethic and the Spirit of Capitalism *early in this century. Like other later explorations of this kind, Weber sought to identify cultural characteristics that determined successful economic performance, making cultural traits "independent variables" (in the parlance of social science) and the resultant economic performance the "dependent variable." As work along these lines continued, it became clear that the characteristics of any highly developed culture are so numerous, ambiguous, and vaguely defined that some of them might be used to explain any level of economic performance, from very poor to very strong. Indeed, in the 1950s Western scholars cited many traditional aspects of Asian cultures as reasons why capitalism had not (and would not) flourish there. Thirty years later, in the 1980s, some of these same characteristics were cited again—this time as reasons why capitalist economies in Asia were so successful. Historians, in particular, now generally shy away from offering culture-based explanations for economic performance.*

Robert Mark Spaulding's essay inverts the previous order of inquiry by beginning with the level of German performance and exploring its role in shaping German national identity. As a preliminary assessment, we can say that the rephrased question "How does economic performance inform German national identity?" has yielded some new and positive insights. Yet past experiences with cultural explanations of economic performance remind us that a word of caution might be in order. The components of communal identity are complex and ambiguous. Can we not easily imagine that in very different cir-

cumstances thirty years hence we might use the same assessments of German economic performance offered here to reach some fundamentally different conclusions about German national identity?

With that caveat Spaulding, an economic and diplomatic historian by training, explores the concept of a national economic identity, using cultural objects, such as popular literature and film, to illustrate his thesis. His essay builds upon Confino's contribution—and even constitutes a response to it. While Confino suggests avenues of inquiry into constructions of national identity based on commercial activities, Spaulding undertakes the actual exploration itself.

On 16 January 1995 the Konrad Adenauer Stiftung published the results of an extensive new survey on the German national identity. In both East and West Germans most frequently cited "the economic system" (*das Wirtschaftssystem*) as the primary reason for identifying themselves with the German nation ("Studie"). Over the past century, and particularly over the past forty years, the German economic identity has been transformed from one of several contributing elements in the national identity into the dominant component of German identity. The evolution of the German national identity into a primarily economic identity is a transformation of far-reaching significance and yet one that remains largely unexplored.[1]

This essay briefly examines the rise and development of the economic component of German national identity in the modern period. This means examining several distinct economic periods: the industrial rise prior to 1914; the troubled 1920s; the rearmament prosperity of 1933–39; the economic miracle of the 1950s; and the industrial growth and financial stability of the 1960s to the 1990s. Although we lack for earlier periods the type of public opinion data now available for the Federal Republic, it is possible to suggest how the economic component of German national identity has evolved in response to changing economic and political circumstances in the past century. That examination might allow us better to assess the large economic component of contemporary German identity by placing it in a longer comparative German historical context.

Meaningful discussion of economic influences on constructions of German national identity can begin only with the achievements of German industrial production in the late nineteenth century. Germany's first economic identity—an industrial identity—came rather late into the mix of images that produced a German national identity in the nineteenth century, perhaps as much as a century later than the cultural identity that began the process of national formation.[2]

Ravaged by the Thirty Years' War in the seventeenth century and then eclipsed by the rise of Atlantic trade in the eighteenth century, the German economy did not distinguish itself in performance until the age of industrial production. Prior to that time traditional economic skills as organized in the guild structure served as the indispensable bases for individual, class, and community identities but not as a contributing source for a German national identity.[3] Not surprisingly, then, descriptions of the German nation in the preindustrial period do not refer to the economic structures or performance of the German inhabited lands as a defining characteristic of the people or the place. Outsiders from Tacitus to Voltaire found the German peoples and lands to be fascinating subjects, but that fascination clearly was not generated by any economic activity then under way in the German territories. Similarly, the most influential insider voices in shaping modern German identity in the preindustrial period— Herder, Fichte, and Hegel—also fail to mention any aspect of German economic life in their respective thoughts on Germanness. Herder's silence on the significance or uniqueness of any German economic activity stands in noticeable contrast to his lengthy, though unsystematic, assessment of German activities in a dozen other fields ranging from literary criticism, aesthetics, philology, folklore, and history to psychology, anthropology, philosophy, and theology.[4]

Not until traditional German skills in design, metalworking, and chemical knowledge had been combined with the new principles of factory organization as developed in England did the German economy begin to command attention, both at home and abroad. Over the course of the nineteenth century the German industrial economy steadily acquired the national and international reputations that served as the bases for a new element in the German national identity. By the close of the nineteenth century German industry had gained worldwide recognition for characteristics that are now so synonymous with German industrial production that they have become integral parts of German national identity: top-quality industrial design, precision manufacture, prompt delivery, and expert installation. Further, Germany's outstanding industrial achievement drew heavily on characteristically German institutions such as apprenticeships and the modern university curriculum, thereby overcoming earlier assertions that an industrial identity was an imported, foreign, or English identity and not a genuinely German one.

By 1900 "Made in Germany" identified a national pride in industrial performance that was felt by both bourgeoisie and workers. In particular, the engineer-entrepreneur (à la Siemens, Daimler, or Mannesmann) was an economic type produced more frequently in Germany than elsewhere and the engineer cum businessman was a self-image conspicuously advanced by the German industrial elite. Despite a political structure weighted in favor of the aristocratic Junkers, tributes to the industrial and commercial activity of the bourgeoisie abounded in imperial Germany. In architecture Ernst Borsig's Renaissance palace on the Vossstrasse in Berlin was imitated at less splendid levels by the numerous upper-middle-class villas built in the Tiergarten and Charlottenburg areas of the capital. The architectural style of official Berlin, embodied, for example, in Georg Hitzig's large Renaissance-decorated Berlin stock exchange building (1859–63), became inextricably identified with achievements of the industrial and commercial bourgeoisie (James 72). In literature two generations of (rather pedestrian) authors such as Berthold Auerbach, Gustav Freytag, Friedrich Spielhagen, and Ernst von Wolzogen championed middle-class commercial productivity as a powerful force in shaping the new Germany.[5]

An ambivalent pride in the German industrial achievement was evident among workers as well, even as genuine *Arbeitsfreude* remained an elusive goal. Two contradictory inputs combined to emphasize to the workers their contributions to Germany's industrial rise. On one hand, flattering tributes to the abilities of German workers flowed from the government in an effort to rally workers to the national community and, hence, to the government via social imperialism.[6] The effort was not without success, at least at the level of forging some connection between workers and the emerging national identity of production, as the outpouring of popular support for the country in the summer of 1914 demonstrated. Social Democratic agitation also stimulated the workers' industrial self-image by continually emphasizing the indispensable role played by the working class in the capitalist arrangement. With the rise of revisionism within the Sozialistische Partei Deutschlands (SPD; Social Democratic Party) in the final decade before the war, the SPD program for Germany acquired an unmistakably patriotic tone, echoing back to Lasallian traditions that had never been completely extinguished in German social democracy.[7] For many workers in the Reich international class identity was gradually transformed into a German industrial identity.

Certainly for Germany's European neighbors, a powerful level of industrial performance had become a central element in the identity of imperial Germany. The British in particular were fascinated by the rise of German productive power, as the spate of turn-of-the-century books investigating the German economy indicates.[8] In the East, Russian patriots assailed German industry's commanding position in the Russian market, while Russian manufacturers found German products essential to modernization.

The progressive intrusion of efficient, high-quality industrial performance as a central element of German national identity was not without problems. Leftist liberal social critics such as author Heinrich Mann decried the "level of materialism to which the nation has sunk," in which "earning money and quieting the workers' movement through social reforms and reprisals so that one can continue earning money," had become "the only thing that seriously occupies Germans of all social groups" (22). On the other side, a growing industrial identity heightened social tensions by opening a deep psychological divide between the new industrial and more traditional agricultural portions of the populations. Those who saw no prospect of inclusion in this new industrial identity sought to deny its growing hold over the German psyche. In desperation a number of aristocratic Prussian estate owners declared flatly in 1893 that agriculture remained the "first Estate" in the Reich and that Prussia could not be considered an "industrial state" (Bundesarchiv; see also Barkin). In rejecting Germany's new economic identity, the nonindustrial portions of society were the first to begin moving toward a new noneconomic German identity based on soil, ethnicity, and race.

Denial of imperial Germany's increasingly industrial character was possible only for that steadily declining nonindustrial portion of the population. On the other side were the numerically advancing groups in society: the commercial and industrial bourgeoisie, the industrial workers, and the white-collar employees. For these groups the Germany economy was an industrial economy or a commercial economy based on industrial exports. By 1914 German economic success in the industrial sector had been so phenomenal as to become part of the definition of the nation.

For a number of reasons the public and private leadership of the Weimar Republic were unable to cultivate further this economic portion of German identity. Gustav Stresemann's 1925 declaration that for Germany there remained only "one area in which we are still a Great Power—our economic power" (434) revealed an appreciation of the role that economic performance might play in both foreign policy and in the national self-image. The performance of the German economy during the 1920s was not good enough, however, to serve as a positive element in the (re)construction of national identity during the Weimar Republic. Framed between the period of postwar dislocations and inflation on one side and the Great Depression on the other, even the "good years" of the republic offered uninspiring economic performances. In 1926, with two million unemployed, real wages in industry remained substantially lower than they had been in 1913–14. The extensive German debate of the 1920s on the need to Americanize German industry highlights the decline of German industrial pride (see Nolan 70 ff.). Weimar's poor economic performance prevented a further development of a positive German identity based on economic performance. The consequences were fatal for republican government and disastrous for the nation. Unable to draw on a positive economic self-image, a significant portion of the population found refuge in other, dangerous images of the nation offered by parties of the far Right.

After 1933 the Nazi government played down the economic component of

German national identity. Although the divergence between a German economy at full employment and other industrial economies still afflicted by depression provided an obvious opportunity to highlight the German economic identity, the Nazi leadership preferred to emphasize the racial definition of the nation. German economic achievements and technological advances were touted by the regime but could never serve as a defining characteristic of the German people. Rather, economic performance could serve only to prove the superiority of the German nation as defined in racial terms. For these same reasons the concept of "German work" as advanced by the regime might help bridge existing divisions between workers and bourgeoisie, but participation in work (of any kind) could never define Germanness during the Third Reich. Workers in particular were encouraged to abandon their economic identities and join the racially defined *Volksgemeinschaft* (folk community). The extent of Nazi success in indoctrinating the masses along these lines has been extensively debated, but there now appears little doubt that at least some movement in the direction desired by the regime was achieved.[9]

Economic influences have played their greatest role in shaping the German national identity in the post-1945 period and most particularly in the Federal Republic. Perhaps no portion of the postwar German experience has been as crucial to the reconstruction of German identity as the economic performance of the Federal Republic. The physical reconstruction of an advanced industrial economy in West Germany was indeed a *Wirtschaftswunder,* a monumental achievement that any society would have eagerly absorbed into the mythology of its national identity.[10] The unusual conditions of post-1945 Germany only magnified this economic achievement in the reconstructed German identity. Because so many traditional portions of the national identity had been expropriated by the Nazis, and thus rendered taboo in the postwar world, this economic portion of German identity now stood alone as a hopeful reflection of the German character, the single available point around which Germans might begin to reconstruct a positive image of the nation.

Allied occupation policies only reinforced the primacy of economics by granting the Germans economic sovereignty before political sovereignty and by integrating West Germany into Europe economically first and politically only thereafter. After 1949 the Federal Republic offered only an anti-identity in politics (not Weimar, not the Third Reich, not the GDR), so that the economics moved to the center of the West German national identity almost by default.

Beginning in the 1970s the German economic identity was enhanced by the addition of a financial element for the first time. As the deutsche mark assumed a secondary role to the dollar as a world reserve currency and gained a reputation as the world's most stable currency, West Germans found a second source of satisfaction in their economic identity. Today most Germans are confidently aware that both German industrial output and German financial stability are essential to the economic future of Europe.[11]

Not surprisingly, the apparent triumph of an economic identity for the Federal Republic provoked a reaction against this industrially based collective self-image. In particular, a younger generation that had never been offered an alternative national identity began to distance itself from the identity of increasing production that had emerged from the West German economic miracle. Werner Fassbinder's 1978 film *The Marriage of Maria Braun* offered a cinematic reprise of Heinrich Mann's turn-of-the-century lament on German preoccupation with production and profit. In the early 1980s critiques of the postwar German economic identity became both more intensive and more extensive as the nation began to perceive the environmental costs of the economic miracle. In literature these worries preoccupied a new generation of poets, such as Sarah Kirsch and Michael Krüger, who adapted the natural lyric tradition of Wilhelm Lehmann and Oskar Loerke in order to write the lyric poetry of a damaged environment. In politics similar concerns boosted the environmental Green Party into the Bundestag in 1983.

How should one react to the rise of economic identity in Germany? I propose, controversial though it might be, that the growing role of economic performance in shaping the German self-image may well be a healthy sign for the present and future Germany, environmental problems notwithstanding.[12] First, an economic identity competes with the racial identity that lingers in Germany. If genuine, an economic identity, as a specific type of sociological identity, ought ultimately to crowd out residual ethnic and racial components of the German national identity. In other words, an economic identity is based on how one behaves (i.e., what one does) as a producer and a consumer; therefore, it must conflict with a racial identity based primarily on inherited physical characteristics (i.e., what one is), however defined. Second, both the historical record and common sense indicate that a strong, positive German economic identity depends on strong, positive economic performance. The structures of the German economy (e.g., physical size, demographic distribution, geographic location, and natural endowments) ensure that economic performance depends, in turn, on cooperation with European neighbors and participation in the world economy and the multilateral institutions that govern international economic relations. Viewed through this series of connections, a strong German economic identity serves as an indirect indicator of the condition of Germany's international economic (and ultimately political) relations. In sum, the strong economic identity recently cited by respondents of the Adenauer Stiftung survey reflects a prosperous German economy participating productively and cooperatively in the European and world economies—all healthy signs for the future of Germany.

NOTES

1. To date, Harold James's *A German Identity, 1770–1990* remains singular in its efforts at including economic elements into a comprehensive discussion of German identity.

2. For this reason I have been wary of accepting Liah Greenfeld's assertions that "the character of [German] national identity was defined during the early phase" of national formation, which she locates as 1806–15 (22), or that "by 1815" the German national consciousness "possessed all the characteristics by which we would know it" (276).

3. On this, see Mack Walker's pioneering and still indispensable *German Home Towns*.

4. See especially bk. 8 of the "Ideas for a Philosophy of the History of Mankind," in which Herder discusses the "occupations" and "modes of life" of the "nations of the world."

5. Freytag's *Soll und Haben* (*Debit and Credit* [1855]) went through six printings in its first two years, thirty in the next fifteen (Carter). Only after the end of the century did the German bourgeoisie come in for penetrating criticisms in the works of Frank Wedekind, Heinrich Mann, and Carl Sternheim, to name a few.

6. One of the many examples that might be cited is Reich Interior Secretary Count Posadowsky's statement in the Reichstag on 6 February 1906: "If Germany has just experienced a vast industrial expansion equalled by no other country in the world during the same time, it is chiefly due to the efficiency of its workers" (qtd. in Dawson n.p.).

7. On the patriotic consequences of revisionism, see Fletcher.

8. Of these, E. E. Williams's *Made in Germany* remains the best known. Equally revealing of British interests and perceptions is William Dawson's book *The German Workman: A Study in National Efficiency,* which sought to "understand the key to all Germany's progress in those practical and material concerns which nowadays increasingly engross the attention of nations" (viii).

9. For a summary of the debate among historians, see Campbell, 379 ff.

10. Perhaps nothing captures the impact of the economic miracle on the German self-image as succinctly as the 1963 English-language title of a collection of Ludwig Erhard's speeches and articles of the previous decade, *The Economics of Success.*

11. In a 28 February 1995 editorial on the financial consequences of the Baring investment house collapse, the *Mitteldeutsche Zeitung* (Halle) commented: "Once again the German Mark will serve as a saving anchor and so become even stronger vis-à-vis other currencies." As the opinion of an undistinguished provincial paper, the comment reveals how widespread the assumed superiority of German financial practices is in contemporary Germany.

12. This is quite different from the "economicization of politics" that Harold James finds so worrying, presumably because that may have retarded the development of strong democratic parties in the imperial and Weimar periods (77–87).

WORKS CITED

Barkin, Kenneth. *The Controversy over German Industrialization, 1890–1902.* Chicago: U of Chicago P, 1970.

Bundesarchiv, R 2/1691.

Campbell, Joan. *Joy in Work, German Work.* Princeton: Princeton UP, 1989.

Carter, T. E. "Freytag's *Soll und Haben.* A National Liberal Manifesto as Best Seller." *German Life and Letters* 21.4 (July 1968): 320–29.

Dawson, William. *The German Workman: A Study in National Efficiency.* London: P. S. King, 1906.

"Editorial." *Mitteldeutsche Zeitung* (Halle), 28 February 1995. Reprinted in *Deutschland Nachrichten,* 3 March 1995, 3.

Erhard, Ludwig. *The Economics of Success.* London: Thames and Hudson, 1963.

Fletcher, Roger. *Revisionism and Empire: Socialist Imperialism in Germany, 1897–1914.* London: Allen and Unwin, 1984.

Freytag, Gustav. *Soll und Haben: Roman in sechs Büchern.* Leipzig: S. Hirzel, 1855.

Greenfeld, Liah. *Nationalism: Five Roads to Modernity.* Cambridge: Harvard UP: 1992.

Herder, Johann Gottfried. *Sämtliche Werke.* Ed. B. Suphan. Berlin: Weidmann, 1877–1913. Vol. 13.

James, Harold. *A German Identity, 1770–1990.* Rev. ed. London: Weidenfeld and Nicholson, 1990.

Mann, Heinrich. Letter to Ludwig Ewers, 10 April 1904. In *Historische Augenblicke. Deutsche Briefe des XX. Jahrhunderts,* ed. Jürgen Moeller. Munich: Beck, 1988.

Nolan, Mary. *Visions of Modernity: American Business and the Modernization of Germany.* Oxford: Oxford UP, 1994.

Stresemann, Gustav. Speech to the Central Committee of the Deutsche Volkspartei, 22 November 1925. Reprinted by Henry Turner in *Vierteljahrshefte für Zeitgeschichte* 15 (October 1967): 412–36.

"Studie sieht wachsende gemeinsame Identität der Deutschen." *Deutschland Nachrichten,* 20 January 1995, 6.

Walker, Mack. *German Home Towns.* 2 vols. Ithaca: Cornell UP, 1971.

Williams, E. E. *Made in Germany.* London: Heinemann, 1896.

CHAPTER 17

Living with Which Past?
National Identity in Post-Wall,
Postwar Germany

Laurence McFalls

When the Federal Republic of Germany and the German Democratic Republic became one nation in 1990 all issues connected with German identity, including most particularly the history of the German nation, were subject to renegotiation. That is to say, new narratives have inevitably been created about the history of the Germanies and "Germany." While Spaulding suggests that economics plays a defining role in such constructions, in the next two essays Laurence McFalls and Daphne Berdahl interrogate the role and relevance of memory in contemporary German political identity. McFalls, a political scientist, argues that, although a common and difficult (i.e., Nazi) past unites eastern and western Germans, their different memories of their respective postwar experiences within opposing political systems continue to divide them.

In developing his analysis, McFalls uses the vocabulary of the "political culture" approach within political science. An outgrowth of the systemic and structural-functionalist theories that dominated American political science in its formative years of the 1950s and 1960s, this approach conceives of political culture as individuals' shared subjective (cognitive, evaluative, and affective) orientations toward political objects or structures. In the original systemic theoretical perspective political culture was functional—that is, it was the subjective grease that allowed the cogs of the political system to keep turning—and hence almost reduced to mere superstructure. Since the 1970s, however, political ethnography (and to a lesser extent poststructuralism) has inspired students of political culture to ascribe it more autonomy and to embrace subjectivism. Although positivist political scientists interested in discovering clear, unidirectional causality have questioned the explanatory value of the political culture approach, its practitioners have generally come to adopt a dialectic concept of culture according to which political culture both reflects and creates political structures, so that, for example, democratic politics simultaneously depends on and creates democratic attitudes within the citizenry.

In his analysis McFalls implicitly adopts this intermediate, dialectical conception of political culture. He suggests that memory, or subjective orientations to the past, including an inherited repertoire of political and social values, is both the functional product of the structural exigencies of the political system and an independent influence on the system. Thus, he argues not only that contemporary eastern and western German political identities, remembered outgrowths of the old GDR and FRG political systems, have become instrumentalized (or functional) within the partisan competition of the new, unified FRG but also that the outcome of the battle for historical memory will determine the value orientation and the objective policy outcomes of German politics in the years to come.

In keeping with the arbitrary magical quality of round numbers, the fiftieth-anniversary commemorations of the end of World War II have raised more public attention and debate in Germany than did the forty-ninth, forty-eighth, or even the fortieth anniversary. Arriving a convenient five years after the fall of the Berlin Wall and just as Germany seems to be overcoming the greatest immediate challenges of unification, the public ceremonies surrounding events such as the liberation of Auschwitz (27 January), the bombing of Dresden (13–14 February), and the capitulation/liberation of the Third Reich (8–9 May) have offered Germans the occasion to reflect on their common past and on the fundamental cause for their forty-five-year division. Ideally, the fiftieth-anniversary commemorations should have permitted the reunited Germans to assume responsibility for their pasts and to forge a common political identity for the future. Instead, it would seem that unification, one precondition for the reconstruction of a common German national identity, has impeded a meaningful confrontation with the Nazi past, another precondition, I would contend, for restoring a common identity.

Many, or perhaps most, Germans (and especially those on the political Right) would deny my latter contention; for them the fiftieth anniversary of 1945 lends itself as the perfect occasion for Germany to put the Nazi past behind itself once and for all and to get on with the future as a "normal" nation. Such, indeed, seems to be the intention of leading politicians, who have in pub-

lic ceremonies called for an end to recriminations and for a grand reconciliation of all now peace-loving nations, as, for example, President Roman Herzog
did in his speech at the Dresden commemorations. While the denunciation of
war and the desire for universal reconciliation may be noble goals in themselves, they conceal a political agenda—namely, the relativization of the inhumanity and scale of German war crimes. The fiftieth-anniversary commemorations have thus become the instrument for the realization of the political
objectives of revisionist historians and German nationalists, who ever since the
Historikerstreit (historians' dispute) of the mid-1980s have openly striven to
"normalize" German history in rendering it qualitatively no different from the
history of any other modern nation (Maier). The restoration of German national
unity in 1990 gave fresh impetus to the revisionist-nationalist cause, for, in formally ending the postwar period and closing the historical parenthesis of puni-
tive national division, unification allowed Germany to reassume its place in the
family of fully sovereign, modern nation-states, a status the commemorations
of 1995 should have served to consecrate.

To be sure, without unification the fiftieth anniversary of the end of World
War II could never have closed the chapter of postwar history, but revisionists,
nationalists, and others are sadly mistaken if they believe that Germany can regain a common national identity by relegating its Nazi past to irrelevant antiquarian history. As Saul Friedländer has observed, the world historic events of
1989–91, including German unification, have resulted in "a complete historicization of the Nazi period" such that the postwar era has replaced the Nazi period as the relevant remembered past (in K. Naumann). That is, in national
memory 1989 has replaced 1945 as the breaking point between past and present. The Germans can thus evacuate the Nazi past and any paralyzing war guilt
from their living collective memory, just as the nationalists and revisionists had
hoped they might. In the process, however, Germans, East and West, find themselves living with very different pasts and hence identities, and they will not be
able to reconcile these identities unless they confront the now-more-distant
common Nazi past that lies at the origin of their divergent recent pasts. Such a
national reconciliation through confrontation with the Nazi past, I shall argue,
however, will be difficult to attain because East and West Germans constructed
postwar identities in opposition to each other and because the opposing East
and West German postwar identities and experiences have become instrumentalized in post-Wall partisan politics.

Postwar German Identities: East and West

The relevant pasts for East and West Germans today may well be their respective experiences of the forty-five-year period of national division, but those
postwar experiences were built on attempts to deny responsibility for the then

immediate Nazi past. The East and West German states and citizenries both formally and informally constructed their postwar identities in mirror image by projecting guilt for the Nazi past onto each other (Le Gloannec chap. 1). With the creation of the FRG and the GDR in May and October 1949, respectively, each of the German states tried to depict the other as the continuation of Nazi Germany under a new name and itself as the better, more democratic Germany. While the East German communist leadership sought to legitimize itself and its new state as the embodiment of the antifascist resistance to Hitler, it denounced the maintenance in the West of political personnel and of the social and economic structures that had allegedly given rise to fascism as proof that Nazi and revanchist forces continued to dominate the FRG. In fact, the West German state did acknowledge itself to be the legal successor of the Third Reich—but only the better to claim, through its *Alleinvertretungsanspruch,* to be the sole legitimate representative of the German people, on whatever territory those Germans might live. West German refusal to recognize the GDR (formally right up until the latter's disappearance) not only sapped the eastern state of legitimacy and of citizens but allowed the equation of the communist leadership with the totalitarian usurper Hitler as it grew ever more repressive in its quest to hold onto its power and citizens.

As time, economic growth, and détente in the Cold War stabilized the division of Germany, the two states based their legitimacy decreasingly on mutual demonizations about the past and increasingly on a more (East) or less (West) conscious evacuation of the national question from the political agenda. In the FRG the official goal of unification became a pious wish expressed only in so-called *Sonntagsreden* (Sunday speeches) that no one took seriously. European integration and the Atlantic alliance preoccupied West German statesmen (Brandt's *Ostpolitik* being no exception, since it sought less to rekindle the national question than to postpone it to a distant future). At the same time, ordinary West Germans virtually ignored the existence of the GDR, except when they had to travel to West Berlin by land or when they remembered some relative at holiday time. In the GDR politicians more quickly dropped the issue of national unification (apparently even sabotaging Stalin's overtures to that end) when they realized that unity would cost them their careers. Since East Germans were less likely than their cousins in the West to forget the existence of another and for them often more attractive German state, the communist leadership had to combat national sentiments openly and aggressively, first building the Wall in 1961 and then expunging ethnicity from public life in a movement that culminated in the disappearance of references to German ethnicity in the new constitution of 1974 (Naumann and Trümpler). Although the East German leadership reversed its anti-ethnic policy in the late 1970s when it revived references to the German and particularly the Prussian past, its attempts to define GDR identity on political rather than ethnic bases marked a significant departure from the German tradition of ethnohereditary nationalism (which continues, moreover, to pose problems in present-day multicultural Germany).

For the vast majority of citizens in East and West, of course, official policies and definitions made little difference for their sense of identity. West Germans built their immediate postwar identity much less around the Cold War posturing of their politicians than around the myth of "Stunde Null," the idea that the end of the war and especially the monetary reform of 1948 had marked a fresh beginning for (West) Germany. Once the introduction of the deutsche mark (since then imbued with magical qualities in popular consciousness) had put an end to the speculation, hoarding, black marketeering, and hence suffering of the war's immediate aftermath, Germans could go about the business of reconstructing their economy unencumbered by questions of guilt or responsibility for what everyone had experienced not as the liberation but as the catastrophe of 1945. Following monetary reform, the FRG's "economic miracle" came, then, as a divine sign of redemption, and West German identity in the 1950s and 1960s grew so closely attached to economic performance that students of political culture questioned whether West Germans were anything more than fair-weather friends of the FRG's democratic institutions (Almond and Verba). The children of West Germany's economic miracle workers, the so-called 68er Generation, also dared to pose the same question. The resulting generational conflict, however, gave rise not only to the terrorism of the 1970s but to a whole new participatory political culture best represented by the Green Party (Baker, Dalton, and Hildebrandt). Because the FRG's political system could not only absorb but respond to such an explosion of participation, West German political culture in the 1970s and 1980s added (to use Jürgen Habermas's terminology) a layer of *Verfassungspatriotismus* (constitutional patriotism) to its earlier *D-Mark-Nationalismus,* that is, confidence in the FRG's democratic institutions joined faith in the social market economy as cornerstones of popular West German identity (Habermas, "Lebenslüge").

Seen from the East, the FRG's political and economic successes undermined the slight antifascist legitimacy the GDR leadership still enjoyed and devalued the GDR's own economic miracle, which may have made its standard of living the envy of the Eastern Bloc but hardly consoled the East Germans who looked westward. Nevertheless, it would be a mistake to conclude that East Germans overwhelmingly identified with the FRG and dreamed of joining it either individually through emigration or collectively through reunification. Just as West Germans forged a sense of identity with the FRG in response to their personal experiences with its economic and political system, so too did East Germans develop a sense of identity with the GDR, though of course not always in the way the leadership might have hoped. After the construction of the Berlin Wall had robbed them of a relatively easy emigration option, East Germans had little choice but to make the best out of life under a regime not of their

choosing. They did so by practicing a kind of internal emigration into the pleasant corners of private life free from state intervention (or into what Günter Gaus,
the FRG's first permanent representative in the GDR, dubbed the *Nischengesellschaft* [society of niches]). They also did so by arranging themselves with
the powers-that-were in morally more or less compromising manners. Thus,
without necessarily identifying with the communist regime, nearly all East Germans learned to mouth the party line at appropriate times, and a minority went
so far as to offer its informal services to the secret police, the Stasi.[1]

Although they may have ideally preferred to live differently, East Germans
nonetheless developed a set of positive values that not only facilitated life under the constraints of "real existing socialism" but also constituted a distinctive
GDR cultural identity. As an adaptive response to the challenges of daily life,
the common, positive values of East German culture concealed or compensated
for the shortcomings, or sometimes just plain ugly reality, of life within state
socialism. Thus, the virtues of modesty and frugality covered up consumer frustration in an economy of perpetual penury, while solidarity put a positive face
on the dependence on the countless connections people had to cultivate, often
speaking out of both sides of their mouths, in order to maintain their modest
well-being. Social equality, as an ideal and by and large as a reality in the GDR,
was the glue that held East German society together, not only because it permitted modesty and solidarity but also because it partially legitimated communist party rule. In addition to these values essential for survival under state socialism, East Germans shared a certain pride in the GDR's economic
accomplishments and social security, which compensated for the inferiority
complex many had toward the West and for the predictability and monotony of
life behind the Wall. As I have demonstrated in an analysis of the relative stability of the GDR before 1989 and of its unexpected collapse that year, the un-
dermining of these GDR-specific values in the late 1980s—primarily through
the rise of a parallel hard-currency economy that destroyed modesty, solidarity,
and equality—motivated popular mobilization against the regime in the fall of
1989 ("Allemagne," *Communism's Collapse,* and "Modest Germans").

Problems of Post-Wall National Identity

Although the erosion of East German cultural values ultimately led to unification, the demise of the GDR did not spell an end to the specific East German
identity. In the year of national euphoria that followed the night of 9 November 1989 and ended the morning after Helmut Kohl's triumphant reelection on
2 December 1990, East and West Germans rediscovered elements of a common
identity. But even the momentous events and consequences of monetary and
political unification in 1990 could not erase forty-five years of cultural divergence. Whereas West Germans had by and large grown up with or into a mod-

ern, liberal-democratic capitalist society, East Germans had cultivated traditional petit-bourgeois values—modesty, solidarity, and equality—that were hardly adapted to a competitive, individualistic consumer society. As East and West Germans began to recognize their differences despite their common heritage, with the easterners appearing to have retained greater "Germanness" in the stagnant security of their niches behind the Wall (Gensicke), even critical intellectuals in East and West embraced the hypothesis that East German society was simply retarded in its modernization and would catch up to the West with time (Habermas, *Revolution;* Brie and Klein).

This hypothesis of East German backwardness, of course, fed into the West German Cold War stereotype of the GDR as the perpetuation of Nazi authoritarianism, a stereotype that regained fashion when xenophobic skinhead violence erupted in the eastern cities of Hoyerswerda in 1991 and Rostock in 1992. The subsequent incendiary murders in Mölln and Solingen in the West, however, proved that racist violence did not have its origins in eastern "backwardness" alone. Indeed, the wave of xenophobic violence that peaked in Germany in early 1993 in no small measure stemmed from the backward-looking concept of ethnohereditary citizenship rights (jus sanguinis) that had allowed the FRG to claim to speak in the name of and to defend the rights of ethnic Germans living in the Eastern Bloc during the Cold War. Such an exclusive definition of citizenship and of the nation certainly cannot have discouraged a climate of tolerance for racist attitudes and acts at a time when the country faced an unprecedented influx of non-German refugees.

Postunification xenophobic violence, however, did not simply spring from a survival or revival of past pernicious values in East and West. Instead, it probably reflected the conflict between the new values that had emerged in both parts of Germany during separation. Hostility toward foreigners may have been a deflection of mutual antagonisms that grew between East and West Germans in the immediate post-Wall years as a result not only of the redistribution conflict that the costs of unification necessarily engendered but also of fundamental cultural misperceptions (McFalls, "Allemagne," *Communism's Collapse* chap. 6). To West Germans the *Ossis* (slang term for "easterners"), who had perfected the economic art of muddling through with scarce resources but with the help of informal networks of cooperation, appeared lazy and inefficient; to East Germans the so-called *Besserwessis* (1991 "neologism of the year" composed from *know-it-all* and *westerner*), who had learned that aggressive self-promotion was the key to success in the postindustrial capitalist economy, appeared arrogant and deceptive. Based on a lack of understanding of each other's previous life experiences, the *Ossi-Wessi* rift widened as a result of the asymmetry of the unification experience: whereas East Germans have had to confront their pasts and to adjust to a radically different way of life, West Germans with few exceptions have come through unification with their pasts and presents unscathed. With such past and present experiences, and hence values, dividing East and West Germans, it has become commonplace in Germany to lament the *Mauer in den Köpfen* (wall in the heads) that replaced the physical Wall, which some even joke about rebuilding, only from both sides and higher.

Because values, cultures, and identities change with experience and time and because East Germans have no choice but to adjust to their new social order, the mental Wall must in the long run crumble from the East, particularly as the economic, social, and psychological shocks of unification begin to wear off. In fact, as I discovered from a new series of interviews conducted in 1994 with 40 of the 202 ordinary East Germans on whose experience I had based my cultural analysis of the GDR's stability and collapse ("Transition," "Partisan Strategy"), East Germans seem to be adjusting increasingly well to life in an individualistic, competitive consumer society. Although I had expected to find them rallying around their GDR identity and the old values of modesty, solidarity, and equality in defense against unemployment, temptations of credit and overconsumption, and Western arrogance, my interview partners expressed confidence in their individual ability to compete on the employment market, satisfaction and security about their standard of living, and good feelings toward their compatriots in the West. East Germans' adjustment to the exigencies of life in the enlarged FRG does not, however, mean that they will become indistinguishable from West Germans in their identity and values. When I indirectly asked my well-adjusted interview partners whether they had completely abandoned their old GDR values and identity, they all claimed—regardless of their ages, which ranged from twenty-one to eighty—that they were too old to give up their GDR identity and that they regretted not being able to keep living by at least some of the positive values from the past, such as solidarity and egalitarianism, in the new order. In other words, in their hearts they clung to values that they knew in their heads to be out of step with the times.

More than merely inconsequential nostalgia, this loyalty to the GDR past continues, despite their adaptation to the FRG present, to distinguish East Germans from West Germans in a politically polarizing manner. Like no other party, the successor to the East German communist Sozialistische Einheitspartei Deutschlands (SED; Socialist Unity Party), the Partei Demokratischer Sozialismus (PDS; Party of Democratic Socialism), has succeeded in positioning itself as the mouthpiece for East Germans who would like to defend their past without necessarily perpetuating it. PDS candidates have attracted support by affirming their biographical continuity with the pre-1989 past and thus reminding voters that they and the candidates share a worthwhile GDR past. At the same time, by being vaguely critical of past errors and ambiguous in its program for constructing democratic socialism in the FRG, the PDS does not menace East Germans' integration into the democratic capitalist order. The PDS must, of course, walk a fine line in seeking to validate East Germans' past without stirring up bad memories or threatening their present and future, but the other political parties have facilitated the PDS's task by discrediting and even disenfranchising East Germans on the basis of their past. Whereas the (western) Social Democrats (SPD) have driven away potential motivated members by rejecting the applications of former SED members, the Christian Democrats (CDU) have offended eastern voters with heavy-handed anticommunist campaign themes, as with their infamous "Rote Socken" poster in the summer of 1994.[2] Even the only other indigenous eastern political force (albeit now formally merged with the West German Greens), Bündnis 90, the successor to the heroic East German dissident citizens' movements, has succeeded in alienating East German voters. Although Bündnis 90 includes many members and leaders with a strong GDR identity, its dissident tradition of moral condemnation of communism and its collaborators leaves the vast majority of East Germans, who made countless petty compromises to arrange themselves with the regime, too uncomfortable to feel at home in a party they nonetheless admire. To be sure, the PDS has not succeeded in winning the votes of a majority of East Germans: its electoral support hovers just under 20 percent in the East. What is more telling is the level of acceptance and legitimacy the party enjoys. For instance, although the PDS won only 17.6 percent of East German votes in the 16 October 1994 Bundestag election, a strong plurality of 48 percent of East Germans welcomed the party's return to the Bundestag as beneficial for the East, and in early 1995 only 22 percent condemned the party as antidemocratic. West Germans, by contrast, cannot understand how their new compatriots can tolerate, let alone support, the PDS. Many complain: "Die Ossis haben immer noch nichts verstanden" (The East Germans still haven't understood a thing). Not surprisingly, anticommunist campaign themes have played very well in the West, where some 62 percent of voters believe the PDS is a threat to democracy.[3]

Fighting for the Past

East and West Germans' diverging attitudes about the PDS signify more than a difference of opinion on the necessity of a separate party to represent East German interests in the Bundestag. Instead, they reflect a deep cleavage in German culture and identity, for the PDS is as much a threat to West Germans' postwar self-image as it is an affirmation of East Germans' post-Wall self-respect. Whether East Germans actually vote for the PDS or not, the party's survival within the unified political system helps validate East Germans' postwar life experience. East Germans must believe that a democratic socialist party could emerge from the dictatorial SED in order to preserve the comforting idea that the founding antifascist myth of the GDR, despite all the subsequent errors and abuses of single-party rule, had a salvageable kernel of democratic, humanistic truth. If the PDS were truly incapable of democratic self-reform, then the entire history of the GDR would have been an abominable perpetuation of Nazi totalitarianism under a new name and any collaboration with or even passive acceptance of the regime an inexcusable personal error. With such a postwar past East Germans could have no voice in post-Wall German politics.

By contrast, the survival of the PDS is just as unacceptable for West Germans' postwar identity as it is necessary for East Germans' self-respect. As a socialist party, of course, the PDS calls into question West Germans' dogmatic faith in the "social market economy" as well as the myth of West Germany's postwar redemption through the economic miracle. More important, however, the possibility that a democratic party could emerge from the SED contradicts the equation of the SED with Hitler's Nazi party (National-Sozialistische Deutsche Arbeiterpartei; NSDAP), and deflates the self-exculpating West German myth that the GDR represented continuity with the Nazi past while the FRG represented rupture. The deflation of this myth would necessitate a reexamination of continuities with the Nazi period in the FRG, and the desire to avoid questioning West German denazification again explains the zeal with which the Western media (led by the central organ of West German self-satisfaction, *Der Spiegel*) have pursued allegations of collaboration with the Stasi, particularly if they involve PDS leaders or other powerful representatives of eastern interests and identity such as Brandenburg premier Manfred Stolpe. Similarly, the discovery of a twenty-four-year-old avowed Stalinist in the ranks of the PDS leadership, Sarah Wagenknecht, has been a godsend for the West, an absurd proof of the party's failure to break with the totalitarian past.

The debate surrounding the PDS's democratic potential that followed the party's return to the Bundestag in October 1994 did not coincide with the debate surrounding the fiftieth-anniversary commemorations of the end of the war by accident alone. To the contrary, the PDS debate served to occult a much more profound debate about postwar German identity. Like the efforts to use the anniversary commemorations to push the Nazi past into politically irrelevant antiquarian history, the PDS debate has sought to obscure the fact that Germans in both East and West built their postwar identities on an ultimately futile attempt to deny responsibility for Nazi crimes and to project it onto the other side of the Wall. With unification, however, the chickens have come home to roost. East and West Germans will be able neither to resolve the PDS debate nor to share a common identity until they recognize their mutual responsibility for the war, for Nazi crimes, and for the division of Germany. Closing the book on the past on the occasion of the fiftieth anniversary of World War II, no matter how magically round the number, will bring Germany no closer to a united, "normal" future. Germans must fight to preserve their unpleasant past, not flee it.

NOTES

1. The numerous more or less admitted and substantiated charges of collaboration with the Stasi leveled against such prominent personalities as Christa Wolf, Heiner Müller, Manfred Stolpe, and Gregor Gysi should not obscure the fact that the overwhelming majority of East Germans (perhaps at least 90 percent) were neither perpetrators nor direct victims of domestic espionage.

2. Conceived in response to the formation of a minority SPD-Green coalition government with the tolerance of the PDS in Sachsen-Anhalt, the poster depicted a red sock pinned to a clothesline with a green peg and was captioned: "Into the future . . . but not on red socks." CDU leaders in the East immediately requested to Bonn headquarters that the red-baiting poster not be distributed in the East, while the PDS profited from the red herring by immediately selling tiny red socks as a fund-raising activity.

3. Opinion percentages drawn from INFAS survey cited on German television (ARD) on 17 October 1994; Forsa survey cited in *Wochenpost* 6, 2 February 1995, 4.

WORKS CITED

Almond, Gabriel, and Sidney Verba. *The Civic Culture: Political Attitudes and Democracy in Five Nations.* Princeton: Princeton UP, 1963.

Baker, Kendall, Russell Dalton, and Kai Hildebrandt. *Germany Transformed: Political Culture and the New Politics.* Cambridge: Harvard UP, 1981.

Brie, Michael, and Dieter Klein, eds. *Umbruch zur Moderne?* Hamburg: VSA-Verlag, 1991.

Gaus, Günter. *Wo Deutschland liegt.* Hamburg: Hoffmann und Campe, 1983.

Gensicke, Thomas. "Sind die Ostdeutschen konservativer als die Westdeutschen?" In *Das Ende eines Experiments,* ed. Rolf Reissig and Gert-Joachim Glaessner. Berlin: Dietz Verlag, 1991.

Habermas, Jürgen. "Die zweite Lebenslüge der Bundesrepublik: wir sind wieder 'normal' geworden." *Die Zeit* (international ed.) 51, 18 December 1992:19.

———. *Die nachholende Revolution.* Frankfurt a.M.: Suhrkamp Verlag, 1990.

Le Gloannec, Anne-Marie. *La nation orpheline.* Paris: Callman-Lévy, 1989.

Maier, Charles. *The Unmasterable Past: History, Holocaust, and German National Identity.* Cambridge: Harvard UP, 1988.

McFalls, Laurence. "Une Allemagne, deux sociétés distinctes: les causes et conséquences culturelles de la réunification." *Revue Canadienne de Science Politique* 26.4 (December 1993): 721–43.

———. *Communism's Collapse, Democracy's Demise? The Cultural Context and Consequences of the East German Revolution.* New York: New York UP; and London: Macmillan, 1995.

———. "The Modest Germans: Towards an Understanding of the East Germans' Revolution." *German Politics and Society* 26 (Summer 1992): 1–20.

———. "Political Culture in Transition: Germany and the Return of the Communists."

In *Russia and Eastern Europe after Communism,* ed. Michael Kraus and Ronald D. Liebowitz. Boulder: Westview Press, 1996. 247–60.

———. "Political Culture, Partisan Strategy, and the PDS: Prospects for an East German Party." *German Politics and Society* 13.1 (Summer 1995): 50–61.

Naumann, Gerhard, and Eckhard Trümpler. *Der Flop mit der DDR-Nation 1971.* Berlin: Dietz Verlag, 1991.

Naumann, Klaus. "Die Sehnsucht des Mitläufers nach dem Schlussstrich." *Die Zeit* (international ed.) 6, 10 February 1995, 16.

CHAPTER 18

Dis-Membering the Past: The Politics of Memory in the German Borderland

Daphne Berdahl

Daphne Berdahl uses the tools of the anthropologist, ethnologist, and historian to offer a unique examination of the construction of identity in contemporary Germany. Like McFalls, she draws our attention to the fate of eastern Germany and East Germans after unification. In discussing recent events, both quotidian and extraordinary, which have occurred in Kella, a small village once part of the restricted "stripe" between the GDR and the FRG, belonging to the former, she offers not "representativeness" (i.e., most former East Germans think like this) but, rather, illustrations of the process of constructing a new identity. She demonstrates that historical memory is dynamic, interactively constructed with great interplay between local and extralocal processes of remembering.

This essay is based on long-term ethnographic fieldwork. Cultural studies' many affinities with ethnography and anthropology stem from these disciplines' focus on the fine-grained details of everyday life; all aspects of a society are worthy of consideration, as all contribute to our understanding of the particularities of that specific culture. Berdahl lived in Kella for two years, with follow-up visits. Her residency began shortly after the fall of the Berlin Wall and the unification of East and West, huge events whose consequences were felt in every household in this town. Both the geographical location of Kella as a border town and the chronology of Berdahl's visit conspired to foreground certain processes of identity formation and negotiation that are particularly visible in moments of social discord. Changes in Kella included not only the economic and social ones (from state socialism to Western capitalism), which all areas of East Germany experienced, but also a radical "geographic" and hence psychic transformation, from a restricted zone at the periphery of the country at its extreme border, to the new center.

Berdahl's training and interest in both history and anthropology have helped her eclipse the traditional limitations of these disciplines. Berdahl developed a sensitivity to and appreciation of cultural difference as an American child living in Germany for several years. She subsequently decided to major in history in college and spent a year after graduation at the Ludwig Uhland Institut für empirische Kulturwissenschaft (Institute for the Empirical Study of Culture) in Tübingen, where she was able to pursue her interest in an emerging dialog between anthropologists and historians. Her graduate degrees are in anthropology. One of the results of her interdisciplinarity is that her work transcends the "village study" paradigm of many anthropological studies of Europe by exploring how long-term and extralocal events are manifested, refracted, and absorbed into local practices and individual actions. Because Berdahl offers a close reading of events that cut to the core of the formation of both personal and national identity, she adds an important dimension to our understanding of German unification.

Werner Schmidt, one of the few "really reds" (*sehr Roten*) in Kella, once told me:

> If you want to conquer a [political] system, and conquer it quickly, then you have to portray this system in the ugliest colors possible. That's how it is. And that can be dirty work.

Werner was commenting on the West German media's frequent comparisons of the GDR to the Third Reich, a portrayal that was part of a general and rapid devaluation of the East German past by dominant West German discourses. As he would frequently share with me during the course of our conversations, Werner himself felt victimized by these attempts at a *Vergangenheitsbewältigung*.[1] Not only did they unjustly connect him, as a devout Party member, to crimes committed by the Stasi (*Staatssicherheit*, or state secret police) and Communist Party leaders, he explained, but the characterization of the East German past as an obstacle—an implicit assumption in the notion of "overcoming the past"— also undermined some of the very foundations of Werner's identity and personhood.

I begin with Werner's perceptive insight, for it suggests several related themes I explore in this essay: the way in which memory is an interactive, infinitely malleable, and highly contested phenomenon; the asymmetrical nature of re-membering in united Germany; and the role of the past in the present.

My essay derives from a borderland situation, in which many of these themes can be observed in particularly bold relief. Kella, the village where I conducted ethnographic fieldwork between 1990 and 1992,[2] is located directly on the former border between East and West Germany, now the boundary between the federal states of Thuringia and Hesse. As part of the Eichsfeld region, for centuries a Catholic enclave in Protestant central Germany, with its origins as an ecclesiastical territory, Kella remained devoutly Catholic despite the socialist state's attempts to root out religion in the GDR. During the period of socialist rule the village's immediate proximity to the border placed it in the highly restricted *Schutzstreifen* (high-security zone). Its six hundred residents needed special passes to reenter Kella, and only with police clearance could they receive visits from East German relatives outside the village. Visitors from the West were prohibited. To deter potential "escapes" to West Germany, all road signs pointing to Kella were removed, and the village was discretely omitted from nearly every map produced in the GDR.

Drawing on the experience of this community, I focus on the construction, production, and negotiation of memory since the fall of the Wall. I concentrate on several arenas in which this production and negotiation take place, including performative ceremonies, national and local discourses of memory, and struggles over the commemoration of the past. More specifically, I analyze two events in the community's recent past that reflect a dialectic of remembering and forgetting that is still occurring throughout united Germany: a parade in honor of German unification in October 1990 and the unsuccessful attempt by village leaders to preserve, as a memorial, sections of the three-meter fence that had surrounded and enclosed Kella between 1952 and 1989.[3] My aim is to examine an interplay between local and extralocal processes of remembering; I argue that memory and its re-presentations[4] both structure and are structured by representations of the past at a broader, often national level. I am interested here in commemorations as well as silences and in the role of the past in negotiating, contesting, and rebuilding the present.

The theoretical and methodological underpinnings of my discussion derive from a long-standing emphasis in anthropology on the fine-grained detail of everyday life.[5] By focusing on the experiences and circumstances of individuals and a community, particularly on "those moments when life is lived most intensely" (Bruner 6), anthropological inquiry explores how larger economic, political, and social processes are manifested, interpreted, negotiated, and contested locally and specifically. Implicit in this approach is the conviction that certain aspects of the macrolevel can best be understood at the micro level. Ethnographic stories, vignettes, or anecdotes thus not only seek to capture a sense of the processes and particulars of historical change, the dramas of social life, identity formation, or the confluence of the global and the local, but also aim to portray the complexity, diversity, and contradictions in social life and thereby avoid certain distancing discourses of generalization that have characterized much of traditional anthropological writing in particular and social scientific inquiry in general (Abu-Lughod; Clifford, "Partial Truths"; Gupta and Ferguson). Such a focus on the processes and particulars of everyday life may demonstrate, for example, that people's experiences of the rapid transformations since the fall of the Berlin Wall have been highly differentiated, even in a tiny border village.

Self Re-Presentations: 3 October 1990

Like many of the unification festivities held throughout Germany on 3 October 1990, Kella's celebration was in many ways a carefully orchestrated media event.[6] It was broadcast on a regional television network that had reported on Kella during the summer of 1990 and had subsequently opted to base its coverage of unification events out of the former *Schutzstreifengemeinde* (village in the high-security zone). Under the glare of media lights, television cameras, and film crews, villagers performed, improvised, and invented a variety of rituals in honor of the historic occasion. Church-related observances, including a candlelight procession to a local pilgrimage chapel on the eve of unification as well as a traditional mass the next morning, had been planned far in advance. Yet, when the television network notified Kella's mayor, two weeks prior to 3 October, of its intention to cover the village's celebration that day, the community was set into motion.

The resulting parade, organized by an informal committee headed by the village mayor, was an elaborate commemoration and display of the village's past, present, and anticipated future, a sort of "definitional ceremony" (Myerhoff 267) in which individuals as well as a collectivity told stories about themselves and itself to others. Throughout the parade these stories were linked to national histories—a way of connecting personal and community biographies to a nationally shared past but also, it seemed, a way to put Kella back on the map.

The procession, which began at the border crossing and circled through the village, contained numerous re-presentations of events and institutions in the community's history that were conceived, funded, and constructed by parade participants themselves. Several women who had worked in the local tobacco factory carried trays of cigars; a few carried signs bearing socialist slogans that had once hung on the walls of their workplace ("My Hand for My Work" [fig. 1]). Similarly, a group of six men carried farming tools and a sign reading "LPG Silberklippe" as representatives of the local collective farm. An old wagon loaded with furniture bore the sign "1952: We Had to Leave" (fig. 2) depicting several families who had been deported from Kella during the

Fig. 1. Kella village unity parade, 3 October 1990. Women from Kella represent a tobacco factory formerly located in the village. Behind them is the group representing the local agricultural cooperative. (Photograph in the collection of Daphne Berdahl.)

Fig. 2. Kella village unity parade, 3 October 1990. Residents of Kella depict several families deported from the village in 1952. (Photograph in the collection of Daphne Berdahl.)

forced evacuation in the spring of that year. On top of an East German Trabant car was a sign that read "Ordered 1964. Received 1990," referring to the long wait involved in obtaining a car in the GDR.

The most popular and loudest exhibit of the village's past was a float containing a reconstruction of the border itself. Across the back of a large, open truck bed, parade participants replicated the border (*Grenze*) by mounting several feet of the former border fence complete with authentic warning signs and barbed wire (fig. 3). On one side of the fence were three young men dressed as border guards; on the other stood several young villagers shouting angrily: "We want out! We want out!" while pounding the ground with sticks, pitchforks, and signs reading, "We want our freedom." A photo of the Communist Party leader Erich Honecker that had once adorned the walls of all public buildings hung on the side of the truck with a caption containing his well-known pledge, "Everything for the good of the people."[7] An adjacent caption contained several villagers' interpretation of the meaning of this slogan after widespread revelations of party leaders' excesses: "I was the people."[8] On the truck's other side hung a banner recalling the *Wende:*[9] "When freedom draws near, not even barbed wire inspires fear!"[10]

In the context of the parade such re-presentations of the past were affirmations of the present. Following the float of the reconstructed border, for example, was a group of participants from East and West symbolically linked by carrying garland arches adorned with red, gold, and black ribbons. Similarly, the wagon of those expelled in 1952 was followed by a car bearing the sign, "Now we can come back again";[11] behind the East German Trabi was a West German Ford. These juxtapositions served to illustrate not only residents' perceptions of positive changes since the *Wende* but also the hardships of life under socialism these changes had overcome. Other representations of the present, referred to as "the new period," included a small basket of East German products next to a large and nearly overflowing shopping cart of western goods, thus contrasting the former socialist economy of scarcity with the abundance of consumer goods in the new market economy. One woman from Kella constructed a large doll figure wearing a pointed cone hood (*Tarnkappe*), which, according to legend, makes those who wear it invisible (fig. 4). "For the people who need to disappear in the new period," she later explained, referring to former Stasi informants and powerful Party members. Her husband's contribution to the parade made a similar critical reference. He carried several spades and a sign that said, "For Sale: Spades to Dig Up Western Relatives," referring to former Party members who had denied having western relatives but who had sought them out after the fall of the Wall.[12]

Accompanied by a marching band and a trumpet choir from the nearby western town of Eschwege, the parade along with its hundreds of spectators made its way to the village soccer field, where the GDR flag was lowered for

Fig. 3. Kella village unity parade, 3 October 1990. Parade participants and the reconstructed border. (Photograph in the collection of Daphne Berdahl.)

Fig. 4.   Kella village unity parade, 3 October 1990. Representing the present, challenging the past: "Magic cap for sale." (Photograph in the collection of Daphne Berdahl.)

the last time and replaced with the West German one. Together with local politicians from the West, Kella's mayor planted a "tree of unity" (*Baum der Einheit*) as a symbol of renewal and a growing together of the two Germanies.[13]

In the tongue-in-cheek ceremony that followed, the GDR flag was placed over a small black casket built especially for the occasion (fig. 5). It was then carried by four pallbearers in mourning dress to its final resting place near the soccer field, where the flag and casket were ceremoniously burned. "They carried the GDR to its grave," one woman later explained.

In addition to demonstrating how quickly the past may be remade into and reshaped by memory, the festivities and many of its performances also reflected

Fig. 5.   Kella village unity parade, 3 October 1990. "Mourning" the end of the GDR. (Photograph in the collection of Daphne Berdahl.)

an emerging discourse of victimization in relation to the community's and nation's socialist past. The reconstructed border, for example, imposed a meaning and memory on the village's experience as a *Schutzstreifengemeinde* by depicting its residents as prisoners fighting for their freedom, using language that would have been unthinkable under socialism, rather than as the relatively complacent citizens that most villagers had actually been. The priest's sermon during that morning's mass reflected a similar use of language: "For forty years we lived in bondage. Let us pray that we don't fall into bondage again." Locals interviewed by the omnipresent television reporters seemed to be telling them what they wanted to hear: "This wasn't a democratic but a dictatorial regime," one villager said, "and I never want to hear of it again!" Another elderly woman, visibly nervous in front of a microphone and television camera, lamented: "They [the communists] took forty years of our lives!"

Like other representations of the past, however, such discourses of victimization have been questioned and contested. While watching a video of this television report over a year later, for example, one woman from Kella became outraged at her fellow villagers' comments. "He never experienced so much hate here! How can he say that? In fact, he earned most of his money from the reds! I simply can't stand to hear such things." Her friend agreed: "How can they say [the Communists] took forty years of our lives? We had our life here, our *Heimat*,[14] and we did a lot in those forty years."

A conversation between a mother and son over afternoon coffee reflected similar contestations over interpretations of the past. The forty-year-old son, Günther Bachmann, cautioned against accepting people's evaluations of the past from today's perspective. "People have a different judgment today than they used to," he explained.

> For example the case of Martin Schneider [a young man from Kella who was sentenced to eighteen months in prison after aborting an attempted escape in 1983]. When that happened and he went to prison, people thought it was bad but the rules were known. The horror and agitation that people display today is new.
>
> We used to sit and work in our garden in Kella, but we never really took note of the fence. It is wrong to say that the population felt oppressed.

His mother vehemently objected: "I always felt unfree, and always had misgivings about the fence. We were always afraid!" But her son reiterated: "It's only after the fact that people feel oppressed. Almost everyone participated passively. Eighty to ninety percent of the population kept the GDR going. The further we come away [from the socialist past], the more we scrub ourselves clean."

From Victimization to Nostalgia: Shifting Discourses of History and Memory

Such discussions at the local, indeed familial, level take place in the context of national debates and discourses about a *Vergangenheitsbewältigung* of the East German past. Largely dominated by the West German press, these debates have focused on a range of issues, including calls for a reevaluation of Germany's Nazi past; debates over what to do with and about East Germany's Stasi heritage that have often compared the GDR to the Third Reich; criminal trials of former border guards and other representatives of the GDR state that have been reminiscent of the Allies' war crimes trials following World War II; and the Christa Wolf debate that called into question the value of GDR culture as well as the apportionment of guilt (see Clifford; Gupta and Ferguson; Abu-Lughod). As one of Wolf's critics, Ulrich Greiner, echoing an argument made by Michael Stürmer during the 1986 historians' dispute, wrote: "This is no academic question. He who determines what was also determines what will be" (Huyssen 51).

At issue were not only questions of history and memory but a reopening and reevaluation of the German national question itself. The need to move beyond a burdened past and create a common history, a central assumption of *Vergangenheitsbewältigung,* was perceived in these debates as being critical to a new understanding of German nationhood and national identity. Implicit in this notion is the assumption that the past is something that must and can be overcome (or at least mastered) in order to "construct an alternative agenda for the future" (Huyssen 52) rather than viewing historical memory as an ongoing process of understanding, negotiation, and contestation.

My aim here, however, is not to analyze the complex and extensive post-unification debates surrounding history and memory, the German nation, or *Vergangenheitsbewältigung.* Instead, I seek to illuminate and contextualize an interplay between local and extralocal processes of remembering. The national debates surrounding Stasi revelations, guilt and responsibility, and *Vergangenheitsbewältigung,* for example, have produced a discourse in which former GDR citizens were either victims or perpetrators, with no gray areas in between. The resulting "rhetoric of accusation and self-righteousness" (Huyssen 37) provided the context for the kinds of representations and expressions of victimization witnessed during Kella's unification festivities (e.g., the *Tarnkappe,* spades, and border reconstruction).

These discourses of victimization have also produced certain images of suffering that emerged after the *Wende.* The exchange between Günther Bachmann and his mother as well as the reconstructed boundary and other references to the border during Kella's unity parade, for example, illustrate how the fence, or the *Grenze* as a whole, quickly came to be a powerful image of suffering af-

Fig. 6.   Kella. New memory symbol merges the fence with the religious symbolism of the Cross, 1992. (Photograph by Daphne Berdahl.)

ter the *Wende,* a metonym for the GDR itself. This was evident not only in the widespread media representations of the fall of the Wall but also in a local merging of the fence's image with the religious symbolism of the Cross (fig. 6). As powerful images of suffering, these "new memory symbols" stand for all that is now regarded as having been wrong with the socialist regime (Jones 161).

Thus, as the old official histories are discredited (see Watson)—in the toppling of socialist monuments, renaming of streets, and rewriting of history books—new histories are constructed, produced, and contested in a variety of ways. The devaluing of the socialist past has been challenged, for instance, by a retreat to nostalgia in the former GDR. In an ongoing dialectic of remembering and forgetting, discourses of victimization have given way to, and continue to oscillate with, discourses of nostalgia and mourning—demonstrating the shifting, multiple, and infinitely malleable nature of memory. At times one discourse may be compelling, at other times not.

The reason for this, it seems to me, lies in the way in which historical memory is interactively constructed (for the gendered implications of this dynamic, see Berdahl, "Where"). During the course of my fieldwork, for example, village residents began responding to West German projections of East Germany (and its citizens) as inferior by reevaluating and reformulating the GDR past. At first voiced in a cautious statement that "socialism wasn't all that bad," early defenses of the former GDR focused on the economic and social security of the socialist system. Gradually, however, these defenses frequently came to be expressed as nostalgia and mourning for an East Germany that had never existed, a "hazy beautification of the past" (Huyssen 47), reflected most recently in an explosion of "Ostalgia" (*Der Spiegel*) for East German products (Berdahl, "Consumer"). In such discourses of nostalgia, metaphors of community and kinship have become increasingly prevalent. "We used to live like one big family here," I was often told, "now no one has time for anyone else."

Rather than focusing on guilt or victimization, these nostalgic discourses of the past may also entail a novel form of willful forgetting, or silence:[15] the choice *not* to know. In the midst of Stasi revelations and "witch hunts" waged largely in the West German press, villagers' initial enthusiasm for obtaining access to the mysteries of the *Stasi* files quickly dissipated. With very few exceptions, residents of Kella have decided not to file for access to their own Stasi files. Although guided by an awareness of the potential risks involved in gaining access to one's personal file (including the possibility that a Stasi informant could be a friend or family member, a revelation that could be particularly disruptive in such a small community), the decision not to know is not merely a pragmatic one. It is also a reaction to the discrediting of the GDR past, a critical resistance to partaking in the construction of new histories and memories. These pockets of subversive silences (Crain) are an important element in an ongoing and interactive negotiation and contestation of historical memory.

Not only can every act of remembering be an act of forgetting; it can also work the other way around.

"This Fence Shall Remain Standing": Dis-Membering the Past

In contrast to many postsocialist societies, in which new histories are being created out of formerly unsanctioned memories of the past (Watson 4), the discrediting of old official histories in the former GDR has been almost instantaneously replaced with the imposition of new ones. The production of historical memory is deeply embedded in the dynamics of East and West German power relations; like other sites of cultural confrontation, remembering in the new Germany has been largely asymmetrical.

Nowhere has this been more evident than in local and national contests over representations and commemorations of the socialist past. As culturally constructed and negotiated events involving struggles over the control and appropriation of historical knowledge (Cohen 246), commemorations may be quite revelatory. In united Germany they have often entailed the construction, reconfiguration, or dismantling of the institutions, symbols, memorials, monuments, and other public memory sites of the former GDR. The removal of the Lenin statue in East Berlin, the renaming of streets and public buildings formerly dedicated to prominent Communist figures throughout eastern Germany, and the nearly complete dismantling of the Berlin Wall are but a few examples of such inverted commemorations. Occasionally, these inverted commemorations have been accompanied by a public ceremony; usually, they are not. The rush to avoid the kind of collective forgetting that characterized post-Nazi Germany by uncovering, confronting, and hence "overcoming" East Germany's burdened past has paradoxically been accompanied by a kind of "organized forgetting" (Connerton 14), an erasure of certain memory symbols and the creation, and contestation, of new ones.

A struggle in Kella between locals and the German federal government over the preservation of the former border fence highlights several of these issues. Demonstrating the asymmetrical nature of remembering in unified Germany as well as the importance of the physicality of memory, this clash between local and official memories entailed contestations over how and by whom the past was to be represented.

Even before plans to dismantle the entire inner German border were announced, village political leaders had submitted applications to *Kreis* (county) officials hoping to maintain the border fencing near Kella as a memorial and potential tourist attraction. Two years after the fall of the Wall, when a subdivision of the Federal Defense Ministry[16] was created to dismantle fully the fencing, guard towers, service roads, and all other structures that had been part of the former border, it became clear that community leaders' plans were threatened. As the encroaching removal of the fence became visible from Kella, the village's mayor, Karl Hartmann, attempted to mobilize the community to combat the dismantling of this intensely symbolic structure (fig. 7). At a large gathering of the local *Heimatverein,*[17] Karl announced the government's intention to "remove the fence and service road . . . and return it to its original state." When the audience expressed its outrage, he continued:

> A part of the border structure should remain as a memorial. In the last few years, many things have been determined too quickly [for us]. And now we want to be the ones to decide about this.

At Karl's suggestion the group passed a resolution to preserve the service road and sections of the border fence near Kella.

The majority, although not unanimous, sentiment entailed not only a concern for memory, for the "symbolic importance" of the border, as one man stressed, or for "preserving the border structure for future generations," as another woman explained. The desire to keep the fence was also an expedient one, based upon the largely misguided anticipation of a burgeoning local tourist industry. The border as tourist attraction was especially stressed by community members working to promote tourism in the region. "That is what really distinguishes our village," one of these men argued. "The border is the first thing visitors want to see when they come to Kella."

Over a period of nearly two years Kella's mayor appealed to county, state, and federal officials to preserve sections of the fence and service road. Together with other supporters of the memorial, he hung hand-painted signs on sections of the fence to mark them for preservation: "This fence shall remain standing."

Stressing orders to dismantle the former border installations "completely" as well as the "not insignificant dangers" the structures allegedly posed to local residents, authorities denied the community's requests.[18] In a move eerily reminiscent of a fenced enclosure of the village pilgrimage chapel in the 1950s—a symbolic and literal demonstration of the socialist state's authority— the border fence was removed from Kella in the summer of 1993.[19]

Local voices were thus ultimately and conclusively silenced in this clash between local and official memories. As David Cohen has noted, struggles over the production of history often entail a "pathology of ownership" (246). What

Fig. 7. Kella. Removal of the border structures, 1992. (Photograph by Daphne Berdahl.)

was being contested here was not only ownership of the actual border fence (a real issue, considering that the land on which it stood had been returned to private ownership) but also ownership of the form, content, and manner of commemoration. It was, in a sense, a contest over the ownership, appropriation, and meaning of this *lieu de mémoire* (Nora), which for locals had been invested with additional meaning after the Wall as an image of suffering.

Conclusion: What Remains

The physical remains of the past in Kella consist of icons of faith and images of suffering—a wooden cross adorned with barbed wire, a renovated pilgrimage chapel, crucifixes that mark community boundaries—set against a backdrop of the recent destruction to the landscape and memory through the removal of the former border fence. The gashes in the earth where the fence and service road were once located will heal, just as vegetation had soon covered and nearly concealed the metal fencing once the political border became obsolete in 1989. As the landscape heals, however, evidence of the past will be increasingly effaced and relegated to museums, the officially sanctioned venue of memory and amnesia.

In the numerous *Grenzmuseen* (border museums) that are now scattered along the former border the past has been neatly arranged, displayed, and distilled.[20] Containing decontextualized objects of the border, including towers, fencing, border police jeeps, observation stands, signs, and deactivated trip wire installations, the museums serve not merely to inform but to legitimate the new German nation-state by providing testimony to the necessity of overcoming Germany's division (fig. 8). Indeed, most border museums contain or are themselves memorials "to the victims of the division of Germany" (fig. 9).[21] The re-membering of the border in this context—the product of its dis-membering in another—exemplifies certain uses of the past in affirming the present. Or, as Paul Connerton has written in an observation uncannily similar to Werner Schmidt's insight quoted at the beginning of this essay: "To pass judgment on the practices of the old regime is the constitutive act of the new order" (7).

The various means and forms of remembering, however—including everyday negotiations of guilt and complicity, alternative memory symbols, and subversive silences—illustrate the inherently interactive, malleable, and contestable nature of memory. What remains of the past in Kella, therefore (as elsewhere in the former GDR), is this ongoing process of production and negotiation, a dynamic that continues to shape and transform people's relationship to their past as it shapes the boundaries, and interstices, of remembering and forgetting.

Fig. 8. Grenzmuseum (border museum) near Bad Sooden-Allendorf, 20 km from Kella. (Photograph by Elmar Mane-gold; used by permission.)

Fig. 9. "To the victims of the division of Germany." Memorial at the Bad Sooden-Allendorf border museum. (Photograph by Elmar Manegold; used by permission.)

NOTES

Funding for this research was generously provided by the Fulbright Commission (1991–92) and the University of Chicago Division of Social Sciences (1990–91). I wish to thank John Baldwin, James Fernandez, Renate Lellep Fernandez, Michael Geyer, and the editors of this volume for their constructive comments on various versions of this essay. Above all, I am grateful to the people of Kella, who so graciously shared their lives with me. Their support, humor, and friendship made my research possible.

1. This term, meaning "overcoming" or "mastering the past," was originally coined in reference to West Germany's attempts to deal with the Nazi past (see, e.g., Maier). Since German unification, however, it is used to refer to East Germany's socialist past as well as the Nazi period. This discursive connection of the socialist with the Nazi past is one of several ways in which the GDR has been compared to the Third Reich.

2. Ethnographic observation, one of the distinguishing features of an anthropological approach, was the primary methodology of my research. As a participant in and observer of most aspects of daily life—including parties, family gatherings, village festivals, church activities, village council meetings, weddings, funerals, shopping, cleaning, gardening, cooking, even pig slaughtering—I conducted both frequent informal interviews as well as taped formal interviews and several life histories. Quotations cited in this essay are drawn largely from taped interviews, involving an average of three two-hour sessions with each person over a period of several months and enhanced by daily interaction with the same individuals during my two-year stay. Although individual names used in this essay are pseudonyms, Kella is not. Most individuals quoted here will be well-known to people in Kella, but I have made every effort to conceal their identity here.

3. The inner German border became impermeable in 1952, nine years before the erection of the Berlin Wall in 1961. Although the actual fencing was changed and fortified several times between 1952 and 1989, it is consistently referred to as "the fence" (*der Zaun*) by village residents, and I have preserved that usage here.

4. I have hyphenated this word to stress a dynamic of agency and performance involved in practices of historical representation. Re-presentations entail the act of presenting something *again* and are thus important elements in the construction of memories and identities. As Bruner has written, experience not only "structures expressions," but "expressions structure experience" (6).

5. See, for example, Geertz on "thick description"; Turner's concept of "social dramas"; Bruner on the "anthropology of experience"; Fernandez's notion of "revelatory incidents"; or Abu-Lughod on "ethnographies of the particular."

6. My account of Kella's unification celebration is based upon the recollections and photographs of numerous participants as well as on a video of the events filmed by the television network Thüringer Fernsehen. I watched this video several times with different groups of people from the village, which enabled me to ask questions of clarification and interpretation in a variety of contexts.

7. "Alles zum Wohle des Volkes."

8. "Ich war das Volk."

9. Meaning "turning point," the term used to refer to the fall of the Berlin Wall and the collapse of socialist rule.

10. "Wenn die Freiheit naht, hilft auch kein Stacheldraht!"

11. "Jetzt können wir wieder kommen."

12. To many villagers whose contact with western relatives had made them subject to certain harassments and scrutiny under socialism—being prohibited from wearing western clothing in school or being questioned or placed under increased scrutiny due to western contacts, for example—this represented the ultimate hypocrisy.

13. The "tree of unity" would later become a symbol of the lost hopes and expectations of German unification: a year later it was dead. A new tree was planted without ceremony several months later, this time surrounded by fencing from the former border fence to protect it, people said, from animals and other elements. This tree, ironically, is thriving.

14. Literally translated, *Heimat* means the "home" or "homeland" but also refers to notions of belonging in which identity becomes grounded in place (see Applegate).

15. I am indebted to David Cohen's stimulating discussion of silences and commemorations, which has influenced my analysis of the Stasi issue here.

16. Gesellschaft zum Abbau und zur Verwendung von Altanlagen und Altlasten (Association for the Dismantling and Use of Old [former border] Installations, Ltd.).

17. A voluntary association dedicated to local culture and the cultivation of *Heimat*. Kella's *Heimatverein* was founded shortly after unification.

18. Letter from *BMV* (Federal Defense Ministry) to *Gemeindevertretung Kella*, 23 July 1992. Karl's last-ditch efforts using ecological arguments were similarly denied when state authorities determined that there would be no damage to the environment by removal of the border structures.

19. The surrounding service road was left intact pending further action, although the rest of this road has been removed along most of the former border.

20. The closest *Grenzmuseum* to Kella is located near the town of Bad Sooden-Allendorf, approximately twenty kilometers away.

21. From a plaque on the Grenzlandmuseum Eichsfeld at Teistungen. A similar commemoration is inscribed on a cross outside the Bad Sooden-Allendorf museum.

WORKS CITED

Abu-Lughod, Lila. "Writing against Culture." In *Recapturing Anthropology: Working in the Present,* ed. Richard G. Fox. Santa Fe: School of American Research P, 1991. 137–62.
Applegate, Celia. *A Nation of Provincials: The German Idea of Heimat.* Berkeley: U of California P, 1990.
Berdahl, Daphne. "Consumer Rites: The Politics of Consumption in Unified Germany." MS.
———. "Where the World Ended: Identity, Differentiation, and Unification in the German Borderland." Ph.D. diss., Dept. of Anthropology, U of Chicago, 1995.
Bruner, Edward M. "Experience and Its Expressions." In *The Anthropology of Experience,* ed. Victor W. Turner and Edward M. Bruner. Urbana: U of Illinois P, 1986. 3–32.
Clifford, James. "Partial Truths." In *Writing Culture: The Poetics and Politics of Ethnog-*

raphy, ed. James Clifford and George Marcus. Berkeley: U of California P, 1986. 1–26.

Cohen, David. *The Combing of History.* Chicago: U of Chicago P, 1994.

Connerton, Paul. *How Societies Remember.* Cambridge: Cambridge UP, 1989.

Crain, Mary. "Poetics and Politics in the Ecuadorean Andes: Women's Narratives of Death and Devil Possession." *American Ethnologist* 18 (1991): 67–89.

Fernandez, James W. *Persuasions and Performances: The Play of Tropes in Culture.* Bloomington: Indiana UP, 1986.

Geertz, Clifford. *The Interpretation of Cultures.* New York: Basic Books, 1973.

Gupta, Akhil, and James Ferguson. "Beyond 'Culture': Space, Identity, and the Politics of Difference." *Cultural Anthropology* 7 (1992): 6–23.

Huyssen, Andreas. *Twilight Memories: Marking Time in a Culture of Amnesia.* New York: Routledge, 1995.

Jones, Stephen F. "Old Ghosts and New Chains: Ethnicity and Memory in the Georgian Republic." In *Memory, History and Opposition under State Socialism,* ed. Rubie Watson. Santa Fe: School of American Research P, 1994. 149–65.

Maier, Charles. *The Unmasterable Past: History, Holocaust, and German National Identity.* Cambridge, MA: Harvard UP, 1988.

Myerhoff, Barbara. "Life Not Death in Venice." In *The Anthropology of Experience,* ed. Victor W. Turner and Edward M. Bruner. Urbana: U of Illinois P, 1986. 261–86.

Nora, Pierre. "Between Memory and History: Les Lieux de Mémoire." *Representations* 26 (1989): 7–25.

Der Spiegel 27 (1995).

Turner, Victor. *Dramas, Fields and Metaphors: Symbolic Action in Human Society.* Ithaca: Cornell UP, 1974.

Watson, Rubie. "Memory, History and Opposition under State Socialism: An Introduction." In *Memory, History and Opposition under State Socialism,* ed. Rubie Watson. Santa Fe: School of American Research P, 1994. 1–20.

CHAPTER 19

How American Is It?
The United States as Queer Utopia
in the Cinema of Monika Treut

Gerd Gemünden

Cultural studies does not merely equal the sum of various apparently disparate methodological components; rather, various different modes of questioning interact, support, and build upon one another. As film studies illustrates, challenges by feminist theory created entirely new lines of questioning and analytical tools. For example, the concept of the gaze is inconceivable without intercourse between film history and feminist theory. Gerd Gemünden's choice in this essay to focus on Monika Treut's films is a particularly felicitous one, because Treut's work is rooted in tradition and yet takes it into new territory. Her scenarios, as Gemünden points out, call into question the stability of numerous binary relationships, most important: male/female and heterosexual/homosexual but also us/them, home/abroad, and American popular culture/German high art. Like cultural studies as a whole, an analysis of Treut's work is more than a sum of its parts. Gemünden shows us how Treut's films challenge the construction of personal, sexual, and national identities as well as of art itself. His reconfiguration of traditional disciplines and methodologies parallels Treut's manipulation of cinematic genres and conventions. What we read here and in other cultural studies projects fascinates us partly because it is a symbiosis of familiar and unfamiliar.

Like Henke and Rogowski, Gemünden is part of a new generation of native Germans who have chosen to do their graduate studies in the United States. His fascination with the interrelation of German and American cultures originates in his (self-described) Americanized upbringing in Germany and attains its urgency from the continuous challenge to straddle more than one culture that living in the United States presents. In his current book project on postmod-

333

ernism in Germany and the United States, Gemünden considers the political and ideological significance of Americanization. The spread of American popular culture, he argues, is far from a simple hegemonic process. Rather, as he shows here in his analysis of Monika Treut's films, the reception of American culture abroad can stimulate acts of subversion or defiance and can produce new and oppositional meanings. Acceptance and imitation are only part of the story.

As in Belgum's exploration of the popular nineteenth-century magazine Gartenlaube, *Gemünden's study of Treut's films implicitly challenges traditional thinking about what is worth teaching in the classroom. While English departments have long offered courses on film, penny romances, and other forms of popular culture, most German departments in this country still resist straying from the traditional canon of literary texts. And those departments offering a film course may well do so in the context of* Verfilmungen *(filmed adaptations of "good" novels). Treut's work specifically draws its energy from American mass media and popular culture; pornography is shown to have a liberating effect on her protagonists. Gemünden's study demonstrates how Treut's filmmaking constitutes an important intervention into the pornography debates in Germany and the United States and how, by considering that intervention, we can come to a deeper understanding of both German and American culture.*

I think going to America was part of a common German dream. The "American Dream" was a dream for me years ago, but by now, especially with New York, I've recently started hating the city, walking around cursing it, and friends say, "Hey Monika, you sound like a real New Yorker now."
—Monika Treut (qtd. in Fox, "Coming to America")

At the end of Monika Treut's film *Jungfrauenmaschine* (Virgin Machine) (1988) we see how Dorothee, a journalist researching romantic love, discards into the San Francisco Bay photographs of couples that she had taken in Hamburg. At the end of *My Father Is Coming* (1991) Vicky, an aspiring German actress living in New York, accidentally drops portrait shots from her acting portfolio onto the sidewalk, and a woman passing by comments, "I think you'll need new photos." For both women the encounter with American culture presents the necessity for change, metaphorically linked in both cases to the changing of an image. Dorothee and Vicky belong to a long list of protagonists of German films who experience the United States. From Luis Trenker's Nazi features *The Prodigal Son* (1934) and *The Emperor of California* (1936) through a wealth of films from the New German Cinema, including Werner Herzog's *Stroszek* (1977), Walter Bockmeyer's *Flaming Hearts* (1978), Herbert Vesely's *Short Letter, Long Farewell* (1977), Volker Vogeler's *Damn This America* (1973), Werner Schroeter's *Willow Springs* (1973), Herbert Achternbusch's *Hick's Last Stand* (1990), and Wim Wenders' *Alice in the Cities* (1974) and *The State of Things* (1982), to Percy Adlon's more recent *Bagdad Café* (1987), *Rosalie Goes Shopping* (1988), and *Salmonberries* (1991), the theme of leaving home for America is a conspicuously popular one with German filmmakers— a fact that has critic Eric Rentschler wondering how much these films have to do with the real America. His reading of *The Prodigal Son, Alice in the Cities,* and *Stroszek* concludes that for the respective travelers of these films "the U.S. plays the role of an imaginary (in the Lacanian sense), a set of possibilities one contemplates and toys with, or put in another way, as a hall of mirrors one passes through while self-reflecting. Confused, inexperienced, and incomplete human subjects gain wisdom and insight in America" (13).

Taking my cue from Rentschler's 1985 article, this essay explores the representation of America in the cinema of Monika Treut. As Treut's films make clear, the answer to the question, "What is 'German' now?" lies in the relationship that those born between 1940 and 1955 (Treut was born in 1954) entertain with the United States. In particular, Treut's works focus on the pivotal role American mass media and popular culture have played and continue to play in shaping the political, social, psychological, and sexual identity of her generation. What matters, therefore, is to understand the political dimension that informs—in often far from obvious ways—the imagined and imaginary community the German filmmaker perceives between her national identity and that of the country into which she sends her protagonists.

Like most of these films, Monika Treut's features *Virgin Machine* and *My Father Is Coming* represent the United States as a country that provides an escape from social and psychological restrictions found at home while also initiating the identity-producing mirror stage Rentschler describes. As is typical for films belonging to this tradition, in Treut's features the foreign country serves as backdrop and catalyst for a professional or personal quest, and the fact that here this quest is for a lesbian sexuality rather than the usual heterosexual one only seems a variation of a familiar theme. After all, the topos of experiencing abroad the pleasures of a transgressive sexuality denied at home is familiar from travel accounts at least since Flaubert's sojourns in Egypt. Yet, unlike the protagonists in most of the narratives cited earlier, the German protagonists in *Virgin Machine* and *My Father Is Coming* do not return home. Thus, Rentschler's argument that in *The Prodigal Son, Stroszek,* and *Alice in the Cities* the entry into the symbolic that follows the mirror stage invariably involves exiting from

Fig. 1.   Female to Male: *Monika Treut.* **(Photograph © Elfi Mikesch, 1990.)**

America does not hold true for Treut. Her narratives are concerned with the process of assimilating into the United States and with the ways national, cultural, and sexual identity are redefined in *this* symbolic order. What is different in the films of Monika Treut, therefore, is not only that the theme of male heterosexual sexual conquest abroad has been transformed into a lesbian one but also the way in which sexuality is here linked to notions of personal and cultural identity in general. By insisting that the most "natural" identity, namely gender, is more of a performance than an essence, Treut's scenarios also call into question the stability of other binaries such as us/them, home/abroad, or American popular culture/German high art, on which so many German literary and cinematic depictions of the United States rely. Treut's gender-bending, cross-cultural scenarios advocate a postmodern collapsing of oppositions, forcing us to rethink identities to a much greater degree than other writers and filmmakers before her (fig. 1). Employing Eve Kosofsky Sedgwick's definition of queer as "the open mesh of possibilities, gaps, overlaps, dissonances and resonances, lapses and excesses of meaning [that can't be made] to signify monolithically" (8) and Alexander Doty's description of queerness as "a quality related to any expression that can be marked as contra-, non-, or anti-straight" (xv), we can understand America in Treut's films as a queer utopia. That is to say, America is not, yet again, a reified exotic Other but, instead, a place that fosters the production of identity through its tolerance of difference. As Alice Kuzniar puts it, paradoxically, it is the very queerness of this land that makes it fit for foreigners. My analysis of Treut's production of queer identity will use as an itinerary three exemplary modes of rehearsing different forms of cross-cultural explorations: pornography, performance, and the work of Camille Paglia. I will conclude with some comments on the styles of this queer cinema and the ways it engages its audience.

I

Unlike the oedipal scenarios of Wim Wenders, whose explorations of German-American relations provide the most exhaustive account of the dialectics of friend and foe, Treut's narratives are lesbian coming-out stories and thus challenge the patriarchal plots and plottings of her male colleague. In *Virgin Machine* Dorothee Müller, a young Hamburg journalist, comes to San Francisco, notepad in hand, to research romantic love and to find her long-lost mother, who once worked here as a stripper. Although her mother has disappeared, this loss is quickly overcome as Dorothee makes the acquaintance of women's erotica activist Susie Sexpert (Susie Bright) and male impersonator Ramona (Shelley Mars). Through them she is initiated into the city's lesbian sex industry, goes to all-women strip shows, and tries (unwittingly) a lesbian call girl service. In *My Father Is Coming* Vicky, an aspiring German actress working in New York, is forced to cover up her lifestyle when her father, Hans, shows up for a surprise visit. While he thinks she is an actress and married, she is, in fact, a waitress and bisexual—a sort of coming-out story in reverse, when at least for the time of his visit she is forced to recreate the straight sexual identity her father knew in Germany. In the end the father proves more tolerant than expected and accepts his daughter's sexual orientation.

As these short plot summaries show, the displacement explored in Treut's films is not only one of continents and cultures but, foremost, one of genders, as her lesbian/bisexual protagonists Dorothee and Vicky move from Germany to San Francisco and New York City, respectively, to escape the heterosexual identities they had in Germany.[1] In both features the emphasis is hardly ever on what the protagonists left behind (even though half of *Virgin Machine* takes place in Hamburg) but, rather, on what they experience abroad. And this experience is commonly described as one of experimenting, of finding out, of choosing options previously not considered. As Chris Straayer has pointed out in regard to *Virgin Machine*—and her argument applies to a lesser degree also to *My Father Is Coming*—it is somewhat misleading to talk about a lesbian coming-out story, for the film has none of the makings typical of the genre. Lacking are the inner torment and suffering of the protagonist; the depictions of society's repressions and reprimands; the slow development from initial decision to come out to a dramatic climax, often followed by some tragic turn of events. In contrast, *Virgin Machine* opposes romantic sentiment—its plot revolves around the very impossibility of experiencing romantic love—and homosexual isolation; it is much more, as Straayer has it, "a coming-in story," as a vibrant and lively San Francisco lesbian community is receptive and supportive of Dorothee's eagerness to join ("Lesbian" 33; fig. 2). Similarly, *My Father Is Coming* introduces us to the gender-bending counterculture of New York's East Village peopled with gays, lesbians, a female-to-male transsexual, a fakir practicing skin piercing, and the flamboyant "post porn" artist Annie Sprinkle, who is running a New Age sex salon—a community that, like the one in San Francisco, encourages everybody "to do their own thing" without apparent fear of oppression and homophobia.

In both films' positive and affirmative portrayal of experimenting with new sexual identities, an important function is assumed by pornography. As I use the term here, I mean it to describe not only "written and graphic, or other forms of communication intended to excite lascivious feelings" (*American Heritage Dictionary*) but also such varied practices and visual pleasures as the S/M couple Dorothee witnesses in her hotel, erotica like Susie Sexpert's dildo collection, the strip shows, the call girl service Dorothee uses, the video of a male stripper that Ben, Vicky's roommate, watches, as well as the sexual practices advocated by sex activists and performers Susie Sexpert, Ramona, and most notably Annie Sprinkle. As we witness how Susie Sexpert explains to Dorothee (and to the viewer, as she unabashedly looks into the camera) the advantages of her dildo collection, we are made to understand that the productive appropriation of pornography has a liberating effect on its consumers. "Penis-to-vagina sex is old-fashioned. Nowadays, there are so many ways to make love." Ironically, this liberating effect becomes especially clear in a scene in *Virgin Machine* that seems to be an affirmation of the quest for romantic love that determined Dorothee's life in Germany. When after a night of passionate lovemaking Ramona presents the bill for services rendered to a startled Dorothee, she realizes that she has mistaken business for love. Significantly, this disillusion does not cause her to despair but, rather, after being momentarily baffled, to burst out in laughter. Realizing her own naïveté, this is a liberating laughter that indicates that she has traded in the last remnants of her search for romantic love that dominated her life in Germany for a notion of sexuality that exercises choices, pursues various options, and is built on equal exchange, namely money for pleasure. In the final scene of the film we witness Dorothee herself dancing as a stripper, while women from the audience slip money under her bra. She is now both consumer and producer in the exchange circuit of pleasure and cash.

Fig. 2.   Monika Treut, *The Virgin Machine.* **(Publicity still, First Run Features, New York, NY.)**

Pornography is also shown to have this liberating effect in *My Father Is Coming.* While Hans initially rejects Vicky's auditioning for a part in Annie Sprinkle's film *Pornutopia,* a visit to Annie's salon, where he is introduced to Annie's peculiar brand of New Age sex, makes him accept his daughter's sexual orientation (fig. 3). We see him checking out the porn theaters on his way home and dropping in on a skin-piercing artist. It must be added, though, that, unlike the sexual experimentation of the prodigal daughters Vicky and Dorothee, Hans's foreign affair, a mixture of genuine character transformation and sex tourism, fits squarely into a long tradition of European travel narratives.

The questions of agency in pornography and sex spectacles, and of its effects on the consumers, that are foregrounded in Dorothee's transformation and in Annie Sprinkle's performance, have been, of course, at the forefront of the heated debate about pornography in the United States throughout the 1980s. Since *Virgin Machine* was made at the height of the *West German* debate about pornography, with *Annie,* a short on Annie Sprinkle's one-woman show "Post-Post Porn Modernist" being made one year later, in 1989, we may understand

Fig. 3.   Monika Treut, *My Father Is Coming.* **(Publicity still, Tara Releasing, San Rafael, CA.)**

the films as a conscious intervention in this debate. I therefore want to digress here for a moment and chart the parameters of that debate in order to reveal the polemic dimension of Treut's sexual politics.

The development of the German debate about pornography is remarkably similar to the one in the United States. It was launched by Alice Schwarzer, editor of *Emma,* in October 1987, and featured the usual half-decade time lag that also marked the transatlantic transfer of discussions about poststructuralism, postmodernism, or, more recently, political correctness. The *Emma* campaign closely followed the argumentation developed by feminist-activist Andrea Dworkin and feminist legal expert Catharine MacKinnon; *Emma*-Verlag published the translation of Dworkin's book *Pornography: Men Possessing Women* and sponsored her appearance in Cologne. The so-called *Emma*-Gesetz (law) discussed in the Bundestag, meant to introduce legislation for litigation to pornography victims, though not approved, was modeled after Dworkin and MacKinnon's proposal for an antipornography civil rights ordinance for Minneapolis (see Struve). Both Schwarzer and Dworkin argue that pornography exploits women by turning them into objects of the male gaze, that it eroticizes violence and thus serves as a blueprint for rape. Dworkin writes: "The pornographers are the secret police of male supremacy: keeping women subordinate through intimidation and assault" (13). But in the United States, and to a lesser degree in Germany, there were also women's groups who defended pornography on the grounds of free speech. The Feminist Anti-Censorship Task Force (FACT) took issue with radical feminists by saying that they overemphasize women's victimization and that they oversimplify the connection between the consumption of pornography and the actual occurrence of violence against women.[2] Among the most outspoken opponents to the German antiporn campaign was a group with which Monika Treut strongly identifies, the lesbian S/M community, because their sexual practices of dominance and subservience were accused of being an eroticization of inequality.

It is not difficult to see this critique of antiporn reiterated in Treut's films. Treut's intervention into the pornography debate, with her defense of women both as producers and consumers of pornography in *Virgin Machine, My Father Is Coming,* and *Annie;* her earlier advocacy of S/M in her feature *Seduction: The Cruel Woman* (codirected with Elfi Mikesch [1985] and based on her research on de Sade and Sacher-Masoch);[3] and her video *Bondage* ([1983] re-released as part of *Female Misbehavior* [1992]), can be seen as calculated provocation to the antiporn movement that was increasingly perceived as a segment of feminist activism aligning itself with (male) reactionary forces. Against the depiction of pornography as degrading to women, Dorothee's adventures in San Francisco emphasize the productive and creative use of popular culture by its consumers. Moreover, and in contrast to Lizzie Borden's *Working Girls* (1986), an early and influential film on prostitution from a woman's perspective, Treut's films do not revolve around the physical and psychological struggle involving prostitution. In other words, they do not attempt to legitimize pornography and prostitution by depicting it as hard work (the prostitutes in Borden's film refer to one another as "working girls") and thereby succumbing to a Protestant work ethic. In Treut the pleasure principle is at work not only in the users of pornography but also in the sex workers themselves, as Ramona and Annie Sprinkle make clear[4]—although it must be emphasized that with Ramona this issue remains more ambiguous than with Annie. While the latter (over)plays on her naïveté and innocence, the former is cunning and calculating and will not let the issue of working for money be bracketed from her performance.

Finally, the fact that both *Virgin Machine* and *My Father Is Coming* are comedies can be seen as a strategy to deflate some of the angry rhetoric that had polarized the opposing parties in this highly charged antiporn debate, and Treut tells us that *Virgin Machine* did indeed have this effect on some of its viewers:

"Some really hard-boiled feminists came to see the film, ready to be angry; by the end, they were laughing and could not hold an anti-porn stance with regard to the film" (Knight 185).

II

As we have seen, Treut's emphasis on the uses of pornography and on the creativity of consumption deflates the essentialist argument that pornography is harmful per se. Once we entertain the possibility of pornography *by* women and *for* women (such as the all-women strip show or Susie Sexpert's dildo collection), monolithic condemnations of the exploitation and reification of women no longer hold true. While it would probably be an oversimplification to call Treut's position anti-antiporn, her work urges us to differentiate between who produces and uses pornography and to reflect on how they do so.

Significantly, all three of Treut's features as well as her documentary *Female Misbehavior* (a four-part compilation film including *Dr. Paglia* [1992], a portrait of Camille Paglia; *Max* [1992], a portrait of a female-to-male sex change; *Bondage* [1983], a portrait of Carol, a member of a New York lesbian sadomasochist group; and *Annie* [1989], a portrait of sex performance artist Annie Sprinkle) make it clear that, as a means to explore and alter sexual identities, pornography is closely connected to the notion of performance. *Seduction: The Cruel Woman* is a film about Wanda, a dominatrix running a gallery specializing in S/M performance art in Hamburg and about the ways in which she exploits the three people who are in love with her: her ex-husband Gregor, her live-in lover Caren, and Justine, a woman visiting from the United States. Wanda's power over the three stems from the fact that for her everything is role-playing and performance, while they seek to have a real relationship with her. Their attempts to break out of the show only strengthen Wanda's position as master of ceremony: when Justine slaps Wanda in the face because she hates all role-playing, or when Gregor shoots Wanda during a live performance but merely hurts her cheek, Wanda considers these acts of revolt part of the performance. The halfheartedness of their attempts demonstrates that they did not really mean it and that Justine and Gregor are now willing to participate in the game. For Wanda there is no outside of role-playing, and her embrace of artifice gives her power over those who still seek the illusion of authenticity. For those using S/M to enact sexual fantasies, role-playing can have a liberating effect, as the example of Herr Mährsch shows: he poses as a journalist but really wants to perform, as he says, "as Wanda's toilet." His pleasure comes from behaving in a helpless and subservient way. As Treut commented, "I'm interested in the liberating possibilities of a play [*Spiel*] which appropriates the images and projections of cruel women to produce pleasure and sovereignty" ("Zeremonie" 135). Interestingly, Treut first encountered this kind of role-playing in the New York group Lesbian Sex Mafia (LSM). Their practices of sado-masochistic role-playing are seen by Treut as a subversive strategy to make sense of a reality where the lines between reality and illusion are increasingly blurred: "In the metropolis of New York City, where like nowhere else reality has become hyper-real, they direct their play: controlled, imaginative, and self-directed" (42). If all authenticity is staged authenticity, the only possible control left is to direct the mise-en-scène of the staging.

Pornography and performance are also linked in *Virgin Machine,* most notably in the figure of Ramona, whose impersonation of a masturbating male amuses the all-female audience. Significantly, her simulation of ejaculation with a beer bottle ends with Ramona's boxer shorts open and empty, suggesting castration and female empowerment. When Dorothee arranges a date with Ramona, Ramona performs so well that Dorothee mistakes it for real love, even though she knows that Ramona is a professional sex performer. The fact that Dorothee laughs after her rude awakening in the scene described earlier shows her recognition and acceptance that everything is performance, and, when we witness Dorothee dancing as a stripper at the end of the film, the scene seems to imply that now for her, too, performance is everything.

My Father Is Coming abounds with performances of all kinds: Vicky is an aspiring but unsuccessful actress who even fails to perform for her father as married woman. The father, in turn, who has no ambition to act, lands a role in a beer commercial. Beyond these more literal examples of performance there is evidence of the performance of ethnicity and gender: the Puerto Rican Lisa says she can pass as a New Yorker, and Joe, the female-to-male transsexual, certainly passes as a "real" male, even though he longs to let Vicky in on his past. The most radical performer is perhaps Annie Sprinkle, featured as narrative agent in *My Father Is Coming* and as a performance artist in the documentary *Annie,* and her example again demonstrates how pornography is tied to performance. In fact, Sprinkle's one-woman performances, such as *Post-Post Porn Modernist,* have thoroughly questioned the distinction between art and pornography. As she said in an interview, "My feminist mother used to come into my room and joke whether I would grow up to be a whore or an artist. She was exactly right!" (qtd. in Williams 176). As Linda Williams has argued, Sprinkle's comment is indicative of a strategy of defusing or going beyond rather than directly confronting familiar oppositions: she is both whore and artist (177).[5] In *My Father Is Coming* Sprinkle also conflates two traditionally opposing views of women; together with Hans, she is as much of a prostitute as she is a mother, both seducing and reassuring and nurturing him. Chris Straayer describes Sprinkle's work as an affirmation of a "fluid identity" that engages a wide variety of discourses including "pornography, feminism, art, spirituality, sex education, advertising, political activism, performance art, body play, and the self-help health, prostitutes' rights and safe sex movements"

("Seduction" 156). For both Williams and Straayer, Sprinkle is an exemplary proponent of queer aesthetics, politics, and sexualities who radically challenges the essentialisms we live by. In the short *Annie* we see how Ellen Steinberg, an unattractive, pudgy woman in her late thirties, turns into her alias Annie Sprinkle by putting on makeup, false eyelashes, black stockings, high heels, etc. "Everybody can achieve this kind of transformation; it's fun and it's easy," she tells us. But in her photo "Anatomy of a Pin-up Photo" (rptd. in Straayer, "Seduction") she reveals the more tortuous, self-disciplining side of dressing up for sexiness. If these two examples blur the lines between "sexy" and "not sexy" people by showing that each person can be both by employing the devices demonstrated in the video and the photo, another example questions the strict division between male and female. When Hans accidentally enters the women's room after spilling Coke on his pants, Annie, unperturbed by his presence, goes about her business and tells him from the toilet seat: "I just love it when we all share the same bathroom. I mean we all have a male side and a female side anyway."

The three examples of Wanda, Ramona, and Annie Sprinkle connect sex to performance, to role-playing, to theater. But the implication here is not that when we're having sex we're putting on a show. Rather, Wanda's S/M show, Ramona's male impersonation, and Annie Sprinkle's performance art suggest that gender itself is a performance rather than an essence and that sexual identity is something we can experiment with, alter, and manipulate. What is at stake in these performances, therefore, is to show that gender is a persistent impersonation and construction and that those who insist on the naturalness of gender often use it to legitimize gender hierarchy and compulsive heterosexuality. The notion of gender as a performative act has been theorized by Judith Butler, who argues that sexual identity is something we institute through a stylized repetition of acts that create the *appearance* of substance (*Gender Trouble*). As Butler makes clear, we should not understand gender as a role that we simply put on to express or disguise an interior self. The selves do not exist prior to the cultural conventions that prescribe the modes of reenactment, since the model of a private internal self and a public external self overlooks "that the ascription of interiority is itself a publicly regulated and sanctioned form of essence fabrication" (Butler, "Performative" 279). Hence—and this is where the comparison to theater roles breaks down—there is no *real* gender outside of performance: "Gender reality is performative which means, quite simply, that it is real only to the extent that it is performed" (278). Since the performances by Wanda, Ramona, and Annie Sprinkle draw our attention to the ways in which we construct our identities, they can be seen as performances of performances—strategies of defamiliarization that reveal as construction site something we believed to be a given. They thereby make visible such distinctions as natural/artificial, surface/depth, inner/outer, through which discourse about genders almost always operates, and they allow us to question these distinctions. Significantly, those performances in *My Father Is Coming* that attempt to cover up, rather than lay open, fail: Vicky cannot trick her father into believing that she is married to Ben, nor can Ben, who is encouraged by Vicky to play a "good butch," pull it off as a straight male. Nor can Vicky cut it as a porn performer at Annie's audition, presumably because she is only doing it, as she tells her father, to pay the rent. There is a reluctance on Vicky's part to give up the notion of separating natural and artificial; she believes in self-styled and self-controlled performances. When Joe asks her if she dresses for sex or for business, she replies: "I dress who I am." Ironically, when she bursts out in anger and tears up Ben's shirt because he's moving in with his lover, Ben compliments her: "You are an actress after all."[6]

Since acts of constituting gender intersect with other discursively constituted identities such as race, class, and ethnicity, gender cannot be considered separately from the political and cultural intersections in which it is invariably produced and maintained. Gender identities are therefore imminently political, and the examples given earlier of subverting these identities have to be seen as political strategies that defy preestablished identities. The possibility of a queer sexuality, of being neither male nor female (or both), may well be the real issue at the core of the antipornography debate, and, not surprisingly, the gay and lesbian community has been the prime target of attack. Consider Sprinkle's experience of being raided by the Cleveland vice squad when giving her performance "Post-Post Porn Modernist" but never being bothered when she performed live sex shows in that same city (see Williams 176). As Butler says, "Performing one's gender wrong initiates a set of punishments" ("Performative" 279).

Clearly, the question of punishment is almost completely bracketed in *Virgin Machine* and *My Father Is Coming,* except for the threat of the *non-du-père* to Vicky's bisexuality. As the double entendre of the title makes clear, the panic caused by the father's visit is deflected once he gets it on with Annie. Both films therefore downplay the political stakes of gender-bending; what is missing from Treut's utopian images of New York and San Francisco is the seedier, violent, and repressive side of the lives of sexual outsiders. Here, for once, Treut comes very close to the affirmative but highly selective portrayal of America that has been present in German culture since the age of Goethe. To discuss further the politics of Treut's queer cinema one has to look at how she engages her audience.

III

Let me, therefore, turn to my third "*p* word," Paglia, who is featured in the twenty-minute sequence, *Dr. Paglia,* the first part of Treut's 1992 compilation documentary, *Female Misbehavior.* Author of the best-selling books *Sexual Personae* (1990), *Sex, Art, and American Culture* (1992), and *Vamps and Tramps: New Essays* (1994) which contains the complete transcript of Treut's film, Camille Paglia is well-known for her attacks on American feminism (and on academia in general), which she promotes in her scholarly and journalistic writings and which she performs in numerous, nationwide lectures on college campuses and appearances on talk shows, news shows, and any other show willing to book her. Her arguments are rather simple and tailored to the message-oriented workings of the media society on which she thrives. They can be summarized like this: the cultural elite, and American feminism in particular, have retreated into an ivory tower of French theory; their continuing loss of touch with reality has allowed conservative Christian organizations to set the terms for an overdue curricular reform of the humanities. We must revitalize the 1960s cosmic vision of sexual and artistic liberation; political radicalism may not be harnessed by political correctness. Paglia's language is one of paganism, of drives and tribes, that values Dionysian exuberance over "the Apollonian office persona" (*Vamps* xii) and "organicism" and "nature" over what she calls social constructionism à la Foucault (not surprisingly, she is deeply opposed to Judith Butler's "unpersuasive and jargon-ridden" [*Vamps* 475] performance theory, quoted earlier).

Discussing Paglia as a further example of Treut's cross-cultural explorations gives a certain twist to the notion of queer, for Paglia's writings on sexuality are very much at odds with scholarship on sexuality and gender of the last twenty years. Hence, queer can be read here to mean something like the German *quer stehen* (to be at odds with something). As an antifeminist feminist who prides herself on her "general obnoxiousness" (*Vamps* 103), Paglia has become a persona non grata not only in the academic circles that she attacks but also among radical women activists such as Susie Bright (the Susie Sexpert of *Virgin Machine*) and Pat Califia, a San Francisco lesbian S/M activist, who calls Paglia "repetitious, hateful, and in the end dreadfully dull" (qtd. in *Vamps* 465). This raises the question why Monika Treut became interested in Camille Paglia and why Paglia now lists Treut as "my most important ally in the international movement for a progressive pro-porn, anti-dogma feminism" (*Vamps* 206–7). Was it the mutual experience of being a lesbian outsider with significant obstacles in the pursuit of their respective careers? (Treut tells us about her problems getting funding for her films in Germany as well as being ignored and attacked by male critics, while Paglia struggled, without success, to find her place in American academia.) Was it Paglia's libertarian sexual politics and her endorsement of pornography? Was it her Davidian eagerness to take on the country's most established, Goliath-like feminist scholars? Or was it simply Camille Paglia's refusal to be "pc," understood by many as a provocative gesture to speak one's mind at a time when political correctness became increasingly experienced as a form of (self-)censorship?

Like *Seduction: The Cruel Woman, Virgin Machine,* and *My Father Is Coming,* Treut's *Female Misbehavior* focuses on the radical potential of pornography and its implication for gender performance, two subjects about which Paglia has a lot to say (in *Dr. Paglia* she describes herself as a "butch bottom" who "some weeks of the month . . . feel[s] very female, others very male. I feel I have a sex change every month" [*Vamps* 247]). Yet, despite the fact that Treut and Paglia agree on many issues, the main use the filmmaker makes of the writer is perhaps more strategic than argumentative. In fact, this is also how Paglia perceives herself in the film: "The value of my work is not just what I am *saying* but rather that I am breaking up all these bunkered positions" (246). Just as *Virgin Machine* can be read as a polemic response to German antiporn feminists such as Alice Schwarzer, the short *Dr. Paglia* is a polemic attack on certain feminists who in Paglia's view have become dogmatic and unwilling to learn from their mistakes. Treut herself describes the four pieces that make up *Female Misbehavior* as "a series of politically incorrect portraits of women in post-feminist times" (Willis 12). The notion of postfeminism implies for Treut neither that the goals of feminism have been achieved nor that they are irrelevant but, rather, that a new kind of feminism has to emerge that would be self-critical of the movement's failures and shortcomings during the 1970s and 1980s. And, like the protagonists of her features, Treut seems to suggest that regarding these issues there is more to be learned in the United States than at home because America's puritanical society creates stronger dissenting minorities than Germany (Fox 64).

Hence, as in Treut's three feature films, there is a transatlantic filter implied in *Female Misbehavior* by virtue of the fact that a German director researches American sexual practices. The sexual experiences made by the American Justine in Hamburg, by Dorothee in San Francisco, by Vicky in New York, and the four people portrayed in *Female Misbehavior* "take on an aura of ethnography as we view the 'strange' events from a distance" (Willis 11). There is, then, a certain pedagogical or instructional dimension to Treut's films as she adroitly educates the less sexually sophisticated. This educational aspect is underscored both by the narrative (Dorothee's profession is that of a journalist doing research on romantic love) and by the use of real-life sex performers and activists such as Susie Bright, Shelley Mars, or Annie Sprinkle whose agency in the narrative is often secondary to the message they relate to the viewers. As so often in documentaries of the New German Cinema and after, the lines between fiction and documentary are blurred. In Treut's films the instructional element is offset by humorous elements. *Virgin Machine* and *My Father Is Coming* are comedies that draw much of their laughter from the fact that sexual and cultural difference are explored in an offhand, entertaining way. Unlike many films on the subject, they completely lack violence; they fail to engage in the portrayal of punishment that for Butler is always connected to a deviant and defiant performance of gender, and they are not sexually very explicit—if they are about pornography, they are rarely pornographic (which has led to criticism from the lesbian community that Treut "doesn't deliver"). In a similar vein it must be added that, in contrast to Treut's explorations of gender, those of culture and nationality remain rather stereotypical, especially of her German characters. Hans is the quintessential Bavarian who comes to New York with a bag of German *Weisswurst* sausages (smuggled through customs), a Dustbuster, and typical German prejudices about cleanliness and the questionable quality of drinking water abroad. Like many Germans of her generation, Vicky feels insecure about her German national heritage and is reluctant to tell her friend Lisa that she auditioned, and failed to get the part, for playing a German tourist.

While I disagree with Treut's uncritical acclaim of Paglia, which bespeaks, I would argue, an outsiders' naive fascination with an oddball whose real oddities escape Treut, I would agree that there is indeed something to be learned from Camille Paglia about the combination of education and entertainment. Paglia has been extremely successful in working the media to get her message across, and this message itself consists of a hybrid concoction of art history and popular culture that explores and subverts how we have traditionally conceptualized "high" and "low." We see an example of this in Treut's short in which she interviews Paglia in a museum shortly after having shown her wandering on Forty-second Street in Manhattan, where she is checking out the porn theaters and adult bookshops. In the museum we watch Paglia standing next to a large black Egyptian tombstone bearing a hawk while she explains how, as a child, she identified with these signs because they suggested a carnivorous and aggressive quality. She then goes on to say that there is an exact correlation between Egyptian signs and advertisement of the late 1940s and 1950s:

> I couldn't read as a child, but I would see images and people doing strange things—you know, people holding a box, or holding a box out like *this* (she demonstrates in the 1950s style of Betty Furness), which later I could read—TIDE SOAP. So I felt since earliest childhood that advertisements were never something that was just popular culture and not to be taken seriously. But rather right from the beginning I saw that there was a connection between ancient pagan culture and the popular culture all around . . . for me the Egyptian hieroglyphics and advertisements are in the same line. And it's *true*. As I went on, I learned that the great pharaohs were *advertising* themselves. That's what they were *doing*—"I am the greatest, I am the most fabulous." Which they've done now. Five thousand years later, we're still reading their signs. (*Vamps* 236–37)

The connections and incongruities explored here between high art, or serious intellectualism, and popular culture are rehearsed throughout the film and most visibly indicated by the film's title, *Dr. Paglia,* a very German way to address a critic and writer that denotes learnedness, respect, and sincerity—as does the museum setting—only to witness how Paglia raps, in a very American way, with breathtaking speed about lesbian and gay sexualities, pornography, sado-masochism, and the "stupidity" of American feminism. While much of what Paglia has to say is arrogant, wildly exaggerated, and even demagogic, her performance is funny and outrageous, and she is keenly aware of how to create and address an audience. Paglia here embodies her credo that "an elitist leftism is a contradiction in terms" (360), and I would argue that this, and not Paglia's regressive antifeminism, is the lesson Treut considers most compatible with her own notion of filmmaking.[7] *Virgin Machine* and especially *My Father Is Coming* have been successful in crossing over into mainstream arthouse audiences through their combination of comedy, pop culture, and a radical sexual agenda—a form of postmodern bricolage that is not afraid to sacrifice aesthetic purity for a chance to reach larger audiences, even if that means drawing criticism from more radical groups who claim that Treut has gone mainstream and sold out. Treut's style can be seen as part of a queer aesthetics that B. Ruby Rich has recently described as "Homo Pomo: there are traces . . . of appropriation and pastiche, irony as well as reworking of history with social constructionism very much in mind. Definitely breaking with older humanist approaches and the films and tapes that accompanied identity politics, these works are irreverent, energetic, alternately minimalist and excessive. Above all, they're full of pleasure" (165–66). Indeed, the pleasure principle informs both Treut's narratives as well as their exuberant styles. Clearly, Treut's outrageous female characters are having fun, and they are fun to watch. The stories of *Seduction: The Cruel Woman, Virgin Machine,* and *My Father Is Coming* are all about the pleasure of finding out about different sexual orientations and practices, and even the most stereotypical German character, Vicky's father Hans, is persuaded into some New Age sex with Annie Sprinkle—a rare depiction of sexual pleasure involving those over age sixty.[8] The point bears repetition that Treut's protagonists enjoy their sexualities without fear of punishment; when punishment seems to be involved as in the sadomasochistic sex of *Bondage,* the protagonist Carol makes it clear that bondage makes her feel "very safe."

A similar transgressive pleasure informs the mixed styles of Treut's films. I have already mentioned the intertwining of documentary and feature film elements and the mixed agenda of teaching and divertissement. Other intertextual references would include the underground film à la Warhol, which was pioneering in its depiction of gay sexuality and use of nonactors, Warhol's Factory superstars. Like Warhol's films, Treut's underground style often takes on the look of a home movie, defending a postmodern dilettantism of "everybody can do it" in which scenes with dead spots or poor use of nonprofessional actors do not end up on the editing room floor. This style transforms the private into the public, thereby insisting that the personal is political. And there are numerous references to Weimar cinema, with its important tradition of queer cinema, its unsurpassed comedies, and films with a strong social and political agenda—all of which are being taken up by both *My Father Is Coming* and *Virgin Machine.* At the end of *Virgin Machine,* for example, the scene of Dorothee racing on her bicycle offers a rewriting of the famous bike sequence in *Kuhle Wampe* (1932; fig. 2). In Brecht/Dudow's left-wing classic we watched young Boenicke participate in the futile rat race for employment soon to be ended by his suicide. In homage to *Kuhle Wampe* Dorothee on her bicycle, donning a very similar kind of 1920s proletarian-looking hat and a similar black outfit, is filmed much in the same angled shots that focus on the spokes and the turning of the pedals, as if to de-emphasize individuality—except that this dyke on a bike is indeed racing toward a better future *because* she has just given up her work as a journalist.

In conclusion, it becomes clear that the queer cinema of Monika Treut questions more than the rigid categories of male and female. As Treut defends the visual pleasures of pornography, as she foregrounds the performance of gender, and as she follows Paglia's anti-elitist collision and collusion of art and popular culture, all kinds of other oppositions start to crumble as well. This postmodern bricolage of multiculturalism and multisexuality can be seen as a striving for the proliferation of difference—yet it also implies the dissolution of a certain German identity. Indeed, her protagonists' eagerness to leave behind—seemingly unproblematically—the confining fatherland can be interpreted as an effacement of national identity that is grafted onto a larger, international identity. Interestingly, Paglia calls Treut an ally in the "*international* movement for . . . anti-dogma feminism" (*Vamps* 206; emph. added) without specifying the scope of this movement any further. One may wonder if Paglia appeals to Treut precisely *because* she is an American (and if Paglia likes Treut because she is *not*). On this issue of nationalities it is also important to note that the two main enablers of transformed identity and sexual discovery—Dominique in *Virgin Machine* and Lisa in *My Father Is Coming*—are both neither American nor German. Dominique is from Uruguay but of Hungarian descent; she conveniently speaks German. Lisa is a Puerto Rican but passes for Anglo. It seems that the blurring of nationality is the prerequisite for transforming one's cultural identity. As Treut says about her audience, no matter whether German, American, Australian, French, or Finnish, "it is always the same kind of person who likes my films. It's like a big family. They read the same books, they like the same movies, they talk about the same things" (Gemünden et al.). In this internationalist frame of reference an imagined community with America is built that has no room for the more troubling sides of urban life in this country. Treut's tales about coming to, coming in, and coming out in America show the utopian potential this country has had, and continues to have, for Germans, but one may wonder if this insight does not present a more accurate description of the country left behind than the one represented on the screen.

NOTES

1. This kind of liberation is also chronicled in Rosa von Praunheim's documentary *Überleben in New York* (Survival in New York [1989]), about three German women whose lives, and particularly sex lives, change after they move to the Big Apple. Von Praunheim introduces us to Claudia, who dumped her German boyfriend for a lesbian relationship with Ryan; to Ulli, who abandoned her rural Swabian background for a life in the American metropolis, where we see her living with her lover in Harlem as the only white woman on the block or, together with a Vietnam veteran, on welfare; and to Anna, a struggling actress like Vicky, who couldn't afford tuition for acting school and began working as a go-go dancer, fell in love with one of the regulars, and later got involved with a lawyer, who changed careers to manage the establishment where Anna works. While their stories are indeed unusual (certainly by non–New York standards), the camera treats the three women with respect and a caring distance and thus refrains from turning them into larger-than-life figures or symbols of an achieved quest for the truth in life. They struggle, they have to make ends meet, but their willingness to take emotional, social, and financial risks in their same-sex, interracial relationships rewards them with unusual experiences.

2. Rick and Treudl's interesting anthology from Austria, *Frauen-Gewalt-Pornographie,* gathers a variety of responses to the debate on pornography and violence.

3. See Monika Treut's book *Die grausame Frau: Zum Frauenbild bei de Sade and Sacher-Masoch,* forthcoming in English from Routledge.

4. As Sprinkle said about her beginnings as a prostitute: "I was working in a massage parlor. For 3 months I worked and didn't even know I was a hooker—I was having such a good time. . . . I just thought of myself as a horny masseuse. I liked having sex with the guys after I gave them a brief massage. When it finally occurred to me that I was a hooker, and I got over the initial shock, I enjoyed the idea" (qtd. in Williams 179).

5. It is interesting to note in this context that traditional definitions of *pornography* such as Webster's rely on the very possibility of separating it from art: "Pornography = obscene literature, art, or photography, esp. that having little or no artistic merit."

6. Ben and Vicky's positions are similar to those of Wanda and Justine described earlier, which illustrate that there is no "outside" of role-playing.

7. It should be noted that, in her scholarly work on de Sade and Sacher-Masoch, Treut draws heavily on French critics such as Deleuze, Foucault, and Derrida whom Paglia despises.

8. Even in Fassbinder's *Ali: Fear Eats the Soul,* in which an older cleaning woman falls in love with a young Moroccan car mechanic, Fassbinder spares the audience a por-

trayal of their lovemaking. An exception is again Rosa von Praunheim, whose *Unsere Leichen leben noch* (Our Corpses Are Still Alive) centers on the sexual and other pleasures of older women.

WORKS CITED

Butler, Judith. *Gender Trouble: Feminism and the Subversion of Identity.* New York and London: Routledge, 1990.

———. "Performative Acts and Gender Constitution: An Essay in Phenomenology and Feminist Theory." In *Performing Feminisms: Feminist Critical Theory and Theater,* ed. Sue-Ellen Case. Baltimore: Johns Hopkins UP, 1990. 270–82.

Doty, Alexander. *Making Things Perfectly Queer: Interpreting Mass Culture.* Minneapolis: U of Minnesota P, 1993.

Dworkin, Andrea. "Against the Male Flood: Censorship, Pornography, and Equality." *Harvard Women's Law Journal* 8 (1985): 1–29.

Fox, Steve. "Coming to America: An Interview with Monika Treut." *Cineaste* 19.1 (1993): 63– 64.

Gemünden, Gerd, Alice Kuznier, and Klaus Phillips. "From *Taboo Parlor* to Porn and Passing: An Interview with Monika Treut." *Film Quarterly* 50.3 (1997): 2–12.

Knight, Julia. "Female Misbehavior: The Cinema of Monika Treut." In *Women and Film: A Sight and Sound Reader,* ed. Pam Cook and Philip Dodd. Philadelphia: Temple UP, 1993.

Kuzniar, Alice. "Comparative Gender: Rosa von Praunheim's and Monika Treut's Cross-Cultural Studies." *Spectator* 15 (1994): 51–59.

Paglia, Camille. *Sex, Art, and American Culture: Essays.* New York: Vintage Books, 1992.

———. *Sexual Personae: Art and Decadence from Nefertiti to Emily Dickinson.* New Haven: Yale UP, 1990.

———. *Vamps and Tramps.* New York: Vintage, 1994.

Rentschler, Eric. "How American Is It: The U.S. as Image and Imaginary in German Film." *Persistence of Vision* 2 (1985): 5–18.

Rich, B. Ruby. "Homo Pomo: The New Queer Cinema." In *Women and Film: A Sight and Sound Reader,* ed. Pam Cook and Philip Dodd. Philadelphia: Temple UP, 1993. 164–74.

Rick, Karin, and Sylvia Treudl, eds. *Frauen-Gewalt-Pornographie.* Vienna: Wiener Frauenverlag, 1989.

Sedgwick, Eve Kosofsky. *Tendencies.* Durham: Duke UP, 1993.

Straayer, Chris. "Lesbian Narratives and Queer Characters in Monika Treut's *Virgin Machine.*" *Journal of Film and Video* 45.2–3 (1993): 24–39.

———. "The Seduction of Boundaries: Feminist Fluidity in Annie Sprinkle's Art/Education/Sex." In *Dirty Looks: Women, Pornography, Power,* ed. Pamela Church Gibson and Roma Gibson. London: BFI, 1993. 156–75.

Struve, Ulrich. "'Denouncing the Pornographic Subject': The American and the German Pornography Debate and Elfriede Jelinek's *Lust.*" In *Elfriede Jelinek: Framed by*

Language, ed. Jorun B. Johns and Katherine Arens. Riverside, CA: Ariadne, 1995. 89– 106.

Treut, Monika. *Die grausame Frau: Zum Frauenbild bei de Sade and Sacher-Masoch.* Basel and Frankfurt a.M.: Stroemfeld/Roter Stern, 1984.

———. "Die Zeremonie der blutenden Rose: Vorüberlegungen zu einem Filmprojekt." *Frauen und Film* 36 (1984): 35–43.

Williams, Linda. "A Provoking Agent: The Pornography and Performance Art of Annie Sprinkle." In *Dirty Looks: Women, Pornography, Power,* ed. Pamela Church Gibson and Roma Gibson. London: BFI, 1993. 176–89.

Willis, Hollis. "Bad Behavior: An Interview with Monika Treut." *Visions* 7 (1992): 10–12.

Part Six

HOW DO WE MEDIATE
THE GERMAN CASE
TO THE PUBLIC?

Cultural studies stresses not only communication across disciplinary boundaries but also among different professions. The authors of the three essays in part 6 argue for the importance of such dialogue by exploring some recent exchanges among museologists, journalists, archivists, diplomats, academics, and others. Their contributions here underscore another tenet of cultural studies: the notion of the politically engaged intellectual. Marrus, Ryback, and Giles affirm the high stakes of the issues they examine, whether they concern the physical condition of Auschwitz, the nature of journalistic work in contemporary society, or the disposition of important Nazi archives. They share in a belief that it is crucial for the public to be well informed and that a collaboration between members of different professions allows for an optimal use of varying skills and methodologies in addressing often intractable problems.

CHAPTER 20

The Future of Auschwitz:
A Case for the Ruins

Michael R. Marrus

The contribution of historian Michael Marrus, which concerns the conservation of the extant Auschwitz camp complex, vividly conveys the manner in which academic discussions reverberate in society at large. Despite charges that the ivory tower is now, more than ever, removed from the "real world"—what with the abundance of scholarly journals (some of them obscure) and the rise of technical parlance—Marrus shows that academics have an important role to play in the public realm. The conference he describes, held at the most notorious site in Poland, engaged issues that affect both our own and future generations in a profound way. We gain a sense of the gravity of the issues by the array of international experts convened for the discussion. One indication that intellectual work resonates in the world at large is precisely that scholars such as Marrus and James Young were included in the deliberations. The challenge for these experts is analogous to the challenge for cultural studies: to communicate historical and cultural knowledge to those who come from another time or place.

As part of a larger dialog among Holocaust scholars about appropriate and effective forms of remembrance, Marrus argues the case for an Auschwitz in ruins. To reconstruct the camp, he contends, would not as effectively evoke the horror of the phenomenon that was the Holocaust as would engagement with a ruined site. Ruins force the visitor's imagination into constructive activity. Marrus himself chooses not to engage the Holocaust deniers and their specious claims that the camp is a fabrication; he is, however, concerned with an issue they have raised—namely, authenticity. Marrus's concern with authenticity is not based on a need to prove that the Holocaust happened. This is a given. What does concern him deeply is the creation of an atmosphere that facilitates the work of commemoration. Marrus addresses the museum officials and offers his insights into their constantly evolving "curatorial plan." As a scholar who has demonstrated the ability to make connections between the specific event of the Nazi genocide and its large historical connotations (see his key 1989 study, The Holocaust in History) *his contribution here represents an effort to mediate between the museologists (who ultimately make the decisions) and the public (i.e., the audience) as well as between past and future generations. The custodianship of Auschwitz, "the largest cemetery in the world," involves stakes that are very high indeed.*

Auschwitz-Birkenau, site of the largest Nazi concentration camp complex and graveyard for more than a million of its victims, is partly in ruins today, decaying and crumbling into the marshy Polish soil on which it was built more than a half-century ago. After decades of neglect or inadequate attention, particularly from the standpoint of the Jewish victims and their survivors, conservation is now proceeding apace—part of the transformation of virtually every aspect of life in Poland following the collapse of communism in 1989. What rules should govern the process now under way? Specifically, might there be a danger of *too much* conservation at Auschwitz—too exhaustive restoration, too aggressive reconstruction, too zealous an effort to recapture in physical form what was the greatest death factory the world has ever seen? These are questions put to the Auschwitz State Museum authorities by a group of about thirty museologists, philosophers, social scientists, historians, and other experts from North America, Western Europe and Israel who assembled in Auschwitz for a three-day conference entitled "The Future of Auschwitz," in August 1993. I offer here a brief personal report on this meeting, in which I participated, together with my own assessment of the broad direction that conservation should follow.

A word, first of all, to underscore what I think was obvious to every participant in our three-day discussion: we were grappling with one of the most difficult of conservation problems, for which there are no easy answers and perhaps no fully satisfactory ones. In its present condition as a memorial, a historical site, and a museum—to which tens of thousands of visitors flock annually, from near and from far—as in its past manifestation as a concentration, slave labor, and death camp, Auschwitz is in a class of its own. Emblematic of the Nazi Holocaust in the West but also the most important center for the commemoration of Polish suffering at the hands of the Nazis during World War II, Auschwitz is a place where several symbolic universes coexist and do not always complement one another.[1] As with the search for its historical significance, so it is with the challenges the camp poses to museologists and conservators: in the case of Auschwitz precedents do not readily apply, and guidelines do not easily suggest themselves. As one of the conference organizers, the British anthropologist and Auschwitz authority Jonathan Webber properly reminded us at a difficult moment in our deliberations, "We are all feeling our way."

Consider just the diverse origins and great scale of the place.[2] Auschwitz-Birkenau is at the center of a huge camp complex, including detention facilities for political prisoners and slave labor camps as well as machinery for mass murder, and which at the height of the Nazi empire included more than forty camps scattered throughout the Upper Silesian countryside, in territory incorporated into the Reich after the defeat of Poland in 1939. Begun in June 1940 with the establishment of *Konzentrationslager* Auschwitz, or Auschwitz I, referred to as the *Stammlager,* or core camp, this system soon extended to a vast enclosure known as Auschwitz II, built on the nearby site of the ruined Polish village of Brzezinka, which the Germans called Birkenau. It was to that camp, beginning in 1942, that Jews from every corner of Europe were deported, almost all of them to be gassed and their bodies burned in specially constructed gas chamber crematorium complexes specially built for the purpose.

The area that came under the jurisdiction of the State Museum at Auschwitz, organized in 1947, amounted to nearly 200 hectares, or 2 million square meters—over 200,000 of these in the *Stammlager,* with its famous "Arbeit macht frei" iron gateway, three-story brick barracks, and reconstructed gas chamber and crematorium; and some 1.7 million square meters within the immense confines of Birkenau, with originally fenced-off interior subcamps, its rows of wooden and also stone barracks, with guard towers, storehouses, and other facilities and with the ruins of four huge gas chamber and crematoria complexes. In 1947 these two camps included over 150 buildings and other structures in various states of disrepair, plus kilometers of barbed wire, ditches, and other grim paraphernalia of Nazi camps.[3] According to the careful investigation of Auschwitz State Museum historian Francizek Piper, as many as 1.3 million people were deported to this place during the period 1940–45, some 1.1 million of whom were murdered—about a million of them Jews but also Poles (between 70,000 and 75,000), Roma-Sinti (Gypsies) (21,000), Soviet prisoners of war (POWs) (15,000), and thousands of many other nationalities (Piper; see also Benz).

Hastily built in 1941–43, originally intended to house Soviet prisoners of war and then devoted to the Nazis' "Final Solution" of the Jewish Question, much of the Birkenau complex was poorly constructed at the start—intended to last only for the short time that it would take to complete the Nazis' murderous project. Wooden barracks, for example, were set directly on the ground rather than on a foundation of stone, gravel, or brick. Many of these huts collapsed or were removed immediately after the evacuation of the camp, with the materials being used for firewood or to construct shelters elsewhere. For more than ten years the remaining structures not only deteriorated due to natural causes but also underwent substantial alteration as a result of the complete or partial dismantling of buildings by former inmates and local inhabitants. Conservation did not begin until more than a decade after the camp was liberated. And even after restoration began parts of the camp complex suffered from more than natural decay. The museum grounds were officially demarcated as state property only in 1958 and a protection zone established around Birkenau as late as 1962.

By 1978, according to Polish authorities in their application to the United Nations Educational, Scientific, and Cultural Organization (UNESCO) for listing as a World Heritage site, fewer than 20 percent of the original structures of Birkenau still survived. Since then the deterioration of the site has continued. Moreover, some of the ruins in Birkenau, notably of the wooden barracks, are not "original" ruins but, instead, structures that had been rebuilt in the 1960s and have subsequently collapsed. The post-liberation perimeter of Birkenau has never been completely closed, and for years people have come and gone for various reasons and cattle have grazed where more than a million people were tortured and slaughtered by the Nazis. Until 1993 unconventional (to us) visitors have remained part of the local landscape at Birkenau. Among the most disruptive have been fictional filmmakers, who not only added their own measure of destruction but who also implanted a few new structures—guard towers and a barracks have been mentioned—intended to round out their picture of the camp during its time of operation. Happily, museum authorities have decided to prevent any such indignity to the camp site in the future by banning such films altogether from the camp grounds.

Is there a comprehensive conservation strategy for Auschwitz-Birkenau? Repeatedly, conference participants put this question to the museum authorities, suggesting that questions about specific issues of preservation could only be answered within the context of what museologists call a "curatorial plan" or "design philosophy," or what lay people might think of as a generally agreed-upon vision about the purpose of place. Such an overarching scheme, several participants insisted, was sadly missing. Wrestling with the problem of hard choices, uncertain sometimes about museum staff priorities, or with strongly held opinions about certain specific issues, these outsiders claimed that it was difficult to move forward in the absence of such a clearly articulated, global conception.[4] Unencumbered by commitments to past decisions at the Auschwitz-Birkenau site, the critics tended to think in terms of broad options and diverse possibilities.

Museum authorities, on the other hand, seemed ill at ease with this line and reluctant to define their guiding principles more narrowly than they have done in the past. My own sense is that the 1978 statement prepared for the UNESCO authorities would have largely applied in 1993 as well: "While conserving its character of a monument to the suffering and struggles of nations, the Museum serves as an historical exhibition and research institute with archives; it is also the largest cemetery in the world. By virtue of its activities, the Museum makes an important contribution to the struggle for world peace and security."

To this one should add the repeated commitment of the museum staff in recent years to take account, in a way that had pointedly not been done before, of the special significance of Auschwitz-Birkenau for Jews. In part owing to the fact that more Jews were murdered in Auschwitz than in any other Nazi camp (although Treblinka, with some 900,000 victims, comes a close second), in part due to the fact that the Jewish victims of Auschwitz came from every corner of Europe, not just from Poland or Eastern Europe, and in part because there are tens of thousands of survivors of the Auschwitz complex and a rich memoir literature testifying to its horrors, this place has become virtually emblematic of the Holocaust—outside the former communist world, at least. In the past, as everyone knows, the failure of the site and the museum to register this significance constituted an important bone of contention and was the subject of protracted, intense polemics in the late 1980s, following the establishment of a Carmelite convent in a derelict building just outside the walls of Auschwitz I (see Bartoszewski). The resolution of this controversy to the satisfaction of most, together with the repeated and sincere statements of museum authorities on this issue, has had the effect of removing the matter from the center of attention. Concerns about balance and emphasis still exist, to be sure, and there may even be continuing unease on this issue in some quarters, but competing views about the place of Jewish victimization at Auschwitz did not seem to have been part of the debate over a comprehensive conservation plan.

My own impression is that the reluctance of the museum authorities to define curatorial goals in the way that was asked springs in part from their discomfort with the notion of a single conception enshrined as official doctrine— an understandable apprehension for an institution emerging from an externally imposed, communist-dominated system that operated within a very strictly defined ideological framework. In reaction to this past the museum seems to have embraced a resolutely pragmatic approach. As one official insisted, there *is* an overall conception at Auschwitz: it is a "mixed conception." *Mixed conception* seems to mean that no single pressure group is allowed sway over the others; no single goal predominates; no single school of conservation thought sets the overall tone.

Two other forces may be at work. The first is a reluctance to rebuke an older curatorial direction—forty years of sometimes painstaking labor on the part of sincere and committed museum employees, operating with insufficient means and in a national environment that treasures any record of Polish creativity and achievement. More than once we were reminded of the many years of constructive work staff members had invested in the museum under difficult conditions—cataloging artifacts, attempting to preserve exhibits, and rebuilding crumbling structures. Rethinking basic goals, the assumption seemed to be, might impugn such faithful service and undermine time-tested, worthwhile efforts at conservation. The other factor is an understandable apprehension of outside criticism, which rains freely on the museum from numerous quarters, national and international, some of them flagrantly insensitive to local concerns and responsibilities. Embracing one philosophy, it might well be feared, particularly one worked out in consultation with intellectuals from outside Poland, would guarantee alienating proponents of other views. It might also diminish the commemoration of the suffering of the Poles themselves at the hands of foreign invaders—a highly sensitive point inevitably raised with the assertion of the Jewish significance of the Auschwitz-Birkenau site. Certainly, the position of the museum officials in the sometimes intense debates over alternative courses was hardly enviable. With resources extremely limited, with a crumbling infrastructure, with lines of authority for decision making sometimes blurred, with powerfully competing interests, it is hardly surprising that the authorities resisted a radical rethinking of their activity. "We're doing the best we can under very trying circumstances," they seemed to be saying.

Sympathetic and understanding as we outside critics may be, I think we owe it to museum officials to press the case for a comprehensive review of existing priorities and to signal our unease about some courses of action that have been proposed or are presently being contemplated. In my own view the failure to work out an overall philosophy of conservation makes it difficult to set what Professor Bohdan Rymaszewski, chairman of the International Auschwitz Council's standing committee on conservation, referred to in our discussions as "a hierarchy of [conservation] tasks." Further, there is danger that some presently contemplated restoration work could disrupt the unique atmosphere of the Birkenau site, in particular, and could interfere with both its commemorative purpose and the interests of historical authenticity. For among the most remarkable aspects of that camp is the mood it evokes because of what Professor James Young of the University of Massachusetts has called "the magic of ruins," places "haunted by the phantom of past events, no longer visibly apparent, but only remembered" ("Reflections"). Many of us felt that serious consideration should be given to preserving at least some of these ruins as ruins, particularly in Birkenau, which presents itself to visitors today as a unique place of horror.

From the guard tower at the southern entrance to that camp, through which the trains of deportees passed in 1944, Birkenau now appears both different than what it was under the Nazis and at the same time evocative of crimes of unimaginable magnitude. To the first-time visitor, in particular, the camp seems vast, empty, desolate, quiet—quite unlike most other tourist sites and capable of communicating to most, I think, a deep sense of loss. Many hundreds of thousands were murdered here, the visitors learn, if they did not know this already. Looking across the empty landscape, one may learn little of how or why this happened, but the scale of the crime probably sinks in, together with another observation: this is a place unlike any other and, therefore, a place where the chatter of explanations may fail, for once, to get to the bottom of it all. The inescapable reaction, I think, is a feeling of awe and horror at what some people did to others.

Starting there, let me recommend a test be applied to any conservation work planned for the camp: do the changes detract in any serious manner from this sense of desolation, from the capacity of ruins to evoke dismay and revulsion in the face of terrible crimes? Will restoration and reconstruction, intended to achieve clarity, make it more difficult to grasp the murderous enterprise as a whole?

Plans to reconstruct the twenty wooden barracks remaining at Birkenau—originally Wehrmacht horse stables intended as makeshift accommodations for inmates and set on the bare ground without proper foundations—are a good example of how a well-meaning effort at reconstruction may fail to meet this test and, indeed, may distract from the search for historical authenticity. According to current plans, the twenty remaining wooden barracks at Birkenau, themselves reconstructions of about a quarter of a century ago and now in very poor condition, are to be turned into literal replicas of the originals through extensive repair and rebuilding. Work has already been completed on one barrack and is now under way for a second. Painstaking and laborious, this project involves careful drawing, photographing, and then dismantling of the structures, the replacement of some wooden elements and the reinforcement of others, and, finally, the setting of the reassembled barracks on solid foundations, intended to prevent deterioration in the future. The entire process takes about six months for each barrack. But the result, from my standpoint, is less than satisfactory: a sanitized, well-reinforced stable—scarcely capable of evoking the filthy, flimsy structures into which inmates were packed like sardines and where they suffered agonies of hunger, illness, and exposure to the elements. The result, indeed, is so remote from the barracks described or remembered by former inmates as to call into serious question whether it is worth the effort. Indeed, unless properly set in context, the result may be deleterious—the introduction of a palpably "fake" element that will detract from the fidelity of the site. The danger is, as James Young puts it, that "even a well-intentioned conservation will begin to infect the surrounding area with the fiction of its own inauthenticity" ("Reflections"). Far better, I conclude, to rely upon the imagination of visitors as it operates amid the present-day ruins, perhaps assisted with models or with photographs available of similar barracks during the Nazi period or at the time of liberation in 1945.

I cite this one example to advance some general opinions about reconstruction at the Auschwitz and Birkenau camps. Over the course of our discussions we heard various plans or proposals for restoration—for the construction, in effect, of replicas of what is known to have existed under the Nazis. Extensive work has been completed on the railway lines and platform built in Birkenau for the arrival of Hungarian Jews in the spring of 1944. For reasons that are unclear to me, expensive restoration has also been completed at one of the camp's sewage treatment systems, and work continues on the second. A second generation of repairs and reconstruction (the first was in the mid-1960s) is proceeding at the "Zentral Sauna," the building through which prisoners allowed to live for a time entered the camp as inmates. Substantial repairs are under way for the stone barracks and other structures. And proposals have been made for the rebuilding of camp kitchens, infirmary barracks, and even part of the system of gas chambers and crematory ovens.

What is the likely effect, one should ask, of all this activity? My own view is that it is a mistake to try to replicate Auschwitz-Birkenau as it was under the Nazis—the apparent intention of much of the work mentioned here. For to state the obvious: even the most faithful and most lavish of reconstructions could not include the mud, the filth, the stench, the noise, the cries, the smoke, the barking of dogs, not to mention the hordes of emaciated inmates and their tormentors. And so the result will invariably diminish the horror, render the place more "familiar" and, hence, more distant from historical reality. Replicas will always be replicas, and we should not invite visitors to evade the challenge to their imagination and confuse our handiwork with the real thing. To be sure there is much that can and needs to be done at Auschwitz-Birkenau. Serious consideration should be given to "freezing" in place some or all of the ruined structures that remain. Some carefully selective reconstruction or the use of models or appropriately placed panels and photographs might help visitors grasp what the original structures looked like and how they functioned. Many of us appreciated museum proposals that pointed in precisely this direction. There are many ways to assist visitors to gain an understanding of the camp, but truth demands that they also appreciate how time and circumstances separate us from when hundreds of thousands suffered and perished in Auschwitz-Birkenau. Perhaps the best piece of advice was offered by several participants, awed by the difficulty of the task and aware that, whatever we do, future generations will contemplate the site differently than we do ourselves: go slowly, cautiously, and do not pretend that we can see or understand it all.

NOTES

1. On questions of conflicting memories, see Webber; Young (*Texture* chap. 5); and Dwork and van Pelt.
2. The best historical orientation to Auschwitz is Gutman and Berenbaum; see especially the articles by Jean-Claude Pressac and Robert-Jan van Pelt. For a chronological account, drawn from archival sources, see Czech. For a bibliographic collection, see Malcowna.
3. United Nations Educational, Scientific and Cultural Organization (UNESCO), Nomination of Auschwitz-Birkenau National Museum to the World Heritage List, Warsaw, 2 May 1978. For important details, see Pressac, *Auschwitz*. There is an excellent collection of photographs in Swiebocka.
4. For an account of some of these issues and the various perspectives on them, see Ryback.

WORKS CITED

Bartoszewski, Wladyslaw T. *The Convent at Auschwitz.* New York: George Braziller, 1990.

Benz, Wolfgang. *Dimension des Volkermords: Die Zahl der jüdischen Opfer des Nationalsozialismus.* Munich: Oldenbourg, 1991.

Czech, Danuta. *Kalendarium der Ereignisse im Konzentrationslager Auschwitz-Birkenau 1939–1945.* Reinbek bei Hamburg: Rowohlt, 1989.

Dwork, Debórah, and Robert-Jan van Pelt. "Reclaiming Auschwitz." In *Holocaust Remembrance: The Shapes of Memory,* ed. Geoffrey H. Hartman. Oxford: Blackwell, 1994. 232–51.

Gutman, Yisrael, and Michael Berenbaum, eds., *Anatomy of the Auschwitz Death Camp.* Bloomington: Indiana UP, 1994.

Malcowna, Opracowala Anna. *Bibliographia KL Auschwitz za lata 1942–1980.* Oświęcim: Wydawnictwo Panstwowego Muzeum w Oświęcimiu, 1991.

Piper, Franciszek. "Estimating the Number of Deportees and Victims of the Auschwitz-Birkenau Camp." *Yad Vashem Studies* 21 (1991): 49–99.

Pressac, Jean-Claude. *Auschwitz: Technique and Operation of the Gas Chambers.* New York: Beate Klarsfeld Foundation, 1989.

Pressac, Jean-Claude, with Robert-Jan van Pelt. "The Machinery of Murder at Auschwitz." In *Anatomy of the Auschwitz Death Camp,* ed. Yisrael Gutman and Michael Berenbaum. Bloomington: Indiana UP, 1994. 183–245.

Ryback, Timothy W. "Evidence of Evil." *New Yorker,* 15 November 1993, 68–81.

Świebocka, Theresa, with Jonathan Webber and Connie Wilsack, eds. *Auschwitz: A History in Photographs.* Bloomington: Indiana UP, 1993.

United Nations Educational, Scientific and Cultural Organization (UNESCO). Nomination of Auschwitz-Birkenau National Museum to the World Heritage List, Warsaw, 2 May 1978.

Van Pelt, Robert-Jan. "A Site in Search of a Mission." In *Anatomy of the Auschwitz*

Death Camp, ed. Yisrael Gutman and Michael Berenbaum. Bloomington: Indiana UP, 1994. 93–156.

Webber, Jonathan. *The Future of Auschwitz: Some Personal Reflections.* First Frank Green Lecture. Oxford Centre for Postgraduate Hebrew Studies, 1992.

Young, James. "Reflections on the Conservation at Auschwitz-Birkenau." Paper prepared for the conference "The Future of Auschwitz: Should the Ruins be Preserved?" Oświęcim, August 1993.

———. *The Texture of Memory: Holocaust Memorials and Meaning.* New Haven: Yale UP, 1993.

CHAPTER 21

The First Draft: Writing History for the General Public

Timothy W. Ryback

After receiving a Ph.D. degree in German from Harvard, Timothy Ryback sub-sequently decided to concentrate on journalistic enterprises. With regular con-tributions in the New Yorker *treating German and Austrian topics as well as features in publications ranging from* ARTnews *to the* Atlantic Monthly, *Ry-back has become an important American commentator on Central European affairs. Many of our academic peers in other fields find out about the German scene by reading Ryback's articles, just as they do by listening to Deidre Berger's radio reports. Both have the public's ear because they tell stories well. Thus, it is important for specialists in the German field to learn how these jour-nalists carry out their work. Ryback's essay here reflects critically on how he mediates the German case to the public.*

Beyond engaging the commonly asked question about the effect that pop-ular writing has on an author, Ryback explores the more difficult issue of taboos. He grounds his discussion in a topic that has long been of interest to him: Na-tional Socialism and the various efforts to come to terms with (or "master") this past. Ryback discerns a bias in the journalistic establishment—primarily among publishers and editors—whereby authors are discouraged from ad-dressing uncomfortable or problematic subjects. He cites as examples the no-tion that some Germans, too, were war victims and that Holocaust deniers, in fact, are occasionally correct in their assertions regarding the way in which the history of the "Final Solution" has been presented to the public. There are myr-iad reasons—many of them good—why the press is so uncomfortable with such subjects, but the net effect has been to curtail discussion and to impose a kind of censorship. Ryback queries whether the public is ready for difficult and dis-turbing journalistic pieces. In answering affirmatively, Ryback still plays the emotions card: at times here he employs rhetoric that rehearses his controver-

sial thesis—with us readers now as the general public. Ultimately, he under-
scores the need for a partnership between journalists and academics so that an
accurate and nuanced treatment of history emerges.

Several years ago, while writing an article on preservation efforts at Auschwitz, I visited the United States Holocaust Memorial Museum in Washington, DC, to meet with museum officials and to tour the exhibitions. Toward the end of a three-hour walk through the museum I found myself before a series of video monitors with black-and-white footage of the concentration and death camp liberations. Each screen was devoted to a separate camp and presented three- to five-minute sequences of the scenes of horror we have all come to know: the abandoned boxcars piled with corpses on a railway siding at Dachau; the gaunt-faced survivors peering from wooden bunks at Buchenwald; bulldozers plowing monstrous tangles of human remains into open pits at Bergen-Belsen.

As I moved from one screen to the next, I noticed a woman in her late sixties standing before a monitor. She watched the flickering images with rapt attention, leaned forward until her face nearly touched the screen, then after an instant leaped back, her hand to her mouth. I watched her repeat this odd sequence of gestures twice before approaching her. Without a word she seized me by the hand and drew me to the monitor. As a group of children came shuffling down a barbed-wire causeway, she indicated herself among these youngest Holocaust survivors.

When I explained to her that I was writing an article on Auschwitz, she related to me, in a voice occasionally trembling with anguish, the story of a young girl brought to Auschwitz, about parents lost to the gas chambers, about the kindnesses of the camp's Soviet liberators, about the double tribulation of being both an orphan and a displaced person, and, finally, about a sojourn to the United States, where she eventually found a new life for herself. When I asked her if it might be possible to conduct a subsequent, in-depth interview, she gave me two numbers: her telephone number in the Los Angeles area and the blue tattooed number on her wrist. I never wrote her story.

I mention this encounter to illustrate the point that the writing of any history, whether scholarly, journalistic, or personal, is based on making choices, selecting which material to include and which to exclude, and that, even when developing a particular line of argumentation that helps "dictate" the information to be used, the selection process remains, to a certain degree, personal, arbitrary, idiosyncratic. I did not include the story of the Holocaust survivor from

Los Angeles for the simple reason that I subsequently encountered another individual whose story was more central to the specific theme of that article. Just as I did not select her story for inclusion, I did not choose the experiences of Primo Levi, Elie Wiesel, Simon Wiesenthal, or a thousand other camp survivors. Not that one survivor's story is any less tragic than another's—each story of suffering and survival would seem to deserve a book of its own—but, in the process of researching and writing, a number of factors come into play that in the end forces one to select particular accounts. This is true in any endeavor to record or interpret history, but it is especially true when writing for the general public. Although I was trained in academia, I have, for the last decade or so, written for a general audience, attempting to make "issues of substance" accessible to mainstream audiences. While the broad exposure can be personally gratifying, one is forced to make many compromises both on the choice of material and the depth of treatment. The numerous constraints (deadlines, space restrictions, readability) compel one to work in what might be considered a form of intellectual shorthand. At its best, however, good journalistic writing brings rigor to the research and writing and can result in lengthy pieces that are enjoyable and intellectually challenging.

In developing a potential article for a general audience, a number of factors come into play that may be of marginal concern in academia. Whereas a scholar can rely on university support or research grants and can turn to diverse venues for presenting one's research—conferences, symposia, professional journals, university presses—the possibilities for serious nonfiction are restricted to a handful of mass-market periodicals and publishing houses. One needs to consider the general editorial policy of a given publication and, in particular, the interest of a given editor with whom one works. A story idea, in short, needs to be compelling enough to compete with literally thousands of other potential story ideas and, often fortuitously, to come to the attention of the "right" editor. Once again the journalist's options tend to be much narrower than those of the academic.

While virtually any aspect of German society, culture, or history is equally viable to the scholar, be it the profane verse of Walther von der Vogelweide, the legal reforms of Frederick the Great, or the *Ostpolitik* of Willy Brandt, when writing for the general public one is restricted to those topics that are relevant to a wide audience or can be presented in a manner that is accessible and engaging to the average reader. In brief, one needs to spark an editor's enthusiasm and, ultimately, to hold a reader's attention.

It happens that my particular area of work, the twelve years of National Socialist rule and its postwar legacy, tends to generate strong public interest. I would suggest there are a number of reasons for the enduring public fascination with this subject. The Nazi era is unquestionably a moment of singular savagery in human history, and we are continually reminded of these events in the perennial cycle of anniversaries—the January liberation of Auschwitz, the February bombing of Dresden, the March *Anschluss* of Austria, the April suicide of Hitler, the May conclusion of the war in Europe, the June invasion of Normandy, etc.—that provides ideal "pegs" for various stories. Further, even though the Third Reich lies a half-century behind us, the many unresolved issues generate ever new controversies. Simon Wiesenthal and others continue to ferret out former SS officers responsible for atrocities. Political leaders both in Germany and elsewhere continue to make notable statements that draw public attention to some aspect of the Nazi past. A handful of German skinheads can make front-page news around the world by desecrating a Jewish cemetery or hurling a firebomb at a synagogue. Even a seemingly tangential event, such as the ethnic cleansing in Bosnia, with its potent images of emaciated figures behind wire fences, can provide impetus for reflection on the era of National Socialist rule.

When treating a serious issue in a manner that is accessible to a wide public, one is inevitably confronted with a tension between that which is sensational and that which is responsible. A journalistic article can spark public debate, set the public agenda for discussion, or, in extreme cases, compel governments to action, as can, in rare instances, scholarly writing. Although journalism can play a role in public dialogue, its fundamental purpose, unlike the purpose of academic writing, is to generate profit. In the end magazines and newspapers sell news that "sells." At its best journalism can engage and educate a reader, but it can also be misused to promote sensational, and divisive, issues.

Let the Holocaust deniers serve as an example. In recent years the Holocaust deniers have made remarkable inroads into the mainstream media and thereby into public consciousness. Although they have moved from the radical fringe to general public attention—through publications, sensational courtroom trials, public access television, talk show appearances, and even the Internet— most serious scholars have refused to engage Holocaust deniers in debate, arguing that such discourse would only lend legitimacy to a bastard science. Given the Holocaust deniers' proclivity for citing statements out of context, the academic community has taken a prudent route in ignoring them. In this context one should mention Deborah Lipstadt's excellent 1993 survey of the Holocaust denier movement, *Denying the Holocaust: The Growing Assault on Truth and Memory.*

Aware of the insidious nature of the Holocaust denier movement, and not wishing to provide them with any additional press, I intended, at the outset of my research on Auschwitz, to avoid any treatment of the Holocaust deniers. Initially, they played no role in my discussion with scholars, Holocaust survivors, museum officials, or experts on preservation. When I visited the site of the former death camp at Auschwitz, however, and began speaking with museum officials, I found that the Holocaust deniers played a significant role in the officials' deliberations on the future of the museum. In response to the claims by Holocaust deniers that Zyklon B had never been used at Auschwitz for the extermination of human beings—a charge the scholars dismiss out of hand—museum officials had sent samples of human hair and pieces from gas chamber walls for testing. Further, the museum officials had deliberated on how to respond to a documentary film, made by a twenty-two-year-old Holocaust denier from California with a hand-held video camera, that offered "proof" that the gas chamber in the Auschwitz *Stammlager* was a "fraud." (It is, in fact, a poorly made reconstruction of a former gas chamber dismantled by the SS in late 1944.)

I had the choice of ignoring the Holocaust deniers—as responsible scholars were doing—or presenting their claims. But because the Holocaust deniers played a significant role in the thinking of the museum officials at Auschwitz, and my article was in fact focused on Auschwitz, I felt compelled to report on their existence, the kinds of issues they raised, and the reactions their behavior elicited. For better or worse I also knew it would make for "great copy."

When I placed calls to several known Holocaust deniers, they proved to be extremely cooperative, providing me with videotapes, publications, photocopied articles, and a copy of Arthur Butz's classic Holocaust denier text, *The Hoax of the Twentieth Century*—a four hundred–page exegesis claiming, with a grotesquely analytical form of technical bean counting, that the crematoria were incapable of incinerating the million or so people who were said to have died at Auschwitz.

What troubled me most about some of the Holocaust deniers' material was the apparent legitimacy of several of their claims. While their basic premise—that the Holocaust never took place—was as absurd as it was repulsive, some of their claims seemed plausible. They objected, as previously noted, that the gas chamber in the Auschwitz *Stammlager* was a reconstruction and a poor one at that. They also noted that the casting of a gas chamber door at the National Holocaust Museum in Washington, DC, was the door to a delousing chamber and not to a chamber used for "homocidal purposes." Their plaint was simple: if you are going to accuse the Germans of perpetrating the most heinous crimes ever committed by man against man, you had better get your facts straight. This, indeed, did not seem to be too much to ask. Another compelling issue that was raised in the Holocaust denier literature was a correlation between the peak use of the Auschwitz crematoria and the outbreak of epidemics, confirmed by the camp medical records.

Initially, I attempted to deal with issues one by one but found some issues so complicated that, without extensive rebuttal, they could give credence to the Holocaust denier arguments. For fear of legitimizing the Holocaust denier position, I dispensed with their arguments in a series of brief, glib remarks. Despite the rather dismissive tone of my article, I subsequently received a letter from the editor of the leading "revisionist" periodical thanking me for my even-handed presentation of their case. I should also note that he paid me the dubious honor of including selected excerpts of my article in promotion materials for the revisionist movement.

In January 1993 the fiftieth anniversary of the Battle of Stalingrad provided an excellent "hook" for a journalistic treatment of a historical issue in a contemporary context. It proved to be an "easy sell" but ended up raising some perplexing questions. In the winter of 1993 Germany rendered quiet and somber homage to the two hundred and fifty thousand soldiers of the German Sixth Army who perished in the worst single military disaster in German history. Since that time a peculiar romanticism, initiated by Nazi propaganda and fostered ever since in countless memoirs, novels, and films, has emerged in Germany regarding the destruction of the Sixth Army at Stalingrad. They are viewed, along with so many others who suffered at the hands of the Nazis—the Jews, the Roma-Sinti, the Poles—as "victims" of Adolf Hitler's fanaticism.

In the autumn of 1992, when I was assigned to write an article on German efforts to bury the remains of thousands of Sixth Army soldiers whose bones still littered the fields to the west of Volgograd—formerly Stalingrad—I was struck by the prevailing attitude among Germans that these soldiers had been victims of National Socialist rule. The evidence for such a notion seemed compelling. In November 1942 the Sixth Army, which consisted exclusively of regular Wehrmacht units, was encircled in Stalingrad by a surprise Red Army offensive. The German military command recommended a strategic withdrawal to save the army; Hitler insisted that they hold their ground. Over the next two months, despite repeated appeals for a withdrawal, Hitler continued to insist that the Sixth Army not abandon the *Festung Stalingrad.* Cut off from virtually all supplies, exposed on the Russian steppes to the bitter winter, the two hundred and fifty thousand soldiers of the German Sixth Army died from exposure, starvation, and enemy gunfire. In the final desperate days soldiers butchered the frozen corpses of their comrades and cooked their flesh on open fires. Only one in every hundred soldiers ever returned to Germany.

As I studied the military documentation regarding the decision-making process, read the various accounts of the battle, and interviewed the surviving veterans, I began to perceive a sense in which these soldiers had been victims of Hitler's blind fanaticism. A remarkable collection of primary source materials confirmed this belief: scores of letters by the German soldiers, written in the final weeks of the siege, that had fallen into the hands of the Red Army. The letters were powerful expressions of human emotion: men faced with certain death writing their last words to parents, wives, children. After two months of intensive research the issue became framed for me by two questions: to what degree was a twenty-two-year-old music student from Leipzig who was drafted into the Wehrmacht and dispatched to the Eastern Front also a victim of Hitler's policies? Did he not, after fifty years, deserve a decent burial?

In early January 1993 I traveled to Volgograd. In the bitter cold of the Russian winter, in a landscape of endless steppes, void of trees or protective hills and swept by a bitter wind, I visited the "bone fields" where the remains of German soldiers littered the fields. It was a scene of unparalleled desolation.

But I also took occasion to visit the graves of the fallen Red Army soldiers, where there were said to be as many as two million war dead—eight times the number of German soldiers. The immensity of Soviet losses, which had not been made public until the Gorbachev era, was overwhelming. Only after I had spoken with Red Army veterans, with the wives and children of Stalingrad fighters who had fallen, after I had had a chance to see firsthand the devastation caused by the German siege, and, finally, after I stood before the mass graves of the Red Army war dead—as many as ten thousand in a mound—did I realize that, for all the suffering of the individual German soldiers, to consider a German soldier a victim made a mockery of the Russian losses. In the end I backed away from my thesis, and, though I still feel sympathy for the German soldiers, their role as victims can in no way be equated with the suffering and the losses of the Soviets. This experience made me realize how important it is to visit the locations about which one writes, to test the ideas on the physical realities of location and on the people who inhabit them. For want of a better term, I refer to the "morality of place."

One of the most perplexing issues I have yet confronted, and one with which I continue to grapple, is that of Sudeten German property claims in the Czech Republic. Although property claims do not have the same evocative power as gas chambers, crematoria, and unburied remains, the Sudeten German "problem" may well be the most significant unresolved issue of the Nazi era. It is certainly the most complex in terms of its historical, legal, political, and moral implications.[1]

In the first two years following the collapse of Nazi rule in Europe—between May 1945 and early 1947—the Czechs expelled an estimated three million Germans from their country, confiscating their land, property, and financial instruments. In the course of these expulsions, referred to by the Allies as "population transfers," at least forty thousand Sudeten Germans—some estimates place the number as high as a quarter million—perished from physical abuse, disease, malnutrition, and exposure.

At the time, the expulsion of the Sudeten Germans from the territory of Czechoslovakia was seen as just retribution for the "betrayal" by the Sudeten Germans who welcomed Hitler's dissolution of Czechoslovakia and for the subsequent seven years of Nazi occupation. During the next half-century the expulsion of the Sudeten Germans was a nonissue. In 1989, following the collapse of communist rule and Václav Havel's call for the Czechs to confront "certain myths" about their past "regardless of the legal or material consequences," the Sudeten Germans began to lobby both in Bonn and Prague for the return of their confiscated property, estimated to be worth hundreds of billions of dollars.

When I began exploring this issue in 1994, it quickly became clear that from a historical and legal perspective the Sudeten Germans had a strong case for reclaiming their property. Germans had first settled the bordering regions of Bohemia and Moravia—known in German as the Sudetenland—as early as the thirteenth century, when they had responded to an invitation by the Czech king. For all intents and purposes the Sudetenland had been "German" land. Further, the laws under which the Sudeten German property was confiscated violated not only international conventions on human rights but also the constitution of the Czechoslovak Republic. From a moral point of view the troubling issue was an "amnesty law," passed in May 1946, mitigating all crimes—including torture, rape, and murder—committed against Germans in the months immediately following the end of Nazi rule.

As with the Sixth Army soldiers at Stalingrad, I was again confronted with the issue of Germans as victims, only this time the situation was more complex. The vast majority of the Sudeten German victims were women, children, the infirm, and the elderly, whose family roots in the region extended back hundreds of years and who had played no personal role in the vicious political developments of the region. There were also thirty thousand Sudeten German Social Democrats who had protested the German occupation of the Sudetenland in 1939. They had subsequently been imprisoned by the Nazis and, following the collapse of the Third Reich, had been expelled by the Czechs, along with the rest of the Sudeten Germans. There were countless eyewitness reports, from German and Czech sources, of the heinous crimes committed against the Sudeten Germans.

"We are seeing atrocities on a scale that equals anything perpetrated by the Nazis," wrote the *Times* of London in the autumn of 1945. One could also cite corroborative statements from the Czechoslovak government, including an admission of "atrocities" by President Eduard Beneš, who greeted the comparison with the National Socialists. "Recently, in the international press we have been criticized for excesses against our German population," Beneš said in November 1945. "They have said that we are simply imitating the brutalities of our former Nazi occupiers. Be that as it may, I state categorically: the Germans will leave our country, and they will leave it once and for all."

In trying to write a responsible treatment of this subject, I have been faced with a complex of historical, legal, and moral questions, at the root of which lies an irrepressible question: even though the Czechs' anger against the Sudeten Germans was understandable, was it any less of a crime for a Czech to seize a six-month-old German infant by the legs and smash its head against a lamppost in Prague than it was for a death camp attendant to force a three-year-old Jewish child into a gas chamber at Auschwitz? The question can barely be articulated, let alone answered. But we can answer that question, and, in fact, we have: each human life lost is a tragedy. Still, violence in a fit of passion *is* fundamentally different from premeditated, institutionalized genocide.

In the end I decided to write three different articles in order to disentangle the historical, legal, and moral issues from one another; the pieces have yet to appear. It is an imperfect solution but seems to be the only way to treat the subject in a fair and responsible manner. As with the German soldiers at Stalingrad, I argued that on balance the injustices committed against innocent German civilians, while reprehensible, were the price that the Germans were forced to pay for the excesses committed in the name of National Socialism. As I do not believe in the concept of collective guilt, or even collective responsibility, I think on balance this is the only honest conclusion that one can reach.

If, as William Randolph Hearst once asserted, journalists provide the "first draft of history," the initial account of past events is by necessity a rough draft, one filled with arbitrary—often fortuitous—encounters and one that generally contains many more deletions than inclusions. It may well be the task of the journalist to raise some of these concerns, to bring them to the attention of the public at large and then rely on scholars to explore the subtleties and complexities of the issues. The journalist and scholar engage in a common cause: the conveyance of information, opinions, and ideas. "If history is to share its insights with a public in need of them, it must practice communication as an art," Barbara Tuchman observed in *Practicing History*. "Research provides the material, and theory the pattern of thought, but it is through communication that history is heard and understood." Theodore Roosevelt put a finer point on the issue back in 1912, when, in a speech before the American Historical Association, he observed: "Writings are useless unless they are read, and they cannot be read unless they are readable." At their best good scholarship and responsible journalism become indistinguishable from each other.

Despite the efforts of the journalist to provide the first draft of history and the efforts of the scholar to fashion, in successive generations, the subsequent drafts, the final word, as we know, is never written. Yet we all remain engaged in the same enterprise: following in the wake of historical events—literary, social, political, economic, historical—sometimes at close range and sometimes from afar, and fashioning from the detritus we collect our own versions of the past. Be it deciding on the Auschwitz experience of Elie Wiesel, Primo Levi, or the Holocaust survivor from southern California, we are, in the end, writing our own interpretations of the past, fact-based fictions, as it were. In recognizing both the limitations and the potential of historical writing—whether it be by the scholar or the journalist—the New York photographer David Levinthal, who has worked extensively with images from the Nazi era, expressed both the futility and the potential of rendering past events when he observed: "History is a past that never was and always will be."

NOTE

1. This essay was conceived and completed long before the signing of the Czech Re-public–German agreement of December 1996. Sadly, that "agreement" does not—at least to date—appear to have resolved the issues Ryback raises here. If anything, it has flamed moral indignation on both sides yet again. For these reasons we have decided not to alter Ryback's original analysis. The editors.

CHAPTER 22

Who Owns the Past? The Surrender of the Berlin Document Center

Geoffrey J. Giles

Regardless of the creativity of the scholar, an empirical foundation must exist in order for the product to be valuable and enduring. Since archival repositories constitute a fundamental part of this foundation, their upkeep and accessibility are crucial to individuals in a variety of disciplines. Historian Geoffrey Giles discusses recent developments regarding the Berlin Document Center (BDC), the archive that houses over seventy-five million pages of documents from the Third Reich. An invaluable resource in the prosecution of Nazi war criminals and now a means of proving German heritage that is sometimes valuable to those wishing to immigrate, the BDC has long elicited ambivalent feelings from the Germans, who have attempted both to master their past and to get on with other projects in their development as a nation. Because of the sensitive nature of these holdings, the transfer of authority from the U.S. State Department to the German Federal Archives stirred controversy not only about the care and management of historical documents but also about "who owns the past." This affair did not remain confined to Americans and Germans, nor to historians and government officials; rather, an impassioned debate raged throughout the world.

Giles chairs the German Studies Association subcommittee on archives, which endeavors to facilitate scholars' access to repositories as well as oversee the physical condition and the organizational schema of their contents. These are issues that are critical to the future of scholarship: governments must be prevented from concealing valuable information; archives must be safeguarded against theft or willful destruction; the physical deterioration (often a problem due to the poor quality and acidic paper used throughout much of this century) must be arrested; and new computer resources must be brought to bear in the ordering and cataloging of ever more voluminous archival materials. As

Giles shows in his essay, the transfer of the BDC involved nearly all of these issues. His contribution, then, constitutes a report both to the academic community and to a general public who look to scholars for information they believe they are not getting from their governments.

Why do people read history books? Many would offer an answer along these lines: history helps us to understand who we are; it teaches us about ourselves and our own society, sometimes through the filter of other people and other societies. Nations take responsibility for preserving important historical documents about their history in archives. Everyone can go to see the Declaration of Independence at the National Archives in Washington, DC. The government would like you to do so. It embodies something quintessentially American: the assertion of freedom against tyranny. In London one can view the Magna Carta, that great charter of personal and political liberty wrested by the barons from King John in the year 1215. It embodies something quintessentially English: the assertion of freedom against tyranny. For many decades Soviet citizens filed past the very body of Lenin, leader of the Russian Revolution, no doubt reflecting as they came face to face with the embalmed corpse that he embodied something quintessentially Russian: the assertion of freedom against tyranny. And so one could continue for other countries. These three examples alone provide us with a telling lesson about history: for here we have a republic, a constitutional monarchy, and a totalitarian state all using historical artifacts in order to emphasize their legitimacy by reminding people just how bad things were before some significant turning point, the heirs of which the (current) government represents.

It is well-known that in communist Eastern Europe the writing of history was unblushingly partisan. If the historical record did not provide the desired version of the truth, then documents were simply altered or written from scratch before being deposited in the archives. As late as 1989, officials in the East German Education Ministry were still insisting to historians, who had gathered to revise history textbooks, that they must not deviate from the maxim "The Party is *always* right!" We like to think that nothing like this could ever happen in the West, but let us remember that a government, like any other institution, sifts and culls its files, so that in many cases a ministry only deposits those documents in an archive that it *wants* historians to read. No wonder that great nineteenth-century pioneer of access to primary sources, Lord Acton, eventually noted in despair, "The documents are liars." Sometimes an institution refuses to surrender its old papers to the archives, knowing that they will then become public. Not so long ago in Vienna an elderly civil servant from the Education Ministry handed over a seriously overdue consignment of files to the National Archives literally one by one, taking leave of each file almost tearfully. And, sure enough, potentially embarrassing documents—for example, on disciplinary infractions by students and teachers—simply did not make it to the archive.

There is a wonderful episode of that devastatingly revealing British comedy series "Yes, Minister" in which the ministry's senior career civil servant, Sir Humphrey, just does not want his minister to see a particular file. When the minister insists, Humphrey finally produces it, and the folder is found to hold a succession of notes explaining that some portions of the materials *formerly* in the file were lost in the move to a new building, others in the floods of 1956, and so on. Apart from these notes, the file turns out to be completely empty. This little vignette will sound very familiar to many historians working today. In the standard scenario for Nazi records one is told that they were destroyed during the war. That is not always true.

At the end of March 1945 an order went out from Berlin requiring all offices affiliated with the Nazi Party to destroy their files, and, indeed, bonfires were built all over Germany. Yet, in the chaos surrounding the German collapse, the sheer bulk of the records, produced by Germany's biggest ever bureaucracy, meant that not all were lost for the historian. In April 1945 American troops found a huge cache of Party documents at a paper mill outside Munich, still waiting to be pulped. Others were discovered inside a salt mine near Berchtesgaden, and gradually several other important collections were captured that had not yet been presorted for posterity. With a view to utilizing them as evidence in the coming war crimes trials, the files were collected in Berlin and by 1947 all stored in one location, an underground, former phone-tapping facility known thereafter as the Berlin Document Center (BDC).

This has subsequently become the single most important center for historical research on Nazi Germany anywhere in the world. Although located in Zehlendorf, a suburb of Berlin, the BDC remained until July 1994 under American control, first of the military government and, from 1953, that of the U.S. State Department. It contains the following major collections:

> The membership master file of the Nazi Party (NSDAP), containing index cards with personal details on some ten million Party members, or 85–90 percent of the total membership. In July 1948 an American committee reported to the military government for Germany (OMGUS) that this collection was of "no historical value." Fortunately for scholars, these utterly invaluable records were nevertheless not turned to pulp.

1.28 million files of Party correspondence with or about members, often highlighting the declared or unspoken aims of various branches and rich in material on personal disputes, sometimes over issues of Party ideology.

53,000 personnel files on SS (Schutzstaffel) officers, following their careers, with related letters of recommendation, criticism, or denunciation.

240,000 files from the SS racial office (RuSHA), containing biographical information both on SS men and on their wives, often with a marriage application form, testifying to the racial purity of both parties.

10,000 files on individual stormtroopers (SA), drawn from personnel records and disciplinary proceedings.

135,000 personnel files for members of various sections of the office controlling cultural affairs (Reichskulturkammer) and the Propaganda Ministry, permitting a rich understanding of cultural policy and of the ideological activities of individual artists and authors.

2.9 million index cards forming the central registry of the immigration office (Einwandererzentralstelle) collections. This was the agency that dealt with the repatriation of ethnic Germans. Its detailed records on individuals, still used extensively today by the German government in determining the eligibility of pension or welfare claimants, amounted to over fifty-two tons of paper. They include 110,000 citizenship application files from the Soviet Union; 100,000 from Poland; 82,000 from Rumania; 73,000 from the Baltic states; 23,000 from Yugoslavia; 14,000 from France; and 700 from Bulgaria. The so-called Rassekartei contains 846,000 index cards documenting the results of racial examinations for the racial suitability of would-be German citizens.

Other categories deal with disciplinary proceedings in the SA (ca. 26,000 records); in the Hitler Youth (HJ) (11,000 records); and in the Party itself, in which some 50,000 case files from the Supreme Party Court have survived (see *Holdings*).

All this, then, represents a source for research into German history that was unparalleled in its bounty, at least until the discovery of the millions of Stasi files in the Normannenstrasse in 1989. To what use were they put, however? Not to portray Germany in the way all governments like—as a great, generous, humane, free society. The only possible result of honest research in these records is to show the country in its worst light. In time this came to be viewed, I would suggest, as a thorn in the flesh of the emerging Federal Republic, which sought to spread good news about Germany.

While the BDC records were being actively used by the prosecutors in the

Nuremberg trials, there was no question of their being returned to the German authorities. Soon, however, American official interest in retaining ownership of all the files appeared to wane. The Berlin Blockade led in 1948 to the airlifting of 288 tons of documents out of Berlin, especially German Foreign Office records, which for that generation of historians provided a main focus of attention. These were evaluated by a team of scholars at Whaddon Hall in England and selected for eventual publication.

This continued a tradition set after World War I, when the German Reichsarchiv had published a long series of volumes of diplomatic documents, in an attempt to prove the nation's innocence in the outbreak of the war. Other countries then felt obliged to follow suit, in order to demonstrate their own peaceloving foreign policy in the decades before 1914. This precedent was followed again immediately after 1939, and now the Allies were attempting to correct the German version of events with the latter's own official documents. These Foreign Office files were not properly part of the BDC's collection, which focused on biographical information about the activities of individuals within the Nazi movement. The new Foreign Office of the Federal Republic of Germany wanted to have them returned to its own safekeeping and began to press the U.S. authorities for a transfer.

When at the beginning of 1952 it was estimated that 250,000 name searches at the BDC might be expected during the course of the year, but only one quarter of them from U.S. agencies, the high commissioner called for a new assessment of the need to retain German records, many further tons of which had been evacuated to Alexandria, Virginia, during the Berlin airlift. By the end of the year a "Statement of Policy regarding the Return of Seized German Documents" was finalized, which agreed to return to the Federal Republic of Germany all files that did not fall under certain categories. Among the reserved groups were:

> Documents tending to glorify the Nazi regime or which are of inherent propaganda character, or which deal with the organization, personnel and operation of Nazi Party institutions, except where such transfer would not jeopardize the democratic way of life in the FRG. . . . All materials which are uniquely a part of the German cultural heritage will, subject to provisions . . . preceding, be returned to the FRG at an early date. (Wolfe xviii)

This, then, established the principle of return as the normal development but also appeared, through the reference to personnel matters, to exclude most of the holdings of the BDC.

The army, which still controlled and bore the expense of running the BDC, realized this and, foreseeing all manner of complaints by the German government, immediately tried to pull out by suggesting that the U.S. State Department should be given control. The army was not interested in history, and its letter of justification reveals where its main concerns lay:

> These records are political in nature and of little current value to the Army in Europe. The Center is expensive to operate and there is a trend toward more foreign utilization. . . . The records contain little or no material of value in the current effort against communism and are of decreasing usefulness in combating right-wing elements. . . . The West German Government is becoming more and more demanding in its effort to obtain custody of the captured records. . . . Any records to be transferred to the United States or otherwise disposed of in such a manner that they will never be returned to the Germans, [should] be acted upon as soon as possible. (Wolfe xix)

The State Department did assume custody of the BDC on 1 October 1953 and moved to return many captured German records outside the BDC (but very few in it) to German control following the acquisition of full sovereignty by the Federal Republic in 1955. Thus, the German Foreign Office records were returned from Whaddon Hall to Bonn between 1956 and 1958, and they in fact included personnel files. This is a crucial case that bears upon concerns expressed by historians in 1994, because the Foreign Office, while answering specific questions from scholars about the contents of these files, consistently *refused* to allow anyone actually to examine them (until 1989). The State Department continued its policy of returning nonbiographical files and handed over to the German Federal Archives (Bundesarchiv) between 1959 and 1962 a considerable collection from the central archives of the Nazi Party (NSDAP-Hauptarchiv) after it had been microfilmed at the Hoover Institution.

In March 1967 word leaked out that the BDC had information on the Nazi activities of the German chancellor, Kurt Georg Kiesinger, causing some tension in relations between the United States and the Federal Republic. A deputy in the German parliament demanded that the whole archive be handed back to the Germans, on the grounds that German voters had a right to know about the Nazi past of public figures. Investigative reporters began bothering the BDC with requests for information about other politicians, and the State Department wondered aloud whether to wash its hands of the entire collection. American scholars raised the alarm, in response to which the State Department promised to microfilm all files of any value to research. Between 1968 and 1972 three biographical collections were, in fact, filmed at a rather sluggish pace, which suited the German government well, so it is rumored. After the Kiesinger affair, and in the radical political atmosphere created by the student revolutions of 1968, the government wanted to head off the embarrassing scandals that the BDC files might unleash and found it quite convenient *not* to have control of the archive for the present. Objections were not raised when the microfilming project fizzled out: "I don't think the Germans really wanted the documents," said [Donald] Kobletz, the former State Department lawyer. "There's a lot of showmanship on both sides of this issue. It's a bit of a hot potato for everybody" (Atkinson).

German scholars, who had to apply to German authorities, not the U.S. State Department, for permission to work in the BDC collections, found their access increasingly denied. Probably as a result of further public pressure, the German government unhurriedly sat down at the negotiating table with the United States in June 1979 for formal talks on the return of the BDC, which were resumed the following year in Washington, DC, and ended in an ad referendum agreement by which the BDC would be given over to the Germans when its entire holdings had been microfilmed. It is important to note the tentative nature of the agreement, which was never formalized by the two governments, nor did the microfilming start up again. The status quo persisted, though consciences had been salved by the agreement that on paper gave the impression of a satisfactory conclusion.

Sleeping dogs continued to lie quite peacefully until the end of 1987, when the question of ownership burst onto the pages of the international press with a vengeance. Some ten thousand documents, bearing the original signature of famous Nazis, especially SS officers, had been stolen over a period of time by at least one BDC staff member and sold to collectors of Nazi and military memorabilia, many of them abroad. This proved to be the turning point. Now the German government could no longer shirk its responsibility. The country's historical heritage, however unseemly, was being bartered away behind the backs of its apparently incompetent American guardians (though in actual fact only one member of the BDC staff, namely its director, was not German). The German government promised in 1988 to provide complete funding for the microfilming project, which resumed in June 1989.

The U.S. State Department wrote in December 1990 that "at our present rate of filming, we anticipate finishing the entire collection in 1995. At that time we will formalize the agreement on the return." In fact, both sides were under pressure to move more swiftly, and the formal agreement on the transfer was concluded in October 1993. When word of this began to percolate through to the scholarly community, there was some concern, principally over continued access to the original documents, should the microfilmed copy prove to be inadequate. Some historians in this country, who had happy memories of the generous cooperation of the BDC in their research, had also experienced a few singularly unhelpful archivists elsewhere in Germany (though never in the Bundesarchiv itself). Moreover, many scholars dislike the eyestrain that long hours in front of a microfilm reader entail and seek to avoid it when the original documents are available.

These concerns exploded with the March 1994 publication in the *New Yorker* of an article by Gerald Posner, entitled "Secrets from the Files." It quoted a number of historians, including myself, expressing their doubts about the continued provision of unrestricted access at the same level that we had hitherto enjoyed. The 1988 Federal Archives Law, while ostensibly supportive of scholarship, was also very firm on personal privacy considerations. That has frequently been interpreted by German archives below the federal level to mean that only *copies* of certain documents shall be given to historical researchers, with the names blacked out, thus sabotaging the inquiry in some cases. Michael Kater was quoted in the article as saying, "The restrictions in the law, coupled with the level of discretion granted to the archivist, worries me." It was reported that even Alfred Streim, one of Germany's leading war crimes prosecutors, had recently been fobbed off by the Bundesarchiv, with documents such as name lists with some of the names blacked out (Posner). The comments in the article of the future German director of the BDC did nothing to allay the fears. Dietrich Krüger noted: "I am bound by the law and must protect the privacy of the person for thirty years after his death. I will sometimes have to reject access to original documents. I believe that this law is the right approach." The fact that access for historians is not guaranteed or codified but is, instead, dependent on the goodwill of the individual archivist of the moment was underlined in his next remark: "If a researcher is interested in a serious treatment of the past, then that is fine. [But] if someone is interested only in finding out whether a politician was a Party member, then that is not historically useful." The specter of the 1968 generation was clearly still exercising a powerful influence. Then Krüger really set the cat among the pigeons by hinting that any American scholar would as a matter of course be denied access to the original documents in the future, if he could not "demonstrate why the microfilm [was] not adequate for his purposes." The National Archives in Washington would have a copy of the entire holdings for the use of American scholars, and therefore, said Krüger, "if there is not a serious need for the original, then they should use the microfilm."

The article closed with remarks by officials of the U.S. Holocaust Memorial Museum, the World Jewish Congress, the Anti-Defamation League, and, finally, from Simon Wiesenthal, who said: "The document center is very important because if you are looking up whether somebody is a Nazi, you can see the whole development of that man, what he says in his own words in his autobiography—those papers simply don't allow people to lie in later years. Those documents are a holy matter" (Posner).

At this signal American citizens from all over the United States are said to have flooded Congress with letters of concern. Congressman Tom Lantos, himself a Holocaust survivor and chairman of the House Foreign Affairs Subcommittee on International Security and Human Rights, scheduled a hearing on Capitol Hill to consider whether to block the transfer at the eleventh hour. Professor Henry Friedlander and I were summoned to testify on behalf of the profession. Essentially, it was too late, because a formal treaty had already been concluded between the United States and Germany, but that did not stop the committee from taking the State Department to task. And the rhetoric rose to a fever pitch in public. Elan Steinberg, executive director of the World Jewish Congress, lamented that "we are transferring away a piece of history that we paid for with the blood of our brave young American boys and Allied soldiers who defeated the Nazi menace" (Fesperman).

There was, indeed, a clear flaw in the treaty negotiated by the State Department inasmuch as it only guaranteed continued access to the original documents for U.S. government officials, meaning principally staff investigating war crimes from the Office of Special Investigations (OSI). The needs of scholars were ignored altogether. Therefore, the chairman of the House sub-committee, Mr. Lantos, insisted that guarantees of access for *all* Americans should be secured from the German government by the State Department—or else. As he put it in closing the hearing, "The alternative is for this issue to go very public with all of the concerns and all of the issues fully debated on the floor of the House of Representatives, and I am sure on the floor of the Senate." That could clearly explode into a major scandal. As Lantos gently hinted, "I do not think it is in the interest of the German government to have a major congressional debate on Germany's Nazi past and the question of possible unwillingness to make available materials to organizations, individuals, scholars, researchers, affected parties in the United States and elsewhere" (Transcript).

Congress, then, had struck a blow for the individual scholar here. Admittedly, the most important clients of the BDC were state and local governmental agencies, who submitted in 1993, for example, twenty-seven thousand requests for information. Private individuals, including scholars and journalists together, investigated only thirteen hundred cases. But there is surely a strong case for stating that it is among those few in the academic world that the greatest advances in our understanding and insight into the nature of the Third Reich arise.

During May 1994 the State Department undoubtedly scurried to prevent potential embarrassment to its leadership but was pipped at the post by independent action from the World Jewish Congress. Ignoring the procedures determined by the congressional hearing in which it had participated, its leaders insisted on their own immediate and private meeting with Chancellor Kohl and Foreign Minister Kinkel, at which they extracted a verbal promise that the conditions of access to the BDC would remain unchanged, at least for the transition period until the full availability of the microfilms in the United States

(Atkinson). As expected, the surrender of the BDC took place on schedule on 1 July but in a cautiously low-key manner. The media were excluded from the transfer ceremony. Only afterward was a news conference held, as the old Berlin Document Center sign just inside the barbed-wire compound was replaced by a more considerable mouthful: "Bundesarchiv, Aussenstelle Berlin-Zehlendorf, ehemaliges BDC" (Federal Archive, Berlin-Zehlendorf Branch, Former BDC). The president of the Bundesarchiv, Friedrich Kahlenberg, told the reporters gathered there: "I believe much of the mistrust as reflected in the U.S. media stems from the fact that too little is known about the work of the Federal Archives. I hope that our work in the future will allay the lack of trust and the fears" (Waetjen). The vice president, Siegfried Büttner, gave an assurance that "the law on posthumous privacy will not pose a problem for users of the BDC" ("Berlin"). Becoming more explicit, he stated: "Requests will be handled in exactly the same way. There will be no changes whatsoever in the availability of records" (Gedye). This seemed to be a reassuring last word on the subject.

Who, then, owns the past? In this case Germany has satisfied the craving for national sovereignty over its (in this case, sordid) past as represented in certain archival records. Yet the United States has a copy of the entire seventy-five million pages, on forty thousand rolls of microfilm. Initially, there were well-grounded fears that some sort of agreement was being negotiated between the U.S. National Archives and the German Federal Archives, whereby the former would respect the posthumous privacy rights of German citizens in granting access to these files. That has proved not to be the case. The Freedom of Information Act, which governs access to records in this country, *can* be used to withhold documents if they would result in the "unwarranted invasion of privacy of a living individual." That would indeed apply to many of the BDC files, which are still used extensively by the German government to check the pension rights of ethnic Germans from the former Soviet Union and elsewhere. Moreover, German practice requires the credentials of each researcher to be approved before he or she is admitted to an archive. Dozens, and possibly hundreds, of West German scholarly historians were kept out of the BDC by the *German* authorities in this way in past decades. The policy of the National Archives in the United States, however, is quite different and follows the British practice. There the name of the national repository of important historical records openly proclaims its policy: the *Public* Record Office. In Britain the public owns the past, and anyone can stop by without any special clearance, fill out an order form, and handle, say, a fourteenth-century manuscript, as many do in pursuit of family history. In the United States, too, the policy on access is an open one. Archivists may not deny entry to any user. This policy has in fact been challenged in the past and has stood firm. In the ringing phrase of the relevant court decision, "Congress granted the scholar and the scoundrel equal rights of access to agency records." Particular records may still be classified and withheld, but, under American law, once a document has been released, it may *never again* be closed or redacted (Kurtz). That means that names could not then be blacked out, as is, and will certainly continue to be, the case in Germany with some of the BDC files.

The good news is that President Clinton signed an order in November 1994 declassifying some forty-four million documents from World War II and the Vietnam War in which were included the entire holdings of the former BDC. Thus, anyone now has open access to these files, as soon as user copies become available. On 12 December 1994 the National Archives released the first batch of almost three thousand rolls of microfilmed SS records. The overall duplication of the master film was completed in May 1996.

In this way the culture of openness that this country espouses has been subtly imposed upon the records of this period of the German past. The more guarded approach to archival policies in Germany has not been allowed to prevail, to the detriment of historical research. In fact, the files are now *more* open than ever. Even the American directors of the BDC occasionally denied access to the archive in the past. I have it on good authority that the British, neo-Nazi historian David Irving was once turned away from the gates in his Rolls-Royce. Henceforth "the scholar *and* the scoundrel" will be able to conduct exhaustive research into the Third Reich. The BDC microfilms will surely lead to a spurt in new research on Nazi Germany among graduate students in this country, who will no longer have to go to the expense of flying to Berlin for extended periods. In a sense this imposes greater responsibilities upon us historians to proceed with our researches in a timely and thorough fashion, in order to demonstrate clearly that this policy and this trust are well placed. In Germany we have for many years sought this trust; we have asked to be treated as conscientious scholars rather than scandalmongers, and the record has shown historians to have acted responsibly in the overwhelming number of cases. It has become a convention to protect the privacy of victims by giving only their initials; this does not apply to the perpetrators, who lose any such rights by their actions. The goal of the historian is to lay bare the truth, and that truth, at least for the Nazi period, is invariably unpleasant. If history is to teach any lessons, then the negative examples it can provide are too important to be hidden. If we believe that, then the Third Reich is not just German history but all our histories.

WORKS CITED

Atkinson, Rick. "Germany Set to Reclaim Files on Its Sinister Past." *Washington Post,* 30 May 1994.

"Berlin Document Center Passes into German Hands; Accessibility Will Remain, Officials Say." *The Week in Germany,* 8 July 1994.

Fesperman, Dan. "Turnover of Nazi Files to Germany Stirs Fear." *Baltimore Sun,* 29 June 1994.

Gedye, Robin. "America Returns Nazi War Archive." *Daily Telegraph,* 2 July 1994.

The Holdings of the Berlin Document Center: A Guide to the Collections. Berlin: Berlin Document Center, 1994.

Kurtz, Michael J. "The Opening of Berlin Document Center Records at the National Archives." In *Archivists and Historians: The Crucial Partnership,* ed. Geoffrey J. Giles. Washington, DC: German Historical Institute. Occasional Paper No. 17, 1996. 29–31.

Posner, Gerald. "Secrets of the Files." *New Yorker,* 14 March 1994, 39–47.

Transcript of Hearing before the Subcommittee on International Security, International Organizations and Human Rights of the Committee on Foreign Affairs, House of Representatives. 103d Congress, 2d Sess., 28 April 1994: U.S.-German Agreement on the Transfer to German Control of Nazi Party Records in the Berlin Document Center. Washington, DC: U.S. Government Printing Office, 1994. 38–39.

Waetjen, Stephanie. "Germany Takes Control of Nazi Document Center." Reuters News Service, 1 July 1994.

Wolfe, Robert. "Preface." In *Holdings of the Berlin Document Center: A Guide to the Collections.* Berlin: Berlin Document Center, 1994. xi–xxii.

Part Seven

TEACHING GERMAN CULTURAL STUDIES

Cultural studies is, as Kacandes points out in her essay, an activist project. Its practitioners aim to make our society better: through mutual understanding of others and their differences; through critical, informed study of power and its manifestations in the products of culture; and through thoughtful, committed teaching. Without the symbiosis between research and teaching, between the library and the classroom, the cultural studies project would produce only desiccated, lifeless facts. The five essays in part 7 concern themselves with aspects of teaching and the profession. Willson underscores the importance of translation for scholarship and especially for the classroom. Henke addresses questions of the canon and the study of materials from older periods and puts forward methodological theses about teaching "the classics" in a cultural studies context. Classroom methods are specifically addressed by Ortmayer in his essay on case study teaching, a means for students and teachers to engage course materials that is as open and contentious and full of negotiation as the cultural studies project itself. Hunt gives the evolutionary history of a model German cultural studies course and reflects on his own role as a teacher of future teachers. And Gilman offers some pragmatic professional suggestions for beginning teachers and scholars of German cultural studies.

CHAPTER 23

Translation in Cultural Mediation and Pedagogy

A. Leslie Willson

This essay is a call to keep in mind the role of the literary realm in the cultural studies project. Key to the success of any interdisciplinary undertaking is the availability of materials for teaching and research. In the study of any aspect of a foreign culture good translations of literary, political, historical, and cultural documents of all types are vital to the success of moving cultural studies work from the library to the classroom, from the desks of scholars trained in one culture's traditions and texts to those of others, and from the campuses of academia into the homes of the general public. Leslie Willson is one of the people who developed the kinds of courses that set the stage for German studies in one of the oldest German departments in the United States (at the University of Texas at Austin). What was so unique about these courses was that they set individual texts into compelling contexts. Though Willson clearly situates himself within the rubric of German studies, without foundational work like his, German cultural studies simply would not be possible. For more than a quarter of a century he edited DIMENSION: Contemporary German Arts and Letters, *a literary magazine that made accessible important new German writing to an Anglophone audience. Willson, a literary translator himself, a Germanist, and a coauthor with John Van Cleve of the polemic work* Remarks on the Needed Reform of German Studies in the United States *(1993), continues his call here for available English-language literary texts for teaching, especially in courses outside of traditional German department literature offerings.*

While the editors understand a cultural studies approach to mean more than simply adding a "literary component" to a "culture course," as Kacandes makes clear in the introduction, Willson's piece rightfully underscores the vital role of literary texts as mediators of cultural knowledge; and Willson calls for us to use English translations of German texts in doing just this. Further-

more, teachers must demand that translations be of high quality and remain in print. Good translations and successful book design do enhance the quality of the reader's experience. This essay is also a plea for what we as scholars must not neglect to do: let publishers know what we need. A fitting message on the bumper sticker sometimes seen in the vicinity of writers' workshops—"People Who Really Love Poetry Buy It"—holds here, too.

In its slow growth to being the most widespread designation for the study of various aspects of Germany—including its political, economic, historic, geographic, philosophical, literary, and linguistic aspects—German studies is still in the process of evolution toward maturation. From the beginning, however, an essential ingredient has been the use of translations in the study of Germany and its many facets. It is, naturally, impossible that every student who turns to German studies, whatever that student's interest, can know the language well enough to read all primary texts in German. The importance of translations for German studies cannot be stressed enough—and possibly no other ingredient can produce equal frustration and perplexity when translations turn out to be flawed or, even worse, simply not there.

Whereas the term *German studies* originally did not include the study of the language and literature of Germany but, rather, focused mainly on sociological, historical, political, and humanistic topics, the term has become more and more preferred for entities in higher education that *do* include the study of language and literature. Departments of German Studies offer courses, in addition to those in language and literature, that concentrate on geography, theater, philosophy, intellectual history, political theory, film, art, music, and literary translation itself. For some reason unfathomable to me, many faculties that offer *cultural* emphases in their curricula sternly omit or deny the importance of and inclusion of literature as a vehicle of mediation in their consideration of what constitutes culture. The word *culture* itself, as in "culture course" (always a vague and thus exceedingly beneficial description, allowing a teacher to examine any subject whatsoever), has been superseded by the term *German studies,* which is more catholic and all-embracing and just as liable to the widest kind of interpretation—which is not a bad thing in itself but which becomes a bad thing only when it is used to limit the vision of any teacher.

In cultural mediation—that is, in German studies courses that consider art, music, philosophy, history, politics, sociological problems (e.g., the role and plight of the guest worker in Germany), the Holocaust, National Socialism, the separation and reunification of the two German states, the Economic Miracle—too many teachers generally have neglected to include a literary component, a grave error, in my judgment. Novels, plays, poems, radio plays, biography, autobiography, and even critical essays on literary subjects often are exemplary in their ability to convey a penetrating depiction relative to those areas generally grouped under the heading of *culture*. The insights of authors and literary critics, and their more than occasional talent in rendering accurate and illuminating portrayals of personal and social behavior, whether in a cosmopolitan or a rural setting, can add compelling dimensions to a factual study of history, politics, and the arts. A teacher of distinction will not omit the reading of literary texts to elucidate a great variety of topics.

During my years of teaching I often offered courses in what can be called German studies in a supraliterary sense: courses with a sociological, political, artistic, or historical content, or a combination of two or more of those and others, but based exclusively on German-authored literary texts in English translation for students whose German was not sufficient to read primary texts.

One course was entitled "The Author/Artist" and introduced students to contemporary authors, along with a short survey of author/artists from the past (from Grimmelshausen to Hesse) who also are graphic artists, who in graphic works make use of their artistic talents to explore, examine, even test and highlight their literary metaphors and themes. Among the twenty contemporary authors discussed in the course were Friedrich Dürrenmatt (who previewed his themes on canvas and drawing paper), Günter Grass (an author whose artistic talents are an indelible part of his creative process), Günter Kunert (whose almost impish illustrations often comment wryly on his themes in prose and poetry), and Peter Weiss (whose fantasy is expanded in original collages, as in those accompanying *Shadow of the Coachman's Body*). The very essence of the artistic temperament and even aesthetic theory and performance, as well as the themes of authors—often political; critical of society; opposed to war; politically, sociologically, or racially biased—were the focal points of students' readings.

Another course was entitled "Society as Reflected in a Poetic Eye" and concentrated on the concerns, problems, and struggles of contemporary German society through the study of German poems in English translation that reflected concerns, problems, and struggles, ranging from horror about war, awe at and fear of the atom bomb, the concern for the poor, and worry about rapacious destruction on our planet through scientific and industrial excesses by contemporary man. The English-language sources for the course were taken mostly from literary magazines, principally *Dimension;* I translated some poems myself specifically for inclusion in the course.

More than twenty years ago I offered a course entitled "The Nazi Experience." Sources were all in English, either translations of various literary and historical works or volumes written in English (e.g., William L. Shirer's famous historical volume, *The Rise and Fall of the Third Reich,* as well as a biography of Hitler). I never enjoyed a livelier and more vibrant class. By sheer accident the class was made up of equal numbers of Jewish and non-Jewish students. Even more incredibly, the father of one student in class had been a Luftwaffe pilot and the father of another a captain on a German U-boat—in neither family was there ever a discussion of the paternal past. Jewish students brought family albums, essentially Holocaust albums, for the class to peruse. I was in terrified awe of one student who had made himself an expert regarding the battlegrounds and war matériel of World War II on the continent of Europe; he did not hesitate to correct my slightest unwitting misrepresentation of a military campaign. For the first and only time during my career in the classroom did my students address me by my seldom used first name, Amos. And I assented humbly to that impertinence.

One course for college freshmen, which included a substantial writing component, was entitled "A Journey up the Rhine" and introduced students to the Dutch Rhine delta, to the course of Germany's greatest river from historical, political, geographic, economic, artistic, and literary perspectives, all the way to its Swiss source. It was truly a voyage of discovery. The possibilities for exploration and discovery were in each instance infinite, and a variety of students availed themselves generously of their freedom to explore and discover. In the required short papers and a final long paper they were encouraged to pursue their own interests, which were broad ranging. One student, a prospective architect, submitted an exquisitely illustrated treatise on the construction of the Cologne Cathedral. Another student researched in great depth the work of a medieval nun, whose name she discovered in our makeshift textbook. The students needed texts in English, which often proved to be a problem. Our principal text was Baedeker's *Rhine* in English. The scarcity of translations available for the course was matched by a lack of material in other media, principally video and film, which made the whole enterprise especially challenging to professor and students.

There is now, and there always has been, a paucity of German works in translation for use in schools and universities. Even extant translations of authors are not always useful; early translations of some philosophers, historians, and other thinkers have turned out to be faulty and often have not been redone, so that a teacher necessarily has to elucidate excessively. Recent translations of Nietzsche have replaced the flawed early ones. The exceedingly poor translations of the work of Kafka, done by a husband and wife who publicly admitted their hatred and disdain for the German language, are at last being replaced. New and improved translations of Rilke are obtainable.

Authors whose works are useful because of excellent translations may well be unavailable because editions have gone out of print and are now not easily accessible for wide use by students. Even works by an author as popular—and useful for political, sociological, historical, and artistic purposes—as Günter Grass are too often simply not to be found on publishers' lists today. For one class I myself resorted to translating Reinhard Goering's *Seeschlacht* (Battle at Sea) for a class that was reading antiwar texts; it had never been translated, as far as I could discover. The extensive work of a monumental author, Nobel Prize recipient Heinrich Böll—whose work, ranging from wartime fables to tales of postwar political, economic, and social conflicts and problems, including the birth pangs of a new German republic, has largely gone out of print—fortunately has found a new publisher, the University of Nebraska Press, which has agreed to reprint everything. The importance of Böll for German studies should be obvious, since his themes include religious perplexities, freedom of expression, feminist sensibilities, and simple and enduring struggles in a society in upheaval.

Other sources for translations useful for the classroom are selected Penguin Books volumes, assorted works under the imprint of George Braziller; New Directions; Farrar, Straus and Giroux; Harcourt Brace Jovanovich; Pantheon (now defunct); several small presses and "little" magazines. The University of Nebraska Press features a series devoted to European women writers. Of great service is Continuum's German Library series: in one hundred volumes (some sixty of which are now available in hardback and paperback) Continuum will eventually offer selected texts and works by Germany's poets, novelists, scientists, philosophers, psychologists, and historians.

The bifurcation of Germany, which divided a nation into two halves with conflicting political and social goals, presented an arena for the scrutiny of a desperate struggle. The works of the late Uwe Johnson and Jurek Becker, as well as those of Christa Wolf, offer fertile ground for the examination of the consciences of those who lived in the East and West. Fortunately, the writings of all three authors are largely accessible in English translation. The East-West division was not eliminated by the fall of the Wall, and the confusion and alienation that remain will furnish stuff for examination and discussion for decades to come. For example, now that authors and others have access to files compiled on them by the former East German State Police, the despised Stasi, a voluminous amount of material will afford a rare glimpse into the inner workings of a state secret police and the enormity of a government's interference in public and private freedom of expression.

A preponderance of German studies courses involve contemporary themes—the enduring legacy of the Holocaust, the rise and fall and sporadic renewal of Nazi ideology, the struggle of a great society to recover from a disastrous past, the rise of new cultural directions, new sociological experiments, new literary styles, and the persistent examination of language and character. Students can benefit from close readings of works that engage such considerations and examinations, but, to close the enormous gap between those who know and are informed and those who are largely ignorant and even uncaring about what goes on in Germany today, there must be texts in English translation.

Teachers who are involved with German studies in its largest sense should become more aware of the availability (and unavailability) of texts in translation and should insist that publishers make such texts available and keep them in print and accessible for classroom use. Teachers who are able should resort to the translation of texts themselves and should encourage the increasing recognition of the work of academicians who approach texts through this closest kind of reading—namely, translation. Teachers who use works in translation should not hesitate to advise publishers when they find a text is so badly translated as hardly to be useful in a class. I make no plea for a canon of specific texts on a variety of subjects; rather, I emphasize the greatest possible freedom of choice as well as an awareness, a constant awareness, by teachers regarding the importance that works in translation have for German studies in general.

I also plead for the realization that literary texts are inherently valuable for use in classes dedicated to the study of topics in politics, art, sociology, philosophy, history, music, law—you name it. A literary ingredient should be present in every such course, simply because the literary author can contribute a point of view, an overview, a reflection of a particular time and place about how human beings react and interact in circumstances that involve the most diverse topics and situations. Nor should any genre of literature be neglected or omitted—libretto, autobiography, saga, poetry, essay, fiction, drama, radio play, humor, travelogue, and film scripts—all genres contain ideas and observations that can illuminate thought on just about any subject. Just one example: the amalgamation of literature and politics is of ancient vintage and should simply be made available to students and incorporated into appropriate classes in German studies and elsewhere in the curriculum.

How can anyone study the effects of deadly political repression and the Holocaust without reading and absorbing and discussing literary works, often autobiographical in nature, in the context of a historical overview? The symbiosis of culture and literature is as ancient as language itself. That symbiosis, when extended to the classroom, can freshen and enliven topics for students and the professors who teach them. A culture course without a literary component is like a house without furniture, with darkened windows and a vacancy sign; a shell in search of the complexity and vibrancy of life.

A BIBLIOGRAPHY OF LITERARY TRANSLATION

Arrowsmith, William, and Roger Shattuck, eds. *The Craft and Context of Translation.* 2d printing. Austin: U of Texas P, 1971. Does not contain the introduction of the first edition.

Bly, Robert. *The Eight Stages of Translation.* Boston: Rowan Tree P, 1983.

Brower, Reuben A. *On Translation.* Galaxy Edition. New York: Oxford UP, 1966. Contains Willa Muir's confession of her loathing of the German language.

Crandell, T. Ellen, ed. *Translators and Translating.* Selected Essays from the American Translators Association Summer Workshops, 1974. Binghamton: SUNY-Binghamton and ATA, 1974.

Delos: A Journal on & of Translation, ed. D. S. Carne-Ross. National Translation Center: U of Texas–Austin, 1968–71. Six issues published. Revival by Boston U, 1993.

DIMENSION: Contemporary German Arts and Letters, ed. A. Leslie Willson. Austin, 1968–94. Ceased publication in late 1994 with vol. 20.

DIMENSION², ed. Ingo R. Stoehr. Kilgore, Texas: Kilgore College. (Began appearing in 1994: three issues per year.) Bilingual, German with English translations. Focus on work by contemporary German authors, their archives, publishers.

Lefevere, André. *Translating Literature: The German Tradition. From Luther to Rosenzweig.* Approaches to Translation Studies, no. 4, ed. James S. Holmes. Amsterdam: Van Gorcum, 1979.

———. *Translating Poetry: Seven Strategies and a Blueprint.* Approaches to Translation Studies, no. 3, ed. James S. Holmes. Amsterdam: Van Gorcum, 1975.

Mundus Artium, ed. Rainer Schulte. Athens: Ohio University. 1967–1985.

Proceedings of the Annual Conference of the American Translators Association. Various editors. Begun 1984. Medford, NJ: Learned Information.

O'Neill, Patrick. *German Literature in Translation: A Select Bibliography.* Toronto: U of Toronto P, 1981.

Rose, Marilyn Gaddis, ed. *Translation in the Humanities.* Binghamton: State U of New York P, n.d.

Steiner, George. *After Babel: Aspects of Language and Translation.* 1975. Reprint. New York: Oxford UP, 1977.

Translation. Columbia U. New York: The Translation Center. 1973–90.

Translation Review, ed. Rainer Schulte. Begun 1978 by the American Literary Translators Association. Richardson, Texas: U of Texas–Dallas.

The World of Translation. Intro. Gregory Rabassa. PEN American Center: New York, 1987. Reprint of 1971 edition, with an introduction by Louis Galantiere.

CHAPTER 24

Cultural Studies, the Eighteenth Century, and the Uses of the German Classics

Burkhard Henke

In this essay Burkhard Henke makes the case for linking the Enlightenment and cultural studies as panoptic enterprises. In the eighteenth century areas of thought were not as sharply divided as they are today, and thus the interplay of philosophy, plastic arts, literary arts, politics, natural sciences, and social life was more lively. In arguing that consideration of the eighteenth century (and early periods in general) should be an integral part of any cultural studies program, Henke is being polemical. As the previous essays demonstrate implicitly, if not explicitly, cultural studies to date has tended to occupy itself with relatively recent history and works of cultural production. As Henke points out, this may be in part because older texts present a language barrier and require more historical reconstruction. Like Willson, Henke makes a plea for excellent English translations to support the cultural studies project.

    Cultural studies by no means "equals" twentieth-century studies, and Henke's essay demonstrates the importance of including material from earlier periods in cultural studies curricula. The broad sense in which culture was understood in the Enlightenment offers a kindred spirit, at least in part, to cultural studies. One must be careful, however, not to ignore or diminish the differences between a cultural studies–based interest in all aspects of a culture and the Enlightenment's universalist ideas. Specifically, Henke argues for the value of including the study of canonical texts. And, faced with the reality of limited time in the classroom, he fears that the introduction of new material through cultural studies necessarily pushes out material (such as eighteenth-century canonical works) that have traditionally been included. What he proposes is a new treatment of the German classics through critical concepts and practices introduced by new historicism and cultural materialism in which literature is viewed as "but one product of culture which is neither central to that culture nor to be viewed in isolation from it." One outcome of such approaches would be that Goethe or Schiller might be taught in a course on "the history of a city" or "everyday life" or "fashion" rather than in an "Age of Goethe" course, as has generally been done to date. Ultimately, Henke wants to include the classics so that we can understand just how and why they came to be considered as such and thus understand better how the social order has been maintained.

As the many recent symposia, conferences, articles, and special journal volumes amply demonstrate, there can be no doubt that German studies in this country finds itself in the midst of a serious and prolonged crisis. The leading indicator of this crisis is the steady decline in enrollments in German language classes at institutions of higher learning. John Van Cleve and A. Leslie Willson sadly preface their *Remarks on the Needed Reform of German Studies in the United States* with a chart detailing the decline of nearly 50 percent, or 100,000 students, between the peak in 1968 and the year 1990 (vii). To be sure, this alarming development has been brought about by a plethora of factors, many of which lie outside the academy and, incidentally, receive little consideration from the authors of the *Remarks*. Such factors include, for example, the decline of the status of foreign languages, literature, and the humanities in general; the changing demographics of the American population; the state of U.S.-German relations in the economic, political, and cultural spheres; and insufficient efforts in presenting things German to the American public. Furthermore, it is worth noting that American colleges and universities themselves—unlike their German counterparts—are highly susceptible to broader cultural and social developments. They are increasingly run like companies that market and sell a commodity, and, because they are heavily influenced by market pressures, they also must possess a great degree of adaptability in order to respond to such pressures. The bottom line, then, is that the problems plaguing our profession are rooted in our discipline, in the academy as a whole, and outside of the academy. If we want to increase enrollments and ensure the well-being of our profession in the future, we must address all three areas. Above all, we must do what other departments and the institutions themselves have already been doing for quite some time: that is, demonstrate an ability and willingness to adapt to the various changes in American culture and society.

Given the necessity of such adaptability and flexibility, both in terms of research and teaching, cultural studies presents the single most attractive option for redefining German studies today. Perhaps most important, its broad, interdisciplinary approach allows us to show undergraduate students that what we offer is relevant to them, that it pertains to other disciplines and courses of study as well as to American culture in general. For that reason alone we ought to offer courses in film, feminism, and popular culture. The perspectives offered by taking a cultural studies approach are not only pragmatic but would also affect the ways the texts themselves are viewed within the discipline. For example, we would not only reclaim Kafka, Nietzsche, Bonhoeffer, Beethoven, and Kirchner from neighboring departments, but we would also adopt select methods used by those departments in confronting them.

As a teacher and scholar of the eighteenth century, I can state provocatively that I feel quite at home working in a cultural studies mode. Certainly, there are many differences between eighteenth-century thought and twentieth-century cultural studies, and yet it is the universalist approach of the European Enlightenment that defined culture in its broadest sense, not just in idealistic terms but also from a decidedly materialistic point of view. The *philosophes* did not, understandably, recognize the division between the humanities and the sciences, which was just beginning to take shape in the late eighteenth century. Indeed, Enlightenment thinkers attempted to interpret past and present very much in the spirit of modern cultural studies. One recognizes this approach, for example, in Goethe's notion of the *Weltganzes* (the world's totality) and in an oeuvre that includes not just literature but also writings on topics as diverse as aesthetics, history, architecture, botany, mineralogy, painting, and color theory. Similarly, one may recall the thorough dissolution of disciplinary boundaries in Herder's programmatic storm and stress collection *Von deutscher Art und Kunst* (*Of German Kind and Art* [1773]), which includes pieces on constitutional law and history, folklore, aesthetics, and architecture and which draws on numerous non-German traditions. Should it surprise us, then, that Voltaire, in his conclusion to *Le Siècle de Louis XIV* (*The Century of Louis XIV* [1752]), has no problem listing mathematicians alongside poets and playwrights to make up the "Catalogue des Écrivains Français" (*Catalog of French Writers*)?[1]

After discussing these issues in light of the current debate on German studies, I will turn to new historicism and cultural materialism as viable models for treating the classics and for assigning them a legitimate space in the new paradigm. I will close with some ideas about bringing all this into the classroom.

1.   Why German Cultural Studies Should Not Be Only Twentieth-Century Studies

I am not a historian by trade, nor can I claim to specialize in contemporary cultural analysis. Rather, I am unabashedly interested in the writings of Dead

White European Males, particularly those specimens who have come to be known as the classical authors of German literature, notably Goethe and Schiller. To me German cultural criticism does not begin and end with modern popular culture, and I would very much like to see German cultural studies be more historically inclusive than current practice and theory would seem to have it. For the time being, however, the academic debate on cultural studies continues to focus on issues of twentieth-century history and culture, thereby ignoring, for the most part, not just the classics and eighteenth-century German literature but all premodern literatures and the select but significant work that has already been done in those areas (e.g., Tatlock). Recent publications, such as Russell A. Berman's book on modern German culture or Rob Burns's introduction to German cultural studies, reflect and further reinforce the pronounced modern emphasis of many symposia and colloquia. In the realm of teaching there are presumably a number of good reasons for that, since, in the struggle to survive the current academic crisis, older literatures seem to have less to recommend themselves to potential students than does twentieth-century culture. Most important, the process of cultural mediation is considerably more difficult. Older texts present a greater language barrier and require a great deal more historical reconstruction. We can assume virtually no prior personal knowledge of, or relationship to, the text on the part of our undergraduates, and only rarely can we utilize modern media to help construct such a relationship. In contrast, twentieth-century German culture is much more accessible to American students, particularly the Nazi era. Even if one may disagree with Sander Gilman's teleological premise that the Holocaust is the "central event of modern German culture, the event toward which every text, every moment in German history and, yes, culture moved inexorably" ("Why" 200–201), there can be little doubt that German studies programs are well served to make the Holocaust and the Third Reich a crucial part of their curriculum. And why should German departments not focus on the National Socialist regime? While a course on Goethe may draw five students—most of whom, I fear, would be unable to pronounce his name—a course on the Nazis is bound to enroll ten times that many.

As warranted as our preoccupation with the Nazis and the Holocaust is, such focus should not lead to the complete blurring of the premodern past. Although the question of focus may indeed be a problem continuously haunting cultural studies, we also have to ask how cultural studies can ever achieve paradigmatic status if it fails to be diachronic in its critical outlook; or, in the German case, if cultural studies is nothing but "Hitler studies"—to borrow from Don DeLillo's novel *White Noise*—rather than German studies. How can we claim to make sense even of the Nazi past if we cannot go back to Fichte and the Romantics to examine nationalism, Otherness, and identity formations? George Mosse has already unearthed strong roots of Nazi ideology in the eighteenth-century cult of friendship; his work, in particular, should stand as a clear warning to any short-sighted approaches. More generally, how can we hope to avoid the pitfalls of a traditional discipline based on national literature and its periodization if we cannot even let go of period categories and find appropriate substitutes for them? Again, it is particularly the "long" eighteenth century (1680–1840) that ought to play a significant role in our curricula, not only for its richness of culture—high and low—but especially for its significant impact on modern thought and culture.

As I mentioned earlier in a provocative vein, the cultural studies approach itself was developed *avant la lettre* in the eighteenth century. With regard to pedagogy one can reasonably assume that most American students will develop an appreciation of eighteenth-century culture once they realize that the discourse of the European Enlightenment is of fundamental importance not only to Europe but to their own history and culture as well. And what better way to illustrate this connection, of course, than the American Revolution and the Constitution of the United States? Already the Declaration of Independence bears the stamp of John Locke, speaks of the inalienable rights of every man, and uses the denial of those natural rights as legitimate grounds for separation from England. The enlightened conception of individual freedom, autonomy, *Mündigkeit* (coming of age, originally in the legal sense), is articulated in the Constitution and has become manifest in the American way of life from the eighteenth century onward. Montesquieu's insistence on the separation of the functions of power for the good of the citizenry found its way into that Constitution, as did Rousseau's call for democracy and the sovereignty of the people. Positing tolerance, freedom, and the fundamental goodness of man, eradicating traditional privileges in favor of equality, doing away with traditional birth rights and replacing them with performance, achievement, and hard work as the sole determinants of social status—these are all demands of the European Enlightenment, realized in a new world that almost immediately became the old world's utopia.

To this day it is striking to see the extent to which the implications of Enlightenment thought (not just of French philosophy but of Kant and of Herder as well) have shaped American consciousness. After all, it is only on the basis of a broader cultural and historical understanding that one can come to terms with Americans' optimistic belief in progress and *Machbarkeit,* or the notion that everything can be done, which is so prevalent in this culture. I, for one, certainly see more of eighteenth-century thought here than in skeptical contemporary Europe. Obviously, the relationship between the European Enlightenment and modern American culture serves as a counterargument to the frequently heard assumption that only modern texts speak to students.

Historians in particular may wonder why cultural studies would be limited to this century when the new cultural history has in fact concentrated on the early modern period. It is difficult to fathom how cultural studies can *not* be more than twentieth-century studies. What is of issue here is not periodization but, rather, perspective, method, and theory. Even if cultural studies were to work best as a critical framework for this century—and it may indeed have become necessary as a means of analyzing the postmodern condition—that hardly restricts the approach itself in terms of its objects of investigation. While cultural studies itself implies an all-inclusive field of study, there is, however, a conspicuous lack of emphasis on premodern Germany. The works of Robert Darnton, Natalie Zemon Davis, Lynn Hunt, and other prominent cultural historians have focused primarily on prerevolutionary France—with Britain (Stone, Thompson) and the Netherlands (Schama, *Embarrassment of Riches*) receiving a fair amount of attention as well—whereas no comparable work has so far been done in early modern German history. Even though the new German cultural history is yet to be written, there is of course no reason to believe that it cannot be written: it simply has not yet been done. Likewise, there has been no analysis yet of the German classics in the context of cultural history. Is there any reason to believe that the new cultural history, with its focus on popular culture, is somehow ill equipped or otherwise unable to deal critically with the classics or canonized literature in general? This leads me to my second concern.

2.   Classics, Canon, and Cultural Studies

In order to answer this question, it may be best first to consider the basic theoretical assumptions of cultural studies and then to consider the function of canonicity within the project.

Not surprisingly, there remains much ambiguity about what cultural studies is or what it should be. This much is clear: the project of cultural studies takes its cue from the poststructuralist and postmodernist debates, which have called into question some of the most basic theoretical assumptions of many disciplines, including that of literary study. At its core poststructuralism insists on the fundamentally linguistic construction of social and psychological realities—even the unconscious is language—and thus renders any object, practice, or experience as a text to be read and interpreted. Cultural studies uses this notion of the text for examining culture as the various representations, images, and symbolic expressions of social behavior. Having crossed the boundaries between high culture and popular culture, between literary and nonliterary texts, cultural studies views the products of mass culture, consumer culture, and popular culture not only as legitimate objects of intellectual inquiry but also as crucial to our understanding of how cultural and national identities are constructed. This, of course, marks a decided difference to the traditional discipline of *Germanistik,* which uses the notion of a national literature as its organizing principle, sees in high literature its primary object of investigation, and, by and large, prefers philology as its main method.[2] *Germanistik* tends to ascribe to the aesthetic a Kantian autonomy and has as the *telos* of its critical inquiry the aesthetic value of a work of literature. It legitimates the results of that inquiry by insisting on the ethical responsibility of any scholar to impartiality and scientific disinterestedness. By contrast, cultural studies does away with the aesthetic as an autonomous discursive realm untouched by ideology. It insists on the political determination of the aesthetic and therefore discards all critical concepts that have been derived from the alleged aesthetic autonomy (aesthetic quality, authorial intention, the imaginary unpolitical reader, etc.). The *telos,* then, of a cultural studies approach will always be the political and the ideological. It asks what is at stake, for whom, and investigates the political function not just of literary texts but of cultural discourses in their totality. That totality includes scholarly discourses themselves. Out of this critical consciousness practitioners of cultural studies will openly—and honestly, some would add—profess their own political position from which they read and analyze texts.

The most important result for our discussion here is the fact that cultural studies has adopted the poststructuralist and postmodernist strategy of decentering any form of authority, be that a discourse, a text, or an author. This has significant ramifications for the construction of a canon—a device that literary critics can hardly do without. Few academic debates have been as fiercely fought as the one about the canon. The emergence of multiculturalism and cultural studies is changing the complexion of the humanities as a whole and is likely to bring about further institutional and curricular reforms. These changes, I believe, ought to be welcomed as tangible results of a diversification process, in the course of which we have learned to listen to those groups who, for a long time, had found themselves on the unheard margins of our profession and who had no say over the terms under which literature, history, and culture were examined. Cultural studies can do much to ensure that we continue this process of democratization, for it offers a unique model for coming to terms with cultural difference.

But, as scholars such as Theodore Ziolkowski have argued rather polemically, there is a price to be paid for the introduction of alterity into the canon. In its efforts to represent the underrepresented, German cultural studies—so far— appears in practice to be able to foreground marginalized texts only by silencing those texts that have hitherto been central to the traditional canon. In other words, German cultural studies runs the danger of, in effect, reproducing the very same mechanisms of exclusion that it set out to abolish in the first place. The all-embracing approach decenters authority, it is true, but it remains unclear whether this move will not merely replace traditional authority with a new one, privilege one discourse over another. If one looks at what cultural studies has managed to do with the classics so far, this does not appear to be an unfounded concern. It is obvious that "merely reversing strategy in curricular design—by valorizing the so-called noncanonical texts and marginalizing canonical ones—has not been an effective remedy" to cure the ills of traditional *Germanistik* (Seyhan 8). It is equally obvious that cultural studies must find a way to deal effectively with the classics, or else it will hardly succeed as the new paradigm in our field.

Before we look at methodology and the various ways in which cultural studies can come to terms with the classics, we need to consider more closely the very vehicle by which the classics have come to carry their ideological weight. What kind of canon is appropriate for German studies? There can be little doubt that the classics ought to be included in any canon. At the same time, it does not follow merely from their traditional reception—a politically determined process at every stage—that "bewährte Klassiker" or "früher geschätzte Meisterwerke" (proven classics or formerly appreciated masterpieces [Ziolkowski 465, 458]) still occupy the central, authoritative position within the canon. What is called for is not a fixed canon for all ages but, rather, a flexible one that remains open to the many different voices of German and German-speaking culture. For the eighteenth century that means the inclusion of women writers from the Gottschedin and Anna Louisa Karschin to Sophie von la Roche and Sophie Mereau-Brentano—all of whom were prominent members of the literary scene in their lifetimes and who owe much of their near anonymity today to nineteenth- and twentieth-century *Germanistik*. A flexible canon also means the inclusion of Jews such as Rahel von Varnhagen and blacks such as Anton Wilhelm Arno. The work and histories of both these figures demonstrate the sorts of contradictions present in enlightened culture that, since then, have often been glossed over by traditional Germanists, who have continually relied on only a few select texts.

In addition to the inclusion of alterity the canon must be malleable according to the particular needs of a course. Ideally, this openness would extend so as to include dissenting student voices. Malleability as such is of utmost importance because it would allow us to go beyond the confines of our discipline and reconfigure the canon at any time according to heuristic concepts relevant to other disciplines. As recent works of cultural history have shown, many such relevant concepts (the body, sexuality, subjectivity, xenophobia, etc.) are contained in eighteenth-century culture, and they are, of course, also present in German classical literature. Institutionally, organizing German courses around these concepts would thus ensure their attractiveness to nonmajors. Intellectually, a canonical focus on such concepts opens the door to the kind of interesting and important interdisciplinary work that makes cultural studies an increasingly attractive option, not just for scholars of modern Germany. Of course, by introducing a given concept relevant to other fields, we are also introducing texts from other disciplines that speak to that complex. A recent anthology such as Sigrid Lange's *Ob die Weiber Menschen sind,* for example, contains numerous eighteenth-century treatises pertaining to the status of women and thereby effectively reconstructs the debates over issues of gender around 1800. The questions lifted from the debate, and posed in the title "Whether Women Are Human Beings," is discussed and answered in contributions drawing on literary, philosophical, social, pedagogical, legal, and medical discourses alike. While Lange's collection is by no means complete, it does more than just sketch the contours of the "controversy." It goes to the heart of the matter and can be read with great profit either by itself or, preferably, in conjunction with literary texts such as *Das Fräulein von Sternheim, Maria Stuart,* or *Penthesilea.* In any case Lange's volume deserves to be part of an eighteenth-century canon that allows nonliterary texts and discourses to play a vital role.

To be sure, there are in eighteenth-century studies a number of Germanists who have investigated nonliterary discourse with outstanding results, but that in itself does not amount to cultural studies. One prominent example is Gerhard Sauder, whose book on *Empfindsamkeit* (sensibility) has been extraordinarily well received and has already been elevated to a sort of standard work on the epoch. In it Sauder examines various discourses (ethical, pedagogical, medical, etc.) but does so in a rather conventional fashion. His method is more akin to a history of ideas than to cultural studies. Whereas Sauder constructs discursive contexts solely for the illumination of works of literature, a cultural studies approach would clearly look for the ideological stakes inherent in the interaction of literary and nonliterary discourses. It would assume—and insist even—that the relationship between the discourses is reciprocal, that literature partakes in the shaping of nonliterary discourses.

Some key examples of German eighteenth-century criticism that better fits the demands of cultural studies include: Barbara Stafford's body criticism, for example (analyzing Winckelmann, Lavater, Lichtenberg, among others, and visual culture in general); Helmut Müller-Sievers's book on epigenesis and Wilhelm von Humboldt; Sander Gilman's history of sexuality; Maria Tatar's studies on mesmerism; Liliane Weissberg's work on cultural studies and on *Geistersprache* (playing on German *Geist* as mind, spirit, and ghost); or Simon Richter's analyses of *Reiz* (irritation, stimulation) and wet-nursing. All these studies explore cultural discourses and the questions of identity, power, politics, and ideology to which they give rise. These studies do not, however, tackle the classical texts in a comprehensive way, thus leaving unanswered the question of what cultural studies can contribute to our understanding of the classics.[3] I have already intimated how a cross-selection of diverse discourses such as Sigrid Lange's volume can be used to elucidate prominent issues in classical texts and, thus, begin to unravel the complex fabric of classical literature, politics, and culture at the time. There are also well-defined and established schools at our disposal to help investigate the participation of the classics in the broader arena of culture and society.

3. New Historicism and Cultural Materialism

Anglo-American literary criticism of the past two decades has produced two models of political criticism that I believe would function well in German cultural studies and that might carry some appeal to both parties.[4] The American *new historicism,* a term coined by Stephen Greenblatt, as well as its more politically activist British counterpart, *cultural materialism,* a term that goes back to Raymond Williams, both originated in English Renaissance studies. Both are concerned chiefly with Shakespeare and thus offer a promising critical practice of coming to terms with classic texts and their uses in culture. Simply put, what distinguishes the two approaches is that new historicism focuses more on the ideological sites and discursive conditions of historical cultural production, while cultural materialism is more interested in the subsequent appropriation and ideological uses of classic texts. Since the work done in the latter area is, of course, less known in this country, it is worthy of attention here.

The premises on which both models rest are very much those of cultural studies. Instead of using traditional critical categories such as aesthetic quality, authorial intention, or critical impartiality, both approaches feature a set of operating assumptions that call for interdisciplinary perspectives as they aim to do justice to the historicity of the text in a new way. Mindful that criticism "does not give access to some unchanging human nature, only to historically specific constructions" (Howard and O'Connor 2), new historicism and cultural materialism insist that neither the aesthetic product nor the aesthetic experience received from it can be adequately explained without locating both in a political context. While new historicism tries to reinsert the literary text into the larger cultural context of the time of its production, cultural materialism, too, assumes an intrinsic link between the literary text and other cultural "texts" surrounding it (social events, cultural practices) but historicizes the literary text by reintegrating it into modern culture. Thus, standard treatments in the history of ideas such as Tillyard's *Elizabethan World Picture,* Lovejoy's *Great Chain of Being,* or Korff's *Geist der Goethezeit* (The Spirit of the Age of Goethe) have been supplanted by a material history that is not "monological," to borrow Stephen Greenblatt's term, and that articulates a variety of ideological positions rather than be "concerned with discovering a single political vision," as the old historicism had been ("Introduction" 5). Instead of looking for that vision—of an intellectual history or a history of ideas—to furnish a stable frame of reference from which we can understand the classic text, new historicists eclectically consider a much wider range of texts, including such "popular" texts as advertisements, business letters, diaries, accounts of dreams, legal documents, and manuals of all kinds, as well as social customs and events, precisely in order to avoid the pitfalls of a predetermined context.

Cultural materialism in many ways holds out the promise of revitalizing and demarginalizing the German eighteenth century, in its radicalism perhaps even more so than the new historicism. Of particular interest to cultural materialists is the circulation of Shakespeare and his texts to political ends, his ideological uses and implication not just in British popular culture but, specifically, the role he is asked to play in British institutions. Very interesting work has been done in this area. Alan Sinfield, for instance, reveals Shakespeare's ideological appropriation in the English school system by analyzing the standardized and state-required questions on the "National Poet" in the O-level and A-level examinations. The title of his article is itself a mocking parody of such questions: "Give an account of Shakespeare and Education, showing why you think they are effective and what you have appreciated about them. Support your comments with precise references." By phrasing the examination questions in such a way as to suggest a logical connection between contemporary cultural and political conditions, on the one hand, and the supposedly eternal truths manifest in Shakespeare's plays, the examinations tend to invite the candidates to "interrogate their experience to discover a response which has in actuality been learnt" (Sinfield 139). Such strategies, Sinfield shows, typically result in the affirmation of bourgeois society, its institutions and its values.

Though they boast an impressive reception history of their own, none of the German classics can these days be said to have quite the same status as is afforded to Shakespeare. In contrast to Britain there is in Germany, for example, no current mandate by the Ständige Kulturministerkonferenz (permanent conference of the ministries of education and culture) to include at least one question on Goethe or Schiller in the various *Abiturprüfungen* (comprehensive high school examinations). It would nonetheless be of great interest to explore the institutional role assigned to the classics in the German educational system. One may well find there what Alan Sinfield has exposed in Britain—that is, a political agenda that dictates the appreciation of the classics as a means of legitimating and reproducing the current social order. Given Germany's recent past and the problems associated with the (dis)continuity of its cultural legacies, such an investigation becomes at once more topical and more troubling.

Sinfield's essay is obviously not so much a new way of looking at the old as it is a new way of looking at how the old is made new. It seems far more concerned with contemporary culture than it is with the Renaissance itself. Can this history of appropriations, or "effective history," still contribute, then, to an understanding of Renaissance literature or, in our case, eighteenth-century texts? Cultural materialism generally tends to furnish a contemporary reading and understanding of those texts, and on phenomenological grounds one could, of course, argue that this is all we ever can do. We always read texts in the present, and we produce their meanings in the present. Like the canon, the texts are in an important sense constructions of the present, contingent upon the reader's present historical and political interests. But there is a difference, nonetheless, if only in critical consciousness. Cultural materialists approach Shakespeare with a thorough grasp of both Renaissance and contemporary culture; the effective history they write is one of dialog and interaction between historically distinct cultural phenomena, in the process of which one illuminates the other.

The degree to which a play such as *Henry IV* or *Macbeth* inherently subverts any forms of authority and thereby resists its own appropriation sharpens our understanding of how contemporary cultural practices are authorized, and vice versa. Shakespeare, as the editors of *Shakespeare Reproduced* point out in their programmatic introduction, "is constantly reproduced in the general discourses of culture and is used to authorize practices as diverse as buying perfume, watching Masterpiece Theater, or dispatching troops to far-flung corners of the globe" (Howard and O'Connor 15–16). Like Shakespeare criticism, criticism of the German classics needs studies that investigate the various reproductions of Goethe and Schiller—their names as well as their words—as authoritative cultural icons in the mass media, in advertising, in political rhetoric, in pop songs, etc. Ignoring such uses of the classics is irresponsible. Not taking them seriously or dismissing them as trivial means "acquiescing in the separation of academia from general culture and it means ignoring, as well, much of what in our time may be of significance to a political and historical criticism" (Howard and O'Connor 16).

It should be clear what is at stake for ourselves as well. If we consider the German case, we will no doubt encounter in contemporary culture an appropriation of Goethe that is similar to that of Shakespeare. Like Shakespeare's, the uses and abuses of Goethe's name, image, and works are plentiful and probably most prominent in advertising. We may complain (or not), yet we in the academy also commodify Goethe. We rarely think twice about using Andy Warhol's print of Goethe to lure students into German departments everywhere, and we have a vested interest in Goethe for securing our existences, scholarly and otherwise. Those who react with moral indignation and outrage to the use of Goethe's image in advertising are likely to be well aware of what is at stake for them when a Goethe other than their own is circulating in our culture.

4.   Conclusion: A Weimar Model for the Classroom

What does this mean with regard to the future of the classics and eighteenth-century literature in German cultural studies? In terms of research the analysis of the ways in which the classics are woven into the fabric of contemporary popular and nonliterary culture remains one important area of work for eighteenth-century cultural studies; reinserting classic texts into the *fluidum* of popular German culture at the time of their production is another. The common ground for both new historicism and cultural materialism is the understanding of literature as but one product of culture that is neither central to that culture nor to be viewed in isolation from it. Similarly, it seems clear that only as part of a larger, interdisciplinary curriculum will we be able to continue the teaching of literature in our "postmodern" undergraduate programs.

As I have argued, the classics ought to remain a vital part within that curriculum. The study of the German classics would then be offered not necessarily in courses on Goethe, the Age of Goethe, or classical drama but in courses on, say, literary monuments or the history of everyday life, fashion, music, and so on. One very specific example may illustrate this. While German Americanists have produced a diverse volume on the cultural history of Washington, D.C. (containing a significant eighteenth-century component [Hönninghausen and Falke]), and, while courses on Berlin and its cultural history are rapidly becoming a paradigm of the cultural studies curriculum, there is no reason why German departments should not also offer courses on the city of Weimar. Like Washington and Berlin, Weimar is in many ways a focal point of national history. A Weimar syllabus could range from the eighteenth-century classicism to twentieth-century modernism, from old Weimar's amateur theater in Ettersburg to the concentration camp just minutes away on the Ettersberg, from the GDR to the present.

It is important to note that Weimar has recently been awarded the title "Culture City of Europe 1999," the smallest city ever to be named one of Europe's annual "Culture Cities." This designation could serve as a convenient springboard for any Weimar cultural studies course, even where the discussion of the cultural-political import of its selection and its ramifications holds little promise; for 1999 marks a number of significant historical anniversaries: the city's first official mention exactly 1,100 years before, the eightieth anniversary of the Weimar constitution and the founding of the Bauhaus, the sixtieth anniversary of the invasion of Poland and the beginning of World War II, the fiftieth anniversary of the founding of the two Germanies, and the tenth anniversary of the fall of the Wall. Incidentally, 1999 also marks Goethe's 250th birthday.

For the sake of the argument I have made here, let us briefly sketch how the latter could figure in a course on the history and culture of Weimar. The format of the course could achieve much of what I have already mentioned. In contrast to a key study such as W. H. Bruford's *Culture and Society in Classical Weimar, 1775–1806,* which provides an excellent social and cultural background but still focuses on high culture in connection with the concept of *Bildung* (cultivation, education), a project like the one proposed here would reinsert Goethe into a cultural context quite different from the one Bruford lays out. It could show how he influenced life in Weimar—his private life, social life, and love life, his position in the service of Carl August, his architectural and landscaping designs, his treatment of his fellow citizens, women and men, his tax status as *classicus* in the original sense of the word—but then put Goethe's influence in perspective by comparing him to his "rival" Caroline Jagemann and the great impact she had on the cultural, social, and political life in Weimar; or to someone like F. J. Bertuch, the most prominent, materialistically ingenious, and immensely successful entrepreneur of his time, who shaped the same cultural space in different ways. To the same end, but perhaps closer to home, we could also venture to include in our syllabus a popular playwright such as August von Kotzebue—someone who managed, after all, to produce more than two hundred plays, nearly half of which Goethe himself put on stage and many of which enjoyed far greater success with the Weimar public than any of Goethe's plays ever did. Not being told what to think of aesthetic quality, our students should be free to pass similar judgment.

Whatever curricular decisions we make, our course would not only show Goethe's participation in Weimar's popular and material culture but also show how the city in turn shaped (or failed to shape) Goethe's literary production. On the whole, the approach would demonstrate the provincial nature of Weimar, debunk the fallacy of a so-called German classicism, and inevitably knock Goethe off the pedestal of national authorship and eternal truths. Literary pieces such as *Torquato Tasso* and *Iphigenie,* but also Thomas Mann's *Lotte in Weimar,* could be read side by side with Goethe's *Dichtung und Wahrheit* (*Poetry and Truth*), his official business correspondence, and numerous other sorts of texts, including Bertuch's popular *Journal des Luxus und der Moden* (Journal of Luxury and Fashion). Integrated into the long history of appropriation from the nineteenth to the twentieth century, the classic texts could be read vis-à-vis the Weimar constitution as well as those of Ettersberg and Buchenwald (a dichotomy that may be tiresome to some of us but eye-opening news to students) or contemporary advertisements.

The issues raised by such contrastive readings would all resonate in the debate about how to celebrate the "Goethe Year," 1999, a critical debate already well under way in Germany. A Weimar course of such scope, organized around a current discussion, affords the kind of flexibility, interdisciplinarity, and openness so crucial to a successful integration of the classics into a German cultural studies program. In general, expanding the base of our offerings entails that we not shy away from teaching German literature in translation and that we actively seek the participation of our colleagues in other fields. For our imaginary course on Weimar it is not difficult to see the benefit of collaboration, be it in the form of invited talks or team teaching. Indeed, such collaboration would do more than safeguard against a monological vision, presentation, and discussion of the material; it would substantively enhance—as would consideration of the classics and of earlier periods—the German cultural studies project.

NOTES

1. Lionel Gossman (26–27) uses this example to point out the changing conceptions of *literature* over time and warns against taking the term for granted. His essay and Lynn Hunt's article on disciplinarity make one of the better cases for maintaining the study of literature as an autonomous discipline.

2. For the history of the discipline, see Hohendahl, *Geschichte;* and Hermand.

3. Alice Kuzniar's *Outing Goethe and His Age* promises to shed much light on new ways of confronting the classics but appeared too late for consideration here.

4. For a critique of new historicism, see Brantlinger; Cohen; and Hohendahl, "Return." The most comprehensive, yet sympathetic critique of new historicism has been formulated by Brook Thomas. Despite the limitations of the approach, I join Anton Kaes and Sara Lennox in welcoming new historicism as a critical, interdisciplinary approach worth adopting in German studies.

WORKS CITED

Berman, Russell A. *Cultural Studies of Modern Germany: History, Representation, and Nationhood.* Madison: U of Wisconsin P, 1993.

Brantlinger, Patrick. "'Post-Structuralist' or Prelapsarian? Cultural Studies and the New Historicism." *Surfaces* 2.4 (1992): 5–21. (Internet anonymous FTP: harfang.cc.umontreal.ca.)

Bruford, W. H. *Culture and Society in Classical Weimar, 1775–1806.* Cambridge: Cambridge UP, 1962.

Burns, Rob, ed. *German Cultural Studies: An Introduction.* New York: Oxford UP, 1995.

Cohen, Walter. "Political Criticism of Shakespeare." In *Shakespeare Reproduced: The Text in History and Ideology,* ed. Jean E. Howard and Marion F. O'Connor. New York and London: Methuen, 1987. 18–46.

Darnton, Robert. *The Forbidden Bestsellers of Pre-Revolutionary France.* New York: Norton, 1995.

———. *The Literary Underground of the Old Regime.* Cambridge: Harvard UP, 1982.

Davis, Natalie Zemon. *Society and Culture in Early Modern France: Eight Essays.* Stanford: Stanford UP, 1975.

DeLillo, Don. *White Noise.* New York: Viking, 1985.

Dollimore, Jonathan, and Alan Sinfield. "Culture and Textuality: Debating Cultural Materialism." *Textual Practice* 4 (1990): 91–100.

———. eds. *Political Shakespeare: New Essays in Cultural Materialism.* Manchester: Manchester UP, 1985; Ithaca: Cornell UP, 1985.

Gilman, Sander. *Sexuality: An Illustrated History Representing the Sexual in Medicine and Culture from the Middle Ages to the Age of Aids.* New York: Wiley, 1989.

———. "Why and How I Study the German." *German Quarterly* 62.2 (1989): 192–209.

Gossman, Lionel. "History and the Study of Literature." *Profession 94.* New York: MLA, 1994. 26–33.

Greenblatt, Stephen J. "Introduction." *The Forms of Power and the Power of Forms in the English Renaissance.* Special issue of *Genre* 15.1–2 (1982): 3–6.

———. "Invisible Bullets: Renaissance Authority and Its Subversion, *Henry IV* and *Henry V.*" In *Political Shakespeare: New Essays in Cultural Materialism,* ed. Jonathan Dollimore and Alan Sinfield. Manchester: Manchester UP, 1985; Ithaca: Cornell UP, 1985. 18–47.

————. *Shakespearian Negotiations: The Circulation of Social Energy in Renaissance England.* Berkeley: U of California P, 1988.

————. "Towards a Poetics of Culture." *Southern Review* 20 (1987): 3–15.

Hermand, Jost. *Geschichte der Germanistik.* Reinbek bei Hamburg: Rowohlt, 1994.

Hohendahl, Peter Uwe. "A Return to History? The New Historicism and Its Agenda." *New German Critique* 55 (1992): 87–104.

————., ed. *Geschichte der deutschen Literaturkritik (1730–1980). Mit Beiträgen von Klaus L. Berghahn et al.* Stuttgart: Metzler, 1985.

Hönninghausen, Lothar, and Andreas Falke, eds. *Washington, D.C.: Interdisciplinary Approaches.* Tübingen: Stauffenberg, 1992.

Howard, Jean E., and Marion F. O'Connor, eds. *Shakespeare Reproduced: The Text in History and Ideology.* New York and London: Methuen, 1987.

Hunt, Lynn. "The Virtues of Disciplinarity." *Eighteenth-Century Studies* 28.1 (1994): 1–7.

————. *Politics, Culture, and Class in the French Revolution.* Berkeley: U of California P, 1984.

Kaes, Anton. "New Historicism and the Study of German Literature." *German Quarterly* 62.2 (1989): 210–19.

Kuzniar, Alice, ed. *Outing Goethe and His Age.* Stanford: Stanford UP, 1996.

Lange, Sigrid, ed. *Ob die Weiber Menschen sind. Geschlechterdebatten um 1800.* Leipzig: Reclam, 1992.

Lennox, Sara. "Feminist Scholarship and *Germanistik.*" *German Quarterly* 62.2 (1989): 158– 70.

Mosse, George L. *Nationalism and Sexuality: Middle Class Morality and Sexual Norms in Modern Europe.* Madison: U of Wisconsin P, 1988.

————. *The Crisis of German Ideology: Intellectual Origins of the Third Reich.* New York: Grosset and Dunlap, 1964.

Müller-Sievers, Helmut. *Epigenesis: Naturphilosophie im Sprachdenken Wilhelm von Humboldts.* Paderborn: Schöningh, 1993.

Richter, Simon. "Wet-Nursing, Onanism, and the Sexuality of the Breast in Eighteenth-Century Germany." *Journal of the History of Sexuality* 7.1 (1996): 1–22.

————. "Medizinischer und ästhetischer Diskurs: Herder und Haller über Reiz." *Lessing Yearbook* 25 (1993): 83–95.

Sauder, Gerhard. *Empfindsamkeit: Voraussetzungen und Elemente.* Vol 1. Stuttgart: Metzler, 1974.

Schama, Simon. *Citizens: A Chronicle of the French Revolution.* New York: Knopf, 1989.

————. *The Embarrassment of Riches: An Interpretation of Dutch Culture in the Golden Age.* New York: Knopf, 1987.

Seyhan, Azade. "Language and Literary Study as Cultural Criticism." *ADFL Bulletin* 26.2 (1995): 7–11.

Sinfield, Alan. "Give an account of Shakespeare and Education, showing why you think they are effective and what you have appreciated about them. Support your comments with precise references." In *Political Shakespeare: New Essays in Cultural Materialism,* ed. Jonathan Dollimore and Alan Sinfield. Manchester: Manchester UP, 1985; Ithaca: Cornell UP, 1985. 134–57.

Stafford, Barbara. *Body Criticism: Imaging the Unseen in Enlightenment Art and Medicine.* Cambridge: MIT Press, 1991.

Stone, Lawrence. *The Family, Sex and Marriage in England, 1500–1800.* New York: Harper and Row, 1977.

Tatar, Maria M. *Spellbound: Studies on Mesmerism and Literature.* Princeton: Princeton UP, 1978.

Tatlock, Lynne. *The Graph of Sex and the German Text: Gendered Culture in Early Modern Germany, 1500–1700.* Amsterdam: Rodopi, 1994.

Thomas, Brook. *The New Historicism and Other Old-Fashioned Topics.* Princeton: Princeton UP, 1991.

Thompson, E. P. *The Making of the English Working Class.* London: Gollancz, 1963; New York: Vintage, 1963.

Van Cleve, John, and A. Leslie Willson. *Remarks on the Needed Reform of German Studies in the United States.* Columbia, SC: Camden House, 1993.

Weissberg, Liliane. *Geistersprache: Philosophischer und literarischer Diskurs im späten 18. Jahrhundert.* Würzburg: Könighausen und Neumann, 1990.

———. "Zur Ausstellung des Fremden: Literatur." In *Wie international ist die Literaturwissenschaft?* ed. Lutz Danneberg and Friedrich Vollhardt. Stuttgart: Metzler, 1996. 499–531.

Williams, Raymond. *Culture and Society, 1780–1950.* Garden City, NY: Doubleday, 1958.

Ziolkowski, Theodore. "Das Neueste aus den USA: Der Text als Feind." *Jahrbuch des deutschen Schillergesellschaft* 39 (1995): 454–59.

CHAPTER 25

Interdisciplinary Teaching with the Case Study Method

Louis L. Ortmayer

Interdisciplinary explorations are inherent in a cultural studies approach and, as such, involve risk. Venturing off in new directions and attempting to hold fast onto slippery new ways of questioning the world do bring dangers: the chance of being misunderstood, the possibility of following false leads into unproduc- tive intellectual territory, and the real potential of being disciplined by acade- micians for one's transgressions. Just as cultural studies invites intellectual risk taking, so too does a cultural studies classroom celebrate such experiments. This volume is dedicated to helping further new ways of thinking about culture and society; teaching ultimately forms the center of any such work. In the fol- lowing essay Louis Ortmayer, a political scientist and former Pew Faculty Fel- low in International Affairs at Harvard's Kennedy School of Government, pre- sents the case study teaching method as an especially apt way of teaching about power, identity, intellectual or cultural territory, and negotiation. Participants in the Pew program learn how to use the case study method from master teach- ers like Ortmayer. Here he explains the method and argues for the special rel- evance of case study teaching in the context of interdisciplinary learning.

Questions with no clear answers can make students nervous, and perma- nently unresolved problems cause them to squirm: they are uncomfortable with unknowns. The case study method privileges messy indeterminacy and open- endedness and forces students to do most of the work of learning. In the case study classroom students carry the burden of working through the implications of the case, with the teacher guiding discussion, not dictating its terms or di- rections or even its outcomes. Case study classrooms are full of controversy, energy, and dynamism—much like the realm of cultural studies.

∞

A case study as used in this essay is a written description of a real situation in which specific and often difficult decisions have to be made by a public official or private individual. Why use cases? Quite simply, case study teachers believe in the method because they believe their students learn more when they are at the center of the process of analysis and decision making. In case teaching, rather than passively taking down lecture notes, students are actively engaged with the course material. The responsibility for learning is theirs. Using cases, students are simultaneously learning a body of material and learning how to learn on their own. Classroom case study learning therefore promotes lifelong learning.

Through the case learning approach students will:

develop critical thinking skills;

apply concepts in an interdisciplinary fashion;

learn through decision-making and role-playing situations;

develop confidence in confronting problems, through interactive discussions, as well as defining, analyzing, and solving those problems;

be encouraged to apply theoretical concepts through the use of practical experience and policy-oriented problem solving;

and exercise skills in discussion, negotiation, group leadership, and persuasion.

Case method teaching supplements the conventional tools of classroom exposition. Teachers can use cases to complement lectures; they can be used comparatively; they can be used for discussion or for simulation; and teachers can provide case discussions to illustrate theoretical concepts (such as power) or to require students to enter into the agonies of political choice ("What would you have done if you were Chancellor Kohl?"). But what the case method of instruction almost invariably enables students to do is to engage and to take responsibility for their own learning and education.

Case method teaching and learning, moreover, fit well with German cultural studies, especially those aspects focusing on politics, political economy, and society. What follows will explain the strengths of case learning and suggest why the approach can be particularly valuable to the cultural studies project.

Case Method Learning

Cases lay out in detail and from varying perspectives the diverse pressures and considerations that an individual must weigh in making a decision and the often incomplete or contradictory information available at the time. For example, a case might address the question of whether the German chancellor should push through legislation enabling the use of German troops in NATO "out-of-area" peacekeeping operations in the post–Cold War era, such as Bosnia, even though such action raises serious questions about its constitutionality under the *Basic Law*. Case method learning has particular applications where critical thinking and decision making must be derived primarily from skillful analysis, choice, and persuasion. The case study method actively engages the participant in these processes: first, in the analysis of the facts and details of the case itself; second, in the analysis and selection of a strategy; and, third, in the refinement and defense of a chosen course of action during discussion preparation often prior to the class (McDade). The case method does not provide a set of solutions but, rather, refines the student's ability to ask the appropriate set of questions and to make decisions based on his or her answers to those questions (see contributions in Christensen and Hansen).

Cases require more preparation and work on the part of the student than the usual reading assignment. For the student to get the most out of a case and for the discussion to be fruitful, the student must immerse him- or herself in the case and attempt to formulate his or her own position and strategy before class, often through small group deliberations and preparation, and participate actively in the ensuing class discussion. Most students find this approach both intellectually interesting and, occasionally, frustrating, especially because the most stimulating cases are ones in which reasonable people might—and, invariably, do—disagree about the appropriate course of action. The fundamental principle behind the case method is that the best lessons are the ones the students teach themselves.

Active Learning and the Case Method

> Perhaps unsettled by our inability to control the outcome of the learning process, . . . we habitually act as if it were entirely the teacher's problem. We develop an *Atlas complex*, shouldering the entire burden of teaching and learning. We concern ourselves with the limits of our own knowledge and focus attention on our own performance. We subordinate process to content and active engagement to coverage. We relegate students to a passive role, making them spectators when they need, and would actually prefer, to be gladiators. (Boehrer, "Spectators" 1)

All too often modern education has relegated students to the galleries, asking them to pursue work that represents others' judgments of what they need to learn and leading them to acquire received wisdom instead of earned knowledge. In an insightful essay Robert Kraft recalls that his own mastery of the bicycle resulted from his personal, very focused quest for quick transportation to the candy store. Reflecting on his college studies, Kraft notes that what he retained from them was not what he was told in class but, instead, the thought he put into writing his papers, the product of his own efforts to construct meaning. His reflection on the connection between self, problem, and learning led him to recognize its importance to—and its usual absence from—his college students' experiences. Active learning seeks to reconnect the student with the problem in creating and maintaining an environment in which students want and learn to work. "Bringing students into the arena" involves a "shift of emphasis from the exposition of knowledge to the recasting of what we know into questions to be resolved, issues to be grappled with, problems to be worked, mysteries to be unraveled" (Boeher, "Spectators" 2).[1]

Cases offer students the opportunity to learn directly from the events described, to face the problems *as if they were one's own,* in effect, to inhabit the case as well as analyze it, to experience the conflict, and, finally, to determine what they might do (or might have done). "Case teaching marries a distinct type of material, essentially narrative, with a certain class activity, group discussion, in which the teacher's major role is that of facilitator" (Boehrer, "On Teaching" 14). The major dimensions of case teaching may be distilled and presented in the following as the material (cases), the activity (case discussions), and role (what the teacher does).

Case Studies/Case Writing

Cases tell stories. Like other stories, they present conflict, character, and situation in some detail. Whatever the story, cases help create a real-world context for doing analysis and applying concepts. Like all good narratives, a successful case should have an interesting plot, one providing compelling, many-layered problems seen from multiple perspectives. It can unfold around an interest or conflict-arousing issue or set of issues. The plot can provide uncertainty and even drama to draw the student into the particulars of the subject matter and the various roles of the actors involved. Narratives also work well when they allow identification, or perhaps even empathy, with the central characters. The personal situation and political context of the central characters become important elements in the decision process articulated through the reading and subsequent discussion of the case. To this end good cases provide access to the principal actors' own insights and positions through quotations that spice up the narrative and supply reflection, color, and anecdote to the progression of the story line (for recent German examples, see Ortmayer, "New 'Berlin Wall'"; and Ortmayer, with Hodges).

Purpose/Focus

The overarching purpose of writing a new case is having a particular teaching function in mind. Cases serve an underlying and conscious "pedagogic utility"

(Robyn; see also Kennedy and Scott). The writer needs to be clear about what learning issues the case will raise, such as the theoretical perspectives that one might derive from the particular sets of events or decision context described in the narrative. In addition, it is instructive for the case writer to have a sense of the case's role as part of a module or course sequence, and not just as an independent vehicle. Acknowledging that pedagogical motives drive the case permits the writer to proceed more efficiently and effectively in determining substantive content, length, and focus of a particular new case. For example, my intent in writing a case about the intense bargaining and negotiations that occurred after the October 1994 German elections was twofold: I wanted to provide the reader with a clear sense of the central issues and players that would dominate the new legislative period, but I also wanted to create a medium through which students could discuss the nature of coalition politics in Germany, the role of party and coalition bargaining, and, more generally, the Federal Republic as a *Parteienstaat* (multiple-party state). Even more broadly, the case could be used as part of a comparative politics module on government formation and party politics in Western liberal democratic societies (see Ortmayer, with Hodges).

The case as narrative is designed to engage the student both in the understanding and the resolution of conflict situations. Stimulating such engagement is the task of the case writer, in choosing the appropriate subject, developing the story of controversy to draw in the reader, and then suggesting avenues of resolution. Although there is a risk in writing cases about current events that have yet to reach a denouement, this type of case finds an eager audience among students, who approach the discussions productively, often in my experience with keen interest, insight, and critical analysis.

Another operational question for the writer, as also in the selection of extant cases, is to decide between two generic types of cases, "retrospective" and "action forcing." My own preference, as a writer, teacher, and student, has been the action-forcing approach. Such cases attempt to put the reader in the shoes of a relevant decision maker faced with a problem or set of problems requiring action. The main body of the case lays out the situation and describes the underlying dilemmas and available options of the decision maker, which then allows the teacher to pose, and requires the student to grapple with, the underlying question, "What would you do in X's place, and why?" In my own work I then usually write a brief sequel, which can be handed out either during or after class, the purpose of which is to describe the action in fact taken and what the general consequences were. I have found that such sequels provide useful vehicles for follow-up discussions and a means to persuade students to reexamine their assumptions developed during the initial case deliberations. By comparison, retrospective cases relate the whole story, constituting the decision point and beyond, including some account of the consequences.[2] I frequently reinforce class case discussions with case-based essay questions on exams; for example, "Formulate and defend an alternative political strategy for the Freie Demokratische Partei (FDP; Free Democratic Party) after 1994 and compare it with the FDP's actual policy in 1969 and 1982." The results have convinced me that case learning enables students to make the jump to the higher-order thinking that we as teachers hope to catalyze.

Case Discussions

What a case discussion most particularly offers students is, first, material containing issues, problems, dilemmas, puzzles, and then the environment in which they can grapple with these concepts individually and collectively. Teaching a case hinges on the ability and opportunity to empower students to wrestle with course material in ways that engage them, challenge them, and inspire them to think critically and productively, and appropriately in the sense of extending themselves and taking risks—in a safe environment.

One of the attractive elements of case teaching is that no two class discussions of a case are the same. Colleagues who teach cases can attest to the variety of possible outcomes inherent in any case discussion. New students bring new dynamics and insights; therefore, case teaching can be as educational for the professor as for the students. "With greater vitality in the classroom, the satisfaction of true intellectual collaboration and synergy, and improved retention on the part of students, the rewards are considerable" (Christensen, "Premises" 15). Essential to the enterprise is the establishment of a "social contract," or a type of teaching/learning contract, which is a matrix of reciprocal agreements that determine the ground rules of behavior for instructor and students alike (Hansen). Students are enjoined to take risks and participate; the teacher defines multiple functions in the exercise of core case teaching skills.

Components of Case Teaching: Questioning, Listening, Response

> The discussion teacher is planner, host, moderator, devil's advocate, fellow-student, and judge—a potentially confusing set of roles. Even the most seasoned group leader must be content with uncertainty, because discussion teaching is the art of managing spontaneity. (Christensen, "Premises" 16)

The responsibilities and roles of the case discussion leader are as varied as the rewards and, like those for all discussion teaching, resist prescription.[3] Preparation for discussion-based classes takes time and energy, because instructors must consider *what, whom,* and *how* they will teach. Moreover, the classroom demands simultaneous attention to process (the flow of activities that make up a discussion) and content (the material discussed), requiring not only intellectual but also emotional engagement. As a guru of the case method, Chris Christensen, distills all the functions of case teaching down to the exercise of the three core skills of questioning, listening, and responding:

> Mastery of questioning does not begin and end with framing incisive queries about the day's material. It requires asking the right question of the right student at the right time. By the same token, true listening involves more than close attention to words: it means trying to grasp the overtones and implications of each participant's contribution with empathy and respect. Response, probably the least understood of the three skills, means taking constructive action—action that benefits each student and the group—based on the understanding that one's listening has produced. ("Discussion Teacher" 154)

All these activities require—but also reward—flexibility. Skills of this order are learned step-by-step, not from a prescribed manual but only in practice. Together the exercise provides the instructor the opportunity to appreciate multiple viewpoints, insights, levels of understanding, and creativity. Learning comes not from the transfer of knowledge, like some commodity, but from the process of the participants themselves framing their own questions, negotiating with other minds and personalities, and reflecting.

Questioning

Questions initiate learning. They are the heart of the case teaching enterprise. Questions can excite or probe, disturb or reassure, discipline or comfort; their purpose is to promote inquiry. In case teaching the careful formulation and skillful asking of questions is what drives a case discussion. On a basic level questions enable a discussion leader to stimulate students to think about and analyze the day's assignment. They also provide a means for testing student preparation and evaluating the validity of their comments.

In case teaching, however, questions have special properties. They make it possible for the teacher to "guide the discussion process along paths that balance the instructor's desire for rigor and thorough coverage of the material with the students' need to explore content freely, in ways meaningful to them" (Christensen, "Discussion Teacher" 157). It is this balance that is critical: a balance between tailoring questions to individual students' needs and interests and to the needs of the whole group while proceeding toward the day's course objectives. Finally, questions help create and maintain the discussion environment of the class; they can promote competition or cooperation. Part of the strategy is to vary and orchestrate the discussion context, in order to keep students engaged while encouraging them to process a variety of tasks.

Generically, case discussion questions may be grouped into several major categories. *Study questions* assigned in advance intend to draw students into the case and help organize their thinking for the subsequent discussion. *Discussion questions* raise issues and help define areas of exploration for the participants. The best sort of questions tend to be those that genuinely intrigue the teacher, who has not yet settled on his or her own response to them. *Facilitating questions* should draw out the more particular meanings of individual contributions and stimulate interaction among the participants, that is, asking them whether they agree or how they might reconcile divergent perspectives or differing positions taken. Finally, questions are a most important *product* of case discussion, since learning, in turn, to ask good questions facilitates student engagement with the material and independent coping with the situations and issues that cases highlight (Boehrer, "On Teaching" 15–16). That is to say, to promote a spirit of inquiry the case teacher should encourage students to question themselves, their peers, the instructor, the organization of the course, and the presented facts and issues of the case in general. My points about types of useful questions can be organized as follows:

Typology of Case Teaching Questions

Open-ended questions:	"What are your reactions to the German asylum policy case?" "What aspects of the problem were of greatest interest to you?" "Where should we begin?"
Diagnostic questions:	"What is your analysis of the coalition's problem?" "What conclusions did you draw from these electoral data?"
Information-seeking questions:	"What was the GNP of Germany last year?" "What was its trade balance?"
Challenge (testing) questions:	"Why do you believe that?" "What evidence supports your conclusion?" "What arguments might be developed to counter that particular point of view?"
Action questions:	"What specific actions does Kohl need to take to keep the coalition intact?"
Questions on priority and sequence:	"Given the government's limited resources, what's the first step Berlin needs to take to overcome the economic downside of German unification?" "The second?" "And the third?"

Prediction questions:	"If your conclusions are correct, what might be the reactions of the German metalworkers' union?"
Hypothetical questions:	"What could Bonn have done had Germany not moved so quickly to recognize Slovenia and Croatia?" "What could the chancellor have done in this particular instance?
Questions of extension:	"What are the implications of your conclusions about Germany's monetary policy under the *Bundesbank* for its European neighbors, particularly those in the European Monetary System (EMS)?"
Questions of generalization:	"Based on your reading of the formation of Germany's coalition government after the 1994 elections, what do you consider to be the major forces that promote cabinet unity?" "Which threaten its long-term viability?"

Listening

Listening is the very active exercise of what seems on the surface to be a passive activity. Indeed, case teaching demands very focused attention to the discussion—to what individual students are contributing, how the others are reacting, what kind of dialog is developing or what potential for dialog there is, and how all this compares with one's original teaching plan. Thus, listening assumes special importance when education aims not only at the transfer of knowledge but also at preparing students to apply that knowledge and to develop critical thinking and speaking skills. When the classroom dynamic shifts from a teacher-student Socratic dialog to a group learning mode, listening becomes central to the process. "The techniques of active listening—paraphrasing what students say, asking clarifying questions, testing understanding, reflecting consensus—all contribute" (Boehrer, "On Teaching" 15). The key to such listening is selectivity. Processing the entire discussion is a daunting task, so the case teacher has to listen selectively for what seems to be critical to the day's teaching and learning targets (Lenard). Keen observation of the mechanics of presentation can add a great deal to the act of listening, as can the use of other senses or intuition to discern and gauge the class's level of preparation, engagement with the material, multiplicity of viewpoints, confidence in their analysis, awareness of conflict, and willingness to bring the discussion to a close. A great deal of energy goes into mediating and guiding the case discussion.

Responding

Response is essential in maintaining the balance between validating student participation and ensuring the integrity of the class's path of inquiry and the learning objectives of the case. It is necessary for the class teacher to foster a climate of respect for individuals while also facilitating a fair but rigorous examination of ideas. Expressing genuine interest in what students are saying, without necessarily evaluating it, is key to creating an environment in which students may venture uncertain thoughts and risk participation (Hertenstein). Validation does not mean casual praise but, preferably, recognition by their peers through their attentiveness, subsequent comments, and statements of agreement or approval. It can be done through writing a student's comment on the board or referring to an earlier comment by the name of the student who made it, inviting further contributions. This connection of student to process is crucial and may contribute to the fact that so many students react positively to case discussions because in such classes, unlike some others, their presence clearly makes a difference (Franko and Boyer).

Maintaining the focus of discussion is one of the case teacher's main functions. Therefore, differentiating responses is critical, since clearly not all student comments are equally worthy or helpful. At times this requires the teacher to insist on relevance or remind the group what the current question is. Assisting the class in maintaining a sense of progress and an organized recall in wide-ranging discussions supports both the students' confidence in the case process and their actual learning. It is highly useful, then, to go beyond merely recording student comments or mediating their interactions to processing what individuals and the group together have said at various points. The case teacher can push this further by asking the students to prioritize a list of key issues or problem factors or to rank a set of options according to feasibility. Finally, responses can be evaluative, provided they are tactful, balanced, and directed toward the usefulness of the analysis or comment, rather than criticism of the quality of thinking. Because case discussion is demanding of students and teachers and requires that all participants take risks, turning to praise before criticism is unlikely to misfire or impede the learning process (Franko and Boyer).

In summary, good case discussions primarily succeed on the basis of a few major, framing questions that require the participants to search their own knowledge and experience, articulate their ideas about the questions and the material, digest and react to one another's views, and subsequently elaborate on their initial comments. These few good questions usually require many facilitating questions (hence the typology for reference), but the fundamental questions set the direction and indicate eventual goals for the case discussion. While the students are offering and processing a multiplicity of viewpoints, the teacher needs time to clarify, connect, extend, and challenge what the students are saying. "A generic sequence of tasks for the class might be observation, analysis, prescription, evaluation" (Boehrer, "On Teaching" 18). In the end, if successful, students have made the connections between self (participation and engagement), problem (the case and wider issues), and learning (constructing meaning for themselves from observation to evaluation).

Case Learning and Undergraduates

At this point one might ask, in an approach developed for professional and graduate school teaching, what can undergraduates, especially those in a liberal arts setting, bring to the table in case discussions? Case teaching takes into account the old truism: "I hear and I forget; I see and I remember; I do and I understand." Engagement, involvement, and participation count.[4]

More specifically, the inherently interdisciplinary approach involved in case teaching encourages, through the articulation of multiple perspectives, the participant to bring the background and concerns that he or she has to the forum. In a case in the area of German cultural studies, therefore, one student might approach the text from exposure to German language and literature, another from an interest in German institutions, a third from simply having lived or traveled in Germany, a fourth from economics, and a fifth from personal involvement in, say, U.S. politics and current events. Even though the latter two may have only a rudimentary background in German studies, they still can provide critical perspectives that can challenge, complement, and extend the viewpoints of their peers. Involvement also means risk taking: "I am not an expert in *X,* but I do have something to contribute."

Involvement can be further structured in a variety of ways to promote active learning. One possibility is role playing—that is, by assigning various roles corresponding to the key actors in the case narrative that the student role players represent in discussion. By having to represent and defend a perspective that they do not personally hold, or only may acknowledge as a possibility, students are encouraged to understand the existence and validity of perspectives that they did not think about previously (Rogers 331–32). Engagement in role-playing and other improvisation can be preplanned as the center of a case class or may be a second pathway for discussion to complement the questioning strategy. This technique can be especially instructive if the teacher finds the discussion has become one-sided, without much controversy. Controversy stimulates engagement, and assigning roles forces some students to look at a problem through a different lens.

Debriefing after role-playing is important because it extends the exercise from a game to an analytical project. While the role-play is instrumental in getting students inside the case, they need to look back at why they portrayed a certain outcome or offered a particular solution and viewpoint. Making the interests of the actors in the case explicit, and perhaps comparing the student outcome to the actual outcome, allows the exercise to become more than simply an expedient and entertaining means of bolstering discussion and generating a policy outcome but also to become material for analysis in and of itself.

Conclusion

Why use cases and the case method of teaching and learning? Case teachers subscribe to the method not only because they believe their students learn more and learn better when they are at the center of the process but also because the teachers themselves find case discussion to be highly stimulating and rewarding. The instructor in the case class is not the teller machine of facts and theories but, rather, the orchestra conductor attempting to elicit each student's personal best. Each student can develop his or her own appropriate context for engaging issues as "foreign" as German political economy or as abstract as German parliamentary behavior and validate those ideas or develop them further in the give-and-take drama of active learning. Good case discussions spill over into the halls and dormitories.

The excitement of the case classroom—the questioning, the engagement, the lively but friendly skirmishing, the sense of collective enterprise—makes straight lecturing less appealing, even boring, for students and teachers alike. With students taking charge of the responsibility for their own learning, they may often take the discussion in directions that the instructor has not predicted or even anticipated. Not infrequently, the outcome of such spontaneity, creatively managed, is that the instructor learns something as well.

NOTES

1. Since 1990 Boehrer has been the director of the Pew Faculty Fellowship in International Affairs, housed at the Kennedy School of Government, Harvard University, and funded by the Pew Charitable Trusts.

2. For instance, David Painter and Kenneth Wolf offer two very interesting and quite different retrospective cases available through the Pew Case Studies in International Affairs program of the Institute for the Study of Diplomacy at Georgetown University; a variant of the decision-forcing genre is the case by Thomas Magstadt.

3. Many of these observations are based on my participation in an intensive workshop as a Pew Faculty Fellow in International Affairs at the Kennedy School of Government, Harvard University, 1990, and as a staff member of the institute in 1993 and 1994.

4. Retention studies support the idea that students' active involvement in their own learning greatly enhances their ability to retain information. Six weeks after a test students retain "10% of what they read, 20% of what they hear, 30% of what they see, 50% of what they see and hear, 70% of what they say, and 90% of what they do and say" (Stice 293).

WORKS CITED

Boehrer, John. "On Teaching a Case." *International Studies Notes* 19.2 (Spring 1994): 13–19.

———. "Spectators and Gladiators: Reconnecting the Students with the Problem." *Teaching Excellence* 2.7 (1990–91): 1–2.

Christensen, C. Roland. "The Discussion Teacher in Action: Questioning, Listening, and Response." In *Education for Judgment: The Artistry of Discussion Leadership,* ed. C. Roland Christensen, David A. Garvin, and Ann Sweet. Boston: Harvard Business School, 1991. 153–72.

———. "Premises and Practices of Discussion Teaching." In *Education for Judgment: The Artistry of Discussion Leadership,* ed. C. Roland Christensen, David A. Garvin, and Ann Sweet. Boston: Harvard Business School, 1991. 15–34.

Christensen, C. Roland, with Abby J. Hansen. *Teaching and the Case Method.* Boston: Harvard Business School, 1987.

Franko, Patrice, Vicki Golich, and Mark Boyer, eds. *The ABCs of Case Teaching: A Manual in Progress.* Washington, DC: Pew Case Study Program, Institute for the Study of Diplomacy, Georgetown U, 1997.

Hansen, Abby J. "Establishing a Teaching/Learning Contract." In *Education for Judgment: The Artistry of Discussion Leadership,* ed. C. Roland Christensen, David A. Garvin, and Ann Sweet. Boston: Harvard Business School, 1991. 123–35.

Hertenstein, Julie H. "Patterns of Participation." In *Education for Judgment: The Artistry of Discussion Leadership,* ed. C. Roland Christensen, David A. Garvin, and Ann Sweet. Boston: Harvard Business School, 1991. 175–91.

Kennedy, David M., and Esther Scott, "Preparing Cases in Public Policy." Cambridge: Harvard Kennedy School of Government Case Program, N15-85-652, 1985.

Kraft, Robert G. "Bike Riding and the Art of Learning." *Change* 10.6 (1978): 36, 40–42.

Lenard, Herman B. "With Open Ears: Listening and the Art of Discussion Leading." In *Education for Judgment: The Artistry of Discussion Leadership,* ed. C. Roland Christensen, David A. Garvin, and Ann Sweet. Boston: Harvard Business School, 1991. 137–51.

Magstadt, Thomas. *Ethics and Emigration: The East German Exodus, 1989.* No. 506-90-O. Washington, DC: Pew Case Studies in International Affairs, Institute for the Study of Diplomacy, Georgetown U, 1990.

McDade, Sharon A. *An Introduction to the Case Study Method: Preparation, Analysis, and Participation.* Cambridge: President and Fellows of Harvard College, 1988.

Ortmayer, Louis L. "A New 'Berlin Wall': German Asylum Policy Change." Forth-
    coming.
Ortmayer, Louis L., with Samantha Hodges. "The End of the Kohl Era? German Poli-
    tics in Transition." Washington, DC: Pew Case Study Program, Institute for the
    Study of Diplomacy, Georgetown U, 1997. Forthcoming.
Painter, David S. *The German Question and the Cold War.* No. 415-94-R. Washington,
    DC: Pew Case Studies in International Affairs, Institute for the Study of Diplomacy,
    Georgetown U, 1988; revised, 1994.
Robyn, Dorothy. "What Makes a Good Case." No. N15-86-673. Cambridge: Harvard
    Kennedy School of Government Case Program, 1986.
Rogers, Carl R. *On Becoming a Person.* Boston: Houghton Mifflin, 1961.
Stice, James E. "Using Kolb's Learning Cycle to Improve Student Learning." *Engi-
    neering Education* (February 1987): 291–96.
Wolf, Kenneth H. *The "Bohemian Corporal" Becomes Chancellor of Germany.* No.
    363-94-N. Washington, DC: Pew Case Studies in International Affairs program, In-
    stitute for the Study of Diplomacy, Georgetown U, 1994.

CHAPTER 26

Teaching Students and Teachers of German Cultural Studies

Richard M. Hunt

There are a variety of ways to explore new methodologies and fields of inquiry: teaching is among the best because the classroom allows for immediate feedback and brings together individuals with varied backgrounds and interests. While scholarship should not be determined by market forces alone, the response of students, like that of professional peers, is an important factor in assessing the merits of an intellectual project. Richard Hunt has taught an extremely popular course at Harvard University on Weimar and National Socialist Germany for over two decades and has recast it several times in ways that, with hindsight, reflect both scholarly innovations and changing public concerns. In the 1960s the course began as straight history; in the 1970s it emphasized the themes of social activism and responsibility; in the 1980s a new interdisciplinarity added literary and filmic resources. These changes did not represent an effort to follow fashion but, instead, reflected receptivity to new ideas and conceptions of what constitutes the subject matter. Flexibility is a hallmark of a cultural studies approach.

Hunt's openness to innovation also manifested itself in a collegiality with graduate students and other associates that is nothing short of legendary. It is no secret that the three editors of this volume all worked with him as teaching assistants: we, like many others involved with the course, felt that our ideas had a discernible impact on both the curriculum and the various pedagogical strategies that were employed. Hunt recruited his assistants from a variety of disciplines, and the weekly meetings that he convened proved a stimulating exercise in interdisciplinary cooperation. His was truly a team-taught course. While individuals were never asked to abandon their disciplinary perspective— which included different methodologies and subject priorities—they were always required to accord their colleagues respect. Hunt told his teaching assis-

431

tants of a metaphor that he used with his own students: that they were all on a joint expedition and that he viewed himself as the seasoned explorer. In fact, this analogy applied to the teaching staff of the course as well and, as we have subsequently recognized, scholarship is an activity that is enriched by this associative effort.

At the beginning I think it appropriate to recall an old epithet: "Those who can, do; those who can't, teach; those who can't teach, teach teachers to teach." And so it goes. The teaching of students and teachers has often been relegated to a second- or third-class status. In the field of modern German cultural studies I think a strong case can be made for special attention to be paid to the task of classroom teaching. Surely in this most provocative and issue-laden area of recent European history, the stakes are quite high for helping our students "get the story straight" and understand some of the deeper issues of the German historical and cultural record.

I was thinking along these lines when I read the observation of a colleague: "The very subject of German cultural studies with all its glorious but also tormented baggage provides—a unique focus of constant self-scrutiny and self-consciousness and sensitivity when we go about doing what we do in our chosen fields." Of course, this focus must pervade our research. I contend that it is all the more necessary, however, when we scholars enter the classrooms of our students and raise the painful problems, quandaries, and moral dilemmas that characterize the German past and present. Self-scrutiny, self-consciousness, and sensitivity are absolutely imperative if we are to reach young inquiring minds as they take our college courses and begin to study German culture. One way for me to proceed is to indulge in some self-reflection about my own experience with German cultural studies. Unlike most graduate students today, my career trajectory into the field of German cultural studies covered a long and sometimes convoluted course. In the end I believe it was the teaching fellows in my course who nudged, pushed, and pulled me into teaching the kind of course I give today to Harvard undergraduates.

Trained in the Harvard history department by William Langer, Franklin Ford, and H. Stuart Hughes, I began to teach a course on "Nazi Germany" to undergraduates in the mid-1960s. Without realizing it at the time, I was giving the kind of course that Arthur Schlesinger Sr. used to call "drum and trumpet" history. By that he meant basically no-nonsense, no-frills, straight, political, military narrative. Most Harvard undergraduate history courses were taught this way in those days. Since my course was actually in the General Education program, I did have some latitude to introduce other, "softer" material. Moreover, I had the good fortune to have been a teaching fellow in David Riesman's General Education course on "American Social Character" (he took pride in giving his students a full picture of what he called "formerly underprivileged orders of data—family life, children, social class, etc.") and also in Erik Erikson's General Education course on the "Human Life Cycle" (he urged his teaching fellows to engage in "creative trespassing" beyond their academic disciplines into other domains such as psychoanalysis, cultural anthropology, and biography). Luckily for me, I had been exposed to broader possibilities in teaching history.

I have to say, however, that in the mid-1960s the pressures to conform to the standards of presenting facts, names, dates, events, and battles were fairly strong. I recall few history courses that introduced novels, slides, or films during the class hour (Franklin Ford's "German History 1815–1945" was an exception). It was almost as if these kinds of extraneous diversions were professionally impermissible. I remember one senior history professor who decried the showing of films in courses because to do so was to display professional insecurity and to sell out one's academic rigor for the sake of trendy student popularity.

Then came the late 1960s. Things changed. It was no accident that events in the United States and the world influenced the content and style of many courses at all colleges. Newly titled "Nazi Totalitarianism" (still in the General Education program), my course quickly expanded to include readings, lectures, and class handouts on topics dealing with the Nazi Party as a social revolutionary movement in the 1920s, youth movements in the Weimar period, the forms of Nazi, Communist, and Social Democratic Party propaganda, and Nazi attacks against "degenerate art." I now asked students to read novels like Remarque's *All Quiet on the Western Front* and Brecht's play *The Resistible Rise of Arturo Ui.* Of course, with a group of increasingly visually adept students, the idea of presenting a variety of film screenings during the term met with student enthusiasm. Leni Riefenstahl's *Triumph of the Will,* Erwin Leiser's *Mein Kampf,* and a Museum of Modern Art selection of Nazi propaganda films including *Hitlerjunge Quex* were the first films shown in the course. I have a vivid memory of a spring evening in 1970, a time of constant student protests and rallies against the Vietnam War. My students and I emerged from Harvard's Burr Hall after watching scenes of street fighting and police clashes with rioters in *Hitlerjunge Quex.* On Quincy Street we were met by a line of Cambridge police spraying tear gas on retreating groups of students and local activists. We had traveled from virtual reality in pre-Nazi Germany to tangible reality in 1970 America; at first it was hard to notice much of a difference.

Students during these years often had difficulties making political distinctions. Student papers sometimes drew parallels between Nixon and Hitler (with the *x* replaced by a swastika), Heinrich Himmler and J. Edgar Hoover, the bombing of Dresden and U.S. bombing in Vietnam. My teaching fellows and I struggled mightily to discourage such counterfeit comparisons. But there could be no denying that Nazi history and culture were very much alive in their minds as powerful cautionary tales.

In 1974 my course, already protean in structure, took on a new identity. Responding to some students and teaching fellows who often raised issues of moral decision, civil courage, and ethical relativism, I redesigned the course to focus on problems in the area of history and practical ethics. "Moral Dilemmas in a Repressive Society: Nazi Germany" became the new title of the course (irreverently dubbed "Krauts and Doubts" by the Harvard *Crimson*), and it offered students the chance to ponder eight real-life moral dilemmas confronting actual historical figures during the Weimar and Nazi periods. They were anti-Nazis, Nazi sympathizers, Nazi ideologues, and non-Nazi ordinary people, all of whom were suddenly thrust into unwanted conflicts in which principles, politics, ambition, ideology, decency, and personal security collided. A fireman in a small town was pressured to join the Nazi Party in 1933 "because it would be good for his career." The mayor of another town had to decide whether to prohibit a Nazi parade in the streets at the same time as a scheduled Social Democratic parade. A physician was asked to do some research for the proposed Nazi euthanasia program. A Catholic cardinal, a Protestant pastor, a Wehrmacht captain on the Eastern Front, young students distributing anti-Nazi leaflets in Munich, all of these Germans, public figures and private citizens, acted out their roles in history with varying degrees of heroism, complacency, and political vengeance. It was the purpose of the course to explore their motives and choices and the consequences of those choices.

Two decades ago in a *New York Times* Op-Ed piece I lamented that some of the students in this class were reacting in puzzling or distressing ways to the material (16 Feb. 1976, "No-Fault Guilt-Free History"). To my chagrin, and I hope not induced by me or by the approach of my teaching fellows, these students were adopting a paralyzing fatalism in their interpretation of the Nazi epoch. I wrote that these students, for one reason or another, had arrived at a "no-fault, guilt-free" judgment about the German people during the Nazi time. Their excuses and exculpations took the form of comments like these: "If I had been there in Germany in those days, I would probably have gone along with the Nazis." "Like everyone else the German people were not able to foresee where Hitler's policies were leading." "The ordinary person could do little or nothing to resist the Nazis." "The German people were locked into their history." For our part, my teaching fellows and I fell into a state of depression when we heard our students lapse into such resigned historical relativism. I remember that we had many meetings to plan how to challenge students out of their philosophical lethargy. We could ask our students many questions. "How do you know you would not have been able to find the courage to resist the appeals of Nazism?" "What do you mean there was no evidence of where Hitler's policies were leading?" "What about *Mein Kampf* published in the mid-1920s?" "Were not Hitler's early speeches ablaze with antisemitism and hatred?" "What about the long record of Nazi terror in the streets in the 1920s?" Finally, "was it not possible for ordinary people to engage in all kinds of decent acts and oppositional deeds that would not necessarily have landed them in concentration camps?" "Do we really have to accept the position that both the German people and the Nazis themselves were passive pawns of fate and the victims of their merciless historical circumstances?"

At any rate I think our challenges worked to some degree because by the late 1970s we heard fewer judgments of this kind from our students. Of course, by this time all of us—students and teachers—were entering the more certain 1980s, and relativism had become less prevalent in various historical inquiries.

In 1984, pushed again by students and teaching fellows who were now coming from disciplines such as German literature, film studies, women's studies, architecture, and fine arts, the course took its latest and present form. Now a Core course in the section under Literature and the Arts, the title became "Culture and Society in Weimar and Nazi Germany." At last it had arrived at a form that might qualify it as a genuine course in German cultural studies. At the time I don't believe my teaching fellows and I recognized it as such, because we never used this term to describe it. In fact, we conceived our task as combining the study of history with the study of works of art and cultural trends. More specifically, this involved relating and comparing historical events and cultural products of two periods of one country's past.

Some students, accustomed at Harvard to studying within discretely defined academic disciplines, found the assignment confusing and frustrating. "What kind of course is this?" they asked. "Is it history or literature or fine arts or what?" Our only answer could be, "All of the above, but in a special combination." In the course syllabus I wrote: "Please note this is a Harvard Core course that conforms to Core guidelines. In studying the social and cultural history of the Weimar and Nazi periods, the course will attempt to enhance the understanding of representative German works of art by considering their historical setting. Conversely, it will use many different artistic works to illuminate the tumultuous historical experience of the German people in the first half of the twentieth century."

In the first year of this particular course my teaching fellows and I recognized several further dimensions to what we were trying to do. First of all, we accepted the interdisciplinary nature of the course. This meant that all of us would have to familiarize ourselves with certain basic concepts in modern art, architecture, music, literature, and filmmaking.

Second, we also wanted to be generalists in drawing our students' attention to how works of art function one way in one society (Weimar Germany) and another way in another society (Nazi Germany). For us it quickly became clear that some interesting discussions could take place in the comparison between those artists who pursued "art for art's sake" and those who, in a later period, were seduced or coerced into producing art for the sake of political propaganda or the advancement of ideology.

Third, we were committed to the risky task of drawing some tentative conclusions about the connections between different artistic expressions in each period and exploring their relation to the historical context. For example, it seemed to us a permissible assumption—most but not all students in the first year agreed—that some ties existed between the disjointed stream of consciousness in Döblin's *Berlin Alexanderplatz,* the increasingly nonrealistic paintings of Karl Schmidt-Rottluff and Wassily Kandinsky, and the twelve-tone musical compositions of Arnold Schönberg. What did they have in common and why? That was to be discussed. It would be easy to find many affinities in terms of style and content in Weimar works of art, but then we also conceived it as an obligation to point out the many variations and deviations from the culture that existed in both the Weimar period and during the Third Reich.

As I look back now on this latest metamorphosis of the course, I am struck again by the enormous expansion of topics and materials now covered in lectures, readings, and films.[1] Some aspects of the course, however, have remained unchanged over the years. I felt strongly, and all the teaching fellows agreed, that narrative history should continue as a central organizing principle of the course. The chronology of both periods went through the influence of World War I, the effects of the 1919 Versailles Treaty, the inflation of 1923, the depression of 1929, the events of the Third Reich at peace in 1933–39, and the history of the Third Reich at war. All of these essentials of historical understanding had to be presented and, we hoped, mastered by students at an early time in the course.

Another ongoing feature of the course that remained unchanged from the first years was the reading of Thomas Mann's powerful novella *Mario and the Magician.* We have always assigned this gripping piece in the first week of the term. Long ago Henry Hatfield, one of Harvard's great scholars of Mann's work, told me that, if a teacher couldn't teach *Mario and the Magician* and get a strong response from students, then he or she couldn't teach anything. This story of the demented magician and hypnotist in a small Italian sea resort offers a marvelous introduction to charismatic leadership and followership. Although Mann wrote the story in an Italian setting several years before Hitler came to power, this allegory about fascist political culture had poignant relevance for the subject matter of the course.

One more unchanging presence on my course reading list over the years has been Primo Levi's searing account of his life in a Nazi extermination camp.

Hundreds of other "I was there" testimonies have appeared in print since the end of the war. Levi's *Survival in Auschwitz* (1959) is, in my opinion, a sensitive, eloquent, and enduring work of world-class literature. I have regularly assigned this book in the course's last week of reading. It is true that it ends the course with a terrible shock of gloom. But few students are unaffected by its message, and, of course, it is a message that needs to be told in a compelling way.

Finally, as I ponder my years of teaching this course, focused on two seemingly very different periods of history, I must mention that I myself have changed the most in my understanding of the inner nature of, and continuities between, the Weimar decade and the Nazi period. Even in the late 1980s my teaching fellows and I almost delighted in finding contrasts between the "golden years" of the German 1920s and the leaden, sordid, violent era of the Nazi record. It was all too easy to compare the cultural brilliance of Weimar artists with the dull propagandistic work of those serving Hitler's regime. Democracy versus totalitarianism, freedom versus dictatorship, individual rights versus Nazi "justice," attempts at peaceful reconciliation versus militarism and total war—these were the political dichotomies that seemed to typify these two periods of twentieth-century German history. Still today, I admit the basic truths of these oppositions.

Yet the more I teach this course the more I find myself thinking about the less obvious underlying continuities running through the Weimar and Nazi periods. My teaching fellows, and the students too, are struck more and more by certain themes that are played out in both periods. As one student, well read in German literature, wrote in his term paper, "in the end there are all too many elective affinities between aspects of Weimar modernism and Hitler's Nazism." A long story needs to be told here. Let me briefly list some of these continuities worth further exploration. My Harvard colleague, Daniel Bell, has done just this on a more general level in his book *The Cultural Contradictions of Capitalism.* Although it requires much qualification and refinement, my thesis is that aspects of Weimar modernism (clearly a term in need of precise definition) resemble certain representations of Nazi ideology in their totalistic rejection of parts of Germany's past: in their contempt for religion; in their pervasive preoccupation with the new; in a revolutionary vision of man and history; in their fascination with violence, crime, war, and anti-intellectualism; in their obsession with death and resurrection; and, finally, in a belief somehow in the possibility and desirability of the transvaluation of all values—moral, political, cultural.

One of the pleasures of teaching my course these past few years has come from challenging teaching fellows and students to explore these ideas, certainly to criticize them and demolish their validity if they can but also to think up other conceptual frameworks. For one thing, it makes for a much more interesting exercise in interpretation, one that can yield more sophisticated understandings than the prevailing light versus darkness and "good guys" and "bad guys" antitheses.

A final note: as a longtime teacher, it is interesting for me to conjecture what will be the future centers of inquiry for the Weimar and Nazi periods. Will deconstruction, semiotics, the history of everyday life, ethnic history, and family history open up new terrain? Or, as it has always done, will the future surprise us with the appearance of unexpected modes of investigating these periods of the German past?

NOTE

1. See Hunt's syllabus in pt. 8.

CHAPTER 27

The Pragmatics of Studying the "German" at the Turn of the Century

Sander L. Gilman

In an academic environment in which not all accusations of dense, jargon-ridden, and self-indulgent prose are off base and in which, to some, professional advancement might appear at first glance to be dependent upon intellectual fashion rather than rigor, Sander Gilman's sensible sketch of how to be a solid scholar is welcome indeed. Gilman served as president of the Modern Language Association in 1995, and here he speaks from this position. He reminds us that we, as teachers and scholars in the humanities and social sciences, control the shape and direction of our profession and of our research interests within it. If we choose to take the study of German literature, German politics, German history, German art, music, culture, and theology to the rich grounds of cultural studies, then we, the practitioners, have the right and the power to do just that. But, Gilman warns, for our new kinds of questions and answers to be useful, for them to help us understand ourselves and our world better, they must conform to the same kind of rigorous scholarly standards by which good work has been judged for generations. Furthermore, like Leslie Willson, Gilman argues for scholarship that is accessible in the context in which it is produced, that is, written in English. Gilman's essay will be especially valuable for young scholars, for he sets out in plain language and with clear examples basic guidelines for what makes scholarly research valuable—valuable enough to be rewarded with tenure. In a polemical, pragmatic, and admonitory way Sander Gilman calls for the kind of scholarship the editors have brought together in this volume and hope will be inspired by it.

∞

In 1989 I shocked many of my colleagues in Departments of German when I published "Why and How I Study the German" in the *German Quarterly,* the official journal of the American Association of Teachers of German. I received calls and letters from colleagues, who said, "Look, I agree with you, but you really shouldn't say this in public for you will anger [the West Germans who are helping pay for our trips to Germany, our films, our book prizes, our fellowships]"—this latter was never stated explicitly but always fearfully implied. My essay had been the basis of a presentation to a conference convened in Philadelphia the year before by the German Academic Exchange Service (DAAD) on the future of German studies. At the meeting I had been even more shocking. I insisted, much to the amusement of the colleagues present, that "where I go, there goes German studies!" This was not at all a narcissistic statement but the obvious (and unrecognized) fact that we—the "certified" members of a profession—at any given time and place determine its structure, direction, and questions. This was the case in 1973, when I began the first German studies major as chair of the German Studies Department at Cornell University, and it is true today in my first years in the newly constituted Department of Germanic Studies at the University of Chicago. In 1995, the year that I served as president of the Modern Language Association, a gathering of scholars across a wide range of disciplines, I thought it appropriate to imagine the pragmatics of what German studies means before the new century dawns. The point of departure for these thoughts was an e-mail letter I had received recently from a younger colleague who had taken part in one of my DAAD summer seminars for college teachers a few years prior. His question was quite blunt and to the point: what is tenure in German studies, and what do I have to do to get it? He is at a research-oriented institution, so my answer began (like it or not) with the question of publications. It is, of course, the production of new knowledge in a field that is what is supposed to set research-oriented institutions of higher learning off against other institutions.

Yes, I know that other institutions, even if not "research oriented," often stress research and that teaching is important, if not vital, for tenure. But, in answering his specific request, I wanted to address the question of the production and dissemination of knowledge in German studies. For what do you teach in the classroom if there is no new knowledge being produced? Do you simply recycle your graduate student notes until they become yellowed with age? And what happens in fields such as German studies in which the very basis of the field has shifted, in which new questions, new approaches, have so altered the inherent structure of the field as to make that option unavailable for those who received their degrees a decade or so ago?

Attacks on the humanities (such as "prof scam") have mocked the role that the humanist, including the teacher of German studies, has in the production of knowledge. What we do as research is labeled as superficial or trivial or meaningless or—even worse—politically correct. All of these labels are an attempt to dismiss the basic research in the humanities as not "pragmatic," as being marginal to the "real" task of higher education: teaching. Humanists teach, like Socrates; scientists do research, like Pasteur. (Even here Pasteur had better spin doctors in his time than did Socrates. Remember, Pasteur published; Socrates didn't.) Basic research in the sciences fares much better today. Few people will attack research in the natural or social sciences that has no obvious "applied" dimension, because we have as a collective hope that such scientific investigations can lead to applied results in an imagined future. Yet the research that we as humanists do has an applied aspect because it directly comes out of or flows into our teaching. Yet the humanist who writes, say, about Esther Dischereit while teaching her work to undergraduates as well as graduates as a means of understanding the role that literature has and has had in post-Wall Germany or the history of the German novel or ethnic writing or the pursuit of an ethical model in culture, is accused of researching topics that are "too ivory tower" (*ivory tower* today can mean too politically correct). How should we present our contributions to scholarship to make it worthwhile and therefore to have it serve as the basis for tenure?

While pondering the request to define the role of publication in the tenure process, there crossed my desk requests to read the scholarly production of younger scholars in German studies who were up for promotion or who intended to apply for competitive fellowships. Here, too, the question of what one must do to get promoted or rewarded within the academy was raised. It is especially important in our field as the standards within and the very definition of the field have so radically shifted in the past decade. In the 1960s it was possible to get tenure in German studies (then *Germanistik*) in the United States by editing scholarly texts. My own work in editing sixteenth-century proverb collections as well as the Storm and Stress writer F. M. Klinger preoccupied a large part of my scholarly life. While I also wrote monographs, it was my editing abilities and interests that marked my early career. Today this would be impossible in any area of the humanities. The premature closing of the Thomas More edition at Yale because the English Department was unwilling to hire anyone to continue it is a salient example. In these cases I could not comment on anything but the projects before me and the publication record of the candidates. I did not know much, if anything, about their teaching and service. Certainly, there were clear guidelines, I thought, that I could write to my younger colleague, guidelines that enabled me to evaluate scholarship. I came up with a five-part answer to my friend and wanted to share it with you (and him). As a scholar in German studies:

1. Publish in refereed books and journals
2. as part of dialogue in the world of ideas

3. and present a new or interesting manner of understanding a problem
4. to a clearly defined audience
5. in an accessible manner.

1.   Publish in Refereed Books and Journals

All judgment of scholarship is subjective, but there are collective norms for judgment that are present in every field at any given time. There is a real difference in North America between vanity publishing and academic publishing, and only some of this has to do with the payment of subventions for publication. There are certainly distinguished presses and series that request subventions, especially in fields in which there is the expectation of limited sales. Such requests are in contrast to the letter that you receive upon defending your thesis (or at least at the moment when the abstract goes on-line) that says, "We will publish your book!" Who will read the book for the press, who will critique it in terms of the wider audience, who will read it for style and content—such questions are important, especially for the first-time author. The authority of the specialist in the field provides some context for the new author's work. Will the "book" be distributed to bookstores, or will it only be announced in a flyer or not at all? Will your book be printed or published? Certainly, there are "famous" cases, such as Friedrich Nietzsche, and different cultures in which vanity publications are understood as valid. In Germany it was and is expected that the dissertation and the *Habilitationsschrift* (second thesis) be published. Presses have arisen to undertake such tasks, and some of them now have expanded into the North American market. In Germany there are even state sources of support for such publications. Many of these presses function as more antiquated equivalents to the University Microfilm on-demand distribution of your dissertation in the United States. You can imagine a certain point in the very near future at which all theses will be on-line (they are now all being written electronically anyway), and we will be able to access each thesis at their university's World Wide Web (WWW) site with illustrations and even quick-time films. There are refereed journals on-line now that have made the breakthrough. Yet we still publish in hard copies of books—make sure the press is not merely printing but is also publishing your book!

2.   Publish Your Work as Part of Dialog
in the World of Ideas

All books in German studies should relate in some meaningful way to the ongoing debates that exist in our world of scholarship. The book can accept these debates and think them further or refute them and show how very wrong they are in root and branch. There are infinite questions that could and have been asked in every field of knowledge. Yet there are always subsets that are important in specific cultures and times. Thus—in German studies today—a much different set of questions is being asked in American German scholarship than in Germanic scholarship in the new Germany itself. Certainly, within American feminist discourse in German studies an entirely different palette of colors is being used than in feminist scholarship in Germany. The very question of the meaning of "gender" is different in Germany. My 1993 book *Freud, Race and Gender* (Princeton UP) appeared with Fischer Verlag as *Freud, Rasse, und Identität*. Indeed, some of the questions here study the kinds of questions now being asked in Germany; they examine why these questions are being asked and how they are being answered.

A generation ago (twenty long years) we in German studies in North America were asking the identical questions to those asked in West Germany. At that time these questions and approaches made sense for us and our students in the United States and Canada. The Cold War was our matrix, and we saw Europe (and Europe saw itself) through certain powerful models. Evidently, if Naomi Schor's essay in the 1992 volume of *Profession* and Alice Kaplan's *French Lessons* are right, this was also the case in French studies at the time. We must become aware of the value of our questions and our ability to generate and frame them. Such questions must arise out of our interest and our positionality. Today the questions and the problems are different, and tomorrow they will again be different. It is not that younger scholars must accept these ever changing models in their scholarship but that the work must respond in one way or another to those concerns of our day. We must not become obsessive about the "outdatedness" of what we do, for at some point every question or paradigm will seem passé; nor would we become "superior" when our fifteen minutes in the academic limelight takes place. All scholarship shifts emphasis over time. Yet at any given moment we need to understand what and why a specific question or text or approach resonates in our scholarly community, a community whose perimeters are also always shifting.

3. Scholarship Must Present a New or Interesting Manner of Understanding a Problem

Scholarship in German studies is a big umbrella; it ranges across all fields and all approaches. Yet there is a quality that has to do with the fascination for the unknown and the interesting. We search in our scholarship for "truths"—for some, truths in our time; for others, absolute truths. But even those who seek after absolute truths know that these truths present different facets at different times. Fashion and taste are not supposed to dictate scholarship, yet they clearly do. Good scholarship speaks to the times and its needs. Thus, work done by great scholars, such as Heinz Politzer's book on Kafka, remain great works of scholarship. Still, as it recently has been elegantly shown, Politzer avoided the question of the materiality of Kafka's life and world, a materiality that would have included his own body. Mark Anderson's brilliant new Kafka book alters our understanding of Politzer's Kafka because it asks questions at a very different point in time. Today, in the age of AIDS, such questions are not peripheral to an understanding of the life and works of an author. We have seen the power of stigmatizing illnesses, especially those imagined to be sexually transmitted, on the world of culture. The meaning of the Jewish body in the 1960s for a German-Jewish exile poet and critic was quite different and much too close to the skin. Did Politzer's work need to be augmented thirty years after its publication? Of course it did, because all scholarship, no matter how great, is never the final word.

Our own awareness as scholars in German studies of how our lives and times help set our scholarly questions must be grounded in our understanding of our own roots and our own desires. Such positions have been articulated in a series of brilliantly written autobiographies by critics in other fields. Scholars such as Eunice Lipton, Marianna de Marco Torgovnick, Cathy Davidson, Alice Kaplan, and Susan Suleiman have reflected on their position as scholars in relationship to the world and to their work. Traditionally, self-reflection of this sort was rarely done by scholars in their prime. These books are not simply the summation of a creative life but, rather, the rethinking of what life events were important to the scholar and why they shaped the choice of scholarly field and object. In an age of identity politics, studying the "German" as a complex object has meant that all of us—whether ethnically German or not—have had to come to terms with why we are undertaking this task. In German studies such self-reflection has rarely taken place for an English-reading audience. (Two German language texts already exist: Jost Hermand's autobiography of his youth under the Nazis and Ruth Klüger's introspective account of surviving Theresienstadt and Auschwitz both could serve as models for so addressing our American experiences as Germanists.) We must undertake such self-examinations, if the critic in German studies is to become aware of the processes within the individual and the society by which scholarship becomes important—and understand that "fashion" in scholarship is a sign of this importance.

4.   Publish for a Clearly Defined Audience

Who do you imagine reading your scholarly work (besides your parents)? More and more, I hear from academic publishers that scholars in German studies have stopped buying their books. The assumption is that they have also stopped reading scholarly books. The very books and essays we produce have to be consumed. Thus, in a small field such as German studies there are by definition limited numbers of readers, yet it has always seemed odd to me that even in the most limited field there were and are always writers who can raise the expectations of the reader and the field above the level of minutiae. Today one can mention Andreas Huyssen, Anton Kaes, Marc Weiner, Eric Santner, Peter Hohendahl, and Maria Tatar as scholars whose recent works have been read by a wide public beyond the boundaries of German studies. Other parallels would include the great academic translators in our field, such as Krishna Winston, who are able to make the complex texts of writers like Grass and Handke available to the English-language reading public. Such work makes our scholarship available to the intellectual reading public—within and outside of the academic setting. Is it possible for this to be at least one of the goals for tenurable scholarship? One hopes so.

5.   Write in an Accessible Manner

It is clear that every profession has its "jargon," the verbal shorthand that makes it possible to communicate complex notions quickly to colleagues working on the same topic. German studies has a number of such ideolects (in both German and English). Accessibility of scholarship might be defined as using such language to communicate directly to other such specialists concerned with your problem. Yet truly great scholarship in German studies usually is great because it has meaning or is useful to scholars across a range of fields. Thus, the work of relatively few professors of German studies, such as those mentioned here, has been as "useful" to students in English, French literature, and intellectual history as to those in German studies. First-rate scholarship should provide a reader with a model for approaching a topic as well as solid and substantial content. Such scholarship is usually especially accessible. Elaine Showalter recently insisted to me that scholarly books be readable books. And I think that this quality would be a requirement for first-rate scholarship.

The language of such scholarship is not incidental. While it is possible that scholars in the Anglophone critical world might well seek to address German colleagues on topics of common interest in German, at least at present, such topics are relatively infrequent. Our critical world should be the world of the Anglophone humanist whose work is of interest and use to scholars and teachers in other fields within our critical universe. It is possible that there are moments of convergence in certain arenas, but the focus should be to speak across the departmental borders at our institutions. Part of this is self-defense. If we speak only to colleagues in Germany and speak to them in German, we lose the potential for dialog with our neighbors. But part of it is the real sense that we have more of a common project in the study of the language, literature, and cultural of a non-Anglophone world with those who study the French or the Italian or the Japanese than with the object of study itself. From Kuno Francke (a paid agent of the kaiser) at the turn of the century to the political and economic refugees of the 1930s through the 1960s, great scholarship was undertaken in the United States in German. But at that point the interests of American and German scholars overlapped more substantially. German studies was defined (by the Germans), and the dialog was among "Germans" in whatever nation (and of whatever nationality and language) they found themselves. This created an illusion of "international Germanistik," which was, of course, rooted in the interests, desires, and financing of the German government. It was (and is) cultural propaganda of the first order. German departments wrote and taught in German for other scholars—who wrote and taught in German. The pragmatic result of this was the linguistic and critical isolation of German departments, which became German-speaking islands in an English-speaking world. While they could have entered into dialog with the broader field, they did not. Quite the opposite is now the case. The very model of German studies that brings all of those working on the object "Germany" (however defined) together means that such scholarship must be accessible across disciplinary rather than geographic boundaries. My hope for the next ten years is that many more books and articles such as my "ideal" type will cross my desk and be read by colleagues in many additional fields to our own. We have now begun to think about the study of the German as a field as complex and fraught with difficulties as, say, American studies—not bad for twenty years of change.

NOTE

A different version of this essay appeared in the Modern Language Association *Newsletter* during 1995.

WORKS CITED

Anderson, Mark, ed. *Reading Kafka: Prague, Politics, and the Fin de Siècle.* New York: Schocken, 1989.

Davidson, Cathy. *36 Views of Mount Fuji: On Finding Myself in Japan.* New York: Dutton, 1993.

Gilman, Sander. *Freud, Race and Gender.* (Trans. as *Freud, Rasse und Identität.*) Princeton: Princeton UP, 1993.

Hermand, Jost. *Als Pimpf in Polen: erweiterte Kinderlandverschickung, 1940–1945.* Frankfurt a.M.: Fischer, 1993.

Hohendahl, Peter. *Prismatic Thought: Theodor W. Adorno.* Lincoln: U of Nebraska P, 1995.

———. *Reappraisals: Shifting Alignments in Postwar Critical Theory.* Ithaca: Cornell UP, 1991.

Huyssen, Andreas. *Twilight Memories: Marking Time in a Culture of Amnesia.* New York: Routledge, 1995.

Kaes, Anton. *From Hitler to Heimat: The Return of History as Film.* Cambridge: Harvard UP, 1989.

Kaplan, Alice. *French Lessons: A Memoir.* Chicago: U of Chicago P, 1993.

Klüger, Ruth. *weiter leben: eine Jugend.* Munich: dtv, 1994.

Lipton, Eunice. *Alias Olympia: A Woman's Search for Manet's Notorious Model and Her Own Desire.* New York: Scribner's, 1992.

Politzer, Heinz. *Franz Kafka: Parable and Paradox.* Rev. ed. Ithaca: Cornell UP, 1966.

Santner, Eric. *Stranded Objects: Mourning, Memory, and Film in Postwar Germany.* Ithaca: Cornell UP, 1990.

Schor, Naomi. "The Righting of French Studies: Homosociality and the Killing of 'La pensée 68'" *Profession* (1992): 28–34.

Suleiman, Susan R. *Budapest Diaries: In Search of the Motherbook.* Lincoln: U of Nebraska P, 1996.

Tatar, Maria. *Lustmord: Sexual Murder in Weimar Germany.* Princeton: Princeton UP, 1995.

Torgovnick, Marianna De Marco. *Crossing Ocean Parkway: Readings by an Italian American Daughter.* Chicago: U of Chicago P, 1994.

Weiner, Marc. *Richard Wagner and the Anti-Semitic Imagination.* Lincoln: U of Nebraska P, 1995.

Part Eight

TOOLS

Part 8 differs from the previous seven in that it does not offer a series of individually authored essays but, rather, various types of materials to aid those readers who would like to begin or to refine their own practice of cultural studies. As emphasized repeatedly in this volume, cultural studies does not have a methodology to call its own. It deploys bricolage, borrowing from many disciplines to create an analysis that seems appropriate for the problem under investigation. What follows, then, is designed to facilitate the reader's ability to make use of various disciplinary practices. This part contains material written for this volume, such as "how-to" handouts for classroom use (a jumping off point into various disciplinary activities); reprints some interdisciplinary course syllabi available elsewhere; and directs readers to other resources and organizations (to the Internet, libraries, professional groups, and several funding and resource organizations). If cultural studies practitioners believe that their work can make a difference, they must commit themselves to collaborative pedagogy and research as transformational tools.

CHAPTER 28

"How to . . ." Classroom Handouts

What follows are handouts that might be used in undergraduate German cultural studies courses. Interdisciplinary by nature, cultural studies requires students and teachers to cross the boundaries of their knowledge and expertise. These short introductions to approaching a specific object of investigation are designed to give students: (1) some basic terms and information about a methodology or discipline; (2) some questions to guide their analysis; and (3) some awareness of the usefulness of a particular discipline to a cultural studies approach. Precisely because cultural studies is a field, rather than a discipline, it is left up to individual practitioners to decide what methodologies to use for analyzing any particular subject. These how-to outlines cannot replace the synthesis required in cultural studies. But it is impossible to achieve synthesis without knowledge of established disciplines and disciplinary practices. Nevertheless, cultural studies has taught us to be wary of authoritarianism. These handouts are by no means definitive introductions. Their styles (in tone, scope, sophistication) vary widely. This range is intended to underscore their provisional nature. The designation *how to* is meant as an invitation into what might be an unfamiliar practice, not as a dictate or restriction. Thus, these eleven handouts are (only) a point of intellectual departure; they should be supplemented, modified, and challenged by teachers and students. It is with this in mind that we invite you to reproduce these as necessary.

A. "how to read a poem" (Judith Ryan)
B. "how to view a building" (Wallis Miller and Scott Denham)
C. "how to view a film" (Gerd Gemünden)
D. "how to listen to western music" (Jean Leventhal)
E. "how to view a painting" (Jonathan Petropoulos)
F. "how to read a play" (Christian Rogowski)
G. "how to view performance" (Heidi Gilpin)
H. "how to read a novel" (Scott Denham and Irene Kacandes)
I. "how to read history" (Omer Bartov)
J. "how to read statistics" (Laurence McFalls)
K. "how to use an archive" (Geoffrey Giles)

A.   How to Read a Poem

Judith Ryan

Poetry in a cultural studies course? Isn't poetry too subjective, too disconnected from history, too much the province of the happy few who have a "gift" for that sort of thing?

Not at all: poetry is no less a cultural document than any other text. Even those who find it intimidating can learn some techniques that will make working with poetry less mystifying, more rewarding, and, above all, more meaningful.

1. The poem and its context.   The more you know about the historical and cultural period in which a poem was written, the more easily you will be able to formulate questions that will help you uncover its secrets. To begin, though, you will need to find out the date when the poem was written or first published. Standard poetry anthologies do not always give this kind of information. In the case of well-known German authors from earlier periods, such as Goethe or Hölderlin, consult the notes to the poet's collected works; in the case of some contemporary poets, such as Karl Krolow or Paul Celan, collected works exist but give only the date of the volume in which the text first appeared; in other instances, you will need to look at the individual volumes themselves. German Romantic poets such as Tieck, Eichendorff, or Brentano are a special case: most of their poems first appeared as *inset lyrics,* songs sung by fictional characters in their novels. Taking the trouble to look at the text surrounding these inset lyrics may produce a big payoff: sometimes the poems turn out to convey a completely different "message" from the one they seemed to have in your anthology.

Once you have a more precise idea of when and where the poem first appeared, it helps to read a brief account of the *period* in which it was written. The articles on various periods and movements in *The Oxford Guide to German Literature* or *Daten deutscher Dichtung* (if you read German) are good places to start. To what extent does this particular poem seem characteristic of the main concerns and themes of the period? In what ways does it diverge from

"How to Read a Poem," from *A User's Guide to German Cultural Studies,* ed. Scott Denham, Irene Kacandes, and Jonathan Petropoulos (Ann Arbor: University of Michigan Press, 1997), may be reproduced as needed.

them? Does it confirm the ideology of its time or present a critique of it? Ask yourself how the poem treats such issues as the rational and the irrational, self and nature, the public and the private self, time and memory. Is there any possibility that the poem refers, perhaps covertly, to an important historical event? If you suspect, for example, that the poem expresses opposition to Nazism, try to find out more about the author's opinions and political stance. Be careful though, with this kind of interpretation. Poems are rarely simple allegories; try to identify various layers of meaning, looking especially for irony and ambiguity.

   2. Cracking the poetic code.   How do you dig down to the deeper levels of a poem? The best way is to concentrate less on what is obvious and more on the parts that seem obscure. Underline these difficult spots in your text and see if they fall into a coherent pattern. This configuration may provide a clue to the poem's underlying concerns.

   Use at least a medium-sized dictionary to look up all the words, even those you think you know. Often a poet plays on secondary or specialized meanings of a specific word. When reading poems in the German original, be aware that sometimes a word acquires a different sense when it has an unfamiliar gender or is used in the plural. Always examine the *syntax* of the poem carefully and make sure you understand it. In German genitive constructions, for example, are a common way of forming metaphors. All poetry takes a certain freedom with the arrangement of the words to construct emphasis and, of course, often to fit the demands of rhythm or rhyme.

   Any word can become an *image.* Arrange the words and phrases in the poem in categories, grouping together such items as references to nature, adjectives of color, or paradoxical expressions. These groupings form the poem's metaphoric network. Does this network confirm or diverge from the typical intellectual and cultural interests of the period in which the poem was written? Would we have different attitudes to these phenomena today?

   Some poems allude to or imitate other poems in the tradition. Sometimes an entire poem is reworked; for example, Günter Eich's famous poem "Inventur" (Inventory) spawned several similar stock-taking poems at later historical junctures. The more familiar you become with the poetic tradition, the more readily you can identify such connections. Browse through the table of contents in an anthology: you may find poems from earlier periods that treat the same topic as the one you are studying. How does Brecht's vision of Germany differ from Heine's a century earlier? Asking this kind of question can add depth to your understanding of a particular poem by understanding better the "dialogue" that it is creating with other poems.

   3. Formal features.   As a student of cultural studies, you are not expected to have a specialist's knowledge of poetics. Nonetheless, you need to inform yourself about some of the basic forms of poetry. A sonnet, elegy, ode, or ballad carries traditional cultural connotations that affect the ideological implications of the poem. You can look up these terms in a poetry handbook, such as the *Princeton Encyclopedia of Poetry and Poetics* (but there are other good ones too).

It is customary to distinguish between the poet and the speaker (or persona) of a poem. The poet selects and arranges the words and images of the text, but the speaker is the person who says "I" in the poem. The speaker may be an invented figure, in which case we can define the poem as a "mask lyric" or "dramatic monologue" (German: *Rollengedicht*); Hofmannsthal's "Der Kaiser von China spricht" is a good example of this kind of poetry. In other cases, such as Mörike's "An einem Wintermorgen, vor Sonnenaufgang" or even Droste's seemingly more autobiographical "Im Grase," the speaker of the poem is not necessarily, or not completely, identical with the real-life author. Sometimes the poet writes in the second-person voice, using the intimate form of address (*thou/du*). Is the speaker addressing a friend or lover, speaking to him- or herself, reaching out to the reader, or are all of these possible interpretations?

A poem's language, or *diction* (choice of words), may be elevated and highly poetic or informal and closer to everyday speech. If the speaker appears to be chatting casually, the style is called *parlando.* This type of language is often deceptively simple, but it is also a good hiding place for irony. Look carefully. Ask yourself why the poet chose one word rather than another; what difference would it have made if the poet had used one of its synonyms instead?

English and German verse depend on *stress,* in other words, on the heavily accented syllables in the line. Certain traditional meters, notably, those used in classical odes and elegies, were derived from Latin and Greek models. Consult a manual on German metrics in order to identify and understand these meters. Be especially careful when using the terms *hexameter* and *pentameter:* they mean something quite different in German than in English. Similarly, the German word *Blankvers* refers only to unrhymed iambic pentameter lines; unrhymed lines of varying length are termed *Freie Rhythmen.*

Much modern poetry is free verse; it often looks like prose cut up randomly into lines. In this—or any other kind of poetry—look carefully at the line breaks. Often these generate ambiguities crucial to the poem's meaning. Contemporary poet Peter Wapnewski illustrates this effect by rearranging his auto mechanic's bill to make it look like a poem. Suddenly, an everyday experience—having to pay a hefty price for a repair—takes on a lighter and wittier tone while, paradoxically, also suggesting something much more sinister: that today's world is dangerously out of alignment.

4. Writing about poetry.   A clearly developed argument is as much an asset in an essay about a poem as in any other kind of written assignment. Move from the background information to the specific details of the text, commenting on as many elements of the poem as you can. Be sparing in your comments about the most evident features of the poem (most readers can identify an *abab* rhyme scheme at a glance, so why insist on the obvious?). Take more time to discuss its divergences from the general pattern it sets up and from the cultural expectations of its epoch. Don't forget that almost any poem depends, to some degree, on "yes, but" structures. Conclude with a brief, but not too reductive, summary that situates the text in its structural context. By following these hints, you will be surprised at all the ideas you come up with, even if you never thought you were really "good with poetry."

REFERENCES

Browning, Robert, ed. *German Poetry from 1750 to 1900.* Foreword by Michael Hamburger. Modern Library, vol. 39. New York: Continuum, 1984.

Forster, Leonard, ed. *The Penguin Book of German Verse.* Harmondsworth: Penguin, 1957.

Garland, Mary, ed. *The Oxford Companion to German Literature.* 2d ed. Oxford and New York: Oxford UP, 1986.

Preminger, Alex, Frank J. Warnke, and O. B. Hardison Jr., eds. *The Princeton Encyclopedia of Poetry and Poetics.* Princeton: Princeton UP, 1974.

Swales, Martin, ed. *German Poetry: An Anthology from Klopstock to Enzensberger.* Cambridge: Cambridge UP, 1987. See esp. "Introduction" (1–27); and "Notes on Individual Poets and Poems" (147–205).

And in German:

Frenzel, Herbert A., and Elisabeth. *Daten deutscher Dichtung. Chronologischer Abriss der deutschen Literaturgeschichte.* Munich: Deutscher Taschenbuch Verlag, 1962.

Gedichte und Interpretationen, 6 vols. Stuttgart: Reclam, 1982–84.

Kaiser, Gerhard. *Augenblicke deutscher Lyrik.* Frankfurt a.M.: Insel, 1987.

Kayser, Wolfgang J. *Kleine deutsche Versschule.* Tübingen: Francke Verlag, 1992.

B.   How to View a Building

Wallis Miller and Scott Denham

Most of us have not thought much about the buildings around us, even though we spend nearly all our lives in them and they affect us far more than we would care to admit. Can I look out a window when I wake up in the morning? Do I share my work environment with another person or ten others or hundreds of others? Is my bank, my classroom, or my town hall made of wood or brick or of glass and steel and marble? How do I arrive at these buildings? Do I pass others that look similar, or do I enter the oddball on the block? Do I enter immediately from the street through an unassuming door or pass through a garden to reach a magnificent portal at the other side? Is the interior designed in a style similar to that of the exterior? How we answer these questions and others like them tells us about our relationship to the immediate world: it tells us how this world has shaped us as well as how we have shaped it. But buildings do not just happen. Many people thought long and hard about the spaces we spend our time in, and when we view a building it is our job to figure out just what they were thinking, why, and if they were right.

When you look at a building you should first ask several basic questions.

Use. What purpose does the building serve? Is it for public or private use? For work, recreation, education, display, production, living, ceremony, or a combination of these things?

Location. Where does a building stand and why does it stand there? Urban or rural, suburban or neighborhood, in a new development or among many older buildings? Does it resemble the buildings around it? From where can the building be seen? Is it easy to reach?

Scale. How does the size and scale of the building determine its relationship to its users? Do you perceive an imposing monolith or a cozy cottage? How do various approaches (stairs, plazas, streets, walkways) mediate between the scale of the user and that of the building? How big is the front door relative to the other elements of the building? To the size of the entire structure?

"How to View a Building," from *A User's Guide to German Cultural Studies,* ed. Scott Denham, Irene Kacandes, and Jonathan Petropoulos (Ann Arbor: University of Michigan Press, 1997), may be reproduced as needed.

Space. How do we move through the building in order to perform specific functions? What do we do when we first enter? When do we move horizontally? vertically? How big are the spaces in which we perform different functions? Are they light or dark, colorful or bland, filled with windows or closed off from the world? How easy is it to find different rooms? Does the arrangement of spaces change the way in which we perform specific functions? Does it make them easier or more difficult to perform? Does it increase the importance of some spaces and diminish that of others?

Style. What sort of messages does a building send out through its appearance? Does a facade resemble those of the temples of ancient Greece? the churches of medieval Germany? the office buildings of twentieth-century New York? Is there a noticeable absence of ornament, and what might this mean? Of what materials is the building made? Are the buildings using their styles as a way to express certain values? What ideas are being communicated by the Greek stoa facade of the Altes Museum on Unter den Linden in Berlin? by the steel and glass of Berlin's New National Gallery?

History. Who designed the building? Who paid for the building? Why did they make it look as it does? For what culture was the building originally built? Has the use of the building or the site changed? Does it change your perceptions to know that your room was once inhabited by Bertolt Brecht? that the eighteenth-century armory in Berlin was used as a German Historical Museum in the twentieth century? or that your Berlin hotel was once the site of Adolf Eichmann's organization?

Type. Finally, think of a building as a type. A building's type is determined by its use. Examples of building types are schools, banks, houses, museums, and city halls. The concept of type allows architects to assess a building as an ideological as well as a practical solution to a functional problem. With use as the common attribute, architects can compare, for example, the nineteenth-century Reichstag to the East German Palast der Republik, in terms of their location, scale, spatial arrangement, and style. Then they can explain the similarities and differences among these buildings as the products of different histories and ideologies: of different cultures, patrons, and architects.

FOR FURTHER READING

Kostof, Spiro. *A History of Architecture: Settings and Rituals.* New York: Oxford UP, 1985.

Frampton, Kenneth. *Modern Architecture.* New York: Oxford UP, 1980.

Miller-Lane, Barbara. *Architecture and Politics in Germany: 1918–1945.* Cambridge: Harvard UP, 1985.

C. How to View a Film

Gerd Gemünden

The film historian Christian Metz once said: "Film is difficult to explain because it is easy to understand." Indeed, since the film image may resemble very much the image of reality as we see it every day, it is easy to mistake representation for reality. Therefore, when we turn to analyzing a film, it is important to focus on how a specific film *constructs* a certain reality: how does it produce meaning on the visual as well as the narrative level? And how does it engage the viewer in producing a certain meaning? Understanding film as a *system of signs,* here is a set of questions that helps us break down that system.

1. Questions Concerning Narrative and Dramatic Development

What does the film's title signify or suggest? What are the film's major narrative units? In what time sequence are they presented (chronological, juggled, with flashbacks/projections; is there a narrative frame)? Are there substantial time gaps between scenes? Are there subplots that comment on the main plot? Is the story presented uninterrupted, or is the story interrupted by songs, chorus, narrator, direct address to the audience (i.e., is the illusion of the film broken)? What are the main locations of the film? In what relationship do they stand to one another? What characters are associated with the different locales? Are characters rounded or flat? What motivates their actions (freedom, money, justice, love, fear)? Does the film give reasons for their acting in certain ways? How is their character revealed to us? Can certain characters be grouped together? Which characters change in the course of the film? How is change brought about? How is the final outcome of the film anticipated? Are there early

---

"How to View a Film," from *A User's Guide to German Cultural Studies,* ed. Scott Denham, Irene Kacandes, and Jonathan Petropoulos (Ann Arbor: University of Michigan Press, 1997), may be reproduced as needed.

signs of what is to come (e.g., foreshadowing)? Are all the strands of the plot resolved, or are there loose ends? What main oppositions are explored in the film?

2. Questions Concerning the Historical and Sociological Context

What is the relationship of the historical time depicted in the film to the time in which it was made? Does the film deal with a conflict still unresolved in our time and culture? Does it consciously present itself as a social statement? Does the film intend to take on controversial matters in a provocative way? Does it offer fictional alternatives to set patterns, or does it merely reaffirm the status quo? To what sort of audience does the film cater? How does the film deal with issues of gender? Do gender roles seem natural or constructed? Do men influence narrative action more than women? Is the female body a particular point of focus? Does the film assume a male spectator? a female spectator? How does the film deal with issues of race and ethnicity? Does the film reaffirm or challenge stereotypical representations of race?

3. Questions Concerning Form and Style

A film introduces its formal trajectory during the first ten shots; it is therefore important to focus on the opening sequence: what expectations does the title of the film arouse (e.g., regarding genre or style)? What do we know about the film beforehand (ads, posters, stars, trailers)? How does the credit sequence lead us into the film (if at all)? What are the signals given during the opening sequence regarding: location; perspective (who is looking at whom?); movement of characters; dialog (who speaks first? to whom? what?); camera movement (outside-inside, from above or below); camera distance (long, medium, or close shot); camera stasis (long or short takes); camera angle (high or low, straight on); lighting (high key, low key, flat); editing (do images flow? are there interruptions?); music (diegetic or nondiegetic); noise and sound? Are there certain images or sounds associated with certain characters? Do certain stylistic and technical devices recur? Do they develop in their repetition? Does the film follow certain conventions (national, generic, historical)? Does it try to play with or subvert our expectations? Does the film quote other films, books, songs, or texts? How likely is it that the audience will "get" these references? Is the film a literary adaptation? How does the film compare to other films by the same director? What is the "realism" of the film: does it aim to construct the impression of the real world, or does it foreground a sense of itself as a framed view of things? Is the film self-reflexive (does it turn back on itself and comment on its working as a fictional product)?

NOTE

This is based on materials by Anton Kaes and Eric Rentschler that were presented and discussed during the Third German Film Institute (1991) at Clark University. Following the spirit of the institute, to encourage and facilitate the teaching of German film, I poach freely from their work, which they generously shared with all participants.

SUGGESTED INTRODUCTORY READINGS

Bordwell, David, and Kristin Thompson. *Film Art: An Introduction.* 3d ed. New York: McGraw, 1990.
Corrigan, Timothy. *A Short Guide to Writing about Film.* 2d ed. New York: Harper-Collins, 1994.
Giannetti, Louis. *Understanding Movies.* 3d ed. Englewood Cliffs, NJ: Prentice-Hall, 1982.
Monaco, James. *How to Read a Film.* New York: Oxford UP, 1977.

D.   How to Listen to Western Music

Jean H. Leventhal

Most of us hear music much of the time and pay little attention to it, whether it is the Muzak in the supermarket or airport, the music accompanying the films we watch, or the background music on our CD or tape players. Many of us actively seek out musical experiences by attending concerts or making music ourselves, but even those who are active rather than passive in their interaction with music may think little about the structures or qualities that distinguish jazz from rock or the music of Wolfgang Mozart from that of Arnold Schönberg. Being aware of some of the possibilities in music will heighten your enjoyment and appreciation of this art.

Purpose. Was this music written for a specific occasion or ceremony, as incidental music for a play, to accompany a ballet, or to entertain royalty? Was it written for performance in a nightclub or in a palace? Different locales and occasions will determine various aspects of the piece: its tone, instrumentation, duration, style. Some music is written for a particular time and place, such as George Frederick Handel's *Water Music* or Johann Sebastian Bach's weekly cantatas for the church services in Leipzig. A piece might be composed on commission from a wealthy person, such as Ludwig van Beethoven's *Rasoumovsky* Quartets, or with a particular performer in mind, like Kurt Weill's songs for his wife, Lotte Lenya. Any of these circumstances puts constraints on the composer. A composer simply writing a piece with the hope that it will be performed at some point by the appropriate forces has much more freedom.

Form. Music is sound organized in time. Does the piece last a relatively long or short time? A lied by Franz Schubert or Hugo Wolf might last a few minutes; an opera by Mozart or Richard Wagner lasts several hours. Are there large sections within the piece, or does it appear to be one unit? Some pieces have subdivisions (operas have acts and scenes that contain *arias* and *recitatives, ensembles* and *solos;* oratorios and cantatas have *choral* and *solo* sections;

"How to Listen to Western Music," from *A User's Guide to German Cultural Studies,* ed. Scott Denham, Irene Kacandes, and Jonathan Petropoulos (Ann Arbor: University of Michigan Press, 1997), may be reproduced as needed.

string quartets, sonatas, concertos, and symphonies have *movements*). Other compositions, like songs and some overtures, are unitary. But even a "unitary" form can have obvious divisions: operas or ballet overtures generally contain clearly demarcated sections, although they are played without pause. *Repetition* is often important in shaping music. A folksong is usually *strophic*, that is, the same music is repeated for every stanza. In a *theme and variation form* a melody may be repeated in one voice, with other voices playing inventive decorations or additional melodies along with the repeated melody. *Sonata-allegro form*, a typical classical form, presents a musical *theme* or themes. In the middle or *development* section the listener is entertained with harmonic, melodic, or rhythmic variation of these themes. Finally, the themes return, more or less in their original form, in the *recapitulation*. In *rondo* form a theme alternates with *episodes* of contrasting music. A rondo appears often as the last movement, or *finale*, of a classical symphony or concerto.

Melody, harmony, and rhythm. How strong are the rhythmic or melodic elements in the piece? Does one of them predominate? What sticks in your head most about the music? What are the emotional or ideological effects of these elements? By *melody* we mean the tune formed by the sequence of *pitches* in music. The melody of a folksong will generally be simpler than that of a lied by Schubert or Robert Schumann. *Harmony* occurs when we hear more than one voice or instrument at the same time (some instruments, such as the violin or the piano, can create more than one "voice" simultaneously). Many *chorales* by J. S. Bach feature simple Lutheran hymn melodies set to complex harmonies. *Rhythm* refers to the pattern of pulses in the music. The drummer in a jazz group is responsible for the rhythmic energy of the performance. Rhythm can be steady, complex, monotonous, or constantly shifting. Sweeping melodic lines and lush harmonies are characteristic of Wagner's operas; lilting melodies and a repeated rhythm are often heard in waltzes by the Strauss family of nineteenth-century Austria.

Tonality. Most pieces give the listener a sense of being "home" whenever the music comes to rest on its *tonic pitch*, especially at the end. The relationship of other pitches in the *scale* to this tonic center contributes to the sense of drama, tension, and movement in music, away from this tonal home base and back to it. The two basic tonalities in most Western music since the seventeenth-century are *major* (a brighter, happier sound) and *minor* (darker, sadder, more introspective). When we say a piece is in the *key* of E major or A minor, we are identifying the home base. J. S. Bach explored all twenty-four keys in each of the two parts of *Das wohltemperierte Clavier* by composing a major and a minor prelude and fugue on each of the twelve notes of the scale.

Tempo. Is the piece fast or slow? Is the tempo steady or varied? Italian words are used frequently to designate the *tempo*, or speed of a piece. Music marked *adagio* or *largo* is quite slow; pieces marked *allegro* and *presto* are quick. Other Italian names designate types of pieces that usually have tempi associated with them: a *scherzo* (Italian for *joke*), for example, is fairly quick.

Meter. Most music you will hear is in a simple meter, in which you can feel the basic pulses grouped as twos or threes. This is called *duple meter (1, 2; 1, 2;* or *1, 2, 3, 4)* or *triple meter (1, 2, 3; 1, 2, 3).* The march is a familiar type of piece in duple meter, the waltz a familiar dance with a strong triple meter. Some pieces change from one meter to another, and modern or folk music may feature irregular meters, such as groupings of seven or five beats.

Other factors. Does the music seem readily accessible or difficult to grasp? What does that say about the composer's assumptions about the audience for which the piece is intended? Is the music *abstract,* to be understood largely in musical terms alone, or *programmatic,* telling a story or describing a mood? Sometimes the title helps the listener to decide: Felix Mendelssohn's "Italian" and "Scottish" Symphonies are more programmatic than Beethoven's Symphony No. 2. The presence of *text* (the lines of a poem in a lied or the libretto of an opera) also provides a programmatic element that shapes a composition. The composition can echo the text or provide a contrasting element. The composer can strictly follow the form of the chosen text or expand the text to provide the music with greater breadth than the poet or librettist ever intended. Music is one place—for instance, in the finale of an opera by Mozart—in which several characters can all "speak" at once. Can you hear references to other compositions or stylistic periods in the music? What does this imply about the composer's relationship with and attitude toward the musical tradition? Imitation and parody are common in music, from the setting of Christian hymns to popular folksongs in the medieval and Renaissance periods to the imitative "baroque" overture to Bertolt Brecht and Kurt Weill's 1928 *Dreigroschenoper* (*Three Penny Opera*). The more music you know, the more you will enjoy this practice.

FOR FURTHER READING

Copland, Aaron. *What to Listen for in Music.* New York: McGraw-Hill, 1988.
Kerman, Joseph, with Vivian Kerman. *Listen.* 3d ed. New York: Worth, 1987.
Yudkin, Jeremy. *Understanding Music.* 3d brief ed. Upper Saddle River, NJ: Prentice Hall, 1996.

E.   HOW TO VIEW A PAINTING

Jonathan Petropoulos

The analysis and explication of paintings is an enterprise with a long and contentious history. There has never been, and in all likelihood will never be, agreement about the most suitable methodology for ascertaining the manifold meanings contained in artworks. The following suggestions, which might be viewed as steps for pursuing a viable interpretation, will not yield an answer to the perennial methodological dilemmas. In fact, if past experience is a guide, these steps will only provoke disagreement. But successful answers to the following questions will provide specific insights and contribute to a more general understanding.

1.   Who is the artist? One might call this homage to Vasari, the Renaissance art historian who was arguably the first of the modern professionals. Beginning with the biographical approach is not only consistent with the history of art history but a logical starting point for further inquiry. Determining the creator of an artwork is also a crucial part of connoisseurship, long the dominant mode of art historical scholarship. By identifying the artist and relating the specific work to a larger oeuvre, the scholar has a strong foundation on which to build a more substantial interpretation. Note that there are often significant limitations to the biographical approach: with certain non-Western cultures, for example, the name of the artist is often of minimal importance.

2.   When was the work created, and to what stylistic epoch, movement, or school does it belong? Relating a work to others in a similar genre is helpful in terms of understanding the broader circumstances as well as contemporary idioms and debates. Artists often worked on similar "projects," such as the Impressionists' exploration of the nature of light. While one should be careful about implying the existence of group decisions, making these connections can help with the biographical and social history of the artists because of the frequency of collaboration and association, within both the academic establishment and avant-garde circles.

"How to View a Painting," from *A User's Guide to German Cultural Studies,* ed. Scott Denham, Irene Kacandes, and Jonathan Petropoulos (Ann Arbor: University of Michigan Press, 1997), may be reproduced as needed.

3. What formal qualities can one discern? Because artists often responded to developments within their discipline, as Clement Greenberg and other critics have argued, an examination of shape, color, materials, and other issues pertaining to the production of a piece offers important information. In discerning trends and the various deviations, one can gain a better understanding of artists' projects. One example is the study of flatness in classical modernism, a crucial concern for many who worked during the first half of the twentieth century.

4. What iconographic and iconological messages are present in the work? Erwin Panofsky, among others, argued for the importance of iconographic investigation, which he defined as the study of the subject matter and meaning of artworks (as opposed to form), and, more specifically, iconological explication, which concerns symbols, myths, emblematic figures, and other encoded messages. In order to ascertain meanings that may be obscure, one might consult a reference source, such as Hans Biedermann, *Dictionary of Symbolism* (1989), or James Smith Pierce, *From Abacus to Zeus* (1977).

5. What are the intentions of the artist? To take a term made famous by Alois Riegl, *Kunstwollen,* or "inner necessity," one should attempt to understand both the motivation and goals of the artist. Riegl, in fact, posited that *Kunstwollen* transcended individual artists and applied to entire cultures. In the latter sense specific cultures collectively drew out elements present in the inherited tradition and, in turn, contributed to art history, which developed in a linear manner. Riegl applied this analysis to Dutch group portraits, examining modifications in certain thematic patterns and formal techniques in such a way as to situate the seventeenth-century Dutch masterpieces in the broader historical context. In short, while issues of intentionality are typically daunting, they often provide interesting points of departure.

6. How might this artwork reflect broader historical or material, political or social, trends? Although crude interpretations positing a correlation between an artwork and the society in which it was produced have been convincingly debunked, it is often the case that the artist meant to address issues beyond formalistic concerns. Certain painters deal with technological and industrial change by depicting trains or cityscapes, while others address contemporary political and military developments, such as Picasso in his masterful *Guernica.* Artists did not work in a vacuum: a knowledge of the historical and social context is important for understanding an artwork. Remember, even an artist's statement "This painting is apolitical" is necessarily a political statement.

7. What can be discovered about the history of a painting's reception? By examining the exhibition venues, critical notices, commercial fate, and subsequent treatment by scholars, one can gain insight into an artwork.

8. How might one's own historic vantage point and subjective views fac-

tor into the analysis? This self-reflective question, while difficult to answer, should be asked. It is naive to think that an interpretation of a painting can be completely objective.

FOR FURTHER READING

Baxandall, Michael. *Patterns of Intention: On the Historical Explanation of Pictures.* New Haven: Yale UP, 1985.

Berenson, Bernhard. *Aesthetics and History in the Visual Arts.* New York: Pantheon, 1948.

Clark, T. J. *The Painting of Modern Life: Paris in the Art of Manet and His Followers.* Princeton: Princeton UP, 1984.

Gombrich, Ernst. *Art and Illusion: A Study in the Psychology of Pictorial Representation.* London: Phaidon, 1977.

Greenberg, Clement. *Art and Culture: Critical Essays.* Boston: Beacon, 1961.

Panofsky, Erwin. *Meaning in the Visual Arts.* Harmondsworth: Penguin, 1970.

Podro, Michael. *The Critical Historians of Art.* New Haven: Yale UP, 1982.

F. How to Read a Play

Christian Rogowski

No matter how strong the impression may be that a play merely mimics real life, nothing in a drama "just happens"; everything has been put on the page (and on the stage) for us by someone. Every element in a drama serves a purpose, has a function. The main question in reading a play should therefore always be "why?" Why does this character say this? Why is this scene set here? Why is this happening now? We can answer such questions only if we share with the makers of a play not only a certain general knowledge about our own culture but also, more specifically, a certain set of assumptions concerning theatrical representation and dramatic enactment. Such assumptions differ widely from culture to culture: we can only appreciate a play if we are to some extent familiar with the particular conventions upon which it is based.

Genre conventions. A play is usually made up of two types of textual material: the *main text* consists of the characters' utterances, the lines to be spoken by actors on the stage; the term *subsidiary text* designates texts not to be heard during a performance, including stage instructions and other peripheral material such as prefaces and author's comments. Information on the setting of a particular scene might be subtly evoked in the main text or elaborately spelled out in the subsidiary text. In our reading we should aim to cull information from both text types so that we are able to hear and see the play in our minds.

The logic of expectation. At the outset of a play, in what is called the *exposition,* a dramatic situation is defined in which the characters are placed and out of which certain tensions and conflicts will develop. At the end of a play, in the *denouement,* the conflicts can be resolved in definitive closure or allowed to linger on in an open-ended, often new way. Plays invite the audience to make conjectures about the development of the plot according to a shared cultural knowledge concerning theatrical and social conventions. Deviations from this logic of expectation are usually charged with significance, re-

"How to Read a Play," from *A User's Guide to German Cultural Studies,* ed. Scott Denham, Irene Kacandes, and Jonathan Petropoulos (Ann Arbor: University of Michigan Press, 1997), may be reproduced as needed.

vealing new facets of the issues involved, challenging our assumptions about human behavior, or introducing subtle levels of irony. We should be attentive to moments of irritation or confusion in our reading, for they may point to unexpected complexities.

Dramatic economy. Most playwrights generally aim to make the intended thematic point or achieve the desired artistic effect with utmost concision. This strategy, known as the principle of *dramatic economy,* implies that, since every detail counts, repetition is a means of highlighting issues that are of special significance. When, in reading a play, an issue turns out to be particularly important, it is usually helpful to go back and trace its first appearance in the text, where the groundwork for its interpretation is laid. Also, underneath the words that appear on the page, there are rich layers of subtext that we have to infer from what the characters are made to say. The lines assigned to characters propel the plot, define their relationships, and affect their interactions. How something is said and in what context is as important as what is said. In speaking, a character in a play wants to accomplish something; any utterance is governed by an underlying motivation, which it is our task as readers to uncover. The printed text of a play is best viewed as the mere tip of an iceberg.

Reading a play should involve at least two phases: first, one should read through the whole text to get a general idea of what is going on. In a second phase one should focus on an aspect that has emerged as crucial in the first reading and trace it through the entire text in all its ramifications. Compared with most other forms of literature, especially novels, plays are relatively short. When we read a play, we have a privilege that is not available to the theatergoer, who watches a performance: we can stop midway, analyze certain passages, and compare them with others. We should make ample use of this privilege.

For Further Reading

Esslin, Martin. *The Field of Drama: How the Signs of Drama Create Meaning on Stage and Screen.* London and New York: Methuen, 1987.
Fischer-Lichte, Erika. *The Semiotics of Theater.* Bloomington: Indiana UP, 1992.
Pfister, Martin. *The Theory and Analysis of Drama.* Cambridge and New York: Cambridge UP, 1988.
Szondi, Peter. *Theory of Modern Drama.* Cambridge: Polity, 1987.

G.   HOW TO VIEW PERFORMANCE

Heidi Gilpin

Performance is a demanding subject: immediately, an enormous range of materials and events come to mind. We could think of dramatic plays, stand-up comedy, musicals, theatrical productions (not based on an already existing text), opera, dance, movement performance, performance art, visual art installations, musical concerts, or spiritual rituals, but we could also consider earthquakes, weather, political campaigning, the zoo, the Home Shopping Network, video games, CD-ROM interactive programs, talk shows, radio, MTV, birthday parties, health clubs, TV journalism, the Internet—the list of what constitutes performance is virtually endless. So, what ties them all together? How do we begin to think about performance, about what it is, what it does, and how it functions?

Let's start with the following proposals:

Performance involves an event of some kind: live or simulated, it gives us the sense that we are witnessing a real, tangible, physical experience. You see the actors standing on a stage before you, you hear them breathing, see the sweat run down their necks. Or you watch newscasters announce the news as they narrate, with graphic imagery, the latest events of the day—murders, trials, wars, sports, political debates and developments on a national and international scale. You believe that they are talking to you right now, even if you know the show was recorded earlier. Or you watch a 3D animation of a voyage through a virtual space—interior or exterior—on the Internet, in a video game, or on a CD-ROM, and you have the sense that this voyage is simulating the real thing. Whether it's a depiction of a fantasy world or an actually existing place, the presence of the movement in relation to you, and the perspective you are offered of the space, convinces you that it exists. It affects you, the viewer, and sometimes it invites your participation.

Performance is a time-based medium. It is about never being able to capture the event or person or thing you are perceiving: the minute you see it or

"How to View Performance," from *A User's Guide to German Cultural Studies,* ed. Scott Denham, Irene Kacandes, and Jonathan Petropoulos (Ann Arbor: University of Michigan Press, 1997), may be reproduced as needed.

hear it or feel it, that moment of performance is already gone, to be followed by another and another. Even if you record a show on TV to watch it later, and you play the video recording over and over, you can never really have it, and it will never be the same, as if it's not really there. The dots or pixels that make up the video screen in front of you change each time you view a recording, even if ever so slightly, so that you are never really watching the "same" thing. Performance is by nature ephemeral. This means that, after the event is over, all we have to work with in thinking about it and discussing it critically is our *memory* of the event, not the event itself.

Performance always involves movement of some kind: physically or in simulation, whether it involves the movement of bodies, objects, or spaces. There is always motion, even if that motion is so specific or minuscule as to be barely perceivable. In a dance performance, whether ballet or breakdance, there are very specific vocabularies of bodily movement that are being employed by the performers, which give us certain kinds of information and which may suggest specific stories or anti-stories, specific moments in time, and particular ideas. Ask yourself how those dancing bodies are communicating with you. What do their gestures convey? Try to be extremely specific in your observations. What kinds of effort, shape, speed, direction, style, or quality of movement is being performed? What does that tell you specifically about the thought, emotion, principle, or context being expressed?

Performance involves representation. Performance is the presentation of a body, a thing, or a place that is not the thing itself but an interpretation, a representation of that thing. By looking very closely at how that representation is constructed, we can begin to understand what composes it and what that particular construction suggests about the thing itself (whatever it is) and our relation to it.

Planned or unplanned, performance is happening all the time. Watch people walking around campus: what are they wearing, how (and with whom) do they move, what are they carrying, what expressions are on their faces? What sort of gestures are they performing with their hands, with their bodies? All these observations give you a lot of information about what these people are doing and how they fit into a certain situation. For example: do they seem powerful? what is their gender, age, or nationality? how can you tell? and how can you be sure? to what racial or ethnic community do they belong? do they make their politics evident in some way through their movement or appearance? what is their cultural background? how do they convey (if at all) their sexual preference, their favorite sport, their life experience, their economic status, their sorority/fraternity, their gang, whether they are new to campus or seniors? how do their movements give you information about who they are and what they want you to know or not know about them? Take a close look, sit down for a while and just watch people. Think about what people say with their bodies, with their clothing, with their haircuts, makeup, hats, shoes, etc. How much information can you collect? How much can you learn about them from their performance of themselves?

No matter what kind of performance you are witnessing, you can teach yourself more about it by asking the following questions:

What do I know about this performance, before I even start to view it? Is there a program, a description, a list of performers, a critical review of an earlier performance of the same production, an instruction manual for a software or CD-ROM program, a list of students in an organization or class?

What issues of time can I pinpoint? Into what time period am I being brought in this performance: am I in the past, present, or future, and what year, what hour of day or night, what kind of time exactly? Or does this performance refer to a timeless moment? Or to a moment that happens all the time or at any time?

What kind of bodies, if any, are there in this performance? How are they dressed? What attributes describe these bodies? Do they represent specific characters or their own "authentic" identities? What kind of information do these bodies convey?

How else is information transmitted? Are there texts of some kind? Are there subtitles or supertitles, banners or menus? Are there words or images visible on the objects, bodies, or spaces? Does the performance involve speech, song, movement, written, sonic, and/or visual information? How does the mode of communication affect my perception of the information? How could that information be transmitted differently? What would be the effect of such changes?

What is the dramaturgy of this performance? How—with what materials, in what forms, in what kind of linear or fragmentary structure—is the message of this event conveyed? How many genres or kinds of cultural production can I discern in the performance I'm watching? Is there artwork of various kinds, and/or are there references to other types of material—film, fiction, media, music, dance, science? What kinds of material are being used to create this performance? How important does this material seem? What sorts of issues are being portrayed and from whose or what perspective? How am I implicated in this event? Who or what is implicating me?

Performance is an inherently multidisciplinary event. In addition to the strategies proposed here, every methodology we use to view, read, or interpret a process or product from another discipline (such as literature, film, anthropology, history, architecture, science, etc.) or from another life experience can contribute to our interpretation of a performance. Performance challenges us to be hyperaware of every element used to construct it and of our relation to it. In order to develop our skills in watching and/or participating in a performance, and to improve our abilities to discuss it critically and from a variety of perspectives afterward, we must collect an enormous amount of information of many different kinds. We must pay close attention, deploying all our senses.

FOR FURTHER READING

Artaud, Antonin. *The Theater and its Double.* Trans. Mary Caroline Richards. New York: Grove, 1958.

ANY (Architecture New York) 5: Lightness (March/April 1994), special issue edited by Greg Lynn and John Rajchman. (Includes critical texts about movement performance, architecture, events, visuality, and philosophy.)

Banes, Sally. *Writing Dancing in the Age of Postmodernism.* Hanover and London: Wesleyan UP and UP of New England, 1994.

Barthes, Roland. *Mythologies.* Trans. by Annette Lavers. 1957. Reprint. New York: Hill and Wang, 1983 (especially "The Face of Garbo," 56–57).

Baudrillard, Jean. *Simulacra and Simulation.* Trans. by Sheila Glaser. The Body, in Theory: Histories of Cultural Materialism Series. Ann Arbor: U of Michigan P, 1994.

Bender, Gretchen, and Timothy Druckrey, eds. *Culture on the Brink: Ideologies of Technology.* Dia Center for the Arts, Discussions in Contemporary Culture, no. 9. Seattle: Bay P, 1994.

Berger, John. *The Sense of Sight.* New York: Pantheon, 1985 (especially "On Visibility," 219–21; "The Place of Painting," 212–18; "The Theatre of Indifference," 68–73).

Blau, Herbert. *To All Appearances: Ideology and Performance.* New York and London: Routledge, 1992.

Colomina, Deatriz, ed. *Sexuality and Space.* New York: Princeton Architectural P, 1992.

Crary, Jonathan, and Sanford Kwinter, eds. *Zone 6: Incorporations.* New York: Urzone, 1992.

de Lauretis, Teresa. *Alice Doesn't: Feminism, Semiotics, Cinema.* Bloomington: Indiana UP, 1984.

Deleuze, Gilles, and Felix Guattari. *A Thousand Plateaus: Capitalism and Schizophrenia.* Vol. 2. Trans. by Brian Massumi. Minneapolis: U of Minnesota P, 1987.

Drama Review: A Journal of Performance Studies, various issues.

Druckrey, Timothy, ed. *Iterations: The New Image.* Cambridge: MIT P, 1994.

Felman, Shoshana, and Dori Laub, M.D. *Testimony: Crises of Witnessing in Literature, Psychoanalysis and History.* New York: Routledge, 1991.

Ferguson, Russell, et al., eds. *Discourses: Conversations in Postmodern Art and Culture.* Cambridge: MIT P, 1990.

Foster, Susan, ed. *Corporealities.* London and New York: Routledge, 1996.

Foucault, Michel. *Discipline and Punish.* New York: Vintage Books/Random House, 1979 (especially "Docile Bodies," 135–69).

Garber, Marjorie, Jane Matlock, and Rebecca L. Walkowitz, eds. *Media Spectacles.* New York: Routledge, 1993.

Goodwin, Andrew. *Dancing in the Distraction Factory: Music Television and Popular Culture.* Minneapolis: U of Minnesota P, 1992.

Kahn, Douglas, and Gregory Whitehead. *Wireless Imagination: Sound, Radio, and the Avant-Garde*. Cambridge: MIT P, 1992.

Kantor, Tadeusz. *A Journey through Other Spaces: Essays and Manifestos, 1944–1990*. Ed. and trans. by Michal Kobialka. Berkeley: U of California P, 1993.

Marker, Chris. *La Jetée: Ciné-roman*. New York: Zone Books, 1992.

Massumi, Brian, ed. *The Politics of Everyday Fear*. Minneapolis: U of Minnesota P, 1992.

Outside the Frame: Performance and the Object, A Survey History of Performance Art in the USA since 1950. Cleveland: Cleveland Center for Contemporary Art, 1994.

Performing Arts Journal, various issues.

Phelan, Peggy. *Unmarked: The Politics of Performance*. New York: Routledge, 1993.

Reinelt, Janelle G., and Joseph R. Roach, eds. *Critical Theory and Performance*. Theater: Theory/Text/Performance Series. Ann Arbor: U of Michigan P, 1992.

Sacks, Oliver. *The Man Who Mistook His Wife for a Hat*. 1985. Reprint. New York: Harper Perennial, 1990.

Sayre, Henry M. *The Object of Performance: The American Avant-Garde since 1970*. Chicago and London: U of Chicago P, 1989.

Schechner, Richard. *The Future of Ritual: Writings on Culture and Performance*. New York: Routledge, 1993.

Wallis, Brian, ed. *Blasted Allegories: An Anthology of Artists' Writings*. Cambridge: MIT P, 1987.

H.   How to Read a Novel

Scott Denham and Irene Kacandes

How do *you* read a novel? Many readers find themselves curled up in a corner of the sofa, warm mug at hand, oblivious to the passing of time or to the presence of others, alive only in the world created by some mysterious connection between the words on the page and an imagination hard at work. Others might be struggling to maintain concentration on a hard oak chair in a vast reading room, pencil and notebook close by, connected to the book only physically. At a most basic level a novel (or short story or novella) is a story, a narrative, and one that is not true—hence, the designation *narrative* or *prose fiction.* And the nature of a reader's identification or involvement or engagement with the story being told has much to do with the experience of reading. For our purposes here, by *novel* we can mean broadly any kind of narrative or epic (from *epos*) fiction, from Homer's *Iliad* to Chaucer's *Canterbury Tales* or some medieval epic, say Gottfried von Strassburg's *Tristan und Isolt,* to the first real novels of the eighteenth century (Fielding, von La Roche, Sterne, du Laclos, Goethe) to the grand nineteenth-century novels of society and psychology (Austen, Dickens, Flaubert, George Eliot, Tolstoy, Melville, Fontane, Stifter, Dostoevsky) to the novels of the modernists (Joyce, Kafka, Proust, Döblin, Svevo, Faulkner, Woolf) to the postmodernists (García Marquez, Pynchon, Grass, Morrison, Calvino, Gordimer)—to name just a few periods and writers.

The narrative. Let us first think about the nature of the novel—or narrative fiction—itself. Any narrative has three elements, what many narrative theorists (narratologists) call story, text, and narration. The *story* is the sequence of events abstracted from their specific telling in the text. A story in this sense has a chronological order that can be reconstructed, regardless how the story came to be known. One story can be told in different versions and by different people at different times. The story can be general, even universal. The *text* (also referred to as *discourse*), on the other hand, is the specific telling of a story: it

"How to Read a Novel," from *A User's Guide to German Cultural Studies,* ed. Scott Denham, Irene Kacandes, and Jonathan Petropoulos (Ann Arbor: University of Michigan Press, 1997), may be reproduced as needed.

is what we read, the words on the page. And the specific process of producing those words by some agent—the narrator—is called *narration*. The narration is something real to the extent that an author wrote the text, but within the world of the text there is also a fictional narrator (or several) who is responsible for the act of narration, for telling the tale to an explicit or implicit *narratee*. The fictional narrator is usually more worthy of our attention than the actual author of a text when we read a novel. It is through the narrator that we are presented not only with the story but also with the text of the narrator—his or her words, in a way. Thus, by focusing on the narration, we have a way to gain insight into the narrator's ideas and attitudes. The complicated relationships between narrators, their narrations, texts, and stories serve to make novels exquisitely dense as carriers of meaning, ideas, and ideology.

Presented with these three aspects of a novel, all of which we learn about only by reading it, we can ask a great many questions. Is the story one already known? Is it a standard type (a fairy tale, a mystery, a love story)? How is the text itself structured; how are the characters portrayed (characterized)? How is the story narrated: through whose eyes and in whose voices? How much do the narrators know or not know about the stories they tell? Are they participants in the action or merely relayers of it? Do they tell the story in their own voice (*first-person* narration) or in a disembodied one (*third-person*)? Or does the narrator tell the story as an address to someone (a less well-known form called *second-person* narration)? Do we sense that we can trust the reliability of the narrator? Why or why not? What difference does it make? Do we find out about the inner life (unspoken thoughts and feelings) of characters, or do we just come to know them from the outside (their actions and words)? Do we know some characters and not others? How does that affect our understanding of the events? And, considering the narration of events: do we get great detail about certain events and none about others? Are certain events elided or told repeatedly? What purpose does the pace of the narration serve?

The Context. There are other questions novels raise that do not necessarily have to do with the internal workings of the book. Novels always have real authors, with real biographies, ideologies, and philosophies (although they may, of course, be unknown or collective authors). To what extent does knowledge of the author affect our understanding of a novel? Does it matter, for example, if a woman or a man wrote a certain kind of story? A native or nonnative speaker of the language in which it was written? Someone with power or someone without it? Similarly, how does a novel's place in history change its import? And what about a book's previous audience and reception? Was it popular, and why? Is it high art or pulp fiction? Who else reads it—only academics and students? everyone but?

The Reader. Finally, what about you, the reader? How do you go about validating or measuring and judging your own feelings and responses to the novel?

If you laugh or cry or are angered or inspired by reading a book, what does this mean? Would others react in a similar manner? Questions about what the reader brings to the text are also central to understanding what a novel means for you. Why are you reading a certain work? What have you been told about why you should read a particular novel? One teacher might have us read Erich Maria Remarque's *All Quiet on the Western Front* to gain some insight into the horrors of warfare, though another might insist that the book has nothing to do with war but should be read as an example of how successful popular, mass-market fiction works. Yet another might say the book is key to understanding a specific German social situation in the 1920s, when the novel was written.

Questions, then, about how a novel functions on its own terms, how it fits into some historical or literary-historical context, and, finally, about how you the reader engage the novel are all productive guides to understanding what cultural work novels do.

For Further Reading

Bal, Mieke. *Narratology: Introduction to the Theory of Narrative.* Trans. Christine van Boheemen. Toronto: U of Toronto P, 1985.

Booth, Wayne C. *The Company We Keep: An Ethics of Fiction.* Berkeley: U of California P, 1988.

Cohn, Dorrit. *Transparent Minds: Narrative Modes for Presenting Consciousness in Fiction.* Princeton: Princeton UP, 1978.

Genette, Gérard. *Narrative Discourse: An Essay in Method.* Trans. Jane E. Lewin. Ithaca: Cornell UP, 1980.

Prince, Gerald. *Dictionary of Narratology.* Lincoln, London: U of Nebraska P, 1987.

Rimmon-Kenan, Shlomith. *Narrative Fiction: Contemporary Poetics.* London and New York: Routledge, 1983.

I. How to Read History

Omer Bartov

Probably anyone who reads has read history. To engage history is to read a newspaper, a novel, a poem, a memoir; it is also to watch a film, look at a painting, walk in a palace, listen to stories by relatives and strangers, visit a concert hall, remember your own past. History claims a monopoly on the past, and countless written, verbal, aural, and visual representations claim a monopoly on history. Yet history is also an academic discipline with certain (increasingly less well-defined and rigid) rules, traditions, and practices. Hence, when we read a text presented to us as belonging to the discipline of history, we should pay attention to several components of that text so as better to evaluate and criticize it.

Sources: We should establish what documentary or secondary sources the text is based on and to what extent the author seems to have made an effort to read a large portion of the available sources and to treat them fairly.

Biases: We should, at the same time, determine what the biases were that made the historian choose the sources and mold the thesis and narrative of the text as presented to the reader. No history can be objective, just as no historian can use all the available sources.

Selection: We should therefore clarify to ourselves what kind of selection was made by the historian concerning the sources, the available historical approaches or methods, and the very subject matter itself. Why is this, for example, a political, or economic, or social, or cultural history? Why, for instance, were diplomatic, military, municipal, regional, or personal archives consulted? For what reason, to take one last example, did certain social classes, geographical locations, urban or rural environments, male or female protagonists, feature more prominently than others?

Thesis and subtext: At this point we should finally examine the relation-

---

"How to Read History," from *A User's Guide to German Cultural Studies,* ed. Scott Denham, Irene Kacandes, and Jonathan Petropoulos (Ann Arbor: University of Michigan Press, 1997), may be reproduced as needed.

ship between the sources, biases, selection, and both the overt thesis of the text and its subtext, that is, what it seems to be saying without telling us that it does.

Paying due attention to the style of the author and the interest the text arouses in us—whether we agree with it or not—we can finally subject it to a critical reading.

FOR FURTHER READING

Burke, Peter, ed. *New Perspectives on Historical Writing.* University Park: Pennsylvania State UP, 1992.

Carr, E. H. *What Is History?* Ed. R. W. Davies. 2d ed. London: Macmillan, 1986.

Gilderhus, Mark. *History and Historians: A Historiographical Introduction.* Englewood Cliffs, NJ: Simon and Schuster, 1996.

Hunt, Lynn, ed. *The New Cultural History: Essays.* Berkeley: U of California P, 1989.

Marius, Richard. *A Short Guide to Writing about History.* 2d ed. New York: Harper-Collins, 1995.

Stern, Fritz. *Varieties of History: From Voltaire to the Present.* 1956. Reprint. New York: Meridian Books, 1960.

J.   How to Read Statistics

Laurence McFalls

Applying statistical methods in cultural studies might sound like a contradiction in terms. While cultural studies engages in qualitative interpretation, seeking to uncover the meaning behind appearances, statistical methods practice quantitative description, inferring causality from the observable regularities of appearances. In fact, cultural studies and statistical methods are complementary, for to paraphrase Max Weber, the founder of interpretive social science, a statistically probable prediction without meaning is as useless as a meaningful interpretation without probability. All too often would-be practitioners of cultural studies evaluate their interpretations of social realities on moral or aesthetic grounds alone and fail to assess their interpretations' correspondence to observable experience. Statistical methods are one technique for judging the empirical validity of cultural interpretations, but only if used properly and critically. Statistics, by their very air of scienticity, enjoy a certain legitimacy and power that should be suspect to any student of culture. The following pointers provide a brief introduction to the proper use of statistical methods and to some of their pitfalls.

Descriptive Statistics

As their name implies, some statistical measures *describe* the characteristics and distribution of *variables*. (The latter are observable phenomena, including expressed subjective states such as opinions, which vary between at least two values. A single event, such as Hitler's seizure of power, cannot be constructed as a variable, but his electoral support from 1924 to 1933 can.) The most common descriptive statistics are the mean, the mode, the median, and the standard deviation.

The *mean*, or the average, is the sum of all observed values divided by the

---

"How to Read Statistics," from *A User's Guide to German Cultural Studies,* ed. Scott Denham, Irene Kacandes, and Jonathan Petropoulos (Ann Arbor: University of Michigan Press, 1997), may be reproduced as needed.

number of observations. The mean can accurately describe a relatively homo-geneous group but can also conceal useful information. For example, during the Weimar Republic the "average" German citizen held moderate political opinions, though we know that German political life at the time was highly polarized.

The *mode* is the most frequent value of a variable. More useful than the mean for describing a distribution that is not centered on the mean, the mode must not be confused with the majority. Thus, for example, while it is true that the Nazis enjoyed the greatest electoral support of any German party in 1933—that is, they were the modal choice of Germans—the majority of Germans never voted for the Nazis.

The *median* is the value of the middle observation in a distribution; that is, half of the observations will have a value above or below the median. Usu-ally close in value to the mean, the median has the (dis)advantage of not shift-ing with changes at the extreme of a distribution. For example, the median level of wealth will not jump, as does the mean, when a rich member of a small pop-ulation suddenly grows much richer.

The *standard deviation* describes how concentrated the values of a vari-able are around the mean. In a "normal," bell-shaped distribution, in which the mean, mode, and median coincide, more than 95 percent of the observations of the variable will lie within two standard deviations of the mean. Because the standard deviation describes how homogeneous (when it is small) or diverse (when it is large) a population is, it is a particularly useful descriptive statistic for cultural studies, which is often interested in questions of conformism and deviation. For example, if a survey of college students produced a large stan-dard deviation from the mean number of sexual partners students had had, then we might expect the student population to be divided between the promiscuous and the prudish.

While descriptive statistics may be useful when we wish to make gener-alizations about a homogeneous population, cultural studies often seeks to ex-plain cultural diversity and/or deviations from cultural norms. Not only are dif-ferences within populations intrinsically interesting, but without divergences we cannot explain anything. For example, we cannot understand cultural con-formism unless we can compare and contrast cultural conformists and deviants, however defined, in order to see which of their characteristics vary and thus might explain their cultural differences. One technique for uncovering such ex-planatory differences is statistical inference.

Statistical Inference

As the name implies, *statistical inference* is the process by which we can infer relations of cause and effect between variables according to statistical measures of their covariation. Although the very notion of causality has been problematic in the philosophy of science for centuries, the standard criterion for establishing the relation of cause and effect between an *independent variable* (the cause) and a *dependent variable* (the effect) is *concomitant variation,* or what John Stuart Mill called the "Methods of Agreement and Disagreement." According to these methods, we can say that *x* is the cause of *y* if *x* is contiguous with and precedes *y* and if *y* always follows whenever *x* is present (agreement) and *y* never follows when *x* is absent (disagreement). Since these conditions of deterministic causality rarely obtain in the realm of human social existence, statistical inference adopts a probabilistic view of causality; that is, it seeks to establish the likelihood that *y* will occur when *x* is present.

Correlation: The standard measure of covariation, or correlation, is called *Pearson's "r,"* a number that ranges between 1 and -1. A perfect correlation of $r = 1$ means that whenever *x* is present so is *y;* a perfect negative correlation of $r = -1$ means that *y* is absent whenever *x* is present; and the absence of correlation ($r = 0$) means that there is no particular tendency for *y* to be either present or absent when *x* is present. As a rule of thumb, r must be greater than 0.3 or less than -0.3 to be substantively significant[1] since the value of *r-squared* suggests the percentage of variation in *y* that might be determined by *x*. For example, if levels of income and education are correlated at $r = 0.5$, then education might explain 25 percent (r-squared $= 0.25$) of the variation in income. Please note, however, that *correlation is not causation,* not even when the correlation is perfect, since statistical correlation between *x* and *y* does not establish whether *x* causes *y, y* causes *x,* or *z* causes both *x* and *y*.

Multiple Regression: Precisely because relations of causality between variables are multiple and interdependent, it is often necessary to use a technique that makes it possible to establish the relative weight of different causal factors, or independent variables. A *multiple regression equation* describes a posited causal relationship between several independent variables (x', x'', x''', etc.) and an independent variable, *y,* in the form $y = ax' + bx'' + cx''' + \ldots + K + E$ (where K represents a constant and E an error term). Although the mathematics of multiple regression equations are relatively complicated, their results are relatively easy to understand: the *standardized coefficients* (*a, b, c,* etc.) of the independent variables (x', x'', x''', etc.) give the relative causal weight of each variable, and the r-squared statistic for the equation indicates the percentage of variation in *y* for which the various variables *x* can account.

Thus, for example, a multiple regression model for racial tolerance might include the independent variables age, education, and income (all correlated among themselves) and determine whether that richer, older, and better-educated people, in that order of independent causal importance, tend to express tolerance for racial diversity. It is important to recall that, even if the r-squared statistic for this equation were relatively high, say 0.6 (i.e., even if the regression model potentially "explained" 60 percent of the variance in tolerance), the explanatory value of any statistical model depends on the *validity* of its measurements and its concepts. The statistical correlation between the numerical values of given variables does not mean that the posited relationship between variables exists if the numerical values do not actually measure the phenomena as the model's author conceived them. For example, if the author hypothesizes that intelligent people are more tolerant and measures intelligence by years of schooling, a correlation between levels of education and tolerance would not confirm the author's hypothesis, since many years of schooling might simply expose those people to more racial diversity and render them more tolerant, regardless of any acquired intelligence. Ultimately, then, the use of statistical methods requires the elaboration of clear concepts and measures and the critical interpretation of findings.

NOTES

1. Note that *substantive significance* is not the same as *statistical significance*. The latter term refers to the probability that an observed statistical relationship might be accidental or due to chance. Thus, a relationship is said to be statistically significant at the level of $p < 0.05$ if there is less than a 5 percent chance that the observed relationship is purely coincidental. Many statistically significant relationships might be considered substantively, practically, or morally insignificant, while some substantively significant findings might not stand up to the requirements of statistical significance.

K.   How to Use an Archive

Geoffrey J. Giles

Know Your Archive

Accommodation away from home can be expensive, and you can use up a lot of precious time during your visit to an archive, simply finding out what it contains. That's even before you submit an order slip for a file, which may take hours to be fetched. So, do as much preparatory work as possible before you travel. There are a number of guides that are readily available. Erwin K. Welsch et al., eds., *Archives and Libraries in a New Germany* (1994), offers general information. There is also an excellent "guide to guides" in the German Historical Institute's publication: Ulrike Skorsetz and Janine Micunek, *Guide to Inventories and Finding Aids at the German Historical Institute, Washington, D.C.* (1995). This also has the merit of giving the address and phone number of each archive that it lists. The booklet gives the titles of all the main, published catalogs of federal, regional, city, and private archives in Germany. The German Federal Archives (Bundesarchiv) itself has published over fifty highly detailed guides (*Findbücher*) to particular collections, which may be purchased relatively cheaply and are invaluable if you are working in that area.

Know Your Archivist

In the old days of the GDR an archivist sat you down and subjected you to an ideological quiz and a little propaganda lecture before allowing you to set foot in the archive's reading room. Those days are gone—think of the archivist now as your friend. When applying to use an archive—do so well in advance, as many are seriously understaffed—you will need to explain in some detail what you are looking for. If you are a graduate student or do not have a regular academic appointment, you may also need a letter of introduction from a profes-

"How to Use an Archive," from *A User's Guide to German Cultural Studies,* ed. Scott Denham, Irene Kacandes, and Jonathan Petropoulos (Ann Arbor: University of Michigan Press, 1997), may be reproduced as needed.

sor or established scholar. You'll be assigned to a particular archivist with expertise in that area (your *Betreuer,* or referent), whose job it is to help you locate the files you need. He or she will generally have some files lined up for you when you arrive and will often point you toward classes of records (*Bestände*) you had not even thought about.

The overseer of the reading room (*Lesesaal-Aufsicht*) is someone with a pretty boring and often menial security job, handing out files and watching to see that no one steals anything from them. *Never* be dismissive or look down on this staff member. He (rarely, she) can be extremely officious, or he can be the best friend you have in the archives, especially in terms of waiving restrictions on, for example, the number of files you can order per day.

Know Your Class

No, this is not an injunction to be aware of your lowly station! A class, collection, group, or *Bestand* is a set of records from a single government ministry or political party or other public or private agency or institution. Perhaps its holdings will be cataloged, sometimes in a *Findbuch,* sometimes in a card index file. The *Findbuch* will only rarely be published in an up-to-date version, so that you will still need to budget some time to consult further finding aids at the archive. Remember that whole *Bestände,* even sixty years old or more, are still arriving at archives and being sorted and cataloged for the first time. The finding aids (*Findmittel*) on the spot will generally be more accurate than any published version, so do not bypass them. They will often contain in addition a helpful, introductory essay about the agency or ministry in question.

Know Your Files

A file with the most promising of titles may contain a single sheet of paper with no useful information at all. On the other hand, you may strike gold in another file with a very vague title. You will often come across the most bizarre items when you are not looking for them. I am probably the only person alive who knows where to find a seventy-year-old condom in the Prussian Secret Archives (outraged members of the Moral Right had written to the government, protesting the ease with which they had been able to acquire the offending article by mail order). If you are going through a dull patch, or items appear to have been removed from the file, do not give up. Go back and talk to your *Betreuer.* If he or she is too busy to see you immediately, suggest that you lunch together in the archive's cafeteria (Dutch treat, of course). Maybe there will be a little more time to chat then. The archivist may think of connections to other files. The original file may have been split up after arriving at the archive. Your *Betreuer* will have access to the concordance. If you treat the archivist as your friend and ally (as most are), the response will usually be a warm one. Above all, you must not play the arrogant scholar for whom the staff of archives are lackeys, simply there to fetch files for you—this does happen, and you can guess the reaction.

Know the Law

Research in Germany is sometimes hampered by the data protection laws (*Personendatenschutzgesetze*). American archives are beginning to protect the privacy of individuals in similar ways, but the law is not nearly so restrictive. And Germany has no Freedom of Information Act. The German archives laws can sound stern: whereas in the United States the rule is that a file should only be withheld if there is a clear invasion of privacy, in Germany a document is not normally released at all, unless thirty years have elapsed since the person's death. And the onus is on you to provide proof of the date of death. Even that does not guarantee access, and sometimes the permission of the children and grandchildren in the matter of access can be declared necessary. If, however, your subject is a public figure or historical personage (although those are rather vague terms), the usual restrictions *may* be waived in the interests of advancing scholarship. On paper the archives laws of the various states are, then, quite friendly toward researchers; in practice much still depends upon the caprice of the individual archivist. The general exception to this is, happily, the Bundesarchiv, which has a reputation for being consistently helpful.

Know Your Time Constraints

You will be eager to move in and out of an archive in as few days or weeks as possible, principally because of lodging expenses. Do not, therefore, attempt to read every document in a file in full. Learn to skim rapidly and identify the more interesting-looking sections in the file. If there is a twenty-five-page report that is clearly crucial to your project but your German is still a little shaky, do not waste two hours reading it then and there—photocopy it, instead. Then you can study it at leisure at home. You need to be aware that most archives will not let you use the copy machines yourself and that photocopies are expensive, compared with the United States. If you ask the archivist to mail the copies on to you after your departure, your request may well be buried for months. So, try if possible to have the copies made while you are still at the archive. This also makes paying for them much easier. Paying foreign bills from the United States usually adds an extra thirty-five dollar fee from your friendly local bank on top of the actual bill. Put in requests for copies as soon as you can after finishing with a file, certainly at the end of each day if this is a short visit. Staff rarely have time to make copies immediately, so give them as much latitude as possible.

If you are lucky enough to have a laptop computer, you can save on photocopying charges by simply typing onto your disk the excerpts that you need. Archives have now generally become computer friendly, though older historians can tell you amusing stories of the early days. Do remember that Germany runs on 220 volts, not 120 volts as in the United States. If you do not have a voltage converter, you will provide great entertainment for your neighbors in the archive by blowing up your laptop before their very eyes, though many of the current generation of computers have been designed to operate around the world under a variety of voltages. And do not forget to backup your files regularly on diskette as you travel.

If you are still making most of your notes on index cards, don't be embarrassed. Probably most of the other users will be doing so as well. There is an important decision to be made here, however, and it comes at the very beginning of your research. Are you going to use American index cards or German ones? They come in totally different sizes, which will not fit in the drawers or holders of the other country. If you decide on American ones and run out of them in Germany, you will have to switch halfway. If you use German *Karteikarten,* then you can replenish when necessary, but you will need to buy a *Kartei* on the spot to store them in back home.

Be aware that some archives will not bring you any new files after 2 p.m., so make sure that you have ordered enough to see you through the rest of the afternoon. Many archives do not allow you to order more than ten files at once. It does not matter whether there are three hundred documents in the file or a single sheet of paper: you may not order fresh files until you have returned some of the original ten. Some archives only collect the order slips once every two hours. Be sure, therefore, to order some for the next morning at the end of the afternoon. Pay attention to the sheet of rules and regulations you will be made to read on arrival (and swear in writing that you accept in full), because these idiosyncrasies will usually be revealed there.

Be Sociable

Archival work is intensive and often exhausting, and it can be lonely. Do not sit with a dazed expression on your face in the cafeteria at lunchtime at your own private table. If you see someone who looks even halfway approachable or friendly, introduce yourself. As likely or not, he or she will have tips to share about the archive in question. And lifelong friendships are often formed out there in the trenches. Another way of meeting people is to find out the names and topics of other visitors in the archive's reading room. Your friend, the reading room attendant, will often be happy to tell you who's who on any given day. There is almost bound to be someone doing work that excites you or a well-known scholar you've always wanted to talk to. And, unless you are blessed with the long opening times of the Bundesarchiv, there are the long evening hours to consider, when most scholars I know are delighted to find companions with whom to exchange news of their interesting discoveries of the day and to sample the local wine or beer.

So remember: you have to read the documents alone, but scholarship should not be a solitary pursuit. You can do no good work without running your ideas past others scholars as you develop them. An archive's reading room can be a silent and forbidding place to the novice, but the camaraderie of researchers outside those walls and the absence of conventional barriers between professor and graduate student are something that make the hard work all the more enjoyable on those trips into the unknown.

CHAPTER 29

German Cultural Studies Course Syllabi: Sources and Examples

Students of German cultural studies are fortunate to have the German Academic Exchange Service (DAAD)–sponsored on-line German studies course syllabus database, organized by Sander Gilman, originally at Cornell University and now administered by the American Institute for Contemporary German Studies (AICGS). Under Gilman's direction the DAAD continues to award prizes for the best German studies course syllabi each year, and all submissions are added to the database, which is accessible via the World Wide Web (WWW) at http://www.jhu.edu/~aicgs.doc/. In addition, most academic departments have their own WWW homepages, many of which also give samples of their course syllabi; with a bit of browsing one can quickly garner a great deal of information. The course syllabi that follow are all accessible in the DAAD/AICGS database, and the Berdahl and Bergerson syllabus was a 1995 second-place winner in the syllabi contest. We offer them to give a taste of the diversity and intensity of cultural studies teaching in German studies today.

Russell Berman introduces a well-known German studies course taught at Stanford; the course is taught in the German Studies Department and satisfies the "Cultures, Ideas, and Values" requirement for Stanford first-year students and is an excellent model of how German studies can be cultural studies. Historian Richard Hunt describes the second course in his essay in part 7 of this volume; it is offered here in its latest incarnation, now a true German cultural studies course. This course is offered in a general education program and has no departmental or disciplinary affiliation; it is designed for undergraduates only, usually those in the first or second year of college. Next we present Daphne Berdahl's and Drew Bergerson's course aimed at more advanced undergraduates or graduate students in history, anthropology, or other interdisciplinary programs. This course, while offering much primary source material on German culture and society itself, engages the theories and methods of "doing cultural studies" more explicitly. Finally, Irene Kacandes's course on the Holocaust, taught originally as an undergraduate culture course in the Department of Germanic Languages at the University of Texas at Austin, concentrates on the texts of survivors, victims, and perpetrators to teach the history and representation of the Holocaust.

A. German Studies
and the General Culture Course:
The Stanford Curriculum

Russell A. Berman

Since the early twentieth century, the liberal arts curriculum at some (but by no means all) leading colleges has included a required general culture course, usually part of the freshman year. To be sure, the history and character of these courses at Columbia, Chicago, Stanford, and elsewhere vary considerably, but, as prominent features of undergraduate education, they are quite significant. From the start this curriculum was linked to ideological concerns, especially as part of an effort to explain the mission of the emerging global power of the United States. Criticized and sometimes canceled in the 1960s or early 1970s, they later came under considerable attack from the standpoint of multiculturalism, given their traditional focus on Western culture. In addition to the complex political field around these courses, however, there are sometimes other agenda articulated in their defense: the putative need for some core or shared first-year student experience, or the remedial claim that such a course makes up for the failings of the high schools, which are seen as no longer providing students with adequate knowledge.

The Stanford requirement is now called "Cultures, Ideas, and Values" (or CIV) and derives from a resolution adopted by the faculty senate. Approximately eight courses, each of which is a full three-quarter sequence, have been approved as CIV tracks. Every first-year student is required to enroll in one of them. The same legislation sets broad guidelines for these tracks and currently includes specific mandates with regard to the diversity of texts. A faculty committee oversees the program and regularly reviews the tracks.

As a freshman at Harvard, I enrolled in a General Education course that entailed a survey of German cultural history and which had quite a large enrollment. The Stanford effort to establish a CIV track based in German studies was in part an attempt to recapture that course, which I had found so invigorating, and to fashion a structure that would allow the departmental faculty to teach more effectively while reaching out to a much larger public than we would

491

normally have. About 125 first-year students (8 percent of the class) enroll in our course each year; some are subsequently recruited into other departmental courses, but all have been exposed to some of the key problems and texts in German culture—and that is certainly the department's mission.

The course, entitled "Myth and Modernity," meets once a week for a one-hour plenum lecture, and each student also participates in a discussion section (two two-hour meetings per week). The organizing theme of the course is reason and its impact on culture: reason as antithesis of myth and reason as itself a mythic force. The first quarter examines, in a generally chronological order, the European Enlightenment and its consequences in the nineteenth century. The second quarter, treating reason and identity, ranges more freely in time and space: Luther is paired with Augustine, Mann with Plato. The third quarter returns to early-twentieth-century Germany, focusing on rationalization in Weimar culture, irrationalism, fascism, and the Holocaust. The syllabus for 1995–96, which follows, was taught by John Heins in the winter, Karen Kenkel in the spring, and me during the autumn.

Myth and Modernity, Stanford University
Department of German Studies

Autumn Quarter

Myth and Modernity is a CIV track sponsored by the Department of German Studies. The course explores the contrasts and interplays between traditional and modern cultural material, raising questions about history, progress, and change. What defines a cultural tradition? How do values change? When does a national past sustain or impinge on the present? These questions are posed with reference to material from Germany, including literature by authors such as Goethe, Brecht, and Kafka, philosophical texts by Kant, Marx, and Nietzsche, and music by Beethoven and Wagner as well as paintings and films. The German works are contrasted with writings by authors from other parts of the world.

The first quarter examines the Enlightenment and its legacy in the eighteenth and nineteenth centuries: the emphatic belief in reason and education, a topic surely central to the university today. The second quarter investigates the relationship between conceptual thought and cultural expression more abstractly and casts a wider historical and geographical net. The third quarter returns to modernism and modern Germany and inquires into the relationship between rationalization and the return of myth in the twentieth century.

The following texts are available at Stanford bookstore (in order of usage):

Lessing, *Nathan the Wise* (Continuum)
Goethe, *Faust* (Penguin)
Burke, *Reflections on the Revolution in France* (Penguin)
Paine, *Rights of Man* (Penguin)
Wollstonecraft, *A Vindication of the Rights of Woman* (Penguin)
Wagner, *Lohengrin* (Riverrun)
Tucker, ed., *The Marx-Engels Reader* (Norton)
Du Bois, *Souls of Black Folk* (Bantam)
Hollingdale, ed., *A Nietzsche Reader* (Penguin)

In addition, several brief photocopied excerpts will be distributed in class.

Class	Topic
1	Introduction: Kant, "What Is Enlightenment?"
2	assignment 1 announced in discussion section
3	Lessing, *Nathan the Wise*
4	assignment 1 due
5	assignment 2 announced
6	Goethe, *Faust*
7	assignment 2 due
8	assignment 3 announced; readings for next week distributed
9	Beethoven, Ninth Symphony; and Schiller's "Ode to Joy"
10	assignment 3 due
11	Mann, excerpt from *Doktor Faustus*
12	Burke, *Reflections on the French Revolution*
13	Paine, *Rights of Man* (33–147)
14	Wollstonecraft, *A Vindication* (77–141, 279–328)
15	Hoffmann, "The Sandman"
16	Wagner, *Lohengrin;* assignment 4 announced
17	*Marx-Engels Reader* (7–8, 71–81, 143–45, 147–75, 294–329, 473–500, 653–64, 735–59); assignment 4 due
18	Du Bois, *Souls of Black Folk*
19	*Nietzsche Reader*
20	exam

Class Organization

One one-hour lecture and two two-hour discussion sections per week. During the quarter you will be required to write several short papers; precise topics will be announced in advance. Your section leader may require additional assignments to help you prepare for discussions. Your grade will depend equally on the written assignments, your participation in discussion sections, and the final examination.

Myth and Modernity

Winter Quarter

The second quarter of this CIV track explores the issues of personal and group identity in a variety of texts from ancient and modern worlds. Last quarter we addressed the issue of reason and self-determination in thinking of the European Enlightenment; this quarter we will take the ideas and tools that we acquired there and attempt to apply them elsewhere, in Western culture before the Enlightenment and in the interface between Western culture and other cultures. The course will be divided into five thematic parts: reason and emancipation, reason in spiritual history, reason in tribal history, reason and love, and reason and suffering. In each part we will attempt to make sense of the texts as documents of cultural identity.

The following texts are available at Stanford bookstore (in order of usage):

The Bible (King James Version)
Ngugi wa Thiong'o, *Weep Not, Child* (Heinemann)
Saint Augustine, *Confessions* (Penguin)
Dilenberger, ed., *Martin Luther, Selections from His Writings* (Anchor)
The Nibelungenlied (Penguin)
William Shakespeare, *The Tempest* (Pelican)
Bartolomé de Las Casas, *The Devastation of the Indies* (Johns Hopkins UP)
Plato, *The Symposium* (Penguin)
Thomas Mann, *Death in Venice* (Vintage)
Franz Kafka, *The Trial* (Schocken)

Several brief photocopied texts will also be distributed in class. There are also two required film screenings.

Class   Topic

Part 1: Reason and Emancipation
1   Introduction; *Exodus*
2   *Exodus*
3   Ngugi wa Thiong'o, *Weep Not, Child*
4   *Weep Not, Child*

Part 2: Reason in Spiritual History
5   Augustine, *Confessions,* bks. 1–3, 7–8; paper 1 due
6   Augustine
7   Luther, "Preface to the New Testament," "The Freedom of a
        Christian," "Sermon in Pleissenburg," "An Appeal to the Ruling
        Class" (pts. 1 and 2 only)
8   Luther

Part 3: Reason in Tribal History
9   *The Nibelungenlied;* film screening, Lang, *Siegfried's Death*
10   *The Nibelungenlied*
11   Shakespeare, *The Tempest;* paper 2 due
12   Bartolomé de Las Casas, *The Devastation of the Indies*

Part 4: Reason and Love
13   Plato, *Symposium*
14   Sappho
15   Mann, *Death in Venice*
16   *Death in Venice*

Part 5: Reason and Suffering
17   *Job;* Epictetus; Diogenes, Buddhist texts; Dogen; paper 3 due
18   Further suffering
19   Kafka, *The Trial;* film screening, Welles, *The Trial*
20   *The Trial*
21   exam

Class organization as in fall quarter.

Myth and Modernity

Spring Quarter

The third quarter of Myth and Modernity will foreground central issues in twentieth-century culture and politics, in particular as they are reflected in the Central European context: the impact of two world wars, the increased rationalization and technologization of life, the explosion of mass culture (particularly film), and the rise of fascism and racist politics culminating in the Holocaust. We will pursue themes developed in fall and winter quarters of individual responsibility and collective identity, of progress and education, while examining forms of irrationalism that emerge from the political and cultural tension of twentieth-century life. Our focus on Central European material allows us to examine the emergence of particular problems that many cultures share, to ask the following questions: How does the experience of German fascism cause us to think differently about other nations and cultures? How do questions of individual responsibility and resistance in relation to the Holocaust and fascism apply more broadly to the modern condition? What are the mechanisms by which a collective identity is established and what are the needs that such an identity meets?

The following texts are available at Stanford bookstore (in order of usage):

Course Reader
Freud, *Civilization and Its Discontents* (Norton)
Brecht, *Three Penny Opera* (Arcade)
Mann, *Death in Venice* (you should already have this from winter quarter)
Kowaga, *Obasan* (Godine)
Arendt, *Eichmann in Jerusalem* (Penguin)

Class	*Topic*
1	Introduction
2	Hitler, *Mein Kampf* (excerpts in course reader); Riefenstahl, *Triumph of the Will* (screening)
3	Benjamin, "The Work of Art in the Age of Mechanical Reproduction" (reader)
4	Eisenstein, *Battleship Potemkin* (screening)
5	Freud, *Civilization and Its Discontents;* paper 1 due
6	Lang, *Metropolis* (screening)
7	articles in reader on primitivism by Marc, Macke; primitivist paintings (reader)
8	photomontages (reader)
9	Freud, "The Uncanny" (reader); paper 2 due
10	Murnau, *Nosferatu* (screening)
11	Brecht, *Three Penny Opera*
12	Musical selections (on reserve)
13	Mann, "Mario and the Magician"; paper 3 due
14	Szabo, *Mephisto* (screening)
15	Kogawa, *Obasan*
16	Kowaga
17	Arendt, *Eichmann in Jerusalem*
18	Arendt
19	Adorno (handout)
20	exam

Class organization as in previous quarters.

B.   CULTURE AND SOCIETY
IN WEIMAR AND NAZI GERMANY:
HARVARD UNIVERSITY CORE PROGRAM

Richard M. Hunt

Course Description

This course explores culture and society in the Weimar Republic (1919–33) and Nazi Germany (1933–45). It focuses on the major shifts in "world outlook" during these two critical periods of German and world history.

During the Weimar period: an infant democracy fighting for its life; political enemies on the Right and Left; after the inflation of 1923 a half-decade of calm and recovery; meanwhile, extraordinary cultural ferment in all of the arts— the so-called Golden Years when modernism, Expressionism, New Objectivity, and experimentation flourished in German literature, painting, architecture, films, and music; then with the Depression of 1929, increasing social and economic strains, along with mounting political crises leading to the appointment of Adolf Hitler as chancellor of the "new Germany" on 30 January 1933.

During the Third Reich of Adolf Hitler: charismatic dictatorship and national unity, political repression, officially sponsored antisemitism, cultural regimentation, press censorship, propaganda, war, the Holocaust, and total defeat resulting in the so-called Zero Hour of complete collapse in 1945.

Please note this is neither a history nor a literature/fine arts course. It is a Core Course and conforms to Core guidelines. In studying the social and cultural history of this era, the course will attempt to enhance the understanding of representative German works of art by considering the historical setting and, conversely, to use artistic works to illuminate the tumultuous historical experience of the German people in the twentieth century.

Film Evenings

As historical documents, films help provide an understanding of the era's ambiance. Since the course encourages insight into both the arts and the history of

Weimar and Nazi Germany, students should treat the films as unique and valuable resources for studying culture.

> Week 2: *The Cabinet of Dr. Caligari* (1919), classic Expressionist film with a controversial political allegory.
> Week 4: *The Blue Angel* (1930), brilliant cinematic attack on the institutions and conventions of Wilhelmine Germany with Marlene Dietrich.
> Week 5: *Metropolis* (1927), Fritz Lang's vision of a future marked by technocratic and urban revolutions.
> Week 6: *Swastika* (1976), with original footage depicting aspects of life and culture in Nazi Germany, including "home movies" of Adolf Hitler and his entourage.
> Week 8: *Triumph of the Will* (1935), Leni Riefenstahl's glorified account of the 1934 Nuremberg Party Rally; also *Der ewige Jude* (*The Eternal Jew*), an original Nazi propaganda film with explicitly antisemitic messages.
> Week 10: *Architecture of Doom* (1989), Peter Cohen's examination Nazi art and artists and their relationship to Nazi ideology.
> Week 12: *The White Rose* (1983), Michael Verhoeven's film about student resistance to Nazism in Munich.

Required Readings

A source book is required for this course and individual handouts will be distributed at certain class meetings.

> Erich Remarque, *All Quiet on the Western Front*
> Hans Fallada, *Little Man, What Now?*
> Peter Gay, *Weimar Culture: The Outsider as Insider*
> Walter Gropius, *The New Architecture and the Bauhaus*
> Bertolt Brecht, *The Jewish Wife and Other Plays*
> Jackson Spielvogel, *Hitler and Nazi Germany,* 2d ed.
> Primo Levi, *Survival in Auschwitz*

Reading period assignment: to be announced
Course Requirements: (1) attendance at lectures, sections, and films; (2) section participation, including two short, ungraded "reflective papers" (25 percent); (3) hour exam given in class (15 percent); (4) term paper (30 percent); (5) final examination (30 percent).
Schedule:

> Week 1: Introduction: 30 January 1933. "Triumph of the Will"
>   The Deepening Crisis: Weimar Germany, 1919–33
>   Mann, "Mario and the Magician"

Week 2: A New Departure: Nazi Germany, 1933–45
  Historical Background; The Legacy of German History
    Levine, *The Apocalyptic Vision,* excerpts (source book)
    Themes and Important Dates of German History (source book)
    Heym and Trakl (source book); film: *Dr. Caligari*
Week 3: The Immediate Past: Second Reich and the Outbreak of World
  War I
    Remarque, *All Quiet on the Western Front*
  The Great War: World War I and Its Aftermath
    Remarque, cont.
    Jünger, *Storm of Steel,* excerpts (source book)
    Brecht, "Germany" poems (source book)
  The Weimar Republic, 1919–33
Week 4: Turmoils of an Unpracticed Democracy
    Fallada, *Little Man, What Now?*
    Weimar chronology and voting statistics (source book)
    Gay, "A Short Political History," in *Weimar Culture,* 147–64
    Fallada, cont.
Week 5: Berlin: A World City
    Film: *Metropolis*
    Friedrich, *Before the Deluge,* excerpts (source book)
    Huyssen, "The Vamp and the Machine" (source book)
    paper 1 due
  The Brilliant Decade: The Bauhaus and Other Accomplishments
    Miller-Lane, *Architecture and Politics* excerpts (source book)
    Bauhaus Manifesto and Curriculum (source book)
    Gropius, *The New Architecture and the Bauhaus*
Week 6: Modernism and the Visual Arts
    film: *Swastika*
    Gay, *Weimar Culture*
    Alfred Döblin, *Berlin Alexanderplatz,* excerpts (source book)
    Kandinsky, *On the Spiritual in Art,* excerpts (source book)
  Music in the Weimar Republic
    Gordon Craig, "Weimar Culture" in *Germany, 1866–1945*
    Brecht, Weimar poems (source book)
Week 7: The Fall of Weimar and the Rise of Hitler and the Nazi Party
    Spielvogel, *Hitler and Nazi Germany,* 1–38
    Nietzsche, *The Gay Science,* excerpts (source book)
    Midterm examination given in class
  The Third Reich at Peace: 1933–39
Week 8: Nazi Revolution
    Spielvogel, *Hitler and Nazi Germany,* 41–122

Chronology, Nazi documents (source book)
Mann, "Exchange of letters" (source book)
Week 9: The National Socialist Ideology
Films: *Triumph of the Will* and *Der ewige Jude*
Spielvogel, *Hitler and Nazi Germany,* 123–53
Major points of Nazi ideology, Program of the Nazi Party (source book)
Nietzsche, "Will to Power," excerpts (source book)
Hitler, "The State" in *Mein Kampf*
Nazi Ideology in the Arts
Spielvogel, *Hitler and Nazi Germany,* 154–91
Miller Lane, *Architecture and Politics,* excerpts (source book)
Hitler's cultural speeches (source book)
Week 10: Music and Drama in the Third Reich
Stefan Zweig, *The World of Yesterday*, excerpts (source book)
Literature in Germany, 1933–45; music (source book)
Brecht, "The Jewish Wife," "In Search of Justice," and
"The Informer," all in *The Jewish Wife*
Week 11: Goebbels and the Art of Propaganda
Film: *Architecture of Doom*
Goebbels, *Michael* (source book)
Fest, *The Face of the Third Reich* (Goebbels) (source book)
Welch, "Propaganda and the German Cinema" (source book)
The Third Reich at War: 1939–45
The Second World War
Spielvogel, *Hitler and Nazi Germany,* 192–231
Chronology and Map (source book)
Paper 2 due
Week 12: Transition from Peace to War
Spielvogel, *Hitler and Nazi Germany,* 232–65
Koonz, *Mothers in the Fatherland,* excerpts (source book)
Craig, "Cultural Decline and the Resistance"
Mass Media and the Propaganda in the Third Reich
"Press and propaganda sections" (source book)
Bonhoeffer, *Letters and Papers from Prison* (source book)
White Rose leaflets (source book)
Hitler, "War Propaganda," in *Mein Kampf*
Week 13: The Holocaust
Dimsdale, ed., *Survivors, Victims and Perpetrators,* excerpts
Chronology of Germans and Jews, documents (source book)
Celan and Sachs poems (source book)

Spielvogel, *Hitler and Nazi Germany,* 266–301

Levi, *Survival in Auschwitz*

From Götterdämmerung to Stunde Null (From Twilight of the Gods to Hour Zero)

Borchert, "The Kitchen Clock," "Rats Do Sleep at Night" (source book)

Brecht poems (source book)

term paper due; exam

C. The Rapprochement of History and Anthropology in Germany (University of Chicago)

Daphne Berdahl and Drew Bergerson

In the last two decades historians and anthropologists have been engaged in a fruitful dialog concerning theory and method. In their studies of everyday life, working-class culture, or village histories, social historians have increasingly turned to the methods of ethnographic analysis and interpretation to study history "from the bottom up." Social anthropologists have similarly rejected their discipline's emphasis on atemporal social reproduction, static cultural systems, and underlying structural models to stress process, agency, performance, and practice in human action and social life.

German social history as well as anthropological studies of Germany have both benefited from and contributed to this trend. Both disciplines face specific challenges in the German context, however, relating to indigenous forms of cultural studies, everyday life under totalitarianism, and the practices of memory. This course will introduce students to specific issues and themes in German culture, society, and politics, past and present, through a close examination of the rapprochement of history and anthropology in Germany. Although the focus of the course is on German cultural studies, we will be alert to the broader implications of our discussions for an ongoing interdisciplinary interaction between history and anthropology beyond German-speaking Central Europe.

The course is divided into three parts. The first part examines some of the pertinent literature on the rapprochement of history and anthropology in general. The second part explores the application and generation of these ideas in the German context, with particular focus on *Volkskunde, Alltagsgeschichte,* and village studies approaches. The final part of the course is devoted to areas of study in which the dialog between history and anthropology has been particularly fruitful and challenging. These include: national identity, gender and the body, everyday life in the Third Reich, representing a burdened past, and German unification.

A general knowledge of modern German history will be presumed; knowledge of German language is helpful but not required. All required readings for discussion will be in English, while lecturers will supplement these sources with translated texts and ethnographic research. The student's grade will be based on: (1) active participation and submission of reading notes for the assigned reading for each seminar and (2) a 15–20-page research paper.

Part 1: Theoretical Introduction (Weeks 1–2)

Session	*Subject*
1	Introduction
2, 3	Discussion: *Rapprochement*
4	Lecture: Structure and Practice

Study Questions:
> Course goals and requirements, our own research.
> What are the historical trends in anthropology and the anthropological trends in history? Are they leading in the same direction?
> A brief introduction to the vocabulary: agency, embodiment, enactment, events, habitus, instantiation, tactics.

Required Reading:
> Cohn, Bernard S. "History and Anthropology: The State of Play." In *An Anthropologist among the Historians and Other Essays,* ed. Bernard S. Cohn. Oxford: Oxford UP, 1987. 18–49.
> Eley, Geoff. "Labor History, Social History, *Alltagsgeschichte:* Experience, Culture and the Politics of the Everyday—A New Direction for German Social History?" *Journal of Modern History* 61.2 (1989): 297–343.
> Medick, Hans. "'Missionaries in a Row Boat'? Ethnological Ways of Knowing as a Challenge to Social History." *Comparative Studies in Society and History* 29.1 (1987): 76–98.
> Ortner, S. "Theory in Anthropology since the Sixties." *Comparative Studies in Society and History* 26.1 (January 1984): 126–66.

Part 2: Various Approaches (Weeks 3–5)

5	Lecture/Discussion: *Volkskunde* and Folklore
6	Ethnography/Discussion: *Heimat*

Study Questions:
> How was popular culture researched traditionally in Germany?
> What are the strengths and weaknesses of the *Volkskunde* approach? (What do you make of "butterfly collecting"?)

What is the enacted relationship between *Volkskunde* and *Heimat* and local or national identity? Why is *Heimat* so compelling a concept? How
can this very localizing concept be reconciled with notions of de-terri-
torialization and globalization today?

What do you think of the idea of a "national character"? Is this something
that can be identified, studied, analyzed?

Ethnography: Heimat and religiosity in postsocialist eastern Germany: the
Seventh Station.

Required Reading:

> Applegate, Celia. *A Nation of Provincials: The German Idea of Heimat.*
> Berkeley: U of California P, 1990. Chaps. 1, 3, 8.
>
> Dundes, Alan. *Life Is like a Chicken Coop Ladder: A Study of German Na-
> tional Character through Folklore.* Detroit: Wayne State UP, 1989.

> 7   Ethnography/Lecture: *Alltagsgeschichte*
> 8   Discussion: *Eigensinn*

Study Questions:

> Is there a working-class culture? Why study it in isolation? With what ben-
> efits or dangers?
>
> How does class consciousness develop? What is the use of *Eigensinn?*
>
> Where can you find sources for the history of workers' everyday life?
>
> *Ethnography:* The Ruhr and Vienna between the wars.

Required Reading:

> Lüdtke, Alf. "Cash, Coffeebreaks, Horse-Play: '*Eigensinn*' and Politics
> among Factory Workers in Germany circa 1900." In *Confrontation,
> Class Consciousness, and the Labor Process: Studies in Proletarian
> Class Formation,* ed. Michael Hanagan and Charles Stephenson. New
> York: Greenwood P, 1986. 65–95.
>
> ———. "Organizational Order or '*Eigensinn*'? Workers' Privacy and
> Workers' Politics in Imperial Germany." In *Rites of Power: Symbolism,
> Ritual, and Politics Since the Middle Ages,* ed. Sean Wilentz. Philadel-
> phia: U Pennsylvania P, 1985. 303–33.

> 9   Village Studies
> 10   Discussion: a village in Württemberg

Study Questions:

> How can you use documents to find culture?
>
> How do historians write village ethnographies? anthropologists?
>
> What did historians take from anthropology?

What are some relationships between class and kinship? What role does kinship analysis play in village studies?

How do we define a "village"? How might we move beyond many of the notions of boundedness that characterize so many village studies?

What do you see as the particular challenges for historical and contemporary village studies?

Required Reading:

Sabean, David. *Power in the Blood: Popular Culture and Village Discourse in Early Modern Germany.* Cambridge: Cambridge UP, 1984.

Part 3: Themes and Problems (Weeks 6–10)

| 11 | Ethnography/Lecture: *Völkisch* Doing: Nationalism and Identity |
| 12 | Discussion: Enacting German Respectability |

Study Questions:

How does one create the experience of feeling German?

Where are the boundaries of this enacted Germany circa 1900?

Where can you find sources to describe informal social practices?

Compare approaches to sources: intellectual history versus cultural anthropology.

What do class, gender, and sexuality have to do with the nation?

Ethnography: student organizations 1900, Hildesheim 1925.

Required Reading:

Mosse, George L. *Nationalism and Sexuality.* New York: H. Fertig, 1985.

| 13 | Gender and the Body |
| 14 | Discussion: Early Modern Doctors |

Study Questions:

Is gender just an issue of women's studies?

Why consider gender as an analytical category in the construction of culture and politics?

How has the intersection of history and anthropology enhanced our understanding of how gender is constructed and negotiated?

How would you evaluate Duden's use of sources? What implications does her study have for a theory of gender?

Required Reading:

Duden, Barbara. *The Woman Beneath the Skin: A Doctor's Patients in Eighteenth-Century Germany.* Cambridge: Harvard UP, 1991.

15　　Ethnography/Lecture: Victims and Villains—Everyday Life under Fascism
16　　Discussion: Resisters versus Collaborators

Study Questions:
What is "normal" about everyday life in the Third Reich?
Where can we find sources to a history of destruction?
Who creates/is responsible for social and political events?
How can everyday life history enhance our understanding of uniquely horrific events?
Ethnography: Gardens in Auschwitz, communists in Hildesheim.

Required Reading:
Peukert, Detlev. *Inside the Third Reich: Conformity, Opposition, and Racism in Everyday Life.* 1982. New Haven: Yale UP, 1987.

17　　Ethnography: Remembering and Forgetting
18　　Discussion: Nasty Girls and Soldier Boys

Study Questions:
What are the different styles of remembering in Germany?
What are their political consequences?
What happens to the rememberer?
Ethnography: An Israeli-German exchange program, 1994.

Required Reading and Viewing:
Huyssen, Andreas. "Monuments and Holocaust Memory in a Media Age." *Twilight Memories: Marking Time in a Culture of Amnesia.* New York: Routledge, 1995. 149–60.
Kertzer, D. *Ritual, Politics, and Power.* New Haven: Yale UP, 1988. 77–101.
Verhoeven, Michael, dir. *The Nasty Girl* (1989).

19　　Lecture: Two Germanies
20　　Discussion: Borderlands

Study Questions:
What notions of Germanness were constructed during Germany's division and how?
What happens to people's identities when a system collapses overnight? What happens when borders disappear?
How would you assess the possible contributions of history and anthro-

pology to understanding the kind of rapid social change experienced after the fall of the Berlin Wall?

Ethnography: Border, Boundaries, and Identities in Kella, (former) East Germany, 1989–92.

Required Reading:

Berdahl, Daphne. "Publicity and the Culture of Secrecy in the Politics of Everyday Life: The Example of a Border Village." *New German Critique,* forthcoming.

Bornemann, John. *Belonging in the Two Berlins: Kin, State, Nation.* Cambridge: Cambridge UP, 1992. 1–118.

D. Survivors, Victims, and Perpetrators: The Literature of the Holocaust (University of Texas at Austin)

Irene Kacandes

It has been argued that the most brutal crime committed against humankind was the "Final Solution," the Nazis' attempted and nearly successful destruction of European Jewry. Sinti-Roma (Gypsies), Poles, Russians, homosexuals, communists, Jehovah's Witnesses, and other groups were also singled out for elimination. Since the end of World War II countless social scientists have tried to describe how and why these genocides occurred. Yet somehow even the best of these accounts fails to communicate fully the essence of the Nazis' madness. By reading poetry, plays, novels, and personal testimonies and viewing several movies, we will attempt to gain insight into the experiences of Holocaust survivors, victims, and perpetrators. Writers to be read include: Ilse Aichinger, Bertolt Brecht, Paul Celan, Anne Frank, Max Frisch, Adolf Hitler, Rudolf Hoess, Gertrud Kolmar, Primo Levi, Nelly Sachs, and Elie Wiesel. Some background readings and lectures are in geography, history, religion, sociology, and psychology.

This course has a substantial writing component.
All readings and discussion are in English.

> Borowski, *This Way for the Gas, Ladies and Gentlemen*
> Brecht, *The Jewish Wife and Other Short Plays*
> Dawidowicz, *The War against the Jews*
> Flannery, *Singer*
> Frank, *Diary of a Young Girl*
> Levi, *Survival in Auschwitz (If This Is a Man)*
> Spiegelman, *Maus*
> *Out of the Whirlwind,* ed. Albert Friedlander
> *Survivors, Victims, and Perpetrators,* ed. Joel Dimsdale, MD

Films: *Shoah; Enemies, A Love Story*

Grading: Attendance, participation, oral presentation of final project, 15 percent; midterm quiz, 15 percent; response papers (four, 2 pp. each; 10 percent each; first ungraded); course diary and media folder, 10 percent; final essay (6–8 pp., first draft, 10 percent; final draft, 20 percent); total writing is 70 percent of grade.

I. Introduction

Week 1: What is genocide? Why study the Holocaust, or how does this relate to me? Overview of course goals and structure

Read in class: "If This Is a Man" (Levi)

Dehumanization, Scapegoating, and Genocide

Read: "Disengagement of Internal Control" (Bandura); "The ABCs of Scapegoating" (Allport); chap. 1: "'An Odious Scourge,'" in *Genocide* (Kuper 11–18)

Write a response to Baruch G.'s video testimony (2 pp., in your own handwriting, ungraded)

Week 2: The History of Antisemitism and the Scope of the Holocaust

Skim: *Macmillan Atlas of the Holocaust* (Martin Gilbert); appendices to *The War against the Jews* (Dawidowicz, 357–403; study maps, xii–xiii; xiv–xv, 113, 126)

Read: "Germans and Jews in Germany—Before 1933" (my handout); chap. 1: "The Nature of the Process" (Hilberg, in *Survivors, Victims and Perpetrators,* ed. Dimsdale 5–54)

(Optional reading: chap. 2, in *Survivors* 55–77; chap. 2, in *War against Jews* 23–47)

II. The Perpetrators

Week 3: The Context of National Socialism and Adolf Hitler

Read: "Chronology of Germans and Jews, 1933–1945" (my handout); "The Perpetrator," in Dimsdale 284–87; chap. 5, in *Hitler and Nazi Germany* (Spielvogel 122–52); chap. 1, in *War against Jews* (Dawidowicz 3–22)

(Optional reading: chaps. 1–3, in *Hitler and Nazi Germany* [Spielvogel 1–81])

Week 4: Nazi Ideology: Hitler's *Mein Kampf*

Read: Chap. 11: "Nation and Race" in *Mein Kampf;* chap. 3: "The Program" in *The Nazi Years* (Remak 27–47)

Write 2-pp. response paper to Hitler's argumentation

Week 5: The Nazi Leadership: Höss, Goebbels, Eichmann

Read: Chap. 11: "Excerpts from *The Autobiography of Rudolf Hoess,*" in Dimsdale 289–304; chap. 12: "Excerpts from *The Di-*

ary of Joseph Goebbels," in Dimsdale 305–15; Chap. 13: "Excerpts from *Eichmann in Jerusalem*," in Dimsdale 317–28; chap. 14: "Destroying the Innocent," in Dimsdale 329–58

Fictional Interlude: Brecht

> Read: "In Search of Justice" and "The Informer," in *The Jewish Wife* (Brecht)

Week 6: The SS

> Read: Excerpts from *Born Guilty: Children of Nazi Families* (Sichrovsky) (everyone read no. 6 ["Susanne"], plus 2 other sections of your choosing)

> Chap. 16: "The SS Yesterday and Today," in Dimsdale 405–56

III. Victims

> The Early Years: The Nuremberg Laws to Reichskristallnacht

> > Read: "The Jewish Wife" (Brecht 9–17); *The Diary of a Young Girl* (Frank, 14 June 1942 to 5 January 1944)

Week 7: Waiting, Hiding, Deportation

> Read: *Diary* to conclusion

> Write 2-pp. response paper to experience of (re)reading Anne Frank

> The Early Years: Other Places, Other Views

> > Read: Section 2 in *Whirlwind* (Friedlander 79–118 [Schwarz-Bart and Aichinger]); chap. 9: "Between Freedom and Ghetto" (Dawidowicz 169–96)

Week 8: Gertrud Kolmar

> Read: selected poems

> The East European Ghettos

> > Chap. 10: "Death and Life in the East European Ghettos" (Dawidowicz 197–222)

> > Read: *Survival in Auschwitz* (Levi 9–98)

Week 9: The Camps

> Read: *Survival in Auschwitz* to conclusion

> excerpt from *Night* (Wiesel, in *Whirlwind* [Friedlander 400–411]); chap. 4: "The Concept of the Survivor," in Dimsdale 113–26

> (Optional reading: chap. 5: "The Concentration Camp Syndrome," in Dimsdale 127–62)

> Scenes from *Shoah*

> For the complete text of the film, see Lanzmann

> Write: 2-pp. response paper to experience of reading Primo Levi

Week 10: Non-Jewish Victims: Poles, Slavs, Blacks

> Read: *This Way for the Gas, Ladies and Gentlemen* (Borowski); "No Blacks Allowed," in *The Other Victims* (Friedman); chap. 6: "The Coping Behavior," in Dimsdale 163–74

> Non-Jewish victims, cont.; Roma and Sinti (Gypsies)

Read: Bubili: A Young Gypsy's Fight for Survival," in *Other Victims;*
"Gypsy History in Germany and Neighboring Lands: A Chronology Leading to the Holocaust" (Hancock)
"Nazi Policies toward Roma and Sinti, 1933–1945" (Milton)
Write and turn in: paper proposal for final essay (1–2 parag., typed)
Week 11: Midterm Quiz
In class listening to Steve Reich's *Different Trains*
Paper proposals returned
IV. Survivors: Responses After the Events
Jews in Germany after the Holocaust
Read: selections from *Strangers in Their Own Land* (Sichrovsky) (everyone read pp. 3–42, plus two selections of your own choosing)
Chap. 7: "Late Effects—Influence on Children, etc.," in Dimsdale 175–204
Write: first draft of final essay
Week 12: Poetry I: Paul Celan
Read: selected poems
Write: continue work on final essay
Poetry II: Nelly Sachs
Read: selected poems
(Optional reading: *Eli, A Mystery Play of the Sufferings of Israel* [Sachs])
Turn in: first draft of final essay (6–8 pp., typed and proofread)
Week 13: Modern Dramatic Responses: The Role of the Roman Catholic Church
Read: Excerpt from *The Deputy* (Hochhuth, in *Whirlwind* [Friedlander 371–89])
First drafts handed back
Film: *Enemies: A Love Story*
(During this weekend you should start to rewrite your longer essay)
Week 14: *Enemies,* discussion; student oral presentations of longer paper (five-minute presentation by each student, five-minute feedback for each student from whole class)
Continue revisions on final draft
Andorra (Max Frisch); student presentations
Week 15: *The Investigation* (Peter Weiss); student presentations
Continue revisions on final draft
Singer (Peter Flannery); student presentations
Week 16: Comics?! *Maus* (Art Spiegelman); student presentations
Turn in: final draft of essay (6–8 pp., revised, typed, proofread)
Share reflections on the semester's work

Turn in: course diary/media folder
Final essays, course diary/media folders, final grades available at my
office

REFERENCES

Allport, Gordon, and Department of Psychology, Harvard U. *The ABC's of Scapegoat-ing.* New York: Anti-Defamation League of B'nai B'rith, 1959.
Borowski, Tadeusz. *This Way for the Gas, Ladies and Gentlemen, and Other Stories.* New York: Viking, 1967.
Brecht, Bertolt. *The Jewish Wife and Other Short Plays.* Trans. Eric Bentley. New York: Grove, 1965.
Celan, Paul. *Poems. A Bilingual Edition.* Trans. Michael Hamburger. New York: Persea Books, 1980.
Dawidowicz, Lucy S. *The War against the Jews, 1933–1945.* 1975. Reprint. 10th anniversary ed. New York: Holt, Rinehart and Winston, 1986.
Dimsdale, Joel, MD., ed. *Survivors, Victims and Perpetrators: Essays on the Nazi Holocaust.* Washington, DC: Hemisphere Publishing Corp. 1980.
Enemies: A Love Story. Dir. Paul Mazursky. Screenplay Roger C. Simon and Paul Mazursky. 1990.
Flannery, Peter. *Singer.* London: Nick Hearn Books, 1989.
Frank, Anne. *The Diary of a Young Girl.* 1952. Reprint. New York: Pocket Books, 1990.
Friedlander, Albert, ed. *Out of the Whirlwind: A Reader of Holocaust Literature.* New York: Union of American Hebrew Congregations, 1968.
Friedman, Ina R. *The Other Victims: First-Person Stories of Non-Jews Persecuted by the Nazis.* Boston: Houghton Mifflin, 1990.
Frisch, Max. *Andorra: A Play in Twelve Scenes.* New York: Hill and Wang, 1969.
Gilbert, Martin. *The Macmillan Atlas of the Holocaust.* New York: Macmillan, 1982.
Hancock, Ian. "Gypsy History in Germany and Neighboring Lands: A Chronology Leading to the Holocaust and Beyond." In *The Gypsies in Eastern Europe,* ed. D. Crowe and J. Kolsti. Armonk, N.Y.: M.E. Sharpe, 1991. 11–30.
Hitler, Adolf. *Mein Kampf.* Trans. Ralph Manheim. Boston: Houghton Mifflin, 1943.
Kolmar, Gertrud. *Dark Soliloquy: The Selected Poems of Gertrud Kolmar.* Intro. and trans. Henry A. Smith. New York: Seabury, 1975.
Kuper, Leo. *Genocide: Its Political Uses in the Twentieth Century.* New Haven: Yale UP, 1981.
Lanzmann, Claude, dir. *Shoah.* Film Aleph; Historia Film; New Yorker Films, 1985.
———. *Shoah: An Oral History of the Holocaust: The Complete Text of the Film.* New York: Pantheon Books, 1985.
Levi, Primo. *Survival in Auschwitz: The Nazi Assault on Humanity.* Trans. Stuart Woolf. New York: Collier Books, 1961.
Milton, Sybil. "Nazi Policies towards Roma and Sinti, 1933–1945." *Journal of the Gypsy Lore Society,* 5th ser., 2.1 (1992): 1–18.
"Rabbi Baruch G." Edited Testimony no. A-50. Videotaped interview. Fortunoff Archive for Holocaust Video Testimony. Yale U. 40 mins.

Reich, Steve. *Different Trains, for String Quartet and Tape.* Kronos Quartet. Elektra Nonesuch CD 9 79176-2, 1989.

Remak, Joachim. *The Nazi Years: A Documentary History.* Englewood Cliffs, NJ: Prentice-Hall, 1969.

Sachs, Nelly. *O the Chimneys: Selected Poems, including the Verse Play Eli, A Mystery Play of the Sufferings of Israel.* Trans. Michael Hamburger. New York: Farrar, Straus and Giroux, 1967.

Sichrovsky, Peter. *Born Guilty: Children of Nazi Families.* New York: Basic Books, 1988.

———. *Strangers in Their Own Land: Young Jews in Germany and Austria Today.* New York: Basic Books, 1986.

Singer, Isaac Bashevis. *Enemies: A Love Story.* New York: Farrar, Straus and Giroux, 1972.

Spiegelman, Art. *Maus: A Survivor's Tale.* New York: Pantheon Books, 1986.

Spielvogel, Jackson J. *Hitler and Nazi Germany: A History.* Englewood Cliffs, NJ: Prentice-Hall, 1988.

Weiss, Peter. *The Investigation: A Play.* New York: Atheneum, 1966.

CHAPTER 30

German Cultural Studies
and the Internet

Daniel E. Rogers

Other than glancing at this book's copyright page, a discussion of the Internet will prove the best way to date the entire book. In fact, given the day-to-day changes in the offerings of the Internet, this material may very well be out-of-date before it even reaches print. But, far from emphasizing this as a disadvantage, perhaps we can use it as a reminder of how quickly the Internet is responding to the needs and desires of the scholarly community and how much we have to look forward to—if we are only willing to do a little searching and be flexible.

Internet itself is a term that many do not understand. It is not a service provided by any entity, either governmental or private. If it is anything concrete at all, it is a system of high-speed telecommunications wires (and satellites) that span the globe. All over the developed world, universities, nonprofit organizations, government agencies, schools, and businesses have attached their computers to this global system of wiring. The result is that a computer user whose own institution or service provider has hooked up to the Internet may access information on any computer linked to the Internet anywhere in the world.

Now that we know that the Internet is nothing more than wires, we should think about how it is we communicate over those wires. Just as the telephone wires in your house could support more than just voice communication (you could play the radio over it or even beep out Morse code if you so desired), the Internet can transmit various kinds of signals. The most common of them we refer to as *e-mail,* or electronic mail. If you have an account on a computer linked to the Internet, you can send e-mail to any other person in the world who has a similar account. This is usually the first exposure to the Internet, and it is alluring, for it offers instantaneous communication that is usually free of any special charge per message.

One way that those new to the Internet who have e-mail accounts can easily learn about German studies is through *mailing lists.* These are groups of e-mail users who have joined a group centered around a common theme. One of the largest is *H-German,* the list dedicated to research and teaching of German history. Its one thousand members all have e-mail accounts, and all receive information contributed by subscribers on subjects of common interest (information on joining H-German may be found at the end of this section, along with information on other Internet resources in German studies).

The most hyped and potentially most valuable way to use the Internet to learn more about things German is via the *World Wide Web,* also known as "the Web" or "WWW." Those with an interest in German studies and information they would like the scholarly world to be able to access have placed pictures and text on computers at their home institution and made them available via the Internet. One special feature of the Web is hypertext links, which are words on the screen that are highlighted; when they are pointed to with a computer mouse, or otherwise highlighted, and then clicked or entered, they immediately take the user to related information on WWW servers throughout the world. For instance, an article on Goethe might mention Weimar, and the word *Weimar* might be highlighted, indicating a hypertext link. Click on that link, and your computer would instantly establish a connection with a computer somewhere else in the world that had information on Weimar. If you don't find what you want, you can always go right back to where you started in your article on Goethe.

To use the information stored on the Web, one needs a computer account that can use software designed for the World Wide Web. The best currently available is *Netscape;* it allows both text and pictures to be transmitted. Other products that will, like Netscape, allow you to access the full range of WWW services are *Mosaic* and Microsoft *Internet Explorer.* A program called *Lynx* is also available to allow users text-only access to the WWW. You must consult the computer technical support person in charge of your Internet-accessible account in order to find out which of these you can use.

Once you have discovered how to begin using the WWW, the most important terms to know are *URL* and *http. URL* stands for "universal resource locater" and is shorthand for the computer address of information stored on the WWW that you are trying to access. For example, the URL for the WWW server of H-German is "http://h-net.msu.edu/~german." To access the *homepage,* or starting point, of H-German's WWW server, you would need to enter this rather long address. Many WWW addresses are this long but do not need to be entered more than once because Netscape and the other programs provide an easy way, called a *bookmark,* to save URL addresses you think you would like to revisit. *Http* stands for "hypertext transfer protocol," and this abbreviation followed by a colon and two slashes (://) begins almost every URL. An annotated list of relevant URLs for German cultural studies will be found at the end of this essay.

Currently, the best way to find information on German cultural studies on the World Wide Web (or any topic, for that matter) is to use one of several search engines, such as Yahoo (http://www.yahoo.com), Webcrawler (http://www.webcrawler.com), or Lycos (http://www.lycos.com). Once you have accessed one of the search engines, you can type in any term (e.g., *German*) and find a list of WWW sites that offer information on German studies or other aspects of German life.

Prior to the development of the WWW the best way to store and retrieve information on the Internet was through software called *gopher* (so named for the mascot of the University of Minnesota, where it was developed). Gophers are fast being replaced by WWW servers, although currently much information on the Internet is still available only via gopher. Fortunately, WWW is fully compatible with gopher; in other words, you can access any gopher in the world while using software designed for the World Wide Web. Alas, the same is not true in reverse; you cannot fully take advantage of the WWW's hypertext links when you are using gopher software. A list of important gopher sites follows at the end of this essay.

Another software program designed to take advantage of the Internet is known as *telnet.* Telnet allows you to use your computer as if it were a computer terminal attached directly to a distant computer. The most common use for telnet in education is to access remote computer library catalogs, also known as Online Public Access Catalogs (OPACs). Just as easily as using a computer terminal in one's own library building, one can use the Internet and the telnet program to search libraries throughout Germany, the United States, and the rest of the world. A full list of available libraries is found at the end of this essay.

Below you will find mailing lists, WWW and gopher sites, telnet addresses, and a few useful e-mail addresses.[1]

Do not be surprised if they don't all work. Remember: the Internet changes by the minute!

Mailing Lists

To join any of these mailing lists, send a one-line e-mail message to the address given for each. That one line message should be:

sub ⟨name of list⟩ ⟨your name⟩, ⟨your institution⟩

For example:

> sub H-German Pat Wilson, Southern Jersey U

List; Address; Description

> 9NOV89-L;LISTSERV@TUBVM.CS.TU-BERLIN.DE; Events around the Berlin Wall (contemporary German politics)
>
> AATG; LISTSERV@INDYCMS.IUPUI.EDU; American Association of Teachers of German
>
> DE-NEWS; LISTSERV@VM.GMD.DE; German News (English version)
>
> GEN-DE-L; LISTSERV@RZ.UNI-KARLSRUHE.DE; German Genealogy
>
> GER-RUS; LISTSERV@VM1.NODAK.EDU; GER-RUS Germans from Russia
>
> GERLINGL; LISTSERV@VMD.CSO.UIUC.EDU; Older Germanic languages (to 1500), their linguistics and philology
>
> GERMNEWS; LISTSERV@VM.GMD.DE; German News
>
> GRAD-L; LISTSERV@VM.UCS.UALBERTA.CA; German Graduate Student Discussion Forum
>
> H-GERMAN; H-GERMAN@H-NET.MSU.EDU; H-NET List on German History
>
> WIG-L; WIG-L@MSA.BERKELEY.EDU; WIG-L-Women in German
>
> German-History (for German historians in the United Kingdom) is a non Listserv list; send to mailbase@ mailbase.ac.uk the one line message: join german-history Jane Doe

WWW Sites

This is just a sample of sites. To gain the best overview, proceed directly to *Deutsche Datenquellen* or the *UNC Greensboro German Studies Trails* (addresses follow).

> *Der Spiegel,* selected articles from the current issue: http://www.spiegel.de
>
> *Deutsche Welle,* current news from Germany's overseas broadcasting service (in German, with pointers to English-language services): http://www-dw.gmd.de/cgi-bin/listfolder/deutsch/news.html
>
> *Simon Wiesenthal Center,* information on the Holocaust and the Los Angeles Museum of Tolerance: http://www.wiesenthal.com
>
> *Deutsche Datenquellen,* located at the University of Heidelberg, this is the starting point for finding WWW and other Internet information in Ger-

many (also available in English): http://www.iz.uni-karlsruhe.de/
Outerspace/VirtualLibrary/index.de.html
UNC Greensboro German Studies Trails, a continually updated set of hy-
pertext links to German studies sites throughout the world via the Ger-
man and Russian Department of the University of North Carolina at
Greensboro: http://www.uncg.edu/lixlpurc/german.html

Gopher Sites

As noted in the text, gopher sites are quickly being replaced by WWW sites.
Nonetheless, college teachers of German studies classes will find the following
address helpful, as will those interested in the American Institute of Contemporary German Studies and the German Academic Exchange Service (DAAD):
jhuniverse.hcf.jhu.edu. Those interested in German history may find items of
interest on the H-Net gopher, which points to both the Holocaust and H-German gophers: hs1.hst.msu.edu. (WWW users may access these gophers by
adding the following to the beginning of each address:gopher://).

Libraries via Telnet

German libraries are rapidly moving away from telnet access and toward
the more user-friendly WWW. These addresses may therefore only be of limited use.

> *Universität Tübingen:*
> (1) Type TELNET OPAC.UB.UNI-TUEBINGEN.DE;
> (2) Login: opacl, password opacl also.
> *Universität Kaiserslautern:*
> (1) Type TELNET AIX2.RHRK.UNI-KL.DE 1000;
> (2) Pick item 7 "Bibliotheken."
> *Universität Erlangen-Nürnberg:*
> (1) Type TELNET FAUI43.INFORMATIK.UNI-ERLANGEN.DE.;
> (2) At the login prompt enter gi;
> (3) At TERM=,type vt100.
> *Universität Heidelberg:*
> (1) Type TN3270 VM.URZ.UNI-HEIDELBERG.DE.;
> (2) On the VM/SP screen, hit TAB twice;
> (3) Type D VTAM on the command line;
> (4) On the Bitte waehlen Sie screen, type cicsub.
> *Universität Karlsruhe:*
> (1) Type TN3270 IBM3090.RZ.UNI-KARLSRUHE.DE;
> (2) Hit RETURN;

(3) At the enter userid prompt, enter OPAC;
(4) Hit RETURN.
Universität Konstanz:
(1) Type TELNET POLYDOS.UNI-KONSTANZ. DE 775;
To exit, type ENDE.
Universität des Saarlandes: (1) Type TELNET UNISB.RZ.UNI-SB.DE;
(2) At the / prompt, type.a logon ub, ub.

NOTE

1. For a more basic guide to the Internet and WWW for beginners, specifically aimed at German language teachers, see Jeff Mellor and Peter Höyng, "Using Internet and World Wide Web: A Practical Guice for German Teachers," *Schatzkammer* 21.1–2 (1995): 135–49; for more extensive lists of German url sites of interest (on-line journals and newspapers; homepages of universities, libraries, governmental, scholarly, and arts organizations; travel and entertainment information), see Werner Kitzler, "WWW-Servers: URL-Adressen für den/die DeutschlehrerIn" *Schatzkammer* 21.1–2 (1995): 150–60.

CHAPTER 31

Practicing German Cultural Studies

The following subsections contain information on German cultural studies resources: professional directories and handbooks, lists of a few of the important professional associations and their journals, and the addresses of several agencies that help support teaching and research in German cultural studies. The information here is by necessity brief and the resources given in the following pages represent only a small portion of the world of German cultural studies. Certainly, the best source of up-to-date information is the World Wide Web.

A. Directories, Resources, and Journals

Adressbuch der deutsch-amerikanischen Zusammenarbeit. Bonn: Auswertiges Amt, Referat Öffentlichkeitsarbeit, 1995. A booklet with addresses and some brief descriptions of a wealth of diverse organizations, everything from German governmental offices to research and academic institutions to binational 4-H clubs to German-language newspapers published in the United States.

Archives and Libraries in a New Germany. Ed. Erwin K. Welsch et al. New York: Council for European Studies, 1994. (For notes on this, see Giles's essay "How to Use an Archive," in this vol.)

DAAD/Monatshefte. *Directory of German Studies: Departments, Programs, and Faculties in the United States and Canada.* Ed. Valters Nollendorfs and Geoffrey S. Koby. New York and Madison: DAAD and U of Wisconsin P; German Studies Information Ltd., 1995. Appearing every five years, the *Directory* is an invaluable source of programs, names, addresses, and contacts in German studies; also contains brief faculty vitae. Based on surveys sent to departments, it presents only the information supplied to the editors voluntarily; fairly complete and comprehensive.

Germanistik in Deutschland. Ed. Dieter Gutzen and Friederike Schomaker. Bonn: DAAD, 1992. A brief guide to German departments and academic requirements in the Federal Republic; addresses and contacts; no faculty descriptions.

German Politics and Society. Quarterly interdisciplinary journal. Occasional special issues, selected book reviews, and a regular "forum" section addressing a timely or contentious subject. Generally more attuned to historical and social science issues, especially good on German elections.

German Studies Review. A quarterly journal published by the German Studies Association (GSA), one of a very few major interdisciplinary organizations. The GSA is composed of scholars from many different humanities and social science disciplines, though its members are primarily Germanists, historians, and political scientists. With occasional special issues and a wealth of book reviews the *GSR* provides a much needed forum for interdisciplinary German cultural studies work.

Guide to Inventories and Finding Aids at the German Historical Institute, Washington, D.C. Ed. Ulrike Skorsetz and Janine Micunek. Washington, DC: German Historical Institute, 1995. (For notes on this, see Giles's essay "How to Use an Archive," in this vol.)

New German Critique. Quarterly journal of German thought. More philosophically oriented than the two previous journals, *NGC* stands in the leftist tradition of the Frankfurt School and is often concerned with social thought and critical theory. Regular special issues; no book reviews.

Women in German Yearbook. Published by the group Women in German (WIG) for over a decade, the *Yearbook* presents a thorough overview of contemporary thought in German studies, with a special emphasis on literature and feminist theory.

B. Funding and Agencies

Scholarships and Funding: Studies and Research in Germany. New ed. 1995–96. Bonn: DAAD, 1996. Booklet with lists and contact information for foreign (non-German) students and scholars. Key resource.

Of special interest are the following agencies, which administer grants or are resource clearinghouses:

Alexander von Humboldt Foundation
1350 Connecticut Ave., NW, Ste. 903
Washington, DC 20036
tel: (202) 296-2990

Administers nearly one thousand grants, fellowships, and prizes for study and research each year. The Humboldt Foundation is especially interested in supporting cooperative and collaborative work. It also administers the ten annual Bundeskanzler-Stipendien—the so-called German Rhodes Scholarship—for future leaders from the United States.

American Association of Teachers of German (AATG)
112 Haddontown Ct., No. 104
Cherry Hill, NJ 08034
tel: (609) 795-5553, fax: (609) 795-9398
e-mail: 73740.3231@compuserve.com

AATG is principally a supporter of German language teaching in the United States, but the website provides many helpful tips regarding German media, professional resources, films, and the like; the AATG is the U.S. distributor of materials from InterNationes, an arm of the German government that publishes (nearly free) everything from German grammar exercises to historical and cultural videotapes about the new federal states or the opening of the Wall. AATG publishes both *German Quarterly,* a journal devoted to German literary studies, which, however, has expanded its focus in recent years, and *Der Unterrichtspraxis,* a journal that addresses aspects of teaching of German as a foreign language.

American Council on Germany (ACG)
14 East 60th St., Ste. 606
New York, NY 10022
tel: (212) 826-3636, fax: (212) 758-3445

A private, independent organization that seeks to further German-American relations, mainly through conferences and meetings, especially for young professionals, often in collaboration with the German Atlantik-Brücke organization. Some fellowships in journalism and environmental studies. The ACG often helps bring high-ranking German politicians to American audiences.

American Institute for Contemporary German Studies (AIGCS)
11 Dupont Circle NW, Ste. 350
Washington, DC 20036-1207
tel: (202) 265-9531, fax: (202) 265-9531

The AIGCS is an affiliate of the Johns Hopkins University and serves to further advanced research and study through seminars, conferences, and meetings on German politics, foreign policy, economics, society, and culture. It also publishes materials and houses a research library.

Aspen Institute
1333 New Hampshire Ave. NW, Ste. 1070
Washington, DC 20036

The Aspen Institute seeks to bring enduring ideas to bear on contemporary problems. Its Berlin branch, Aspen Institute Berlin, hosts intimate international conferences, seminars, study groups, and workshops on major contemporary issues, especially those concerned with European-American and East-West relations, and economic, cultural, and intellectual life in Germany and Berlin.

> Austrian Cultural Institute (ACI)
> 950 3d Ave., 20th floor
> New York, NY 10022
> tel: (212) 759-5165, fax: (212) 319-9636
> e-mail: desk@aci.org

ACI is the clearinghouse for anything and everything Austrian, especially concerning current cultural events, news, and the arts; information about study and research in Austria is also available through the institute. ACI will soon occupy a new award-winning building on East 52d St.

> Bertelsmann Stiftung
> Carl-Bertelsmann-Straße 256
> D-33335 Gütersloh

Works with the Council on Foreign Relations in New York on a Euro-American Strategy Group that looks at the future of transatlantic relations. The foundation also supports U.S.-German-Israeli teacher exchanges, journalism workshops, and various other educational projects.

> Deutscher Akademischer Austauschdienst (DAAD)
> German Academic Exchange Service
> 950 3d Ave. at 57th St.
> New York, NY 10022
> tel: (212) 758-3223, fax: (212) 755-5780
> e-mail: daadny@daad.org

The New York office of the DAAD administers programs and activities for North America, distributes information and publications, publishes various newsletters, and is the U.S. liaison office for the German University Rectors Conference, the German Research Society, and the Max Planck Society. DAAD offers a wide array of study and research grants at the graduate and postgraduate levels; it also administers Fulbright study and research grants to Germany.

The European Forum of the European University Institute
Villa Schifanoia, Via Boccaccio 121
I-50133 Florence, Italy
tel: 39-55-4685.537/521, fax: 39-55-4685.575
e-mail: divry@datacomm.iue.it

Awards European Forum Fellowships and Jean Monnet Fellowships to scholars pursuing research on various comparative or historical aspects of Europe.

Friedrich Ebert Foundation, Inc.
1155 15th St., NW, Ste. 1100
Washington, DC 20005
tel: (202) 331-1819, fax: (202) 331-1837

Supports cooperative research projects and exchange programs and gives grants for young leaders in politics and organized labor. Topics supported include: the German unification process, images of Germany in the United States, European unification, changes in Eastern Europe, social and educational reform, trade policy, and labor relations.

Friedrich Naumann Foundation
1759 R St. NW
Washington, DC 20009
tel: (202) 667-4885, fax: (202) 332-6819

Informs American political leaders and journalists through meetings and seminars about important political developments in Germany and Europe, especially with respect to trade and economic issues and educational and social policy.

German-American Academic Council
1055 Thomas Jefferson St., NW, Ste. 2020
Washington, DC 20007
tel: (202) 296-2991

The council, established in 1994, serves to strengthen German-American collaboration in science, engineering, and the humanities. Several conferences and programs serve to help young German and American scholars network in their areas of expertise.

Deutsches Historisches Institut
German Historical Institute
1607 New Hampshire Avenue, NW
Washington, DC 20009
tel: (202) 387-3355, fax: (202) 483-3430
bitnet: DHIUSA@GWU

The German Historical Institute promotes transatlantic exchange of people and ideas in history and the humanities. It organizes conferences, seminars, workshops and lectures and publishes handbooks, reference guides and occasional papers.

German Marshall Fund
11 Dupont Circle, NW
Washington, DC 20036
tel: (202) 745-3950

The German Marshall Fund develops its own programs as well as supports other initiatives that bring together Americans and Europeans to further mutual understanding through solving problems together. Political planners, journalists, and academics work on common projects in the areas of regional and community development, economic development, environmental protection, immigration policy, and political integration.

Institut für die Wissenschaften von Menschen
Institute for the Human Sciences
Spittelauer Lände 3
A-1090 Vienna, Austria
Tel: 43-1-313-58-0, fax: 43-1-313-58-30
e-mail: iwm@iwm.univie.ac.at

An independent, interdisciplinary institute for advanced study made up of permanent, corresponding, and visiting fellows who devote their attention to European ideas, history, and culture, especially with respect to contemporary changing European institutions and policy.

Konrad Adenauer Foundation
20005 Massachusetts Ave. NW
Washington, DC 20036
tel: (202) 986-9460, fax: (202) 986-9458

Supports conferences, seminars, and meetings on basic issues of foreign policy, security policy, and the economy.

Max-Planck-Gesellschaft zur Förderung der Wissenschaften
Hofgartenstrasse 2
D-80539 Munich
tel: (089) 2108-0, fax: (089) 2108-1111

Though primarily concerned with supporting natural science research at its various institute branches, the Max-Planck-Gesellschaft does support research in several areas of comparative law as well as in economic systems and the history of science.

Robert Bosch Stiftung
Heidehofstr. 31
D-70184 Stuttgart, Germany
Postfach 10 06 28
D-70005 Stuttgart, Germany
tel: (0711) 46-0840, fax: (0711) 46-2086

Supports German-American relations through a program of grants for young American leaders.

United States Institute of Peace
1550 M St. NW, Ste. 700
Washington, DC 20005-1708
tel: (202) 457-1700, fax: (202) 429-6063

Offers dissertation fellowships for projects addressing international conflict and ways to prevent it.

Volkswagen-Stiftung
Kastanienallee 35
D-30519 Hannover
Postfach 81 05 09
D-30505 Hannover
tel: (0511) 8381-0

Offers various grants for doctoral students and recent Ph.D. graduates in the social sciences working on contemporary German or European topics; also supports guest professorships and a European-American cooperative project on nuclear history.

CHAPTER 32

Selected, Annotated Bibliographies on German Cultural Studies and on Cultural Studies in General

German Cultural Studies

Burns, Rob, ed. *German Cultural Studies: An Introduction.* London: Oxford UP, 1996. This book was designed as part of a series (French cultural studies, Spanish cultural studies, etc.). It offers an interesting survey of German cultural history, chronologically organized, beginning with imperial Germany and ending with Unification, with the focus clearly on the post–World War II period. It aims at a student audience or general readers who would like to know more about Germany. Its content is intelligently put together in a true "cultural studies" vein, in that it looks at politics, visual art, mass media, etc., and the contributors are well versed in the British cultural studies and Frankfurt School traditions. The short introduction offers a lucid reading of Adorno and Horkheimer's foundational essay, "Kulturindustrie. Aufklärung als Massenbetrug" (The Culture Industry: Enlightenment as Mass Deception" [1944]). The explication of this essay sets the stage for a survey of German cultural history in the service of the "culture industry" thesis, that is to say, chapters "chart the growth of (or reaction against) modernism, outline the diversification (or centralization) of the institutions of cultural production, and trace the extent to which culture in any given period functions as an instrument of ideological manipulation or critical enlightenment." What it does not do, and appears not to have intended to do, is to expose, explicate, and analyze the methods of the cultural studies approach itself.

Czaplicka, John, ed. *German Politics and Society* 32 (Summer 1994). Special issue on "Cultural Transformations and Cultural Politics in Weimar Germany." Centered on the culture and society of the Weimar Republic, the essays in this volume each show the exploratory and interdisciplinary nature of German cultural studies. Concerns with gender identity, social power relations, the symbolic historiography of World War I in art, and consumer culture, among other things, are examined in six thoughtful essays by Bernd Wittig, Maria Tatar, Sabine Hake, Neil H. Donahue, David Frisby, and Jonathan Petropoulos. A useful introduction to the depth of German cultural studies topics within a specific historical context.

Czaplicka, John, Andreas Huyssen, and Anson Rabinbach, eds. *New German Critique* 65 (Spring–Summer 1995). Special issue on "Cultural History/Cultural Studies." This special issue contains the papers that were presented at a conference on cultural history at the Center for European Studies at Harvard University in the spring of 1994. The conference itself was noteworthy for the way it brought historians and Germanists, Europeans and Americans, together. Conference participants included Geoff Eley, Helmut Lethen, Anton Kaes, Michael Diers, Peter Jelavich, Suzanne Marchand, Michael Geyer, and Russell Berman. Jan Assmann and Sigrid Weigel were not in attendance but contributed to the journal issue. The volume's introduction by Czaplicka, Andreas Huyssen, and Anson Rabinach offers some fascinating reflections not only on the relation—often antagonistic—between cultural history and cultural studies but also on the role of *New German Critique* itself in bringing German cultural history center stage in the U.S. academy. The introduction and several of the essays sound warnings about the need for adequate attention to disciplinarity, suggesting that cultural studies practitioners need to "fully account for the position from which those [disciplinary] crossings began." Berman makes a plea for greater discrimination about what specific subjects one chooses to study, arguing that some topics are simply more significant than others. Of the many helpful clarifications of definition and agenda in the volume, Eley's description of cultural studies as "a set of proposals with which to think" should perhaps be singled out. The level of all essays is high, and one is grateful for much attention to Aby Warburg, someone whose ideas clearly deserve a central place in cultural studies approaches.

Geyer, Michael, and Konrad H. Jarausch, eds. *Central European History* 22.3–4 (September–December 1989). Special issue on "German Histories: Challenges in Theory, Practice, Technique." Required reading for German cultural studies practitioners: key essays on the state of German historiography by Geyer (national histories), Jarausch (postmodernism and interdisciplinarity), Jane Caplan (postmodernism, poststructuralism, deconstruction), Isabel Hull (feminist and gender history), John Boyer (boundaries: Austria, Germany, Central Europe),

Rudy Koshar (Germany historiography before the linguistic turn), Peter Jelavich (contemporary literary theory and historiography), Thomas Childers (political sociology and the linguistic turn), David Crew (Alltagsgeschichte [the history of daily life]), Eric Johnson (quantitative social history in contemporary contexts), and Jere Link (a very useful protocol of the discussion). All the essays pay special attention to the influence of contemporary literary and social theory—deconstruction, feminist theory, poststructuralism, postmodernism—on the writing of German history.

Hartman, Geoffrey, H., ed. *Holocaust Remembrance: The Shapes of Memory.* Cambridge, MA: Blackwell, 1994. To single out a collection of essays and reflections on the Holocaust and memory might seem beyond the scope of a brief, general annotated bibliography, but Hartman's volume is a model of German cultural studies work. Not only does the book bring together scholars, writers, and artists from wide-ranging fields and present their diverse and insightful wrestlings with a difficult topic; it also addresses the single most fundamental and defining feature of Germanness and German culture of our age. The twenty-one contributors have vastly different agendas and ways of writing, yet all circle around the problem of how to remember the Holocaust. The volume could serve especially well as a case textbook in any kind of course on cultural studies and could obviously have a place in a well-rounded German cultural studies survey, for it presents creative, aesthetic modes of inquiry (e.g., R. B. Kitaj on his own painting, a poem by Abraham Stutzkever, and autobiographical essays by Aharon Appelfeld and Leo Spitzer) alongside exhaustive scholarly treatments of related issues and problems (e.g., David Tracy, Lawrence Langer, Deborah Dwork and Robert Jan van Pelt, Sara Horowitz, and Hartman). Hartman argues passionately for cultural studies and interdisciplinarity when he says that "it will require both scholarship and art to defeat an encroaching anti-memory."

Huelshoff, Michael, and Andrei S. Markovits, eds. *German Studies Review.* Special issue on "DAAD Special Issue 1990." Proceedings of the DAAD-sponsored "German Studies Conference for Political Scientists and Sociologists," held at the fall 1989 American Political Science Association meeting. Essays on political economy, comparative politics, German-German relations, women in the two Germanies, Germany and European integration, and voting behavior, all conceived with an interdisciplinary methodology in mind. Essays by Jutta A. Helm and Markovits address specifically the place of political science in German studies.

Janes, Jackson K., and Helene L. Scher. *Mixed Messages: A Report on the*

Study of Contemporary Germany in the United States. Submitted to the German Marshall Fund of the United States. 2d ed. 1987. A useful survey of German studies in the U.S., covering teaching and research (in German, history and various social science departments) and the "demand for expertise on contemporary Germany" (mostly business, law, media, and various government offices). The report also includes a descriptive listing of study and research opportunities for contemporary German studies as well as bibliography, useful addresses, and the like. Slightly out of date but still valuable.

Lützeler, Paul Michael, and Jeffrey Peck, eds. *German Quarterly* 62.2 (1989). Special issue on "Germanistik as German Studies: Interdisciplinary Theories and Methods." Proceedings of the first of three DAAD-sponsored conferences on new trends in German studies, especially interdisciplinary approaches, in this case on German literary studies. The others are edited by Geyer and Jarausch for historians and by Huelshoff and Markovits for political and social scientists. Together these three special issue volumes should be required reading for students and teachers of German cultural studies. The *German Quarterly* volume contains important statements by Hinrich Seeba (intercultural German studies), Sara Lennox (feminist scholarship and Germanistik), Jeffrey Peck (identity and "topography" in German studies), Sander Gilman (studying "the German"), and Anton Kaes (new historicism and German studies). Individual responses to these scholars' essays and summary comments as well by Michael T. Jones, Azade Seyhan, Arlene Teraoka, Leslie Adelson, Steven Taubeneck, and Peter Uwe Hohendahl.

McCarthy, John A., and Katrin Schneider, eds. *The Future of Germanistik in the USA: Changing Our Prospects.* Nashville: Department of Germanic and Slavic Languages, Vanderbilt U, 1996. Proceedings of a DAAD-sponsored symposium, fall 1994. Sections on "professional profile and visibility," "curriculum matters," "(re)shaping the discipline." As the title implies, much in the volume simply revives the Germanistik debates of the last decades. There are, however, several especially relevant essays: Wolfgang Natter on cultural studies theories, Frank Trommler on disciplinary practices, Alice Kuzniar on gender studies in German cultural studies, and Peter Uwe Hohendahl and Lynne Tatlock on foreign versus nativist and insider versus outsider influences on the practice of German studies and especially literary studies in North America.

Timm, Eitel, ed. *Challenges of Germanistik: Traditions and Prospects of an Academic Discipline/Germanistik weltweit? Zur Theorie und Praxis des Disziplinrahmens.* Munich: iudicum, 1992. Mainly concerned with shifting emphases in German literary studies, this modest volume of eight essays presents some sophisticated perspectives on the state of German studies; especially helpful are theoretical analyses by Hans-Joachim Schulz ("intercultural hermeneutics" of German studies) and Ingeborg Hoesterey ("postmodern condition" of German studies).

Trommler, Frank. "The Future of German Studies or How to Define Interdisciplinarity in the 1990s." *German Studies Review* 15.2 (May 1992): 201–17. In an appeal to get beyond the bickering prevalent at the departmental level and to pay real attention to the methodological and theoretical demands of interdisciplinary work, Trommler concludes: "If the success of interdisciplinarity in the natural and social sciences over the last decades can teach the humanities anything, then it is the insight that an interdisciplinarity that neglects the active structuring of its practice remains mere academic window dressing."

———, ed. *Germanistik in den USA: Neue Entwicklungen und Methoden.* Opladen: Westdeutscher Verlag, 1989. An attempt to educate the German academy about the state of affairs in the United States. The contributors include some of the most important voices in German literary and cultural studies in North America: Wulf Köpke, Henry J. Schmidt, Egon Schwarz, Jeffrey Sammons, David Bathrick, Russell Berman, Biddy Martin, Robert Holub, and Albrecht Holschuh. This most useful information about theoretical, practical, and pedagogical aspects of German studies is written in German only.

Trommler, Frank, Michael Geyer, and Jeffrey Peck. "Germany as the Other: Towards an American Agenda for German Studies. A Colloquium." *German Studies Review* 13.1 (1990): 112–38. Papers from a 1989 German Studies Association panel, these three essays offer critiques and suggestions for change in German studies. Trommler "redefines the importance of the encounter with the foreign text for a viable pragmatics of German studies"; Geyer looks at American historiography of Germany "in an era of diminishing returns from the traditional historical narrative"; and Peck assesses "the established notions of 'the authentic' and 'the native' as obstacles" to real understanding and interaction with a foreign culture and its productions.

Cultural Studies

Bathrick, David. "Cultural Studies." In *Introduction to Scholarship in Modern Languages and Literatures,* ed. Joseph Gibaldi. New York: MLA, 1992. 320–40. In this sophisticated essay Bathrick focuses on the specific ways in which cultural studies diverges from traditional literary studies; he pays particular attention to popular literature and mass culture. He situates the development of cultural studies briefly, but effectively, in intellectual as well as social developments in North America, Britain, and on the Continent. Bathrick sees cultural studies playing an important role in the canon controversy and in the (global) renegotiations of national identity issues. This volume also contains some helpful, related essays on "interdisciplinary," "feminist and gender," "ethnic and minority," and "border" studies.

Brantlinger, Patrick. *Crusoe's Footprints: Cultural Studies in Britain and America.* New York: Routledge, 1990. In this concentrated and readable study Brantlinger surveys the development of cultural studies with emphasis on its British origins. He also identifies many of the varied kindred spirits: Althusser, Foucault, Gramsci, and Habermas, among others. He launches this helpful introduction to cultural studies with a review of the "humanities in crisis" and shows how the North American academy has responded. The summaries of theoretical developments are particularly thorough and clear. Brantlinger is passionate about his subject and makes a strong case for what cultural studies as a "loosely coherent group of tendencies, issues, and questions" has to offer.

During, Simon, ed. *The Cultural Studies Reader.* London: Routledge, 1993. If one had time to read only a single book on cultural studies, this should probably be it. During's concise introduction manages to cover the history and main theoretical developments of cultural studies in twenty-five pages. He reviews the several genealogies of the field and then reprints twenty-seven essays that display the range of concerns and analytic practices of cultural studies. From Adorno and Horkheimer's foundational essay on the "culture industry" to a selection from Barthes's *Mythologies* to de Lauretis on feminist theory, Spivak and Gunew on multiculturalism, Ross on pornography, and Radway on popular romance, During has gathered together many of the texts that are referred to over and over. In trying and largely succeeding to convey the nature of cultural studies work, During perhaps underrepresents the contributions of the Birmingham School. But even this decision productively serves to foreground the anticanonical nature of cultural studies as a field. During's short introductions to each of the essays helpfully situate the thinkers and the ideas.

Grossberg, Lawrence, Cary Nelson, and Paula A. Treichler, eds. *Cultural Studies.* New York: Routledge, 1992. This tome (788 pp.) grew out of a large international conference held in 1990. The flavor of the conference is partly conveyed through inclusion of some of the discussions that followed paper presentations. The physical awkwardness of the book and a perusal of the table of contents powerfully communicate Stuart Hall's point that cultural studies includes "many different kinds of work." In addition to the impassioned, useful introduction (mainly more theoretically and politically oriented than During's), the editors suggest sixteen topics to guide a reader through the volume's embarrassment of riches. These topics include: "Gender and Sexuality," "Nationhood and National Identity," "Colonialism and Postcolonialism," "Popular Culture and Its Audiences," "The Politics of Disciplinarity," and "Science, Culture, and the Ecosystem." The fact that many essays appear under more than one category underscores the hybrid nature of cultural studies. With forty essays the volume offers readers an even wider range of voices than other anthologies. Contributors consist overwhelmingly of academics from the British Commonwealth and North America.

Inglis, Fred. *Cultural Studies.* Oxford: Blackwell, 1993. This critical introduction to British cultural studies serves first to set the stage for cultural studies work in the postmodern era. The utopian scientistic, teleological, and technocratic Enlightenment project failed during the age of modernism (1914–89), says Inglis, and the new relativist, postcolonialist, post-Enlightenment world will need cultural studies theories and methods to survive. Following a thorough review of the history of cultural studies and its development from the work of Leavis, Williams, Hall, Adorno, Gramsci, and Geertz, among others, Inglis then moves into a theoretical explanation of why cultural studies is always necessarily politically oppositional, in its critiques both of science and of capitalism, for it works best when it studies power. The book's final section addresses the question of "how to do cultural studies" and insists on the importance of art and biography as objects of study. It is decidedly British—Inglis is professor of cultural studies at Warwick—and has less to say about the emphasis that literary studies has had on cultural studies in the North American context. This book is a necessary synthesis and call to action for students of cultural studies.

Thwaites, Tony, Lloyd Davis, and Warwick Mules. *Tools for Cultural Studies: An Introduction.* Melbourne: Macmillan Australia, 1994. This volume distinguishes itself from others mentioned here because it is designed as a practical undergraduate textbook. The book is organized around a series of topics that are introduced through clear definitions and expanded discussions of key terms (e.g., *sign, text, institution, discourse, hegemony, habitus*). Each chapter includes not only illustrations (reprinted short texts and images) but also exercises for students to do that promote interaction with the key concepts just introduced. The brief definitions are occasionally overly reductive or inaccurate, but this is compensated for by the careful and subtle expansions that follow and the excellent suggestions for further reading. With a field as broad as cultural studies this book provides a viable place to begin with one's students. One can, of course, quibble with the authors' choice of terms to focus on in this "first step," but such objections attest to the breadth and energy of the field and to the indispensable role of the teacher in the classroom.

Turner, Graeme. *British Cultural Studies: An Introduction.* Media and Popular Culture, vol. 7. New York, London: Routledge, 1990. This book, too, is aimed at undergraduates. It can be read productively, however, by graduate students or anybody interested in a succinct account of the main ideas and the history of British cultural studies. In addition to a survey of the "idea of cultural studies" and the history of developments in Britain, Turner chooses to focus on "Texts and Contexts," "Audiences," "Ethnographies, Histories, and Sociologies," and "Ideology." As Turner admits in his introduction, his analysis reveals a textualist/structuralist bias. But he offers this book as a "kind of map that will organize the territory at least provisionally," and he invites the production of other maps. Like Brantlinger, Turner summarizes particular scholars' contributions well.

Notes on Contributors

Celia Applegate is Associate Professor of History at the University of Rochester. Her research and teaching centers on the political culture of modern Germany, especially with respect to the history of German nationalism and national identity. She is author of *A Nation of Provincials: The German Idea of Heimat* and is currently working on a project about German music in the nineteenth century and the significance it accrued for Germans in search of a national identity.

Angelika Bammer is Associate Professor in The Graduate Institute of the Liberal Arts and the Department of German Studies at Emory University, where she teaches courses on history and fiction, women's and minority issues, and national culture. She is the author of *Partial Visions: Feminism and Utopianism in the 1970s* and editor of *Displacements: Cultural Identities in Question* and is currently working on the shifting location of concepts of Germanness in modern German culture.

Omer Bartov is Professor of History at Rutgers University. He is the author of *The Eastern Front, 1941–1945: German Troops and the Barbarisation of Warfare; Hitler's Army: Soldiers, Nazis, and War in the Third Reich;* and, most recently, *Murder in Our Midst: The Holocaust, Industrial Killing, and Representation.* Bartov is currently writing a book titled *Imagining Destruction in the Age of Total War,* a study of French, German, and Jewish attitudes to war and genocide since 1914.

Kirsten Belgum is Associate Professor in the Department of Germanic Studies at the University of Texas at Austin. She is author of *Interior Meaning: Design of the Bourgeois Home in the Realist Novel* and articles on feminist aesthetics, nineteenth-century German literature, and national identity in culture. Her contribution to this volume is derived from her book manuscript *Popularizing the Nation,* which examines the production of identity in the popular press of nineteenth-century Germany.

Daphne Berdahl is Lecturer on Anthropology at Harvard University. Her forthcoming study of an East German border village after the fall of the Berlin Wall is titled *Where the World Ended: Identity, Differentiation, and Re-unification in the German Borderland.* She is coeditor of a forthcoming volume, *Altering States: Ethnographies of the Transition in Eastern Europe and Russia,* and has written on publicity and secrecy in the GDR, dilemmas of ethnographic research in postsocialist societies, and historical memory in American culture.

Deidre Berger has worked for National Public Radio since 1980. She has reported for the network from Germany since 1986. Her knowledge of Germany and Europe also led to radio work for Monitor Radio and to television work for Deutsche Welle Television in Cologne. She has a B.A. degree in art history from Bryn Mawr College and an M.A. degree in journalism from the University of Missouri. She contributed the chapter on Germany in the recently published *American Jewish Yearbook 1996.*

Andrew Stuart Bergerson is currently an adjunct faculty member at Columbia College in Chicago and a lecturer at the University of Chicago. In 1997 he will defend his dissertation on the history of conviviality in Hildesheim from 1900 to 1950 for the Department of History at the University of Chicago. He has written on history and memory.

Russell A. Berman is Professor of German Studies and Comparative Literature at Stanford, where he has taught since 1979. He has published widely on modern German literature and culture and is author of *Cultural Studies of Modern Germany.* He is currently working on a project on community and individuality in Germany and the United States.

Alon Confino is Assistant Professor of History at the University of Virginia. He recently completed a book about the construction of regional and national memories in imperial Germany and is now at work on a study of the transformation of the past into a commodity for mass and tourist consumption in twentieth-century Germany.

David F. Crew is Associate Professor of History at the University of Texas at Austin. His publications include *Town in the Ruhr: A Social History of Bochum, 1860–1914* and the forthcoming book *Germans on Welfare, 1919–1933.* He has also edited *Nazism and German Society, 1933–1945.* His current research interests include German popular and mass culture in the twentieth century, the history of sexuality, and the politics of commemoration. He is a member of the editorial boards of *Social History* and of the monograph series "Social History, Popular Culture, and Politics in Germany" and is a corresponding member of *WerkstattGeschichte.*

John Czaplicka is an art historian and cultural historian currently affiliated with the Center for European Studies at Harvard. There he cochairs the German Cultural History Study Group and the Study Group on the Culture and History of Central Europe. He has written, spoken, and curated exhibitions on pictorial representations of Berlin, pictorial satire, Edward Hopper, images of America in Wilhelmine Germany, Austrian exile artists, and contemporary commemorative practice in Germany. He is currently completing a book on public commemorative practice in twentieth-century Germany and preparing a conference and a publication on Berlin as the German capital.

Scott Denham is Associate Professor of German at Davidson College. He is the author of *Visions of War: The Ideology and Imagery of War Fictions in German Literature before and after the Great War* and has written and lectured on theories of modernism, Walter Gropius, Weimar literature, Kleist, German studies pedagogy, and recent German film. He is currently writing a critical cultural history of Gropius and the Bauhaus and beginning a book on Ernst Jünger.

Gerd Gemünden is Associate Professor of German and Comparative Literature at Dartmouth College. He is the author of *Die hermeneutische Wende: Disziplin und Sprachlosigkeit nach 1800* and coeditor of *Wim Wenders: Einstellungen* and *The Cinema of Wim Wenders: Image, Narrative, and the Postmodern Condition.* He has published widely on German film and is currently completing a study of American popular culture and postwar German literature and film.

Geoffrey J. Giles is Associate Professor of History at the University of Florida. He is author of *Students and National Socialism in Germany.* He has published and spoken widely on German social history, especially on youth culture, education, the history of sexuality, and the Holocaust, and is currently writing *A Social History of Alcohol in Germany, 1870–1945.* He chairs the Archives Committee of the German Studies Association and is a member of many editorial and executive boards.

Sander L. Gilman is the Henry R. Luce Professor of the Liberal Arts in Human Biology at the University of Chicago, where he holds positions as Professor of Germanic Studies and Professor of Psychiatry and is a member of the Fishbein Center for the History of Science and the Committee on Jewish Studies. He is a cultural and literary historian and the author and editor of over forty books, the most recent in English on the culture of medicine, *Picturing Health and Illness,* and on Kafka, *The Jewish Patient.* He is a past president of the Modern Language Association.

Heidi Gilpin is Assistant Professor of Dance History and Theory at the University of California, Riverside. Since 1989 she has worked as a dramaturge for William Forsythe and the Frankfurt Ballet and directed numerous workshops in multidisciplinary theory and composition in Eastern and Western Europe. Gilpin lectures and publishes on critical and cultural studies in performance, with an emphasis on issues of embodiment, new media technologies, architecture, and literary and film theory. She is presently engaged in electronic media and Internet projects and is completing a book titled *Traumatic Events: Toward a Poetics of Movement Performance.*

Burkhard Henke is Assistant Professor of German at Davidson College. He has written and lectured on Weimar classicism, Schiller, dramatic theory and political discourse, aesthetics, computer-aided instruction, and hiring in the profession. He is currently writing a book on Schiller and Shakespeare and is coediting a volume provisionally titled *Unwrapping Goethe's Weimar.*

Richard M. Hunt is Senior Lecturer in Social Studies and University Marshal at Harvard University. He has a Ph.D. degree in History from Harvard, where he did his early research on Joseph Goebbels. He teaches a core course on Weimar and Nazi Germany and also courses in social studies on leaders and followers in politics. He is on a number of boards of directors, including Scudder New Europe Fund, Scudder First Iberian Fund, the American Council on Germany, the Council of the U.S. and Italy, the American Field Service, and the International Council of the Museum of Modern Art in New York.

Irene Kacandes has taught at Harvard and the University of Texas at Austin and is currently Assistant Professor of German Studies and Comparative Literature at Dartmouth College. Trained in comparative literature, she has published and lectured on the Holocaust, orality and literacy, ethnography and James Clifford, feminist linguistics, narrative theory, postmodernist fiction, Goethe, Günter Grass, Monika Maron, pedagogy issues in German studies, and violence and sexuality in Weimar culture. She is currently completing a book on oral strategies in twentieth-century prose fiction.

Jean H. Leventhal is Assistant Professor of German at Wellesley College, where she teaches German literature, culture, and language. She has published *Echoes in the Text: Musical Citation in German Narrative from Theodor Fontane to Martin Walser* and continues to work on music and literature of the nineteenth and twentieth centuries, with a special interest in Austrian cultural relations.

Michael R. Marrus is Professor of History at the University of Toronto and a fellow of the Royal Society of Canada. Among his books are *Vichy France and* *the Jews,* coauthored with Robert Paxton; *The Unwanted: European Refugees in the Twentieth Century;* and *The Holocaust in History.* He has just completed a book on the Nuremberg War Crimes Tribunal.

Laurence McFalls teaches at the Université de Montréal and has lectured and written on political culture in France and Germany, European politics, post-communist transformation processes, and on the relations between culture and politics. He has published *Communism's Collapse, Democracy's Demise? The Cultural Context and Consequences of the East German Revolution* and is currently working on a cultural analysis of the 1995 Quebec referendum on sovereignty.

Wallis Miller is an Assistant Professor in the College of Architecture at the University of Kentucky, where she teaches courses on the history and theory of architecture, architectural design, and the humanities. She has written on the 1987 International Building Exhibition in Berlin, on architectural education in the U.S. and Germany, and is currently completing a dissertation at Princeton University about architecture and its popular audience during the Weimar period.

Norma Claire Moruzzi is Assistant Professor of Political Science and Women's Studies at the University of Illinois at Chicago. She works in political theory and feminist theory, and she has published on intersecting issues of French feminism, national identity and political agency, Western representations of Islamic women, and marginal ethnicities and colonialism. She is currently completing a book on the construction of social identities in Hannah Arendt's political theory.

Louis L. Ortmayer is Professor of Political Science at Davidson College. He is the author of *Conflict, Compromise and Conciliation: West German-Polish "Normalization," 1966–1976* and has written on German politics and foreign policy, European integration, and international political economy. He is currently completing a book titled *Decisions and Dilemmas: Case Studies in American Foreign Policy* and serves as Chair of the Active Learning in International Affairs Section of the International Studies Association.

Jeffrey M. Peck is Professor in the Center for German and European Studies and in the German Department at Georgetown University. He works on topics such as the history of German studies in the United States, cultural studies, racism and ethnicity, and East German responses to the Holocaust, contemporary Jewish-German relations, and cultural studies and foreign policy. He has recently coedited *Culture and Contexture: Explorations in Anthropology and Literary Studies* and has completed *Sojourners: The Return of German Jews* *and the Question of Identity in Germany,* a collaborative book and video project on German Jews who returned to postwar Berlin. His current book project is "German Cultures/Foreign Cultures: The Politics of Belonging," a collection of essays on Jews and other minorities in Germany.

Jonathan Petropoulos is Associate Professor of History at Loyola College in Maryland. He has written and lectured on art and politics during the Third Reich, Nazi cultural policies, German and Austrian émigré issues, Berlin, the Holocaust, and German studies pedagogy. He has helped prepare museum exhibitions and is the author of *Art as Politics in the Third Reich.* He is currently writing a book on the Nazification of the art professions and has begun work on a history of the aristocracy in Germany.

Daniel E. Rogers is Assistant Professor of History at the University of South Alabama. He is author of *Politics after Hitler: The Western Allies and the German Party System* and is currently working on constructions of public memory through a comparative history of major incidents in the history of dealing with the Holocaust in Germany since 1945. He is editor of *H-German,* an Internet forum for scholars of German history.

Christian Rogowski is Associate Professor of German at Amherst College. He is author of two books on Robert Musil and has published articles on, among others, Ingeborg Bachmann, Heiner Müller, Wim Wenders, and Thomas Brasch. His current research projects focus on the Medea myth and on the popular culture of the Weimar Republic.

Judith Ryan is the Robert K. and Dale J. Weary Professor of German and Comparative Literature and Chair of the Department of Germanic Languages and Literatures at Harvard. Her teaching and research interests are in nineteenth- and twentieth-century literature, especially poetry and the novel. She is author of books on Rilke's poetry, *Umschlag und Verwandlung;* on postwar German novels, *The Uncompleted Past;* and on the relation of literature to empiricist psychology, *The Vanishing Subject.* She has written and spoken widely on authors such as Franz Kafka, Paul Celan, Christa Wolf, and Günter Grass. Her current research project is a study of Rilke's intertextual relations.

Timothy W. Ryback is the Director of the Salzburg Seminar, an independent, educational institution based in Salzburg, Austria. Ryback has written on European politics and culture for numerous publications including the *Atlantic, New Yorker, New York Times, ARTnews,* and the *Christian Science Monitor.* He is the author of *Rock around the Bloc: Rock Music in Eastern Europe and the Soviet Union.* Ryback has a Ph.D. degree in German from Harvard University.

Robert Mark Spaulding studied Geschichte and Politische Wissenschaft at the University of Cologne before completing his doctorate in History at Harvard University. He is currently Assistant Professor of History at the University of North Carolina at Wilmington. Spaulding's articles on German and international political economy have appeared in numerous edited collections as well as in the journals *International Organization* and *Diplomatic History*. He is the author of *Osthandel and Ostpolitik: German Foreign Trade Policies in Eastern Europe from Bismarck to Adenauer.*

Arlene A. Teraoka is Associate Professor of German at the University of Minnesota. She is the author of *East, West, and Others: The Third World in Postwar German Literature* and *The Silence of Entropy or Universal Discourse: The Postmodernist Poetics of Heiner Müller* and coeditor of a special issue of *New German Critique* on minorities in German culture. Her current work focuses on Turkish-German literature and minority discourses in Germany.

A. Leslie Willson is Emeritus Professor of German at the University of Texas at Austin, cofounder of the American Literary Translators Association, past president of the American Translators Association (1991–93), and a translator of plays, poems, and fiction by contemporary German-speaking authors. He has translated novels by Michael Krüger, Gerhard Kopf, and Ulla Berkewicz. He edited *Dimension,* a literary magazine of contemporary German-language literature in English translation, from 1968 to 1994. Willson is a corresponding member of the Darmstadt and Mainz Academies and a recipient of the Bundesverdienstkreuz Erster Klasse and the Goethe Medaille.

Susanne Zantop received her Ph.D. degree in Comparative Literature from Harvard University and is currently chairing the Department of German Studies at Dartmouth College. In addition to working on history and literature (*Zeitbilder: Geschichte und Literatur bei Heinrich Heine und Mariano José de Larra* [1988]), literature and painting (editor, *Paintings on the Move: Heinrich Heine and the Visual Arts,* 1989), and women's writing (*Bitter Healing: German Women Writers from 1700 to 1830,* coedited with Jeannine Blackwell [1991]), she has just published a book on German colonialist fantasizing, *Colonial Fantasies: Conquest, Family, and Nation in Precolonial Germany (1770–1870)* (1997).

Index

Absence, 214
Achternbusch, Herbert, 335
Ackermann, Irmgard, 72, 73, 75
Active learning, 419–20
Adelson, Leslie, 75
ADFL Bulletin, 125
Adlon, Percy, 335
Adorno, Theodor, xii, 6, 8, 43
Advertising, 48, 150
Aesthetics: as category, 10–11, 12, 14, 17, 22, 42, 50, 72, 79, 80, 118, 142, 152, 153, 154, 162; in literature, 404–5
Africa, xiv, 73, 115, 178, 180
African-American, 68, 69, 71, 75, 91, 123; studies, 10
Africans, 190, 195, 197
Afro-Germans, 69
Agencies, supporting German cultural studies, 522–27
Ajami, Fouad, 81, 90
Alber, Siegbert, 70
Albertinaplatz (Vienna), 258, 269–71
Alexander von Humboldt Foundation, 522
Allgemeine musikalische Zeitung (Leipzig), 148, 159
Allies, 101, 102, 105
Allport, Gordon, 509
Alltagsgeschichte. See History, of everyday life
Alter, Peter, 177, 179
Alterity, 83, 207
Althusser, Louis, 6
American Association of Teachers of German (AATG), 25, 68, 77, 440, 523
American Council on Germany (ACG), 523
American Institute of Contemporary German Studies (AICGS), 489, 523

Americanization, in Germany, 334
American Political Science Association (APSA), 23
American Revolution, 403
Amherst College, 114, 127
Anderson, Benedict, 31, 35, 38, 67, 143, 175
Anderson, Mark, 444
Anniversaries, historical, 298, 306, 370
Anschluss, 267
Anthropology, xiii, 7, 8, 12, 46, 47, 49, 55, 67, 77, 79, 80, 122, 137, 140, 163, 309, 502
Anti-Semitism, 42, 86, 87, 109, 130, 151–52, 165, 175. *See also* Jews
Appadurai, Arjun, 55
Applegate, Celia, 504
Arab problem, 212
Arc de Triomphe, 238
Architectural History, 227
Architecture, 456–57
Architecture of Doom (1989), 498
Archives: availablity of, 377, 385; and governments, 378–79, 385; purpose of, 18, 378–79; using, 483–87, 521
Archiv für Fremdenverkehr, 186
Arendt, Hanna, 43, 127–34, 496
Aristocracy, 135, 144, 146, 148
Arndt, Ernst Moritz, 168–69
Arnim, Achim von, 36
Arno, Anton Wilhelm, 406
Arnold, Matthew, 12, 65
Articulation, 10
Art, visual, 257, 464–66
Asia, 5, 115
Askari, 192
Aspen Institute, 523–24

Associations: fraternity, 176; musical, 147–48; tourist, 185–86
Asylum seekers, 189, 190
Athenäum, 42
Attali, Jacques, 153
Attie, Shimon, 40, 43
Atwood, Margaret, 3–5, 13, 19, 21–22
Audience, publishing for, 444
Auerbach, Berthold, 290
Auerbach, Erich, 35, 36, 42
Augustine, Saint, 494
Auschwitz: as cemetery, 358; conservation of, 358, 360, 362–64; convent at, 361; experience of, 368; feeling of, 363; and Holocaust deniers, 370–72; liberation of, 298; as museum, 358, 360–62; people murdered at, 359; reporting on, 368; ruins of, 363–64; survivors of, 368–69, 444; as symbol of the Holocaust, 358–59; teaching about, 506, 508–13. *See also* Concentration camps
Ausländer. See Foreigners, in Germany
Australia, xiv, 22, 165, 171, 179
Austria, Republic of, 257, 281
Austrian Cultural Institute (ACI), 524
Auswärtiges Amt. *See* German Foreign Office
Autobiography, 37, 128, 137, 444
Ayim, May, 69

Bach, Carl Philipp Emanuel, 148, 159
Bach, Johann Sebastian, 139–60, 461, 462; Germanness of, 155, 157; and Protestantism, 157
Bach, Wilhelm Friedemann, 148, 159
Baedecker guides, 186
Bammer, Angelika, 190
Barkin, Kenneth, 55
Barthes, Roland, 6, 7
Bate, Walter Jackson, 15
Bathrick, David, 533
Bauhaus, 243, 499
Bavaria, 70, 168
Baxendall, Michael, 153
Becker, Jurek, 37–40, 395
Beethoven, Ludwig van, 131, 149, 153, 159, 461, 463
Behrendt, Walter Curt, 255
Beidermann, Hans, 465
Bell, Daniel, 437
Belle-Alliance Platz (Berlin), 239
Benjamin, Walter, 6, 47, 50, 122, 182–83

Berdahl, Daphne, 507
Bergdoll, Barry, 254
Berlin, 20, 39–40, 73, 79–90, 97–99, 104, 106–10, 114, 134–35, 139–60, 207, 210, 214, 224, 228, 230, 231, 238–39, 290, 298, 300, 323, 411, 499
Berlin, University of, 148
Berlin Document Center, 377–87; documents sold from, 383; transfer of, 386
Berliner Allgemeine musikalische Zeitung. See Marx, Adolf Berhard
Berlin Singakademie, 139, 141, 144, 148–50, 152, 157
Berlin Wall. *See* Wall, The
Bernhard, Thomas, 258, 266
Bertelsmann Stiftung, 524
Bertuch, F. J., 411
Betzingen, 166–68, 183
Bible, 494
Bibliographies, annotated, 529–36
Biedermeier, 133–44
Bielefeld School, 48
Biermann, Wolf, 39
Bildung, 20, 67, 140–41, 143–44, 152, 159
Birkenau. *See* Auschwitz
Birmingham Centre for Contemporary Cultural Studies, xi, 6, 8, 47, 82, 91
Bismarck, Otto von, 175
Bitburg, 86
Black Forest, tourism in, 168, 182
Blacks, 510. *See also* African-American; Afro-Germans
Bley, Helmut, 199–200
Blue Angel, The, 498
Blue Book, 193, 197
Blume, Friedrich, 141, 158
Bochum, 45
Bockmeyer, Werner, 335
Body language, 53
Boers, 195–98, 204
Bokel, Franz, 49
Böll, Heinrich, 103, 216–17, 395
Bombing, 100–102, 104, 106, 124. *See also* Dresden, bombing of; Hiroshima; Nagasaki
Bonhoeffer, Dietrich, 500
Borchert, Wolfgang, 501
Borden, Lizzie, 341
Borders, 506; cultural, 169; experience of, 311; national, 169–70
Bornemann, John, 507

Borowski, Tadeusz, 510
Borsig, Ernst, 290
Bourdieu, Pierre, 6, 11, 47
Bourgeoisie, 49–50, 65, 144, 147–48, 152,
    159, 290–91, 409
Brandenburg Gate, 81, 83, 88–89
Brandt, Willy, 300
Brantlinger, Patrick, 8–9, 22, 534
Brasch, Thomas, 114
Brazil, as immigrant country, 165, 171–74,
    177–78
Brecht, Bertolt, 117, 350, 433, 463, 496,
    498–500, 510
Brentano, Clemens, 36, 452
Bright, Susie, 337
Broadcasting. *See* Media
Brodhead, Richard, 65
Broszat, Martin, 221–23
Brubaker, Rogers, 174
Bruford, W. H., 411
Buchenwald, 368
Büchner, Georg, 69, 117
Bundesarchiv. *See* German Federal Archives
Bundestag, 306
Bündnis, 90, 305
Burke, Edmund, 493
Burns, Rob, 22, 24, 529
Burschenschaften. See Fraternities
Bush, George, 83, 88
Büttner, Siegfried, 386
Butz, Arthur, 371

Cabinet of Dr. Caligari, The, 498
Cameroon, 192
Canetti, Elias, 266
Canning, Kathleen, 24, 48, 50, 52
Canon: flexibility of, 405; high school exami-
    nations and, 409; literary, 10, 14, 20, 65–67,
    74, 163; musical, 140–42; rejection of, 10,
    66, 163; study of, 11–12, 22, 37
Caroline Islands, 192
Case study method, in teaching, 417–28; com-
    ponents of, 422; and cultural studies, 418;
    discussions with, 422; listening with,
    425–26; pedagogic utility with, 421; ques-
    tioning in, 423–25; rationale for, 418; re-
    sponding with, 426; and undergraduate
    teaching, 427–28
Catholicism, 50, 129
Celan, Paul, 224, 452, 500, 511

Censorship, 160
Centers of Excellence, 90
Central European History, 23, 45, 530
Chartier, Roger, 47, 49
Chicago, University of, 440, 491
Christensen, Chris, 423
Christian Democratic Union (CDU), 305
Citizenship, 39, 70. *See also* Identity
Civil rights, 65, 123
Clark, T. J., 257
Class, 11, 18, 49–52, 54, 65, 68–69, 140,
    143–48, 159, 165, 289–90, 345, 433, 505
Class consciousness, 504
Clifford, James, 19, 21, 67
Clinton, Bill, 79–90, 387
Clinton, Hillary Rodham, 85–86, 90
Clubs. *See* Associations; Fraternities
Cohen, Peter, 498
Cohn, Bernard S., 503
Cold War, 65, 80–81, 88, 246, 284, 301
Colonialism, 189, 191–202; and Britain,
    194–96, 203; and France, 194; German role
    in, 192–93, 199, 202; Herder's critique of,
    194; and Spain, 194–95
Colonial legend, 191–92
Colonies, German, 115, 178, 189–202
Columbia University, 491
Commerce, 145–46
Commercialization. *See* Consumer Culture
Communism, 19, 50, 52, 81, 107–8, 305, 382,
    506
Communist party, German (KPD), 56
Computers. *See* World Wide Web
Concentration camps, 40, 99–101, 103, 116,
    131, 133, 298, 358, 360–64, 368–69,
    370–72, 444, 508–13. *See also* Auschwitz;
    Buchenwald; Dachau; Mauthausen; Sach-
    senhausen; Stutthof; Theresienstadt;
    Treblinka
Concert. *See* Performance
Confino, Alon, 288
Conjuncture, 10
Connerton, Paul, 326
Conrad, Joseph, 40
Conservatism, 75, 119
Consumer culture, 47, 182–87; and national
    identity, 185
Consumption, tourism as, 183–84
Cornell University, 440
Craig, Gordon, 499

Crew, David F., 23, 210
Cuisine, 70, 85, 166
Culler, Jonathan, 122
Cultural anthropology, 505
Cultural history, 49, 404
Cultural materialism, 400, 407–10
Cultural studies: British, 8, 10, 24; and the
    canon, 11–12, 399; definitions of, 7–13, 22,
    46, 54, 94, 122, 133–34, 404; of the eigh-
    teenth century, 407; and the Enlightenment,
    399, 403; and German history, 50; and mu-
    sic, 142; and the political, 9; and popular
    culture, 46; resources, 533–36; teaching,
    411–12; and texts, 8, 81–82; and traditional
    disciplines, 7, 82, 122, 133
Culture: comparing, 109–10; consumer,
    181–87; definitions of, 7, 55, 70; German,
    as asset, 172; local, 166; mass, 94, 176,
    182; mediation of, 392–93; musical, 145;
    national, 142, 165, 172; popular, 11, 46, 49,
    51–52, 54–55, 164–65, 187, 189, 408
Curtis, Tony, 114
Czaplicka, John, 18–19, 529–30
Czech Republic, 373–74, 376

DAAD (Deutscher Akademischer Austauschdi-
    enst), xiv–xv, 13, 15, 24, 440, 489, 521, 524
Dachau, 103
Dahrendorf, Ralf, 41
Darnton, Robert, 47, 404
Davidson, Cathy, 444
Davidson College, xiv–xv, 24
Davis, Lloyd, 535
Davis, Natalie, 47, 404
Dawidowicz, Lucy S., 509, 510
Dawson, William, 294
de Certeau, Michel, 47
Decolonization, 19, 21, 65, 67, 72, 189, 191
Deconstruction, 82–83
de Las Casas, Bartolomé, 494
Deleuze, Gilles, 40, 67, 351
DeNora, Tia, 159
Der ewige Jude [*The Eternal Jew*], 498
Derrida, Jacques, 351
Deutsche Akademie, 41
Devrient, Eduard, 143–44
Diction, 454
DIMENSION (journal), 391
Dimsdale, Joel, 500, 509, 510
Directories, 521

Discussions, in class, 422
Döblin, Alfred, 436, 499
Dolff-Bonekämper, Gabi, 253
Drama, studying, 467–68
Drechsler, Horst, 199
Dresden, bombing of, 100–102, 299. *See also*
    Bombing
Droste-Hülshoff, Annette von, 454
Droysen, Johann Gustav, 140, 154, 157
DuBois, W. E. B., 493
Duden, Barbara, 505
Duke University, 17
Dundes, Alan, 504
During, Simon, 22, 534
Dürrenmatt, Friedrich, 393

Economic influences, on identity, 287–94
Economic Miracle. See *Wirtschaftswunder*
Economic periods, in Germany, 288–90
Eichendorff, Joseph von, 452
Eichmann, Adolf, 284, 509, 510
Eighteenth-Century studies, 407
Einsatzgruppen, 198
Elbe, 100
Eley, Geoff, 6, 50, 53, 55, 503
E-mail, 515–16
Emigration, 170
Emma (magazine), 340
Empathy, 214–16, 228
Enemies, A Love Story, 511
Enlightenment, 151, 156, 172, 399, 403
Enzensberger, Hans Magnus, 35, 42,
    200–201
Epic, 474
Erikson, Erik, 433
Erotic, 8, 47, 333. *See also* Sexuality
Ethnic cleansing, 5
Ethnicity, 70
Ethnography, 8–10, 65, 67, 80, 166, 169–72,
    174, 177, 297, 309, 311, 329, 503
Eurocentrism, 18, 65–66, 68–69
European Forum of the European University
    Institute, 525
Examinations, high school, canon for, 409
Exile, 115
Expositions, 182–83
Expressionism, 497

Fallada, Hans, 498, 499
Fasch, Karl Friedrich, 148

Fascism, 66, 84, 94, 116, 264, 267–68, 275, 300, 506; in Austria, 267–68; rise of, 300

Fashion, 48, 94, 166

Fassbinder, Rainer Werner, 218, 220–21, 293, 351

Federal Republic of Germany. *See* Germany, Federal Republic

Feminist: debates about pornography, 340–42; historiography, 45, 48–49, 51–52, 54, 56; theory, 10, 21, 47, 65–68, 71, 91, 333, 350. *See also* Paglia, Camille

Fest, Joachim, 500

Festivities, unification, 312, 320. *See also* Parades

Film, 12, 14, 17, 20, 51, 95, 114, 118, 218–21, 334–51; documentary, 342; studying, xiii, 48, 54–55, 458–60

Final Solution. *See* Auschwitz

Flannery, Peter, 511

Flugblätter, 17

Folklore studies, 502

Fontane, Theodor, 163

Ford, Franklin, 432

Foreign Affairs, 81

Foreigners, in Germany, 63, 70, 190–91; hostility toward, 303

Foreign policy, 41–42, 79–90

Forkel, Johann Nikolaus, 147, 156

Forssmann, Eric, 254

Foucault, Michel, 6–7, 47, 80–81, 351

France, 94, 96–100, 129, 134, 144, 146, 166, 168, 221, 257, 404

Francke, Kuno, 445

Frank, Anne, 510

Frankfurt School, 6, 8, 47

Fraternities, 176

French Revolution, 47, 151

Freud, Sigmund, 496

Freytag, Gustav, 163, 290, 294

Fried, Erich, 266

Friedlander, Albert, 511

Friedlander, Henry, 385

Friedländer, Saul, 221, 245, 299

Friedman, Ina R., 510

Friedrich, Otto, 499

Friedrich Ebert Foundation, 525

Friedrich I, King of Prussia, 141, 144, 152, 160, 235, 254

Friedrich Naumann Foundation, 525

Friedrich Wilhelm III, King of Prussia, 231, 235

Frisch, Max, 511

Fulbright study and research grants, 524

Fulbrook, Mary, 43

Funding, for German cultural studies work, 522–27

Gartenlaube, Die, 137, 164–79

Gastarbeiter, 38, 63

Gates, Henry Louis, Jr., 67

Gay, Peter, 498

Gay and lesbian studies. *See* Gender studies

Gay protesters, 265

Gdansk, 116

Geck, Martin, 144, 154

Geertz, Clifford, 67, 80–81, 85, 140, 152–53

Gender studies, 10, 20, 54, 67, 505

Genocide, 124, 200, 375, 509. *See also* Holocaust

Geography, 163–79. *See also* Space

Georgetown University, 79, 85, 90

Gerhard, Ute, 70

German Academic Exchange Service. *See* DAAD

German-American Academic Council, 88, 525

German cultural studies: and anthropology, 311; curriculum in, 37–41, 405; definition of, xi, 13–15, 21, 22–23, 401, 405; journals in, 521–22; methods, 451; and National Socialism, 402; range of, 115, 402–3; resources for, 521–27, 529–33; structure of, 37, 123, 401; teaching, 489–90. *See also* Cultural studies

German Democratic Republic (GDR): end of, 312, 317, 319; history of, 39, 49, 53, 66, 84–85, 106–9, 253, 304, 323; leadership of, 300; life in, 319; and National Socialism, 297; and the Neue Wache, 246; *Nischengesellschaft* in, 302; nostalgia for, 320, 322; political parties of, 304–6; values of, 302

German East Africa, 192

German Federal Archives, 382, 386, 483

German Foreign Office, 41

German Historical Institute, 483, 526

German Historical Museum, 246, 249, 255

Germanistik, 14–15, 17, 23, 31–41, 63, 66, 72–74, 82; Americanization of, 119, 445–46; differentiated from cultural studies, 404; feminization of, 119; in Germany, 71, 74; intercultural, 64, 72; in North America, 67–68, 80, 113–24; publishing in, 441

German Marshall Fund, 526
Germanness, xiv, 33, 37, 39, 42–43, 91, 102, 113, 115–16, 142, 164, 166, 170–72, 174, 183, 292; of East Germans, 303; and economic identity, 292–93; and Jewishness, 210; reporting on, 95; studying, 502–7; and work, 292. *See also* Identity
German Politics and Society, 16, 258, 522, 529
German Quarterly, 23, 440, 532
German Samoa, 192
German Southwest Africa, 192, 196–97
German studies: definitions of, 13, 392, 440; jargon in, 445; journals in, 521–22; methods, 451; origins of, 392; role of, 32, 66, 440; resources for, 521–27, 529–33; scholarship in, 443, 445–46; teaching of, 392–93, 432, 489–90; tenure in, 440. *See also* German cultural studies
German Studies Association, 16, 23, 55, 66, 377
German Studies Review, 16, 23, 522, 532
Germany, Federal Republic of, 34, 41, 49, 53, 71, 74, 216, 218, 292–93, 297, 421; *Alleinvertretungsanspruch* of, 300; and the Berlin Document Center, 380–86; and the German Democratic Republic, 297
Gerstäcker, Friedrich, 170
Geyer, Michael, 13, 15, 19–20, 22, 24, 530, 533
Gilbert, Martin, 509
Gilman, Sander L., 21, 113, 407, 489
Goebbels, Joseph, 500, 509, 510
Goering, Reinhard, 395
Goethe, Johann Wolfgang, 17, 42, 135, 141, 148–49, 151, 159, 400, 401, 410–12, 452, 493
Goethe Institute, 41
Gopher, internet sites via, 519
Görres, Joseph, 36
Gossman, Lionel, 412
Göttingen Conversations on Historical Studies, 49, 55
Gottsched, Johann Christoph, 36, 42
Graduate school, 119
Graff, Gerald, 4
Gramsci, Antonio, 6, 47
Grass, Günter, 35, 216, 218, 393, 395
Great Depression, 497
Greenblatt, Stephen, 408

Greenfeld, Liah, 294
Green Party, 70, 293
Greiner, Ulrich, 320
Grimm brothers (Jacob and Wilhelm), 15, 36
Gropius, Walter, 498, 499
Grossberg, Lawrence, 9, 11, 19, 22, 25, 534
Grosz, Paul, 263
Grützmacher-Tabori, Ursula, 39, 43
Guattari, Felix, 40, 67
Gypsies. *See* Roma and Sinti
Gysi, Gregor, 307

Habermas, Jürgen, 49, 145–47, 281
Habitus, 10
Haider, Jörg, 94, 265, 283–84
Hall, Stuart, 6, 8, 16
Hancock, Ian, 511
Handel, George Frederick, 461
Handke, Peter, 266
Hannover, University of, 49
Hansen, Miriam, 55
Hapsburg, 177
Hartman, Geoffrey, H., 531
Harvard University, 15, 17, 24, 258, 417, 431, 497
Hatfield, Henry, 436
Hausbesetzer, 264
Hauser, Franz, 157
Hearst, William Randolph, 375
Hebdige, Dick, 11, 52
Hegel, Georg Wilhelm Friedrich, 141, 150, 154, 156
Hegemony, 10
Heidegger, Martin, 134
Heidelberg, 134
Heimat, 139, 175, 184, 319, 329, 504
Heimat (film). *See* Reitz, Edgar
Heine, Heinrich, 69, 155
Heins, John, 492
Heldenplatz (Vienna), 258
Heller, Agnes, 43
Herder, Johann Gottfried, 15, 36, 42–43, 193–94, 198, 201, 401
Herero uprising, 197
Hermand, Jost, 444
Herrnstein Smith, Barbara, 22, 143, 145
Herzog, Roman, 299
Herzog, Werner, 218, 335
Heym, Georg, 499
Hilberg, Raul, 509

Hillgruber, Andreas, 221–23
Hiroshima, 106, 124
Hispanic, 68–69
Historikerstreit (historians' dispute), 23, 185,
281, 299, 320
Historische Anthropologie, 49
History: Austrian, 267; continuity of, 255; of
everyday life, 45, 48, 50, 53, 54, 56, 57, 58,
59, 61, 95, 502; German, 50, 115–16, 211;
of the Holocaust, 221–23; of ideas, 408;
image of, 263, 267; and memory, 229–30;
social, 48, 52–53; studying, 477–78; of
tourism, 182–87
Hitler, Adolf, xii, 53, 100, 102, 104–6, 120,
258, 267–68, 283, 300, 372, 402, 497, 500,
509. *See also* National Socialism
Hitlerjunge Quex, 197, 433
Hitzig, Georg, 290
Hobsbawm, Eric, 179
Hochhuth, Rolf, 511
Hoffman, E. T. A., 140, 146
Hoffman von Fallersleben, Heinrich, 169
Hofmannsthal, Hugo von, 454
Hogan's Heroes, 118
Hoggart, Richard, 6–7, 91
Hohendahl, Peter U., 13–15, 445
Hölderlin, Friedrich, 117, 452
Holland, Agnieszka, 224
Holocaust: and colonialism, 199–200; deniers,
370–72; in film, 219; history of, 52, 85,
103–4, 116; influence of, 113–14, 117,
123–24, 133, 191, 193, 199; Memorial
Museum, United States, 368; miniseries
(1979), 102; representation of, 20, 32–34,
38, 40–41, 212, 221, 274–75; teaching
about, 20, 395, 435–37, 500, 508–13. *See
also* National Socialism
Homosexuality, 10, 65, 75, 91. *See also*
Gender studies
hooks, bell, 67
Hoover Institution, 382
Horkeimer, Max, 6, 8, 264
Höss, Rudolf, 509
Howe, Irving, 22
"How to . . ." handouts, 451
Hoyerswerda, 189, 190
Höyng, Peter, 520
Hradlicka, Alfred, 257–85
Huelshoff, Michael, 531
Hughes, H. Stuart, 432

Humanism, 12, 65, 122
Humanities, xii–xiii, 4, 8, 17, 81, 82, 119, 128,
440–41
Humboldt, Wilhelm, 154
Humboldt University (Berlin), 88
Hunt, Lynn, 7, 47, 54, 404, 412
Huntington, Samuel, 81
Huyssen, Andreas, 18, 19, 445, 506, 530

Identity, xiii, 10, 91; Austrian, 282; colonial,
193; economic, 185, 287–93; East German,
299–300, 310; English, 289; German, 31,
34–35, 41, 71, 116–18, 143, 152, 165, 185,
207, 246, 289; Jewish, 128–35, 152, 198;
national, 39, 43, 70, 130, 135, 142–43, 165,
175, 297–306, 310, 333; perceptions of, 95;
personal, 128, 333; political, 297; post-
Wall, 302, 310; postwar, 299; Prussian, 235,
243; sexual, 333; studying, 502–7; West
German, 299, 301
Ideology, 10
Image, 453
Images, tourist, 186
Immigration, xiv, 34, 70–71, 82, 119, 123,
129, 131, 171, 175, 189, 380
Imperialism, 175, 190, 193, 200, 202–3
Industrialism, 99–100, 105, 288–93
Inflation, 51
Inglis, Fred, 535
Institute for the Human Sciences, 526
Institut für die Wissenschaften von Menschen,
526
Intellectual history, 505
Interdisciplinarity, xiii, 14–16, 17, 123; in
teaching, 417–28, 435, 451
Internet, 515–20
Iraq, 100
Islam, 70
Israel, 33, 110, 121, 129–30
Italy, 94, 131

Jageman, Caroline, 411
Jahn, Friedrich Ludwig, 36
James, Harold, 185, 294
James, William, 187
Janes, Jackson K., 531
Jankowski, Karen, 72
Jarausch, Konrad, 13, 15, 19–20, 22, 24, 530,
533
Jaspers, Karl, 43, 134

Jefferson Memorial, 238
Jelavich, Peter, 24, 52
Jewish, 38–40, 66, 91, 109, 128–35; body,
    444; communities in Berlin, 84–86;
    Mendelssohn as, 151–52; question, 212;
    students, 394. *See also* Identity; Neue
    Synagoge (Berlin)
Jews: absence of in Germany, 207, 213–24; in
    Austria, 258; and colonialism, 198, 203;
    compensation for, 283; in Germany, 103,
    209–24; representation of, 265, 275, 278,
    285; as victims, 101–4, 106, 358
Johnson, Uwe, 395
Jones, Garth Stedman, 47
Jones, Michael, 66
Journalism: history writing as 367–76; music
    in, 146; National Socialism in, 367, 369–70;
    popular, 164; radio reporting as, 93–111
Journals, 442; for German cultural studies,
    521–22
Jud Süss, 198
Jünger, Ernst, 499
Jus sanguinis, 70

Kaes, Anton, 413, 445, 460
Kafka, Franz, 67, 394, 443–44, 494
Kahlenberg, Friedrich, 386
Kaltenbrunner, Ernst, 284
Kamenko, Vera, 37–39, 41
Kandinsky, Wassily, 436, 499
Kant, Immanuel, 154
Kaplan, Alice, 443, 444
Kater, Michael, 384
Keifer, Anselm, 118
Keil, Ernst, 165
Kella (Thuringia), 311, 507
Kenkel, Karin, 492
Kennedy, John F., 80–81, 83, 86–88
Kertzer, D., 506
Kiaochow, 192
Kibbutz, 129–30
Kiesinger, Kurt Georg, 382
Kiessling, Martin, 255
Kift, Dagmar, 48
Kinkel, Klaus, 385
Kluge, Alexander, 114, 218
Klüger, Ruth, 444
Knobelsdorff, Georg, 232
Koberstein, August, 36
Kocka, Jürgen, 185

Kohl, Helmut, 81, 82, 84, 86–88, 97–98, 113,
    120–21, 246, 302, 385
Kollwitz, Käthe, 249, 251, 253
Kolmar, Gertrud, 510
Königsplatz (Berlin), 239
Konrad Adenauer Foundation, 526
Koonz, Claudia, 500
Kornfeld, Melvin, 40
Kosseleck, Reinhard, 253
Kotzebue, August von, 412
Kowaga, Joy, 496
Kracauer, Siegfried, 249
Kraft, Robert, 419
Kreis, Wilhelm, 255
Kretzer, Max, 163
Kristallnacht, 85
Krolow, Karl, 452
Kronen Zeitung, 285
Krüger, Dietrich, 384
Kuhn, Anna, 67
Kunert, Günter, 393
Kuper, Leo, 509
Kuzniar, Alice, 413
KZ. See Concentration camps

Landscape. *See* Space
Langer, William, 432
Lange, Sigrid, 406
Langewiesche, Dieter, 177
Langhans, Carl Ferdinand, 232
Language, foreign, teaching of, 68, 72, 88,
    171, 400
Lantos, Tom, 384–85
Lanzmann, Claude, 510
Lasker-Schüler, Else, 38
Law, and archives, 485
Leftist, 190
Leggewie, Claus, 70
LeGoff, Jacques, 228
Leipzig, 107–8, 148, 156
Leiser, Erwin, 433
Leisure, study of, 46
Lennox, Sarah, 21, 67, 193, 201, 202–3, 413
Lenya, Lotte, 461
Lenz, Siegfried, 216
Le Pen, Jean Marie, 94
Lesbian and gay studies. *See* Gender studies
Lesbian Sex Mafia, 343
Lessing, Gotthold Ephraim, 36, 42, 493
Levinthal, David, 375

Levi, Primo, 369, 375, 436–37, 498, 501, 509
Levy, Sara Itzig, 159
Liberal arts, 119
Liberalism, 50, 164–65, 169, 174–75
Libraries, via internet, 517, 519–20
Libya, 99–100
Liechstenstein, 257
Lincoln Memorial, 238
Linguistic turn, 45–46, 49, 52, 54–56
Link, Jere, 23
Lin, Maya, 40, 43
Lipton, Eunice, 444
Listserv. *See* Mailing lists
Literary history, 36
Literature: classics of, 404; conceptions of,
    412; minority, 40, 69; national, 36, 42, 69;
    popular, 163; representation of history in,
    216; study of, 32–33, 35, 37, 64, 67, 82,
    163, 393–96, 474–76; teaching, 406; trans-
    lation of, 393, 395–96
Loebell, Wilhelm, 157
London, 47, 378
Lüdtke, Alf, 50, 504
Luther, Martin, 22, 494
Lützeler, Paul Michael, 532

Maase, Kaspar, 49
Maier, Charles, 185, 245, 255
Mailing lists, via internet, 516, 517–18
Mann, Heinrich, 293
Mann, Thomas, 33, 163, 412, 436, 494, 496,
    498
Mariana Islands, 192
Markovits, Andrei S., 531
Marlitt, Eugenie, 163
Marshall Islands, 192
Marssolek, Inge, 48–49
Marx, Adolf Berhard, 140–41, 143, 146,
    150–51, 153–54, 156
Marx, Karl, 493
Marxism, 6, 9, 10, 46, 50, 66, 75, 209. *See
    also* Communism
Mason, Tim, 209
Mass culture, 11, 46, 49–52, 54–55, 118, 165,
    187, 404, 408. *See also* Popular culture
Mauthausen, 260, 274
Max-Planck-Gesellschaft zur Förderung der
    Wissenschaften, 527
Mazursky, Paul, 511
McCarthy, John A., 532

McCracken, Grant, 184
Media: news, 96; study of, 46, 49, 51
Medick, Hans, 503
Mellor, Jeff, 520
Memorials, 31, 33–34, 41, 43, 84–85, 207,
    228, 238, 240, 246, 255, 311
Memory, 34, 101, 105, 113, 115, 117–18,
    132–33, 228, 230, 251, 255, 506; construc-
    tion of, 311; national, 33–35, 40–41, 299;
    post-Wall, 311; symbols of, 84, 322
Mendelssohn, Fanny, 149–50, 157
Mendelssohn, Moses, 42, 152
Mendelssohn-Bartholdy, Felix, 139–43,
    149–60, 463; as Jew, 151–52
Menzel, Wolfgang, 36
Metropolis, 498
Metz, Christian, 458
Meyer, Hannes, 243
Michigan, University of, 17, 24
Middle-class, 145
Mies van der Rohe, Ludwig, 243–45, 255
Mikesch, Elfi, 341
Military, 34, 101–3, 216, 231–32, 235,
    238–39, 243, 245–46, 251, 255, 372
Mill, John Stuart, 187
Miller-Lane, Barbara, 499, 500
Milton, Sybil, 511
Minghi, Julian, 168
Mitscherlich, Alexander and Margarethe, 105
Mitteldeutsche Zeitung (Halle), 294
Mitterand, François, 96–99
Modernity, 18, 53, 116
Modern Language Association, 440
Modleski, Tania, 11
Mommsen, Hans, 221–23
Monoculturalism, 5, 19, 53, 63–66, 68–69, 72.
    See also Multiculturalism
Monument against War and Fascism (Vienna),
    257–85
Monuments, 33–34, 40, 43, 175, 260
Moretti, Franco, 115
Mörike, Eduard, 454
Morrison, Toni, 71
Moscow Declaration, 267
Mosse, George L., 402–3, 505
Mozart, Wolfgang Amadeus, 153, 461
Mules, Warwick, 535
Müller, Heiner, 118, 307
Müller, Herta, 37–39
Müller-Sievers, Helmut, 407

Multiculturalism, xii, xiv, 5–6, 17, 19–21,
32–43, 63–75, 84, 86, 124. *See also* Mono-
culturalism
Multidisciplinarity, 14; in performance, 471.
See also Interdisciplinarity
Museums, 40, 85, 106, 147, 231, 249, 270,
326, 357–65, 368, 370–71, 433
Music, 12, 17, 49, 70, 88, 95, 120, 137,
139–60, 166, 167, 499; studying, 461–63
Musicology, 139–44, 147–48, 152, 158, 160
Mysorekar, Sheila, 191
Mythology, 25, 34, 36, 106, 127, 129, 175

Nagasaki, 106, 124
Nägeli, Georg, 154
Nama uprising, 197
Napoléon I (Bonaparte), Emperor of France,
231
Narrative, 35, 37–38, 50, 53, 115–16, 130,
132, 157, 168, 171, 175, 274, 279, 282, 337,
343, 420, 421, 474–75
Nasty Girl, The, 506
National Archives (Washington), 384
National character, 504
National Endowment for the Arts, 4
National Endowment for the Humanities, 4
Nationalism, 36, 67, 165, 177, 301
National Public Radio, 93, 95–96
National Socialism: archives concerning,
379–80; in Austria, 258, 267–68, 283; and
colonialism, 197; concentration camps under (*see* Concentration camps); economy
during, 291–92; end of, 298; experience of,
37–41, 70, 93–94, 103–6, 116–21, 129, 131;
and the GDR, 310; heirs of, 306; history of,
xiii, 15, 48–56, 99–100, 113, 211, 213–14,
221, 246, 251, 433; and mass culture,
49–50; in the media, 99–100, 213; and the
Neue Wache, 246; and propaganda, 55; resistance to, 106–7, 281; and the SED, 306;
teaching about; 433–37, 497; and tourism,
186. *See also* Neo-Nazi; World War II
National space, 166, 251
Native, as concept, 172
Native Americans, 114, 124, 171–72, 174,
190, 195
NATO, 100
Nazi; Nazi Party. *See* National Socialism
Nelson, Cary, 9, 11, 19, 22, 25, 534
Neo-Nazi, 94, 103, 109, 117

Neue Synagoge (Berlin), 82, 84–88, 90
Neue Wache, 85, 228–53
Neuschwanstein, 117
New cultural history, 46, 48, 50
New Forum, 107
New German Cinema, 335
New German Critique, 16, 24, 66, 258, 522,
530
New Guinea, German, 192
New historicism, 10, 400, 407–10
New Objectivity, 497
New York, 129, 135
New Yorker, xiii
Ngugi wa Thiong'o, 494
Nibelungenlied, 494
Nicolai, Friedrich, 36, 42
Nietzsche, Friedrich, 40, 394, 493, 499
Nobel Prize, 71
Novalis, 36
Novels, studying, 474–76
Nuclear weapons, 121

Office of Special Investigations, 385
Ohm Krüger, 195–97
Oklahoma City bombing, 94
Online public access catalogs (OPACs), 517,
519–20
Opera, 144, 159
Operation Barbarossa, 198
Opitz, Martin, 36, 42
Opitz, May Ayim. *See* Ayim, May
Oranienburg, 198, 203
Orpheus, 279
Ortner, S., 503
Ostpolitik, 300

Paglia, Camille, 342, 345–49
Paine, Thomas, 493
Painting, studying, 464–66
Panovsky, Erwin, 465
Parades, 33, 50. *See also* Festivities
Paris, 108, 144–45, 157, 160
Parties, Austrian, 264, 265, 269–70, 283
Party of Democratic Socialism (PDS), 304–6
Patriotism, 170, 301
Paul, Gerhard, 55
Peck, Jeffrey, 16, 21, 29, 67, 73–74, 532, 533
Pedagogy. *See* Case study method, in teach-
ing; Teaching
Performance, 83, 139–41, 149–50, 152, 157,

159; definitions of, 469–70; and pornography, 343; studying, 469–73
Pergamon Museum, 85
Petro, Patrice, 48, 51
Peukert, Detlev, 53, 506
Philology, 82, 90
Photography, 51, 53–56, 334–35
Picasso, Pablo, 465
Pierce, James Smith, 465
Plato, 494
Plays, studying, 467–68
Poelzig, Hans, 243
Poetry: reading, 13, 38, 67, 114, 452–55; teaching, 452–55; in translation, 393
Poland, 33, 38, 40, 50, 116, 121, 358–65. *See also* Auschwitz
Political correctness, 4, 340, 441
Political culture, 82, 297–98
Political readings, 405
Political science, 10, 14, 18, 23, 64, 67, 79–81, 82, 97, 127–28, 134, 163; statistics in, 479–82
Politzer, Heinz, 443
Popular culture, 11, 46–52, 54, 88, 118, 137, 163–76, 187, 408. *See also* Mass culture
Pornography: debate about, 340–42; definitions of, 338, 351; Paglia's views of, 346; role of, 337
Posner, Gerald, 384
Postcolonial gaze, 191
Postcolonial studies, 65, 91, 115, 137, 189
Postmodernism, 18, 22–23, 45–48, 52, 53, 54–55, 340, 349; in the classroom, 410
Poststructuralism, 10, 54, 66, 340
Power, 8, 10–11, 16, 19, 34–35, 68, 72, 143, 218, 221, 228, 230, 239, 268, 291, 300, 323, 389, 403, 407, 417, 418
Pratt, Mary Louise, 19, 20, 21, 25, 172
Praunheim, Rosa von, 351
Pressac, Jean-Claude, 365
Presses, academic, 442
Prisoners of war, 98, 131, 359
Profession, 443
Professional concerns, 389
Protestantism, 144, 151, 155–57, 160
Prussia, 20, 115, 139, 146, 148–49, 152, 165, 177
Prussian Academy of Arts, 148
Psychoanalysis, 9, 66, 118, 121
Public sphere, 145

Publishers, of German literature in translation, 395
Publishing, in German studies, 441–46
Pundt, Hermann, 254

Queer, as concept, 336–37

Raabe, Paul, 163
Rabbi Baruch G., 509
Rabinbach, Anson, 18, 19, 530
Race, 5, 10, 18, 42, 63–70, 73–74, 164–65, 174, 345, 380
Racism, 81, 83–84, 86, 94–95, 102, 109–10, 191, 221
Rademacher, Norbert, 40
Radio, 49, 54, 93–110
Radtke, Frank-Olaf, 70
Radway, Janice, 11
Ranke, Leopold von, 215
Reagan, Ronald, 83, 88
Reception history, 263
Red Army, 102, 104, 372. *See also* Soviet Union
Red Army Faction, 105
Redslob, Edwin, 255
Reformation, 115
Regions, geographical, 168
Reich, Steve, 511
Reichstag, 83, 239
Reitz, Edgar, 218, 219–20, 224
Rellstab, Ludwig, 146, 157
Remak, Joachim, 509
Remarque, Erich Maria, 433, 498–99
Renovation, 228, 230, 235, 240, 246
Rentschler, Eric, 198, 335, 460
Representation, 10
Resistance, 106–7, 246, 267–68, 279, 281, 300, 322–23
Resources, for German cultural studies, 521
Reunification. *See* Unification
Revolution of 1848, 115, 162, 165, 175
Rezeptionsgeschichte, 263
Rhine (river), 177, 394
Richter, Simon, 407
Riefenstahl, Leni, 433, 498
Riegl, Alois, 465
Riehl, Wilhelm Heinrich, 175
Riesman, David, 433
Rilke, Rainer Maria, 394
Ritual, 87, 130. *See also* Festivities

Robert Bosch Stiftung, 527
Roma and Sinti, 372, 511
Romanticism, 36, 132, 134, 139, 156, 158, 160
Roosevelt, Theodore, 375
Rosenhaft, Eve, 51
Rousseau, Jean-Jacques, 129
Ruhr valley, 504
Rumania, 38–39, 115
Rumley, Dennis, 168
Russia, 104

Sabean, David, 505
Sachsenhausen, 40, 198, 203. *See also* Concentration camps
Sachs, Nelly, 500, 511
Sachs, Wolfgang, 49
Safire, Willism, 99
Said, Edward, 67; and Maire, 42
Salinger, J. D., 129
Salons, 132, 145–46, 150, 152, 160
Sanders-Brahms, Helma, 218
Santa Monica, 115
Santner, Erich, 121, 445
Sauder, Gerhard, 407
Schama, Simon, 47, 175, 181, 404
Scharnhorst, Gerhard von, 231
Scharping, Rudolf, 88
Scheessel (Lower Saxony), 184–85
Scheffler, Karl, 255
Scher, Helene L., 531
Schiller, Johann Christoph Friedrich von, 12, 69, 402, 410
Schindler's List, 20, 25
Schinkel, Karl Friedrich, 228–53; Altes Museum, 231; Bauakademie, 232; Friedrich-Werderische Church, 231; Momument at Kreuzberg, 238; Neue Wache, 230; Packhof, 231–32; Schauspielhaus, 231
Schlegel, August Wilhelm, 36–37, 42, 154
Schlegel, Friedrich, 36–37, 42, 154
Schleiermacher, Friedrich, 88, 141, 154, 157
Schlesinger, Arthur, Sr., 432
Schlöndorff, Volker, 218
Schlüpmann, Heide, 48–49
Schmitt-Rottluff, Karl, 436
Schneider, Katrin, 532
Scholarship, in German studies, 443
Schönberg, Arnold, 436
Schor, Naomi, 443

Schroeter, Werner, 335
Schubert, Franz, 159, 461, 462
Schumann, Robert, 462
Schutztruppe, 192
Schwarz, Egon, 282
Schwarzer, Alice, 340, 347
Search engines, for internet, 517
Sedgwick, Eve Kosofsky, 336
Seeba, Hinrich, 20, 21
Semiotics, 48, 81, 88
Şenocak, Zafer, 71
Sexpert, Susie. *See* Bright, Susie
Sexuality, 10, 18, 47, 51, 55, 69, 335, 505
Shakespeare, William, 409–10, 494
Shanghai, 115
Shoah, 510
Sichrovsky, Peter, 510, 511
Siegessäule (Berlin), 239
Sieg, Katrin, 190, 192
Singer, Isaac Bashevis, 511
Sinowatz, Fred, 266
Skinheads, 191
Slavery, 114, 123, 171
Sloterdijk, Peter, 35, 43
Smithsonian Museum, 106
Social Democratic Party (SPD), 50, 88, 290, 305
Socialism, 50, 97, 107–8, 116, 302, 309, 312, 315, 319, 322
Socialist Unity Party (SED), 304, 305, 310, 315
Social theory, 7–9, 12
Sociology, 23, 55, 175
Soja, Edward, 175
Sonderweg, 53
South Africa, 199
Soviet Union, 121, 372
Space: colonial, 178; imagination and, 175; national, 168–69; understanding of, 175
Spector, Scott, 24
Spiegelman, Art, 511
Spielberg, Stephen, 20
Spielhagen, Friedrich, 290
Spielvogel, Jackson, 498, 499, 509
Spivak, Gayatri, 67, 71
Spohr, Louis, 159
Sprinkle, Annie, 338, 339–40, 341, 343–44
Squatters, 264
Stafford, Barbara, 407
Stalingrad, battle of, 372–73

Stanford University, 24, 73–74, 491
Stasi (GDR secret police), 306, 310, 322, 395
State Department, United States, 382, 383
Statistics, studying and using, 479–82
Steinberg, Ellen. *See* Sprinkle, Annie
Stockholm, 115
Stock-im-Eisen-Platz (Vienna), 268
Stoiber, Edmund, 70
Stolpe, Manfred, 306, 307
Stölzl, Christoph, 249
Stone, Lawrence, 404
Storm, Theodor, 163
Straayer, Chris, 337
Strauss, Botho, 113, 118–20
Streim, Alfred, 384
Ströhmfeld, Gustav, 183–85
Structuralism, 9, 47–48, 55, 66, 79, 82, 88
Strukturgeschichte, 48. *See also* Bielefeld
    School
Student movement, 66–67, 118, 121, 433–34
Students. *See* Teaching
Stürmer, Michael, 320
Stutthof, 116
Sudeten Germans, expulsion of, 373
Suhr, Heidrun, 71
Suicide, 108
Suleiman, Susan, 444
Swabia, 183
Swastika, 498
Switzerland, 21, 115, 118, 257
Syberberg, Hans-Jürgen, 218
Syllabi. *See* Teaching
Synagogues. *See* Jewish
Syntax, 453

Tabori, George, 37–41, 43
Tatar, Maria, 51, 407, 445
Teaching, xi–xii, xiv, 10, 12, 20–22, 31–32,
    37–41, 63–74, 82, 103–4, 113–14, 123–24,
    389, 406, 440; with case study method,
    417–28; course syllabi for, xiv, 12, 15, 24,
    37–38, 489–90; handouts, 451; methods,
    449; teachers, 431; team, 431
Television, 95–96, 99, 102, 114, 118, 120,
    469–70
Telnet, 517, 519–20
Tenure, 440–42
Terrorism, 121
Tessenow, Heinrich, 240–43, 245, 249, 255
Texas, University of, at Austin, 391

Text, 8–9, 81
Theater, studying, 467–68
Theresienstadt, 133
Theweleit, Klaus, 51
Thibaut, Justus, 160
Third Reich. *See* National Socialism
Third World, 201
Thirty Years' War, 115
Thompson, E. P., 7, 47, 404
Thwaites, Tony, 535
Tieck, Ludwig, 157, 452
Timm, Eitel, 532
Togo, 192
Tomb of the Unknown Soldier (Arlington), 238
Torgovnick, Marianna de Marco, 444
Tourism, 84, 137, 172, 182–87
Trabant, 315
Tragedy, 223
Trakl, Georg, 499
Translation, 39–40, 42–43, 49, 391–96, 445
Treblinka, 361
Treichler, Paula A., 22, 534
Trenker, Luis, 335
Treut, Monika, 207, 333–51
Triangular thinking, 190, 192–94, 198
Triest, J. F. K., 156
Trinh T. Minh-ha, 63, 64
Triumph of the Will, 498
Trommler, Frank, 69, 533
Tübingen, 166
Tuchman, Barbara, 375
Turks, 17, 39, 69–71, 73, 201
Turner, Graeme, 536
Turner movement, 36
Tyrol, 169, 177

Unification, 19, 23, 37, 73, 97, 99, 105,
    107–10, 297–306, 312; festivities, 320
United Nations Educational, Scientific and
    Cultural Organization (UNESCO), 360, 365
United States Institute of Peace, 527
United States of America: experience of, 335;
    influence of, 334–35, 348
Unter den Linden (street), 232, 234
URL (univeral resource locator) addresses, for
    internet. *See* World Wide Web

Van Cleve, John, 68, 119, 391, 400
Van Pelt, Robert-Jan, 365
Varnhagen, Rahel, 127–28, 132–35, 406

Venezuela, 177
Verdun, 97–98
Vereine. See Associations
Vergangenheitsbewältigung, 103–6, 116,
   118–19, 121–22, 124, 310, 320, 329
Verhoeven, Michael, 506
Versailles Treaty, 102
Vesely, Herbert, 335
Vico, Giambattista, 230
Victims, 216, 223–24, 319–20, 322, 372–73
Vienna, 36–37, 160, 257–82, 504
Vierhaus, Rudolf, 49
Vietnam war, 40–41, 43, 121, 123, 200, 238
Village studies, 504–5
Vogeler, Volker, 335
Volga Germans, 115
Volk ohne Raum, 210
Volkskunde, 502, 503
Volkswagen-Stiftung, 527
Voltaire, François-Marie Arouet de, 401
Von Saldern, Adelheid, 48–49
Vranitzky, Franz, 263

Waeldler, Alfred, 171
Waffen-SS, 94
Wagenknecht, Sarah, 306
Wagner, Martin, 255
Wagner, Richard, 43, 139, 152, 155, 158, 461,
   493
Waldheim, Kurt, 263, 265–66, 269, 283–84
Walker, Mack, 294
Walkowitz, Judith, 47
Wall, The: construction of, 300, 301, 311; ex-
   perience of, 310, 329; fall of, 20, 73, 81,
   104, 107–10, 207, 298, 309, 311, 507;
   preservation of, 323–26; as symbol, 326
War criminals, 103–4, 106, 120
Warhol, Andy, 349, 410
Washington, D. C., 40, 96, 411
Washington University, 67
Weber, Max, 287
Weber, William, 144–45, 155
Weill, Kurt, 461, 463
Weimar, 141, 151
Weimar classicism, 411
Weimar Republic, 48, 50, 53, 56, 116, 240;
   economy of, 291; film in, 51; history of, 51,
   433; similarities to Nazi Germany, 437;
   teaching, 433–36, 497–501

Weiner, Marc, 445
Weinrich, Harald, 72
Weiss, Peter, 393, 511
Weissberg, Liliane, 407
Welch, David, 500
Welsch, Erwin K., 483
Wende, Die, 315. *See also* Unification
Wenders, Wim, 38, 75, 218, 335, 337
Werckmeister, Otto Karl, 257
WerkstattGeschichte, 48
West, Cornel, 65
Whitehead, Rachel, 283
White Rose, 500
White Rose, The, 498
Widdig, Bernd, 48, 51
Wierlacher, Alois, 72
Wiesel, Elie, 369, 375
Wiesenthal, Simon, 369, 384
Williams, E. E., 294
Williams, Raymond, 6–8, 11, 47, 91, 408
Williams, Rosalind, 181
Willson, A. Leslie, 68, 119, 400, 439
Winston, Krishna, 445
Wirtschaftswunder, 121
Wisconsin, University of, 67
Wittenberg, 151
Wolf, Christa, 307, 320, 395
Wolf, Hugo, 461
Wollstonecraft, Mary, 493
Wolzogen, Ernst von, 290
Women in German, 66–67, 522
Women's studies. *See* Gender studies
Woolf, Virginia, 38–39
Workers, 49–56, 66, 91, 290–91
Working class culture, 504
World War I, 41, 45, 51, 97, 102, 115, 123,
   131
World War II, xii, xiii, 20, 34, 38, 65–66, 85,
   94–95, 98, 100–107, 110, 120–23, 216
World Wide Web (WWW), 489, 516–17,
   518–19
Worms, 168
Württemberg, 182
Würzburg, 132–33

Xenophobia, 37, 42, 81, 189, 190

Yale University, 86
Yiddish, 40

Young, James, 31–34, 41, 239, 255, 357, 362
Yugoslavia, 5, 38–39

Zeldin, Theodore, 185
Zelter, Karl Friedrich, 141, 148–50, 154

Zero Hour, 497
Zilk, Helmut, 260, 263, 269
Ziolkowski, Theodore, 139, 405
Zionism, 129–30
Zweig, Stefan, 500